Software Process Improvement for Small and Medium Enterprises:
Techniques and Case Studies

Hanna Oktaba
Nacional Autonomous University of Mexico, Mexico

Mario Piattini
University of Castilla–La Mancha, Spain

INFORMATION SCIENCE REFERENCE

Hershey · New York

Acquisitions Editor:	Kristin Klinger
Development Editor:	Kristin Roth
Senior Managing Editor:	Jennifer Neidig
Managing Editor:	Jamie Snavely
Assistant Managing Editor:	Carole Coulson
Copy Editor:	April Schmidt
Typesetter:	Cindy Consonery
Cover Design:	Lisa Tosheff
Printed at:	Yurchak Printing Inc.

Published in the United States of America by
Information Science Reference (an imprint of IGI Global)
701 E. Chocolate Avenue, Suite 200
Hershey PA 17033
Tel: 717-533-8845
Fax: 717-533-8661
E-mail: cust@igi-global.com
Web site: http://www.igi-global.com

and in the United Kingdom by
Information Science Reference (an imprint of IGI Global)
3 Henrietta Street
Covent Garden
London WC2E 8LU
Tel: 44 20 7240 0856
Fax: 44 20 7379 0609
Web site: http://www.eurospanonline.com

Library of Congress Cataloging-in-Publication Data

Software process improvement for small and medium enterprises : techniques and case studies / Hanna Oktaba and Mario Piattini, editors.
     p. cm.
  Summary: "This book offers practical and useful guidelines, models, and techniques for improving software processes and products for small and medium enterprises, utilizing the authoritative, demonstrative tools of case studies and lessons learned to provide academics, scholars, and practitioners with an invaluable research source,"--Provided by publisher.
  ISBN 978-1-59904-906-9 (hbk.) -- ISBN 978-1-59904-908-3 (e-book)
  1. Computer software--Development--Management. 2. Computer software industry--Management--Case studies. 3. Small business--Data processing--Case studies. I. Oktaba, Hanna. II. Piattini, Mario, 1966-
  QA76.76.D47S66354 2008
  005.1--dc22
                                         2008001869

British Cataloguing in Publication Data
A Cataloguing in Publication record for this book is available from the British Library.

All work contributed to this book set is original material. The views expressed in this book are those of the authors, but not necessarily of the publisher.

Table of Contents

Chapter I
Organizational Analysis of Small Software Organizations: Framework and Case Study 1
    Jesús Zavala-Ruiz, Metropolitan Autonomous University – Iztapalapa, Mexico

Chapter II
The Application of International Software Engineering Standards in Very
Small Enterprises 42
    Claude Y. Laporte, École de Technologie Supérieure, Canada
    Alain Renault, Centre de Recherche Public Henri Tudor, Luxembourg
    Simon Alexandre, Centre d'Excellence en Technologies de
        l'Information et de la Communication, Belgium

Chapter III
Practical Experience in Customization for a Software Development Process for
Small Companies Based on RUP Process and MSF 71
    Valerio Fernandes del Maschi, Universidade Paulista, Brazil
    Mauro de Mesquita Spinola, Universidade Paulista, Brazil
    Ivanir Costa, Universidade Paulista, Brazil
    Alexandre de Lima Esteves, Universidade Paulista, Brazil
    Luciano S. Souza, Universidade Paulista, Brazil
    Wilson Vendramel, Universidade Paulista, Brazil
    Jorge Pirola, Universidade Paulista, Brazil

Detailed Table of Contents

Chapter I

    Jesús Zavala-Ruiz, Metropolitan Autonomous University – Iztapalapa, Mexico

This chapter contains an overview on the complexity of a software organization focusing on the around software engineering and project management as disciplines in crisis and their underlying management paradigm. The author considers opening it to those related disciplines and presents a framework to support this change of paradigm.

Chapter II

    Claude Y. Laporte, École de Technologie Supérieure, Canada
    Alain Renault, Centre de Recherche Public Henri Tudor, Luxembourg
    Simon Alexandre, Centre d'Excellence en Technologies de
        l'Information et de la Communication, Belgium

This chapter is focused on the new ISO project proposed to facilitate access to, and utilization of, its standards in SMEs by means of developing profiles and providing guidance for compliance with ISO software engineering standards.

This chapter shows the methodology, strategy, main phases, and procedures to the implantation of a customized software engineering process in a SME.

This chapter shows some foundations of the discipline of software testing and fragments of some successful test process defined using a proprietary process definition language and presents two case studies realized in Mexican SMEs that show the economic impact of the testing process.

This chapter presents a low-cost process evaluation method especially designed for SMEs that has been successfully apply in several organizations and provides ways to be more competitive.

This chapter presents a comparison of some process assessment and software process improvement methods for SMEs. This will lead towards development of a standardized software process improvement model for small and medium sized software development organizations in the future.

This chapter presents the CMM Fast-track Toolkit (CMMFT) that provides a faster and cheaper method of obtaining CMMI capability for SMEs, increasing quality of their software products and gaining competitive advantage.

This chapter resumes the process model (MoProSoft) and its assessment method (EvalProSoft) and shows their most important features. It also includes the results of their application in four small Mexican enterprises.

This chapter presents the framework Agile SPI, designed to motivate SMEs towards improving and certifying their software development processes, which is based on the integration of software processes on small and medium organizations context and culture.

This chapter presents common agile practices as the way to address the daily problems that may appear in a process improvement initiative. Authors explain how these practices can reduce the efforts and cost, and contribute to realize benefits sooner, in a motivational way.

This chapter presents the COMPETISOFT project and its framework for improving software process in Latin-American SMEs. This framework is composed by a reference process model, an assessment model, and an improvement model, and it is based on other previous solutions, especially in the MoPro-Soft project.

This chapter presents a study of assessment-based improvement in more than 20 SMEs during five years; its results show how improving frameworks can affect the organization and its business.

This chapter shows the validated methodology used in a factory oriented at free software development. This incremental methodology is based on a prioritization of functionalities development according to needs and has features of both cathedral and bazaar developing styles.

This chapter proposes a methodological framework to promote strategic alignment, improve execution through a better communication, and understand IT projects that will help to make better IT decisions for offering a competitive edge to companies based on a better management of the strategic IT portfolio.

This chapter identifies a model to characterize knowledgeable assets and their relationships in a software organization, and it sets the basis for defining a transversal process of knowledge management at the organization.

This chapter describes a framework implementation experience in an accounting office by showing how its process definition allows for progressively putting a work model into practice for implementing a process model with continuous improvement.

This chapter contains a proposal for project estimation of software used in a Mexican SME, based on the Karner's use case point estimation method. Two methods are compared to provide conclusions.

This chapter presents how resources have been managed according to recommendations of the MoProSoft reference model in a governmental organization and presents some lessons learned from this case study.

Foreword

There is little disagreement within the software community about the need for addressing process improvement within small businesses and projects. Small businesses in the software industry represent a significant amount of the resources applied to software problems around the world. These businesses sometimes plan on staying small, but often they hope that they will grow with success. Particularly for those who plan on growing, understanding how processes that are well-conceived, described, and used can contribute to their success in the business world is critical to attain and sustain competitiveness.

As important as this is, small businesses often find there are many more "urgent" concerns that claim their attention. This is exacerbated by the perception that defining, training, and following disciplined processes is too much work in comparison to the benefit today. Because small businesses are so often worried about day-to-day survival, thinking about how processes can help them tomorrow is often at the bottom of their priority list. Not to mention, small software companies rarely have the internal expertise and resources to perform process definition and improvement activities themselves. This means added cost that is rarely considered in the survival-level business plan.

Governments across the world have taken note of these challenges for the small businesses within their economies and have instituted a variety of approaches to encourage and support their small software businesses in taking process improvement seriously. One of the most ambitious of these government initiatives is Mexico's MoProSoft initiative. This initiative built a national norm (in the U.S., it would be called a standard) that is explicitly targeted at the *pequeña* (tiny) software organizations in Mexico. The MoProSoft team looked not only at the process topics covered in other common international standards and guides, but they also identified the need in these small organizations to deal explicitly with business strategy issues, a unique contribution to the process improvement community. It is one of the several techniques that Hanna Oktaba and Mario Piattini have included in this volume.

MoProSoft does not intend to replace more widely used process improvement standards like ISO 9001 or CMMI. However, it does fill a gap for those organizations that are ready for "some" type of improvement, but that are still sufficiently taken up with business survival issues that they do not feel ready to take on the more prominent standards fully. In my conversations with Hanna and other authors of the norm, it is clear that their dedication to encouraging productive improvement activities in organizations that normally would not engage in improvement is a goal that they hold dear. This book covers both the challenges that led to solutions like MoProSoft as well as other productive approaches to improving processes in small settings.

If you are in an organization trying to approach improvement with limited resources and few people, you will find useful guidance and experience reports in this book. If you are working with small organizations who are reluctant to try process improvement, you will find some ammunition for encouraging those organizations to think more seriously about process improvement. If you are working with frameworks like CMMI or ISO 9001, you will find ideas on ways you might adapt your implementation to account for some of the issues commonly present with the smaller organizations you work with. In any case, we all have much to learn from both the successes and the struggles of small organizations working to adopt improved processes that are provided here.

SuZ Garcia is a senior member of the technical staff at the Software Engineering Institute of Carnegie Mellon University in Pittsburgh, PA, USA. She currently works in the Integrating SW Intensive Systems initiative. Her research in this area is focused on creating processes, tools and techniques to support complex systems of systems engineering. From June 2001 to Oct 2006, she worked in the technology transition research area, with 3 of those years focused specifically on transition support of process improvement for small settings. From Nov 1997-May 2001, she was the Deployments Manager for aimware, Incorporated's US customers, focusing on using technology to accelerate organizational improvement. The 5 years prior to this were spent at the SEI working in various capacities on all the Capability Maturity Models the Institute was involved in. She spent the previous 12 years in multiple improvement-related roles at Lockheed Missile and Space Co. She is co-author of CMMI Survival Guide: Just Enough Process Improvement, a book that focuses on the skills and practices needed to establish and support process improvement programs in small and other constrained-resource settings. Education: BA, Ergonomics, 1980 from University of California, Santa Barbara; MS, Systems Management, 1988 from University of Southern California.

Preface

From the very beginning of the 1990s onward, the software engineering community (industry and researchers) has expressed special interest in software process improvement (SPI). This is evidenced by the growing number of books, articles, and conferences that deal with the topic of SPI and the great number of international initiatives related to SPI such as CMM®, CMMI®, ISO/IEC 12207, 15504, and ISO 90003, among others.

Nevertheless, these standards and models are conceived for big organizations like USA DoD, NASA, multinational software factories, and so forth. In fact, there is a widespread tendency to emphasize that the success of SPI is only possible for large companies that have enough resources to tackle these types of practices. This perception is based on the fact that SPI programs are just not viable for small and medium enterprises (SMEs) because of their organizational structure and the high costs that are involved. However, the software industry in most countries is made up mainly of SMEs which favor the growth of national economies. Most software development organizations (nearly 90%) are SMEs which contribute to very valuable and widespread products.

Almost all the experts agree that the special characteristics of SMEs mean that process improvement programs must be applied in a way that is particular to them and visibly different from how this is done in the large organizations. This is not as simple as just regarding these programs as scaled down versions of those applied in big companies. In fact, the assessments conformant to the international standards are expensive and time consuming, difficult to perform in small companies, their process model structure is too complex, and the return of investment undertaken has to be seen from a long-term perspective.

The first International Research Workshop for Process Improvement in Small Settings organized by the Software Engineering Institute (October 2005), the new ISO/IEC JTC1 SC7 Working Group 24, which was created (2006) to develop the "Software Life Cycle Profiles and Guidelines for use in Very Small Enterprises (VSE)," and several other initiatives have demonstrated the increasing interest for new proposals and experiences in software improvement for SMEs. SMEs have become concerned about how to improve the capability of their software processes, as a fundamental element to increase product quality, addressing two main concerns: the first one has to do with their image, which is a key factor in order to be able to export software and hence enter the global marketplace; and the other concern is related to the efficiency and effectiveness of software process management.

Also, different countries like Mexico, Spain, Australia, Brazil, Colombia, and so on have developed local programs to promote the improvement of their software industry, especially focused on SMEs. As a result, several maturity and improvement models have been developed and successful experiences have been carried out. Therefore, in this context, we present this book, the main objective of which is to provide practical and useful guidelines, models, and techniques for improving software processes in SMEs and collecting real case studies and lessons learned, as successful examples of experiences in improving software process capability.

The book consists of 18 chapters. The chapters seek to provide a critical survey of the fundamental themes, problems, arguments, theories, and methodologies in the field of software process improvement in SMEs. Each chapter has been planned as a self-standing introduction to its subject.

Therefore, in Chapter I, "Organizational Analysis of Small Software Organizations: Framework and Case Study," Jesús Zavala Ruiz realizes an overview on the complexity of a software organization focusing on software engineering and project management as disciplines in crisis and their underlying management paradigm. He considers opening it to those related disciplines and presents a framework to support this change of paradigm.

Claude Y. Laporte, Alain Renault, and Simon Alexandre, in Chapter II, "The Application of International Software Engineering Standards in Very Small Enterprises," present the new ISO project proposed to facilitate access to, and utilization of, its standards in SMEs by means of developing profiles and providing guidance for compliance with ISO software engineering standards.

In Chapter III, "Practical Experience in Customization for a Software Development Process for Small Companies Based on RUP Process and MSF," Valerio Fernandes del Maschi, Mauro de Mesquita Spinola, Ivanir Costa Alexandre de Lima Esteves, Luciano S. Souza, Wilson Vendramel, and Jorge Pirola, show the methodology, strategy, main phases, and procedures to the implantation of a customized software engineering process in a SME.

Chapter IV, "The Impact of Software Testing in Small and Medium Settings," by Luis Vinicio León-Carrillo, shows some foundations of the discipline of software testing and fragments of some successful test process defined using a proprietary process definition language. He presents two case studies realized in Mexican SMEs that show the economic impact of the testing process.

Sarah Kohan, Marcelo Schneck de Paula Pessôa, and Mauro de Mesquita Spinola present "QuickLocus: A Software Development Process Evaluation Method for Small-Sized Organizations" (Chapter V). This is a low-cost process evaluation method especially designed for SMEs that has been successfully apply in several organizations which provide ways to be more competitive.

In Chapter VI, Deepti Mishra and Alok Mishra present "A Study of Software Process Improvement in Small and Medium Organizations," in which some process assessment and software process improvement methods for SMEs are compared. This will lead towards development of a standardized software process improvement model for small and medium sized software development organizations in the future.

"CMM Fast-Track: Experience and Lessons Learned," Chapter VII, by Hareton Leung and Yvette Lui, presents the CMM Fast-track Toolkit (CMMFT). This program aims to provide a faster and cheaper method of obtaining CMMI capability for SMEs, increasing the quality of their software products and gaining competitive advantage.

Chapter VIII, written by Hanna Oktaba and Ana Vázquez, presents "MoProSoft: A Software Process Model for Small Enterprises." This chapter resumes the process model and its assessment method (EvalProSoft) and shows their most important features. It also includes the results of their application in four small Mexican enterprises.

Julio A. Hurtado, Francisco J. Pino, Juan C. Vidal, César Pardo, and Luis Eduardo Fernández present "Agile SPI: Software Process Agile Improvement: A Colombian Approach to Software Process Improvement in Small Software Organizations" in Chapter IX. This framework (Agile SPI), designed to motivate SMEs towards improving and certifying their software development processes, is based on the integration of software processes in small and medium organization contexts and cultures. Knowledge regarding the organization and its main features let processes generate profits and increase the intellectual capital of the organization.

In Chapter X, John Gómez and Alejandro Núñez present "Agile Practices in Project Management." In this chapter, both authors present common agile practices as the way to address the daily problems that may appear in a process improvement initiative. They explain how these practices can reduce the efforts and cost, and contribute to realize benefits sooner, in a motivational way.

A framework for improving software process in Latin-American SMEs is being developed by the COMPETISOFT project. This framework is composed by a reference process model, an assessment model, and an improvement model, and it is based on other previously solutions, especially in the Mo-ProSoft project. COMPETISOFT is shown in Chapter XI, "COMPETISOFT: An Improvement Strategy for Small Latin-American Software Organizations," written by Hanna Oktaba, Mario Piattini, Félix García, Francisco J. Pino, Claudia Alquicira, Francisco Ruiz, and Tomás Martínez.

Chapter XII, "SPI Long-Term Benefits: Case Studies of Five Small Firms," written by Aileen Cater-Steel and Terry Rout, presents a study of assessment-based improvement in more than 20 SMEs during five years. The results show how improving frameworks can affect the organization and its business.

Oswaldo Terán, Johanna Alvarez, Blanca Abraham, and Jose Aguilar show in Chapter XIII, titled "An Incremental Functionality-Oriented Free Software Development Methodology," the validated methodology used in a factory oriented at free software development. This incremental methodology is based on a prioritization of functionalities development according to needs and has features of both cathedral and bazaar developing styles.

"How to Align Software Projects with Business Strategy" (Chapter XIV) by Gustavo Ricardo Parés Arce, proposes a methodological framework to promote strategic alignment, improve execution through better communication, and understand IT projects. It will help to make better IT decisions for offering a competitive edge to companies based on a better management of the strategic IT portfolio.

Chapter XV, "A Model to Classify Knowledge Assets of a Process-Oriented Development," written by Raquel Anaya, Alejandra Cechich, and Mónica Henao, identifies a model to characterize knowledgeable assets and their relationships in a software organization, and it sets the basis for defining a transversal process of knowledge management at the organization.

Alicia Mon, Marcelo Estayno, and Patricia Scalzone describe a framework implementation experience in an accounting office in Chapter XVI, titled "Practical Application of a Software Development Framework in an Accountant Office." They show how their process definition allows progressively putting a work model into practice for implementing a process model with continuous improvement.

Chapter XVII, "Estimate of Effort in Software Implementation Projects" by María Julia Orozco Mendoza, Evaristo Fernández Perea, and Claudia Alquicira Esquivel, contains a proposal for project estimation of software used in a Mexican SME. This is based on Karner's use case point estimation method. Two methods are compared to provide conclusions.

In "Improving Resource Management: Lessons from a Case Study in a Middle-Range Governmental Organization," Chapter XVIII, Juan M. Luzuriaga, Rodolfo Martínez, and Alejandra Cechich present how resources have been managed according to recommendations of the MoProSoft reference model in a governmental organization. They present some lessons learned from this case study.

In summary, these chapters constitute evidence of the importance of software process improvement in SMEs. These are intended to be useful to a wide audience, including CEOs, CIOs, software engineers, software process engineers, quality specialists, consultants, and software students.

We hope that the practical vision and experience presented in this book will provide the reader with useful guidelines, models, and techniques for improving software processes in SMEs. In this sense, we wish to contribute to increase the quality of the processes and products of SMEs.

Acknowledgment

This work has been funded by the "Process Improvement for Promoting the Competitiveness of Small and Medium Iberoamerican Software Enterprises – 506AC0287 COMPETISOFT" project financed by CYTED (Cooperación y Tecnología para el Desarrollo). We would like to thank Suz García for writing the foreword, for which we are truly grateful. We would also like to thank Tomás Martínez of UCLM for his support during the development of this book.

Hanna Oktaba and Mario Piattini, editors
Mexico/Ciudad Real

Chapter I
Organizational Analysis of Small Software Organizations:
Framework and Case Study

Jesús Zavala-Ruiz
Metropolitan Autonomous University – Iztapalapa, Mexico

ABSTRACT

The intention of this chapter is twofold. On the one hand, I illustrate the complexity of the small software organization, because it is not a reduced version of a large company. Rather, it has very important advantages and challenges. Then, I use organization studies as a multi-disciplinary and multi-paradigmatic link between disciplines, able to reconcile those distinct visions. On the other hand, I open the discussion on the state of crisis affecting software engineering as a discipline. For that, I try to sensitize the reader to the facts surrounding this crisis, but also to the most promising alternative, which is the redefinition of software engineering as a discipline. One of the possible options for that paradigmatic change requires a multi-disciplinary orientation because their positivist roots and the adoption of a constructivist ontology and epistemology facilitating the inclusion of visions non-qualified for a systematic, disciplined and quantitative approach. My position is that only by opening up this discussion is it possible to begin transforming and consolidating software engineering as a strengthened and more terrain-attached discipline because of its powerful theoretical and practical explanatory capacity.

INTRODUCTION

In modern society, service-related activities are growing in importance. Software is playing a preponderant role. More and more, organizations depend on data-processing processes and on the abilities of highly skilled and scarce personnel. They have been named *knowledge workers* and this kind of organization is named *knowledge intensive firms* (Alvesson, 2004, p.5ss) or *postmodern organizations*. Software organizations are a paradigmatic case of intensive-knowledge organizations for many reasons, but principally because its main work is symbolic or non-material in nature and because it is non-standard work for its labour conditions.

Paradoxically, most software organizations are not characterized as applying to themselves what they promote for others. A closer, detailed look inside them frequently reveals a totally different situation: while in the business, most productive, administrative and management processes are candidates for automation, in software organizations, these processes still continue to develop in a craft-like and chaotic manner. The same thing happens in the systems department of any organization. Software production and the most of the work relating to information technology have succumbed to the culture of urgency and competition typical of management. Business cycles decrease and everything is in constant change, with the rising pressure of changing information systems.

Management in software organizations, in a process of imitation, has attempted to adopt the same management recipes applied in business. In this way, it has succumbed to management fads. One of these clearly is *total quality management* (TQM), adopting the name of the normative standards of that moment. Many TQM initiatives have failed miserably in practice in small businesses as well as in large ones. However, in implementing these organizational models, organizational limits exist for their full application, most importantly in small and medium enterprises (SMEs). Resource constraints in SMEs at all levels (monetary, human, time, opportunity, etc.) make it impossible to adhere completely to such prescriptions. Additionally, those organizational characteristics, such as size, diversity, structure and formalization, impose specific restrictions since causes can be manipulated, but not effects. Possibly, the consideration of formal-informal structure duality is the most important, because it provokes both structures to distance themselves from each other, making a close attachment of the informal one to the formal one practically impossible and expensive. But this structural duality is present in all aspects of the organization and software projects become chaotic because of that, among others. To analyze this organizational complexity, which is magnified in small organizations, a framework has been developed based on organization studies and with a social constructionism approach.

This chapter is organized into three parts. In the first part, I provide an overview of the organizational paradigms that allow estimating the complexity of the organization conceived as a social construct beyond its classical mechanics and simple vision. This way, the organization appears as complex, multi-dimensional and multi-paradigmatic. Additionally, I provide an overview the three disciplines that support software production: management, project management and software engineering. I end with a recounting of facts pointing to software engineering as a discipline in crisis, and the causes of that crisis identified.

In the second part, I propose that, if software engineering is in crisis, a paradigmatic change as a discipline is required and I propose three alternatives for that change. In addition, based on Kenneth Gergen's arguments, I assume that all paradigmatic change can only be possible by means of abandoning the current paradigm, adopting a critical attitude with a new discourse and arguments, and then promoting a new paradigm. This part ends with positing the conceptual tools that constitute a framework for doing organizational analysis in software organizations. It is exemplified by a study case of a small outsourcing software company in Mexico City. In addition, I reflect briefly on the scope and utility of this framework. The application of this framework demonstrates that the use of a distinct paradigm other than software engineering for studying software organizations is possible. Finally, in the third part, I explore some of the main trends I consider promising for research in the short term.

BACKGROUND

Organization in an Organization Studies Approach

In their essay *Organizations, Organization and Organizing*, Steward R. Clegg and Cynthia Hardy (1996) give the most commonly accepted definition of *Organization Studies* as "a series of conversations," in particular those of organization-studies researchers who help to constitute organizations through terms, "derived from paradigms, methods and assumptions, themselves derived from earlier conversations" (p. 3). In other words, organization studies are "a place of meeting", "a crossroads," of disciplines and discourses as Luis Montaño Hirose observes (Montaño, 2005). Therefore, organization studies embrace disciplines like engineering, management, economics, psychology, sociology, anthropology and human sciences, among others, all revolving around organizations. Similarly, an *organization* is:

"a collective with a relatively identifiable frontier, a normative order, levels of authority, systems of communications and of coordination; this collective exists in a continuous way in an environment which is involved in activities that are related in general around a group of goals; the activities throw results for the members of the organization, the same organization and the society." (Scott, 1992, p. 25)

In an organization studies approach, according to Clegg and Hardy (1996), *organizations* are conceived as "empirical objects" (p. 3) and "sites of situated social action more or less open both to explicitly organized and formal disciplinary knowledges [...] and also to conversational practices embedded in the broad social fabric" (p. 4). In other words, organizations are social constructs depending on the participants and the approach used to study them. Two related concepts are *organization*, conceived as a "theo-retical discourse," and *organizing*, as a "social process" (p. 3). It is still an on-going debate, but it shows a multi-dimensional arrangement of all organizations.

Now I'll review the most common paradigms accepted in organizations. In his essay *Organizational Theorizing: A Historically Contested Terrain*, Michael Reed (1996) has provided an instructional account of the analytical narratives and the ethical discourses shaping organization studies. The overview of organization theory has been structured using Reed's framework. It captures the complete array of theorizing to date and provides a useful guide for a more sophisticated exploration. 'Organization', 'human being' and 'management' have been chosen as central categories for the ontological characterization of each paradigm. In an epistemological point of view, the most representative theories or approaches close to each paradigm have been cited, being illustrative rather than exhaustive. In this sense, Reed parses organization theory into six analytical *metanarratives*, in a progressive and historical approach.

Reeds' (1996) first paradigm is *rationality*, illustrated with the phrase "from night watchman state to industrial state." It conceives *organization* as a *rationally constructed* artefact for resolving collective problems of social order and administrative management (p. 29). In other words, organization is conceived as a *tool* or *instrument* for pursuing collective goals through the "design and management of structures" directed toward administering and manipulating organizational behaviour (p. 30). In this rational paradigm, *human beings* are "raw material," transformed by modern organizational technologies into "well ordered, productive members of society" (p. 30). *Management* translates highly contestable, normative precepts into universal, objective, immutable and, hence, unchangeable laws. Therefore, efficiency and effectiveness permeate all, including human beings. In other words, management transforms "an intuitive craft into a codified and analyzable" science (p. 30). Taylorism is "an important component of the philosophical outlook of modern industrial civilization" (p. 29) quite close to the rational paradigm. *Epistemology* is supported by bounded rationality, administrative behaviour and decision-making theories. Strategic analysis inscribes in this way also. This paradigm has been the most dominant in the past and at present.

Reed's (1996) second paradigm is *integration* ("from entrepreneurial capitalism to welfare capitalism"). The ontologies of this paradigm are *organization* conceived as a *social system* that facilitates the integration of individuals into society. *Human beings* are discovered as more social and psychological, that is, rational, emotional, and social rather than only rational, and *management* is reinforced by social engineering and flexible design. *Epistemology* is supported by sociotechnical systems and contingency theories, among others, always in a structural-functionalist and systems approach (pp. 31-32).

Reeds' (1996) third paradigm is *market* ("from managerial capitalism to neo-liberal capitalism"). This paradigm conceptualizes *organization* as a unitary social and moral order in which individual and group interests are fitted and lead by suprahuman and live market forces. *Human beings* are cooperative agents rewarded by material, economic and moral incentives. *Management* leads invisible market forces oriented to visible organizing. *Epistemology* uses agency and firm theories grounded in this paradigm (pp. 33-34).

Reeds' (1996) fourth paradigm is *power* ("from liberal collectivism to bargained corporativism"). In this paradigm, *organization* is conceived as a place of "conflicting interests and values constituted through power struggle" and power is responsible for success and failures in organizations. *Human beings* are immersed in the domination logic as dominant or as dominated, that is, involved in a power game. *Management* is based on episodic, manipulative and hegemonic power using institutional and political discourses. *Epistemology* utilizes Weberian and Foucauldian

approaches widely, and labour-process theory and total quality management emerged from this paradigm (pp. 34-35).

Reeds' (1996) fifth paradigm is *knowledge* ("from industrialism/modernity to post-industrialism/post-modernity") that conceives ontologies as follows: *organization* as "a socially constructed and sustained 'order' necessarily grounded in the localized stocks of knowledge, practical routines and technical devices" (p. 36), that is, as result of "the condensation of local cultures of values, power, rules, discretion and paradox" (Clegg, cited by Reed, 1996, p. 36). The *glocality* (impact globally, act locally) is a common discourse. *Human beings* are the new *skilled workers,* empowered by knowledge but in conflict with management (e.g., computer programmer). *Management* is faced with the challenge of managing empowered knowledge workers as experts without destroying their innovative initiatives in a cultural global/local environment. *Epistemology* favours ethnomethodology, postmodernist, neorationalist, actor-network and poststructuralist approaches (pp. 35-36).

Reeds' (1996) sixth paradigm is *justice* ("from repressive to participatory democracy"). Ontology in this paradigm conceives the *organization* as an institutionalized structure of power and authority surrounding the localized micropractices of organizational members (p. 37), but tending to be a paradoxical and chaotic, but ordered new post-modern organization. *Human beings* are institutionally and organizationally mobilized, but historically and culturally grounded, and professionalism is promoted. *Management* is reinforced by social and economic governance. *Epistemology* utilizes neo-institutionalism and postmodernism intended to address complexity using an inclusive, multi-disciplinary approach. Positivist/constructivist philosophical and epistemological debate occurs (p. 39).

In my opinion, Reed's (1996) framework may be extended to a seventh paradigm: the *human* paradigm. This paradigm may be expressed as *from fragmented life to integrative life.* This paradigm conceives of an *organization* as a social construct and discourse, a place for economic purposes but also for social and personal growth too. In other words, *organizations* are built by human beings for human beings serving humanity, not serving against them. *Human being* includes rational, emotional, sentimental, social, objective, subjective, quantitative, and qualitative, among other complimentary human facets, all in action. *Management* is conceived as paradoxical, favouring innovation, liberty, and commitment. It abandons a fragmentary and disciplinary control paradigm, and business firms turn into real ethical and socially responsible organizations. *Epistemology* is based on multi-disciplinary human sciences.

As I illustrated in the brief review of organization theory, the complexity of the organization is evident when each paradigm is added to the previous one and the organization has been conceived as an object of study much more complex, because previous visions have not been abandoned but have been incorporated into current ones.

SOFTWARE ORGANIZATION: A POST-INDUSTRIAL FACTORY OR A POST-MODERN SHOP?

Software organization or software firm, also known ironically as *software factory*, may be conceived in different ways: (1) a *production factory* of interchangeable parts (McIlroy, 1969), or rational paradigm; (2) complex strategic management and production infrastructure *facilities* (Laporte, Papiccio, & Trudel, 1998, p. 1), or power paradigm; (3) a manufacturing, product development, and automation *flexible factory* (Griss & Wendtzel, 1994, p. 48), or market paradigm; or (4) an *experience factory* (Basili, Caldiera, & Rombach, 2002, p. 8), or knowledge paradigm. The final definitions of software organization are close to the logic of an organization as an evolution

of manufacturing with mass production lines in the rational and mechanistic management paradigm, Taylorian Scientific Management, but they are simplistic because organizations are so much more than production functions alone. The rational approaches adopted only "achieve" descriptions and quantitative calculus, but they are unable to successfully address the complex organizational and management issues involved in software development, because cause-effect schemes are not so clear in practice. In other words, the software organization may be conceived better as a social construct, not a thing that is not governed by linear cause-effect laws but rather by social, non-predictive and irrational organizational behaviour (social process or social interaction) as illustrated by Reed's (1996) paradigm framework and the constructionism approach has proposed (cf. Burr, 2003, p. 1ss; Hibberd, 2005, p. 2ss).

But a clear characterization of the current software organization, adapted in a literary organizational perspective, was depicted in masterfully by Moschedai Ben-Ari (1998). He narrates an imaginary visit to an ancient twenty-first century software factory in the year 2300. The most common characteristics of interest in this discussion are as follows.

First, according to Ben-Ari (1998), the *production model* of software organization is Taylorist, that is, a disciplinary system in a wide sense oriented toward controlling employees, process and product using authoritarian bureaucratic management:

In those pioneering days of the computer industry, there was apparently a strict division between professional engineers who knew how to design and build a computer, and another class of workers who adapted these computers to specific applications. […] They were called 'programmers' or 'software developers.' (p. 89)

The coordinator of the factory […] was usually called 'president' or 'manager,' which were euphe-

mistic terms applied to someone who functioned as an authoritarian dictator of the factory. (p. 90)

Second, Ben-Ari (1998) states that software organization, frequently is immersed in the "high performance culture" based on the cheapest, disciplined, half-educated and inexperienced, but reckless, young workers. The *business model* of software organization has a high-profit, short-term orientation. The productive consequences of this are high turnover rates, skilled-worker "piracy" between firms, the overexploitation and precariousness of the labour workforce, short productive work life, deficient software quality and "mercenary" behaviour, I consider:

Recently discovered historical documents show that the workers were forced to labour for fourteen to sixteen hours a day, six or seven days a week. (Ben-Ari, 1998, p. 90)

The result of using mass [cheapest and disciplined] *labour was that the factory output was extremely high, but since it was produced by half-educated, inexperienced even reckless young workers, it was of such low quality that large numbers of workers were employed fixing flaws in the products.* (p. 91)

Third, the *personal and social impact* exhibits anomie, out of balance, fragmentation and loss of meaning in social, personal and work life (Sievers, 1994, pp. 12-46), as well as work addiction (workaholism):

Not only was this extremely detrimental to their physical health, but therapists have shown that this leads to a complete breakdown of family and community life. Divorce was rampant and children of these workers showed high levels of psychological trauma resulting from parental neglect. (Ben-Ari, 1998, p. 90)

Finally, Ben-Ari describes a *management style* centred on a culture of excellence as a management paradigm facilitating enrollment of new employees and personnel management, but generally causing stress and burn-out:

Forensic psychologists believe that many people attracted to this discipline had infantile personalities, and resisted efforts to place it on a sound economic footing. (Ben-Ari, 1998, p. 89)

One theory holds that a psychological technique called 'brainwashing' was used to convince software factory workers that labour under these conditions was spiritually rewarding and that selective admission to this prestigious profession was a mark of superiority. The theory is plausible, because the alternative that workers voluntarily accepted these conditions is outrageous. (p. 90)

Moschedar Ben-Ari's literary description of software factory, in my opinion, ties into the characteristics of the typical software organization. In some aspects, management style in software organizations is similar to the *psychic management* or *managinary management* (managinary derives from a linguistic contraction of "management" and "imaginary") that was found in France by Aubert and Gaulejac (1993, parts 2-3) and Aubert (1994). This management style gets the psychic energy from its members, until the members burn-out. It occurs in large firms, but frequently also in SMEs. Asterion, who probably was a burned-out software worker when he wrote this message in his blog, illustrates it:

"July 18, 2005
I'm tired.
I'm fed up with my work.
I'm tired of programming like this, patching and tying everything with wire. I'm fed up of everything being for yesterday, everything burning, always urgent. Of programming "as it turns out,"

discarding optimal solutions in favour of those taking less development time, without planning anything. Here [in Argentina] *the expression 'software architect' we've never heard even the name of. Everything is improvised, with more or less degree of luck.*

In our 'software factory' we are all equal. Rotten. And that's the problem. People talk bad about the company, of those leading it, there's bad vibes. There are meetings, comments, coteries. And I'm tired of that climate, tired of being hostage of those rumours of war.

We're like a defeated army, perhaps the 'wasted procession' of which John Dryden spoke.

Our work place is any old thing. It's a house, far from downtown. We are packed like sardines. In the Winter we freeze and in the Summer the opposite. There are too many people together in a very small space.

The worst thing of all is that there is no outlook of change. It's always going to be like this, per secula seculorum, ad nauseam.

All these things, though I don't want them to, affect me. They take away my desire to do things.

[...]

They sent me to work at another company, for several months.

The place is fantastic. It's a modern, spacious office, very well set up.

But what really killed me is the labour climate. People come to work in good mood, awake, and apparently happy with the destiny they were lucky to get.

I have to go. Life doesn't wait." Asterion (2005)

This burn-out phenomenon demonstrates that an organization is a complex social system in which people work, create, desire, love, enjoy and live, but also destroy, hate, suffer and "die" (psychically speaking). When workers enroll in the organization, they interweave their own stories with the story of the organization. This specificity makes each organization unique in its existence and for studying it: history, owner, leadership, entrepreneurship, management, people, production process, work, labour relations and culture, among others. There are no universal recipes for addressing that. The reader can appreciate that the multi-dimensional nature of the organization makes it very complex because it includes aspects such as economics, entrepreneurial aspects, management, work organization, coordination and communication, personnel management, relationship management, politics and sustainability, among others. Next this complexity will be analyzed.

THE COMPLEXITY OF THE SMALL IN SOFTWARE ORGANIZATION

Two important size aspects influencing the organizational complexity are the size of the firm and the size of the workgroup. Categories of *firm size* depend on the research objective but, independently of this, in studying software organizations, one must similarly focus on a measure equivalent to a full-time worker, because personnel turnover is high, among other issues. The appropriate organizational size for software firms is not yet fully addressed and requires further in-depth research. There is no universal classification of firm size. Therefore, the criterion of both the Organisation for Economic Co-operation and Development (OECD) and the European Union may be appropriate. Formally, the definition of small and medium enterprise (SME) is:

non-subsidiary, independent firms which employ fewer than a given number of employees. This number varies across countries. The most frequent upper limit designating an SME is 250 employees, as in the European Union. However some countries set the limit at 200, while the United States considers SME to include firms with fewer than 500 employees. (OECD, 2002, p. 7)

Table 1. SME firm size criteria (Source: European Commission 2005, pp. 13-14)

Enterprise category	Headcount	Turnover	Balance sheet total
Medium	< 250	≤ € 50 million	≤ € 43 million
Small	< 50	≤ € 10 million	≤ € 10 million
Micro	< 10	≤ € 2 million	≤ € 2 million

Throughout the world, SMEs represent a large percentage of enterprises (up to 99%), economic output, employment (up to 70%) and innovation share (up to 60%), and provide flexibility to the economy (OECD, 2002, pp. 7-11). The most important aspect, due to SMEs' economic vulnerability, is financing strategy during start-up, the most vulnerable stage. SME owners appeal to diverse financing sources, such as credit unions, leasing companies, as well as personal and family relations (p. 19).

Small companies differ from large ones in four major aspects: (1) *territorial scope of action and mobility* (small firms concentrate on local markets in contrast to multinational companies (MNC) because of their asymmetric power); (2) *innovation and organizational change* (small firms are important sources of innovation and have innovative advantages in several respects: they spend less on research and development because of their limited available resources); (3) *regulations* (compliance costs are relatively higher for SMEs); and (4) *capital–labour ratio* (SMEs usually require more labour-intensive work, labour productivity tends to be lower and unit labour costs are higher) (Traxler, 2005, p. 300). Due to these differences, it is comprehensible that large firms and small firms may have distinct and even conflicting interests (p. 301). Some precise observations about SME characteristics are necessary: (1) small firms are essentially different, that is, not just smaller versions of large ones (Mugler, 2004, p. 2); (2) overwhelming evidence shows that smaller companies, in general, are not inferior to

larger units on economic performance and firm size (Aiginger & Tichy cited by Traxler, 2005, p. 300); (3) entrepreneurs and entrepreneurship play an important role, and entrepreneurship theory may be an alternative approach for studying SMEs (Mugler, 2004, p. 2); (4) the personality of the entrepreneur is often more critical; and (5) the owner of an SME generally will not replace himself/herself in cases of failure (Mugler, 2004, p. 5). In short, for small firms, four groups of variables play a decisive role: (1) the environment of the firm, (2) the resources of the firm, (3) the personality of the entrepreneur, and (4) the management system adopted (Mugler, 2004, p. 7).

In SMEs, strategy and decision making are wide-ranging. A business owner uses direct observation, oral communication, direct sensing from the social environment (friends, family members, key employees, or quasi-family members), market, partners, and competitors, including professional analysts and consultants (Mugler, 2004, p. 5), among others. Day-to-day activities in the organization differ greatly from those roles, stereotypes, and functions proposed by classic management, as Henry Mintzberg demonstrated. Two famous works caveat the most robust pillars of management, that is, manager's work and decision-making: *The Manager's Job: Folklore and Fact* (Mintzberg, 1975) and *Decision Making: It's Not What You Think* (Mintzberg & Westley, 2001), showing there is not universal truth on managerial roles.

There are few studies on software organizations that study firm size and performance. Carmel and Bird (1997) made a statistical study with a sample of 74 software firms in the business of software package development. The authors classify them as: (1) *embryonic* (1-19 employees), (2) *small* (20-100 employees), and (3) *medium-to-large* (over 100 employees). These authors focused on the organization workgroup and found that only 11 of 74 cases diverge from the "small team" (1-9 employees) and only 5 diverge by more than 50% (larger than 15) (paragraph: Measures). Alfredo Hualde (2004) studied the software industry linked to the *maquila* concept and the off-shore outsourcing phenomenon in Baja California, Mexico. He used a cluster perspective and confirms the small as the most common property, with a percentage of 75% of the sample ranked five employees or less (p. 15).

With regard to *team size*, it is frequently demonstrated that *small teams* of skilled developers can develop innovative complex applications on-time and on-budget, with high levels of quality and customer satisfaction (Carmel & Bird, 1997, paragraph: Team Size & Group Size; Greenfield & Short, 2003, p. 16). Software firms depend on highly skilled individuals, highly integrated and mature teams, and highly capable managers. In Bangalore, a study determined that, in the software industry, the organization's dependency on individuals' capacity is greater and that an organization's competency in the market is determined by the nature of its workforce (Ilavarasan & Sharma, 2003, p. 6).

But, what does small mean? A team size defined as *small* is relative. According to E.F. Schumacher, who popularized the phrase "small is beautiful" in 1973, advocating small teams is a key factor in success and innovation for everything from corporate committees, government units, to technical-design activities (Carmel & Bird, 1997, paragraph: Team Size & Group Size). These authors, in an in-depth study of software firms, coined that *a work team of 10 or above is a violation of the "small is beautiful" rule*. They remark that organization structure, communications and

coordination are a challenge as the organization grows, which has been confirmed by organization theory since the Woodward and Pugh studies in the fifties. Carmel and Bird found that, in all cases, the work teams studies tended to be small in size, following the "small is beautiful" rule. They considered that the best sub team structure and size has not yet been addressed, but frequently find that the rule of thumb is to "split up into sub teams of five plus/minus two" and conclude that this requires more research (Carmel & Bird, 1997, paragraph: From Size to Structure). The reason they argue for the complexity of the organization is intercommunication between team members.

Two basic team structures are common in software organizations: the *permanent team* and the *ad hoc team*. In the *permanent team*, members "are involved throughout the entire development cycle" and may even "see the product through several development cycles." Members are "empowered with decision-making responsibilities" and with "ownership of the product," as a result of members' long tenure and decision-making responsibilities. Such teams generally have a very high level of commitment. On the other hand, in an *ad hoc team* "the project manager may be one of the few people involved throughout the entire development cycle," and other team members "may be involved for short periods, or just briefly every day" like a matrix organization. Because of this flexibility, "managers can optimize personnel assignments and provide more varied and stimulating work to employees." In both permanent and ad hoc teams, the "small is beautiful" rule was observed.

Generally speaking, team boundaries were usually quite clear for smaller teams, but tend to become more ambiguous with larger ones, and these team boundaries were a function of the "style and culture of the firm, the personal proclivities of the team members and of its management" (Carmel & Bird, 1997, paragraph: From Size to Structure). However, concluding that management style and culture are responsible for non-accountability may be problematic and simplistic, I consider. For that reason, it should be considered more carefully.

The final discussion exhibits that a work team or project may be considered as an analysis unit with the appropriate dimensioning because of the fully organizational properties it possesses. In conclusion, optimal team size and optimal organization size have not yet been fully addressed by organization theory. There is no in-depth research on SMEs, then, qualitative case studies looking for detailed descriptions, and explicative analyses are required.

ORGANIZATION DIVERSITY AS A SOURCE OF COMPLEXITY

Diversity is the main characteristic of biological and social life. It provides sustainability to the whole as a live and social ecosystem. In social science, ecological approaches to organization have been developed, too. Although it is not dominant today, the analysis of organizational diversity is based on an ecological concept: *isomorphism* as a process constrainer that forces a unit in a population to resemble other units facing the same environmental conditions (DiMaggio & Powell, 1983, p. 149). In an institutional approach, three general *mechanisms of isomorphism* are conceived: (1) *coercive*, when an organization is compelled to adopt structures or rules, (2) *mimetic*, when one organization copies another, often because of uncertainty, and (3) *normative*, when the organization adopts forms because professionals claim they are superior (pp. 150-154), but in spite of this theoretical isomorphism, in practice, there is huge organizational diversity.

DiMaggio and Powell (1983) argued for three types of *conformity mechanisms*: (1) *structural*, such as institutional rules, government regulation, environmental uncertainty, desire for legitimacy, hiring personnel from successful firms or hiring consultants, and accreditation programs, among others; (2) *procedural*, as many of the "rational

myths," for example, total quality programs, PERT charts becoming standard procedure, and professional groups; and (3) *personnel*, for example, specialized roles filled by certified professionals, hiring of specific types of personnel, licensing or accreditation as "qualified" personnel, certification and educational requirements (pp. 150-154).

ORGANIZATIONAL STRUCTURE AS A SOURCE OF ORGANIZATIONAL COMPLEXITY

Many organizational typologies are used as ideal models, similar to Weberian ideal types (Heckman, 1983, pp. 121-123), for contrasting reality with its ideal model. For example, based on Burns and Stalker's studies on firms in England, organizational literature distinguishes two basic organization structures and two types of management style: *mechanistic* and *organic*. *Mechanistic organizations* are associated with the so-called rational organizations conceived as instrumental and tend to be rigid, formalized, non-specialized, routinized work, undifferentiated horizontally with more hierarchy, among other features. *Mechanistic styles* were found in more stable environments (managers broke down tasks into specializations with precise job descriptions and hierarchical interaction with management). On the other hand, *organic firms* were found in unstable systems where adaptation to their specific context is required. Job roles are redefined continuously, and workers had to perform their jobs using their own knowledge. Communication occurs more laterally than through hierarchical structures. Organic organizations are closer to knowledge organizations, consisting of more flexible, informal, highly specialized, not routinized and creative work with decentralized and flatter structures (Boje, 1999, Table 1). But mechanistic/organic structures are not unique and there is no full consensus.

The most common framework for studying organizational structure, not exempt from criticism, are the *organizational configurations* proposed by Henry Mintzberg (entrepreneurial organization, machine, professional, diversified, innovative or adhocracy, missionary, and political organization). This framework consists of six basic parts and six coordinating mechanisms (Mintzberg, 1979). Mintzberg's configurations should be considered ideal models in a Weberian sense, but empirical research gives us more insight on organizational variety. For example, Aaen, Bøtcher and Mathiassen (1997), after reviewing the organizational structures proposed for software factories based on Mintzberg's model, conclude that the appropriate organizational form for a software firm is the *professional bureaucracy*, in which professional competence is viewed as more important than standardized procedures and advanced technologies (p. 431). Ensmenger (2001b) explored professionalism as a form of predicting the organizational behaviour but his study is not conclusive. In other empirical research, Meijaard, Brand and Mosselman (2005), based on the study of a stratified sample of 1,411 small Dutch firms, found more diversity based on Mintzberg's configuration criteria: (1) entrepreneur with a "submissive" team, (2) co-working boss with an open structure, (3) entrepreneurial team, (4) boss-loose control, (5) boss-tight control, (6) singular structure, (7) u-form, (8) matrix organization, and (9) m-form (pp. 17-18). These organization configurations were constructed based on terms of three-year persistent sales growth performance.

In conclusion, organizational structure is an important feature, but this is generally associated with the formal structure of the organization and it is a partial view of that because organizations are made up of formal and informal structures. A *formal structure* is that in which the social positions and relationships between members have been explicitly specified, and positions are defined independently of the personal characteristics of the participants occupying these positions (Scott, 1992, p. 18). This structure is closer to a mechanistic or bureaucratic organization. The formal structure is formally established by means of the organizational vision, mission, chart, statutes, laws and regulations, policies, procedures and plans that establish and assign authority and resources for completing goals by projects or programs. In short, formal structure is *"how things should be."* The formal structure is useful for planning or other formal procedures, but clearly it does not correspond to reality.

On the other hand, an *informal structure* is the non-written structure built by individual participants or groups that shape ideas, expectations and agendas, and participants and groups bring to them distinct values, interests and abilities (Scott, 1992, p. 54). But, more important, the informal structure is always developed in a parallel manner to the formal one, but differs. It is transformed by asymmetrical power correlations in authority, subordination, insubordination, trust and distrust, among others, in a political manner. The informal structure is called *"how things are."* Every organization really operates by the combination of both formal and informal structures. For example, when the formal structure blocks operations, workers consciously still make decisions and work against the formally established procedures and policies to resolve that contradiction or paralysis.

Of course, the last formal-informal abstraction is an oversimplification of the complex organizational reality because the informal structure is developed at different levels: individual, group and whole organization, involving complex dynamics of economics, labour, power, social, political, affective and psychic relationships and interests that are interwoven among all members, including the owner and the manager. The formal-informal duality is a feature close to human, social, and organizational life, as it was exemplified by Goffman (1993, p. 31) in his work on social performance. This complex structure is manifested in the organizational culture that organization is, not has, as shared practices, beliefs, values, fears, myths, phantasms. This complexity moves organizations toward the simple, mechanistic and predictable production system only operating for profit.

This formal-informal structure has implications for every organization, not only bureaucracies. The most evident implications for software development are important. Now, it is clear that the structure that should be modelled in software is the informal one, because it is the *"how things are"* structure that really operates, but in practice, the requirement analysts not use organization charts and manuals, among other documents (formal organization) as the primary sources for developing a software system in the organization. It was confirmed by IEEE Computer Society (2004, pp. 2-5) in the *Software Engineering Book of Knowledge* (SWEBOK):

"[the] software engineer needs to acquire, or have available, knowledge about the application domain. This enables them to infer tacit knowledge that the stakeholders do not articulate, assess the trade-offs that will be necessary between conflicting requirements, and, sometimes, to act as a 'user' champion." (IEEE Computer Society, 2004, pp. 2-5, emphasis mine)

This confirms that informal structure corresponds to the *tacit knowledge* or *expertise* of the members of the organization which software engineers are urged to assess during requirement elicitation. This knowledge acquisition and transfer as power is disputed by software engineers, software managers and business managers, and is one of the most important sources of conflict between management and software workers. Then, *software* may be conceived in an organizational approach as the partial model of the operative facet of the organization, as the "modern implementation of the rules, policies and business procedures, in a wide sense." (Zavala, 2004, p. 4)

Another implication of this formal-informal structure and dynamics is its universal occurrence. Therefore, is there any guarantee that a small software organization (supposedly formalized by any procedure) really adheres to it during day-to-day work? It is not possible because of cost and practical concerns, I think. Formalization requires an extra effort to maintain the closest relationship between formal and informal procedures, and consumes many of the SME's scarce resources (economic, time and human in nature). Therefore, formalization is the most practical organizing limit.

Formalization derives from the bureaucratic organization theorized in-depth by Max Weber (Miller, 1970, pp. 91-92). Weber found that rules and policies give certainty in behaviour by means of standardization (e.g., diagrams, workflows and organization charts) and behaviour regulation (working and making decisions following formal procedures). Bureaucracy is a rational model, a mechanistic model and a disciplinary system which is predictive, but provokes the so-called "vicious circles" when members use rules to defend themselves against the system and other members as well. In all organizations, members are "obligated," (informally) by their superiors or by situations, to violate formal rules to resolve organizational paralysis. This generates a *paradoxical management* but is tolerated by the hierarchy, always with a discretional and self-convenient basis. This universal violation of formal rules (procedures, policies, structures) is, to an extent, responsible for organization manuals always being outdated. Cornelius Castoriadis, for example, showed notably that "if workers strictly applied the methods and rules of the bureaucratic organization, it wouldn't operate one minute more" (free translation, cited by Enriquez, 1992, p. 129).

Another distinct approach to SMEs is developed by Rosa (2000).

THE ORGANIZATIONAL NATURE OF THE SOFTWARE PRODUCTION PROCESS

Approaches to the software-development process take two opposite postures: software work is routinized or it is not. The first position states that *software work is routinized* like any other traditional manufacturing work by successfully implementing neo-Taylorian principles in the software organization. This view is criticized for its political bias and lack of understanding of the nature of software work (Ilavarasan & Sharma, 2003, p. 1). However, in this approach, routine in software work is attempted by normative isomorphic mechanisms such as standard programming languages, programming, and analysis and design techniques (Unified Modelling Language, UML, for example), certification, training, learning, total quality management models (like Capability Mature Model, CMM and CMM-I, promoted by Software Engineering Institute), process standards (such as ISO 12207, ISO 15504 and others in progress by the Standard International Organisation), and quality standards (such as ISO 9001:2000). Specifically, quality models assume that quality is guaranteed by process and that it is objectively reflected in a quality product, but there are still many unsolved controversial conceptual and practical issues (Hackman & Wageman, 1995; Tuckman, 1994) more clearly in software organization. In spite of this, these models are used as prescriptive organizational models for universal adoption, attempting the standardization sought (Mutafelija & Stromberg, 2003).

This routinized view is called a *software engineering approach* that call for the application of "precise" engineering methodologies and techniques for software development in a "systematic" and "disciplined" manner. However, in day-to-day practice, there are many facts to the contrary. Moreover, not all organizations have adopted these normative models. Microsoft, a large organization, for example, does not adopt many of the structured software engineering practices commonly promoted by organizations like the SEI and ISO (Cusumano & Selby, 1997, p. 52) and many SMEs neither.

Tore Dybå (2001) studied software firms in Norway and concluded that rather than "'best practice' approaches such as the CMM, which rely on a predictable sequence of events," organizational members should favour an organizational culture oriented toward organizational learning based on improvisation, where technical procedures can prosper instead of imitating technical procedures (pp. 259-260). Dybå's conclusion is more important for smaller firms, I consider. In a similar way, the challenge in software organizations is to find ways to improve organizational skills that require firms to balance two seemingly contradictory ends: efficiency and flexibility. This is the conclusion of Aaen, *et al.* (1997, p. 431).

Regarding the implementation of quality systems, a study in Bangalore found that managerial control is not enhanced by quality certification procedures (Ilavarasan & Sharma, 2003, p. 6). Carmen Bueno (2000) used an anthropological approach to study a quality system implantation in a manufacturing plant in Mexico. She discovered that when getting a quality certification becomes a matter of a firm's survival, this goal becomes instrumental and an end-in-itself. Therefore, a certification process becomes a "great theatrical performance" for managers, workers, and auditors, in which everyone acts out his/her own role. In this performance, innovations and non-permitted procedures contravening the certification requirements are intentionally hidden from the auditor's scrutiny. On the other hand, numeric indexes are specified in such a way that they allow for manoeuvring and inventing them (pp. 43-46). As a result, well-filled-in forms, well-calculated numbers and indexes are available, but they become an end-in-themselves and no longer reflect the quality measure they intended to achieve, and the quality system has, in practice, destroyed itself.

The second approach contends that the nature of software work is a more creative, unroutinizable, complex, and intellectual activity than clerical work. In this approach, the software process is defined as mental-intensive labour such that the worker can solve the problem in many possible manners with enough leeway to use his/her creativity and imagination. Software workers clearly are knowledge workers that are not fully differentiated into conception or execution workers, and control over work is distributed among workers and managers not managers alone. In conclusion, software work seems to be unroutinizable at the moment and it will continue to be so for quite a long time (Ilavarasan & Sharma, 2003, pp. 1, 5, 6).

According to Dybå's (2001) conclusive study, it is clear that "organizational issues are as important in firm improvement as technology, if not more so" because *"the large literature on organizational theory, developed in non-software settings, has more relevance to software development than previously been recognized in software engineering"* (p. 269, emphasis added). Dybå provides insight into the most important issue underlying software production: how to improve it. It has yet to be fully addressed. My own hypothesis in this respect is that, in small business, adopting rigid and very quantitative procedures and management models is not recommended. Instead of those, more flexible and qualitative procedures and management models are recommended because they do not destroy the SMEs' competitive advantage centred on flexibility, improvisation, rapid response to the environment and efficient resource allocation, among others. This implies the necessity of a paradigmatic change of management from 'control' to 'that will facilitate learning' (Dybå, 2005, p. 420). Therefore, when adopting a quality system, it should not be an end-in-itself because it destroys itself, subsequently requiring a progressive, real effort to improve all organizational processes, that is, a practical formalization so as to be useful rather than normative, alone,

because this is the real danger of some formalized (bureaucratized) initiatives, I consider.

Finally, the *"software paradox"* shows a contradiction in software organizations because, while the factory assembly line has been automated by "software engineers," ironically, they "have done a good job of automating everyone's work, but their own" (Mahoney, 2004, p. 15). This is relatively constant in many software organizations and it makes the software organization closer to a post-modern shop than a post-modern organization.

MAIN THRUST OF THE CHAPTER

Issues, Controversies, Problems

Management: A Management Paradigm in Crisis

During the sixties, the mass-production paradigm or the so-called *Fordist production system* was on a rise throughout the world. So it is understandable that, since the *NATO Software Engineering Conference* in Garmisch in 1968, Taylor's Scientific Management basic principles have been adopted as a management paradigm for the incipient software industry (Mahoney, 1990, p. 329). Since that time, it has been attractive to have an automated software factory with production lines and standardized and interchangeable software components, including interchangeable standardized workers as another production factor. For example, M.D. McIlroy's "mass-produced software" factory was considered the software factory on the other side of the Industrial Revolution (p. 331).

According to Frederick W. Taylor, the father of the Scientific Management the primary obligation of that was to determine the scientific basis of the task to be accomplished, based on four main duties:

- First. To develop a science for each element of a man's work, replacing the old rule-of-thumb method. The famous *one best way* acquired by management up to that point.
- Second. Scientifically select and then train, teach and develop the work force, instead of doing as in the past, when each one chose his own work and taught himself as best he could.
- Third. Heartily cooperate with the men so as to insure all the work being done in accordance with the principles of the science that have been developed.
- Fourth. There is an almost equal division of the work and the responsibility between the management and the workmen, the famous 'fifty-fifty' management rule. The *management takes over all work* for which they are better fitted than the workmen, while in the past almost all of the work and the greater part of the responsibility were thrown upon the men. (Mahoney, 2004, pp. 13, 14).

In addition, Taylor's system conceives monetary incentives only as a fixed and variable wage because "[h]igh wages give the workmen the spur needed to induce them to quit loafing on their jobs and to turn out more goods. The wage systems [...] usually consists of two parts: a base wage and a bonus. The base wage is customarily the same as the prevailing rate for the work in the community, while the bonus is a percentage of the base" (Keir, 1918, p. 528). Simplified, Scientific Management is the *one best way* of doing work. This implementation of this management system is called *Taylorism* and, ever since it came out, it has being criticized as ideologically biased, unscientific but scientific-discourse justified, extremely and mechanistic instrumented, not well-suited for universal application, and as a dehumanized production system. But despite this, Taylorism continues to fascinate and influence day-to-day management. Taylor's ideas persist as the roots of management theories and practice.

At present, it is clear that since sixties, style management has undergone its so-called fashions (Abrahamson, 1991, p. 255), fads (Clarke & Clegg, 1998, pp. 15-19) and "silver bullets" (Brooks, 1995, pp. 179-226). For example, Business Process Reengineering (BPR) and TQM had been become management fads (Miller & Hartwick, 2002, p. 26; Stewart, 2006, p. 84; Turner & Müller, 2003, p. 4) and did not fulfil their promise of providing a solution for predictive and successful management. In spite of failure in practice and criticism of the concepts underlying them (e.g., Hackman & Wageman, 1995; Tuckman, 1994), management fads still continue to be promoted, trying to prove their friendliness. Unfortunately, such miraculous solutions do not exist.

In the so called, humanist management, a different perspective than traditional management, Omar Aktouf promoted the idea that, in the ever-changing world of today, a new management type is needed which undertakes the challenge of utilizing the creative energy of all members of an organization, rather than focusing on the disciplinary aspects of behaviour on the job.

Survival in the future is to be able to mobilize, to the benefit of the organization, all intelligence, all brains and all energy, taking care of the environment to the maximum. It is to be able to achieve everyone working for himself and adopting an attitude of constant improvement, serenely, if possible, enthusiastically. And that can only be obtained by a proper climate, with job security, with an effective sharing of luck, good or bad. (Aktouf, 1998, p. 604, free translation)

An example of these new approaches distinct than Taylorist ones, appears in the work *Le management ludique: Jouer et travailler chez UbiSoft* [*Playful Management: Play and Work at UbiSoft*], discovered by Laurent Simon in a software organization in Montreal. He did not use a software engineering focus, but rather one of social sciences. Specifically, he used ethnomethodology and participant observation to understand what he was observing and human sciences to interpret it. He made an in-depth observation and description of the software-game work process, studying managers and workers in action. Here are some of his illustrative conclusions:

The project is not a game, which goes without saying, but its structure, so similar to the structure of the game, can certainly welcome phenomena of a ludic type. (Simon, 2002, p. 387)

Finally, the will to create the capacity to auto-organize itself could be put effectively in parallel with the need to create and maintain a world environment "sufficiently good" that allows everyone to experiment, create and express themselves. (p. 392)

One of the most important consequences of this management approach is the possibility of fully developing creativity, and a conscious and voluntary commitment to work and a management conception:

The ludic logic of the légaliberté opens the way of a total, conscious and voluntary engagement in the double action of the possibility of a serene réflexivité on the value and the relevance of the action. The ludic conception of work also lends the activity a human value oft overlooked: one commits oneself because one wants to, because one can express itself and grow while learning, because one can hope and be oneself. (Simon, 2002, p. 397)

This ludic reading of the organization is not without consequence on management. It clears on a necessary recognition of the 'constructed' and 'situated' character of the organized activity, on a disclosure of its rules. If the game is product of the rule, to play the game well requires a good knowledge of the real rule, but especially the spirit of the game implies consenting to the game.

[...]The game to which one is obliged to play loses its character of game. Ludic liberty, supposes an engagement knowingly and voluntarily agree to, the sole guarantor of the motivation to play and to play well. (p. 406)

In conclusion, this playful management approach transforms bureaucratic control into innovative and creative committed work, giving meaning to work and life-sense itself for workers and managers.

Lethbridge, Sim and Singer (2005), recently made a comprehensive compilation of techniques for studying software engineers, many of which were qualitative in nature. Similarly, a group of European researchers found evidence that main issues in software organizations are organizational in nature, not technical. A review of their research topics yields illustrative: improvisation (Dybå, 2000), empirical knowledge, evidence-based software engineering (Dybå, Kitchenham & Jorgensen, 2005), and culture and organizational aspects (Dybå, 2002, 2003). Sharp and Robinson (2004), for example, did *An Ethnographic Study of XP Practice* in the United Kingdom, attempting to be explicative. These authors use quantitative but predominantly qualitative observations based on knowledge management, learning organization and other organizational related theories. Much of this research is far removed from the dominant positivist software engineering approach which considers these "related disciplines" unacceptable because they are not quantitative. Simon's work clearly showed the power of social-science interpretive approaches and in-depth qualitative case studies as methodologies for studying software organizations and for management theorizing. They favour theorization because they are based on a set of richly detailed empirical observations. Unfortunately, often, both social-science and qualitative observations had been excluded by rational approaches, accusing them of being invalid and unscientific because of their distinct nature.

Software Project Management: A Social Constructivism Approach Required?

For software production, project management is the concrete exercise of management and it is the most difficult and problematic area of software engineering. It remits us to the infamous "software crisis" and to the project-failure phenomenon (Zavala, 2004, pp. 7-11). According to Harrison and Winch (cited by Hodgson, 2004, p. 85), the use of project management models and techniques has proliferated since they came into popularity in the late fifties following their use in high-profile technical endeavours such as the Manhattan Project and the Apollo space programmes. In this context, I consider that the adoption of software engineering as a project-oriented discipline at the Garmisch Conference in 1968 is no surprise.

Technically speaking, *project management* is "the application of knowledge, skills, tools and techniques to project activities to meet project requirements," accomplished through the application and integration of project-management processes of "initiating, planning, executing, monitoring and controlling, and closing" (Project Management Institute [PMI], 2004, p. 8). Also stated is that the project manager, in collaboration with the project team, is responsible for determining the appropriate rigor for each process and technique (p. 37). Project management promises frameworks and management techniques (Hodgson, 2004, p. 85) for *coping with technical and managerial challenges*, but most important, it offers *to predict and control people behaviour* by means of a strong bureaucratic control system (p. 88).

Project management draws upon the rhetoric of empowerment, autonomy and self-reliance, central to post-bureaucratic organizational discourse but, at the same time, immersed in a traditional bureaucratic essence producing much conflict. Project management is rooted in Taylorian Scientific Management and Fayolian administrative process, the hardest management approaches.

Turner and Müller proposed conceiving *project* as a *temporary organization*. They base this on the assumption that project pursues the organization's objectives and is managed by an opportunistic manager in conflict with the principal (Turner & Müller, 2003, p. 3). This instrumental approach is based on *agency theory* dating from the seventies, which is nowadays considered incomplete. Agency theory, rooted in the rational paradigm, is criticized because it is not be fully appropriate for addressing the complexity of organization. Of course, project management may be conceived as a temporary organization similar in complexity to every organization, with additional characteristics such as uncertainty, urgency, risk and highly dependent on the work team, manager and management. To this end, a more explicative and open organizational approach than agency theory is required. For example, I used organizational analysis in a socioeconomic approach to study the information technology department in a municipality in Mexico, with good results (Zavala, 2006).

"Software crisis," linked to software-project failure, has many justifications: (1) not carrying out a financial feasibility study, benefits being overestimated, and costs and time underestimated, frequently without solid bases for estimating (Haigh, 2001, pp. 79, 80, 89), (2) others (organizational causes) (Pinto & Mantel, 1990), (3) "software crisis" as a crisis of programming labour (Ensmenger & Aspray, 2000, p. 140), and (4) "software crisis" as a management crisis (Ensmenger, 2001a, p. 30).

Last new position that argues that "software crisis" is a management crisis is based on the fact that the "software crisis" solution most frequently recommended by managers is the elimination of rule-of-thumb methods (i.e., the old-time "black art of programming" or the "tacit knowledge" in present-day managerial discourse), among other principles of Scientific Management of an earlier era (Ensmenger, 2001a, p. 99). The author considers that real concern about "software crisis" was the emergence of *the programmer as a new uncontrolled privileged knowledge worker.* Therefore, *"software crisis" is a management crisis* because of its inability to manage traditionally in a non-traditional industry.

"The apparent unwillingness of programmers to abandon the 'black art of programming' for the 'science' of software engineering was interpreted as a deliberate affront to managerial authority [...] The reinterpretation of the software crisis as a product of poor programming technique and insufficient managerial controls suggested that the software industry, like the more traditional manufacturing industries of the early twentieth century, was drastically in need of a managerial and technical overhaul." (Ensmenger, 2001a, p. 30)

The promised "scientific" managerial recipes of Scientific Management have become very attractive to software management because, as Dick H. Brandon pointed out, "the anarchic nature of programming meant that *management had to depend on the workers* to determine the pace of a project and that the insatiable market for programmers meant that *management had little control at all over the wage structure*" (cited by Mahoney, 1990, p. 333, emphasis added). The keyword in management has been *discipline* and the promise has been "to achieve managerial control over product, process and worker" (*idem*).

By now, the failure of project management to establish standards for selecting and training programmers is legendary. Despite Taylor insisting productivity was a 50/50 proportion, management played its role through selection, training, and supplying tools and materials relatively well. From the sixties to now, the science of management (whatever that might be) has not been able to supply what the science of computing (if there be such) had failed to establish so far, called a scientific basis of software production. (Mahoney, 1990, p. 333)

I also agree with Ensmenger that, despite more than four decades of managers having tried to settle down and rationalize software development as traditional manufacturing, developing software remains a distinctively craft-oriented and idiosyncratic discipline. Nevertheless, complaints about "the quality and reliability of software still plague software developers" and the "rhetoric of crisis continues to dominate discussions about the health and future of the industry" (Ensmenger, 2003, p. 174). In my opinion, software engineering is still in crisis but as a discipline, because of its management part.

Criticism of project management and of the management theory underlying it and its practice has occurred recently. Growing criticism of the intellectual and philosophical foundations of the discipline are rarely made explicit in project-management textbooks and publications (for example, Thayer (1997) is free of that) (Winter & Smith, 2006, p. 15), but are coming out. According to Mark Winter and Charles Smith, from the conclusions to *Rethinking Project Management EPSRC Network 2004-2006 Conference* was criticized: (1) that "conventional project management theory remains wedded to the epistemological and ontological foundations of the 1950s-1960s, with *its emphasis on machine-like conceptions of organizations and projects* (for example, Thayer, 1997), (2) that realistic assumptions about 'organisations' and 'projects' as entities existing 'out there' independently of the people involved" (*idem*). For these authors, three paradigmatic changes were considered relevant at this conference:

1. *Projects as social processes,* not mechanical ones, toward "concepts and images which focus on social interaction among people, [...] the flux of events and human action, and the framing of projects... within an array of social agenda, practices, stakeholder relations, politics and power." (Winter & Smith, 2006, p. 5).

2. *A multidisciplinary approach*, not isolated, toward "concepts and approaches which facilitate: broader and ongoing conceptualization of projects as being multidisciplinary, having multiple purposes, not always predefined, but permeable, contestable and open to renegotiation throughout" *(idem)*.

3. *A reflexive practitioner*, not a narrow one, toward "learning and development which facilitates the development of reflexive practitioners who can learn, operate and adapt effectively in complex project environments, through experience, intuition and the pragmatic application of theory in practice" *(idem)*.

Surprisingly, previous recommendations by project management practitioners and theorists are oriented toward a reflective practitioner, only possible with broad knowledge and experience, as Aktouf (1998, p. 607) suggested, and far from the classic Master's in Business Administration (MBA) curriculum, as Stewart proposed (2006, pp. 86-87). The final criticism is against the rational paradigm underlying project management from a clear social constructivism or interpretive position, not explicitly assumed. This constitutes a change in discourse that facilitates a breakdown in its traditional position and implicitly proposes a paradigm change, in my opinion. This opens up project management to those theoretically, practically and ideologically "related disciplines" supporting a distinct discourse. *The most important consequence of that is the emergence of a necessary paradigmatic change in management, project management and software engineering*, I consider.

Now it is the moment to analyze software engineering as a discipline in crisis.

Software Engineering: A Discipline in Crisis Itself

Because of the "software crisis," it was argued that a new discipline for solving problems was needed when software engineering was invented in 1968:

In the late 1960s, in the wake of the 1968 NATO Conference, a new model for situating the pro-fessional programmer was invented. Software engineering emerged as a compelling solution to the software crisis in part because it was flexible enough to appeal to a wide variety of computing practitioners. (Ensmenger, 2001a, p. 30, emphasis added)

The term *software engineering* was indeed provocative, if only because it left all the crucial terms undefined (Mahoney, 2004, p. 9; Naur & Randell, 1969, p. 13). As conference organizers suggested, the solution to the "software crisis" was to convert the "black art" of programming (the programmer's tacit knowledge) into science, similar to what Scientific Management supposedly did, now with a worker's knowledge. Central to this "scientific" approach was programming activity. Software engineering's offer was very attractive because it "seemed to offer something to everyone: standards, quality, academic respectability, status and autonomy" (Ensmenger, 2001a, p. 31), besides the possibility of controlling the development process when the laws of causation were discovered. Finally, the hoped-for "silver bullet" was invented, but that promise has not come through:

[...] for software developers to adopt 'the types of theoretical foundations and practical disciplines that are traditional in the established branches of engineering'. In the interest of efficient software manufacturing, the "black art" of programming had to make way for the "science" of software engineering. (Ensmenger, 2003, p. 165)

Since the early days, software engineering was established as a goal to achieve (Ludewig, 1996, p. 25), but not as a legitimization and institutionalization of a genuine professional practice, because it lacked of widely accepted theory, practices and professional culture, among others. This was demonstrated by the failed second and last NATO Software Engineering International Conference held in Rome in 1969. Some of that criticism of software engineering persists until today.

Results from the Garmisch Conference were determinant in both institutionalizing software engineering as a discipline during the seventies and in creating conditions for *a new stream of thinking* oriented toward *discovering those principles*. It is supposed that this new discipline should exist, but was never defined, nor posited as such, ever since it was born in 1968 until 1976. Since those early days, all these efforts have been oriented by managerial goals, but dressed in engineering discourse. In agreement with Nathan L. Ensmenger, a better approach to understanding software-engineering is to consider it a *movement*, "to better understand why it *succeeded* (*on a rhetorical level, at least, if not in actual practice*) where other systems and methodologies have failed miserably" (Ensmenger, 2001a, p. 30, emphasis added).

Thinking about the invention of a discipline as a series of interconnected social and political negotiations, rather than an isolated technical decision about the "one best way" to develop software components*, provides an essential link between internal developments in information technology and their larger social and historical context.* (Ensmenger, 2001a, p. 30, emphasis added)

A clear example of these political negotiations is the current "marriage and divorce" between computer science and software engineering as disciplines, as suggested by academicians and practitioners (Denning, 1998; Parnas, 1998).

Since the Garmisch Conference, both software engineering and management are looking for a miraculous solution that will finally resolve both the inherent complexity of software itself and of its production, and that will permit managing them.

In Fred Brooks' words, they are looking for the "silver bullet" to "kill the monster."

Of all the monsters who fill the nightmares of our folklore, none terrify more than werewolves, because they transform unexpectedly from the familiar into horrors. For these, we seek bullets of silver that can magically lay them to rest. The familiar software project has something of this character (at least as seen by the non-technical manager), usually innocent and straightforward, but capable of becoming a monster of missed schedules, blown budgets, and flawed products. So we hear desperate cries for a silver bullet, something to make software costs drop as rapidly as computer hardware costs do. (Brooks, 1995, pp. 180-181)

Software engineering emerged at Garmisch as the silver bullet for the "software crisis". But it is not a problem of shortcoming in computer science, technology or software innovation, but rather a managerial one. In 1986, Brooks stated that "… as we look to the horizon of a decade hence, we see no silver bullet" concluding that "*[t]here is no single development*, in either *technology* or *management technique*, which by itself promises even one order-of-magnitude improvement in productivity, in reliability, in simplicity" (Brooks, 1995, p. 181, emphasis added). This last sentence was valid for the decade between 1986 and 1995, as predicted, but, incredibly, it continues being valid for the two decades even to 2006. *Perhaps, it continues being valid because the management or social dimensions are the most complex issues in software production,* I would think. This confirms once again that the "software crisis" is one of management.

The official technical definition of *software engineering* states that it is "(1) The application of a *systematic*, *disciplined*, *quantifiable* approach to the development, operation, and maintenance of software; that is, the application of engineering to software. (2) The study of approaches as in (1)" (IEEE Computer Society, 2004, p. 1-1; Institute of Electrical and Electronic Engineers, 1990, p. 67, emphasis added). Other definitions are similar. Barry Boehm proposed that formal definition of software engineering in 1976; and more recently, in his paper *A View of 20th and 21st Century Software Engineering in the ICSE '06 Conference* (Boehm, 2006), he upholds his same 30 year-old position. Since the 1968 NATO Conference, surprisingly, definition and discourse has not budged from its proclaimed (but not fully demonstrated) 'systematic', 'disciplined' and 'quantitative' intention, notwithstanding empirical evidences to the contrary (Lewerentz & Rust, 2000; Ludewig, 1996; Smith & McKee, 2001).

Although Bohem had said he himself is convinced that software engineering is and should continue being an engineering discipline, he considered it as "distinct" one, because its features definitively identify it as *a multidisciplinary discipline* which is oriented toward people. That "implies that the *relevant sciences* include the behavioural sciences, management sciences, and economics, as well as computer science" (Boehm, 2006, p. 12). Unfortunately, in practice, many of these "related" or "relevant" disciplines are not incorporated into software engineering, because many of them are not considered to be 'systematic', 'disciplined' and 'quantitative' as software engineering *pretends to be* and because they have an opposing epistemological and ontological discourse, definitively I consider. For example, in the Software Engineering Body of Knowledge (SWE-BOK), in the chapter on Software Requirements (IEEE Computer Society, 2004, chapter 2), there is reference to them. They erroneously, continue being disciplines "related to" not "part of" software engineering. When they *are* incorporated, it is partially, only if they do not contravene the software engineering's central discourse. If they do, they are ignored. Finally, simply, I ask: why, are many of these "related disciplines" more social than technical in nature? Why would they have to

be 'systematic', 'disciplined' and 'quantitative' if they deal with different study objects?

As previously shown, the "software crisis" was a rhetorical term used by proponents at the Garmisch Conference to interest the audience in the emerging software industry (Naur & Randell, 1969, p. 13). Since they emerged, data and statistics (and managerial discourse) have tried to support this catastrophic vision, but they are not very conclusive (Glass, 2006, p. 16). Today, it is wiser to consider the "software crisis" as an institutionalized myth (a common term used in neo-institutional analysis of organizations) subsuming the management crisis. This permits reinforcing both software engineering and management discourses urging the industrialization (in the manufacturing sense) of software production. However, software engineering is trapped in management (and software engineering) fads and fashions, too as management is.

Software engineering as discipline has being characterized by an unusual discursive stability, trying to consolidate itself since it emerged some forty years ago. This, from a Kuhnian perspective, may be interpreted as a paradigmatic hegemony trapped in its own paradigmatic myth: the "software crisis" and its 'systematic', 'disciplined' and 'quantitative' terms in its definition. So, it is pertinent to explore software engineering and its foundation so as to reinterpret them, because perhaps software engineering is considered improperly.

Next I shall analyze those facts associated with present-day software engineering.

- *Fact 1. The IT Paradox is a symptom of the failure of software engineering.* The so-called *Information Technology Paradox (IT Paradox)* has shown that organization productivity is not caused solely by information technology, as the data partially supports, except for large companies (Brynjolfsson, 1994; Brynjolfsson & Hitt, 2000, p. 45, 2003).

- *Fact 2. Software engineering as defined today has failed, because it has no clear theoretical roots.* First, we need a theory explaining software development more universally, not as exceptions valid only in particular firms. Second, software engineering and computer science are competing for ownership of the theoretical foundation, and this has led to an uncomfortable relationship between them. Third, perhaps it is time to recognize the pertinence of agreeing that so-called bodies of knowledge (BoK), such as Software Engineering Body of Knowledge (SWEBOK), are *ideal models* (in a Weberian sense) and they should be used as such, instead of being used for normative ends, as they are today. Fourth, radical criticism is emerging, questioning the project management epistemological and ontological foundations underlying software engineering (Winter & Smith, 2006, p. 5). This is the first open criticism of the project management paradigm from within the field in an international setting.

- *Fact 3. Disciplines related to software engineering are excluded.* In spite of the wide recognition of the need for a multidisciplinary approach to be successful in software engineering, in practice, many of those "related" or "relevant" disciplines are not incorporated, for example, they are not in the Software Requirements chapter in SWEBOK (IEEE Computer Society, 2004, chapter 2). Recently in Europe, a research current has emerged which is evidencing that classical software engineering approaches ones are not better for studying software development and software organizations. Tore Dybå is a good example of using a hard quantitative approach, combined with a qualitative one, in an organization learning approach (Dybå, 2001).

- *Fact 4. The institutionalization of software engineering does not mean a mature discipline.* SWEBOK justifies "unmistakable trends indicating an increasing level of maturity"

with the increasing of software engineering education programs at universities, accreditation boards, professional societies, quality formal models and professional licensing, but this only confirms that an institutionalization process is underway, not disciplinary maturity. The application of a *systematic, disciplined, quantifiable* approach to the development, operation and maintenance of software is far from what practitioners really do around the world.

- *Fact 5. Software engineering is not engineering as such.* Fred Brooks is overwhelming when he proposes the essential nature of software (their conceptual, abstract construct) (Brooks, 1995, p. 199) and he declares that no software engineering or management technique would solve it. Neither client nor software analyst knows how to understand and tame the "beast" when organization becomes software. Both managers and software professionals are looking for the miraculous "silver bullet," but, unfortunately, all these initiatives have led to business fads marked for failure because the organizational nature of software in abstraction and production is not considered (Winter & Smith, 2006, p. 5). Software abstracts the operation in the organization, but it is so complex. Brooks (1995, p. 199) reveals a truth that many of us are very well aware of: clients do not know what they want, but software analysts do not comprehend the complex nature of the organization being modelled, neither do software requirements and software design, the most difficult key areas. From the perspective of software production process, there is broad consensus that it is not routine, but rather a creative process based on technical, business and managerial knowledge not easily formalized like some crafts that have become automated industrial processes.

- *Fact 6. Traditional management has failed to support software engineering.* Scientific

Management sounded so promising because of its supposed 'scientific' and 'disciplinary' characteristics for controlling "the anarchic and non disciplined nature" of programmers. Unfortunately, management has not been able to discover, as promised, a magic formula for achieving managerial control over product and development process. It does not exist, as Fred Brooks remarked twenty years ago. In a more critical sense, management is a myth (Stewart, 2006). Finally, some paradigmatic approaches appeared such as *management ludique* (Simon, 2002) and humanist management (Aktouf, 1998).

SOLUTIONS AND RECOMMENDATIONS

Software Engineering Requires a Paradigm Change

Considering the preceding, there is much evidence pointing to the fact that software engineering, as currently defined, is partially mistaken in its definition, tools and techniques and, far from being a type of engineering in the style of classical engineering. Ever since software engineering was invented, it has been unable to satisfactorily address its central objective: predict the software production process. The lack of professionalism in software engineering, as explored in-depth by Ensmenger (2001b), but it is not the problem, rather: "*software engineering has not progressed far beyond its roots*" (Mahoney, 1990, p. 335). Bound to its definition and perhaps the development of software engineering, it is not an engineering discipline, but a management one. This hypothesis is appropriate because software production is close to an organizational phenomenon and social in nature, and therefore, the theoretical and practical has not been fully addressed by the current software engineering approach. *Software engineering is an exhausted discipline* due to its reductionist conception, because the complexity of reality is huge compared to its narrow concepts, tools and techniques. It is time to reconsider the evidence emerging, which tries to support the wisdom of a more multidisciplinary approach, rather than its rigid 'systematic,' 'disciplined' and 'quantitative' one.

Software engineering needs a revolution (in the Kuhnian sense) that will achieve a transformation of the discipline itself and that develops a theoretical, practical, reality-based body of knowledge applicable to large software organizations and to small ones. We cannot continue looking for the "silver bullet," hoping that, some day in the future, miraculously, it will adapt reality to theory. We should embrace a different paradigm, conceived in short as those values, beliefs and techniques shared by the scientific community, in Kuhn words (Kuhn, 1971, chapter I), a new scientific theory explaining current reality should being created.

Experiments validating current theory are not possible because they are social experiments in nature and are "not fully controllable." But, each case, each organization is a live experiment itself and an opportunity for studying the concrete reality that will possibly permit building the respective explanatory theory. We should create a theory explaining current reality, not the one that we want or speculate should be. Therefore, we should be looking for what software engineering practitioners really do, just as Thomas S. Kuhn did when he proposed the decisive role of science history in formulating an adequate concept of science by looking at what scientists (software engineering theoreticians and practitioners, in our context) do, rather than what they say they do (*idem*).

I consider that an answer to that complexity, necessarily points to the roots of software engineering, to its definition, because perhaps it would be another kind of discipline, not necessarily engineering in nature and its current conceptual framework, methodologies and tools are inappropriate. If software engineering as a discipline does not open up to this discussion, it will possibly be replaced by those "related disciplines" that demonstrate understanding and solving the object of study better than a discipline that promised and failed to solve something. Such paradigm change is a necessity, not a whim. This change implies that the software engineering movement will restructure itself, based on changing its basic paradigms, scope, practices and institutionalization, as well as on a new discourse, practice and education.

Complementing and going beyond Kuhn, Gergen (1996, chapter 1), in a Social Constructionism approach, provides a useful analytic framework for conceiving paradigmatic change. His model of nucleus of intelligibility has three elements: (1) *theory,* conceived as the explicit version of the world, that is to say, "what is it?" (2) *method,* providing us tools to learn about this socially constructed world, and (3) *metatheory,* basic assumptions on the nature of the knowledge on which the whole model rests. The most important consequence of Gergen's framework is to consider that adopting a new paradigm necessarily requires abandoning the current one, looking for another discourse and using different arguments. Then, from outside, criticize and question the abandoned paradigm, make new formulations and promote the emergence and eventual adoption of the new paradigm. However, this transformation occurs only if those three elements of the nucleus of intelligibility (theory, methodology and metatheory) change. If they do not, you did not leave the initial paradigm behind.

Social constructionism is based on the following suppositions: (1) terms used to define the world are not provided by the object itself, neither are they part of things, but are the product of agreements or naming them, privileging certain interpretations and not others (Gergen, 1996, p. 72); (2) terms used to describe the world and ourselves are the result of the social interaction of people living in historically and culturally located communities (p.

73); (3) the degree to which a way of naming the world remains over the time does not depend on its empirical capacities or its empirical strength, but on the vicissitudes of the social and historical process (p. 75); (4) concepts do not have meaning in and of themselves, their meanings are derived from language games and their associated rules (p. 76); (5) the unique way in which we understand the world is to acquire another conceptual framework because it is sole possibility of seeing something different from what we are accustomed to seeing, understanding and naming in that new reference system (p. 78).

Therefore, I propose that paradigm change in software engineering could be made using one of four alternatives:

1. *Giving more emphasis to "related disciplines"* as "part-of" its own body of knowledge, (including organization studies, as a central one), being "tolerant" of discursive contradictions, because their not 'systematic', 'disciplined' and 'quantitative' definition and contradictions with. If not, it will prolong the current state of crisis without resolving it. If software engineering, as a discipline does not open up to this discussion, it may be replaced by those "related disciplines" that prove to understand and solve the object of study better than software engineering promised and failed.

2. *Splitting its present range* into two complimentary, well-known disciplines. The first is *software engineering,* but redefined as a technical discipline, focusing on the technical aspects of software programming and replacing current 'systematic', 'disciplined' and 'quantitative' features with broader "scientific" far beyond any positivist or post-positivist classic approach. The second discipline might be *software management* or *software sociology,* focusing on the management, organizational and social aspects of software production conceived as a multidisciplinary and multiparadigmatic field. It focuses on the

software production process, embracing all necessary, present-day "related disciplines" such as management, linguistics, anthropology, sociology, psychology, psychoanalysis, labour studies, cultural studies, organization studies, and science and technology studies, among others. With this division, software analysis and design could be redefined into two separate, but complimentary, areas: one defined by business requirements and another by software modelling.

3. *Creating a new discipline: software sociology.* If software engineering does not choose either of the last two options, then the unique solution is to create a new discipline that focuses on studying software as social fact. This discipline, necessarily multidisciplinary and multiparadigmatic in approach, would address the implied organizational complexity. The discipline would exclude technical aspects of software production, approaching it in a social, organizational and management manner, incorporating whatever disciplines it needs for an adequate study and understanding of that so complex object of study. Quantitative and qualitative approaches are accepted as complimentary support.

My conclusion is clear. Software engineering is in crisis principally because the object of study is too complex to be approached with the current narrow mechanical conception of organizations, software production and software itself. Software engineering is trapped by its own definition (its management component and its disagreement with computer science) and by its myths ("software crisis" as management crisis and the "software factory" as a non traditional factory but managed using a traditional approach), but it is fundamentally trapped by its own underlying paradigm: Scientific Management. Presently, it is clearly accepted that such a vision is insufficient. Software engineering as a discipline has succumbed to managerial whim and to the ac-

celerated inertia of business, based on a financial logic of the short term, competition and economic war making economic and social progress unsustainable. I am not against management, rather for its transformation toward something that allows profit, but at same time permits development of the organization, employees and society in which it operates. In other words, management should turn into administration and serve humanity, not the other way around.

FRAMEWORK FOR SOFTWARE ORGANIZATIONAL ANALYSIS

Using Gergen's (1996) analytic scheme, I assumed the pertinence of using social constructionism as the metatheory, permitting to state basic assumptions for the conception of the world and the way of approaching it. The ontology of organization used in this framework is organization as action, as a verb, as a process of organizing, as a discourse, as Clegg and Hardy (1996, p. 3) suggested. I use an organizational change epistemology using process studies as narratives of actions and activities by which collective endeavours unfold, as Van de Ven and Poole (2005, p. 1387) and Tsoukas and Hatch (2001, pp. 984-985, 996-1007) suggested. In this sense, narratives are our main resource for studying organization.

Organizational analysis should be conducted without any prior hypothesis to be tested, but the object of study (the software organization) should be constructed progressively during social interaction between organization members and researcher. Therefore, progressive and cumulative research is pertinent, in an attempt to discover regularities, contradictions, events, sequences and actors by opposing all points of view, from owner, administrative workers to base workers.

In practice, *ethnomethodology* and *participant observation* would be used when possible, trying to observe and describe organization as detailed as possible. At same time, superficial and in-depth interviews of representative individuals in a semi-structured approach, oriented toward the subjects in question around in a *life-story* approach (Bertaux & Singly, 1997, pp. 31-50), are appropriate. In general, interviews explore meanings involving personal, academic and labour trajectories, engagement and identity as a member of a company, and as participant in work activities and projects; immediate and midterm expectations regarding work and profession; the opinions of bosses and owners regarding the problems and solutions proposed, reasons and causes why someone is leaving the company. We should encourage individuals to narrate each topic, looking for places, times, events, sequences, actors and situations as precisely as possible. Therefore, we articulate these distinct individual narratives or life-stories, each explaining its own point of view or position, but the stories are interwoven in agreements and disagreements. A sequential reconstruction of organization history, looking for events that shaped the present-day organization, is suggested.

Accordingly, I had proposed three conceptual tools for analyzing software organizations in an organization studies approach. The *first conceptual tool* is a *typology for classifying software organizations*. Jorge Carrillo and Arturo Lara, as well as Arturo Hualde, proposed that *maquiladoras* (industrial in-bond companies near Mexico's northern border) evolve through a generational typology based on Weberian ideal types. Each category has been defined as a "generation" from first to fourth. They considered the next generation to be more competitive than the previous one (Carrillo & Lara, 2005, pp. 7-12; Hualde, 2003). Carrillo and Lara considered an ideal work-evolution process to be as follows: *Manual Work → Rational Work → Creative Work → Not Material Work - Coordination Work* (Carrillo & Lara, 2005, p. 29). Similar to *maquiladoras*, I consider that software organizations may develop these, but there is no research on this yet. Software organizations support industrial firms that are adopting

information technology for business operations. There is even a large Mexican software company that identifies itself as a *software maquiladora* and international advocates conceive software development as *maquila* (i.e., manufacturing) (Hualde, 2004, p. 19; Sinclair, 2003) because it involves the off-shore software business.

Considering Carrillo and Lara's typology, software organizations could not be fully classified into any of the four *maquiladora* categories. However, because the type of work (from a managerial point of view) and labour conditions, it would be classified as third or fourth generation. The software-organization typology, inspired in maquiladora-generation typology, considers only a few organizational variables based on theory and practice (Table 2). It is only a descriptive tool because only an in-depth organizational analysis would give us greater insight into understanding its internal structure and dynamics.

The *second conceptual tool* uses the analogy of the ice-cream cone to simplify understanding

Figure 1. Metaphoric organization studies as a multidisciplinary approach

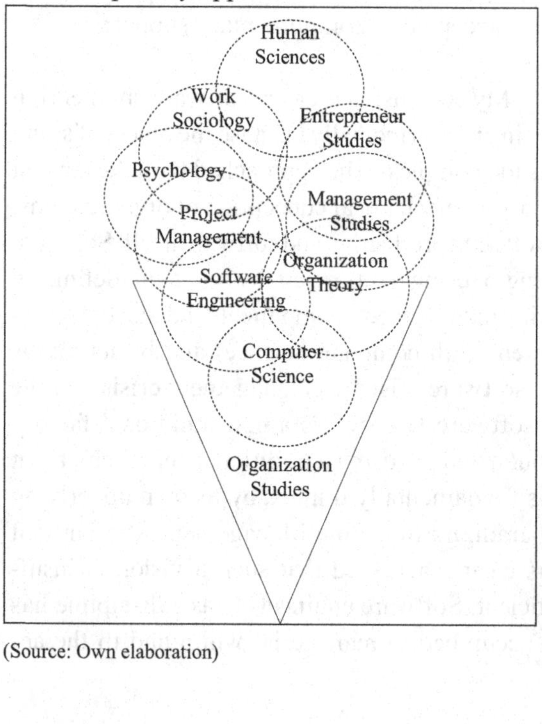

(Source: Own elaboration)

Table 2. Typology for classifying software-organization generations

Dimension	1st Generation Software Firm	2nd Generation Software Firm	3rd Generation Software Firm	4th Generation Software Firm
Software Engineering Focus	Programming	Testing	Analysis & design + Project Management	Project portfolio
Market	Local	Regional	National	Global
Rewarding	Material	Training	Career	Life
Organizational Paradigm	Rational	Integration	Knowledge	Humanist
Management Focus	Product	Process	People	Culture
Management	Command	Technology, Project	Creative Process	Professional & New Approaches
Main Analysis Level	Individual	Group	Project	Organization
Knowledge	Basic Individual	Techniques, Process and Methods	Project Methodologies	Multi-disciplinary Research
IT Infrastructure	Incipient or Manual	Basic Planning	Encourage Design (Creativity)	Knowledge Management (Industrial)
Annual Turnover ($USD)	0.25 thousand	1 million	50 million	> 50 million
Human Resources	Cheap & New	Consultants	Highly Skilled Experts	Highly Skilled Researchers & Innovators
Full-Time Employees (equivalent)	< 50	50 – 99	100 – 500	> 500
Flexibility on Labour	Little	Functional	Projects	Workgroups
Firm Age (years)	1-5	5-10	10-20	> 20
Entrepreneurship	Venture	Survivor	Consolidated	Growing
Main Competence	Software Programming	Project Management	Software Design	Knowledge Production & Management
Business Focus	Relationships	Marketing	Invitation	Competence
Work	Manual & Craft	Rational & Specialized	Creative & Expert	Non-material, Symbolic & Professional
Sub teams/Projects Number	1 – 5	6 – 10	11 – 50	> 50
Managerial Control	Supervision	Delegation	Coordination	Self- Organization
Labour	Freelance, Halftime, Precarious	Fulltime with Social Security	+ Limited Stock Participation	+ Partnership, Decent Work
Formal Degrees	Studying and Bachelor's	+ Bachelor's in-hand	+ Specialization & Master's Degree	+ Doctorate
Experience (Full-time years)	< 2	2 – 5	5 – 10	> 10
Apprentice	Novice	Apprentice	Mentor, Consultant	Expert
Stock Ownership	Single	Family	Partnership	Social
Organizational- Size Category	Micro & Small	Small	Medium	Large

(Source: Own elaboration)

the multidisciplinary approach of organization studies. The wafer represents organization studies and the scoops of ice cream the disciplines participating in a dialogue regarding the object of study, each contributing its own flavour (paradigm, discourse, theory and techniques), looking for coincidences and divergences that allow achieving a more complete understanding of the object. (See Figure 1) Disciplines can be added as needed.

The *third conceptual tool* is a framework for the *organizational analysis* of software organizations, inspired in the idea that there are many levels of analysis similar to Enriquez (1992). This framework is conceived as an ideal type, not existing in the real world. I propose five levels of analysis (psychic/symbolic, individual, group,

organization and inter-organization), three ideal actors or roles (engineer, project manager and owner) and three disciplines (software engineering, project management and entrepreneur theory) for addressing software organizations analysis (See Table 3).

In Table 3, each column corresponds to a principal role: *engineer* (skilled workers: brand-new or student trainees, junior and senior consultants, experts, non-technical workers and administrative staff), *managers* (project manager, program manager, technical leader) and *owners* (partners, top management, stockholders, managers, proprietors). In tune with these actor roles, a main discipline provides discourses, theories, methodologies, practices, techniques and tools for addressing its concerns. From left-to-right

Table 3. Framework for the organizational analysis of software organizations

Analysis Level	Ideal Organizational Actor		
	Engineer	Manager	Owner
Inter-Organization (Network)	Job Prospecting Career Development (Mercenary Work)	Political Relationships	Entrepreneur Networks, Strategic Alliances (Business Relationships)
	Competence	*Support*	*Trust*
Organization	Engagement & Commitment (Organizational Knowledge)	Technical & Managerial Leadership (Project Management)	Organizational Culture, Leadership & Management (Social Rewarding)
	Rewarding	*Leadership*	*Power*
Group / Team / Project	Work Group, Social Relationships (Membership & Mentoring)	Personnel Management, Work Organization (Leadership)	Discourse, Ceremony & Goal
	Task	*Goal*	*Business*
Individual	Learning & Knowledge (Expertise)	Rewarding & Group Relationships	Business Management
	Software	*Project*	*Enterprise*
Psychic / Symbolic	Values, Beliefs, Fears, Myths (Psychic Commitment)	Work, Challenge & Responsibility	Entrepreneurship, Owner Personality & Family Support
Discipline	Software Engineering (Software Development)	Project Management (Software Management)	Entrepreneur Theory (Venturing/ Entrepreneurship)
Organization Studies (OS) (Other disciplines needed, as part of OS)			

(Source: Own elaboration)

and from bottom-to-top, cumulative complexity is taken into consideration, not as a linear or causal pattern, but rather as a continuous, complex one. For example, *Project Manager* at *Individual Level* is surrounded by eight quadrants. Then its analysis may include both: the three *Software Engineer* (left quadrants) as well as the three *Project Manager* (right quadrants) and both upper and lower quadrants. Obviously, the topics in each quadrant are illustrative, not unique, and one should include others as needed. Between each level of analysis is a transitional object (real or conceptual) that acts as an attractor between contiguous levels and materializes the analysis. For example, Software permits materializing the internal creative energy (the so-called Freudian *pulsion* of the individual aspects: learning, knowledge, expertise) and its psyche (values, beliefs, fears, psychic commitment). Only the symbolic level permeates all the other levels, manifested in each individual as culture, in this case, as the organizational culture that software organization is, not has. At once, there expose briefly the obtained results of applying the framework in the organizational analysis of a small software organization.

SMALL SOFTWARE ORGANIZATIONAL ANALYSIS: A CASE STUDY

The case study analyzed is a small Mexican software organization. It was studied, carrying out an organizational diagnosis oriented toward evaluating the adoption of a CMMI quality model. The software company is located in Mexico City, has fewer than 50 employees and it develops software for large private firms. The target of the organizational analysis was that it was allowing define the strategies towards the implantation of the quality model CMM. Only the main findings using the organizational analysis framework are presented at each level of analysis. I quoted representative or illustrative words, phrases and concepts obtained from the interviewed people.

Inter-organization level. At this level, I discovered two main actors: the owner and the project manager. Both people use their relationships with the managers of client firms for project concourses, contracting and development, as for prospects for other business deals. The inclusion of the client makes labour and production relationships more complex. The small software firm's business model clearly was based on high project-profitability because it contracts non-expert people who are outsourced as experts. The client firm and the provider (the software firm) are aware of this, but both client and provider "cloak them in mutual complicity": the client turns a blind eye and provider does "extra work" outside the scope of the contract. This is a power game, as "blackmail hoping for another project contract." The owner has a broad relationship network with business partners, friends, ex-workmates and others. This contact-network data is updated monthly through phone calls, business breakfasts, lunches or dinners, attending tech events, as well as other social events. These meetings are formal or informal in nature. In conclusion, at this level, political and social relationships are vital to doing business.

Organizational level. At this level, many elements were discovered. Using the "interiorized charts," as I named them, I discovered as many organization charts as there are members in the organization. Each one reflects the structure of authority or control which each individual believe exists (or perceives). Only the one drawn by the owner reflects the "official chart." Using this technique, it was possible to analyze the "real" organizational operation (informal structure), specifying the area to which the interviewee belongs. Later, this and other paper-based techniques were used to interpret the software-project dynamics, based on concrete examples, not idealized ones.

An organization incongruity was discovered, manifested in two completely divergent discourses: public and private. The public discourse depicts a great company: the best, the winner, a unique one with the best technology and best employees, the one that has done major projects (and to demonstrate such, exhibits on its website the logos of companies that were clients at some time, be they good or bad results, but already part of the firm's past and current curriculum). The size, image and discourse frequently contrast with reality. On the other hand, the internal discourse directed to employees for the purpose of producing a common image about the firm is not contrary to the inner reality of the day-to-day labour reality. For example, in practice, workers are not as important as the public discourse says and incentives are not paid out as promised, among others inconsistencies.

The owner of the business, himself defined as "partner-president," exercises an "authoritarian" management style with little delegation to his immediate subordinates (managers) and a prize/penalization system against wages to "indemnify" the firm in cases of "unacceptable acts" or "non-compliance with commitments" by employees. Notwithstanding this punitive control style, it frequently does not obtain the desired behaviour by employees. This is widely sensed by the owner, but he considers it "appropriate." Owner argued that his punitive (carrot-and-stick) management style was "humanist" and that it was learned it when he studied his MBA in a main business school in Mexico City some years ago. Some employees resist managerial control, allowing the penalization, but not changing to the behaviour desired by management. The owner is undergoing a leadership crisis and personal discrediting, though he is considered as a "good technician." None of the immediate subordinates trusts him. One of them demanded he be "directed by his boss." Engineers use the "cycle of terror" (letter of resignation) as a weapon for negotiating a pay raise with owner, believing that they put him into a corner. Employees do not feel comfortable using it, but it works, they argued.

The reward system is solely "money-centred," based on a *homo economicus* conception that supposes that money is the main stimulus for employees. However, they look for "friendship, companionship, solidarity, love, recognition," among other rewards in the organization, because "money by itself is cold." This demonstrates the non-validity of this punitive style. This reward system is based on a fixed, plus variable-wage, calculation. The variable rate is much more important and it produces anxiety and behaviour oriented toward formally satisfying the "quality-assessment form" and the client's project manager, because he fills out the form as an act of power, rather than one of real quality control, then "quality is anything he wants."

Managers (project managers, technical managers, department heads or managers) are the technicians with the most time in the company and they have been promoted to their positions by the owner. Two of them have no formal (academic or business) education for the position they hold. One manager with management training is considered generally grateful and successful by his subordinates and client managers; the other two, not so much. Frequently managers' authority is harmed by the director giving contrary orders. Coordination, delegation and leadership, as well as education, are the main problems faced.

Group/Team/Project level. At this level, I have focused on the production system. The engineer works at the client's office. Sometimes it is an office with furniture, computers and network services for "consultants" (software programmers or software developers), "project leaders" and "technical leaders" (rarely same person). This produces tension within the work team. Other times, the client conditions large rooms or surplus facilities with a minimum of investment. Tables, chairs, electricity and communication cables are in disarray and aesthetically ugly. There are bad working conditions. It is hot or cold, according to the season, and no climate control. Rooms have no ventilation and no windows. Sometimes there are cooling apparatuses, but they do not circulate fresh air. Other times, the development team works in meeting rooms fitted as work places.

People are physically lined up in symbolic production lines, frequently made up of several work teams belonging to different suppliers and all operating physically and emotionally apart from the other workmates, even though they work together in the same place. Consultants, as they name them-self, do not have Internet access for peer-to-peer communication (chat), e-mail or web browsing. When searching for technical databases, tips, files and other information resources, workers use Internet cafés or other Internet facilities.

Work organization is based on "its own private methodology," says the public discourse. In reality, it does not exist. Project management is one of the organization's main problems. There is ambiguity in control, coordination and authority, because of the conflicting roles between project and technical leaders, among others. Frequently, a labour conflict becomes a personal one. Project and technical leaders compete for leadership and control over the work team and project. Frequently, the "leader-leader" (the "real leader") recognized by work team is the technical leader instead the project leader. Although there is a weekly report, what is portrayed in such reports frequently does not correspond to reality, but managers say they have projects "controlled" (through the reports), even though they are really behind. Project cost is "controlled" by penalizing the variable wages of managers and consultants, "against them" as employees say.

In day-to-day work, consultants do not use commonly known software-system-development methodologies. Rather, each ones does their work as "they can" and "they achieve goals," using their "own methodology" (whatever it be).

Individual level. At this level, a labour cycle was found. Employment in the organization is competitive, but recruiting process is quite expensive; so that recommendation by organization members is preferred. It produces better

performance and forms a "sense of group" when it is finally set up. Unmarried young candidates and those "hungry for learning" are looking to be recruited as trainees. Thereafter, managers offer the next positions progressively: "*associate consultant*", "*junior specialist consultant*" or "*senior specialist consultant*". The "*junior manager*" and "*senior manager*" positions are exclusive those "privileged" by the owner. This career path occurs in a progressive engagement-conflict game cycle, called "cycle of terror" by employees. It consists of being involved in a project, becoming a critical "resource" in day-to-day work, threatening resignation, negotiating a pay increase, and getting a new position or a pay increase, or leaving the company if the strategy fails.

This career path is not conceived as for the real progress of employees, but rather as a means for intensifying work according to high profits and short-term business logic. The business model is clear, because it is based on hiring non-experts for "sale" (outsourcing) as experts. The entrance wage is $450 U.S. (2005), with maximum hikes of 20% per year, assigned discretionally in the power game before described. This wage has always been the crux of the matter ever since the company started. It is "planned" that a worker will stay on nearly six years to get to earn $1,650 U.S. (a relative decent wage) as senior specialist consultant, if not fired earlier. During this period, the worker has already "attempted" leaving the company several times, always using the "cycle of terror." Around the sixth year working at the company, a consultant begins to be less dependent on his parents because he lives alone or forms his own family, and income growth becomes critical. Perhaps he will leave the company. If not, he may fall victim to economic pressures, computer illnesses (neurosis, colitis, gastritis, among the more serious ones), and have a shattered family life because of work. For six years now, he has being working "without a labour contract" or "paid by the job" as a freelancer (but working for a single employer). Perhaps, he may now realize he has no any benefits, such as getting a loan or applying for a housing loan. Perhaps he realizes he has lost a lot by having a job without benefits. If a worker leaves the company, there is more uncertainty and precariousness outside than inside. Now he has the experience, but he looks forward to from three to six months of temporary jobs and low wages. He does not really have a competitive professional career.

Psychic/Symbolic Level. At this level of analysis, I concentrated on the inner aspects that individuals express about themselves, the organization, work and co-workers. It has been discovered that, once an individual knows the mechanics allowing him to obtain positions, wage differentiation and discretionary assignment of positions and wages, he becomes "disenchanted with the company" and begins to look for alternatives. At that moment, a wage-negotiation process begins that will continue on for a long time. Individuals are aware of attempts at manipulation by managers from the first or second time promises are not kept. Therefore, trust in the system and in individuals is lost and both enter into a game of power and mutual convenience until such time as someone does not accept something and the relationship breaks down.

I found little identification with and commitment to the company. It is for being trained, but not for making a career: "it is not for making a career it is for three or four years. It doesn't last any longer" or "it doesn't even pay anything." The company's values and the individual's do not coincide completely. No company values are interiorized by workers. Those come from their families.

Identification with the company as a common project does not occur. The company only offers money, though it is not enough and does not provide any human warmth: "money is cold." The company and its worker are separate entities: "I work for myself" [not for the company], then there isn't a serious courtship. Employees do not "fall in love" with the company.

Employee commitment is achieved when an individual is appreciated as a member of a select group (the company), it trusts him, assigns him responsibilities, he transfers his commitment over to the client, and the commitment is achieved when the company represents the ideal the person is looking for.

This analysis of a small software organization uncovers aspects that should be resolved at each level: non-quantifiable and impossible to acquire from a software engineering approach. In this case study, I carried out semi-structured interview using, as attractors, the concepts expressed in Table 3 between levels of analysis. As result of this organizational analysis, problematic technical aspects were limited to a lack of practical application of programming methodologies and to a need of technical mastery of the technologies used. In the end, they succumb to the pressure of time and the client. On the other hand, management-related aspects turned out to be more important, permeating all activities in the organization. The dynamics of the organization are tinged by management aspects.

The apparent urgency to achieve CMM-I is really the owner's desire, based on the assumption that once certification is achieved, the company will be more attractive on the market. Another assumption by the owner is that the production process will become predictable and independent of workers, because "process drives work." The promise of a quality model does not always give results. After the owner has made various attempts over several years, it has not been possible to implement even small effective control policies and practices, because they are discretionary in nature. This confirms that there is a real practical limit in the level of formalization because of the high consumption of resources. Managerial control does not control anything in day-to-day, except wages, because weekly reports do not substitute control. It is an illusion.

In this organization, there are many managerial contradictions because of management style.

However, the owner's immediate past reflects a different work style, similar to mentorship. Although management should generate favourable conditions, liberating the creative energy of all the members of the organization and channelling it toward work, it is not occurring in this company. This repressive management style has already become institutionalized. Managers, project mangers and technical managers practice it, occasionally magnified by a possibly disproportionate exercise of power when they do not get the desired behaviour from subordinates. This rational or rather punitive management system, inspired in classic American management, produces individuals who are never really committed to the organization, neither to the managers or owner. For example, workers with more than 5 years of experience in the company are not convinced of staying and making it a career because the business model pushes them out. If management substitutes them for other cheaper workers, they would stay. After both monetary and emotional acts cancel each other out between manager and worker, the balance is zero. There is no gift, debt, gratitude or received favours that have to be given in the future, therefore there is no commitment. In addition, the company promotes values that are contradictory in practice, so that the labour relationship transcends the economic value, and the lack of emotional aspects employee-employer are transferred to the client. Since the consultant and client are involved in a recognition-commitment game, the boss only represents the role of paymaster and wage negotiator. This demonstrates that the *Principle of Gift*, proposed by the social anthropologist Marcel Mauss at the beginning of the twentieth century, and expressed by means of three obligations: to give, to receive and to return (goods, obligations, symbols, etc.) (Mauss, 2002[1924]) has full validity in this type of organizations. I conclude that the symbolic aspects come out the monetary ones and that "the substitution of a rational economic system for a system in which exchange of goods was not a mechanical but moral transaction, bringing about and maintaining

human, personal relationships between individuals and groups" (Mauss, 1970, p. ix).

The personnel manifest a big desire to achieve balance and justice within the company. They say they suffer anxiety to a greater or lesser degree. Management does not listen to employees and acts against itself by destroying the trust between both.

This analysis confirms that many aspects, except software development methodologies, are management in nature: labour and management discourses, labour relationships, power games, incentives, leadership, reward system, management style, work conditions, project management, career management, involvement and commitment, trust, symbolic aspects, among others. Therefore, organizational analysis is appropriate.

The first conclusion is that, under these particular conditions, any attempt to implement quality models is risky. While the company is trying to achieve certification, the personnel will stay to learn, but, once granted, they will look for better job offers outside the organization. They do not have a future (as they have seen from other co-workers fired) or they freelance because they earn better wages but are less committed. If a "software engineer" decides to freelance after a frustrated round of wage negotiations and this frustration is repeated, he will behave as a *mercenary worker,* always looking for better paid jobs instead of working more committed. This learning experience is more significant for younger workers because they have seen a "bad example" of work cooperation, a competitive work "organizational culture" instead of a cooperative one. Possibly, when they leave the company, they will believe all software organizations are the same, thereby producing, non-cooperative power-game behaviour.

I have found this framework useful in studying organizations. Six successful diagnoses of the organization of small software organizations using this framework confirm this (one described in Zavala, 2006). This framework has evolved since first conception and may still evolve.

In my consulting practice, I have found that every organization should be considered distinct. There are no universal recipes, at least in this practice.

FUTURE TRENDS

Disciplines are opening up their own paradigms toward a more inclusive and more multidisciplinary approach. For example, medicine today accepts and includes homeopathic medicine and alternative, traditional, sacred or natural medicine in official medicine, as occurs in Mexico recently. This shows a paradigm shift. These epistemological and ontological issues are major concerns that research should address. However, it still has not happened in the so-called "hard," "rational" or "empirical" disciplines such as engineering, because they are tied up in the most pure objectivism and reject contributions made by "soft" sciences such as the social sciences and humanities when they contradict their "hard" discursive positions. Surprisingly, it is beginning to be accepted in engineering disciplines that the positivist approach is not the only one valid and that it has serious constraints. Software engineering is an example of a discipline that has not been able to consolidate itself because of its roots. More research is needed on the ontology and epistemology of this discipline. Law is another case of a hard discipline, where we can see how a scenario is frequently interpreted different ways, and the verdict is the result of political voting, cloaked in legal language. Where is the so-called objective action? Language is so important and linguistics is another discipline of concern and of promise to software-engineering research.

Research in science and technology is needed to uncover (not discover) how software development really occurs. Research methodology based on extremely restrictive rationalism is unable to address that complexity which is not measurable or quantifiable. I believe this will provide space for better qualitative appraisals and case studies or for using another qualitative methodology. Qualitative research, with no previous hypotheses to prove and rich in detailed observations, has been able to demonstrate the falsehood of stereotypes or beliefs, even building a new theory. Henry Mintzberg and Laurent Simon are examples. Therefore, one of the most promising fields for research is *action research*. The contributions of human sciences as disciplines are slowly being discovered as the "other" disciplines, for example, in management, the emergence of concerns of ethics and social responsibility in corporations.

Given the criticism arising among practitioners and academic groups, mainly in management and project management, it is possible that, in the short term, research on software projects, software engineering and management will multiply and, as a result, organizational issues will gain in importance.

Another promising field of research is that allowing us to create specific theories, techniques and methodologies. Research done in Australia and Europe demonstrates this. Latin America is a virgin field because of the specific conditions for developing particular software organizations.

CONCLUSION

The main conclusion is that software organization is not only a function of profit, but a complex social system, far from a simple rational system that can be analyzed from a powerful perspective, as is illustrated by the organization paradigms cited. However, this requires a multidisciplinary outlook such as organization studies. Software organization is a paradoxical post-modern organization, because of the nature of software, production and economics, but is closer to a post-modern workshop, because of its production system.

Generally speaking, small organizations and small software organizations are particularly complex because its challenge is to compete

competing with large companies. Conditions are favourable, with the ability to innovate and the capacity to make quick changes, but, most important, their organizational formalizing limit is their most important constraint to an attempt at implementing any rational managerial system. Therefore, formalizing should be the result of an organizing process, instead of a prescriptive end in and of itself. Discovering the equilibrium point specific to each organization is the most important challenge for any discipline attempting to do so.

Recognition of the specific formal-informal structure and the organization dynamics of each organization is an issue of major importance because of the profound implications they have on organization-formalizing dynamics and its practical limits, software abstraction and software-engineering theory and practice.

Software production (development and maintenance) is a social process or, more precisely, organizational in nature. It includes a technical facet and has profound implications for software-engineering education requiring reforms to education curricula.

The rational management paradigm has limited application in present-day software organizations because they are different in nature: people and production process are not like industrial manufacturing, where even this paradigm has limited success. New humanistic-oriented management styles are apparently more appropriate for these knowledge organizations and their scarce, highly skilled knowledge workers. It is clear that project management, as a management discipline, requires a paradigmatic shift too, oriented toward more humanistic concerns.

Using a science and technology studies approach, I have demonstrated that software engineering is an invented discipline, built on the "software crisis" rhetoric. Limited real advances in software engineering as a discipline are clear. It has only been successful in a discursive way, but, in methodologies, techniques, theory and practice,

it has failed miserably. Software engineering has trapped itself, because it attempts to solve a concern that is not technical in nature, as has been demonstrated. This obliges us to conceive software engineering as organizational in nature, with profound implications. Therefore, software engineering should change its current paradigm, accepting those "related disciplines" as "part of" itself. It should be reshaped, redefined, excluding its supposed management scope, so as to guarantee its so-called "quantitative, disciplined and systematic" properties, or succumb to those successful disciplines.

The framework proposed has resulted in a powerful conceptual tool for analyzing software organizations. But alas, for you to use it and interpret the distinct facts, histories and narratives, a paradigm change in you yourself is needed. From my own experience, this was a prerequisite. I abandoned my rigid thought as an engineer when I immersed myself into organization studies as a new and strange discipline. It has being the most complicated intellectual task I have attempted. Only after that, was it possible to reconsider my prior engineering knowledge and reincorporate it as another discipline, not as the main one, because that does not exist any more. After that change in paradigm happened, I was immersed in a multidisciplinary world. The complex, real world has always been so, but now it is in shades of colour. It is urgent to do a distinct research, because current research is not appropriate and entrepreneurs must loose their fear of academia. Really, we don't bite.

ACKNOWLEDGMENT

The author wishes to express his love and gratitude towards Ixchel Xaman Ek, Akira Itzamaná, and Marulis for their support during the research and composition of this chapter.

REFERENCES

Aaen, I., Bøtcher, P., & Mathiassen, L. (1997). Software factories. In L. Mathiassen (Ed.), *Reflective systems development* (Vol. II, pp. 407-433). Aalborg, Denmark: Aalborg University, Institute for Electronic Systems, Department of Computer Science. Retrieved December 5, 2007, from http://www.cs.auc.dk/~larsm/Dr_Techn/Volume_II/17.pdf

Abrahamson, E. (1991). Managerial fads and fashions: The diffusion and rejection of innovations. *The Academy of Management Review, 16*(3), 586-612.

Aktouf, O. (1998). *La administración entre tradición y renovación.* Cali: Artes Gráficas Univalle-Gaëtan Morin Éditeur.

Alvesson, M. (2004) Knowledge Work and Knowledge-Intensive Firms, New York: Oxford University Press.

Asterion. (2005). Tríptico: Preludio. *Zahir blog.* Retrieved December 5, 2007, from http://www.zonalibre.org/blog/zahir/archives/081847.html

Aubert, N. (1994). Du systeme disciplinaire au systeme managinaire: L'emergence du management psychique. In J.P. Bouilloud & B.P. Lécuyer (Eds.), *L'invention de la gestion. Histoire et pratiques* (pp. 119-136). Paris: L'Harmattan.

Aubert, N., & Gaulejac, V. d. e (1993). *El costo de la excelencia: del caos a la lógica o de la lógica al caos?* Barcelona: Paidós.

Basili, V. R., Caldiera, G., & Rombach, H.D. (1994). The experience factory. In J.J. Marciniak (Ed.), *Encyclopedia of software engineering* (Vol. 1, pp. 469-476). New York: John Wiley & Sons. Retrieved August 5, 2006, from http://wwwagse.informatik.uni-l.de/pubs/repository/basili94c/encyclo.ef.pdf

Ben-Ari, M. (1998). *The software factory.* Paper presented at 10th Annual Workshop of the Psychology of Programming Interest Group, PPIG 1998, Knowledge Media Institute, Open University, UK. Retrieved December 5, 2007, from http://www.ppig.org/papers/10th-benari.pdf

Bertaux, D., & Singly, F.d. (1997). *Les Récits de vie: perspective ethnosociologique* (Collection 128, 122). Paris: Nathan.

Boehm, B. (2006). A view of 20th and 21st century software engineering. In D. Osterweil, D. Rombach, & M.L. Soffa (Eds.), *Proceedings of the 28th International Conference on Software Engineering ICSE '06* (pp. 12-29). New York: ACM Press.

Boje, D.M. (1999). The storytelling organization game. Retrieved December 5, 2007, from http://business.nmsu.edu/~dboje/between.html

Brooks, F. P. (1995). *The mythical man-month: Essays on software engineering.* Reading, MA: Addison-Wesley.

Brynjolfsson, E. (1994). Information assets, technology, and organization. *Management Science, 40*(12), 1645-1662.

Brynjolfsson, E., & Hitt, L.M. (2000). Beyond computation: Information technology, organizational transformation and business performance. *The Journal of Economic Perspectives, 14*(4), 23-48.

Brynjolfsson, E., & Hitt, L.M. (2003). *Computing productivity: Firm-level evidence* (MIT Sloan Working Paper 4210-01, eBusiness@MIT Working Paper 139). Cambridge, MA: MIT Sloan School of Management. Retrieved December 5, 2007, from http://ebusiness.mit.edu/erik/cp.pdf

Bueno, C. (2000). QS9000: Calidad en la diversidad. *Revista Mexicana de Sociología, 62*(3), 29-49.

Burr, V. (2003). *Social Constructionism.* London: Routledge.

Carmel, E., & Bird, B.J. (1997). Small is beautiful: A study of packaged software development teams. *Journal of High Technology Management Research, 8*(1), 129-148.

Carrillo, J., & Lara, A. (2005). Mexican maquiladoras: New capabilities of coordination and the emergence of new generation of companies. *Innovation: Management, Policy & Practice, 7*(2/3), 256-273.

Clarke, T., & Clegg, S.R. (1998). *Changing paradigms. The transformation of management knowledge for the 21st century.* London: Harper and Collins Business.

Clegg, S.R., & Hardy, C. (1996). Organizations, organization and organizing. In S. Clegg, C. Hardy, & W. Nord (Eds.), *Handbook of organization studies* (pp. 1-28). Thousand Oaks, CA: Sage.

Cusumano, M.A., & Selby, R.W. (1997). How Microsoft builds software . *Communications of ACM, 40*(6), 53-61.

Denning, P.J. (1998). Computer science and software engineering: Filing for divorce? *Communications of the ACM, 41*(8), 128.

DiMaggio, P.J., & Powell, W.W. (1983). The iron cage revisited: Institutional isomorphism and collective rationality in organizational fields. *American Sociological Review, 48*(2), 147-160.

Dybå, T. (2000). Improvisation in small software organizations. *Software, 17*(5), 82-87.

Dybå, T. (2001). *Enabling software process improvement: An investigation of the importance of organizational issues* (NTNU 2001:101, IDI Report 7/01). Unpublished doctoral dissertation, Norwegian University of Science and Technology, Trondheim, Norway. Retrieved December 5, 2007, from http://www.idi.ntnu.no/grupper/su/publ/phd/dybaa-dring-thesis-2001.pdf

Dybå, T. (2002). Enabling software process improvement: An investigation of the importance of organizational issues. *Empirical Software Engineering, 7*(4), 387-390.

Dybå, T. (2003). Factors of software process improvement success in small and large organizations: An empirical study in the Scandinavian context. *ACM SIGSOFT Software Engineering Notes, 28*(5), 148-157.

Dybå, T. (2005). An empirical investigation of the key factors for success in software process improvement. *IEEE Transactions on Software Engineering, 31*(5), 410-424.

Dybå, T., Kitchenham, B.A., & Jorgensen, M. (2005). Evidence-based software engineering for practitioners. *Software, 22*(1), 58-65.

Enriquez, E. (1992). *L'Organisation en analyse.* Paris: Presses Universitaires de France.

Ensmenger, N.L. (2001a). *From "black art" to industrial discipline: The software crisis and the management of programmers.* Unpublished doctoral dissertation, University of Pennsylvania.

Ensmenger, N.L. (2001b). The "question of professionalism" in the computing fields. *IEEE Annals of the History of Computing, 23*(4), 56-74.

Ensmenger, N.L. (2003). Letting the "computer boys" take over: Technology and the politics of organizational transformation. *International Review of Social History, 48*(Supplement), 153-180.

Ensmenger, N.L., & Aspray, W. (2000). Software as labour process. In U. Hashagen, R. Keil-Slawik, & A.L. Norberg (Eds.), *Proceedings of the International Conference on History of Computing: Software Issues* (pp. 139-165). New York: Springer-Verlag.

European Commission. (2005). *The new SME definition. User guide and model declaration.* Europe: Enterprise and Industry Publications.

Gergen, K.J. (1996). *Realidades y relaciones. Aproximaciones a la construcción social.* Barcelona: Paidos.

Glass, R.L. (2006). The Standish report: Does it really describe a software crisis? *Communications of the ACM, 49*(8), 15-16.

Goffman, E. (1993). *La presentación de la persona en la vida cotidiana*. Buenos Aires: Amorrortu.

Greenfield, J., & Short, K. (2003). Software factories: Assembling applications with patterns, models, frameworks and tools. In R. Crocker & G.L. Steele (Eds.), *Companion of the 18th Annual ACM SIGPLAN Conference on Object-Oriented Programming, Systems, Languages, and Applications* (pp. 16-27). Anaheim, CA: ACM Press.

Griss, M.L., & Wendtzel, K.D. (1994). Hybrid domain-specific kits for a flexible software factory. In H. Berghel, T. Hlengl, & J. Urban (Ed.), *Proceedings of the 1994 ACM Symposium on Applied Computing 1994* (pp. 47-52). Phoenix: ACM Press.

Hackman, J.R., & Wageman, R. (1995). Total quality management: Empirical, conceptual, and practical issues. *Administrative Science Quarterly, 40*(2), 309-342.

Haigh, T. (2001). The chromium-plated tabulator: Institutionalizing an electronic revolution, 1954–1958. *IEEE Annals of the History of Computing, 23*(4), 75-104.

Heckman, S.J. (1983). Weber's ideal type: A contemporary reassessment. *Polity, 16*(1), 119-137.

Hibberd, F.J. (2005). *Unfolding Social Constructionism*, New York: Springer.

Hodgson, D.E. (2004). Project work: The legacy of bureaucratic control in the post-bureaucratic organization. *Organization, 11*(1), 81-100.

Hualde, A. (2003). ¿Existe un modelo maquilador?: Reflexiones sobre la experiencia mexicana y centroamericana. *Nueva Sociedad, 186*. Retrieved December 5, 2007, from http://www.iztapalapa.uam.mx/amet/debate/modelomaquilador.html

Hualde, A. (2004, August). *Proximity and transborder networks in the US Mexican border: The making of a software cluster*. Paper presented at the *4th Congress on Proximity Economics: Proximity*. Marseille: Université de la Méditerranée, Groupe de Recherche Dynamiques de proximité. Retrieved December 5, 2007, from http://139.124.177.94/proxim/viewabstract.php?id=82

IEEE Computer Society. (2004). *Guide to the software engineering body of knowledge (SWEBOK)*. Los Alamitos, CA.

Ilavarasan, P.V., & Sharma, A.K. (2003). Is software work routinized? Some empirical observations from Indian software industry. *The Journal of Systems and Software, 66*(1), 1-6.

Institute of Electrical and Electronic Engineers. (1990). *IEEE Std 610.12-1990. IEEE Standard glossary of software engineering terminology*. Los Alamitos, CA.

Keir, M. (1918). Scientific management simplified. *Scientific Monthly, 7*(6), 525-529.

Kuhn, T.S. (1971). La estructura de las revoluciones científicas. Argentina: Fondo de Cultura Económica.

Laporte, C.Y., Papiccio, N.R., & Trudel, S. (1998). *A software factory for the Canadian government Year 2000 Conversion Program*. Paper presented at Software Process Improvement 98, Monte Carlo. Retrieved December 5, 2007, from http://www.lrgl.uqam.ca/publications/pdf/701.pdf

Lethbridge, T.C., Sim, S.E., & Singer, J. (2005). Studying software engineers: Data collection techniques for software field studies. *Empirical Software Engineering, 10*(3), 311-341.

Lewerentz, C., & Rust, H. (2000). Are software engineers true engineers? *Annals of Software Engineering, 10*(1-4), 311-328.

Organizational Analysis of Small Organizations

Ludewig, J. (1996). Software engineering: Why it did not work. In A. Brennecke & R. Keil-Slawik (Eds.), *History of software engineering* (pp. 25-27). Dagstuhl Seminar, Paderborn University. Retrieved December 5, 2007, from http://citeseer.ist.psu.edu/rd/0%2C229833%2C1%2C0.25%2CDownload/http://coblitz.codeen.org:3125/citeseer.ist.psu.edu/cache/papers/cs/2159/ftp:zSzzSzftp.dagstuhl.dezSzpubzSzReportszSz96zSz9635.pdf/history-of-software-engineering.pdf

Mahoney, M.S. (1990). The roots of software engineering. *CWI Quarterly, 3*(4), 325-334. Retrieved December 5, 2007, from http://www.princeton.edu/%7Emike/articles/sweroots/sweroots.pdf

Mahoney, M.S. (2004). Finding a history for software engineering. *Annals of the History of Computing, 26*(1), 8-19.

Mauss, M. (1970). *The Gift: Forms and Functions of exchange in Archaic Societies*, London: Routledge.

Mauss, M. (2002[1924]) *Essai sur le don*, Retrieved May 12, 2006, from http://socioeconomie.free.fr/MAUSS/essai_sur_le_don.pdf

McIlroy, M.D. (1969). Mass produced software components (and discussion panel). In. P. Naur & B. Randell (Eds.), *Software engineering: A conference sponsored by the NATO Science Committee.* Garmisch, Germany: NATO Scientific Affairs Division. Retrieved August 15, 2006, from http://homepages.cs.ncl.ac.uk/brian.randell/NATO/nato1968.PDF

Meijaard, J., Brand, M.J., & Mosselman, M. (2005). Organizational structure and performance in Dutch small firms (SCALES-paper N200420). Netherlands: EIM Business and Policy Research: Scientific Analysis of Entrepreneurship and SME. Retrieved December 5, 2007, from http://www.eim.net/pdf-ez/N200420.pdf

Miller, D., & Hartwick, J. (2002). Spotting management fads. *Harvard Business Review, 80*(10), 26-27.

Miller, J.P. (1970). Social-psychological implications of Weber's model of bureaucracy: Relations among expertise, control, authority, and legitimacy. *Social Forces, 49*(1), 91-102.

Mintzberg, H. (1975). The manager's job: Folklore and fact. *Harvard Business Review, 53*(4), 49-61.

Mintzberg, H. (1979). *The structure of organizations.* Englewood Cliffs, NJ: Prentice Hall.

Mintzberg, H., & Westley, F. (2001). Decision making: It's not what you think. *MIT Sloan Management Review, 42*(3), 89-93.

Montaño, L. (2005). ¿Qué son los estudios organizacionales?, conference presented at the *Coloquio Internacional: Los Estudios Organizacionales en México: Una Década de Investigación, formación y vinculación,* Universidad Autónoma Metropolitana – Iztapalapa, September 27th, 2005, Mexico City.

Mugler, J. (2004). The configuration approach to the strategic management of small and medium-sized enterprises. In *Proceedings of the Budapest Tech Jubilee Conference.* Budapest: Budapest Tech. Retrieved December 5, 2007, from http://www.bmf.hu/conferences/jubilee/Mugler.pdf

Mutafelija, B., & Stromberg, H. (2003). *ISO 9001:2000 – CMMI v1.1 Mappings.* Pittsburgh, PA: Carnegie Mellon University, Software Engineering Institute. Retrieved December 5, 2007, from http://www.sei.cmu.edu/cmmi/adoption/pdf/iso-mapping.pdf

Naur, P., & Randell, B. (Eds.). (1969). *Final report from software engineering: A conference sponsored by the NATO Science Committee.* Garmisch, Germany: NATO Scientific Affairs Division. Retrieved December 5, 2007, from http://homepages.cs.ncl.ac.uk/brian.randell/NATO/nato1968.PDF

Organisation for Economic Co-operation and Development. (2002). *OECD small and medium enterprise outlook 2002*. Paris: OECD Publications Service.

Parnas, D.L. (1998). *Software engineering: An unconsummated marriage*. Paper presented at McMaster University, Hamilton, Ontario, Canada. Retrieved December 5, 2007, from http://www.cs.utexas.edu/users/software/1998/parnas-19981208.pdf

Pinto, J.K., & Mantel, S.J. (1990). The causes of project failure. *IEEE Transactions on Engineering Management, 37*(4), 269-276.

Project Management Institute. (2004). *A guide to the project management body of knowledge (PMBOK guide)*. Newton Square, PA.

Reed, M. (1996). Organizational theorizing: A historically contested terrain. In S. Clegg, C. Hardy, & W. Nord (Eds.), *Handbook of organization studies* (pp. 25-50). Thousand Oaks, CA: Sage.

Rosa, A. d.e la. (2000). La micro, pequeña y mediana empresa en México: Sus saberes, mitos y problemática. *Revista Iztapalapa, 20*(48), 183-220. Retrieved December 5, 2007, from http://148.206.53.230/revistasuam/iztapalapa/include/getdoc.php?rev=iztapalapa&id=656&article=667&mode=pdf

Scott, W.R. (1992). *Organizations: Rational, natural, and open systems*. Englewood Cliffs, NJ: Prentice Hall.

Sharp, H., & Robinson, H. (2004). An ethnographic study of XP practice. *Empirical Software Engineering, 9*, 353-375.

Sievers, B. (1994). *Work, death, and life itself: Essays on management and organization*. Berlin: Walter de Gruyter.

Simon, L. (2002). *Le management en univers ludique: Jouer et travailler chez UbiSoft, une entreprise du multimédia à Montréal (1998-1999)*. Doctoral thesis, École des Hautes Études Commerciales, Université de Montréal, Montréal, Canada.

Sinclair, B. (2003). Can Mexico develop a software maquiladora industry? *Infoamericas Tendencias Latin American Market Report, 38*. Retrieved December 5, 2007, from http://tendencias.infoamericas.com/article_archive/2003/038/038_industry_analysis.pdf

Smith, J., & McKee, P. (2001). Troubled IT projects: Prevention and turn around (IEE Professional Applications of Computing Series, 3). England: MPG Books.

Stewart, M. (2006, June). The management myth. *The Atlantic Monthly, June,* pp. 80-87. Retrieved December 5, 2007, from http://www.edst.educ.ubc.ca/courses/EADM532/Stewart.management.myth.pdf

Thayer, R.H. (Ed.). (1997). *Software engineering project management*. Piscataway, NJ: Wiley-IEEE Computer Society Press. Retrieved December 5, 2007, from http://media.wiley.com/product_data/excerpt/08/08186800/0818680008.pdf

Traxler, F. (2005). Firm size, SME and business interest associations: A European comparison. In F. Traxler (Coord.), *Small and medium sized enterprises and business interest organisations in the European Union*. Europe: European Commission, DG Employment. Retrieved December 5, 2007, from http://www.ueapme.com/docs/projects/Project%20Business%20Associations/study_final.pdf

Tsoukas, H., & Hatch, M.J. (2001). Complex thinking, complex practice: The case for a narrative approach to organizational complexity. *Human Relations, 54*(8), 979-1013.

Tuckman, A. (1994). The yellow brick road: Total quality management and the restructuring of organizational culture. *Organization Studies, 15*(5), 727-751.

Turner, J.R., & Müller, R. (2003). On the nature of the project as a temporary organization. *International Journal of Project Management, 21*, 1-8.

Van de Ven, A.H., & Poole, M.S. (2005). Alternative approaches for studying organizational change. *Organization Studies, 26*(9), 1377-1404.

Winter, M., & Smith, C. (2006). *Rethinking project management (EPSRC Network 2004-2006)* (Final Report). United Kingdom: Engineering and Physical Sciences Research Council. Retrieved December 5, 2007, from http://www.mace.manchester.ac.uk/project/research/management/rethinkpm/pdf/final_report.pdf

Zavala, J. (2004, February). ¿Por qué fracasan los proyectos de software? Un enfoque organizacional. Paper presented at *Congreso Nacional de Software Libre 2004*. February 11th, 2004, Mexico City. , Retrieved December 5, 2007, from http://www.consol.org.mx/2004/material/63/por-que-fallan-los-proy-de-soft.pdf

Zavala, J. (2006). *Dinámica organizacional en el área informática de una organización pública de México*. Unpublished master's dissertation, Universidad Autónoma Metropolitana–Iztapalapa, Mexico City, Mexico.

Chapter II
The Application of International Software Engineering Standards in Very Small Enterprises

Claude Y. Laporte
École de Technologie Supérieure, Canada

Alain Renault
Centre de Recherche Public Henri Tudor, Luxembourg

Simon Alexandre
Centre d'Excellence en Technologies de l'Information et de la Communication, Belgium

ABSTRACT

The software industry recognizes the value of very small enterprises in contributing valuable products and services to the economy. As the quality of software increasingly becomes a subject of concern and process approaches are maturing and gaining the confidence of companies, the use of ISO/IEC JTC 1 SC7[1] standards is spreading in organizations of all sizes. However, these standards were not written for development organizations with fewer than 25 employees and are consequently difficult to apply in such small settings. A new ISO/IEC JTC1 SC7 Working Group, WG24, has been established to address some of these difficulties by developing profiles and providing guidance for compliance with ISO software engineering standards. A survey was conducted to question these very small organizations about their utilization of ISO/IEC JTC1 SC7 standards and to collect data to identify problems and potential solutions to help them apply these standards. Over 400 responses were received from 32 countries. Results from the survey are discussed.

INTRODUCTION

This chapter presents a new ISO project which proposes to facilitate access to, and utilization of, ISO/IEC JTC1 SC7 software engineering standards in very small enterprises (VSEs). VSEs are organizations with fewer than 25 employees. In Europe, for instance, 85% of the information technology (IT) sector's companies have between 1 and 10 employees. In Canada, the Montréal area was surveyed, as illustrated in Table 1, and it was found that close to 80% of software development companies have fewer than 25 employees (Laporte, April, & Renault, 2006), and over 50% have fewer than 10 employees. In Brazil, small IT companies represent about 70% of the total number of companies (Anacleto, von Wangenheim, Salviano, & Savi, 2004). Finally, in Northern Ireland (McFall, Wilkie, McCaffery, Lester, & Sterritt, 2003), a survey reports that 66% of companies employ fewer than 20 software development staff.

There is a need to help these organizations understand and use the concepts, processes, and practices proposed by the International Standard Organization's (ISO's) international software engineering standards. A new ISO/IEC JTC1 SC7 Working Group, WG24, has been established to address some of these difficulties by developing profiles and providing guidance for compliance with ISO software engineering standards. A profile is defined as a set of one or more base standards and/or international standard profiles (ISP), and, where applicable, the identification of chosen classes, conforming subsets, options, and parameters of those base standards, or ISPs, necessary to fulfill a particular function (ISO/IEC TR 10000-1, 1998).

This chapter is divided into six sections. In the first section, the ISO/IEC JTC1 SC7 organization's mandate and collection of standards are described. In the second section, a history of the recent events that led to an ISO/IEC JTC1 SC7 project proposal for very small organizations is presented. In the third section, a few centers and institutes focusing on small and very small software enterprises are described. The results of an IEEE survey performed to obtain feedback from software engineering standards users are discussed in the fourth section. The analysis of survey data, conducted by WG24, is presented in the fifth section. In the last section, we present the future work of WG24.

OVERVIEW OF THE ISO/IEC JTC1 SC7 MANDATE AND COLLECTION OF STANDARDS

In this section, we present the mandate of ISO/IEC JTC1 SC7, an overview of the collection of standards produced and maintained by this committee, and a description of the ISO standard development process. During 1987, the International Organization for Standardization and the International Electrotechnical Commission (IEC)

Table 1. Size of software development companies in the Montreal area (Laporte et al., 2006)

Size (employees)	Software Companies		Jobs	
	Number	%	Number	%
1 to 25	540	78%	5,105	29%
26 to 100	127	18%	6,221	36%
over 100	26	4%	6,056	35%
TOTAL	**693**	**100%**	**17,382**	**100%**

joined forces and put in place a joint technical committee called Joint Technical Committee 1 (ISO/IEC JTC1) with the following mandate: "Standardization in the Field of Information Technology: Information technology includes the specification, design, and development of systems and tools dealing with the capture, representation, processing, security, transfer, interchange, presentation, management, organization, storage, and retrieval of information" (Coallier, 2003). The mandate of subcommittee SC7, within JTC1, is to standardize processes, supporting tools, and supporting technologies for the engineering of software products and systems.

Figure 1 illustrates the evolution of the ISO/IEC JTC1 standards that are maintained and published under the responsibility of SC7.

Within the portfolio of SC7 standards, a number of international standards are grouped together in a category called "Software and Systems Engineering Processes." These standards describe good software and systems engineering practices, as well as standards assessing them. Within this group, there are four key ISO/IEC standards:

- ISO/IEC 12207 Software Life Cycle Processes (ISO/IEC 12207, 1995)
- ISO/IEC 15288 Systems Life Cycle Processes (ISO/IEC 15288, 2002)
- ISO/IEC 15504 Software Process Assessment series (ISO/IEC 15504, 2003-2005)
  - ° As an example, the Capability Maturity Model[®2] Integration[SM3] (CMMI[®]) conforms to ISO/IEC 15504
- ISO/IEC 90003 (ISO/IEC 90003, 2004) Guidelines for the Application of ISO 9001 (ISO 9000, 2000) to computer software

The relationships between these standards are illustrated in Figure 2.

Although these standards are well known in large software and systems engineering organizations, the current SC7 Life Cycle standards are a challenge to use in VSEs, and compliance with them is difficult, if not impossible, to achieve. Consequently, VSEs have few, or a very limited number of, ways to be recognized as organizations producing quality software systems.

Figure 1. Evolution of published ISO/IEC JTC1 SC7 software and systems engineering standards (SC7, 2006)

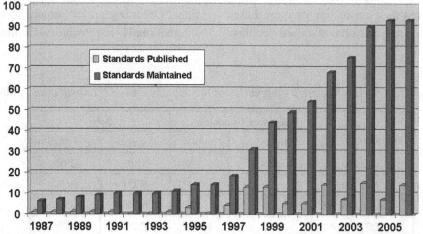

Figure 2. Relationships between key SC7 standards (Coallier, 2003)

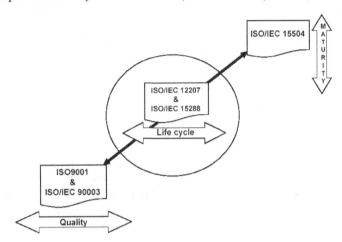

HISTORY LEADING TO AN ISO/IEC JTC 1/SC7 PROJECT PROPOSAL FOR VERY SMALL ORGANIZATIONS AND RECENT ACHIEVEMENTS

In this section, a history of events leading to the creation of the new ISO/IEC SC7 Working Group, WG24, is presented. This section will also describe the mandate of WG24.

Plenary Meeting of ISO/IEC JTC 1/SC7 – Australia

At the Brisbane meeting of the SC7 in 2004, Canada's representatives raised the issue of small enterprises requiring standards adapted to their size and maturity level. The current software engineering standards target (or are perceived as targeting) large organizations. Australian's delegates supported Canada's representatives' position in this regard, and the two national bodies took action to investigate possible ways forward. A meeting of interested parties was held with delegates from five national bodies (Australia, Canada, the Czech Republic, South Africa, and Thailand) at which a consensus was reached on the general objectives:

- To make the current software engineering standards more accessible to VSEs
- To provide documentation requiring minimal tailoring and adaptation effort
- To provide harmonized documentation integrating available standards:
  - Process standards
  - Work products and deliverables
  - Assessment and quality

  Modeling and tools
- To align profiles, if desirable, with the notions of maturity levels presented in ISO/IEC 15504

It was also decided that a special interest group (SIG) be created to explore these objectives and to better articulate the priorities and the project plan. The participants felt that it would be possible, during 2004, to draw up:

- A set of requirements
- An outline of key deliverables and the associated processes to create them (e.g., how to create profiles)
- A terms of reference document for the working group
- An example of a simple profile

First Special Working Group Meeting – Thailand

In March 2005, the Thailand Industrial Standards Institute (TISI) invited a Special Working Group (SWG) to advance the work items defined at the Brisbane meeting. The meeting was attended by delegates from the following countries: Australia, Belgium, Canada, the Czech Republic, Finland, South Africa, South Korea, the USA, and Thailand.

A key topic of discussion was to clearly define the size of a VSE that would be targeted by the working group. The working group used a paper published by the Centre for Software Process Technologies (McFall et al., 2003) to help define the size of small organizations. McFall et al. presented the various perceived priorities and areas of concern for different organization sizes.

As illustrated in Figure 3, the priorities and concerns of organizations with fewer than 20 employees are quite different from those of larger organizations. As an example, medium and large organizations rank process adherence higher than do small organizations. For the latter, managing risk is of great concern while larger organizations rank managing risk as priority number 8 only. Conversely, for small organizations, consistency across teams is less of a concern, while for larger organizations it is a top-priority issue.

A consensus was achieved by the members of the SWG on this study and a consensus was reached on defining our target VSE as IT services and organizations and projects with between 1 and 25 employees.

A list of actions that could be undertaken by a future ISO/IEC SC7 working group was developed at this meeting. The proposed action items are:

1. Validate the work products produced by the working group
2. Prepare, conduct, analyze, and communicate survey results
3. Search for other centers/organizations focusing on SMEs and VSEs
4. Assemble a complete list of characteristics of VSEs and projects
5. Generate multiple profiles from the standards mentioned above
6. Prepare communication material to inform VSEs about the work performed by the WG

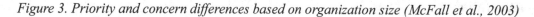

Figure 3. Priority and concern differences based on organization size (McFall et al., 2003)

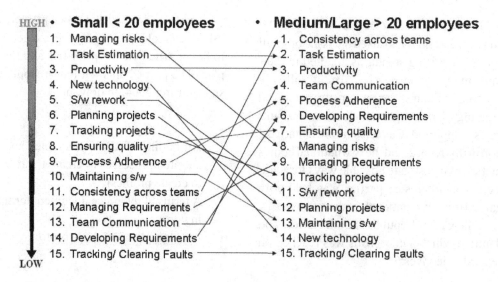

7. Develop business cases for the adoption and deployment of work products developed by the WG
8. Develop one or more ISO 12207 roadmaps
9. Pilot roadmaps, using an approach similar to the trials conducted by the ISO/IEC 15504 (SPICE) project

The major output of this one-week meeting was a draft list of new work items, as described later. A work schedule has also been developed for the new working group. As illustrated in Figure 4, the top row shows the standard steps for the development and approval of an ISO standard. The lower part of the figure illustrates the actions that would need to be performed, as well as their expected date of completion, in order to obtain a CD 1 (Committee Draft) by the end of 2007.

The major output of this one-week meeting was a document that has since been presented and discussed at the Helsinki SC7 meeting held in May 2005. The document was essentially a draft list of the new work item that was approved by ISO/IEC in September 2005. This document is presented later.

Plenary Meeting of ISO/IEC JTC 1/SC7 Meeting – Finland

The document developed in Thailand was reviewed during a meeting of one of the WGs at the 2005 SC7 plenary meeting in Helsinki. A resolution was approved as follows: "*JTC1/SC7 instructs its Secretariat to distribute for letter ballot an updated version of New Work Item Proposal for the development of Software Life Cycle*

Figure 4. Proposed work schedule for the new working group

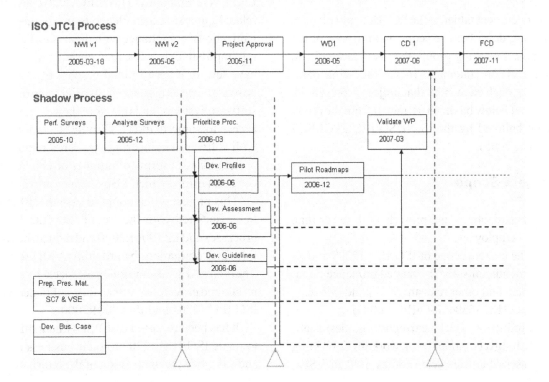

Profiles and Guidelines for use in Very Small Enterprises (VSE) by 20 June 2005 (ISO/IEC JTC1/SC7 N3288, 2005).

Balloting on this document was open until September 21, 2005. Over 12 countries voted in favor of the NWI Proposal, and the following countries indicated a commitment to participate in the new working group: Belgium, Canada, the Czech Republic, Ireland, Italy, Japan, Korea, Luxemburg, South Africa, Thailand, the UK, and the USA. As a result of this vote, the project was approved and the new working group, WG24, was established as follows:

- Mr. Tanin Uthayanaka (Thailand) was appointed convener.
- Mr. Claude Y. Laporte (IEEE Computer Society) was appointed project editor.
- Mr. Jean Bérubé (Canada) was appointed secretary.

Proposed Project Tabled at ISO/IEC JTC 1/SC7

The document tabled at the SC7 Helsinki plenary meeting describes the scope and purpose of the proposed working group, the justification for it, and a vision statement. In the following paragraphs, each element of that project is presented. The text below has been extracted from the document balloted by the ISO (ISO/IEC JTC1/SC7 N3288, 2005).

Project Scope

- Organizations and projects with fewer than 25 employees.
- The current scope of ISO/IEC 12207 and its amendments, the associated guidance document and other relevant SC7 standards (e.g., ISO/IEC 15504, ISO/IEC 90003).
- Production of technical reports (guides) establishing a common framework for describing assessable life cycle profiles used in VSEs, including small software systems development departments and projects within larger organizations.
  - ° Guides to be based on ISPs identifying which parts of the existing standards are applicable to VSEs at a specific level and for a specific domain.
  - ° Guides which can be applied throughout the life cycle for managing and performing software development activities; the ultimate goal is to improve the competitiveness and capacity of VSEs.

Purpose and Justification

The software systems industry as a whole recognizes the value of VSEs in terms of their contribution of valuable products and services. The majority of software organizations fall within the VSE size category. From the various surveys conducted by some of the national bodies that initially contributed to the development of this NWI list, it is clear that the current SC7 Life Cycle Standards (ISO/IEC 12207 and the related guide) are a challenge to use in these organizations; compliance with them is difficult (if not impossible) to achieve. Consequently, VSEs have few, or a very limited number of, ways to be recognized as organizations producing quality software systems, and therefore they do not have access to some markets. Currently, conformity with software engineering standards requires a critical mass in terms of number of employees, cost, and effort, which VSEs cannot provide.

This project will attempt to ease the difficulties associated with the use of ISO/IEC 12207 processes and ISO 9001:2000 and reduce the conformance obligations by providing VSE profiles. The project will develop guidance for each process profile and provide a roadmap for compliance with ISO/IEC 12207 and ISO 9001:2000.

It has been reported that VSEs find it difficult to relate ISO/IEC 12207 to their business needs and to justify the application of the international standards in their operations. Most VSEs cannot afford the resources for, or see a net benefit in, establishing software processes as defined by current standards (e.g., ISO/IEC 12207). A liaison will be established between the proposed work and other SC7 work; specifically, the progress of ISO/IEC 12207 will be tracked.

Vision Statement

This project will:

- Provide VSEs with a way to be recognized as producing quality software systems without the initial expense of implementing and maintaining an entire suite of systems and software engineering standards or performing comprehensive assessments.
- Produce guides which are easy to understand, affordable, and usable by VSEs.
- Produce a set of profiles, which build on or improve a VSE's existing processes, or provide guidance in establishing those processes.

- Address the market needs of VSEs by allowing domain-specific profiles and levels.
- Provide examples to encourage VSEs to adopt and follow processes that lead to quality software, matching the needs, issues, and risks of their domain.
- Provide a baseline for how multiple VSEs can work together or be assessed as a project team on projects that may be more complex than can be performed by any one VSE.
- Develop scalable profiles and guides so that compliance with ISO/IEC 12207 and/or ISO 9001:2000 and assessment become possible with a minimum of redesign of the VSE's processes.

Referenced Documents

As illustrated in Figure 5, a number of documents have been identified as pertinent inputs to this project: ISO 90003, ISO/IEC 12207, ISO/IEC 15504, Capability Maturity Model Integration

Figure 5. Referenced documents (ISO/IEC JTC1/SC7 N3288, 2005)

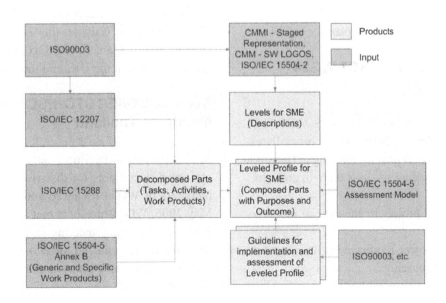

(CMMI) and the Software Capability Maturity Model (SW-CMM).

Second Special Working Group Meeting – Thailand

In July 2005, the Thailand Industrial Standards Institute (TISI) sent out a second invitation to participate in the Special Working Group held in September 2005 in Bangkok. The main objective of the meeting was to prepare material that would be presented to WG24 in order to facilitate the start-up of the working group. The main outputs of the meeting were:

- Proposed requirements for ISPs based on Technical Report ISO/IEC TR10000-1
- A proposed survey on VSE exposure and needs for software development life cycles
- Proposed approaches to profile development and architecture
- Proposed business models, that is, how organizations profit from software (Iberle, 2002), such as custom systems written on contract, custom systems written in-house, commercial products (mass-market), and consumer software
- Proposed agenda for the first WG24 meeting
- Proposed draft strategic plan for WG24

First ISO/IEC JTC 1/SC7 WG24 Meeting – Italy

In October 2005, Italy hosted the ISO/IEC JTC1 SC7 Interim Meeting 2005. WG24, officially established at the SC7 plenary meeting in Helsinki, held its first working sessions there in order to:

1. Present the project to the official members of WG24
2. Finalize project requirements to constitute the project baseline

3. Gain consensus and commitment of WG members regarding the project
4. Process the NWI comment disposition
5. Liaise with other related working groups (i.e., WG7 and WG10)
6. Define the profile creation strategy
7. Define situational factors, that is, the attributes of a business model, such as the criticality of the software under development, that influence the selection of software practices (Iberle, 2002) and business models
8. Build survey material in order to validate project requirements and collect missing information for the industry

Discussion on the material presented in order to start building consensus led to the updating of some input documents and the validation of the project baseline. The new work item list was updated in order to take into account relevant comments received during balloting, and the requirements were validated by WG members. Furthermore, some VSE business models were identified (i.e., custom on contract, custom in-house, commercial products, mass-market software, firmware), as well as a strategy for creating profiles. Finally, WG24 designed a survey in 2006 to collect relevant information from VSEs around the world. Twelve countries committed to participation in WG24: Belgium, Canada, the Czech Republic, Ireland, Italy, Japan, Korea, Luxemburg, South Africa, Thailand, the UK, and the USA.

Second ISO/IEC JTC 1/SC7 WG24 Meeting – Thailand

In the previous meetings, national delegates presented documents for discussion, which the members of WG24 reviewed and discussed. In May 2006, WG24 members met at the ISO/IEC JTC 1/SC7 plenary meeting in Thailand. Two new countries, India and Mexico, sent delegates to WG24. The three main outputs of the meeting were:

1. Analysis of the survey responses:
- 345 responses were collected from 26 countries.
    ◦ 219 responses were received from enterprises with 25 or fewer employees.
    ◦ Over 67% indicated that it was important to be either recognized or certified (e.g., ISO, market).
    ◦ WG24 decided to prioritize the development of profiles and guides for organizations with 25 or fewer employees (total staff). These profiles and guides should also be usable for projects and departments with 25 fewer employees.
- WG24 decided to propose separate profiles for:
    ◦ Enterprises with fewer than 10 employees and
    ◦ Enterprises with 10 to 25 employees.
- WG24 decided to focus first on enterprises with fewer than 10 employees.
2. Evaluation of documents tabled by national delegations.
3. Selection of the Mexican Standard (NMX-059-NYCE, 2005) as an input document for the development of profiles and guides. (The Mexican standard is presented later.)

Centers and Initiatives Focusing on Small and Very Small Software Enterprises

In this section, we describe the work performed by a few centers and initiatives that focus their activities on small and very small enterprises. Most software engineering research centers, such as the Software Engineering Institute, dedicate their resources mainly to large organizations. Even though there seems to be a certain awareness of those needs for VSE solutions, these are still quite unusable by companies with 25 or fewer employees. We discuss their objectives and accomplishments in helping these enterprises become more competitive, since WG24 will try to benefit from the experience gained by these centers.

Centre for Software Process Technologies

The Centre for Software Process Technologies (CSPT)[4] is a research and knowledge transfer organization hosted by the Faculty of Engineering at the University of Ulster. Its activities cover a wide range of areas affecting the quality and effectiveness of both software development processes and products, from process measurement, through business process co-evolution, to object oriented software complexity metrics. The CSPT recently published the results of its first six assessments in small- and medium-sized enterprises (SMEs) using its express process appraisal (EPA) method (Wilkie, McFall, & McCaffery, 2005). EPA is a class C method that complies with the appraisal requirements for CMMI (2002). The EPA model assesses six of the seven process areas at maturity level 2: requirements management, configuration management, project planning, project monitoring and control, measurement and analysis, and process and product quality assurance. The authors reported that the EPA method requires approximately 45 person-hours of the appraised organization's time and 42 person-hours of the CSPT appraisal team's time over a two-week period.

The CSPT also published a paper (McFall et al., 2003) in which the authors present the various perceived priorities and concern areas for different sizes of organizations. As illustrated in Figure 3, the priorities and concerns of organizations with fewer than 20 employees are quite different from those of larger organizations. As an example, for small organizations, managing risk is of great concern, while for larger organizations, this only ranks as priority number 8. Conversely, for small organizations, consistency across teams is less of a concern, while for larger organizations, this is the top-priority issue.

British "Toward Software Excellence"

Toward Software Excellence (TSE)[5] provides a self-assessment "health check" facility and corresponding guidance on best practices (the Route Map) and is based on the ISO/IEC TR 15504 International Standard. It proposes an interesting mix of functionalities and characteristics that can explain small organizations' success: it uses business language and addresses the business perspective of the process issue, aiming at solving business problems first and highlighting the importance of customer relationships. TSE is, in fact, much more than an assessment tool, as it helps to explain issues to people using a language they can understand. This one (with the Belgian Gradual Framework) is probably a good example of how to make tough topics accessible to all.

European Software Institute – IT Mark

The European Software Institute (ESI) is a technological center with an aim to contribute to developing the information society and to increase industry competitiveness by means of knowledge, innovation, continuous improvement, and the promotion and dissemination of IT.

The ESI commercially promotes and delivers the ESI's products and services to the European and Latin-American market in the first phase and at the worldwide level in the second phase. It has established a network of partners, called ESI@net, with companies in which activities are related to SPI (software process improvement) and IT in general.

The ESI Centre Alliance has launched the IT Mark Certification[6] worldwide, which is aimed at certifying the quality and maturity of the processes in SMEs (up to 250 workers) that develop and maintain IT systems. IT Mark assesses and certifies the quality of SMEs in three main areas: business management (overall management: strategic, commercial, financial, marketing, etc.); information security management; and software and systems processes (maturity).

In matters relating to business management, the reference used is the 10^2 model that was developed to assess venture capital applications. For information security management, the reference model used is ISO 17799 (ISO/IEC 17799, 2005), and for software and systems processes, a lightweight version of CMMI® (2002) is used.

SataSPIN

SataSPIN (Varkoi & Mäkinen, 1999) is not a methodology or a solution for assessing or improving software processes, but rather a regional network for software SMEs wanting to make improvements. The authors' main goal is to set up an SPI program in each of the participating companies with a view to establishing a network of companies promoting good software practices in a region. The project provides the participating companies with training and consultation on subjects related to software processes. An essential part of the project is the process assessment. Companies can also obtain assistance in planning and implementing the improvements. Training activities within the project are targeted to support improvement of the software processes and enhance the skills of the personnel. All the activities are tailored separately for each company to ensure flexibility in participation and alignment with business goals.

The core of the SataSPIN project is to help software SMEs develop their operations using international software process models. The project uses the ISO/IEC 15504 standard as the software process assessment tool and improvement framework (which requires public funding as an enabler). The project is based on the cooperation of the participating enterprises, and offers a wide variety of courses and seminars in the area of software engineering and management.

SataSPIN[7], located at Tampere University of Technology of Finland, offers the following services:

- Training and expert services for software process improvement
- Process assessments, improvement planning, and results evaluation
- Training and expertise in software management, methods, and technologies

Two SataSPIN projects have involved 20 software SMEs and over 400 IT professionals.

NORMAPME

NORMAPME[8] (2006) is the European Office of Crafts, Trades, and SMEs for Standardisation. It is an international nonprofit association created in 1996 with the support of the European Commission and the only European organization focusing on small enterprise interests in the European standardization system. Its members represent over 11 million enterprises in all European countries, including all EU and EFTA member states, and its mission is to defend the interests of all of them. This mission is of crucial interest, as SMEs represent over 90% of European companies, and they employ nearly 81 million people, which is 66% of Europe's total employment.

Standards are essential for SMEs today, as they are for any company operating in an internal market. The application of standards adoption guarantees them several advantages, such as enlarging the potential market for products, facilitating product acceptance, lowering transaction costs, achieving economies of scale, reducing external effects (like environmental impact), interoperability, improving management systems, and so on. Thus, standards definition cannot be a privilege enjoyed by big companies alone. SMEs must be represented. However, SMEs lack knowledge with respect to standards and standardization, and they need some support to help them implement existing standards, as well as have a voice in the standardization process.

The European Commission (EC) has supported NORMAPME during its first years of operation. Currently, NORMAPME is party to an EC contract offering standardization services to SMEs.

The principal and most important activity of NORMAPME is participation in the standardization process: experts recommended by member SME organizations participate in the work of technical committees at the European standardization organizations (CEN, CENELEC, ETSI) and at the ISO.

Second, NORMAPME collects information on new directives, directives under review, and standardization works. Essential parts of this information are published in simple language by means of newsletters, specific circulars, a Web site, seminars, and the like. All publications are translated into six languages (English, French, German, Spanish, Italian, and Polish) in order for them to be accessible by the largest number of Europeans.

NORMAPME members, and all SMEs and their organizations, have the opportunity to formulate proposals for the improvement of standards and directives. These opinions are debated in the expert groups in order to draft SME representative positions. Once these positions are finalized, they are promoted in the standards organizations, in European institutions, and through the media by publishing articles and through the press.

Software Quality Institute

The Software Quality Institute, Griffith University (Australia), developed the rapid assessment for process improvement for software development (RAPID) method in conformity with ISO/IEC 15504 (Rout, Tuffley, Cahill, & Hodgen, 2000). RAPID was developed for SMEs with limited investment of time and resources. The model includes eight ISO/IEC 15504 processes: requirements gathering, software development, project management, configuration management, quality assurance, problem resolution, risk management, and process establishment. The scope of the model is limited to Levels 1, 2, and 3, although capability ratings at Levels 4 and 5 are possible. The organizations assessed in Queensland ranged in size from 3 to 120 employees, with an average size of 10 to 12 employees.

ESPRIT – ESPINODE Initiative

An assessment methodology has been developed by ESPINODE for Central Italy, with the aim of using rapid software process assessment as a way to promote innovation for SMEs (Cignoni, 1999). The methodology is based on a two-part questionnaire compiled by experts who interview representatives of the enterprise. Part 1 is conducted by phone, and Part 2 is completed in a direct audit meeting.

Rapid-assessment meetings to allow enterprises to "taste" SPI and awareness and training events are used as a way to establish the very first contact with the enterprises and to present the opportunity of a rapid software process assessment as a free service. The specific goals of the subsequent assessment program are:

- To stimulate interest in software process assessment and improvement
- To contribute to the definition of specific improvement plans
- To collect data and statistics about software process maturity

Being "rapid," the methodology developed is also approximate. Due to time constraints, the scope and accuracy of the assessment are sacrificed, since the assessment meeting is limited to half a day, including time for discussion. In particular, a very general assessment is made of the 35 processes, and some more accurate questions are formulated on just three processes belonging to two of the five SPICE process categories. Moreover, the accuracy of the assessment is limited to the answers given by the enterprises,

and the answers are neither cross-checked nor validated.

The rapid assessment procedure offered through awareness and training events shows that, in very many cases, identifiable benefits can be achieved via focused SPI projects. The offer of a free (rapid) assessment is a way to both diffuse process quality concepts and propose actual improvement paths to enterprises.

Mexican Approach

In Mexico, it was felt that standards such as ISO/IEC 12207, or models such as CMMI, were either too general or too costly for Mexican enterprises. A Mexican standard was therefore developed at the request of the Ministry of the Economy. It provides the software industry there with a model based on international practices and on the following characteristics:

- It is easy to understand.
- It is easy to apply.
- Adopting it is economical.
- It provides the basis on which to achieve successful evaluations with other standards or models, such as ISO 9000:2000 or CMMI®.

The Mexican standard (NMX-059-NYCE, 2005) is divided into four parts: Part 1, Definition of Concepts and Products; Part 2, Process Requirements (MoProSoft); Part 3, Guidelines for Process Implementation; and Part 4, Guidelines for Process Assessment (EvalProSoft).

The Process Model

The process model MoProSoft uses ISO/IEC 12207 as a general framework. It was developed considering integration between software processes and business processes and borrows practices from ISO 9000:2000 and CMMI®. It also incorporates practices from the Project Management Body of Knowledge (PMBOK, 2006) and the Software Engineering Body of Knowledge (SWEBOK) (ISO TR 19759, 2005). In addition, MoProSoft addresses the process model requirements of ISO/IEC 15504-2 (ISO/IEC 15504-2, 2003). The percentage of coverage by MoProSoft with respect to these practices is as follows:

- ISO 9001:2000   92%
- ISO/IEC 12207
    (Amendments 1 and 2)   95%
- CMMI level 2   77%

MoProSoft focuses on processes and considers three basic organizational or structural levels under which processes are organized: top management, management, and operations.

- The top management category contains the business management process. Its purpose is to establish the reason for the existence of an organization, its goals, and the conditions required to achieve them.
- The management category consists of process management, project portfolio management, and resource management.
- The operations category consists of specific projects management and software development and maintenance.

In addition, MoProSoft highlights informative data, added to the normative part, and proposes tailoring guides for each process. This is a very helpful feature and one requested by VSEs in the survey.

The Assessment Method

The Mexican standard also proposes Guidelines for Process Assessment, EvalProSoft, based on ISO/IEC 15504-2. The process assessment model defines five levels of capability and their associated attributes, as illustrated in Figure 6. For VSEs, WG24 will develop profiles, guides, and templates for capability levels 1 and 2. After reaching level 2, a VSE should be mature enough to make appropriate decisions about future improvement activities.

The Association of Thai Software Industry (ATSI)

The Association of Thai Software Industry (ATSI) developed the Thai Quality Software (TQS) standard[9] (2005) to provide Thai VSEs with a way to improve their process quality using a standard as a reference model. TQS is a staged

Figure 6. Capability dimensions of ISO/IEC 15504-2

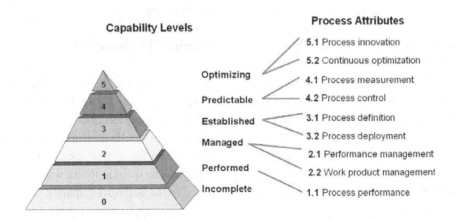

implementation of ISO/IEC 12207, where different processes are implemented at each of five capability levels, and each level has different requirements (L1=records; L2=procedures, plans; L3, L4, L5=more processes).

TQS was developed to respond to the following issues:

- Thai SMEs are not ready to implement the entire ISO/IEC 12207 standard.
- Not all ISO/IEC 12207 activities are suitable for SME operations.
- There is no assessment model for the ISO/IEC 12207 standard.
- Most software developers are not document-oriented.

To address those issues, ATSI proposed the following guidelines for the creation of a framework:

- Break down the ISO/IEC 12207 standard into stages or levels in order to fit all sizes of SMEs.
- Modify ISO/IEC 12207 activities to suit SME operations: product and project based on type of business.
- Develop a set of checklists for use by assessors.
- Provide templates and examples.

The TQS standard has the following characteristics:

- It has been adapted from the ISO/IEC 12207 Software Life Cycle Standard.
- It is divided into five stages.
  ○ Each stage ensures that software organizations use international standards for producing software.
  ○ Software organizations are assessed for certification at each stage.
- It comprises three main processes:

  ○ Primary Life Cycle Process
  ○ Supporting Life Cycle Process
  ○ Organizational Life Cycle Process

Table 2 illustrates the breakdown, from level I to level V, of the development process.

By March 2005, 43 Thai software organizations had already been certified at TQS level 1, and 11 software organizations had been certified at TQS level 2. However, in spite of the effort made to stage the standard and make it a step-by-step approach, most companies (VSEs) still found it too complicated and difficult to implement, and few of them managed to do so.

Centre d'Excellence en Technologies de l'Information et de la Communication

The Centre d'Excellence en Technologies de l'Information et de la Communication (CETIC),[10] located in Wallonia (Belgium), focuses on applied research and technology transfer in the field of software engineering and electronic systems. CETIC is a connecting agent between academic research and industrial companies. At the University of Namur, a software process improvement approach dedicated to small development structures has been developed. The method, called Micro-Evaluation, has been used and improved in collaboration with CETIC and the Department of Software and IT Engineering at the École de Technologie Supérieure (ÉTS, Québec, Canada).[11]

Gradual Framework

At the first stage, a very simplified questionnaire, called the Micro-Evaluation, is used to collect information about the current software practices in small structures and to make people sensitive to the importance of software quality aspects. The questionnaire was mostly designed based on the Software Capability Maturity Model

Table 2. Breakdown of the development process

12207	12207 Processes & Activities	Level I	Level II	Level III	Level IV	Level V
5.	*Primary life cycle processes*					
5.3	Development process	Process implementation	Process implementation	Process implementation	Process implementation	Process implementation
		Software requirements analysis	Systems requirements analysis	Systems requirements analysis	Systems requirements analysis	Systems requirements analysis
		Software architectural design	System architectural design	System architectural design	System architectural design	System architectural design
		Software coding and testing	Software requirements analysis	Software requirements analysis	Software requirements analysis	Software requirements analysis
		Software acceptance and support	Software architectural design	Software architectural design	Software architectural design	Software architectural design
			Software coding and testing	Software detailed design	Software detailed design	Software detailed design
			Software installation	Software coding and testing	Software coding and testing	Software coding and testing
			Software acceptance and support	Software integration	Software integration	Software integration
				System qualification testing	System qualification testing	System qualification testing
				Software installation	Software installation	Software installation
				Software acceptance and support	Software acceptance and support	Software acceptance and support

(Paulk, Curtis, Chrissis, & Weber, 1993) and on the ISO/IEC 15504 (SPICE) reference model and uses an interview method. It covers six key axes selected on the basis of former experience with SME and VSE evaluation as the most pertinent and the most important to the targeted organizations. These axes are quality management, customer management, subcontractor management, development and project management, product management, and training and human resources management.

The Micro-Evaluation was first tested on a sample of 20 organizations in Wallonia (Laporte, Renault, Desharnais, Habra, Abou El Fattah, & Bamba, 2005). Figure 7 shows the global maturity profile of the small enterprises involved in the first

Micro-Evaluation round. Subsequently, 7 of the 20 companies reevaluated their practices and one performed a third Micro-Evaluation.

In 2004, 23 micro-evaluations were performed in Quebec, Canada. The average number of employees in the companies concerned was about 13, and the average number of years the companies had been producing software was about 12. Figure 8 shows that small organizations were performing, with a score of about 3 out of a maximum of 4, requirement formalization, project planning, problem management, and verification and versioning activities. A number of weaknesses can also be noted: very low scores on commitment to quality, change management, product structure, human resources management (i.e., training), and project tracking. It is also interesting to note that project planning scored significantly higher (3.0) than tracking. It seems that VSEs develop a plan, and then, once in development, the plan is forgotten while the "fire" of the day is put out.

The ÉTS is currently conducting experiments with some of its graduate software engineering students. As part of their academic courses (Software Quality Assurance and The Case Study), they are required to perform evaluations, identify one or two practices to improve and transfer the practice(s) to the organization. Since some of the students already work for VSEs, it is easy for them to sell their management on the idea of a small team of two or three students investing a few hundred hours of their own time into improving an area of the VSE development process.

The second step of the OWPL (Observatoire Wallon des Pratiques Logicielles) gradual approach is the OWPL assessment based on a light reference model adapted from SW CMM. The OWPL model has been designed with respect to the particular context of small businesses, to help them improve their software practices. The structure of the OWPL model involves processes, practices, and success factors. It defines

Figure 7. Evolution of profile over three micro-evaluations

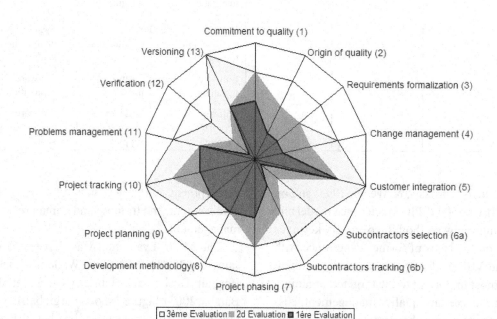

Figure 8. First micro-evaluation round in Québec

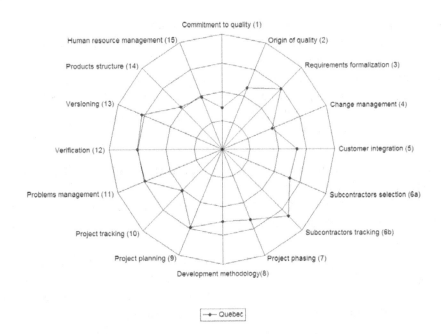

10 processes (requirements management, project planning, project tracking and oversight, development, documentation, testing, configuration management, subcontractors management, quality management, and experience capitalization), each of which is decomposed into a number of practices (from 3 to 12). It is also supported by success factors. Each of the above processes is assigned a general goal in accordance with the organization's defined objectives. It involves a number of practices and is supported by a number of success factors. Each practice is defined by its goal, its inputs and outputs, the resources assigned to support it and its weight. This last attribute is an indicator of the importance of the practice to improving the process as a whole.

Software Engineering Institute

The Software Engineering Institute (SEI) has launched a project titled "Improving Processes in Small Settings (IPSS)."[12] For this project, small settings are defined as companies with fewer than

100 employees, organizations with fewer than 50 people, and projects with fewer than 20 people (Garcia, 2005). The IPSS project will assemble small businesses, governments, large businesses, advocacy organizations, universities, and industry associations from around the world to jointly explore the unique challenges and opportunities of applying process improvement strategies in small businesses. The SEI seeks to achieve the following objectives:

- Increase awareness of process excellence as an enabler of global competitiveness
- Demonstrate effective approaches to process improvement for the small business
- Provide tools for process improvement that are easily applied by small businesses

The ParqueSoft Organization of Columbia

The Software Technology Park Foundation[13] (Fundación Parque Tecnológico del Software),

ParqueSoft, is a not-for-profit organization established in December 1999 for the purpose of creating and developing enterprises providing goods and services to the IT market. ParqueSoft is consolidating Southwestern Colombia's Science and Technology Corridor, integrating 12 software technology parks located in Cali, Popayán, Pasto, Buga, Tuluá, Palmira, Buenaventura, Roldanillo, Cartago, Armenia, Manizales, and Pereira.

To date, ParqueSoft and its network of software technology parks house more than 200 VSEs where more than 800 software engineering professionals specializing in the industry's latest technologies, along with 200 other professionals, provide support in administrative and business development processes. These VSEs have, on average, six employees each.

ParqueSoft has created an innovative support model encompassing five macro objectives supported by 16 synergistic strategies to promote enterprise development and research and development (R&D). The macro objectives and their corresponding strategies are listed in Table 3.

ParqueSoft has completed the implementation of its quality management system based on ISO 9001:2000. This certification turns ParqueSoft into the first enterprise incubator in Colombia to certify its quality processes. This is also being achieved by 14 of its VSEs. The next goal is to certify all ParqueSoft VSEs in the next four years.

Common Features of These Initiatives

Dozens of universities, research centers, and associations have tried to find their own answers to one issue facing most VSEs. However, at this point, no one has been able to propose an answer that fits whatever the context and taking into account all previous experience and knowledge as valuable input.

Obviously, all the VSE initiatives listed had the following statements in common:

Table 3. ParqueSoft's objectives and strategies

• Objective 1. To provide an infrastructure for business development and support
   o   Competitive infrastructure
   o   Technological support (Telco, networking, videoconferencing, data center)
   o   Effective communications (Internet, Intranet, and media)
   o   Intellectual property and legal support

• Objective 2. To develop the best people in the industry
   o   Empowerment of human talent
   o   Preparation for the software industry
   o   Develop seedbeds of research and entrepreneurship

• Objective 3. To become more innovative and provide reliable and competitive products   o   Build with quality (products, processes)

• Objective 4. To develop a financial strength
   o   Entrepreneurship promotion funds
   o   Risk-capital funds
   o   Savings

• Objective 5. To support enterprise development
   o   Market intelligence
   o   Creative marketing
   o   Business knowledge
   o   Business development
   o   Business support and updating

- VSEs require low-cost solutions.
- VSEs require additional effort in communications, in standardizing vocabulary.
- VSEs require a staged approach.
- VSEs require ways to identify potential quick wins.

FINDINGS OF THE IEEE STANDARDS SURVEY

In 1997, the Technical Council on Software Engineering responsible for the IEEE Software Engineering Standards (SES) conducted a survey to capture information from software engineering standards users in order to improve those standards (Land, 1997). They gathered 148 answers, mainly from the USA (79%) and large companies (87% of them having more than 100 employees). The main application domains of the survey respondents were IT (22%), military (15%), and aerospace (11%). (It should be noted that the purpose of this section is not to systematically compare the two sets of survey results.)

Even though the IEEE survey objectives differ from those of the ISO/IEC survey, there are some interesting common findings. In response to the question concerning the reasons why their organization does not use standards, 37% said that the standards were not available in their facilities, while 37% explained that they use other standards. In fact, the IEEE survey underscores the fact that ISO/IEC standards are often used in organizations, rather than the IEEE standards.

The IEEE survey underlined the difficulties regarding IEEE standards use reported by the respondents. The two main difficulties were a lack of understanding of the benefits (28%) and a lack of useful examples (25%). The survey also revealed how IEEE standards are used in organizations. Most of the organizations (35 answers) claimed to use IEEE standards for internal plan elaboration.

The IEEE survey gathered several new requirements about IEEE standards being requested by the respondents. These were principally examples and templates of deliverables (about 32 responses), support for metrics and measurement (about 30 responses), help on life cycle process definition (about 23 responses), and a training course and support for small, rapid application development efforts.

ANALYSIS OF SURVEY DATA CONDUCTED BY WG24

The WG24 survey was developed to question VSEs about their use of standards and widely recognized documents, such as the CMMI, and to collect data to identify problems and potential solutions to help them apply the standards and become more competitive. From the very beginning, the working group drew up several working hypotheses regarding VSEs. The survey was intended to validate some of these, such as:

- The VSE context requires light and well focused life cycle profiles.
- Particular business contexts require particular profiles.
- There are significant differences in terms of available resources and infrastructure between a VSE employing 1 to 25 people and an IT department of the same size in a large company.
- VSEs are limited in both time and resources, which can lead to a lack of understanding of how to use the standards for their benefit.
- Benefits for VSEs may include recognition through assessment or audit by an accredited body.

The working group also wanted to know: the reasons for using standards, or for not using them, which standards were used, the problems/barriers encountered when using them, and how we can facilitate their adoption and utilization.

An introductory text (see Appendix A) and a questionnaire were developed by a graduate student and members of WG24 and translated into nine languages: English, French, German, Korean, Portuguese, Thai, Turkish, Russian, and Spanish. The survey (see Appendix B) is made up of 20 questions structured in five parts: general information, information about standards utilization in VSEs, information about implementation and assessment problems in VSEs, information about VSE needs, and information about justification for compliance to standard(s).

A Web site, hosted by the École de Technologie Supérieure,[14] was developed to maximize the number of responses and facilitate data collection and analysis. A mailing list was created using WG24 members' contact networks. We also contacted centers and software engineering professors focusing on the concerns of small software enterprises, such as the CETIC[15] Center in Belgium, the Centre de Recherche Public Henri Tudor in Luxembourg,[16] the Thai Software Industry Promotion Agency (SIPA[17]), The European Software Institute (ESI[18]), the Colombian Parquesoft[19] organization, the Japan Information Technology Promotion Agency (JITEC[20]), the Irish Enterprise Ireland,[21] and the Software Process Improvement Networks (SPIN[22]) worldwide. Access to the Web-based survey was protected, as suggested by Kasunic (2005), to prevent unauthorized individuals from participating and to prevent duplicate submissions by a single respondent. The survey software, produced by Quask,[23] was satisfactory. Its weakness was that it was not capable of supporting double characters. These characters are used in languages such as Thai, Korean, and Russian. To remedy this problem, we provided the survey questionnaire to the respondents from these countries as a Word document.

One of these organizations, Thailand's SIPA, also acted as a host for the 2006 ISO/IEC JTC1/SC7 plenary meeting. The SIPA organized a series of free tutorials for their members the week before the SC7 meeting. One condition for a SIPA member to participate in the tutorials was to respond to the survey. This resulted in over 58 responses from Thai VSEs (see Table 4). In Colombia, ParqueSoft designated an individual to solicit VSEs and help them complete the survey. Since there are over 100 VSEs in the Parquesoft group, this explains the high number of responses received from that country.

Respondents were informed that it would take a maximum of 15 minutes to complete the survey. They were also informed that all data would be kept confidential and that only summary results and project data that could not be matched to a specific VSE would be included in the published results.

In order to increase participation in the survey, WG24 promised to send all respondents a report presenting, on an anonymous basis, the survey results. The survey was launched in February 2006, and, as of as of June 2006, over 392 responses had been collected from 29 countries.[24]

Categorization of the Sample According to the Size Criterion

In order to avoid developing profiles that would not meet the needs of VSEs, WG24 defined what VSEs are in terms of size. At the time, there was no official definition of the VSE, while the concept of the small- and medium-sized enterprise (SME) had already been clearly defined in Europe (fewer than 250 employees or with a turnover $\leq$ €50 million) and in the United States (fewer than 500 employees). The Organization for Economic Cooperation and Development (OECD) subdivides the SME category into several subcategories: micro (0[25]-9 employees); small (10-49 employees); and medium (50-250 or 500 in the United States). In Europe, micro enterprises represent 93% of the total number of companies (56% in the United States) and 66% of total employment [9].

Of the 392 responders, 228 were enterprises

with 0 to 25 employees (58%), as illustrated in Figure 9. These 228 VSEs constitute the sample for this study. The following paragraphs present findings common to the 228 VSEs, identifying correlations inside the sample and findings that differ from those of the bigger companies that contributed to the survey.

This categorization and several studies underscore the differences between micro-, small-, and medium-sized enterprises in terms of available resources. WG24 decided to focus on the first category (micro enterprises with 0-9 employees) and on a subpart of the small enterprise category (10-25 employees).

General Characteristics

Here, we draw attention to some weaknesses of the sample itself. Since the survey was initiated through WG24 contacts without building a true random sample, the survey results may have been impacted. The first observation about the respondent sample, as illustrated in Table 4, is

the geographical distribution of the responses. We collected a high number from Latin America (46%), mainly from Colombia (22%) and Brazil (17%).

At the same time, we received only a few responses from European countries (48), Japan (3), and the United States (3). Possible reasons for this are:

* The invitation to participate in the survey was not distributed in some countries.
* Many SPIN members are employed in larger companies not directly targeted by this survey.
* Most SPIN members already use CMMI, and they may not be interested in ISO standards.
* Most VSEs do not care about IT standardization, so only those aware of it took the time to contribute.

Our results might, therefore, only generalize to the broader populations of projects in each region

Figure 9. Number of employees in the enterprises surveyed

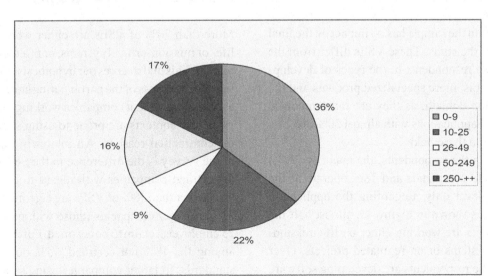

Table 4. Number of survey responses per country, as of June 2006

Country	Number of Responses	Country	Number of Responses
Argentina	2	Italy	2
Australia	10	Japan	3
Belgium	10	South Korea	4
Brazil	70	Luxembourg	2
Bulgaria	3	Mexico	20
Canada	9	New Zealand	1
Chile	1	Peru	4
Colombia	109	Russia	4
Czech Republic	3	South Africa	10
Dominican Republic	1	Spain	3
Ecuador	9	Taiwan	1
Finland	13	Thailand	58
France	4	Turkey	1
Germany	1	United Kingdom	2
India	57	United States	3
Ireland	10		

to the extent that this sample represents them. Moreover, we have no evidence that participating companies are representative of the situation in their own countries. Conclusions drawn from these survey results should be confirmed with additional responses. To achieve this objective, WG24 plans to keep the survey Web site online and launch another survey blitz.

The strong representation of Latin American countries in the sample has no impact on the final results of the study. These VSEs differ from the rest of the respondents in the types of development, that is, more specialized products and the application domain, as they are more involved in critical applications with almost 50% of VSEs working on these fields.

Among the respondents, the majority (79%) are private companies and 78% operate at the national level only. Regarding the application domain, as shown in Figure 10, almost half the respondents are working either on life/mission-critical systems or on regulated projects. Over 40% of the respondents are developing software

for life/mission-critical systems and 34% on regulated developments.

With regard to the types of software development, the majority control customized or tailor-made software and specialized products, as shown in Figure 11.

Features of the VSE Results

More than 70% of VSEs are either working on life- or mission-critical systems, or in a regulated market. This underscores our hypothesis concerning the awareness of the participating companies, as it is assumed that companies working on these particular contexts are prone to using standards for contractual reasons. An interesting finding of the survey is the difference in the percentage of certified companies with regard to company size: fewer than 18% of VSEs are certified, while 53% of larger companies (those with more than 25 employees) claim to be certified. Furthermore, among the 18% not certified, 75% do not use standards. In larger companies using standards,

Figure 10. Application domain

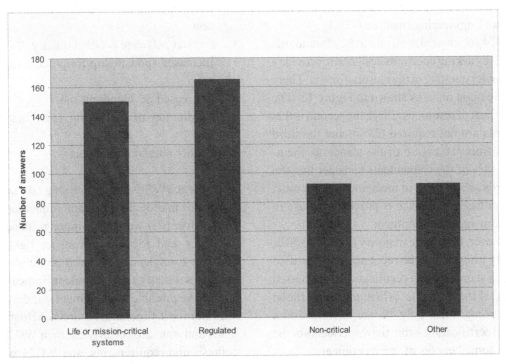

Figure 11. Types of software development

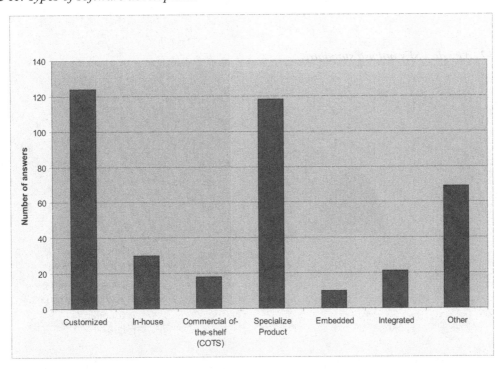

two families of standards and models emerge from the list: ISO standards (55%) and models from the Software Engineering Institute (47%).

WG24 anticipated the limited use of standards by VSEs by asking questions designed to provide a better understanding of the reasons for this. There are three main ones, as shown in Figure 12. The first is a lack of resources (28%); the second is that standards are not required (24%); and the third derives from the nature of the standards themselves: 15% of the respondents consider that the standards are difficult to meet and bureaucratic, and insufficient guidance is provided for use in a small business environment.

However, for a large majority (74%) of VSEs, it is very important to be recognized or certified against a standard. ISO certification is requested by 40% of them. Of the 28% requesting official market recognition, only 4% are interested in a national certification. From the respondents of the survey, some benefits of certification are:

- Increased competitiveness
- Greater customer confidence and satisfaction
- Greater software product quality
- Increased sponsorship for process improvement
- Decreased development risk
- Facilitation of marketing (e.g., better image)
- Higher potential to export

However, VSEs are expressing the need for assistance in order to adopt and implement standards. Over 62% would like more guidance with examples, and 55% are asking for lightweight and easy-to-understand standards complete with templates. Finally, the respondents indicated that it has to be possible to implement standards with minimum cost, time, and resources. All data about VSEs and standards clearly confirm WG24's hypothesis and requirements, and WG24 will use this information to develop profiles, guides, and templates to meet VSE needs.

Figure 12. Why do VSEs not use standards?

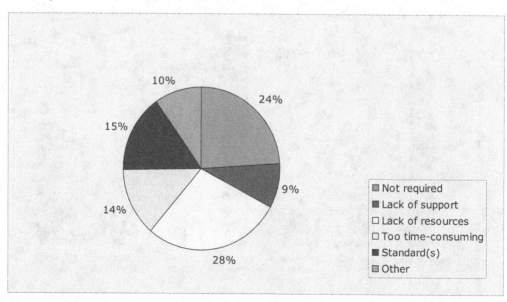

FUTURE WORK AND CONCLUSION

The software industry recognizes the value of VSEs in contributing valuable products and services to the economy. As software quality increasingly becomes a subject of concern, and process approaches are maturing and gaining the confidence of companies, the use of standards is spreading in organizations of all sizes. However, existing standards were not written for small or very small organizations (development organizations with fewer than 25 employees), and are consequently difficult to apply in such settings, though small and very small companies can represent from 50 to 85% of a local economy in some regions of the world.

A large number of universities, research centers, and associations have tried to find their own answers to this issue being faced by most VSEs, and are proposing software process models dedicated to small companies. However, at this point, no one has been able to propose a one-size-fits-all solution for any context and taking all previous experience and knowledge into account. Most potential solutions are still too complicated and cannot be applied to VSEs as defined in the scope of this project.

A new ISO/IEC JTC1 SC7 Working Group, WG24, has been established to address those difficulties by developing profiles and by providing guidance for compliance by very small organizations with ISO software engineering standards. A survey was conducted to ask these very small organizations about their use of ISO/IEC JTC1 SC7 standards and to collect data to identify problems and potential solutions to help them apply standards. Over 400 responses were received from 30 countries. The survey was intended to validate working hypotheses regarding VSEs drawn up by the working group.

Based on this feedback, the working group will start tailoring existing solutions (i.e., the Mexican standard) to adapt them to the requirements expressed by VSEs taking part in the survey. This will enable WG24 to propose profiles, guides, and templates for the 0-9 employee category and the 10-25 employee category that really take the concerns of VSEs into account and fit them into their particular context. The working group's key challenge will be the selection and tailoring of processes from existing standards (mainly ISO 12207) for VSEs.

The next stage will be to undertake pilot projects. These will be conducted within real projects to assess the artifacts developed by WG24, providing the working group with key information to update them and move towards international balloting and publication by the ISO. We will conduct pilot projects in different environments in order to gain confidence that their results will be applicable to a wide spectrum of VSEs. These projects will be coordinated and monitored by the members of WG24. The fact that the members of this working group are located on many continents should enable us to conduct pilot projects in different cultural contexts.

ACKNOWLEDGMENT

The authors would like to thank Mrs. Karine Bluteau, a graduate software engineering student at the ÉTS, who was instrumental in developing and conducting the survey and the establishment of the survey Web site. The authors would also like to thank all those who helped translate the survey and invited VSEs to respond to it.

REFERENCES

Ad Hoc Report. (2004, May). Software engineering standards for small and medium enterprises. ISO/IEC JTC1/SC7/N3060. Retrieved December 12, 2007, from http://www.jtc1-sc7.org/

Anacleto, A., von Wangenheim, C.G., Salviano, C.F., & Savi, R. (2004). Experiences gained from applying ISO/IEC 15504 to small software companies in Brazil. In *Proceedings of the 4th International SPICE Conference on Process Assessment and Improvement*, Lisbon, Portugal (pp. 33-37).

Cellule Interfacultaire de Technology Assessment CITA. (1997). *Utilisation des Systèmes d'Information Inter-Organisationnels [SIO] par les PME Belges* (SIO Research Report). Cita-Computer Sciences Department, University of Namur.

Cignoni, G.A. (1999). Rapid software process assessment to promote innovation in SME's. In *Proceedings of Euromicro 99*, Italy.

CMMI. (2002). CMMI for systems engineering and software engineering (CMMI-SE/SW, V1.1): Continuous representation (CMU/SEI-2002-TR-001). Software Engineering Institute.

CMMI. (2002). CMMI for systems engineering and software engineering (CMMI-SE/SW, V1.1): Staged representation (CMU/SEI-2002-TR-002). Software Engineering Institute.

Coallier, F. (2003). *International standardization in software and systems engineering. Crosstalk, Journal of Defense Software Engineering*, 18-22.

Garcia, S. (2005). *Thoughts on applying CMMI in small settings*. Presentation to Montréal SPIN.

Iberle, K. (2002). But will it work for me? In *Proceedings of the Pacific Northwest Software Quality Conference*, Portland, WA.

ISO/IEC 12207. (1995). *Information technology: Software life cycle processes*. Geneva, Switzerland: International Organization for Standardization/International Electrotechnical Commission.

ISO/IEC 15288. (2002). *Systems engineering: Systems life cycle process*. Geneva, Switzerland: International Organization for Standardization/International Electrotechnical Commission.

ISO/IEC 15504. (2003-2005). *Information technology: Process assessment* (Part 1-5). Geneva, Switzerland: International Organization for Standardization/International Electrotechnical Commission.

ISO/IEC 15504-2. (2003). *Information technology: Process assessment* (Part 2: Performing an assessment). Geneva, Switzerland: International Organization for Standardization/International Electrotechnical Commission.

ISO/IEC 17799. (2005). *Information technology: Security techniques* (Code of practice for information security management). Geneva, Switzerland: International Organization for Standardization/International Electrotechnical Commission.

ISO/IEC 90003. (2004). *Software engineering: Guidelines for the application of ISO 9001:2000 to computer software*. Geneva, Switzerland: International Organization for Standardization/International Electrotechnical Commission.

ISO/IEC 9001. (2000). *Quality management systems: Requirements*. Geneva, Switzerland: International Organization for Standardization/International Electrotechnical Commission.

ISO/IEC JTC1/SC7 N3288. (2005, May). *New work item proposal: Software life cycles for very small enterprises*. Retrieved December 12, 2007, from http://www.jtc1-sc7.org/

ISO/IEC TR 10000-1. (1998). *Information technology: Framework and taxonomy of international standardized profiles* (Part 1: General principles and documentation framework, 4th ed.). Geneva, Switzerland: International Organization for Standardization/International Electrotechnical Commission.

ISOTR19759-05. (2005). *Software engineering body of knowledge: Technical report ISO/IEC PRF TR 19759*. Geneva, Switzerland: International Organization for Standardization/International Electrotechnical Commission.

ITMark. (2006). Retrieved December 12, 2007, from http://www.esi.es/en/main/iitmark.html

Kasunic, M. (2005). *Designing an effective survey* (Handbook CMU/SEI-2005-HB-004). Software Engineering Institute.

Land, S.K. (1997, June 1-6). Results of the IEEE survey of software engineering standards users. In *Proceedings of the Software Engineering Standards Symposium and Forum: Emerging International Standards (ISESS 97),* Walnut Creek, CA (pp. 242-270).

Laporte, C.Y., & April, A. (2006a, January). Applying software engineering standards in small settings: Recent historical perspectives and initial achievements (CMU/SEI-2006-Special Report-001). In *Proceedings of the 1st International Research Workshop for Process Improvement in Small Settings* (pp. 39-51). Software Engineering Institute, Carnegie Mellon University.

Laporte, C.Y., April, A., & Renault, A. (2006, May 4-5). Applying ISO/IEC software engineering standards in small settings: Historical perspectives and initial achievements. In *Proceedings of the SPICE Conference,* Luxembourg (pp. 57-62).

Laporte, C.Y., Renault, A., Desharnais, J.M., Habra, N., Abou El Fattah, M., & Bamba, J.C. (2005, May 27-June 1). Initiating software process improvement in small enterprises: Experiment with micro-evaluation framework (SWDC-REK). In *Proceedings of the International Conference on Software Development,* University of Iceland, Reykjavik, Iceland (pp. 153-163).

McFall, D., Wilkie, F.G., McCaffery, F., Lester, N.G., & Sterritt, R. (2003, December 1-10). Software processes and process improvement in Northern Ireland. In *Proceedings of the 16th International Conference on Software & Systems Engineering and their Applications,* Paris, France. ISSN: 1637-5033.

NMX-059-NYCE. (2005). *Information technology-software-models of processes and assessment for software development and maintenance* (Part 1: Definition of concepts and products, Part 2: Process requirements (MoProSoft), Part 3: Guidelines for process implementation, Part 4: Guidelines for process assessment (EvalProSoft)). Mexico Ministry of Economy.

NORMAPME. (2006). Retrieved December 12, 2007, from http://www.normapme.com/

Parquesoft Brief. (2006). Cali, Colombia: Parquesoft.

Paulk, M., Curtis, B., Chrissis, M.B., & Weber, C. (1993, February). Capability maturity model for software (Version 1.1, CMU/SEI-93-TR-24, DTIC No. ADA263403). Software Engineering Institute.

PMBOK. (2006). Project management body of knowledge. Retrieved December 12, 2007, from http://www.pmi.org/publictn/pmboktoc.htm

Resolutions. (2005, May). Presented at the JTC1/SC7 Plenary Meeting (ISO/IEC JTC1/SC7 N3274), Helsinki, Finland.

Rout, T., Tuffley, A., Cahill, B., & Hodgen, B. (2000). The rapid assessment of software process capability. In *Proceedings of SPICE 2000,* Limerick, Ireland (pp. 47-55).

SC7 Secretariat Presentation. (2005, May 25). ISO/IEC Advisory Group Planning Meeting, Helsinki, Finland.

SC7 Secretariat Presentation. (2006, May). Bangkok, Thailand.

Software Technology Park Foundation. (2006). Retrieved December 12, 2007, from http://www.parquesoft.com

Thai Quality Standard. (2005, March). Association of Thai Software Industry presentation to the Special Working Group Meeting, Bangkok, Thailand.

Varkoi, T., & Mäkinen, T. (1999). Software process improvement network in the Satakunta region: SataSPIN. In *Proceedings of the EuroSPI'99*, Pori, Finland.

Wilkie, F.G., McFall, D., & McCaffery, F. (2005, April 27-29). The express process appraisal method. In *Proceedings of 5th International SPICE Conference (SPICE 2005)*, Klagenfurt, Austria (pp. 27-36). Austrian Computer Society. ISBN 3-85403-190-4.

ENDNOTES

[1]   ISO/IEC JTC 1/SC7 stands for the International Organization for Standardization/International Electrotechnical Commission Joint Technical Committee 1/Sub Committee 7.

[2]   CMMI and CMM are registered with the U.S. Patents and Trademarks Office by Carnegie Mellon University.

[3]   Capability Maturity Model Integration is a service mark of Carnegie Mellon University.

[4]   http://www.infc.ulst.ac.uk/informatics/cspt/

[5]   http://www.softwareexcellence.co.uk/

[6]   http://www.esi.es/en/main/iitmark.html

[7]   http://www.tut.fi/public/

[8]   http://www.normapme.com/

[9]   http://www.atsi.or.th/atsi_th

[10]   http://www.cetic.be

[11]   http://profs.logti.etsmtl.ca/jmdeshar/SiteWQ/index.html

[12]   http://www.sei.cmu.edu/iprc/ipss.html

[13]   www.parquesoft.com

[14]   www.etsmtl.ca

[15]   www.cetic.be

[16]   www.tudor.lu

[17]   www.sipa.or.th

[18]   www.esi.es

[19]   www.parquesoft.com

[20]   www.ipa.go.jp

[21]   www.enterprise-ireland.com

[22]   http://www.sei.cmu.edu/collaborating/spins

[23]   www.quask.com

[24]   As of October 2006, 430 responses had been collected from 32 countries.

[25]   Company formed by its founder without any additional employees (e.g., consultant).

Chapter III
Practical Experience in Customization for a Software Development Process for Small Companies Based on RUP Process and MSF

Valerio Fernandes del Maschi
Universidade Paulista, Brazil

Mauro de Mesquita Spínola
Universidade Paulista, Brazil

Ivanir Costa
Universidade Paulista, Brazil

Alexandre de Lima Esteves
Universidade Paulista, Brazil

Luciano S. Souza
Universidade Paulista, Brazil

Wilson Vendramel
Universidade Paulista, Brazil

Jorge Pirola
Universidade Paulista, Brazil

ABSTRACT

The quality in software projects is related the deliveries that are adjusted to the use, and that they take care of to the objectives. In this way, Brazilian organizations of software development, especially the small and medium ones, need to demonstrate to future customers whom an initial understand of the business problem has enough. This chapter has as objective to demonstrate methodology, strategy, main phases and procedures adopted beyond the gotten ones of a small organization of development of software in the implantation of a Customized Software Engineering Process and of a Tool of Support to the Process in the period of 2004 to 2006 on the basis of rational unified process (RUP) and in the Microsoft solutions framework (MSF).

INTRODUCTION

Most Brazilian software development companies focus on the customer's needs, thus creating cells dedicated to these customers both for products that have been built or that are being built. Furthermore, they normally lack the financial resources necessary for investments in specialized technologies and professionals, leading them to use processes that do not adhere to the market's best practices, such as object-oriented technology and standard development methods and procedures, for example, rational unified process (RUP), unified modeling language (UML), Microsoft solutions framework (MSF), quality models proposed by the Software Engineering Institute/Capability Maturity Model Integration (SEI/CMMI), and the International Standardization Organization/Standard CMMI Appraisal Method for Process Improvement (ISO/SPICE). This chapter describes the general concepts of the low and high complexity software development processes and models, the steps that a small Brazilian software development company followed to achieve maturity, parting from a research and development initiative in the aforementioned processes, and finally creating and instituting the customized software engineering process (CSEP[1]) and the process supporting tool (PST[2]). An economic/financial overview of the Brazilian market for software development is also presented, besides historical data concerning the projects before and after the implementation of the processes and tool, as well as the success obtained, and lastly the emerging trends in Brazil's software development market.

BACKGROUND

One of the factors that determine the competitiveness of the companies is the definition of the target market. Customer companies of different sizes, who need software based products or systems, expect to receive quality solutions that meet the defined requirements. Besides the agile models, the proposals made by Rational, such as the RUP, and Microsoft's MSF will be described, which although similar, clearly display differences regarding complexity and level of depth in relation to specific subjects, thus justifying the combination of both processes.

In the following sections, the authors cover the processes and methods that stand out in the Brazilian market and that would support software development companies individually, capable of making them competitive. In the subsection 1.2.4, a better detailed vision about the flexibility and its level of customization will be presented. This approach shows the project staff how complex or simple the process can be for each project according tailoring activities. In this way, the project portfolio can cover projects with any level of complexity.

Rational Unified Process

The rational unified process is a software engineering process aimed at establishing tasks and responsibilities within a software development organization in a disciplined manner. Its objective is to ensure the production of high quality software that satisfies the needs of its stakeholders within predictable deadlines and costs. The RUP uses some of the best current practices in software development, aimed at providing service to a large number of projects and organizations. Although the RUP is widely customizable, it is considered to be a complex and heavy process, especially applicable in large development teams and large software projects. According to the RUP, it has two dimensions, as shown in Figure 1 (Kruchten, 2003):

The horizontal axis represents the time and shows the life cycle aspects of the process during its development. This axis represents the dynamic aspect of the process when it is approved and is expressed in terms of phases, interactions, and macros.

The vertical axis represents the disciplines, which group the activities in a logical manner, according to their nature. This axis represents the static aspect of the process, as described in terms of components, disciplines, activities, workflows, artifacts, and process roles.

The RUP has four basic components: roles, activities, artifacts, and disciplines. A role is an abstract definition of a set of executed activities and the respective artifacts. The roles have a set of coherent activities accomplished by them. These activities are closely related and combined in terms of functionality, and it is recommendable that they be executed by the same person. The activities are strongly related to the artifacts. The artifacts provide the input and output for the activities and the mechanism by which the information is transmitted between the activities. Artifacts are products of the final or intermediary work produced and used during the projects. The artifacts are used to capture and transmit the

project's information. An artifact can be one of the following elements:

- A document, such as a business use case diagram or software architecture document
- A model, such as the use case model or the design model
- An element of the model, in other words, an existing element in a model, such as a class or a subsystem

A discipline is a set of activities related to an "area of interest" that is important to the entire project. The main objective of grouping activities into disciplines is to help understand the project from a cascading perspective, a vision of the traditional software development model. For example, generally it is more common to execute certain requirement activities directly coordinated with the analysis and design activities. The separation of these activities into distinct disciplines makes

Figure 1. RUP phases and disciplines (Rational Unified Process, IBM Rational, 2004)

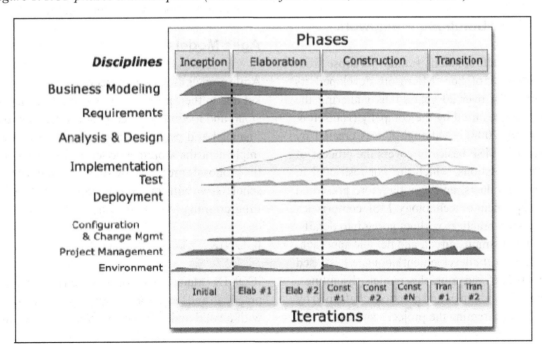

them easier to understand, although programming becomes more difficult. As occurs in other workflows, the workflow of a discipline is a semi-organized sequence of activities that are carried out to reach a certain result. The semi-organized nature highlights the fact that these workflows cannot display the true nuances of the programming of the actual work, since they are unable to represent the potential options of the activities or the interactive nature of the projects. Nevertheless, they are valuable as a means to understand the process by dividing it into lesser "areas of interest." Each "area of interest" or discipline has one or more models associated with it, which in turn are composed by associated artifacts. The most important artifacts are the models that each discipline produces: uses case models, design model, implementation model, and set of tests.

In order to allow the development of a complete software system to be managed, the artifacts are organized in sets that correspond to the disciplines. Many artifacts are used in several disciplines, for example, the risk list, the software architecture document, and the interaction plan. These artifacts belong to the set that was initially produced.

Microsoft Solutions Framework

The Microsoft solutions framework arose from the analysis of how Microsoft developed its products for over 20 years, thus gathering the best practices used by the company (Hansen & Thomsen, 2004). Although it was created by Microsoft, MSF basically covers the process of building solutions, which are not restricted to its own products, and it is therefore presented as independent of technology. MSF comprises a set of good practices without going into details, allowing a simple, direct, and flexible approach, regardless of the development language. It is based on a set of defined principles, models, disciplines, concepts, guidelines, and practices confirmed by Microsoft, targeting the project's success.

Microsoft does not classify MSF as a methodology, but rather as a discipline. Basically, it serves as a large guide and comprises a set of good practices without going into details, allowing a simple, direct, and flexible approach, regardless of the development language. It is based on a set of defined principles, models, disciplines, concepts, guidelines, and practices confirmed by Microsoft, targeting the project's success. Although the lack of details in MSF might seem to be a deficiency, it was this characteristic that allowed creating a simple and direct approach, which is also flexible and can be adapted to meet the needs of any software and IT infrastructure development project, regardless of size and complexity (Microsoft Corporation, 2003).

One of the models suggested by MSF is that of processes that foresee the life cycle of a project (the MSF process model). Every project goes through a life cycle. The main function of a life cycle model is to establish the order in which the project activities are executed. The appropriate life cycle can speed a project and help to ensure that each step brings the project closer to a successful conclusion. A simple view of the life cycle of the MSF process model is presented in Figure 2.

Agile Models

Agile models are gaining acceptance in the market due to their proposal of providing service to small and medium size companies that lack the financial and personnel resources necessary to implement the aforementioned models. Among the proposals presented by software engineering scholars, we will cover the ICONIX and eXtreme Programming (XP) proposals.

ICONIX

ICONIX (Maia, 2005) is considered to be a pure, practical, and simple, although powerful, process with a solid and effective problem analysis and representation component. As a result, ICONIX is characterized as effective and was developed by ICONIX Software Engineering. The ICONIX process is not as bureaucratic as the RUP, in the sense that it does not generate so much documentation, and although it is a simple process, it leaves nothing to be desired in terms of analysis and design and stands out as a powerful software analysis process. This process also uses UML and has an exclusive characteristic called traceability of requirements, more precisely meaning that its mechanisms "oblige" us to check if the requirements are being met during all the phases.

The ICONIX approach is flexible and open, meaning that there is no problem if another UML resource needs to be used to complement the resources used in the ICONIX phases. ICONIX is composed of the following phases:

- Domain Model
- Use Case Model
- Robust Analysis
- Sequence Diagram
- Class Diagram

This process is divided into two large sectors, which can be developed in parallel and in a recursive way. The models are static model and dynamic model. The static model is formed by the domain diagrams and the class diagram that belong to the static division since they model the system's operations without any user dynamics or interaction; in other words, it is the opposite of the dynamic model that always shows the user interacting with the system through actions in which the system presents a response to the user during execution time. The static model shall be refined incrementally during the successive interactions of the dynamic model. It does not require formal project macros for refining, which is carried out naturally during the project.

Extreme Programming

According to Teles (2004), XP is a software development process intended for:

- Projects of which the requirements are vague and change frequently.

Figure 2. Model for MSF processes (Microsoft, 2003)

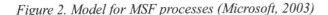

- Development of object-oriented systems.
- Small teams, preferably up to 12 developers.
- Incremental (or interactive) development, where the system starts to be implemented right at the start of the project and gains new functionalities as time goes by.

XP is organized around a set of values and practices that work in a harmonic and coherent manner to ensure that the customer always receives a high return on the investment in software. XP is composed of the following values and practices:

- XP Values:
- Feedback
- Communication
- Simplicity
- Courage

XP Practices:

- On-Site Customer
- Planning Game
- Stand Up Meeting
- Pair Programming
- Test-Driven Development
- Refactoring
- Collective Code
- Standardized Code
- Simple Design
- Metaphor
- Sustainable Pace

Background Discussion

Currently there are several methodology proposals ranging from extreme simplicity to highly complex processes. Targeting flexibility to meet the requirements of customer companies' projects calls for definition of a process, and consequent support from a tool, that meets the needs of the customers' software development projects, wheth-

er extremely simple or extremely complex. The objective here is to improve the competitiveness of the companies sustained on the productivity and quality of the software development projects by making the severity of the processes that will be used more flexible.

Figure 3 shows this chapter authors' view concerning the classification of the proposals presented above, as well as CSEP's proposal to make flexibility feasible.

CHARACTERISTICS OF SMALL SOFTWARE COMPANIES IN BRAZIL

The micro and small software companies (SSC) are part of a new sector that stands out in the field of information science. There are a series of definitions formulated with the objective of characterizing these companies, however, according to the Ministry of Science and Technology (MST), the SSC are classified according to their gross annual revenue (MST, 2001):

- Micro companies: Up to R$120 thousand
- Small companies Above R$120 thousand up to R$720 thousand

In the same document, the MST[3] suggests another classification based on the companies' effective workforce:

- Micro companies – from 1 to 10 employees
- Small companies – from 11 to 50 employees

Martins and Von Wangenheim (2002) report some of the characteristics of the SSC in their article:

- Generally very new companies, with little accumulated experience, are frequently immature in terms of production process and organizational aspects.

Figure 3. Gradient of simplicity and complexity of the processes according to the authors

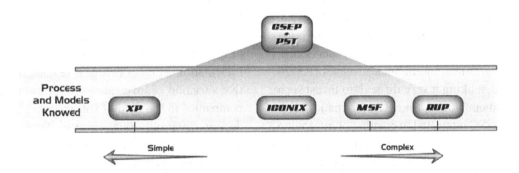

- These companies have small teams and therefore require their employees to take on more than one role in the company's development and management process, thus dividing their time between technical, administrative, and, in some cases, organizational activities.
- Display internal organization faults caused by excess informality in the organization structure and information flow.
- The company is focused on external activities (finishing the product as soon as possible, promote the product in marketing and sales activities, create strategic alliances, etc.) and does not dedicate the attention necessary to improve the development, management, and quality process.
- They are still very susceptible to influences from investors, customers, or the market itself.

As a result, the company maintains a constant process of adjusting what it does and how it does. These problems, which are also faced by medium and large companies, are experienced by micro and small companies to the extreme. On the other hand, with the objective of solving or minimizing the aforementioned negative characteristics, these companies seek methods that target the produc-

tion of quality software, although this is when the small companies face difficulties:

- Financial
- Specialized labor deficit
- Talent retention

Financial Difficulties

In order to allow the SSC to achieve quality improvements in their final product, thereby meeting higher requirement levels, they must implement a processes management model or a quality stamp.

Since March 1997, the ITS (Software Technology Institute) has set out to support national software companies in terms of capitalization, business promotion, creation of new companies, qualification of the software companies, development of research and development (R&D) projects, besides marketing and communication (ITS, 2006a). In one of its publications, this institute affirms that a national company located in the city of Uberlânida in Minas Gerais state invested close to R$400 thousand over an 18 month period to obtain Level 2 certification in the CMMI of the SEI (ITS, 2006b). It is worth noting that this company invoiced R$7.5 million in 2005. Currently, this company develops software products in the fields of telecommunications, finance, industry, and services with activities in Latin America, Europe, and the Middle East. However, this is not the reality of the SSC. As previously mentioned, the PES have a maximum annual revenue of R$720 thousand, making it very difficult to invest such a large amount (or anything close to that). Therefore, the SSC interested in creating or improving their software processes search for new ways to implement quality software processes, although at a cost that is accessible to them.

Specialized Labor

A good example that characterizes the deficit of specialized labor for working with software is the effort that the city of Blumenau, in Santa Catarina state, aware of this gap, is making to increase the volume of people qualified for the information technology (IT) sector. US$500 thousand are being invested in the qualification of 400 young employees between 16 and 29 years old who participate in information science professionalizing courses over the next two years (ABES, 2006a).

Another good example of our scarcity of qualified professionals comes from the interview in *Valor Econômico* newspaper with the CEO of India's TCS subsidiary in Brazil, Sérgio Rodrigues, in which he calls attention to the lack of investments in preparing qualified professionals, which in turn may represent a bottleneck for accomplishing the government's goal of exporting US$2 billion in software and IT services in 2007. "It's not just a question of reducing taxes, but rather the country's strategy. Where are the people for us to export US$ 2 billion? We do not have sufficient qualified professionals to achieve this goal," he said (ABES, 2006b).

Talent Retention

According to a study made by the Brazilian Association of Software Companies, Brazil's software and services market occupies the twelfth position

in the global market, with financial transactions of approximately US$7.41 billion in 2005. These figures account for Brazil's leadership in the Latin American ranking, corresponding to 41% of this market (ABES, 2006c). Other important information in this document reveals the positive variation of investments made by the large companies in the field of software and services during 2004 and 2005: close to 23.9%. These figures suggest that the growth of investments in this market will develop a demand for specialists in the performance areas of the software and services market, for example:

- Applications
- Development environments
- Infrastructure
- Consulting
- Systems integration
- Outsourcing
- Support
- Training

On the other hand, as highlighted in the previous topic, there is a deficit of specialized labor for working with software, thus generating an even greater gap for these jobs and creating a strong market demand for these professionals. This fact calls attention to the difficulties faced by the companies to retain their intellectual capital through qualified professionals. A study made by the MST says that some companies appear to be undisciplined in relation to the process of implementing the CMMI stamp, and one of the great difficulties is the high rotation of the participants of the software process (Bezerra, Carneiro, Nibon, Carneiro, & Araújo, 2006).

A SOFTWARE DEVELOPMENT MODEL FOR SMALL BRAZILIAN COMPANIES

The model proposed is based on the needs of a small Brazilian software development company and the software engineering concepts preconized by the RUP, MSF, and agile modeling. The model was created with four phases that define the life cycle of the software development projects. In each phase, there is a set of activities to be performed culminating in approval marks, which provide subsidies to transpose each phase. The project phase mark can lead to the project's cancellation or temporary hold up.

The disciplines perform with greater or lesser intensity during the entire life cycle of the process, collaborating towards the accomplishment of the activities. At each cycle of the project, a new set of document and software artifacts is delivered to the customer. The project phase provides technical subsidies to assist making commercial proposals to eventual customers, performing all the necessary analyses. The approval mark of the project phase must contain the artifacts that indicate the understood business problem, the survey of the customer's needs, and a vision of the technological solution involved. As a result, the project scope is well defined between the parties, customer, and development company. The specification phase defines technical subsidies that will serve as a base for the development of a technological solution, and its approval mark must foresee that the development environment was constituted and is stable and, if there are graphic interfaces, that they have been approved by the customer and that a software architecture was specified. The development phase targets the development, testing, and approval of the technological solution, and its approval mark requires the solution to be coded with all tests and validations successfully concluded as well as its approval by the customer. The delivery phase concludes the product's development process and delivers the final technological solution to the customer, whose approval mark checks if the projects final evaluation has already been made, whether innovations were proposed for the next version of the product and whether the technological solution and the artifacts agreed on in the project phase were delivered.

Figure 4. CSEP life cycle

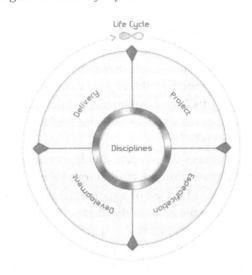

The prescriptive procedures of the proposed process, understood as disciplines, must be followed during the entire project, assisting its progress as required, regardless of the phase. The resources must always be attentive to the disciplines, which are connected through roles so that they can be started whenever necessary. The disciplines are occurring at any moment in the project with greater or lesser intensity. As already mentioned, their exact moment of occurrence is impossible to describe. There will be moments when some disciplines will not be used. During phases or even projects, the resources involved are responsible for this type of decision. The disciplines must be explained in terms of their concept and how they can be employed. A workflow that sequences event and group activities is also defined, which is represented by input and resulting artifacts, as well as the roles that execute them. Six disciplines are proposed: *coordination, documentation, requests, environment, risk and test,* and *approval.* The roles of disciplines did not appear on the flows because any role can be done its.

Methodology

The great concern in the elaboration of the process of engineering of customized software was to allow that the paradigm of simplicity X complexity could be treated by the organizations to allow through a tool the configuration of the devices resultant of the activities to be used without the instituted process was modified. The alternative to the scene of the projects with bigger adopted simplicity was to register in the target log book the justification of not use of some described macro-activities in the flows of the phases. The project phase is the only one that cannot have discarded activities. The RUP was used as a base to create the process, disciplines, and roles, while the life cycle originated from the RUP and MSF.

Process

- Subdivision of the cycle of life of the projects in phases
- Use of the discipline concept for activities of support to the development of the product
- Use of macro-activities for the grouping of a set of activities
- Use of the paper concept, activities, and devices for the activities that add value to the product, as well as of support to the development
- Iterative and incremental development

Disciplines

The disciplines were created using the main MSF concepts.

Roles

With the concept of roles praised for the RUP, human resources with diverse technician attributes exert the polyvalence, or either can play diverse roles, as it is very common in the Brazilian market. With this, small companies who make use of a limited amount of human resources obtain to balance stated period, cost, and effort; therefore, the process was constructed taking in account the profile of the professionals of the domestic market and also the agility that the projects need, due to the almost always urgent customer demands.

Phases of the Customized Software Engineering Process

In the following subsections, the objectives, scope, phase flow, and a summary of the details of the flows of the main phases will be described, as well as the activities and artifacts.

Project Phase

Objective

Provide the technical subsidies to assist the elaboration of proposals, performing all the necessary project analyses.

Scope

- Provide the team necessary to perform the procedures of the phase.
- Understand the business problem together with the customer.
- Conduct a high level survey of the customers' needs, including infrastructure and current systems analysis, limited to the business problem.
- Propose a technological solution, considering the needs raised in the survey.
- Provide an estimate of the deadline and quantity of resources based on the proposed technological solution.

Project Phase Approval Mark

The approval criteria of this mark requires that:

- The list of the survey team must be complete.

- The business problem was understood.
- All the customers' needs were raised.
- A technological solution was proposed.
- The deadline and resources were estimated.

Project Phase Artifacts

Type	Artifacts
These artifacts are deliverable and must be closed.	- High Level Use Case - Use Case Diagram - Vision/Scope - Phases Plan - State of the Surveyed Infrastructure - List of Actors

Figure 5. Project phase flow

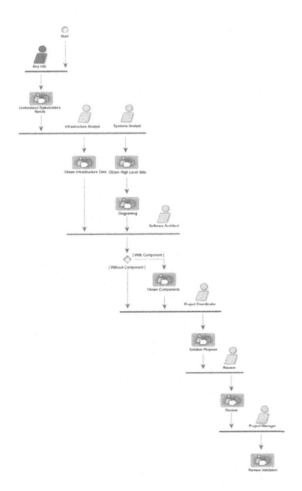

These artifacts are deliverable and must be open and available for the next phase.	- Risk List - Glossary
These artifacts are undeliverable and must be closed.	- Document of Understanding - List of Reutilization of Components - Interaction Plan - Service Order - Revision Registration - Resources for the Project - Infrastructure for the Project
These artifacts are undeliverable and must be open and available for the next phase.	- Team List

Specification Phase

Objective

Specify technical subsidies that will serve as a basis for the development of the technological solution.

Scope

- Specify the entire high level survey performed in the preproject phase.
- Specify the software architecture.
- Define the software's graphic interface.

Specification Phase Approval Mark

The approval criteria of this mark requires that:

- The development environment was established and is stable.
- Everything that was high-level in the first phase was specified.
- If graphic interfaces exist, they were approved by the customer.
- A software architecture was specified.

Figure 6. Specification phase flow

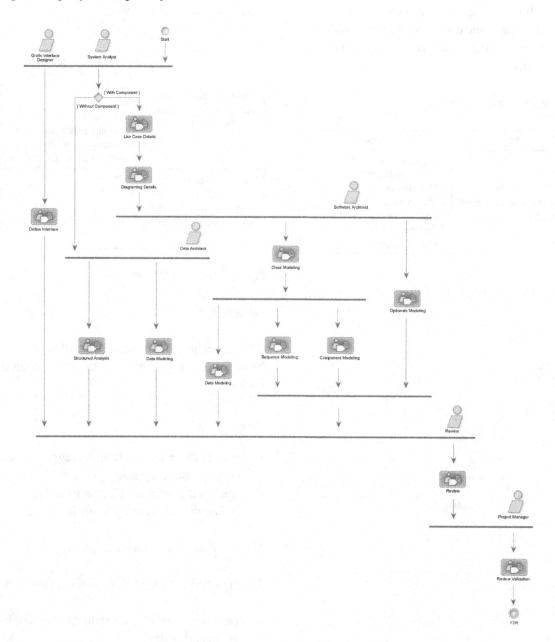

Specification Phase Artifacts

Type	Artifacts
These artifacts are deliverable and must be closed.	- Data Model - Prototype (Optional) - Classes Diagram - Components Diagram - Sequence Diagram - Any UML Artifact - Use Case Specification - Data Flow Diagram - Flowchart - Any Structured Analysis Artifact - Software Architecture Document - Use Case Diagram - Acceptance Document
These artifacts are deliverable and must be open and available for the next phase.	- Risk List - Glossary
These artifacts are undeliverable and must be closed.	- Infrastructure for the Project - Request for Change - Interaction Plan - Service Order - Revision Registration - Integrated Test Plan - Business Test Plan
These artifacts are undeliverable and must be open and available for the next phase.	- Team List

Development Phase

Objective

Develop, test, and approve the technological solution.

Scope

- Code the technological solution based on what was specified.
- Test all the functionalities.
- Approve the technological solution presented for the business problem.

Development Phase Approval Mark

The approval criteria of this mark requires that:

- The solution was codified and is stable.
- All tests and validations were satisfied and completed.
- The technological solution was accepted by the customer.

Figure 7. Development phase flow

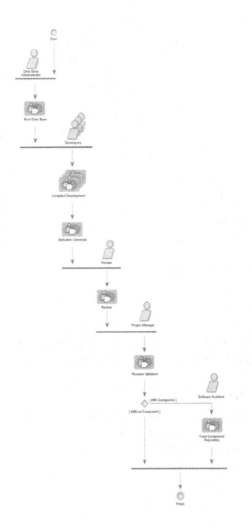

Development Phase Artifacts

Type	Artifacts
These artifacts are deliverable and must be closed.	- Source Font - Acceptance Document
These artifacts are deliverable and must be open and available for the next phase.	- Risk List - Glossary
These artifacts are not deliverable and must be closed..	- Components Repository - Compiled - Component Source Font Repository - Software Repository Artifacts - Database - Project Infrastructure - Integrated Test Plan - Business Test Plan - Test Report - Iteration Plan - Job List - Review Records - Change Solicitation - Module - Application
These artifacts are deliverable and must be open and available for the next phase	- Staff List

Delivery Phase

Objective

Conclude the development process of the product and deliver the technological solution.

- Scope
- Plan how the product will be distributed.
- Build the product's manuals.
- Final evaluation of the project.
- Propose innovations for the next version of the product.

Delivery Phase Approval Mark

The approval criteria of this mark requires that:

- The solution was coded and is stable.
- All tests and validations were satisfied and completed.
- The technological solution was accepted by the customer.

Figure 8. Delivery phase flow

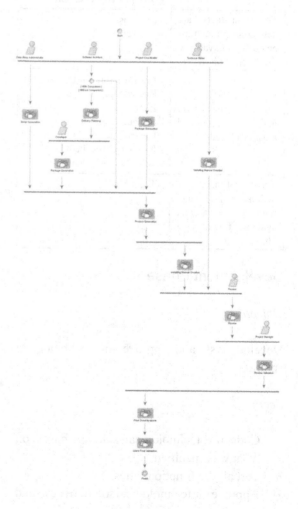

Delivery Phase Artifacts

Type	Artifacts
These artifacts are deliverable and must be closed.	- Data Script - Product - User Manual - Installation Manual - Inovation Proposed Documents - List of Risks - Glossary - Acceptance Documentation
These artifacts are deliverable and must be open and available for the next phase.	N/A
These artifacts are not deliverable and must be closed.	- Distribution Plan - Installation Package - Documents Package - Final Evaluation Package - Iteration Plan - Job List - Records Review - Project Infrastructure - Staff List - Change Solicitation
These artifacts are not deliverable and must be open and available for the next phase.	N/A

Disciplines

Disciplines are prescriptive procedures that must be followed during the entire project, as required, regardless of the progress of the phases, assisting the project's progress. The resources must always be attentive to the disciplines, which are connected through roles, so that they can be started whenever necessary.

As already mentioned, the disciplines are occurring at any moment within the project. However, it is not possible to describe the moments when they can occur, since they will be performing with greater or lesser intensity between the phases and the projects, although for this to occur, the resources must know how they work; otherwise it will be impossible to employ them correctly. It is also worth noting that as the disciplines can occur with greater or lesser intensity, there may be moments when some disciplines might not be used. During phases or even projects, the resources involved in the project are responsible for this type of decision.

The disciplines in the software engineering process are described by:

- **Introduction:** Discipline proposal and explanation of how it works and can be employed.
- **Flow:** A typical sequence of events, which reveals how the discipline's workflow operates, expressed in terms of flow details. A flow detail is a group of activities that will be accomplished "together" represented by input and resulting artifacts and the roles they execute.

The six disciplines in the CSEP are *coordination, documentation, requests, environment, risk and test,* and *approval,* as detailed below, but without roles.

Coordination Discipline

Description

The purpose of this discipline is to plan and manage the project. It is responsible for managing interactions during the entire life cycle. The service orders are generated in these interactions, thereby making this discipline responsible for the project's management regarding the deadlines and tasks to be executed by the resource. Furthermore, at every new interaction, this discipline recommends an analysis if the project continues within the scope and deadline, managing the risks that eventually arise from this analysis. This discipline is also responsible for the entire revision process of the artifacts generated, in addition to validating these revisions.

Documentation Discipline

Description

The purpose of this discipline is to level out the knowledge between the project team and all external stakeholders. If terms that are not common to all those involved with the project arise during its life cycle, these terms must be documented, thus allowing easier reference, since they will be centralized in a single document. This documentation involves technical and business terms alike.

Request Discipline

Description

The purpose of this discipline is to manage all the requests made by the customer during the project's

life cycle. All requests made by the customer must first be screened by the coordinator, recording those that are relevant and declining those that are not. From the moment a request is recorded, it is analyzed by some resource that has greater knowledge about the request in which this resource evaluates the impact of such a request and the time required to put it into practice. Last, the project manager approves or declines the implementation of this change. If approved, the coordinator takes the necessary attitudes, through the coordination discipline, so that this request is incorporated into the development process.

Environment Discipline

Description

The purpose of this discipline is to provide the environment necessary for the team during the

Figure 9. Coordination discipline flow

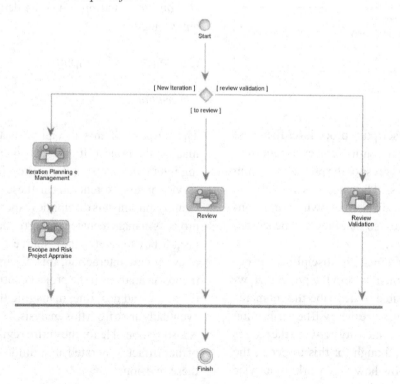

project's life cycle. The project coordinator, when faced with a certain need that requires a request for some sort of environment element for the project, whether a hardware or software element, uses this discipline to make the requests necessary to meet these needs.

Risk Discipline

Description

The purpose of this discipline is to evaluate the risks continuously and use them to influence decision making during the project's entire life cycle. Each risk that arises must be treated with

Figure 10. Documentation discipline flow

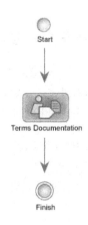

Figure 11. Request discipline flow

Figure 12. Environment discipline flow

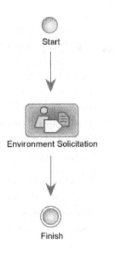

Figure 13. Risk discipline flow

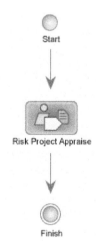

due care, from the simplest to the most complex. This avoids unpleasant surprises arising during the life cycle of a project. Therefore, through this discipline, the risks are continuously evaluated, monitored, and actively managed, attributing levels of severity to the risks that arise. This management takes place until the risk is solved or becomes a problem to be handled.

Figure 14. Test and approval discipline flow

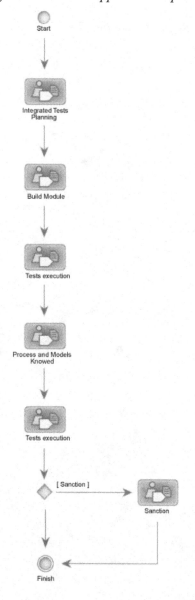

Test and Approval Discipline

Description

The purpose of this discipline is to control the project's entire test and approval process. The management of the tests and approval operates as a cycle, going from the initial planning of the tests to the approval by the customer. The coordinator must take care to always use this discipline, especially during the development phase, since it allows controlling what is being developed and also allows guaranteeing quality in everything that is produced, through strict and uniform control.

Implementation Strategy Proposal

In order to make the proposed activities operational, we must base ourselves on an implementation strategy according to the following steps:

- Do not change the life cycle of eventual ongoing projects
- Reutilization of assets from existing projects
- Maintain the current quality of the projects, at least
- Transfer the knowledge in a short space of time

APPLICATION OF THE MODEL AND RESULTS

The proposed model is based on an actual necessity and its implementation, the project of which was conceived and concluded in four months (July to October 2003) in a small company. After its approval, there was a significant improvement in the company's software development projects, which began to use the new process in a unique manner, starting a process of maturity of the organization, reducing costs and deadlines in the

Figure 15. Implementation strategy

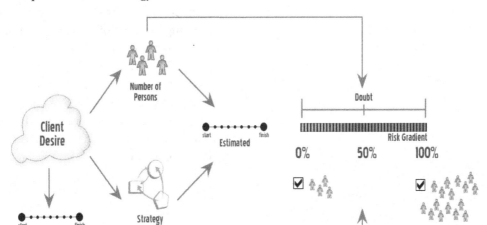

projects, and consequently maximizing revenue. The implementation of the process demanded the development of a collaborative tool in a Web environment that tactically and operationally supports the described software development process. The results from the practical use of processes and tools in some projects developed for customer companies will be described in the following sections, utilizing and not utilizing the instituted processes and tools developed to support the process. Competitiveness aspects resulting in the reduction of estimated and accomplished deadlines and costs in the projects will be emphasized, as well as the measurement of defects and the background history of several projects. All data were collected and consolidated according to the CMMI ML 2 Measurement and Analysis Process Area.

Reduction of Deadlines and Costs

The reduction of deadlines and costs explains a scenario that is increasingly desired and necessary for organizational survival, especially regarding its competitiveness in the market. Through the implementation of the CSEP combined with the FSC, the software projects are followed up in

detail. The cost and the deadline become easier to manage as the quality procedures are effectively applied. The institutionalization of the CSEP in software development centers or factories allows improving productivity, since the functionalities developed tend towards a low rate of defects. This is possible through the implementation of procedures defined for the specification of the requirements, standardized development for a pre-established architecture, unit tests and application of the tests plan focusing on the fulfillment of the business rules, and the nonfunctional requirements. The visualization of problems becomes clearer and the decision making to trace an improvement action is faster, contributing towards a strong management of the delivery time.

The rework, which is a factor that generates impacts on the deadlines and costs, is reduced, since the resources are directed to maintain their work coherent to the needs of the software development process. The nonconformities are detected by the constant measurement and analysis of the process and the product, ensuring that the process is actually being followed and understood as established. As a result, the effort during the tests phase is reduced, filtering the occurrences, since many problems are detected and corrected during

Figure 16. Competitiveness pillars

the project, avoiding accumulation of defect correction activities. With increased productivity and visible improvement of quality, the organization becomes more competitive in the market, allowing it to offer highly reliable products, with agile decision making, meeting the customer's needs and managing the occurrence of problems. In order to be competitive, it is necessary to guarantee the sustainability of the quality and productivity pillars (Figure 16).

Figure 18. Defects percentage chart

Figure 17. Productivity chart

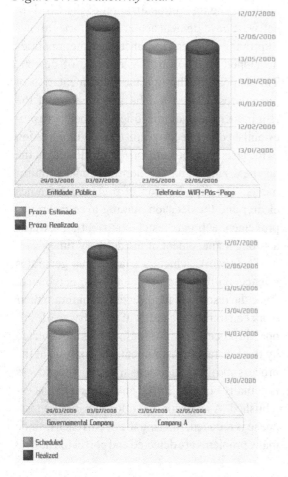

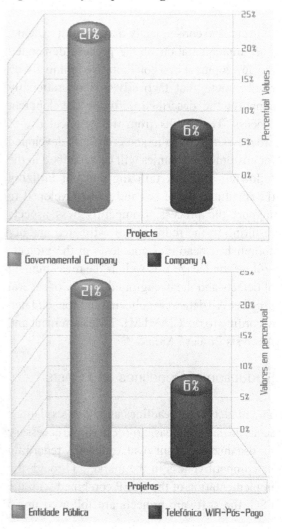

Example of Measurement to Reduce Deadlines and Costs

The chart below represents the estimated time and the accomplished time of two projects, the first in a public entity without using a formal process and the second for a private initiative company, using CSEP together with FPS. A significant difference was identified in productivity between the two projects, as shown in the data represented (Figure 17).

Defects Chart

Analogously, the chart below represents the percentage of defects according to their respective severity levels (Figure 18).

Based on the analysis of the charts displayed, we verified that a significant reduction in the deadline and cost was observed when using CSEP and FSP.

Background History of Projects from 2004 to 2006

We briefly present the scope of a few projects carried out during 2004, 2005, and 2006. These projects were developed using CSEP together with FSP.

Figure 19 show in an objective way the estimated and accomplished conclusion dates of these projects.

FUTURE TRENDS

The search for development processes that apply best practices is becoming a reality among Brazilian software companies, due especially to the pressure imposed by the market for them to produce software faster, although cheaper and with higher quality, thereby making them competitive. The use of object-oriented technology together with the concept of software reuse has been boasted as being the solution that most supports companies in their quest for a competitive edge. However, reuse can only be achieved with the application of the concepts of components, which is already taking place for many decades in other engineering disciplines. However, software engineering is only just starting its journey towards this daring proposal and will demand much research and practices until it reaches these objectives. Certain steps must be established and followed:

- Establish a practical process for the development of software components without compromising quality.

Figure 19. Projects delivered

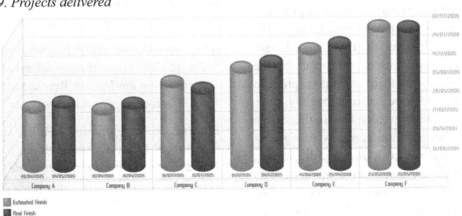

- Create tools that support the developers in their discovery, specification, construction, and recovery of software components.
- Create an administration model capable of managing the distribution of the components and control their use and maintenance.
- Disseminate this development technology in both computer science academies and the Brazilian software production market, aimed at preparing Brazilian developers in these new approaches and technologies.

As a result, the current electronic commerce will be based on a service-oriented model offered intracompanies situated at a higher abstraction level and will add flexibility to the customer-service model that greatly benefited from the object-oriented technology over the past decade.

CONCLUSION

The evolution of the software engineering process and the developed Web tool, during 2004 and 2005, was considerably dynamic. The increase in demand for software development projects has been growing and continues to grow, justified by the conception and institutionalization of the CSEP and FSP, which translate the reality regarding the flexibility in applying the severity of the software development processes. The investments necessary to reach CMMI level 2, a worldwide reference in software maturity models, are incompatible with the financial reality of the PES in Brazil. However, the Brazilian software market is booming, which in turn encourages the companies to improve their processes to produce higher quality software and consequently grow. The CSEP and FSP revealed how in this case a small Brazilian software company can gradually improve its competitiveness and dream with broader and more competitive markets, thus envisaging a significant increase in revenue. The success of the implementation of this model led

the company that is the object of this study to create a software factory. A considerably expressive result, in terms of maturity supported by the process and tool mentioned, can be seen in the favorable report issued by the SEI for CMMI level 2 obtained in April 2006. The software factory is currently experiencing growth and expansion, which justified the creation of a PMO (project management office) and a superintendent of software products, which today also commercializes services in the fields of consulting, customization, implementation, and technical support for CSEP and FSP for the Brazilian market. To achieve this, investments are being directed to the continuous improvement of the processes and tools. In July 2006, the project charter for the project "On the Way to CMMI Maturity Level 3" was approved and its evaluation is foreseen to be made in July 2007.

REFERENCES

ABES[4]-Associação Brasileira das Empresas de Software. (2006a). *Blumenau (SC) faz esforço para formar mão-de-obra.* Retrieved December 12, 2007, from http://www.abes.org.br/templ3.aspx?id=232&sub=21

ABES-Associação Brasileira das Empresas de Software. (2006b). *TCS diz que Brasil não tem técnicos para cumprir meta de exportação.* Retrieved December 12, 2007, from http://www.abes.org.br/templ3.aspx?id=232&sub=19

ABES-Associação Brasileira das Empresas de Software. (2006c). *Mercado brasileiro de software – panorama e tendências.* Retrieved December 12, 2007, from http://www.abes.org.br

Bezerra, C.I.M., Carneiro, D.M.R., Nibon, R.T., Carneiro, R.M.R., & Araújo, S.A. (2006). *Capacitação em melhoria de processo de software: uma experiência da implantação do SW-CMM em um grupo de pequenas empresas.* Ministério de Ciência e Tecnologia (MCT). Retrieved December 12, 2007, from http://www.mct.gov.br/upd_blob/2641.pdf

Hansen, J.E., & Thomsen, C. (2004). *Enterprise development with visual studio: NET, UML, and MSF*. New York: Apress.

ITS (Instituto de Tecnologia de Software). (2006a). *Institucional*. Retrieved December 12, 2007, from http://www.its.org.br/default.aspx?portalid=LJFK QNUL&navid=351

ITS (Instituto de Tecnologia de Software). (2006b). *TQI conquista CMMI nível 2*. Retrieved December 12, 2007, from http://www.its.org.br/default. aspx?pagid=EMMCUMUL

Kruchten, P. (2003). *Introdução ao RUP*. Rio de Janeiro: Ciência Moderna.

Maia, J.A. (2005). *Construindo softwares com qualidade e rapidez usando ICONIX*. Retrieved December 12, 2007, from http://www.jugmanaus.com

Martins, A.F., & Von Wangenheim, C.G. (2002). *Caracterização da gestão de conhecimento em micro e pequenas empresas de software*. LQPS - UNIVALI - CES VII, São José, SC, Brasil.

Microsoft Corporation. (2003). *Microsoft solutions framework version 3.0 overview*. Retrieved December 12, 2007, from http://download. microsoft.com/download/2/3/f/23f13f70-8e46-4f44-97f6-7dfb45010859/MSF_v3_Overview Whitepaper.pdf

MST (Ministry of Science and Technology). (2001). *Pesquisa nacional de qualidade e produtividade no setor de software brasileiro – Caracterização das organizações*. Retrieved December 12, 2007, from http://www.mct.gov.br/index. php/content/view/4913.html

Rational Unified Process. (2004). *IBM Rational*.

Teles, V.M. (2004). *Extreme programming*. São Paulo: Novatec.

ENDNOTES

[1] CSEP – Customized Software Engineering Process

[2] PST – Process Support Tool

[3] MCT – Ministério da Ciência e Tecnologia

[4] ABES – Brazilian Association of Software Enterprises is a respected and known association of the Software Enterprises in Brazil – www.abes.org.br

Chapter IV
The Impact of Software Testing In Small and Medium Settings

Luis Vinicio León-Carrillo

e-Quallity Corporation[1] and ITESO University, Mexico

ABSTRACT

In the U.S. alone, the cost of faulty software ranges in the tens of billions of dollars per year; the costs of inadequate testing infrastructure are estimated between $22.2 and $59.5 billion, one half paid by the developers and the other half by the users. Albeit the criticality of a good testing process (the inadequacy of which would kill many small enterprises, in particular Latin American ones), many times the testing process is misapplied or not applied at all. We provide here some foundations of the discipline of software testing and present fragments of a variation of a test process used successfully by e-Quallity Corporation (a firm specialized in software testing) in commercial projects, defined formally using a small proprietary process definition language. We present also two case studies of projects with Mexican small and medium enterprises showing concrete economic impacts of the use (and misuse) of this testing process.

INTRODUCTION

It is estimated that the costs (in the industry) of faulty software in the U.S. range in the tens of billions of dollars per year, representing approximately just under 1% of the gross domestic product (Tassey, 2002). Although testing is an activity that could help reduce this significantly, it is frequently considered a cost-only activity. As a result, there is a tendency in software organizations to reduce it to the minimum, sometimes treating it as a second-class activity. Consequences from this tendency can be seen, for example, in organizations that have testing teams composed of people who "have not done it elsewhere"; people who do not have the appropriate qualifications to be testers and are not being properly trained to develop tests; or testing groups that are wrongly positioned in the organization chart, typically under the project manager who is in turn under the product manager who is in turn under the chief information officer (CIO). Such a configuration easily generates the situation of unheard or mis-understood test results by the CIO and the CEO (chief executive officer) and a lack of authority of the testing team in the decision of accepting or rejecting a product. Usually the testing teams in these organizations receive the system under testing at the end of the development cycle, frequently with only a few days (and nights!) left for testing before the release date. In such a situation, the testing team will always be wrong: if it accepts testing at the end with little time, it will probably miss catching many bugs, so it will be said that "the testing team did not do its job correctly"; if it does not accept the time constraint and demands the authority to approve or reject the product, then it will be said that "the release was delayed because of the testing team." We believe that this view of testing is mainly due to a lack of understanding of its cost-benefit relation within the software development process and to an underestimation of its complexity and impact.

In this chapter, we present foundations and economics of software testing, as well as frag-ments of a formally defined test process used successfully in commercial projects, together with two real case studies showing concrete economic impacts that the use (and misuse) of this process had in projects with two Mexican small- and medium-sized enterprises (SMEs). The process was applied in these two projects by e-Quallity Corporation[2] (referred to as "e-Quallity" from here on), a firm specialized in software testing. We start this chapter by setting up a conceptual framework; we then present the testing process and develop the case studies. Finally, we reveal some conclusions.

THE PROBLEM AND SOME SOLUTIONS PROPOSED

We will present here the problems justifying the discipline of software testing and other related approaches; we then propose a definition and describe some concepts involved in it, providing the point from which we view and analyze the case studies developed in this chapter. Finally, we present data concerning the relative cost of software testing, which will be important in later sections.

A "Software Crisis"

There is a debate in the literature between authors stating that there has been a decades-long chronic crisis in the software industry (e.g., Scientific American, 1994), and some say that such a crisis has already been overcome. One can agree with one or another viewpoint, but one can easily perceive that in this industry:

• We have an ever-growing number of applica-tion areas.
• Software systems become bigger and more complex.
• There is a growing demand for quality in software products.

Regarding the last problem, some approaches to reduce the problem have been developed besides testing, for example:

• Quality models such as the Capability Matu-rity Model Integration (CMMI[®3]) (Chrissis, 2006) and MoProSoft (Ventura-Miranda & Peñaloza-Báez, 2006) with the underlying idea that high-quality *processes* will generate high-quality products.
• Quality "philosophies" such as total quality management for software (TQMS) (Schul-meyer, 1993), which emphasizes the role of qualified and motivated *people* in the devel-opment of high-quality software.
• Formal methods (Gabbar, 2006) with an emphasis in the (full) *automation* of software development by means of formal languages (in the sense of Rozenberg & Salomaa, 1997) to obtain "bug-free software."

Testing focuses on the quality of the *product* in opposition to models like CMMI® which usually put more emphasis on the *process* (although there are some process areas dealing with related practices like validation and verification); in this sense they are complementary. We believe they are also complementary in time: process improvement is usually a relatively expensive and medium-term effort, while a product improvement is a rather cheaper and short-term one; the quick benefits of testing could be used to support the mentioned medium-term process effort.

TQMS approaches are broad and usually include areas like validation, verification, or even testing explicitly with a certain emphasis on the qualification and motivation of the people who perform these activities. TQMS is usually applied in medium and large organizations. Testing is a discipline and a profession in itself now, so it can complement TQMS with the details in specialized testing skills and knowledge.

With formal methods, testing shares the emphasis on the quality of the *product*. A significant difference is the denial of the big goal of generating "bug-free software" for the more pragmatic one of finding the majority of the most pernicious bugs as early as possible in the development cycle. Both approaches can be combined in a project, applying formal methods in the critical parts of a system and testing in the rest.

Adoption of international quality models like CMMI® is usually pushed by clients demanding such a qualification. For small (and some medium) organizations, the costs and time involved in such a project are often prohibitive. TQMS is not popular in technological SMEs mainly because it is a rather general, long-term effort. They require approaches with short-term results. Compared with formal methods, the application of testing in SMEs today is by far a more common practice in the industry, mainly because of the mathematical knowledge required to apply them and the lack of tool availability and support.

Specially for small organizations, the liberation and commercialization of an immature product can have catastrophic economic results: on one hand, it would obstruct market penetration; on the other hand, the maintenance of such a product would be difficult and costly. We firmly believe that, in order to reduce significantly and effectively the costs of faulty software produced by SMEs, a short-term and economically accessible *product*-oriented approach is necessary that includes software testing as one of its central practices.

Software Testing

Initially confused with debugging, software testing was performed to gain confidence that a system would behave correctly. Myers (1979) was one of the first people who changed this view when he stated that the goal of testing was to detect anomalies. This conceptualization generated a discipline of its own and provided the basis for a new profession. We will consider software testing to be:

A process parallel to the development one, performed to detect, as early as possible, in as many places as possible, where the system under testing (SUT) does not meet the requirements, especially the critical ones. To do this, stimuli (test cases) are designed and applied in a systematic way to the SUT, sometimes with the support of specialized software tools known under the acronym CAST (Computer Aided Software Testing). (e-Quallity, 2006)

When discussing the testing process, it is usual to make a reference to the "V-Model" (as in Black, 2002). In this model (see Figure 1), test cases start to be developed (although with many left incomplete) when the requirements are being defined, continuing this way through design and coding (left line of the "V"); these test designs are then completed and applied after the system components are executable (right line of the "V").

Following this process, one can use the information provided by testing about the maturity of the product and the value earned along the whole development effort to manage risks that could cause delays and budget surpassing, as well as the one related to the liberation of an immature product. Unfortunately, it is not common to see that testing starts in the requirements phase. It is usually sent to the end (as in the waterfall model) and only with little time prior to product liberation, leading to very expensive and difficult bug removal with the consequence of a complex and costly maintenance phase, usually the longest (and most expensive) one.

As already stated, test case design should be approached systematically; this is shown in the next example (a classic from Myers, 1979): Let us suppose a very simple and small SUT has three integers as input, representing (possibly) the three sides of a triangle and as output one of the following messages: "It is not a triangle, isosceles, equilateral, or scalene." Let us further assume the integers range from 1 to 100,000 (10^5). We would have to apply 10^{15} test cases to be sure that the SUT always behaves correctly ($10^5 * 10^5 * 10^5$). If we could apply one test case every second, this would take us more than $31.7 * 10^6$ years, an impossible task in practice; no organization would invest in it.

Instead of trying to verify that a SUT *always* behaves correctly (which is impossible for the vast majority of software systems), testing has the less aggressive objective of generating the smallest set of test cases with the highest probability to detect *most* of the bugs. Test cases must be therefore designed using engineering methods like the ones described in Burnstein (2003), Jorgensen (2002), and Patton (2006). These methods can be classified using several criteria. According to León-Carrillo (2005a), three common criteria are:

- Size of the SUT, leading to the following approaches:
  - o **Unit testing:** Each organization defines what are considered atomic parts of a SUT (subroutines, objects, components, etc.), which are tested separately.
  - o **Integration testing:** The correct interaction between units is tested.
  - o **System testing:** Overall and transversal aspects of the whole system are tested, like reliability and performance.
  - o **Acceptance testing:** Done (usually with the customer) to review requirements satisfaction.
- Degree of knowledge that the tester has about the internal elements of the SUT. There are several approaches:
  - o **Transparent-box testing:** Initial testing usually performed by the developer who knows that part of the SUT very well.

Figure 1. The V-Model

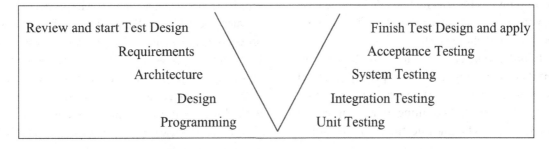

o **White-box testing:** Performed usually by a tester with development background who has access to design and source code information.

o **Grey-box testing:** Performed by a tester who has access to part of the design and source code information, for example, the database design.

o **Black-box testing:** Performed by a tester who has neither access to design nor to source code information; the main input for this activity is the requirements documentation.

- Times the test cases are reapplied:

o **Progressive testing:** First application of cases after they are designed.

o **Regressive testing:** When a new version with corrections is delivered, the reapplication of a (eventually proper) subset of the "progressive" test cases is necessary to verify on one hand that the bugs were really eliminated and on the other to see if the corrections did not introduce new bugs.

It is the job of the tester to determine the combination of these (and other techniques) to achieve the goal stated above in such a way that it represents a (close to) optimal cost-benefit relation in terms of time, money, and bugs found (or left). At e-Quallity, one applies the rule that testing should receive at least 20% of the whole software development effort (León-Carrillo, Ruelas-Minor, & Castillo-Hernández, 2004). This amount has been published, and it is confirmed with our experience: although in a few projects the amount has been as high as 66% (in the case of critical systems), in most of them it achieves a good cost-benefit relation.

In order to be effective, it is also very important that the testing team is properly positioned on the organization chart, avoiding the situation we described at the beginning of the chapter. No combination techniques, testing team, or effec-

tive metric would be enough if the test results are not heard and properly used by the right people in the organization. A good place for the testing team would be, for example, in a QA department, depending directly from the CEO.

THE TESTING ORGANIZATION AND PROCESS

The process we will present here is part of a variation of the one institutionalized at e-Quallity, a firm specialized in software testing with an integrated service portfolio that includes:

- Evaluation of software products.
- Consulting in software testing (particularly maturity assessment of testing organizations).
- Training in software testing.
- Start-up of testing organizations.
- Sourcing of testers in the clients' facilities.

This testing-only focus, together with its specialization level, is very appreciated by its customers: since e-Quallity does not commercialize software development, its objectivity is not called into question, and the latent problems of confidentiality and intellectual property regarding the SUT are easily solved. e-Quallity does develop software with its teams of white-box testers (who have a strong background in software development) but only to construct internal tools. e-Quallity provides its services to individual SMEs, clusters (regional organizations typically gathering SMEs), as well as to government and multinational firms such as IBM, Siemens, FreeScale, and Softtek. We will describe the test process in question using a formal notation; a variation of this process was recently assessed by the specialized dutch firm Polteq[4]. A testing company with comparable assessment results is hard to find in the world. Only companies in high-risk industries, e.g. pharmaceutics, defense and aviation, achieve higher scores.

A Notation for Process Definition

The V-Model we described earlier has the advantage of being intuitive, but it lacks the necessary detail to be operative in a real test organization. On the other hand, process documentation is a demanding activity: if one adds sufficient detail, documents can easily become incomplete and/or inconsistent when one tries to update them. Following the seminal idea presented in Osterweil (1987), we see processes as something that can and must be defined by means of a formal language. Programming languages are developed to permit the precise definition and modularization of computational processes (algorithms and heuristics) and automatic processing with compilers. Today we have also specialized process definition languages (PDLs), which facilitate the definition, modularization, and automatic processing of software development processes; with this, the activity of defining and maintaining big process descriptions becomes more manageable.

At e-Quallity, we use a small PDL of our own to specify our processes (León-Carrillo, 2005b). We will present here a specification in BNF (Garshol, 2006) of a subset of the language with terminals marked in bold and "λ" denoting the null string; the nonterminals written *<Like_this>* are not relevant for our explanation and thus will not be further defined. The PDL is rather procedural and Pascal-like, enabling the definition of a hierarchy of processes. For reasons of space and readability, the lexical definition is oversimplified, and, among other things, we omit the definition of the type system (primitive types and constructors) and the specification of the parameter passing mechanisms. For the same reasons, templates for the activities are also left out. We include some explanations in the next language specification.

Process_Documentaton →
   main process Identifier (*<Parameters>*) ;
   Body

Body → Subprocesses
   Activity_Sequencing

Subprocesses → **process** Identifier (*<Parameters>*) ;
   Body
   Subprocesses
   | λ

Any process, whether the main process or a process, has a name and parameters (its "signature"), may contain a hierarchy of subprocesses (process is a recursive concept) and *must* include a sequence of activities defining the process.

Activity_Sequencing →
   sequence Activities **end_q**

Activities → Activity
   | Activity Activities

Activity → λ
   | *<Task_definition>* ;
   | Assignment ;
   | Subprocess_Call ;
   | Activity_Sequencing
   | Activity_Alternation
   | Activity_Repetition
   | Activity_Parallelization

Activity is also a recursive definition with four base cases (first four lines). An activity can be nothing (null string), a *task*, an assignment, a call to another process, or a sequence, alternation, repetition, or parallelization of activities. A *task* in this PDL is a relatively simple activity that does not require further refinement so that the associated text in natural language fully defines it (in technical terms, *<Task_definition>* is a base case of the recursive definition of activity). If the activity is more complex than a task, then it should be defined as a (sub)process to be refined further.

Assignment → Identifier := *<Expression>*

Subprocess_Call → Identifier (*<Parameters>*)

Activity_Alternation →
   if (*<Condition>* **)** Activities Else **end_i**

Else → **else** Activities | λ

Activity_Repetition →
   while(*<Condition>* **)** Activities **end_w**

Activity_Parallelization →
   paralellize Activities **end_p**

We will write comments in our process definitions /* like this */.

A Test Process

The costs of inadequate testing infrastructure have severe impacts in industry. In the U.S. alone, they are estimated to be between $22.2 and $59.5 billion (Tassey, 2002); one half is paid by the developers and the other half by the users. An appropriate test process synchronized with the development process that could rapidly detect and locate bugs as they are introduced would help to reduce these costs. We will use our PDL to specify parts of a variation of a test process applied successfully at e-Quallity. We have seen that this process represents a much better basis for the development of an operational test process than the V-Model because it provides more detail and a richer structure.

We consider that a project is an instance of a process in several ways, just as an object is an instance of a class: organizations specify the way they do things in the form of a process, a rather static documentation; when a project takes off, a group of people takes this process and incorporates real data into it, completing and customizing it and generating a more dynamic entity. This viewpoint is reflected in our next process specification, in which we structured the definition in a way that makes explicit the project phases and areas presented in the PM-BoK (Project Management Body of Knowledge,[5] Project Management Institute, 2000). In the specification, we will use "..." after a process signature to mean that the definition of its body is not presented here, mainly because it is not relevant for our presentation.

This process specification has more detail than the V-Model and provides a good basis to guide the execution of a real testing project in the context of SMEs.

The detail is introduced in the form of a hierarchy of subprocesses as well as sequences, cycles, and alternations of activities related to testing; this provides a richer structure than the V-Model, which is rather plain. As we mentioned before, *when* the testing subprocess takes off in a project can be determinant. Ideally, it should begin when the requirements are being established, and it should synchronize with the development process. These considerations will be important in the next sections.

CASE STUDIES

We now present two case studies that show the impact that testing can have on a software project. For each case study, we first describe some relevant characteristics of the organizations that hired the testing activities (a software buyer and a software developer, respectively), as well as the projects involved; then we explain their main problems regarding testing and the approach e-Quallity applied to test. We finally compare the results obtained in both projects.

Even though one can find limitations in the Man-Month metric, we will use it here because it will facilitate the comparison between the two case studies. Furthermore, in order to be able to make a comparison between the two projects, we will take the size of 20 Man-Months as the unit of measurement and will show the testing

Figure 2. A test process

```
main process test(); /* Progressive test only */
    process start();
        process establish_scope();... /* 1 area of PM-BoK*/
        process define_deliverables();  ...
            /* Typical ones: test cases; test results;
                graphics showing value earned and product
                maturity */
        process define_test_strategy ();
            process establish_termination_criterion();...
                /*Specify when testing should stop; examples
                    are "until the test cases have caused a
                    certain percentage of the code to be
                    excecuted", and "until the critical
                    requirements have been covered with at
                    least one test case" */
            process establish_regression_criterion();
                /* Which test cases should be re-excecuted
                    in the regression testing */
            sequence
                if (Total_regressions>0)  /* Zero means no
                                regression cycles are required */
                    if (SUT is a critical system)
                        regression_criterion =
                                Apply_all_Test_Cases;
                    else
                        regression_criterion =
                                Apply_Test_Cases_exposing_Bugs;
                    end_i
                else
                    regression_criterion = Null;  end_i
            end_q
            ...
        Sequence  /* define_test_strategy */  ...
            /* Define regression and termination criteria as
                well as the combination of techniques to be
                used (white-/black-box testing; α-/β-testing;
                unit/interaction/system testing; Automation)*/
        end_q /* define_test_strategy */
    sequence    /* start */
        paralelize
            stablish_scope();
            define_deliverables();
        end_p
        define_test_strategy ();
        establish_regression_criterion ();
    end_q   /* start */
```

continued on following page

Figure 2. continued

```
    process plan();
        process estimate_effort();...
            /* Estimate testing effort
                (>= 20% of the whole)*/
        process establish_time_management();...
            /* Establish time management plan */
        process establish_personnel_management();...
            /* Establish human resources management plan */
        process establish_procurement_management();...
            /* Establish procurement management plan */
        process establish_risk_management(); ...
            /* Specially contingency plan */
        process establish_quality_management();...
            /* Specially change control mechanism(s) */
        process establish_communication_management();...
            /* Establish communication */
        process establish_cost_management();...
            /* Establish cost management */
    sequence    /* plan */
        estimate_effort();
        paralelize /* 3 areas of PM-BoK */
                establish_time_management ();
                establish_personnel_management ();
                establish_procurement_management ();
        end_p
        paralelize /* 3 areas of PM-BoK */
                establish_risk_management();
                establish_quality_management();
                establish_communication_management();
        end_p
        establish_cost_management(); /* 1 area of PM-BoK */
    end_q  /* plan */

    process reproduce_SUT_context(); ...
        /* Set up a computational environment similar
            to the one the SUT is going to execute on */
    process set_up_tools(); ...
        /* Set up the testing tools that will be used */
    process design_test_cases(); ...
        /* Using one or more techniques */
    process apply_test_cases(); ...
    process report_statistics_and_supervise(); ...
        /* Statistics should include: number of test cases;
            Bug distribution; test cases/bugs */
    process manage_anomalies(); ... /* Track bugs */

    process close();
        process close_contract(); ...
                    /* Close with client */
        process close_project(); ...
                    /* Close in one's organization */
        process document_lessons_learned(); ...
                    /* For knowledge management */
    sequence  /* close */
        close_contract();
        close_project();
        document_lessons_learned();
    end_q  /* close */
```

continued on following page

Figure 2. continued

```
sequence  /* test */
    /* In the best case, the two first phases should
       Coincide with the same phase of the development
       project. In other words: the testers should
       participate in the start and plan activities
       together with architects, analysts and
       programmers */

       start();     /* 1st phase in PM-BoK */
       plan();      /* 2nd phase in PM-BoK */

            /* 3rd and 4th phases in PM-BoK:
               excecution and control*/
       reproduce_SUT_context();
       set_up_tools();

       while (not Termination_criterion)
           /* This cycle is synchronically and repeatedly
              executed in the development phases of
              requirements, design and programming, as
              shown in the V-Model */
           design_test_cases();
           apply_test_cases();
           report_statistics_and_supervise();
           manage_anomalies();
        end_w
       close();     /* 5th and last phase in PM-BoK */
end_q  /* test */
```

results proportionally to this unit. For reasons of confidentiality, we will only mention the name of one of the hiring organizations.

The Case of Acquiring Software Without Testing

Our first case study refers to a medium-sized firm (around 100 people, 10 of which belong to the IT Department) from an expanding industrial sector in Mexico, which required the automation of part of its business processes with a kind of enterprise resource planning system; we will call this firm the "Acquirer." It subcontracted the development of the system to a company we will here refer to as the "Developer."

During two years, the Acquirer's CIO in turn received several modules of the system (it resulted in a development of several Man-Years). With every delivery, the Developer said something like "Here is your Module-X of *n* Man-Months and here is the corresponding invoice. If you find bugs in the next *m* months, they will be corrected without charge; after that, any correction will have a price." The Acquirer had neither the infrastructure nor the know-how to validate that the quality of the modules it received was the hired one. (This is a common situation in non-technological SMEs but can also be seen in some technological SMEs, especially if they are small.) In these two years, the Acquirer had three CIOs in a row; then a third came in. After a couple of months in charge, he realized that the software had at least "small" quality problems. He looked for an independent and specialized assessment of the software product and hired e-Quallity.

The life cycle of this development effort was rather waterfall-like with testing at the end of the process. Our test process adapted without problem to the project with the subprocess start beginning when the product was already coded (and in operation). To gain an overview of the system's maturity, a module considered one of the most stable ones was chosen and tested; we will refer to it here as SUT_1. e-Quallity applied integration testing using both black- and white-box testing techniques; no regression testing was needed. There were no requirements documentation, so a pre-assessment was performed to set the termination criteria, which was the amount of test cases necessary to cover most of the processes automated by SUT_1. The testing was in fact an autopsy: it was performed at the end when the software was in operation, and it showed both wrong design and programming decisions, along with their negative consequences. Paradoxically, several months after the testing project, the Developer was assessed to have CMM level 3.

The Case of Delivering Tested Software

The second case study comes from a project with SIAC Software,[6] a small software development firm (less than 10 people) that was beginning to develop a new and innovative product for the financial sector in the Mexican and Latin American region. SIAC Software wanted to launch a mature product into the market (we will call it SUT_2) and decided to invest in testing from the beginning to know at any time in the project the quality of the subproducts generated, as well as the value earned. This data should permit it to make decisions like rejecting a subproduct or adjusting the planning.

This situation is a standard in innovative small development firms: when they first conceptualize an interesting product, they usually realize that in order to strongly and constantly penetrate the market, they must develop a very mature product so that its maintenance will not consume the time, money, and attention that should be rather invested in marketing and sales. Furthermore, it is usually the case that if this goal is not achieved,

the firm would face a really bad financial situation; sometimes they are conscious about it. Also a standard in small firms is that the strategy of hiring testers to form an internal testing team is out of the question because it would deviate the organization from its core business. A good alternative is to subcontract a specialized firm in testing and remain small, which was the choice taken by SIAC Software in our case study; it hired e-Quallity to perform the testing.

In a way, this case represents a minimal development project: one single expert developer with certifications in the technology he would use, one single expert in the application domain, and one small senior testing team. One would think, "In a team so small and with such ample expertise, misunderstandings should not be an issue." Even under such favorable circumstances, critical bugs were found, both technical and domain-related ones; the good part is that most of them were corrected in early development phases, saving time, money, and intangible assets like customer confidence (which in turn has impact in market penetration).

The development life cycle was rather incremental. Our subprocess start began early enough in the project (just after the requirements were known), and the development and test planning almost overlapped, which facilitated the synchronization of testing and development. This early involvement of testing permitted the testers to review the requirements for consistency, completeness, and testability, and to question and challenge the proposed architecture. The risk of delays was reduced by considering time and resources for bug elimination. Error-prone and critical parts of the SUT were identified and the test resources distributed accordingly, minimizing the risk of leaving critical bugs undetected.

e-Quallity applied integration as well as system testing, using both black- and white-box techniques. The termination criterion for testing was an amount of test cases covering the requirements for SUT_2. Regressive testing was first planned when the results of the progressive ones were available. The regression criterion was a compromise: on one hand, the testing team should not apply all the test cases again, but on the other hand, it should apply not only the ones that discovered bugs. So, related test cases that would disclose bugs originated by the "corrections" were also applied. At the end of the first regression, the product showed good behavior so that no other regressive cycle was needed.

A Comparison

The test results obtained for both SUTs are shown in Table 1.

Bugs were considered to have one of the following levels of criticality:

- **Low:** If it does not impede normal program execution, like that of orthographic bugs, or of colors in the GUI.
- **Medium:** If it impedes normal execution of the SUT but there are alternatives to continue.
- **High:** If it is impossible to continue using the SUT without abnormally terminating it.

Note that, although the SUTs have a similar number of bugs overall, SUT_1 has a higher concentration of medium and high criticality. Since testing was performed when SUT_1 was already in operation, its bugs were found only in program execution. For SUT_2, bugs were found also during requirements definition and system design.

Suppose now that these two SUTs with equal size also had similar complexity and that their development costs were similar, too; let us assume for simplicity that this cost is $100.

Remember that we mentioned in our introduction that for testing to be effective, it should receive at least 20% of the total resources of the project. Another way to obtain this is calculating 25% of the resources of the project that do not include testing.

Table 1. Test results

Criticality	SUT$_1$ Bugs found in Execution	SUT$_2$ Bugs in Requirements & Design	SUT$_2$ Bugs found in Execution
Low	106	179	127
Medium	257	29	92
High	296	98	95
SubTotal	659	306	314
TOTAL	659	620	

For SUT_1, the Acquirer paid $100 and received a faulty system which was put in operation. He had to pay $25 additionally for the testing to obtain a maturity assessment of the product (25% * $100) due to the problems it started to detect. This cost was not considered at the beginning of the development project.

The assessment exposed the bugs shown in Table 1. Correction was a complicated issue because the Acquirer did not want to pay for the corrections, and the Developer had considered neither the time nor the money to perform them. This was a very important topic for both parties: for the Developer, because as we know, correction after liberation is significantly more expensive than during development; and for the Acquirer, because maintaining a faulty system can become a very complicated and expensive task. After a complicated negotiation, some corrections were done; the system ended up with 534 bugs (81% of the total) after an investment of $125 (ignoring the costs of correction).

For SUT_2, the client knew from the beginning that he would pay $125 for the development with testing included. The testing team made clear it would have to plan time and resources for the correction of the bugs; there were no hidden costs. Timely, it had the opportunity to make the decision of which bugs to correct and when. The number of bugs overall was 620; some of them were found, and most of them corrected, in the early development phases, and others were corrected in the last phase, as shown in Table 1. There remained 71 bugs to be fixed in the next release (11% of the total). They were not corrected for a combination of reasons, including difficulty to detect and correct, and probability that they would cause problems to the user.

Now suppose we were lucky with SUT_1 so that, after testing and correction, 50% of its bugs were concentrated in one of its five modules which represents 20% of the system. We could upgrade its quality significantly by rebuilding the "buggy module" from scratch. This would leave SUT_1 with "only" 267 bugs in the best case, albeit increasing the total cost by at least \$20 (20%*\$100). At the end of the two projects, we would have the situation described in Table 2.

In addition to having invested \$20 more than the developer of SUT_2, the Acquirer of SUT_1, that paid late for testing, will have to live with a "buggier" system.

Even if no investment was made to test SUT_1, and it was discovered that in 20% of the system 50% of the bugs are concentrated. The overall investment would be similar to the one in SUT_2 after eliminating these bugs (in fact \$5 lower), as shown in Table 3.

Money was saved, but SUT_1 has significantly lower quality than SUT_2 (making the sales more difficult), so its maintenance will be more expensive; these costs are usually determinant for small development enterprises.

As we already mentioned, a very important point that made a big difference between the two projects was *when* testing took place.

In SUT_2 (the one from the small enterprise), this happened since the beginning, so problems were detected in early development phases, and corrections could be made before advancing to the next phase, diminishing a cascade effect. The costs of maintenance were moderate and permitted investment into more resources in marketing and sales to have a higher market penetration.

That was not possible with SUT_1 (the one for the medium enterprise) because testing took place at the end. The costs of correction and maintenance were high, and the productivity of the users was relatively low. Fortunately, the Acquirer was in an expanding market with high profit margin, and its size permitted it to absorb such costs. Performed early, testing would have helped even with this "buggy" system: after testing the first module that was received, the Acquirer could have refused to pay and could demand it to be corrected or rebuilt.

Mainly because of the limited resources related to its size, the development firm of SUT_1 would

Table 2. First situation

	Development	Testing	Redevelopment	Total Investment	Bugs left
SUT_1	\$100	\$25	\$20	**\$145**	**267**
SUT_2	\$100	\$25		**\$125**	**71**

Table 3. Second situation

	Development	Testing	Redevelopment	Total Investment	Bugs left
SUT_1	\$100		\$20	**\$120**	**330**
SUT_2	\$100	\$25		**\$125**	**71**

have had serious financial difficulties if it had not tested from the beginning and had ended with 620 bugs. Its quality would have been lower, and its maintenance would have stolen resources from marketing and sales; this would have impact in user acceptance to the product and would have made the market penetration more difficult. These financial risks are common to small (and some medium) development enterprises, so we believe they all could profit from using testing as a tool to manage their projects.

LESSONS LEARNED

We hope we presented enough data to encourage software developers (especially small ones) and buyers to apply testing to save time and money and to reduce risks. Our study resulted in some final reflections:

Unless the SUT is of little relevance for the buyer or developer, testing should not be avoided in any project. Impacts in both directions were shown using the case of the buggy SUT_1 and the "minimal development effort" of SUT_2.

Testing should be performed as early as possible in the development process to obtain higher benefits for the same cost, as shown in our case studies.

Testing makes explicit the need for time to correct bugs, adding realism to the planning and reducing the risks of delays.

The process presented here was a good framework for testing in the two case studies presented here; its adaptation was easy in both cases, but variations of this process have been useful in the operations of e-Quallity, so it represents a good operational basis in general.

The use of our PDL proved to be beneficial at e-Quallity, increasing the readability and simplifying the adaptation and maintenance of its test processes. It was important that the PDL was kept simple and small to facilitate its use.

Testing can be a good tool for software project management because it provides objective and fresh data regarding product maturity and value earned, useful to manage risks like delays and budget surpassing.

To achieve better results in an effort of process improvement, special attention should be placed in the testing activity at the beginning in order to obtain rapid profits from product improvement.

Testing is a discipline in itself, and this profession requires particular profiles, somewhat different from the ones for software development.

FUTURE WORK

Although our PDL has been used successfully in testing projects, it could be applied to define other software processes in order to gather more information to improve it. Companies should try to use PDLs in testing tools so that at least partial process documentation is automatically generated. This would add value to the tools and would be helpful in a process improvement effort. Nonprocedural constructs should be (systematically) included in PDLs, enriching their definition mechanisms and providing another perspective. More statistical evidence is needed about the savings and losses when performing testing early or late in the development process. Much work remains to be done so that time for corrections is taken into account, making planning more realistic and reducing several risks. This could impact positively and directly the whole software industry and, in an indirect way, other industries that consume software development.

REFERENCES

Black, R. (2002). *Managing the testing process*. Wiley Publishing Inc.

Burnstein, I. (2003). *Practical software testing: A process-oriented approach*. New York: Springer.

Chrissis, M.B., Konrad, M., & Shrum, S. (2006). *CMMI: Guidelines for process integration and product improvement.* Addison-Wesley.

e-Quallity. (2006). *Prueba de Software: una Definición.* Retrieved December 12, 2007, from

http://www.e-quallity.net/def.php

Gabbar, H.A. (Ed.). (2006). *Modern formal methods and applications.* Berlin-Heilderberg: Springer-Verlag.

Garshol, L.M. (2006). *BNF and EBNF: What are they and how do they work?* Retrieved December 12, 2007, from http://www.garshol.priv.no/download/text/bnf.html#id1.1

Jorgensen, P. (2002). *Software testing: A craftman's approach.* CRC Press.

León-Carrillo, L.V. (2005). Caracterización de la Prueba de Software. *Software Gurú, 1*(5), 49.

León-Carrillo, L.V. (2005). *La Especificación de un "Process Definition Language"* (Reporte interno). Guadalajara, Mexico: e-Quallity.

León-Carrillo, L.V., Ruelas-Minor, E., & Castillo-Hernández, A. (2004). *Métricas de Proyecto y de Proceso* (Internal Report). Guadalajara, Mexico: e-Quallity.

Myers, G. (1979). *The art of software testing.* John Wiley & Sons.

Osterweil, L.J. (1987, March). Software processes are software too. In *Proceedings of the 9th International Conference of Software Engineering,* Monterey, CA (pp. 2-13).

Patton, R. (2006). *Software testing.* Sams Publishing.

Project Management Institute. (2000). *A guide to the project management body of knowledge.*

Rozenberg, G., & Salomaa, A. (Eds.). (1997). *Handbook of formal languages.* Berlin-Heilderberg: Springer-Verlag.

Schulmeyer, G.G., & McManus, J.I. (Eds.). (1993). *Total quality management for software.* New York: Van Nostrand Reinhold.

Scientific American. (1994). *Software's chronic crisis.* Retrieved December 12, 2007, from http://www.cis.gsu.edu/~mmoore/CIS3300/handouts/SciAmSept1994.html

Tassey, G. (2002, May). *The economic impacts of inadequate infrastructure for software testing* (Final Report). National Institute of Standards & Technology.

Ventura-Miranda, M.T., & Peñaloza-Báez, M. (2006). *MoProSoft: modelo de procesos de software hecho en México.* Retrieved December 12, 2007, from http://www.enterate.unam.mx/Articulos/2006/marzo/moprosoft.htm

ENDNOTES

[1]   The company is called "e-QuALLity" because of the names of the founders (it is a *"planted* bug").

[2]   e-Quallity can be visited at www.e-quallity.net.

[3]   CMMI® is a service mark of the Software Engineering Institute.

[4]   PolTeq can be visited at www.polteq.com

[5]   PM-BoK is a trademark of the Project Management Institute.

[6]   SIAC Software can be visited at www.siac.com.mx.

Chapter V
QuickLocus:
A Software Development Process Evaluation Method for Small–Sized Organizations

Sarah Kohan
Carlos Alberto Vanzolini Foundation, Brazil

Marcelo Schneck de Paula Pessôa
Escola Politécnica da Universidade de São Paulo, Brazil

Mauro de Mesquita Spinola
Escola Politécnica da Universidade de São Paulo, Brazil

ABSTRACT

Many small-sized organizations have a significant role in the software business. A good software development process is the best way to assure quality to software products. Audits and evaluations are commonly used to verify implementation and certify the development process. This chapter describes the development and application of **QuickLocus**, *a special-purpose evaluation method of software process developed to be applied in small-sized organizations.* **QuickLocus** *has been successfully applied since January 2003 by more than 50 organizations in process improvement programs. The reason for* **QuickLocus** *success is its low-cost methodology and its capability to output reliable information for kicking off a software improvement process.* **QuickLocus** *will provide organizations ways to be more competitive—producing better products at lower costs faster—ready to compete in the international software market. This chapter is organized in three parts: foundation, method, and results. The first one is theoretical and presents how the method was developed. The second part details the method itself, and the third part presents the method application results.*

INTRODUCTION

Computers and software have increasingly become a key component for business operations, and today they are part of critical mission management activities in many companies. For some industries, for instance, banking, the daily operations are heavily supported by complex information systems. Many other industries are also heavily dependent on information technology. Software is the cornerstone for what has become known as the information technology.

The traumatic experience IBM went through in the 1960s while developing the OS/360 Operating System is a case study in this regard. According to Watson and Petre (1990, p. 339), the concept for the System/360 was chartered in December 1961, and "hundreds of programmers had to deliver millions of machine language code. Nothing like that had ever been tried before and the engineers lived under constant deadline pressure." The same authors still report the following:

As the delays in delivering the software got bigger, more programmers were added; by 1966 we had two thousand programmers and the software development costs were already higher than the costs for developing the hardware. We learned, in the school of hard knocks, one of the biggest secrets in software engineering: you don't speed up a software development project by filling up office space with programmers. (p. 342)

Following this same line of thoughts, several authors write about the importance of software and the controls required during its development to assure quality and reliability as well as the ability to forecast the resources required for project execution. Literature is very abundant on making the point that the identification of software development process status (process evaluation) is important to the organization overall improvement processes, contributes to problem reduction during software creation and help develop better products. Sometimes the word assessment is used with similar meaning of evaluation.

Jones (2000) highlights the requirements for research that adds accuracy to software development. For Jones (2000), software process evaluation is a practice that contributes to the delivery of better products. Process evaluations can contribute to the reduction of problems during software development, helping organizations pinpoint improvement opportunities in the process that contribute to the development of better products. Software Engineering Institute (1997) states that an effective change program requires understanding the current situation and mentions two sayings:

The Chinese Saying: "If you do not know where you are heading to, any road will do."
Humphrey's Saying: "If you do not know where you are, no map will help you."

The "Chinese Saying" forces us to think about the clarity of goals. The demand exists for improvements in software process, both in large- and small-sized organizations. While it is a fact that big organizations are reasonably well served by existing solutions, we do not see it happening for the small ones. The requirement of an evaluation feature, as a process improvement tool, for the great number of small-sized organizations suggests the development of a method for evaluating the software process delivering on two must-have prerequisites. First, the evaluation results are the foundation for a process adjustment or improvement plan. Second, the costs associated to applying the evaluation are in line with the means and resources available for such organizations.

This chapter describes **QuickLocus** (Kohan, 2003), an evaluation method for software processes aimed at small-sized organizations. Evaluation is one of the most important activities for implementation of software quality processes improvement programs. Process models, techniques, and tools are easily found in the literature and in the market. The challenge is to integrate all the concepts in one adequate methodology to be understood and executed by all personnel involved with such activities. A good evaluation method is to "take a snapshot" of the process compliance, to not only its definition breadth and model adherence but its use adoption by everybody as well.

QuickLocus details the setting and the managing of the evaluation for the software process covering two factors: behavioral and technical. **QuickLocus'** main features are:

- Evaluation in small-sized organizations: up to 50 people[1]
- Evaluation of a reduced scope of the model: up to three process areas
- Evaluation of up to four different software development processes from the organizational point of view
- Size of evaluation team: three people
- Data gathering from two sources: questionnaires and interviews
- Duration of work at the organization: 1 day
- Rating model/reference standard practices with higher level of detail

The objective of this chapter is to provide the reader with information on the concepts and directions that might lead to the utilization of the **QuickLocus** method.

FOUNDATION

The Research Developed

Many evaluation methods for software development process are available. While each of these methods has specific features, they share in common the requirement for substantial time commitment (days or weeks) and a trained team for the engagement. As a result, they are budgeted as costly activities that interfere not only with daily activities for the development team but the whole organization as well. The level of interference and costs can be assimilated by organizations with a great number of developers (because they are more risk averse) or those with tradition in software development (because they are more familiar with the risks in this activity). Direct and indirect costs and annoyances in the organization workplace are the key factors that make the process evaluation activity a tough decision for many companies. In spite of a growing recognition, these factors inhibit the dissemination of methods for software processes evaluation in small organizations.

The demand for software process improvement exists in both large and small organizations. While the large organizations are reasonably well served by the existing solutions, we see the opposite for the small organizations. It is clear that the starting point for improvement projects should be, according to Humphrey's saying (Humphrey, 1989), to monitor the software development process, which means one thing: evaluation. The requirement for good software development processes for all organization sizes inspired this research, but with our eyes set on the small organizations.

Theoretical Concepts

This section presents concepts related to the evaluation process execution and short descriptions from methods found in the literature. Evaluation, according to Jones (2000), is a formal and structured method of examine the way how software projects are built and maintained. The ISO/IEC 15504 standard (ISO/IEC, 2004, 2003, 2004a, 2004b, 2006) defines the process evaluation as "systematic evaluation of an organization software process, as defined in a reference model." Humphrey (1989) identifies three phases in a process evaluation: readiness, evaluation, and recommendations. In the readiness phase, the organization to be evaluated is defined, as well as the team to execute it and the management sponsorship. The evaluation phase has its own three steps: assembling and training the evaluation team, programming and developing the evaluation. The recommendation phase steps are delivering the conclusion report, the activities plan (including the milestones for following up), and establishing new priorities for continuous improvements.

On the other hand, Zahran (1998) defines the following phases: pre-evaluation/preplanning, evaluation, and postevaluation. Although they have different names, the phases of both the authors have almost the same feel. It has an exception for the evaluation final report where Humphrey (1989) includes it in the phase of recommendations, and Zahran (1998) includes it in the evaluation phase. Product quality improves when process quality improves and process improvements can be measured through evaluations. The definition for quality found on IEEE STD 610-90 has two topics (IEEE STD, 1991):

1. Measurement of how much one system, component, or process complies with predefined requirements

2. Measurement of how much one system, component, or process complies with requirements or expectations from customers or users

According to Paulk, Weber, Curtis, Chrissis, et al. (1995), organization may be defined as "one unit, inside a company or other entity in which several projects are built concurrently. Every project inside one organization practices the same policies and top level management." Based on the results from evaluations, improvement plans for the software development process are put in place. The software process as defined by ISO/IEC 15504 is the following: "the process or combination of processes used by one organization or project to plan, manage, execute, follow up, control, and improve their activities related to software."

Development process improvement programs aim to improve process capacity and maturity. Juran (1992) defines process capacity as "the intrinsic capability of a process to replicate its

Figure 1. Dimensions for the process evaluation strategies adapted from Nielsen and Pries-Heje (2002)

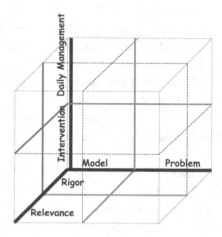

results in a consistent way, during multiple cycles of operations"; and in Paulk et al. (1995) we find the following definition for process maturity: "the process maturity for software represents a dimension where a specific process is meticulously defined, managed, measured, controlled, and efficient."

Executing an evaluation is an important element for knowing a process, planning its improvement, and as a consequence for obtaining better software products and better budget control. Some approach criteria for definition of an evaluation strategy can be used. According to Nielsen and Pries-Heje (2002), these approach criteria or underlying strategies oppose each other. (See Figure 1) We have three strategic dimensions: one based on enforcement or in relevance, the second based on model or problem orientation, and the third based on intervention or on daily management:

1. **Strategy based on rigor vs. strategy based on relevance:** An evaluation strategy that collects data and uses them to reach conclusions is called strategy based on rigor. The opposite is a strategy based on relevance

that focuses on the extraction of relevant data for one or more sponsors. A strategy based on relevance cannot reach complete, total, or enforceable results; instead, it can deliver results and conclusions related only to the organizational roles involved.

2. **Strategy based on model vs. strategy oriented to problems:** A strategy based on model focuses on best practices models and models for software process common problems. A strategy based on problems focuses on what people who execute the software process and their managers think the problem might be.

3. **Strategy based on intervention vs. strategy based on daily management:** Strategy based on intervention is supported by external consultants who evaluate the organization. It is planned as a specific project with a start and finish date. The day-to-day management approach implements worky assessments into the routine work of the organization.

By combining these three basic strategies, Nielsen and Pries-Heje (2002) defines eight possible strategy categories, as follows:

1. Strategy focused on rigor, with intervention and based on model—Assisted evaluation
2. Strategy focused on rigor, with intervention and based on problem—Assisted metrics program and benchmarking
3. Strategy focused on rigor, with daily management, and based on model—Evaluations that are independent from specific projects
4. Strategy focused on rigor, with daily management, and based on problem—Program with independent metrics based on projects
5. Strategy based on relevance, with intervention, based on model—Assisted evaluation, based on model (small sample)

6. Strategy based on relevance, with intervention, based on problem—Problem assisted diagnosis
7. Strategy based on relevance, with daily management based on model—Independent self-evaluation, based on models
8. Strategy based on relevance, with daily management based on problem—Independent self-evaluation, based on projects

Figure 1 shows the dimensions for the software process evaluation basic strategies as described by Nielsen and Pries-Heje (2002).

The following paragraphs describe the analysis of some methods found in the literature.

Appraisal Requirements for CMMI, Version 1.1—ARC V1.1

Phases and principles of evaluation methods that comply with ARC V1.1 requirements (CMMI Product Team, 2001) are compatible with those defined by Humphrey (1989). ARC V1.1 has introduced method classes A, B, and C. This innovation allows the development of evaluation methods with a better fit for the sponsor's specific needs. The provided flexibility allows for creation of faster and less expensive methods that in turn can evolve to more sophisticated methods by adding new requirements, while still keeping compatibility with the original methods.

Standard CMMI Appraisal Method for Process Improvement Version 1.1— SCAMPI V1.1

Since method SCAMPI V1.1 (Assessment Method Integrated Team, 2001) is compatible with ARC V1.1 requirements, it is organized in three phases and it is compliant with Humphrey's (1989) evaluation principles. It is a well structured method that unites best practices and features found in several methods. The phase steps cover a lot of ground, and if properly used, SCAMPI V1.1 provides the evaluation sponsor with good results.

Guidelines for Quality and/or Environmental Management System Auditing—NBR ISO 19011

The NBR ISO 19011 (ABNT, 2002) phases correspond to those defined by Humphrey (1989); NBR ISO 19011 phases 1, 2, and 3 correspond to Humphrey's (1989) setup phase; phase 4 corresponds to the evaluation phase, and phases 5, 6, and 7 correspond to the recommendations phase.

Software Engineering—Process Assessment—Part 2: Performing an Assessment - ISO/IEC 15504-2

ISO/IEC 15504-2 (ISO/IEC, 2003) defines the evaluation method requirements in a similar way as ARC V1.1 does, but it does not predefine the model process, which is considered a parameter from the evaluation method. So, it is a more generic set of requirements then SEI's, which already incorporates a definition for the process reference model. We can establish a comparison between the requirements from methods compatible with ISO/IEC 15504-2 and the phases from evaluation methods defined by Humphrey (1989) and Zahran (1998) and conclude they comply with the concepts from these authors.

Systems Engineering Capability Model—Appraisal Method—EIA/IS-713-2

The EIA/IS-713-2 method (Electronic Industries Alliance, 1998) complies with the principles and phases defined by Humphrey (1989). Since it is a method suited for improvement efforts, phase 3 is rich in details as defined by Humphrey (1989), such as developing action plans, plan milestones, creation of time schedule, and establishment of

improvement priorities. The basic activities are the same in the CBA IPI (Dunaway & Masters, 2001) method to evaluate the CMM staged model. The EIA/IS-713-2 was used as a base for the development of requirements for evaluation methods of CMMI (ARC V1.1) models. It has the same structure as those of CBA IPI V1.2, SCE V3.0, and SCAMPI V1.1 methods, with more steps, and was published in 1998.

Proprietary and Custom-Made Methods

The specific needs from project or organizations led some institutions to develop evaluation methods with special characteristics. One of these characteristics is the low cost of operation; one of its most common objectives is to use these results to jump-start improvement processes. One can find descriptions for these methods in articles from trade journals, without a high level of detail. Some of these methods are:

- **Rapid Assessment for Process Improvement (RAPID):** RAPID was developed at Griffith University, Queenland, Australia and was published by Rout, Tuffley, Cahill, and Hodgen (2000). It was created to support small and medium organizations that cannot afford to pay for evaluations that would take three or four days. It complies with ISO/IEC 15504, and it is assumed it will be conducted by experienced evaluators; its main objective is to support process improvement.

- **Quick TOPS evaluation to motivate process improvement for SMEs:** The TOPS project (Toward Organised Process in small and medium enterprises) has been created by the European Community to promote best practices for software. The project developed a quick evaluation method, published by Bucci, Campanai, and Gignoni (2000), adapting the SPICE (ISO/IEC 15504) and providing evaluation at no cost for companies that join the project.

- **Project SataSPIN, A Detailed Evaluation Method for Software SME:** started in 1998 in Satakuta, in western Finland, was published by Mäkinen, Varkoi, and Lepasaar (2000). The project objective is to help small and medium enterprises (SMEs) develop their operations using international models for software process. The model complies with SPICE (ISO/IEC 15504) and has been adopted according to small enterprises needs and tested in several evaluations.
- **SEI Progress-Assessment method:** The SEI Progress-Assessment method, as described by Daskalantonakis (1994), is exclusive for Motorola and was first used by an organization with 1,000 software engineers in the Cell Phone Infrastructure Group and then by other Motorola groups.

Research Method

According to Bryman (1989), the research methodology has two approaches: quantitative and qualitative. These approaches create two method types: qualitative methods and quantitative methods. According to Nakano and Fleury (1996), quantitative methods are known as traditional methods while qualitative methods are known as nontraditional. According to Bryman (1989), the main characteristic for quantitative research is the focus placed on the subject under study (whether it is an individual, organization, or process). The quantitative method is driven by a predefined set of questions (extracted from proper theory or literature). On the other hand, qualitative research goes against the notion the researcher is the "source" of what would be relevant and important, trying to bring up whatever the subject under study elects as important, according to its own perspective (Table 1).

According to Nakano and Fleury (1996), the experimental research and survey are the methods more frequently associated to the quantitative research (traditional); participant research, research action, and case study are associated to the qualitative research (nontraditional). A case study, according to Yin (1994), is the process of investigating a contemporary phenomenon, within a real context, where the boundaries between the phenomenon and the context are not clear, and uses multiple information sources. The main research methods can be summarized according to approach described in Table 2.

According to Yin (1994), three conditions define which research method should be used:

1. The question type proposed in the research: "who," "what," "where," "how," and "why."
2. The level of control the researcher has over behavioral events: when the researcher can

Table 1. Research approaches

| Reseach Metodology | Qunatitative methods (traditional): theory identification |
| | Qualitative methods (nontraditional): perspective from the person under research |

Table 2. Research methods by approach type

Main approach	Research method
Quantitative (traditional)	Experimental
Quantitative (traditional)	Survey
Qualitative (nontraditional)	Participant
Qualitative (nontraditional)	Research-action
Qualitative (nontraditional)	Case Study

directly, precisely, and systemically manipulate the behavior.

3. The degree of focus on historical facts compared to contemporary facts: when the researcher is dealing only with the past and there is not one person to explain, even in retrospect, what happened, the focus is mostly directed to the historical facts.

This research analyzes contemporary facts (within an organization that develops software), and the key question becomes: *how to evaluate the status of software development and maintenance processes for small organizations* and do not allow for manipulation of behavior in any way (like under lab controlled conditions). A project like this can use the case study as its research methodology. **QuickLocus** was developed according to the case-study research methodology as a master degree dissertation: comprising a bibliography survey, the construction of a guideline (theory) to accomplish assessments, field testing, and review of outcome data. Adjustments in theory were made and a new evaluation method, named **QuickLocus**, was built. Five steps were covered:

1. Comprehensive research and comparative analysis of evaluation methods found in the literature;
2. Partially structured interviews with renown and experienced auditors and evaluators;
3. Development of a theory and draft for the case study;
4. Use of the draft applied to a specific case; and
5. Based on results from this field test, making the necessary adjustments and development of the method.

THE QUICKLOCUS METHOD

QuickLocus is a method for evaluating software development for small-sized organizations. The method's objectives are:

- To be the foundation for an improvement or adjustment plan for the software development process
- To be low cost
- To generate reliable results
- To interfere the least with the organization daily activities
- The **QuickLocus** method has three phases:
  - Readiness
  - Evaluation
  - Postevaluation

QuickLocus requires the role of a coordinator as well as an organization sponsor and an evaluation team leader. The evaluated organization must be small with up to 50 people involved with the software development process, according to the classification criteria for small-sized organizations as defined in Brazil by the National Foundation for Quality Award (FPNQ, 2002). Although the definition used was for small-sized organizations, the enterprise itself can be a large company, but the software organization involves up to 50 people. For this reason, some authors use the term small settings for this specific situation. The evaluation results can be used to be the starting point for a process improvement plan or to monitor its implementation.

QuickLocus Overview

Figure 2 presents an overview for **QuickLocus**. The evaluation method is comprised of three different phases: readiness, evaluation, and postevaluation.

During the readiness phase, the scope and the model or standard to be used as reference are defined, and the field activities are planned in detail.

During the evaluation phase, two different sources are used: questionnaire and interviews; results are rated and a preliminary report is presented.

Figure 2. Overview of the evaluation process

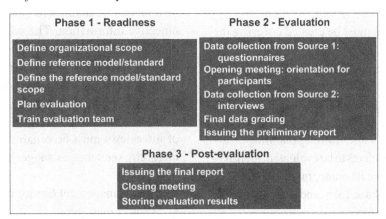

During the postevaluation phase, the results are presented, an agreement about the results is established, and the results are stored.

The next paragraphs detail each phase.

QuickLocus—Phase 1

Phase 1—Readiness—takes care of activities that allow for the understanding of the evaluation context and to prepare the day of activities at the organization. It has five steps:

- Define the organizational evaluation scope
- Define the model/standard to be used
- Define the model/standard evaluation scope
- Plan the evaluation
- Train the evaluation team

Defining the Organizational Scope, Reference Model, and the Reference Model Scope

The first three steps for Phase 1 are the definition for three scopes: the organizational scope, the reference model, and the scope within the reference model. They must be defined jointly with the organization. The *organizational scope* definition must represent the development processes, or the most important area from the business organization standpoint. If the scope becomes bigger that what is understood as a small-sized organization, in this case, 50 people, this scope can be split to be executed in more than one evaluation. The scope must encompass the processes representative from development (no more than four different processes in one evaluation). The *reference model* definition depends on the organization's objectives related to its improvement plan. Commercial or market requirements are legitimate and very common in defining a model (e.g., a certain customer may force the use of a specific model by the organization).

The selection of the scope within the reference model must take into account the reduced time for executing the activity. Selecting up to three process areas is a basic **QuickLocus** condition/restriction to deliver on its objectives. The selection process must take into consideration the specific organization conditions at the moment of the evaluation. For example, an area that is recognized as deficient can be better understood through an evaluation. On the other hand, one area considered efficient can also be analyzed to better understand its strengths and possible replication to other areas. Templates 1 and 2 must be sent to the organization and filled out (see Appendix).

Planning the Evaluation

An evaluation plan must be created covering the following items at a minimum:

- The company and the organization
- Evaluation objectives
- Sponsor identification
- Team assembly and training planning
- Selection of projects to be evaluated, identifying for each one its name, manager, process, development phase, roles, and names of people per role in the project
- Selection of participants with their names, project, and project role, position in the organization, and immediate manager
- Definition of main guidelines and orientation for participants
- Planning the interviews and the parts of the model scope to be covered in each interview
- Defining the overall schedule for the evaluation and the day of activities at the organization
- Planning the evaluation logistics

Responsibility and role for each team member must be defined during the evaluation team selection. The team must have three people, at least one of them belonging to the organization. Designated roles include the leader, members, process area monitors, the time keeper, and the facilitator. Observers can watch the work but must keep a distance to not interfere with the team's performance. The role must be clearly defined to prevent activities gaps or overlapping.

The selected projects must have no more than two different development processes. In the case of three or four processes, it can be split in two project groups (Group 1 and Group 2). In all cases, the participants must have a key role in the project. People are interviewed in groups, according to their role. The evaluation complexity increases as the number of evaluated processes also increases.

It is very important to select the right person to be interviewed in order to quickly get direct and objective information. The schedule for the day of activities at the organization must start with an opening meeting (duration: 30 minutes), followed by five interviews, teamwork meetings, consensus meeting to create a preliminary report, and lunch break. Based on people availability, schedule of interviews must be organized in a top-down hierarchy sequence as suggested below:

- Top Management (senior management)
- Project managers
- Developers

or, as an alternative:

- Top Management
- Project managers from Group 1
- Project developers from Group 1
- Project managers from Group 2
- Project developers from Group 2

It is very important to follow the interviews hierarchical order, from top to bottom. This allows for checking what top management declares against what technical personnel reports. Inconsistencies between management expectations and what the team delivers and the process actually used become clear. The evaluation schedule must provide dates for:

- Delivering/receiving the forms for collecting data from the organization and process
- Delivering the preliminary evaluation plan
- Organization approval for the plan (including time schedule)
- Evaluation activities at the organization (including time schedule)
- Delivering the final report to the organization for approval
- Meeting to present final results (including time schedule)

The earlier definition of a time schedule and discipline regarding each activity time are key to the execution of all activities at the organization during this phase to keep disruption of daily routines to a minimum. Strict discipline regarding time and keeping last minute improvisation to a minimum contribute to a respectful and professional image for the whole activity.

An example of a time schedule for the day of activities is found in Table 3. Duration of activities was defined based on past experience. For instance, an interview with top management must be fast and objective (40 minutes maximum) as this group is very busy and has little time available to participate. Interviews with project managers must be limited to 60 minutes. For interviews with a big group of people (more than five participants) allow for a longer time period. Another important suggestion is to reserve some time right after each interview so the evaluation team can register all information, discuss the covered topics, and use it as a buffer time to accommodate possible delays.

Table 3. **QuickLocus** *schedule of activities at the organization*

Time	Activity
8:00	Opening meeting
8:30	Evaluation team alignment meeting
8:45	Interview 1—top management
9: 25	Closing for Interview 1
10:05	Interview 2—project managers Group 1
11:05	Closing for Interview 2
11:45	Interview 3—project managers Group 2
12:45	Lunch break
13:45	Closing for Interview 3
14:25	Interview 4—project developers Group 1
14:55	Closing for Interview 4
15:15	Interview 5—project developers Group 2
15:45	Closing for Interview 5
16:05	Final rating and preparation of preliminary report
17:05	Organization of working material from the team
17:30	Closing of the day of activities

When planning for the logistics at the organization, the complete infrastructure required by the activities must be provided. This includes the meeting room for the opening and closing meetings, the interview room (big enough to fit the team and the interviewed), as well as computers and projection equipment for the presentations. The opening meeting presentation and orientation must discuss the following topics with the participants:

- Leader presentation to emphasize the importance of this evaluation
- Thanks for the company's support for the execution of the evaluation
- Introducing the evaluation team
- Evaluation objectives
- Evaluation method overview, detailing:
  o What is already done: responses to the questionnaires and plan preparation
  o What will be accomplished during the day of activities (the interviews and team meetings)
  o Follow-up activities: preparation and validation of final report, date and time of closing meeting
- Highlight the confidentiality status for the disclosed information
- Highlight the team focus: on processes, not on people
- Highlight the activities following the evaluation: support from top management in driving the improvement plan and its implementation
- Switch the meeting over to the organization top management and/or sponsor/coordinator

The evaluation plan can be created following Template 3 and the orientation message in accordance with Template 6 (see Appendix).

Training the Evaluation Team

The evaluation team must get trained.[2] Other people from the organization can participate along with team members. Training must cover the following topics:

- Basic concepts: process measurement, measurement methods, method to be used, attributes and responsibilities for the evaluator (leader and team members).
- **QuickLocus** phases: describing the steps for each phase, highlighting the most important ones and defining the role for each team member.
- Discuss the behavior and posture for the evaluation team regarding "patrolling," politeness, respect for the interviewed, confidentiality of the information, recording evaluation data, and no people attribution.

Qualifying and Defining Roles for Evaluation Team Members

Every member of the evaluation team must have been trained in the **QuickLocus** method and be familiar with the reference model as well as the evaluation scope. The team leader must have at least a 10-year professional experience, management experience (two years), and participated on at least two evaluations as a **QuickLocus** team member or at a similar evaluation process. The leader experience is very important, particularly when delicate subject relationships or some type of polarization inside of the team is dealt with or in the evaluated organization. Evaluation team members must be experienced professionals in software development for at least five years, with software engineering knowledge. The desirable personal attributes for the evaluation team members include good observation skills and a sharp eye for details (to objectively conduct the interviews while looking for practices still not covered in the model). Ethics and a conciliatory

and receptive attitude are important qualities to keep confidentiality issues as well as the cordiality during any tense situation that may occur as part of the activities. Beyond the skills described above, team members must have some other traits that will guarantee the evaluation process evolves smoothly: communication and relationship skills, analysis and judgment skills, objectivity, and a sense of organization. The team roles assigned to the team are:

- Leader—leads and orients the activities
- Member—executes the assigned activities
- Process Area Monitor—in charge of collecting data covering the process(es) area(s)
- Timekeeper—makes sure the activities do not exceed their planned duration
- Facilitator—helps with the infrastructure required by the activities at the organization and keeps track of people so they do not miss their scheduled appointments
- Observer—person that observes the evaluation process only without interfering in the activities. Generally, observer is someone being trained in this kind of activity.

The leader selects the team members and defines each one's roles. Team members can be designated to more than one role.

QuickLocus: Phase 2

Phase 2—Evaluation—comprises the preliminary data collection (Source 1) as well as the activities for the activity day at the organization. It comprises five steps:

1. Data collection from Source 1: questionnaires
2. Opening meeting: orientation for participants
3. Data collection from Source 2: interviews
4. Final rating of data
5. Preliminary report issued

Data Collection from Source 1: Questionnaires

Data collection from Source 1 is executed by the organization filling out Template 4 (see Appendix). Each process area belonging to the reference model scope must have its own questionnaire, in a way that a direct correspondence exists between questions and the scope practice. The goal is to determine which model practices are present in the organization, from its point of view. This data must be reported on Template 5 in the Source 1 column.

Activities at the Organization

The next four steps are to be executed during the day of activities at the organization. To get to the expected results during that day, one should assume that:

- The evaluation team knows the reference model scope in detail.
- The monitor for each process area has prepared, in writing, his/her list of questions for the interviews.
- The evaluation team has studied the evaluation plan and knows the organization chart, the detailed scope organization chart, the scope of the projects, and the schedule of activities for the day.
- The evaluation team has had preliminary access to the information provided by the organization through the forms, such as the organization profile, the initial information about the software development process, and the responses to the questionnaires.
- Data collected in the preliminary questionnaires are already reported in the mapping table for each process and had been passed along to the team members.
- Each evaluation team member has received the scope organization chart, the schedule of activities for the day, interview forms to take

notes during the conversation, and the form for mapping each process area containing already rated questionnaire data.

- The team leader has access to, besides the material for each of the team members: attendance list of participants for the opening meeting, opening meeting minutes form, check list to guide the opening meeting or the presentation slides for the meeting, responses for the previously sent questionnaires, forms for mapping each process area containing already rated questionnaire data, and the preliminary report template.

The opening meeting must be lead by the leader, as defined on Template 6 (see Appendix).

Opening Meeting: Orientation for Participants

The orientation for the participants during the opening meeting is planned to last for 30 minutes. The following group of people (at least) must be present at the meeting:

- All persons to be interviewed
- The evaluation team
- Top management for the organization scope

Besides this group, it is always desirable to have the greatest number of representatives from the organization in the opening meeting, following the priority scale below:

- Top management from areas not covered by the evaluation scope (for example, the finance director, sales director, and others)
- Members from the selected projects who will not be interviewed
- Project managers that belong to the organization scope, that, nevertheless, were not selected to be interviewed
- Members from the projects included in the organization scope that were not selected to be interviewed

- Project managers out of the organization scope

The orientation session is conducted as described in the in a check list or slides prepared during the evaluation planning, according to Template 6. The opening minutes must be created and the presents should sign a list using the appropriate forms shown on Template 8 (see Appendix).

Data Collection from Source 2: Interviews

The evaluation team must meet to align attitudes and actions to be taken during the day of activities before collecting data during the interviews. Topics to be covered during this preparatory meeting are the organization, the length of the interviews, and the sequence of the questions to be formulated by team members. Data collection from Source 2 comes from five interviews, as planned during Phase 1. The interview is divided in two parts:

- Interview properly said—its length is determined by the hierarchic level from the person or group being interviewed:
- Top management interview: 40 minutes
- Project manager interview: 1 hour
- Developer Interview: 30 minutes
- Closing the interview—the time allocated for this depends on the profile of the interviewed:
- For top management and project managers: 40 minutes
- For developers: 20 minutes

During the closing, the leader checks the mapping tables that display greater detail from the reference model (for the CMMI, the specific and generic practices), while the team rates each practice for that interview, in consensus, based on the evidence shown (CMMI Product Team, 2001a.) The interviews with top management,

usually represented by the board of director (duration: 40 minutes), should have the following suggested script:

- Leader salutes all and explains the objectives of the interview
- Leader invites all persons to be interviewed to talk about their daily activities (total: 15 minutes)
- Leader presents, for five minutes, the planned questions
- Each team member has five minutes for his/her planned questions
- Leader makes his/her comments or complementing questions and opens for questions or remarks from the group interviewed (10 minutes)
- Leader thanks all and closes the interview

The interviews with project managers from Group 1 and Group 2 (duration: one hour), should have the following suggested script:

- Leader salutes all and explains the objectives of the interview
- Leader invites each manager to be interviewed to talk about their daily activities (10 minutes for each development process)
- Leader asks questions about work processes for each group of managers (15 minutes)
- Team members have 10 minutes to ask the specific questions about each process area; Questions are made by the process area monitor and complemented by the other members
- Leader makes his/her comments or complementing questions and opens for questions or remarks from the group interviewed (five minutes)
- Leader thanks all and closes the interview

The interviews with developers from Group 1 and Group 2 (duration: 30 minutes), should have the following suggested script:

- Leader salutes all and explains the objectives of the interview
- Leader invites each developer group to talk about their daily activities (five minutes for each development process)
- Leader asks questions about work processes for each group of developers (five minutes)
- Team members have five minutes to ask the specific questions about each process area; Questions are made by the process area monitor and complemented by the other members
- Leader makes his/her comments or complementing questions and opens for questions or remarks from the group interviewed (five minutes)
- Leader thanks all and closes the interview

Final Data Rating and Issuing the Preliminary Report

Final data rating can be done simultaneously with the issuing of the preliminary report. It lasts for one hour—20 minutes for each process area. The leader should refer to a reference model mapping template and a template for issuing the report with one line for each practice with the greater detail degree in the reference model (for the CMMI, the specific and generic practices) (CMMI Product Team, 2001a.) The leader conducts the final rating by reading each model practice and coordinating the opinions from team members, to get to a consensus for each rate based on data from questionnaires and from interviews. The team should check if the scope has been totally covered. If not, additional data must be collected. Each practice with greater detail degree in the model must be rated using the semaphore analogy as follows:

E—practice exists (green)
M—practice exists and should be improved (yellow)
N—practice does not exist (red)

As the consensus is formed for each practice, the preliminary report can be finished. The preliminary report will have the following topics:

- Identification information about the organization
- Identifying the evaluation method: **QuickLocus**
- Date and location
- Scope (organization and projects)
- People involved
- Objective: identifying the reference model and the model scope
- List with all practices with highest degree of detail from the model scope and its associated rating scale

The preliminary report should be delivered at the end of the day of activities to the organization coordinator, according to Template 7 (see Appendix). The organization final remarks and report acceptance can be done later.

QuickLocus: Phase 3

Phase 3—Post-evaluation—covers the evaluation closing activities. It has three steps:

- Issuing the final report
- Closing meeting with presentation of final results
- Storing evaluation results

Issuing the Final Report

The report should be prepared by the team leader according to Template 10 (see Appendix). Team members should review it before delivering the report to the organization coordinator. The final report should contain, at least, the following topics:

- The company and the organization identification

- Evaluation objective, identifying the sponsor, reference model the scope within the reference model
- Evaluated projects—project list
- People involved in the evaluation efforts—list of evaluation team members, identifying the leader, and list (with number) of people to be interviewed, by role in the projects, and total number of people to be interviewed
- Rating the results—practices rated as E—practice exists; practices rated as M—practice exists and should be improved; practices rated as N—practice does not exist
- Another way to organize the results, if necessary
- Aggregated Results—to make it easier for the top management to view the results with tables and graphics to display the results.
- Acceptance—section where the organization and all members of the evaluation team sign accepting the results.

Organization Acceptance of the Final Report

The final report must be delivered to the organization coordinator. The team leader should have a preliminary (informal) acceptance for the report content before delivering the final report. The acceptance can be obtained in a meeting, by phone or e-mail, for instance. Upon delivery of the final report, the organization and the team should sign the document, as a sign of a formal acceptance. Two copies should be signed, one for the organization, delivered to the sponsor, and the other to be person in charge of filing the evaluation info obtained by the **QuickLocus** method.

Closing Meeting with Presentation of Final Results

The closing meeting should be set up in advance and have the greatest participation of people from the organization. The same recommendations about the participants for the opening meeting apply.

The closing meeting should cover the following topics:

- Organization and evaluated projects
- Evaluation objective
- Involved professionals: team and interviewed people
- Practices with greater degree of detail from the reference model are rated as E—practice does exist, M—practice exists and should be improved and N—practice does not exist.
- Notes, if necessary.
- Graphics and tables

The presentation of final results session is conducted as described in the in a check list or slides prepared according to Template 9 (see Appendix). The closing minutes must be created and people sign a list using the appropriated forms shown on Template 8 (see Appendix).

Storing Evaluation Results

The evaluation results, as well as all the material used for planning and developing the activities must be stored in order to assure the confidentiality of proprietary data from the organization. There must be a person in charge for the information confidentiality and there must be procedures to assure it to the evaluated organizations. The evaluation sponsor is in charge of keeping confidentiality of information included in the final report copy delivered to the organization. The formalization shown here and in several topics in this method is very important since it associates credibility to the activity, clarifies next steps, and contributes to get similar results when the same activity is performed by different team/organization members.

Table 4. **QuickLocus** *evaluation method: Phase 1*

1   Phase 1 – Readiness
  1.1   Define the evaluation organizational scope
    1.1.1   Define the organization to be evaluated
  1.2   Define the process reference model/standard to be used
  1.3   Define scope within the process reference model/standard
  1.4   Plan the evaluation
    1.4.1   Identify the evaluation sponsor
    1.4.2   Define the evaluation team
    1.4.3   Plan the evaluation team training
    1.4.4 Select the projects to be evaluated
    1.4.5   Select the participants who will participate in the evaluation
    1.4.5.1 Collect their names
    1.4.5.2 Plan the orientation for participants
    1.4.6   Plan the interviews
    1.4.5.1   Plan the portion of the scope model to be covered in each interview
    1.4.7   Prepare the evaluation schedule
    1.4.8   Plan the evaluation logistics
    1.5   Train the evaluation team

Table 5. **QuickLocus** *evaluation method: Phase 2*

2   Phase 2 – Evaluation
  2.1   Collect data from source 1: questionnaires
  2.2.   Opening meeting – orientation for the evaluation participants
  2.3   Data collection from Source 2: interviews
    2.3.1   After each interview: consolidate and validate data and notes, and rate each practice from the process reference model/standard scope details as follows:
    ⇒ E – the practice exists
    ⇒ M – the practice exists and should be improved
    ⇒ N – the practice does not exist
  2.4   Data final rating
    2.4.1   Rate each practice from the process reference model/standard scope details as follows, according to the collected data:
    ⇒ E – the practice exists
    ⇒ M – the practice exists and should be improved
    ⇒ N – the practice does not exist
    2.4.2   Summarize data rating defining whether the model is compliant or
  2.5   Issue the preliminary report
2.5.1   Get rating "approval" from the evaluation sponsor/team in the organization

Table 6. **QuickLocus** *evaluation method: Phase 3*

3   Phase 3 – Post evaluation
  3.1   Plan and issue final report
    3.1.1   Issue final report
    3.1.2   Deliver report to the organization
    3.1.3   Get final report approval from the organization
  3.2   Present the results
    3.2.1   Closing meeting – present the final results from the evaluation
  3.3   Storing the evaluation results
3.3.1   Storing notes and reports to assure the information confidentiality

QuickLocus in a Nutshell

The three phases and 13 steps from the **QuickLocus** evaluation method are summarized in Tables 4, 5, and 6.

QUICKLOCUS RESULTS

Application Example

CMMI-SW v1.1 model was chosen to present an example of **QuickLocus** utilization due to its wide use by software development companies (CMMI Product Team, 2001a.) The selected organization pursued and got CMMI level 2 and **QuickLocus** was applied twice: the first at the beginning of the improvement program and the second just before the SCAMPI A appraisal. The CMMI implementation project began in March and the defined scope covered the software factory with 26 programmers. This organization reported directly to the vice president of technology and its main product is an ERP application. The software factory is a technical department dedicated to both small and large ERP customization tasks. Table 7 presents

Table 7. Global evaluation schedule

Activity	Date	Time
Form handling: collecting organization data	03/12	
Form handling: collecting process data	03/19	
Collecting filled out forms with organization information	03/19	
Collecting filled out forms with process information	03/25	
Sending of evaluation preliminary plan	03/26	
Organization agrees with plan	03/30	
Training of evaluation team	03/25	8:30AM-11:00 AM
Evaluation activities at the organization	04/08	08:00AM -12:55PM 02:00PM-07:00PM
Sending final report for organization approval	04/19	
Final meeting: presentation of results—all involved meeting	04/13	11:00AM-12:00 noon

Table 8. Interviewed people by role

Role	Number
Senior Management	2
Project Management	5
Developers	16

Figure 3. Percentagens by rate

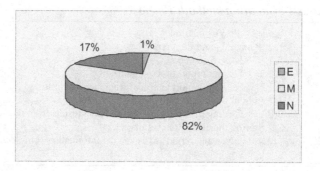

the global evaluation schedule and activities found in the first **QuickLocus** evaluation plan.

Six interviews were planned with 23 interviewed people for the first **QuickLocus** evaluation. Their roles are described in Table 8.

Figure 3 describes the adherence after the final rating of the first **QuickLocus** evaluation.

QuickLocus corresponding to the end of the implementation was applied in December when the software factory had 30 programmers reporting to a manager who, in turn, reported to the vice president. The evaluation lasted two and a half working days since all (seven) CMMI level 2 process areas were evaluated. The schedule for

Table 9. Second working day and second evaluation on December 22,

Time	Subject	Activity	People
8:00	Interview # 5	Interview # 5—Project leader	Evaluating team Interviewed: Mauro
9:00	Closing # 5	Closing Interview # 5	Evaluating team
10:00 AM		*Coffee Break*	
10:15 AM	Interview # 6	Interview # 6—Project Leader	Evaluating team Interviewed: Celina
11:15 AM	Closing # 6	Closing Interview # 6	Evaluating team
12:15 PM		*Lunch Break*	
01:30 PM	Interview # 7	Interview # 7—Project Leader	Evaluating team Interviewed: Waldir
02:30 PM	Closing # 7	Closing Interview # 7	Evaluating team
03:30 PM		*Coffee Break*	
03:45 PM	Interview # 8	Interview # 8—Developers	Evaluating team Intervieweds: Roberto, Cristina, Rosa
04:45 PM	Closing # 8	Closing Interview # 8	Evaluating team
05:45 PM		Closing of working day	Evaluating team

Table 10. Interviewed people by role

Role	Number
Senior Management	3
Project Management	4
Developers	3
Quality	1

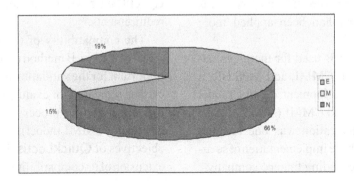

the second working day of the second evaluation is presented in Table 9.

During the second evaluation, 11 people were interviewed. Each leader was interviewed individually to prepare him/her for the SCAMPI formal appraisal. The roles of interviewed people are shown in Table 10, and the pie chart of the results is presented in Figure 4.

An action plan was put in place to analyze the 34% of noncompliant practices. The result was a full CMMI implementation and a successful SCAMPI evaluation in May of the following year. Using **QuickLocus** during the initial and final steps of the project was the key to the implementation project: in the initial steps, it is important to plan the implementation itself, defining work priorities and strategies and, at the final steps, to clarify the gaps related to the model, adjust the improvement plan, and finish the project with success. One of the best features for this method is the fast turn around for the evaluation and the easiness for top management to understand its results, without the need to deep into technical details.

Critical Analysis after Applying the Method in Several Organizations

As mentioned before, **QuickLocus** was developed as a master degree dissertation in 2003, and it has been used ever since. During this research, the method was applied in an organization in order to be compared to other methods available at the time. Since then, the method has been used several times, and at the time this document was written, **QuickLocus** had been applied more than 50 times.

The reference models used for these evaluations were SW-CMM, CMMI, and MPS.BR, a Brazilian software development quality model based on ISO 12207 and CMMI (ABNT, 1997). Another specific application was one adapted model created to evaluate implementation of security processes in one leading finance company.

After using this method several times, we came to the following conclusions:

- **QuickLocus** has proven to be effective to be used at the beginning of process improvement implementation projects. No change to the method is required, since the results are consistent and precise.
- Evaluations done close to the end of software process improvement program, that is, with most of the processes already implemented, showed the need of an improvement. **Quick-Locus** lacks a more systematic activity that would analyze the documentation for the organization processes, for both the procedures already in place and the documents created by the processes.

An analysis of **QuickLocus** in relation to the requirements of the ARC V1.1 Class B method shows that there are a few remaining requirements for it to be totally compliant; even so, this compatibility has not been a premise for its development. To satisfy all the missing requirements, any additional step is demanded for **QuickLocus**. In some cases, the documentation of the proper method will have to be detailed, specifying more clearly the responsibilities and papers of the sponsor and leader of the team; additional data will be required to plan the evaluation. This can be performed by modifying the two forms concerned with data for elaboration of the evaluation plan. Another requirement to be added is the risk analysis in the evaluation plan. With these improvements, **QuickLocus** will satisfy all ARC V1.1 Class B requirements.

The compatibility of the **QuickLocus** with ARC V1.1 Class B method requirements becomes important for the validation of the method, as this class is indicated for evaluation in organizations that are initiating process improvement activities (using CMMI model), and this is one of the objectives of **QuickLocus**. In this direction, the extension of its compatibility with ARC V1.1 Class

B requirements is a good measure of its quality as evaluation method. SCAMPI A (compliant to all ARC V1.1 Class A method) is used for official evaluations and requires greater depth of analysis. ARC V1.1 Class C methods compliant are simpler so it is less precise and reliable.

CONCLUSION

QuickLocus can offer small-sized organizations access to best practice processes for software development. There are several methods that apply to specific projects for small-sized organizations such as TOPS used in central Italy, as published by Bucci et al. (2000); project SataSPIN, applied at Finland and published by Mäkinen et al. (2000); and RAPID used in Australia and published by Rout et al. (2000). These methods focuses on organizations considered small in their countries and indirectly shed light on the importance that small enterprises have in the software business. **QuickLocus** can, just like these other methods, be adopted in an improvement program for software products, enabling the first step for every program: evaluation of software development and maintenance processes for small-sized organizations. Several small-sized organizations play an important role in the software business. **QuickLocus** can offer them greater competitiveness—creating better products at a lower price, faster—and allowing the possibility to compete in the software marketplace worldwide. We believe that a reader interested in this subject will be able to execute one **QuickLocus** evaluation using the method and the templates described here.

REFERENCES

Associacao Brasileira de Normas Técnicas. (1997). *NBR ISO/IEC 12207/1997 Tecnologia de Informação—Processos de ciclo de vida de software.* Brazil.

Associacao Brasileira de Normas Técnicas. (2002). *NBR ISO 19011 Diretrizes para auditorias de sistema de gestão da qualidade e/ou ambiental.* Brazil.

Bryman, A. (1989). *Research methods and organizational studies.* England: Urwin Hyman Ltd.

Bucci, G., Campanai, M., & Gignoni, G.A. (2000). *Rapid assessment to solicit process improvement in SMEs.* In Annals from EuroSPI 2000: European Software Process Improvement. Retrieved December 12, 2007, from http://www.iscn.at/select-newspaper/assessments/italy.html

Byrnes, P., & Phillips, M. (1996). *Software capability evaluation* (Version 3.0: Method description (SCE V3.0), CMU/SEI-96-TR-002). USA: Carnegie Mellon University, Software Engineering Institute. Retrieved December 12, 2007, from http://www.sei.cmu.edu/pub/documents/96.reports/pdf/tr002.96.pdf

CMMI Product Team. (2001). *Appraisal requirements for CMMI* (Version 1.1 (ARC, V1.1), CMU/SEI-2001-TR-034). USA: Carnegie Mellon University, Software Engineering Institute. Retrieved December 12, 2007, from http://www.sei.cmu.edu/pub/documents/01.reports/pdf/01tr034.pdf

CMMI Product Team (2001a). *Capability Maturity Model Integration (CMMI)* (Version V1.1 CMMI for systems engineering and software engineering (CMMI-SE/SW, V1.1): Continuous representation CMU/SEI-2002-TR-001). USA: Carnegie Mellon University, Software Engineering Institute. Retrieved December 12, 2007, from http://www.sei.cmu.edu/cmmi/models/v1.1se-sw-cont.doc

Daskalantonakis, M. (1994, July). Achieving higher SEI levels. *IEEE Software*, pp. 17-24.

Dunaway, D.K., & Masters, S. (2001). *CMM-based appraisal for Internal process improvement* (CBA IPI, Version 1.2: Method description CMU/SEI-2001-TR033). USA: Carnegie Mellon University, Software Engineering Institute. Retrieved

December 12, 2007, from http://www.sei.cmu.edu/pub/documents/01.reports/pdf/01tr033.pdf

Electronic Industries Alliance. (1998). *Systems engineering capability model appraisal method EIA/IS-731.2.* Electronic Industries Alliance, Engineering Department.

Fundação para o Prêmio Nacional da Qualidade. (2002). *Critérios de Excelência—O estado da arte da gestão para a excelência do desempenho e aumento da competitividade.* Brazil: FPNQ (National Foundation for Quality Award). Retrieved December 12, 2007, from http://www.fpnq.org.br

Fundação para o Prêmio Nacional da Qualidade. (2002). *Instruções para Candidatura - Prêmio Nacional da Qualidade—2003.* Brazil: FPNQ (National Foundation for Quality Award). Retrieved December 12, 2007, from http://www.fpnq.org.br

The International Organization for Standardization and the International Electrotechnical Commission (ISO/IEC) (2004). *ISO/IEC 15504-1:2004 Information technology—Process assessment—Part 1: Concepts and vocabulary.* Suisse, Geneve: ISO.

The International Organization for Standardization and the International Electrotechnical Commission (ISO/IEC) (2003). *ISO/IEC 15504-2:2003 Information technology—Process assessment—Part 2: Performing an assessment.* Suisse, Geneve: ISO.

The International Organization for Standardization and the International Electrotechnical Commission (ISO/IEC) (2004a). *ISO/IEC 15504-3:2004 Information technology—Process assessment—Part 3: Guidance on performing an assessment.* Suisse, Geneve: ISO.

The International Organization for Standardization and the International Electrotechnical Commission (ISO/IEC) (2004b). *ISO/IEC 15504-4:2004 Information technology—Process as-*
sessment—Part 4: Guidance on use for process improvement and process capability determination. Suisse, Geneve: ISO.

IThe International Organization for Standardization and the International Electrotechnical Commission (ISO/IEC) (2006). *ISO/IEC 15504-5:2006 Information technology—Process Assessment—Part 5: An exemplar Process Assessment Model.* Suisse, Geneve: ISO.

Jones, C. (2000). *Software assessments, benchmarks, and best practices.* USA: Addison-Wesley.

Juran, J.M. (1992). *A Qualidade desde o Projeto—Novos Passos para o Planejamento da Qualidade em Produtos e Serviços* (N. Montigelli Jr., Trans.). Brazil: Pioneira Thomson Learning.

Humphrey, W.S. (1989). *Managing the software process.* USA: Addison-Wesley Publishing Company.

Kohan, S. (2003). **QuickLocus**: *Proposta de um método de avaliação de processo de desenvolvimento de software para pequenas organizações.* Master's dissertation, Instituto de Pesquisas Tecnológicas, São Paulo, Brazil.

Mäkinen, T,, Varkoi, T., & Lepasaar, M. (2000). *A detailed process assessment method for software SMEs.* Annals from the EuroSPI 2000: European Software Process Improvement. Retrivied December 12, 2007, from http://www.iscn.at/select-newspaper/assessments/tampere.html

Members of the Assessment Method Integrated Team. (2001). *Standard CMMI appraisal method for process improvement* (SCAMPI, Version 1.1: Method definition document CMU/SEI-2001-HB-001). USA: Carnegie Mellon University, Software Engineering Institute. Retrieved December 12, 2007, from http://www.sei.cmu.edu/pub/documents/01.reports/pdf/01hb001.pdf

Nakano, D.N., & Fleury, A.C.C. (1996). Métodos de Pesquisa na Engenharia de Produção (CD-

ROM). In *XVI ENEGEP—Encontro Nacional de Engenharia de Produção, Annals.* Piracicaba: UNIMEP/ABEPRO.

Nielsen, P.A., & Pries-Heje, J. (2002). A framework for selecting an assessment strategy (pp. 185-198). In L. Mathiassen, J. Pries-Heje, & O. Ngwenyama (Eds.), *Improving software organizations from principles to practice.* USA: Addison-Wesley.

Paulk, M.C., Weber, C.V., Curtis, B., Chrissis, M.B., et al. (1995). *The capability maturity model: Guidelines for improving the software process.* USA: Addison-Wesley.

Rout, T.P., Tuffley, A., Cahill, B., & Hodgen, B. (2000). *The rapid assessment of software process capability.* Australia: Software Quality Institute. Retrieved December 12, 2007, from http://www.sqi.gu.edu/~terryr/RAPID_SPICE2000.pdf

Software Engineering Institute. (1997). *Introduction to the capability maturity model: Participant notebook.* USA: Carnegie Mellon University, Software Engineering Institute.

Software Engineering Standards Commitee of the IEEE Computer Society (1991). *IEEE STD 610-90 IEEE Standard Computer Dictionary.* United States: IEEE.

Watson, T.J., Jr., & Petre, P. (1990). *Pai, Filho & CIA. A História da IBM* (M.C. Fittipaldi, Trans.). Brazil: Editora Nova Cultural Ltda.

Yin, R.K. (1994). *Estudo de Caso—Planejamento e Métodos* (D. Grassi, Trans.). Brazil: Bookman Companhia Editora.

Zahran, S. (1998). *Software process improvement.* USA: Addison-Wesley.

ENDNOTES

[1] Small and micro organizations: up to 50 people in the workforce is the criteria according to FPNQ 10/03 Rev.0—nov.02 (FPNQ - FUNDAÇÃO PARA O PRÊMIO NACIONAL DA QUALIDADE - The Brazilian National Foundation for Quality Award)

[2] This is a training to prepare the evaluation team, to be conducted by an experienced leader.

APPENDIX

QuickLocus Template Examples

The templates presented in this chapter support an evaluation using the **QuickLocus** method. They are presented in the same order they are used, so it is easier to prepare the evaluation. After the first contact with the organization, a coordinator is assigned who will interact with the **QuickLocus** team leader. The **QuickLocus** team leader sends the coordinator the forms: Templates 1 and 2. After those forms are filled out, they are sent back to the leader who will create Template 3. Once the initial draft for the plan is created, the leader sends it to the coordinator who will check the activities plan as well as provide the required resources. Usually one or two additional meetings (or call conferences) are required, so all details are sorted out and the plan can be accomplished by everyone involved, according to the planned activities and agenda.

Planning includes sending the form and getting it back to gather information from source 1. A form as described in Template 4 is sent for each process model within the evaluation reference model scope. After the leader receives data from source 1, Template 5 is used to map the data. The leader should prepare:

- An opening presentation meeting as described on Template 6 (or a check list to guide the leader)
- A draft of the preliminary report as shown on Template 7
- Copies of the mapping table to team members
- The leader also should provide sufficient copies of Template 8:
- To register the opening and closing minutes of meetings
- For every participant to sign in at meetings
- For every team member to register all interviews

Once the on-site planned activities are finished, the leader issues a draft of Template 10 and sends it to the coordinator, and they interact until get an agreement about the report. The leader prepares the closing meeting presention as described on Template 9 and prints two copies of the final report that are properly signed and formally delivered during the closing meeting.

Finally, the leader must provide the storage of the evaluation material in order to assure the confidentiality of proprietary data from the organization.

Template 1. Company Profile

Company_____ Organization_____ Date:_____

	Date of Company foundation	
2	Amount of employees	
3	Industry	
4	Is software a Company business?	
5	Annual Sales Income	

	Up to U\$60.000	From U\$60.000 up to U\$360.000	From U\$360.000 up to U\$1.250.000	Higher than U\$1.250.000	
6	How long Company is in the software development business?				
7	How long Company is selling software?				
8	How many people is concerned with software business (Process, Requirement, development, Implantation and other concerned activities)				
9	Software concerned activities				
	Software for own deployment				
	Software packages				
	Customizing Software				
	Embarked Software				
	Software for internet				
	Software distributor				
10	The market of the Software:				
11	There is (or there was) any other initiative to improve the process of software development?				
12	Which?				
13	Acquaintance of software development improvement standard				

		CMM/CMMI	ISO 9001	ISO 15504	ISO 12207
	Systematic knowledge				
	Acquainted with; starting to deploy				
	Acquainted with; no deployment				
	Not acquainted with				

Comentários adicionais:

Template 2. Data Required for Creating the Evaluation Plan

Company_____ **Organization**_____ **Date:**___

The information described below will be used to plan the activities for the software development process evaluation. The evaluation will be done by one or two external evaluators and one representative from the organization. The activities will be completed in one working day (eight hours) according to the schedule created using information provided in this form and agreed to by the organization.

1	Organization Chart

Data for Planning the Activities in the Organization

2	Evaluation sponsor:
3	Evaluation objectives:
4	Evaluation scope (areas):
5	Reference model:
6	Model processes to be evaluated:
7	Projects in development:
8	Projects in maintenance:
9	Projects being implemented:
10	Number of differents software development processt (describe):

11	Representative from organization that will be part of evaluation team	
	Name	Role
	Time at this role	Time at the organization
12	Training date:	
13	Blanked out days for the evaluation activities	
	Week Days	
	Calendar Days	

14 Project team:		
Project:	Project manager:	
Phase:	Process:	
Role:	Number of participants:	Name of participants:
Analyst		
Developer		
...		
Total number of project participants:		

Project:	Project manager:	
Phase:	Process:	
Role:	Number of participants:	Name of participants:
Total number of project participants:		

Additional Notes:

Template 3. Evaluation Plan

The evaluation plan template is a document that will have around 15 pages after being filled out. The table of contents for the evaluation plan is shown in Template 3.

1   ASSESSMENT OBJECTIVE
2   ASSESSMENT PARAMETERS
2.1 Reference Model
2.2 Scope In The Model
2.3 Assessment Sponsor
2.4 Organizational Scope
2.5 Scope Organization Chart
3   PROJECT SELECTION FOR THE ASSESSMENT
3.1 Project Development Processes
3.2 Selected Projects For The Assessment
4   GENERAL ASSESSMENT SCHEDULE
5   ASSESSMENT PARTICIPANTS
6   ASSESSMENT TEAM
6.1 Data Gathering Strategy
6.2 Team Members Responsibilities
7   SCHEDULE OF THE ACTIVITIES IN THE ORGANIZATION
8   ORGANIZATION RESPONSIBILITIES
9   NECESSARY INFRASTRUCTURE
10   PREMISES FOR THE PLAN ELABORATION
11   PLAN APPROVALS
ANNEX 1—CONTACTS RELATION

Template 4. Source 1: Data Collecting Form

Data colleting via source 1 must be done using one form for each process area to be evaluated. See an example below for the CMMI-SW V1.1 Requirement Management process area.

CMMI – Capability Maturity Model Integration

Preliminary Data Collecting

Company Organization		Date:	

REQM - Requirements Management

		Yes	No	I don't Know	N/A	Commentaries
1	An understanding on the requirements is done with the project solicitant?					
2	The project team compromises itself to the project requirements?					
3	Changes made in the requirements throughout the project are controlled?					
4	Does a traceability exists between the requirements and between requirements and products produced by the project?					
5	Inconsistencies between project plan, work products and requirements are identified?					
6	If yes, are corrective actions taken?					

Additional Commentaries

Template 5. Mapping Table

The mapping table is used to rate the reference model into the organizational process. The Requirements Management of CMMI-SW V1.1 is shown in Template 6.

Level 2 - Process Area: REQM - Requirements Management				Legend:						
				E - practice exists						
Enterprise/Organization		Date		M - practice exists and can be improved						
				N - practice does not exist						
	Specific Practices by Goal	Source 1	I 1	I 2	I 3	I 4	I 5	Final		
SG1	Manage Requirements									
	Requirements are managed and inconsistencies with project plans and work products are identified.									
SP1.1	Obtain an Understanding of Requirements									
	Develop an understanding with the requirements providers on the meaning of the requirements.									
SP1.2	Obtain Commitment to Requirements									
	Obtain commitment to the requirements from the project participants.									
SP1.3	Manage Requirements Changes									
	Manage changes to the requirements as they evolve during the project.									
SP1.4	Maintain Bidirectional Traceability of Requirements									
	Maintain bidirectional traceability among the requirements and the project plans and work products.									
SP1.5	Identify Inconsistencies between Project Work and Requirements									
	Identify inconsistencies between the project plans and work products and the requirements.									

Template 6. Opening Meeting

The template document to support the opening meeting is an eight-slide PowerPoint file for which the content is described below: The first slide identifies the evaluation method and the scope of the organization; the second slide has the title "Opening Meeting" and the organization logo and date; the third slide has the initial topics that should be addressed by the leading evaluator (acknowledgments, meeting objectives, top management support, information confidentiality, focus on the process instead of on people, attitude—add value). The fourth slide should be filled out with the following information: organization, projects to be evaluated, define where the activities will take place in the organization, date, and assigned representatives. The fifth slide presents the evaluation objectives. The sixth and seventh slides list the **QuickLocus** method steps to describe the activities already completed, those that will be conducted in the short term, and those that will happen in the long term. Finally, the last slide brings the meeting to a close.

Template 7. Preliminary Report

The template for the preliminary report contains, besides the slides for the opening meeting, the rating slides for rating each of the analyzed practices and notes collected during the interviews. Due to time constraints for the activities in the organization, the preliminary report must be prepared previously by the leader so the only required activities will be filling out the rating for each practice and recording the notes and suggestions reported during the interviews.

Template 8. Supporting Forms

Three forms are available to support the activities in the organization. Those forms are described below. The meeting minute form, the list of participants' form (used during the opening and closing meetings) and the interview data collecting forms.

Meeting Minute

Company	Date	Page /
Organization	Starting time:	Ending time:
Opening meeting ( ) Closing meeting ( )		

Notes

List of Participants

Company	Date	Page /
Organization		
Opening meeting ( ) Closing meeting ( )		

Name	Company/area	Phone	Signature

The meeting minutes and list of participant forms to be used during the opening and closing meetings are the same. The purpose of the meeting must be specified in the form. During the interviews, the evaluation team write down the questions and answers for mapping purposes. Such notes must be as close as possible to what is said, to register everything interviewees say. The objetive is to map the executed process to the reference model. The **QuickLocus** method has two different interview data collecting forms: one for the first page form of notes and other for the next ones. The first interview data collecting form is:

Interview

Company		Date		Page /
Organization				Interview #
Project role		*Starting time:*		Ending time:
Interviewed:				

Item	Note

The next interview data collecting form is:

Organization	Interview #	Page /

Item	Note

Template 9. Closing Meeting

The template for the closing meeting contains, besides the slides for the preliminary report, some slides describing the reference model used and the aggregated results. The objetive is to show to the people involved with the program of process improvement the evaluation results (which contains improvements needed, strengths, weakness, and some suggestions).

Template 10. Final Report

The final report is comprised of several pages created based on the template defined by **QuickLocus**. The typical report contents of the final report are:

FINAL CONSIDERATIONS

QuickLocus can be considered a software development process metric that has shown to be effective as all conducted evaluations were not contested. Hence, the results can be considered reliable.

Chapter VI
A Study of Software Process Improvement in Small and Medium Organizations

Deepti Mishra
Atilim University, Turkey

Alok Mishra
Atilim University, Turkey

ABSTRACT

Presently, the majority of software development, including outsourcing, is carried out by small and medium size software development organizations all over the world. These organizations are not capable to bear the cost of implementing available software process improvement models like CMMI, SPICE, ISO, and so forth. Therefore, there is a need to address this problem. In this chapter, various software process assessment and software process improvement models for small and medium scale organizations are discussed and compared. This will lead towards development of standardized software process improvement model for small and medium sized software development organizations in the future.

INTRODUCTION

Quality models and standards have been developed to improve product quality. Software quality is defined as all characteristics of a product that bear on its ability to satisfy explicit and implicit needs of the user (ISO/IES 9126, 1991). According to Pressman (2002), software quality is defined as conformance to explicitly documented development standards and implicit characteristics that are expected of all professionally developed software. Therefore, this definition suggests three requirements for quality assurance that are to be met by the developer (Galin, 2004):

- Specific formal requirements, which refer mainly to the outputs of the software system.
- The software quality standards mentioned in the contract.
- Good software engineering practices (GSEP), reflecting state-of-the-art professional practices to be met by the developer even though not explicitly mentioned in the contract.

The way with which we develop software impacts the quality of the software and hence software process is one of the most crucial factors in determining the quality of the software. A software process is a set of activities, together with ordering constraints among them, such that if the activities are performed properly and in accordance with the ordering constraints, the desired result is produced. The desired result is high quality software at low cost. As each software development project is an instance of the process it follows, it is essentially the process that determines the expected outcomes of a project (Jalote, 2002). Improving the process automatically results in improved quality of the product (software).

Today only few software organizations around the world achieve a high quality level for their development process. A considerable amount of software is produced worldwide by small and medium sized enterprises (SMEs) ranging from 1 to about 50 employees (Gresse von Wangenheim, Punter, & Anacleto, 2003). In this context, the German and Brazilian software market of these companies was around 77% and 69% during 2001 (Ministerio da Ciencia e Tecnologia, 2001). This is further supported by Richardson (2002) that there is need for small software companies in the Irish sector to improve their software process. The term *small setting* has been defined as an organization or company of fewer than approximately 100 people and a project of fewer than approximately 20 people (Software Engineering Institute, n.d.). As mentioned on the Software Engineering Institute (SEI) Web site for small settings, a major aspect

to be considered in these environments is that the amount of resources used to support a process improvement effort would be a large percentage of an organization's operating budget. Johnson, Johnson, and Brodman (1998) define a small organization as fewer than 50 software developers and a small project as fewer than 20.

A vast majority of software producers, which have not yet implemented a methodology for software process improvement, are paying high costs of production and systems maintenance, and therefore being displaced from the global market, not being on the same competitiveness level as companies that possess a process improvement method (Herrera & Trejo Ramirez, 2003). There are several models for software process improvement, such as the Capability Maturity Model Integration (CMMI), the software process improvement and capability determination (SPICE), and the ISO 9000 norms from the International Standardization Organization (ISO). These models provide quality patterns that a company should implement to improve its software development process (Herrera & Trejo Ramirez, 2003). Unfortunately, the successful implementation of such models is not generally possible within the context of small and medium-sized software organizations because they are not capable of bearing the cost of implementing these software process improvement programs. The proper implementation of software engineering techniques is difficult task for small organization as they often operate on limited resources and with strict time constraints. Cultural issues like resistance to change from the employees or management who regard the extra work required for quality assurance as a useless and complicated burden put on the developing team. According to Biro, Messnarz, and Davison (2002), national culture also affects the process improvement methods. Due to budget constraints, services of a consultant organization to improve the software quality is not possible; still the need for a good quality assurance program is becoming more evident, and managers are striving to achieve international quality standards that, in the long run, result in lower production cost (Herrera & Trejo Ramirez, 2003).

The remainder of this chapter is organized as follows: The following sections discuss some software process improvement models for small and medium scale organization. Later, these models are compared. Finally, the chapter concludes with directions for future research in this area.

SOFTWARE PROCESS IMPROVEMENT MODELS FOR SMALL AND MEDIUM ORGANIZATIONS

In order to get an edge in the ever-growing highly competitive software development world, it is significant for an organization to regularly monitor the software process. It is important for an organization to continuously improve its software process on the basis of feedback from various stakeholders. Some software process improvement models for small and medium scale organizations are discussed in this section.

A METHODOLOGY FOR SELF-DIAGNOSIS FOR SOFTWARE QUALITY

The first step to implement any software process improvement strategy is to assess the current quality level of process and finding the potential areas of improvement. This methodology for self diagnosis is based on concepts, goals, and activities defined by the Capability Maturity Model (CMM) which can be used by a small or micro organization as a part of internal audit plan before the official appraisal. It is difficult for a small or medium scale organization to assess its current capabilities by using SCAMPI A (the only method in CMMI product suite that can result in

a rating) appraisal method because it takes more time and consumes more resources. It is costly to hire lead appraisers and also company's own staff has to spend time for these appraisals away from work which is costly for the company. This methodology can generate a simple diagnosis or help generate an action plan. This methodology has tried to adapt CMM for small scale organizations by adding some additional questionnaires to help the organizations to understand their current status and find out the areas for improvement. With the help of these questionnaires, small and medium scale organizations will be able to use CMM. The main goal of this methodology is to gather facts that help in taking a "snapshot" of the current processes implemented by the organization, so it is possible to understand it, and then the goal is to identify strengths and areas of improvement, thus determining the degree of completeness of every one of the KPAs (key process areas) of the CMM model. In order to gather this information related to the current processes of the organization, researchers have created three questionnaires (Herrera & Trejo Ramirez, 2003):

- The extended maturity questionnaire (EMQ)
- The goals, activities, and responsibilities matrix (GAR)
- The directed questionnaire

The CMM describes activities and practices required to achieve a maturity level within the software developing processes. A company that wishes to improve its processes through CMM must achieve the mentioned levels in a progressive, continuous, and ascending manner; that is, the lower levels are the basis for the upper levels. The first step is to assess the maturity level of the organization and for this purpose, official questionnaires are designed as a list of nonhierarchical, binary questions so that figuring out the maturity level of the company is straightforward. Once the current maturity level is known, this model helps to identify the key practices required to increase the maturity of processes.

The Extended Maturity Questionnaire

EMQ is based on the maturity questionnaire developed by SEI. This questionnaire includes some questions about specific KPAs, allowing for "yes," "no," "I don't know," and "not applied" as answers. All questions are related to goals and commitments for each KPA, but not to specific activities which should be performed to achieve such goals. The direct application of the maturity questionnaire in small and micro organizations results in a great majority of questions answered with a "no." The main reason for this tendency is that many of the goals proposed in the questionnaire are only partially achieved. Therefore, EMQ is modified by researchers, allowing for "yes," "no," and "partially" (for describing incomplete goals) as answers. The purpose of EMQ is to guide the system's administrator of a small organization so that he or she can answer the questions in a way that reflects more accurately the status of the organization. With this questionnaire, the administrator is capable of identifying the goals and commitments that are being only partially fulfilled so that they can be included in the improvement plan by the audit leader in charge of the self-diagnostic process.

The Goals, Activities, and Responsibilities Matrix

The success of a model based on CMM depends on the complete achievement of certain goals and commitments for every KPA. These goals include measuring, documenting, reviewing, and validating activities for software quality assurance. There is a close relationship among goals, activities, and abilities, which are not that immediately apparent from the 344-page description of the CMM standard (Bush, 1995). It is obvious, then, that

assimilating and interpreting this amount of information is a long and difficult process. In order to facilitate the task of the software administrators, a matrix is proposed. This matrix includes the relationship between abilities (variables), activities (practices and subpractices associated to each KPA), goals, and commitments (objectives to achieve in each KPA) as well as the responsible individuals (the client, the requirement analyst, the software engineering group, the manager, the quality assurance group) for each KPA.

When this matrix is used as a control within the life cycle of the project, it works not only as a diagnosis on the quality of the project, but also as a guide of action that helps the project manager to correct deficiencies and achieve the goals required by the KPA, thus providing an improvement in the overall process.

The GAR matrix can be automated by means of an expert system by transforming the relationships between rules, the responsible person (the person concerned), and activities into inference rules that can be triggered by a knowledge base consisting on the answers given to the questions inside the matrix. The expert system could help an internal or external auditor in evaluating the maturity of the development processes by determining the degree of satisfaction of each KPA according to CMM. In this way, by having the knowledge base and by filling the questionnaire, we could get a rating of the state of the organization with no extra work, except for the documentation of activities. The original CMM is representing as a text. The GAR provides a visual representation, which simplifies comprehension of the vast amount of information required for the evaluation of goals.

The Directed Questionnaire

The last format of the self-diagnosis methodology is a direct questionnaire with which a lead auditor can construct a knowledge base. This questionnaire has the essence of the original maturity questionnaire from CMM, but in this case, each new question is generated based on the answer of the previous questions, so a new question may be directed to complement information obtained earlier or to confirm such information. In any case, useless questions are discarded.

Evaluating the Result of the Self-Diagnosis

The results obtained from the questionnaires answer the basic question: Are the key process areas required by CMM for a certain level achieved? For each KPA, there are four possible answers: The KPA is either fully achieved, partially achieved, not achieved, or it does not apply. The KPAs that are partially achieved or not achieved are the areas of opportunity for improvement and that should be part of an action plan.

SOFTWARE PROCESS MATRIX MODEL

The SPM provides the organization with a ranked list of actions which can be input to their software process improvement strategy. SPM is based on quality function deployment (QFD). This model helps the organization in finding the relative importance of software processes. For the high priority processes, the practices that need to be worked on are determined by software process matrix. The SPM model uses self-assessment within the organizations and demonstrates the following characteristics (Richardson, 2002):

- Relates to the company's business goals
- Focuses on the most important software process
- Gives maximum value for money
- Proposes improvements which have maximum effect in as short a time as possible
- Provides fast return on investment (ROI)
- Is process oriented
- Relates to other software models
- Is flexible and easy to use

The SPM can be used to establish an improvement strategy based on QFD. QFD is a way to assure the design quality while the product is still in the design stage (Akao, 1990, p. 4) and as a "quality system focused on delivering products and services that satisfy customers" (Mazur, 1994). In order to collect and maintain the voice of the customer throughout the production life cycle, QFD uses a series of matrices which convert the customer's voice into a final product. Different models are available for use, and according to Cohen (1995), the model adapted by American Standards Institute (four-phase model) and containing four matrices (Hauser & Clausing, 1988) is probably the most widely described and used model in the United States. The SPM is based on the first matrix of this model, the house of quality.

Initially, the "voice of the customer" is collected, and the relative importance of each customer requirement is measured. In the house of quality matrix, these requirements are used to identify design characteristics which have the greatest impact on customer requirements. Although QFD consists of many matrices, the main focus is often this matrix, as using it alone can have a significant effect on the product development process (Fortuna, 1988). The matrix is normally broken down into six rooms:

- Customer requirements (WHATs)
- Design characteristics (HOWs)
- Overall importance of customer requirements
- Relationship between customer requirements and design characteristics
- Importance of design characteristics
- Inter-relationships between design characteristics

Using QFD, the software process model is treated as the customer where software processes are the customer requirements. These processes were identified from the software process literature. Examples of processes are:

- Define and document processes.
- Systematic assessment of suppliers' software process suitability.
- Systematic implementation of software design.
- Systematic planning of project workflow and estimates.

The design characteristics are the practices which must be followed for processes to be successful. These practices were also identified from the software process literature. Examples of practices are:

- Test the customer's operation before software implementation.
- Prototype or simulate critical elements of the software.
- Maintain and trace product item histories.

A crucial part of the development of the software process matrix was to identify the relationships between processes and practices. Those which are explicitly mentioned in the literature were easily identified. Using expert opinions and various statistical techniques, other relationships between processes and practices were identified, resulting in the development and verification of the software process matrix which was then validated in the industry.

For a small company to use any software process model to its advantage, it is imperative that the effort expended is minimal. The SPM provides it with a generic section that has been completed previously and can be used in the company. A questionnaire is provided to assess the current performance, planned future performance, and importance to the company for every process. From the company's point of view, all they need to provide are the measurements for calculating the overall importance of the software process considering the following (Richardson, 2002):

- Current capability as assessed using a self-assessment questionnaire.

- Future capability as input from management.
- Importance of software process to the business.
- Competitive analysis
- Market leverage for company specific requirement, for example, ISO certification.

Allowing management to choose whether or not to include figures for competitive analysis and market leverage allows flexibility within the model. Using standard QFD calculations and referring to Table 1, which contains specific company data, the Importance of Process (D) is calculated as $[1+ (B - A)*0.2]*C$ (adapted from Richardson, 2002).

In the example given in Table 1, it can be seen that they are ranked from most to least important as:

1. Development of detailed design
2. Development of system requirements and design
3. Systems acceptance testing

Using the value of the relationships between processes and practices, the importance of each practice is calculated as:

$\sum$ Importance of process * Relationship value

which, in the case of "user requests determine requirements," is

$(3.6 * 9) + (7.0 * 9) + (2 * 0) = 95.4.$

This provides the following prioritized list of practices:

1. User requests determine requirements
2. Define interfaces of the software system
3. Develop and document unit verification

145

Table 1. Specific company data (adapted from Richardson, 2002)

Practices Processes	User requests determine requirements	Define interfaces of the software system	Develop and document unit certification	Current achieve ment (1 – 5) A	Future achievement (1 – 5) B	Improvement to company (1 – 5) C	Importance of process (1 – 5) D
Development of system requirement and design	•	•		2	3	3	3.6
Development of detailed design	•		∘	2	4	5	7
Systems acceptance testing		∇	∇	3	3	2	2
Importance of Practice	*95.4*	*34.4*	*14.6*				

Practices with the highest values are the most important, and therefore it is suggested that these should be worked on first in the organization. From this, the priorities to be included in any software process improvement action plan are established and can help the organization to determine its improvement strategy. The complete SPM provides the organization with a ranked list of actions which can be input to their software process improvement strategy. This ranked list can be combined with cost figures and time-effective calculations, thus taking these factors into account when determining the action plan for the organization.

AN APPROACH FOR SOFTWARE PROCESS ESTABLISHMENT IN MICRO AND SMALL COMPANIES

An ASPE-MSC is defined by integrating and adapting existing approaches (Ahonen, Forsell, & Taskinen, 2002; Becker-Kornstaedt, 2001; Becker-Kornstaedt, Hamann, & Verlage, 1997; Curtis, Kellner, & Over, 1992; Kellner et al., 1998; Madhavji, Holtje, Hong, & Bruckhaus, 1994; Scott, Zettel, & Hamann, 2000; Gresse von Wangenheim, 2006) to the characteristics of small

software companies. As illustrated in Figure 1, the principal phases of the approach are diagnosis, strategic analysis, definition, and implementation, which can be executed in an iterative and incremental way in order to establish step-by-step one or more process(es) within an organization. In addition, the approach also covers the management of the establishment of the software process(es), including planning, monitoring, and control and postmortem. The establishment of the process in the context of small companies is done by a process engineer, typically an external consultant, if the company does not have competence in this area. In this case, one employee of the organization should be assigned (at least part-time) as process engineer assistant in order to enable knowledge transfer and to facilitate the process establishment. Other participants are the sponsor, typically one of the directors of the company, and all process performers, who are involved in the respective process(es).

The principal phases of the approach are (Gresse von Wangenheim, 2006):

Planning. In the beginning, the process establishment is planned on a high level. Later on, during strategic analysis, the plan is revised, completed, and adapted in accordance with the decisions made. During planning, all involved

Figure 1. Overview on ASPE-MSC approach (adapted from Gresse von Wangenheim, Weber, Hauck, & Trentin, 2006)

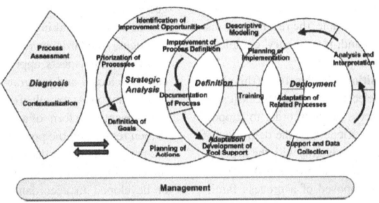

parties are informed and motivated and commitment should be obtained. If necessary, the process engineer assistant is trained with respect to basic aspects of software process establishment and improvement.

Phase 1: Diagnosis. The objective of this phase is to contextualize the organization and to obtain a high-level snapshot of the actual software process in place. Such a baseline can be established through a software process assessment using, for example, MARES (Gresse von Wangenheim, Anacleto, & Salviano, 2006), an ISO/IEC 15504 conformant process assessment method tailored to small companies. Assessment results specifically relevant for the process establishment may include:

- A context description on the organization
- A high-level description of the actual software process indicating which processes are executed and how
- Target process capability profiles indicating high-priority processes and their capability level to be achieved in order to meet the organization's business and improvement goals

- Observations and/or assessed process capability profiles and strengths and weaknesses of the software process(es) identified, including the indication of potential risks and improvement opportunities.

Phase 2: Strategic analysis. The objective of this phase is to specify the scope and to prioritize candidate processes to be established based on the results of the diagnosis and in accordance with the organization's business and improvement goals. This can be done by using, for example, an adaptation of the SWOT (strengths/weaknesses/opportunities/threats) analysis technique (Johnson, Scholes, & Sexty, 1989) relating the importance of processes and their assessed/estimated capability. Based on the decisions made, measurable goals are defined to be achieved by the establishment of the selected process(es) in accordance with the business and improvement goals of the organization. Actions are planned, revising and completing the plan. This includes also the definition of measures necessary to monitor progress in accordance with the defined goals, using, for example, the GQM approach (Basili, Caldiera & Rombach, 1994a). The strategic analysis is typically done by the director(s) of the company and guided by the process engineer and assistant. In each iteration cycle, decisions should be revised. If any of the information or artifacts to be produced in phase 1 and 2 is already available, the results may just need to be revised and, if necessary, completed or updated.

Phase 3: Definition. The objective of this phase is to define the selected software process(es) in the form of a process guide in order to support process performers. Generally, the definition of the selected process(es) begins with the descriptive modeling of the actual process(es) in place. This activity is composed of a process familiarization phase and a detailed elicitation phase (Becker-Kornstaedt, 2001). During the process familiarization phase, an overview of the software process and its general structure, interaction, and sequence is obtained and documented, for example, in a process flow diagram. In a next step, roles, competencies, and responsibilities related to each activity are identified. Associated work products are identified and templates for these artifacts are elicited. The objective of the process is defined in quantifiable terms identifying measures in accordance with quality and management goals, as well as the goals to be achieved by the process establishment. This includes also the definition of performance characteristics for the process and associated work products. The initial process representation is then completed during the elicitation of details on the process, such as entry/exit criteria, techniques and tools used, tailoring guidelines, examples, warnings for potential problems, required infrastructure, checklists, and so forth. This is done by the project engineer and assistant in close cooperation with all process performers in order to capture their understanding and know-how on the process through interviews, observations, or workshops (Ahonen et al., 2002; Becker-Kornstaedt, 2001; Moe, Dingsoyr, & Johansen, 2002) and the examination of existing artifacts. Once defined, an initial version of the process as-is, the process representation can be analyzed, restructured, com-

pleted, or adapted, aiming at the improvement of the process in accordance with the organization's goals (Scott et al., 2000). Alternative solutions can be identified taking into consideration best practices, standards, or reference models. Analyzing various aspects, appropriate alternative(s) can be selected and integrated into the process representation. As a result of this phase, the process is represented in form of a process guide, which is then revised by the process performers. Once the process has been defined, tools used during the execution of the process have to be adapted or developed in accordance with the process definition. In addition, related processes, such as management processes, have to be revised and, if necessary, adapted. This phase may have to be repeated several times until a satisfactory process representation has been defined and/or reiterated in order to continuously adapt and improve the process representation.

Phase 4: Implementation. First, the evaluation of the defined process(es) is planned in parallel to their implementation. This includes the revision and/or definition of measures in order to monitor and determine the effectiveness and suitability of the process(es) and whether the expected benefits are achieved. The implementation plan is also revised and refined. Required resources, information, and infrastructure are made available and allocated. Process performers are motivated and trained with respect to the process(es) to be implemented. In the beginning, the process engineer and assistant closely follow the implementation, provide support, and collect data in accordance with the planned evaluation. The collected data and experiences are analyzed and interpreted. Based on these insights, the process representation may be improved or new cycles started repeating the diagnosis phase and/or strategic analysis. Captured experiences on how the process definition is being adapted to specific projects may also serve as a basis for the continuous evolution of tailoring guidelines. In the context of small companies, we do not explicitly separate between a pilot and organization-wide deployment, as piloting in most cases, due to its small size, already takes place across the whole company. The only difference here is a stronger focus on assistance and data collection in the beginning of the implementation of the process(es), which continually evolves into a less intensive routine monitoring and maintenance.

Monitoring and control: The complete establishment of the process(es) is monitored and controlled. Therefore, data are collected and analyzed by the process engineer and assistant. If necessary, corrective actions are initiated and the plan is updated.

Postmortem: Once a complete process establishment cycle is terminated, the process establishment approach is evaluated as a basis for continuous improvement. This is done by collecting and analyzing feedback from process performers, sponsor, and the process engineer and assistant in a feedback meeting or by questionnaires.

PRISMS: An Approach to Software Process Improvement for Small to Medium Enterprises

PRISMS is an action research project, with a team of three researchers working alongside managers and developers in participating companies advising and assisting with the planning and implementation of software process improvement programs over a three-year period. The PRISMS process model is summarized in Figure 2.
The key features of the process are (Allen et al., 2003):

- The existing process, however informally defined, is examined, and if resources permit, an explicit model is created. (This often leads to heated discussion as different interpretations of the existing process specification are uncovered.)

- Early in the PRISMS program, the business goals are defined by management. These goals drive much of the subsequent activity, especially the selection and prioritization of key process areas for improvement and the selection of measurements.

- A consultation exercise is carried out, involving all members of development teams. This is a useful exercise which plays to the strengths of small, flexible teams found in smaller organizations. A brainstorming session, and/or questionnaire-based survey, helps the developer's team to take ownership of the SPI program and to be involved in the program from the earliest stage.

- A tailored version of the CMM assessment is carried out by members of the research team, primarily to help identify key process areas for improvement. This also indicates the CMM level of the software process, which is often of less immediate usefulness to SMEs but still

Figure 2. The PRISMS process (adapted from Allen, Ramachandran, & Abushama, 2003)

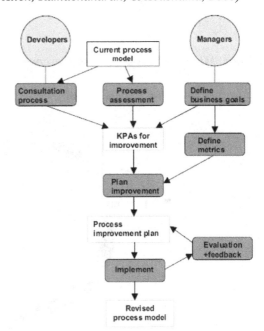

useful as a baseline from which to measure future progress. This is in agreement with the observation of Paulk (1998) that maturity levels should be measures of improvement not goals for improvement.

- Using these inputs, the KPAs for improvement are identified and prioritized. The main criteria here should be the extent to which the KPAs are likely to contribute to the identified business goals. One company has found a weighted selection approach of the type described by Martin (2002) to be useful. The process/practice matrix approach described by Richardson (2001) could also be used.

- Measurements are defined as an integral part of the SPI planning process. Managers are generally keen to have more precise ways of tracking key resource and quality indicators. The goal question metric paradigm can be used to measure selected attributes based on the business goals defined for the SPI program (Briand, Differding, & Rombach, 1996).

- The SPI plan is periodically reviewed, and mechanisms are put in place to collect feedback from stakeholders.

MESOPYME

MESOPYME is a continuous software process improvement method (Calvo-Manzano et al., 2002). It is oriented to SMEs and provides a working guide to implementing improvement. MESOPYME has been defined, taking into account a generic SPI model defined by ISPI (ESSI, 1994) with four stages. The objectives are similar to those of the IDEAL model (McFeeley, 1996) from the SEI.

- **Stage 1: Commitment to improvement**. Its objective is to obtain the support of senior management to carry out the improvement project.

- **Stage 2: Software process assessment**. Its objective is to obtain strengths and weaknesses of the process assessed with respect to a software process model—CMM. From this assessment, processes (usually one to three) to be improved are selected.

- **Stage 3: Improvement solution**. Its objective is to provide the needed infrastructure to carry out improvement (in selected processes)

Figure 3. MESOPYME's process improvement method (adapted from Calvo-Manzano et al., 2002)

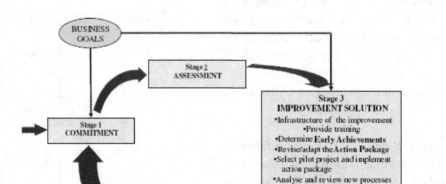

and to create the plan to follow in order to define and implement improvement in these selected processes. The *improvement solution* stage is performed through the application of a generic set of components that we have called an action package. An action package is a general solution to a particular software process area that should be customized to a company, taking into account its business goals and assessment results. An action package is implemented in some selected pilot projects.

- **Stage 4: Institutionalize**. Finally, improvement must be institutionalized.

Goal Question Metric Lightweight

The main idea behind this model is "software measurement is a necessity for controlling software projects and improving quality (Gresse von Wangenheim, 1995.)" This model is based on GQM. "GQM Lightweight" is a customized GQM

model that combines the existing model adapted to specific characteristics and limitations of small software companies. The goal question metric paradigm (Basili, Caldiera, & Rombach, 1994b; Basili & Rombach, 1998; Basili & Weiss, 1984) has been proposed as a goal-oriented approach for the measurement of products and processes in software engineering. It is a mechanism for defining and evaluating a set of operational goals, using measurement. GQM represents a systematic approach for tailoring and integrating goals with models of the software processes, products, and quality perspectives of interest, based upon the specific needs of the project and the organization. This model is a result of adapting the existing GQM process models to the specific characteristics and limitations of small software companies. GQM lightweight is based on Gresse von Wangenheim (2002) and Gresse von Wangenheim, Hoisl, and Wüst (1995) with respect to its principal phases and activities. However, each of these activities has been customized keeping in view limited

Figure 4. Architecture of the action package (adapted from Calvo-Manzano et al., 2002)

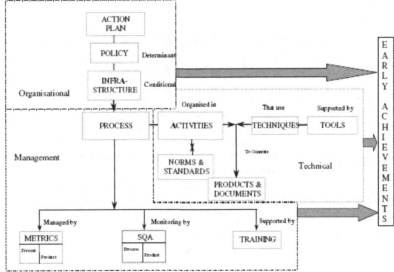

resources and predominant informality in small software companies.

The planning phase prepares the establishment of software measurement in the organization. In SMEs, no separate measurement team will be established due to the small number of employees and informal structures of the organizations. Kick-off session is important to get the approval and opinion of all the people. A feedback session can be helpful towards motivation. According to Gresse von Wangenheim et al. (2003), identification and selection of measurement goals is easier in SMEs due to the fact that less people are involved in the pilot project and often the goals definition process is more restricted.

During the data collection phase, the data are collected according to the procedures specified in the measurement plan. By developing suitable data collection instruments and integrating into the software process, effort can be reduced substantially. The interpretation phase aims at the periodic analysis of the collected data and interpretation during feedback sessions involving project personnel following the GQM plan bottom-up. In the packaging phase, the measurement results, including the collected data and its interpretation, are analyzed, packaged, and stored in a way suited to the organizational context so

that this knowledge can be reused in future software projects and measurement programs. Here focus should be on documenting the GQM plan, the results of the feedback sessions, and cost and benefits report.

DISCUSSION

As these SPI models are difficult to compare due to their divergent characteristics, we have tried to find out some significant but common attributes so that we can find a comparative view of all available SPI models. These models for small and medium organizations are based on some existing methods like CMM, GQM, QFD, and so forth. These approaches are adapted and simplified either by incorporating some additional questionnaires (in the self-diagnosis model) or matrix (in the SPM model) or process guides (in ASPE-MSC) or action packages (in MESOPYME) so that they can be used by small and medium scale organizations. One key point is that all methods except self-diagnosis model considers business objectives of the organization while making the SPI plan. Moreover, these methods (excluding self diagnosis) are flexible enough that although methods for identifying and prioritizing areas of improvement

Table 2. Overview of GQM Lightweight (adapted from Gresse von Wangenheim et al., 2003)

Phases	Approach for SMEs GQM Lightweight
Planning	Introduce measurement program
Definition **[Reuse of Quality & Resource Models]**	1. Define measurement goals, Goal formalization 2. Define questions 3. Define metrics 4. Produce GQM plan, Define data collection procedures, Define data instruments 5. Produce data collection plan, Create metrics base
Data Collection	1. Collect and validate data 2. Store data collected
Interpretation	1. Data analysis 2. Data interpretation, Feedback session

Table 3. Comparison of various SPI models for small and medium scale organizations

Models → / Criteria ↓	Self-diagnosis	SPM Model	ASPE-MSC	PRISMS	MESOPYME	GQM Lightweight
Based on	CMM	Quality Function Deployment	Integration and adaptation of many existing approaches	CMM and GQM	CMM	Goal Question Metric
Key question	Where am I? What should I do?	What needs to be improved? How to improve?	Where am I? What needs to be improved? How to improve?	Where am I? What needs to be improved? How to improve?	Where am I? what needs to be improved? How to improve?	What should I do? How to do?
What is new?	EMQ questionnaire for assessment. Also, relationship among abilities, activities, goals, and commitments for every KPA in matrix format is given which can be automated with expert system.	SPM (software process matrix) that identifies practices needed for software processes	Iterative-incremental approach for assessment, identification, and implementation of SPI plan.	Adapting CMM by incorporating business objectives with the help of GQM paradigm	Emphasis on SPI implementation step with the help of action packages developed by problem domain experts.	It enhances GQM by including planning, reuse of quality and resource models, data collection, interpretation, and packaging phases.
Implementation details	First, the current situation of the company is assessed with EMQ questionnaire. This can help to identify which KPAs are partially achieved or not achieved at all to attain a particular CMM level. Once KPAs for improvement are identified, goals and commitments for every KPA can be found out with the help of GAR matrix.	First, prioritized list of processes for software process improvement according to the business objectives and other factors are made. Then a ranked list of actions is made with the help of SPM to improve above-mentioned processes.	First diagnosis of current process capabilities is done, then prioritized list of candidate processes is made according to the diagnosis and business objectives and improvement goals. Later, these processes are defined in the form of a process guide. Thereafter, implemented with the help of their process guide and evaluated continuously.	First, current process is examined and assessed. Then KPAs for improvement are identified based on current capabilities, business goals given by the management and after consultation with developers. Later, process improvement plan is made and implemented.	First, current process is assessed and then action package for each process area consisting of action plan, infrastructure needed, techniques, tools, metrics, etc. is developed according to the business goals and assessment results. Later, this action package is implemented in some pilot projects. Finally, improvement is institutionalized.	First, measurement goals, questions, and metrics are defined. Then, GQM plan is developed. Later, data collection procedures, data collection instruments are defined. Afterwards, metrics base is created and data are collected, stored, and analyzed for future reuse.
Flexibility	Not flexible. Defined methods and tools. Elimination is not preferred.	Flexible Company is not required to include all factors of measurement for overall importance of software processes and only processes important for company need to be considered for improvement.	Flexible Methods for assessing current capabilities and to prioritize processes are suggested but organization can use other methods also. Only processes important for company need to be considered for improvement.	Flexible Methods to identify and prioritize KPAs for improvement are suggested but organizations can use other methods also.	Flexible Can be tailored to the specific need of an organization	Flexible Can be tailored for the specific need of a project or organization

Table 3. continued

Models → / Criteria ↓	Self-diagnosis	SPM Model	ASPE-MSC	PRISMS	MESOPYME	GQM Lightweight
Practitioner's knowledge level	Does not need much experience. Easy to use.	Needs considerable experience to assess current capabilities and planned future performance of a software process and importance of process to company.	Needs considerable experience to assess current process capabilities, prioritization, process definition, and implementation.	Needs considerable experience to assess current process, identify KPAs for improvement. Also development and implementation of process improvement plan requires experienced person.	Does not need much experience as action packages are developed by domain experts according to the organizations' business goals and current capabilities.	Certain measurement experience is required.
Continuous / phased	Phased	Continuous	Continuous	Phased	Continuous	Phased
Main focus	On CMM standards.	On business objectives of the organization and processes most important to the business	On business and improvement goals	On business objectives	On business goals and organizations' current capabilities	More likely to address the specific needs of an organization than universal models
Outcome	Actions, goals that needs to be achieved for software process improvement	Ranked list of actions for software process improvement	Process guide for processes selected for improvement that contains entry/exit criteria, techniques, and tools to use, examples, required infrastructure, checklists, etc.	Process improvement plan and later revised process model after implementation of process improvement plan.	Action package for each process area consisting of action plan, infrastructure needed, techniques, tools, metrics, etc. according to the business goals and assessment results.	Information after analysis of collected data that can be reused to take decision for future improvement
Constraints	Can only be used for internal assessment before official assessment by CMM. If the CMM adoption is not intended, then its application is limited.	Measuring the importance of software processes needs considerable experience	Considerable experience is needed for process assessment, process prioritization and development of process guides.	Considerable experience is needed to identify current process model and process improvement plan.	Needs assistance of domain expert to develop action package according to the organizations' business goals and current capabilities	Reuse is done in an ad hoc informal manner. Knowledge management and organizational learning should be systematically integrated.
Origin	Latin America	Ireland	Mexico	Britain	Spain	Germany and Brazil

are suggested but organizations can choose any other method also. Also, organizations have the flexibility to select processes more important to them for the SPI plan. These methods not only detect what needs to be improved but also provide the roadmaps for how to improve.

These SPI models are specifically developed for SMEs as these organizations do not have the resources and cannot bear the cost to implement CMMI, SPICE, and so forth, but whether a small or medium scale organization can implement these methods without the help of some external quality consultant is yet to be proven. As far as the practitioner's knowledge level is concerned, self-diagnosis and MESOPYME do not require much experience, while other models need much knowledge and experience to assess current capabilities of the process. Small and medium scale organizations generally do not have people dedicated for quality work alone. A person has many roles in these organizations; for example, people who are doing software development are also responsible for the SPI initiative. These individuals may or may not have experience dealing with the SPI initiative, so it is not easier for them to use any of these models without the help of some external consultant. The self-diagnosis method is easier to use as it gives the list of KPAs that are partially achieved or not achieved at all to attain a particular CMM level. To achieve these KPAs, a list of actions can also be generated by the GAR matrix but how to implement these actions is not discussed in this method which may be problematic for a small or medium scale organization. It can only be used for self-assessment before an official appraisal.

CONCLUSION

Small and medium size software development organizations are facing severe problems in ensuring quality due to their limited resources for investment in providing such infrastructure.

Existing software process models are not easily applicable in small and medium organizations and requires extensive infrastructure. In this context, we had studied available software process improvement models for small and medium software development organizations and compared their significant characteristics. Each model has its benefits and limitations. Organizations should select the specific process model keeping in view their objectives, constraints, and expectations. Further work in this area is directed to perform case studies and empirical validation in real software development settings. It would be interesting to study the impact and comparison of these approaches on software process quality.

REFERENCES

Ahonen, J.J., Forsell, M., & Taskinen, S.K. (2002). A modest but practical software process modeling technique for software process improvement. *Software Process Improvement and Practice, 7,* 33-44.

Akao, Y. (1990). QFD: Integrating customer requirements into product design. Portland, OR: Productivity Press.

Allen, P., Ramachandran, M., & Abushama, H. (2003, November 6-7). PRISMS: An approach to software process improvement for small to medium enterprises. In *Proceedings of the 3rd International Conference on Quality Software (QSIC '03)* (pp. 211-214). Dallas, Texas.

Basili, V., Caldiera, G., & Rombach, D. (1994a). Goal question metric paradigm. In J. Marciniak (Ed.), *Encyclopedia of software engineering* (vol. 1, pp. 528-532). New York: Wiley.

Basili, V., Caldiera, G., & Rombach, D. (1994b). The experience factory. In J. Marciniak (Ed.), *Encyclopedia of software engineering* (vol. 1, pp. 469-476). John Wiley & Sons.

Basili, V., & Rombach, D. (1998). The TAME project: Towards improvement-oriented software environments. *IEEE Transactions on Software Engineering, 14*(6), 758-773.

Basili, V., & Weiss, D. (1984). A methodology for collecting valid software engineering data. *IEEE Transactions on Software Engineering, 10*(6), 728-738.

Becker-Kornstaedt, U. (2001). Towards systematic knowledge elicitation for descriptive software process modeling. In *Proceedings of the 3rd International Conference on Product Focused Software Process Improvement (PROFES)* (pp. 312-325). Germany.

Becker-Kornstaedt, U., Hamann, D., & Verlage, M. (1997). Descriptive modeling of software processes (IESE-Report 045.97/E). Germany: Fraunhofer Institute IESE.

Biro, M., Messnarz, R., & Davison, A.G. (2002). The impact of national cultural factors on the effectiveness of process improvement methods: The third dimension. *Software Quality Professional, 4*(4), 34-41.

Briand, L., Differding, C., & Rombach, H.D. (1996). Practical guidelines for measurement-based process improvement. *Software Process: Improvement and Practice, 2*, 253-280.

Bush, M. (1995). *The capability maturity model: Guidelines for improving the software process* (SEI Series in Software Engineering). Carnegie Mellon University, Software Engineering Institute. Addison-Wesley.

Calvo-Manzano, J.A., et al. (2002). *Experiences in the application of software process improvement in SMES. Software Quality Journal, 10*, 261-273.

Cohen, L. (1995). *Quality function deployment: How to make QFD work for you.* USA: Addison-Wesley.

Curtis, B., Kellner, M.I., & Over, J. (1992). Process modeling. *Communications of the ACM, 35*(9), 75-90.

ESSI. (1994, February). *IBERIA, LAE, SPIE: Software process improvement and experimentation* (ESSI Project No. 10344).

Fortuna, R.M. (1988, June). Beyond quality: Taking SPC upstream. *Quality Progress, 21*(6), 23-28.

Galin, D. (2004). *Software quality assurance, from theory to implementation* (1st ed.). Pearson, Addison-Wesley.

Gresse von Wangenheim, C. (2002). *Planning and executing GQM based software measurement* (Tech. Rep. No. LQPS001.01E). Sao Jose, Brazil: UNIVALI.

Gresse von Wangenheim, C., Anacleto, A., & Salviano, C.F. (2006, January/February). Helping small companies assess software processes. *IEEE Software, 23*(1), 91-98.

Gresse von Wangenheim, C., Hoisl, B., & Wüst, J. (1995). *A process model for GQM based measurement* (Tech. Rep. No. STTI-95-04-E). Software Technology Transfer Initiative, University of Kaiserslautern, Germany.

Gresse von Wangenheim, C., Punter, T., & Anacleto, A. (2003). Software measurement for small and medium enterprises: A Brazilian-German view on extending the GQM method. Retrieved December 12, 2007, from http://www.sj.univali.br/prof/Christiane%20Gresse%20Von%20Wangenheim/papers/ease2003.pdf

Gresse von Wangenheim, C., Weber, S., Hauck, J.C.R., & Trentin, G. (2006). Experiences on establishing software processes in small companies. *Information and Software Technology, 48*, 890-900.

Hauser, J.R., & Clausing, D. (1988, May-June). The house of quality. *Harvard Business Review*, 63-73.

Herrera, E.M., & Trejo Ramirez, R.A. (2003). A methodology for self-diagnosis for software quality assurance in small and medium-sized industries in Latin America. *The Electronic Journal on Information Systems in Developing Countries, 15*(4), 1-13.

ISO/IES 9126 (1991). *Information technology: Software product evaluation, quality characteristics and guidelines for their use.*

Jalote, P. (2002). *An integrated approach to software engineering* (2nd ed.). Narosa Publishing House.

Johnson, D.L., & Brodman, J.G. (1998). Applying the CMM to small organizations and small projects. In *Proceedings of the 1998 Software Engineering Process Group Conference,* Chicago, IL.

Johnson, G., Scholes, K., & Sexty R.W. (1989). *Exploring strategic management.* Englewood Cliffs, NJ: Prentice Hall.

Kellner, M.I., Becker-Kornstaedt, U., Riddle, W.E., Tomal, J., & Verlage, M. (1998). Process guides: Effective guidance for process participants. In *Proceedings of the 5th International Conference on the Software Process* (pp. 11-28).

Madhavji, N.H, Holtje, D., Hong, W., & Bruckhaus, T. (1994). Elicit: A method for eliciting process models. In *Proceedings of the 3rd International Conference on the Software Process* (pp. 111-112).

Martin, S. (2002). *Business process improvement.* McGraw-Hill.

Mazur, G. (1994, November). QFD for small business: A shortcut through the "maze of matrices." *Transactions from the 6th Symposium on Quality Function Deployment*, Michigan (pp. 375-386).

McFeeley, B. (1996, February). *IDEALSM: A user's guide for software process improvement* (Handbook CMU/SEI-96-HB-001). Software Engineering Institute, Carnegie Mellon University.

Ministerio da Ciencia e Tecnologia. (2001). *Quality and productivity of the Brasilian software sector* (in Portuguese). Brazil: Ministerio da Ciencia e Tecnologia.

Moe, N.B., Dingsoyr, T., & Johansen, T. (2002). Process guides as software process improvement in a small company. In *Proceedings of the EuroSPI Conference* (pp. 177-188). Germany.

Paulk, M. (1998). Using the CMM in small organizations. In the *Joint 1998 Proceedings of the Pacific Northwest Software Quality Conference and the Eighth International Conference on Software Quality*, Portland, Oregon (pp. 350-361).

Pressman, R.S. (2002). *Software engineering: A practitioner's Approach* (6th ed.). McGraw-Hill.

Richardson, I. (2001). Software process matrix: A small company SPI model. *Software Process: Improvement and Practice, 6*, 157-165.

Richardson, I. (2002). SPI models: What characteristics are required for small software development companies? *Software Quality Journal, 10*, 101-114.

Scott, L., Zettel, J., & Hamann, D. (2000). Supporting process engineering in practice: An experience based scenario. In *Proceedings of the Conference on Quality Engineering in Software Technology (CONQUEST)* (pp. 160-169), Germany.

Software Engineering Institute. (n.d.). *Improving processes in small settings: A research initiative of the SEI's IPRC.* Retrieved December 12, 2007, from http://www.sei.cmu.edu/iprc/iprc-overview.pdf

Chapter VII
CMM FastTrack:
Experience and Lessons Learned

Hareton Leung
Hong Kong Polytechnic University, Hong Kong

Yvette Lui
Hong Kong Polytechnic University, Hong Kong

ABSTRACT

This chapter presents the Capability Maturity Model Fast-track Toolkit (CMMFT) programme which aims to provide a faster and cheaper method of obtaining Capability Maturity Model Integration (CMMI) capability with the end goals of increasing quality of software products and gaining competitive advantage as software development practices are recognised internationally. The programme is specifically designed for helping software SMEs (small- to medium-sized enterprises) in Hong Kong to "fast track" their quality and process improvement effort. We first present an overview of the CMMFT programme, including its expected benefits, project deliverables, and project plan. Then, the results of our project are summarised. Finally, we outline the key lessons learned and future work. It is hoped that others can learn from our experience in assisting SMEs to enhance their development capability and become more competitive.

INTRODUCTION

Small- and medium-sized companies often face budget, time, and resource constraints when they approach process improvement. Compounded to these challenges, they also lack the experience and skills in starting the "quality improvement journey" (Mondragon, 2006; Revankar, Mithare, & Nallagonda, 2006). Although senior management or middle managers in these organisations realise the benefits of process improvement and are willing to devote effort, they lack guidelines of effective approach for the improvement project.

This chapter presents the Capability Maturity Model Fast-track Toolkit (CMMFT) programme which aims to provide a faster and cheaper method of obtaining CMMI capability (SEI, 2001a; 2001b; 2001c; 2001d) with the end goals of increasing quality of software products and gaining competitive advantage as software development practices are recognised internationally. The programme is specifically designed for helping software SMEs (small- to medium-sized enterprises) in Hong Kong to "fast track" their quality and process improvement effort.

This project builds on a prior project initiated in 2000. The Hong Kong Software Quality Assurance (HKSQA) project aimed to help Hong Kong companies improve software quality by providing companies with a set of ready-to-use procedures, forms, and tools (Ko & O, 2002). The HKSQA model provides an intermediate step to capability maturity model (CMM) with the key objective of achieving maturity level 2. Based on the experience with HKSQA and other models, we believe that the CMMFT programme can help more SMEs to get on the "process improvement train."

The second section presents an overview of the CMMFT programme, including its expected benefits, project deliverables, and project plan. The third section presents the results of our project. Finally, the last section outlines the key lessons learned and future work.

CMMFT PROJECT

The SME Development Fund (SDF) of Hong Kong Special Administrative Region (HKSAR) aims at providing financial support to projects to enhance the competitiveness of Hong Kong's SMEs in general or SMEs in specific sectors. SDF is administered by the Trade and Industry Department of the Hong Kong government.

In 2004, the Hong Kong Computer Society, with the support of nine local IT professional associations and in collaboration with the Hong Kong Polytechnic University, proposed the CMMFT programme to the SDF. The main objective of the project is to provide a fast-track means for Hong Kong software SMEs to reach development capability assessed to maturity level 2 (Repeatable) and 3 (Defined) of CMMI (Chrissis, Konrad, & Shrum, 2003). When developed, the CMM Fast-track Toolkit can serve as an effective means of communication during software development between software SMEs in Hong Kong and partnering software companies located in the Pearl River Delta region (Southern China), encouraging wider collaboration and cooperation. The increase in software quality of a significant proportion of SMEs will also in turn benefit the Hong Kong software industry as a whole as it becomes better regarded in the region and internationally.

Benefits to SMEs

For SMEs participating in the CMMFT programme, the major benefits that can be derived from this project include:

1. Faster and cheaper method of obtaining CMMI capability.

    The traditional method of achieving CMMI capability consists of hiring CMMI assessors and consultants to evaluate existing practices of the target software organisation against CMMI, followed by more work to fill in the CMMI required gaps to reach a specific CMMI level of software development capability before a formal assessment takes place. Apart from the lengthy period required, typically 18 months to achieve CMMI maturity level 2 from 1 or 3 from 2, the associated high costs excludes the majority of Hong Kong SMEs from considering this approach.

    In contrast, our project recognises the specific needs of Hong Kong SMEs on speed and costs to achieve CMMI capability without compromising quality, since the developed Fast-track Toolkit can be fully verified and tested before use. Insofar as the Fast-track Toolkit is tailored to the specific needs of SMEs, larger software organisations with more complex structure and established practices are likely to also find it useful as a reference guide.

2. Increased quality in software products developed by a significant proportion of SMEs
The number of Software SMEs that are estimated to benefit from increased quality in software products resulting from achieving CMMI capability eventually can reach 80 (10%) assuming a total Hong Kong software SME population of 800. As the toolkit is designed for ease of use by software SMEs, we expect software SMEs adopting the toolkit to reach development capability in approximately 6 to 9 months compared to 18 months in the traditional way.

3. Gain competitive advantage as software development practices are recognised internationally
One of the main areas of emphasis in the project is to increase software development competencies in Hong Kong software SMEs in an expedient manner. Through this project, development staff can be exposed to software quality and process improvement concepts, practices, and technology with CMMI know-how applied directly into their working environment in the most efficient manner by means of a Fast-track Toolkit. The resulting knowledge acquisition and sharing in software quality and process improvement can help accelerate the growth of software quality specialists which in turn can increase the overall competitiveness of the Hong Kong software industry internationally.

Project Deliverables

The major deliverables of the CMM fast-track project was a toolkit consisting of:

- An *Introductory Guide* to serve as an introduction to the toolkit and a reference to other supporting pieces of documentation in the overall delivery package;
- A *Procedure Manual* that details the procedures that are required to be followed to reach maturity or capability levels 2 and 3 in the most expedient manner;
- A *Technical Guidebook* that provides guidelines, templates, and techniques that should be used in adhering to the procedures in the Procedure Manual;
- An *Implementation Guide* that describes the steps that should be followed and critical success factors in implementing and using the overall toolkit.

The toolkit is available on the project Web site for downloading. Before an SME can access the project material, it must complete a registration form and sign a nondisclosure agreement to protect the interests of Hong Kong. The content is primarily in English.

Apart from the toolkit, two public seminars were also organised. The first seminar was arranged in the early stage of project to publicise the objectives of the project and to invite software organisations to participate in the project. The other seminar was arranged after the toolkit has been developed to announce the readiness of CMMFT Toolkit for use.

Project Plan

The project began with gathering existing information and acquiring knowledge of development practices of software SMEs in Hong Kong, classifying them into common characteristics of business operation and requirements. The results of this exercise were used to define a "generic" or "model" SME organisation in Hong Kong for CMMI consideration.

Based on knowledge and experience of CMMI and other software process improvement standards like the HKSQA model, the CMM accelerated model, and so forth, a CMM Fast-track Toolkit was developed for this "generic" SME organisation to achieve development capability assessed to CMMI levels 2 and 3.

The major tasks for developing the CMM Fast-track Toolkit are provided below:

1. Initiate and set up the project organisation and steering committee
    To ensure broader exposure and maximum contribution to the project, an advisory committee was also formed at the start of this project, to provide suggestions on the project plan and ideas to address issues surfaced in carrying out ongoing activities of the project. The members of the committee included senior members of the Hong Kong Computer Society and representatives from local IT associations. See Figure 1 for the project organisation.
1. Gather information and acquire knowledge of development practices of software SMEs in Hong Kong, classifying them into common characteristics of business operation and requirements. We conducted a survey of the SMEs.
2. By analysing the information collected, define a "generic" or "model" software organisation

that best represents the characteristics of a typical software Hong Kong SME in business nature, mode of operation, and requirements for CMMI consideration. These common characteristics are likely to be present for a significant number or a majority of software SMEs.

3. An example that characterises many Hong Kong software SMEs is one where the SME thrives in a "division of labour" development environment in which design and project management tasks are assigned to staff in Hong Kong, while coding and testing tasks are assigned or outsourced to staff in Mainland China. Accordingly, common characteristics that are present in a significant number of software SMEs were selected for use in developing the CMM Fast-track Toolkit.

4. Gather and review available information references on subjects that have bearing on speeding up the CMMI assessment process, for example, the accelerated CMM model developed by QAI India and the HKSQA model developed in collaboration with HKSPIN.

5. Launched in July 1999, the HKSQA model provides a standard for local software organisations in Hong Kong to bridge to other international standards including CMM. As such, valuable information can be obtained

Figure 1. Project organisation

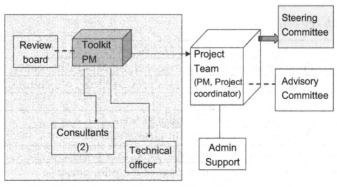

Toolkit development team

from understanding the structure and contents of the HKSQA model. Similarly, the same principles can be applied on the use of other reference models to build the CMM Fast-track Toolkit.

6. Select about five software SMEs to participate as reviewers and pilot group for the CMM Fast-track Toolkit. Mini-assessments were carried out for these selected companies to determine their development capability at the onset of the project.

7. Identify and obtain commitment of qualified reviewers, which included CMMI lead assessors and process improvement specialists in the software industry for the CMM Fast-track Toolkit.

8. With the input, requirements, and involvement of participating software SMEs, external reviewers and in collaboration with the Hong Kong Computer Society and the Hong Kong Polytechnic University, define and develop the CMM Fast-track Toolkit.

9. On an ongoing basis, review, evaluate, revise, and improve the CMM Fast-track Toolkit and/or components of it with feedback obtained from the qualified reviewers and the participating software SMEs to ensure the quality and practical effectiveness of the developed toolkit.

10. Evaluate results of the reviewers and make revisions/improvements to all deliverables of the CMM Fast-track Toolkit.

11. Conduct a post-implementation review on the pilot group to evaluate whether any development capability improvements have taken place since mini-assessments.

12. Prepare, promote, and conduct awareness seminars to SMEs on the availability, structure, and content of the CMM Fast-track Toolkit.

To assist the pilot group to adopt the CMMFT, we also organised several process briefings to explain the process guides and answer their concerns. Our original plan is given in Table 1. Although we planned to complete the project in 18 months, it turned out that we took 24 months to complete all deliverables.

PROJECT RESULTS

The CMMFT programme officially commenced in December 2004 with the solicitation of software SMEs to join the pilot group. The pilot group comprised seven companies for ease of manageability and in anticipation that some may become inactive. In this section, we first highlight the results from the initial survey and mini-assessment, then, a brief description of the CMMFT is provided, followed by the findings from the post-implementation review.

Table 1. Project plan with key deliverables

Dates	Key Deliverables
12/2004	Forming steering committee and project organisation
5/2005	Information gathering and survey of SME companies
5/2005	Selection of pilot group
7/2005	Mini-assessment of the pilot group
2/2005	Project announcement and promotion
12/2005	First draft of the HK CMM Fast-track programme
9/2006	Post-implementation review of the pilot group
3/2006	Promotion and marketing

Initial Survey and Mini-Assessment

During the period of January to May 2005, we e-mailed, phoned, and contacted over 200 software companies. Those software SMEs that showed interest in our programme were invited to participate in our survey. Twenty-one companies returned the survey questionnaires. Based on the survey results, it was observed that the majority of the industry agreed that software quality improvement should be part of the organisation's business strategy or objectives, and they are interested in improving their software development processes.

However, the software quality assurance practice of the industry is low as compared with other countries in the region (e.g., India). The majority of the industry has not instituted process and provided sufficient resources for SQA. The resources invested in SQA practices by the Hong Kong companies are far below the international benchmark; namely, 50% of software product cost should be allocated to software quality work including quality assurance, software testing, and training.

China plays and continues to play an increasing role for the Hong Kong software development industry. China is the largest external software application market for Hong Kong. Also, China provides low-cost computer workforce for the Hong Kong software development companies. Software development functions characterised by labour intensive work tend to move to China; these functions include programming, testing, implementation, and support and maintenance.

The software SMEs have the following characteristics:

- Their clients are not confined to a specific industry although they lean more towards trading and manufacturing software applications.
- Internet based applications, enterprise management systems, and database applications are in big demand.
- Most of them employ fewer than 50 full-/part-time staff.
- Their annual gross turnover is below US$2 million.
- For a typical project, the project duration is 3 to 6 months with 5 staff, 18 person-months, and project value of US$80,000.
- More than 40% of the companies have set up offices in Mainland China.
- The size of the Mainland China office is larger than the local office.
- In terms of development practices, most companies lack measurement, contractor management, and a quality assurance (QA) process.
- Their main focus is to remain competitive by offering timely delivery of products and services. There is less focus on management, control, documentation, and other quality-related processes.

In order to benchmark the ability of the pilot companies, a mini-assessment (also known as gap analysis) was conducted with each company separately at their premises, in order to obtain an impression of the organisations' business and daily operations. The mini-assessment questionnaire developed by the CMMFT team (a snapshot of which is depicted in Figure 2) was based on the practices from the CMMI ® Version 1.1.

The rundown of this assessment was in the format of a short programme overview for the whole company, and then face to face interviews with selected members of the organisation. These individual members were hand-picked by the point-of-contact of each SME. Representatives were roughly divided into senior management, project managers, and developers/engineers, and had separate dialogues in order to obtain an unbiased view of their perception of current processes and workflows of the entity.

To maintain confidentiality of data, assessment results of the companies are aggregated and then reported below. Where particular companies are mentioned, they are represented by alphabets,

Figure 2. Snapshot of mini-assessment questionnaire

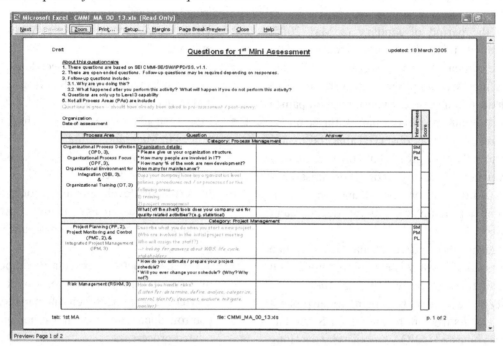

that is, companies "A" through "I." Results of the *mini-assessment* were quantified, and data were input into an in-house developed program "CMM Online Assessment Tool" (COAT). Scoring was given by the same CMMFT project team member throughout the project to maintain consistency of results. Moreover, scores were occasionally slightly amended after visiting more SMEs and further clarifying findings with the company in question. Individual company's results were sent back to the particular SME for its in-depth understanding of where it stood at that point in time in order to obtain a benchmark result.

Scoring within the COAT system ranged from 0 to 3, with "0" meaning an activity was *never*

performed, while "3" represents an activity was *always* performed. Scores were tallied into four broad categories: process management, project management, engineering and support, covering different process areas (see Table 2).

Despite a couple of companies claiming to have ISO 9001 in place, or in process of acquiring such certification, generally speaking, all of the assessed companies were found to be weakest in the process management category with an average of 0.9 and scores ranging from 0.0 to 1.5. This actually comes as no surprise, as this category comprises "metalevel" procedure(s) that instruct staff how to write processes and procedures.

Results in other categories did not fare better, with project management at 1.4, engineering at 1.8,

Table 2. Coverage of process areas under different categories

CATEGORY	PROCESS AREAS
Process Management	OPD, OPF, OT, OEI
Project Management	PP, PMC, IPM, RSKM, SAM
Engineering	OEI, PP, PMC, IPM, RSKM, SAM, REQM, RD, CM
Support	PP, PMC, IPM, IT, TS, PI, V&V, MA, CM, DAR

while support was 1.3. Generally speaking, SMEs did best in the engineering category with one of the companies obtaining a score of 2.5, most probably because it had a fairly well-established process in place (rapid unified process).

During the course of the programme, two of the SMEs (companies A and F) were deemed "dropped out," as they were nonresponsive to our e-mails and never attended the numerous process seminars which we organised. To acquire sufficient data for analysis in order for the results not to be so frivolous, we subsequently invited two more companies to join the pilot group.

Table 3. Toolkit objectives and target readers

Documents	Objectives	Target Readers
Introductory Guide	• Provides the background of CMMI ® and the CMMFT programme; • Gives an idea of what to expect when embarking on the process improvement journey	• CEOs of IT SMEs • IT Heads in large organizations • Sponsors of CMMI ® in IT SMEs or large organizations with IT Departments • People who are interested in CMMI ® implementation, but are not sure how to get started.
Implementation and Improvement Guide	• Provides details of how to implement CMMI ® in an IT SME setting	• IT Heads in large organizations • Project Managers • People who are interested in CMMI ® implementation, but are not sure how to get started.
Technical Guidebook	• Has templates for use • A companion to "Procedure Manual"	• Project Managers • Engineers
Procedure Manual	• Allows readers to follow detail step-by-step of processes	• Project Managers • Engineers

Figure 3. CMMFT Toolkit

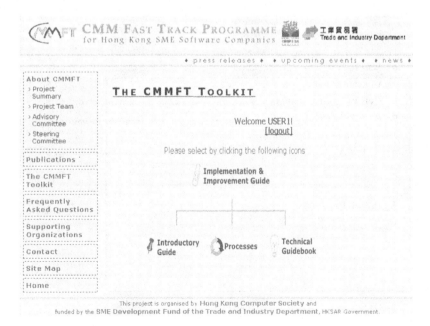

Table 4. Mapping process areas to process guides

Process Guides	Process Areas (PAs)
Configuration Management Process Guide	Configuration Management (CM)
Decision Process Guide	Decision Analysis and Resolution (DAR)
Integrated Development Process Guide	Integrated Teaming, IPPD (IT)
	Organizational Environment for Integration, IPPD (OEI)
Metrics Management Process Guide	Measurement and Analysis (MA)
Organizational Process Guide	Organizational Process Focus (OPF)
	Organizational Process Definition (OPD)
Product Development Process Guide	Technical Solution (TS)
	Product Integration (PI)
Project Management Process Guide	Project Planning (PP)
	Project Monitoring and Control (PMC)
	Integrated Project Management (IPM)
	Risk Management (RSKM)
Quality Assurance Process Guide	Process and Product Quality Assurance (PPQA)
Requirements Process Guide	Requirement Management (REQM)
	Requirements Development (REQD)
Supplier Management Process Guide	Supplier Agreement Management (SAM)
	Integrated Supplier Management (ISM)
Training Process Guide	Organizational Training (OT)
V&V Process Guide	Verification (VER)
	Validation (VAL)

Figure 4. Generic structure of process guide

1 PURPOSE 2
2 SCOPE 2
3 POLICY 2
4 EVOLUTION OF THIS DOCUMENT 2
5 [NAME OF PROCESS] DEFINITION 3
5.1 OVERALL ROLES AND RESPONSIBILITIES 3
5.2 ENTRY CRITERIA / MAJOR INPUTS 3
5.3 EXIT CRITERIA / MAJOR OUTPUTS 3
5.4 [NAME OF PROCESS] FLOW AND PROCEDURES 3
6 MEASUREMENTS 4
7 VERIFICATION 5
8 EVIDENCE OF COMPLIANCE 5
9 REFERENCES 5
10 GLOSSARY OF TERMS 5
APPENDIX A: [SAMPLE TEMPLATE PLACED HERE] 5

TABLE OF FIGURES

Figure 5.4: Illustrative Work Flow (Style: Caption) 4

CMMFT Toolkit

The CMM Fast-track Toolkit consists of an *Introductory Guide,* a *Procedure Manual,* a *Technical Guidebook*, and an *Implementation Guide.* The objectives and target readers of these documents are given in Table 3. All of them are available on the project Web site (www.cmmfasttrack.hk), as shown in Figure 3. The implementation guide consists of a number of process guides, capturing the process areas of CMMI levels 2 and 3. The mapping of the process areas to our process guides is shown in Table 4. All process guides follow the generic structure shown in Figure 4.

Results of Post-Implementation Review

At the end of the programme, we conducted a post-implementation review with the still active pilot companies. Six of the seven (86%) active SMEs responded. All of them admitted that joining the CMMFT programme provided some benefit to their organisations. Moreover, they were still very enthusiastic about the programme and would like to continue with it. Most of them (83%) said that the toolkit is the most useful to their organisations, while others (50%) said that the process briefing sessions were useful. It is noted that in their opinion, everything provided by the CMMFT team (toolkit, briefings, Web site, and assessments) are useful. Nearly all of them (5 out of 6) perceived the benefit of joining the programme as "greater awareness of the importance of process," while others found that increased knowledge of software development practice and obtaining a set of usable process for future reference as important. However, currently, they do not notice a higher rate of productivity but believe that their companies will achieve higher productivity in the future.

As to how we can assist their organisations to further their process improvement journey, most of them requested that we could provide consulting help at a low cost. This goes in tandem with a plea to help obtain a grant/subsidy to cover some of the implementation cost of doing process improvement. Although process briefings are well-received, some felt that the seminars are still too broad and not case-specific enough. In addition, all of them did not specify a need for a Chinese version of the toolkit, as (1) the staff knows English and (2) they have dealings with overseas partners, and documentation are written in English.

Regarding implementation status, only Companies C and D (33%) revealed that they had partially followed the *Requirements Process Guide.* This was mainly because a process briefing had been conducted on requirements management, thereby increasing SMEs understanding of process *per se* instead of how to conduct requirements gathering; and SMEs could then trial the procedure at the start-up of a new project. Company C commented that they have similar requirements procedures at a branch office; hence they used the best of both worlds and adapted the CMMFT Toolkit for the Hong Kong branch.

Company B stated that its staff had commenced to using the *Configuration Management Process Guide,* as they already have similar processes in place and thus found the guide relatively easy to understand and follow. The rest of the SMEs had not yet implemented any processes; the top two reasons cited are mainly lack of funding support and therefore lack of workforce. They understand that they need a budget to handle process improvement activities, but this amount is not small. Two other companies mentioned that they would like to see a more complete "picture," as they still feel lost and lack understanding of CMMI.

In retrospect, although the toolkit was designed to be "one-size fits all," nevertheless, on implementation by the various SMEs, they found that they still require some tailoring and amendment to the developed procedures before the processes can be used within their organisations. Moreover, procedures cannot be designed in a vacuum, nor can they be thrown over a silo after development.

All of the SMEs had the same sentiment—that they appreciated very much the free-of-charge process guide briefings organised by the Hong Kong Polytechnic University. Despite this, they also understood that they still require some hand-holding by a quality expert.

In summary, the CMMFT programme exhibited some benefits to participants, which included a set of process guides and workable procedures which they could customise and use within the company. Despite the perceived huge start-up cost and workforce usage, all of them agreed that embarking on the process improvement journey is worthwhile, and they would continue on this path, preferably with some support in terms of funding.

CONCLUSION AND FUTURE WORK

From working with the pilot group, we observe the following main challenges facing SMEs trying to implement CMMI:

- Lack of resources (people and time) to implement CMMI
- Language and process culture barrier
- Difficult to disseminate CMMI concepts and importance
- Very steep learning curve for people new to process culture

In working with the SMEs, we learn several key lessons, as shown below:

1. Process improvement will always be lower priority compared to the day-to-day project work. It is unrealistic to expect the SMEs can achieve improvement in a short time.
2. A process champion in the SMEs should be identified and coached on how to drive the improvement activities. Without this person, it is hard to obtain strong participation in the improvement project.

3. SMEs cannot afford staff taking long time off work due to their heavy workload. Thus, training must be planned carefully to minimise the impact to their daily work. In particular, training duration should to be kept within one day at a time.
4. The training should focus more on practical implementation, rather than concepts and benefits.

Based on feedback from the pilot group, we plan to organise more process training in the near term, as this can provide direct benefits to the SMEs. In addition, we will further enhance the toolkit based on their feedback. In the medium term, we are considering the following:

- Assist the SMEs to obtain CMMI certification based on the CMMFT Toolkit
- Translate the CMMFT Toolkit into Chinese as many SMEs have branch offices or partners in China and we have received some requests from Chinese organisations
- Set up a certification scheme based on CMMFT, as a "stepping stone" to full CMMI implementation

ACKNOWLEDGMENT

The CMMFT project is funded by the SME Development Fund of the Trade and Industry Department, HKSAR Government.

REFERENCES

Chrissis, M.B., Konrad, M., & Shrum, S. (2003). *CMMI guidelines for process integration and product improvement*. Addison-Wesley.

ISO9001 mapping to CMMI. http://www.sei.cmu.edu/cmmi/adoption/iso-mapping.html

Ko, R., & O, J. (2002). *HKSQS model: An implementation tool for CMM.* Paper presented at the SEPG Conference on Tour.

Mondragon, O.A. (2006). Addressing infrastructure issues in very small setting. In *Proceedings of the 1st International Research Workshop for Process Improvement in Small Setting* (pp. 5-11).

Revankar, A., Mithare, R., & Nallagonda, V.M. (2006). Accelerated process improvements for small settings. In *Proceedings of the 1st International Research Workshop for Process Improvement in Small Setting* (pp. 117-126).

SEI. (2001a, September). Capability Maturity Model® (SW-CMM®) for software. Retrieved December 14, 2007, from http://www.sei.cmu.edu/cmm

SEI. (2001b, September). CMMI publications and transition materials. Retrieved December 14, 2007, from http://www.sei.cmu.edu/cmmi/publications/pubs.html

SEI. (2001c, September). CMMI product suite. Retrieved December 14, 2007, from http://www.sei.cmu.edu/cmmi/products/products.html

SEI. (2001d). CMMI tutorial. Retrieved December 14, 2007, from http://www.sei.cmu.edu/cmmi/publications/stc.presentations/tutorial.html

Chapter VIII
MoProSoft®:
A Software Process Model
for Small Enterprises

Hanna Oktaba
Universidad Nacional Autónoma de México, Mexico

Ana Vázquez
Asociación Mexicana para la Calidad en Ingeniería de Software, Mexico

ABSTRACT

This chapter introduces MoProSoft as a new software process model specific for small enterprises and EvalProSoft as its corresponding assessment method. It resumes the reasons for its creation and the basic characteristics of both. It also includes the results of four pilots in very small Mexican enterprises, as well as its selection as the base documents for the development of an international standard. The authors wanted to share this experience to make clear that software process improvement in small enterprises is possible through simplified versions of good practices created by and for big transnational companies.

INTRODUCTION

A total of 92% of software companies in Mexico have less than 100 people, therefore most of the times it is difficult to perform software process improvement (SPI) "by the book" in our companies. First of all, there is almost no SPI literacy available on the bookstore shelves in Mexico; our engineers have to learn SPI in expensive books which have to be bought through the Internet and are written in English, narrating experiences of huge transnational companies. The same happens with standards, which are written by wealthy countries and address the needs of their big companies. Developed and wealthy countries like the USA and Japan are always leading standards creation, while Latin-American countries almost never have representation there. Those books and standards are written by companies with plenty of financial resources and hundreds of employees with huge projects for customers like the Department of Defense of the U.S., while a successful story of a company with only 10 employees with only one client and almost no resources to perform SPI is almost never known.

In this context, the Mexican government launched a program to promote the software industry in 2002; and one of its challenges was to perform massive process improvement for very small companies with limited resources, funding, and people. At that time, the average process capability level of the software development companies was 0.9 in 0 to 5 ISO/IEC 15504 (ISO/IEC, 2003) scale (Secretaría de Economía, 2004). A formal selection of a process model to improve these levels was performed, but there were no standards or models suitable for the Mexican industry, which led to the creation of a new one. In the following sections, we describe the highlights of the history.

THE SELECTION OF A STANDARD

The government and the industry defined the selection criteria which were applied to evaluate the suitability of the most popular standards and reference models in Mexico at that time: SW-CMM® (SEI, 1995), CMMI® (Chrissis, Konrad, & Shrum, 2003), ISO/IEC 12207 (ISO/IEC, 2002), ISO 9000 (ISO, 2000), and ISO/IEC 15504 (ISO/IEC, 2003).

The suitability criteria for the software process reference model and assessment method were defined by the Mexican industry as:

C1. Proper for small and medium enterprise (SME) with low processes maturity level.
C2. Not expensive in adoption and assessment.
C3. Permissible as a national standard.
C4. Specific for software development and maintenance organizations.

C5. Defined as a set of processes based on internationally recognized practices.

Those criteria were applied to evaluate the suitability of the selected standards and models. Table 1 resumes the evaluation results. The "Yes/No" value means that the standard or model fulfills/does not fulfill the criteria. The question mark (?) means that there is no evidence to make the decision.

The ISO 9000 is not specific for software development organizations (C4) and it is not defined as a set of processes (C5). On the other side, there exist examples of its adoption by Mexican SMEs with reasonable costs (C1, C2) and it is already a national standard (C3). SW-CMM or Capability Maturity Model Integration (CMMI) models fulfill the criteria C1, because they apply to organizations of any size, independent of the organization's maturity level starting point. Also they are specific for software development entities (C4) and defined as a set of (key) process areas (C5). Nevertheless, the cost of its adoption and assessments is one of its drawbacks (C2). Finally, due to Mexican bylaws, those models cannot be accepted as national standards (C3).

The problem with ISO/IEC 12207 and ISO/IEC 15504 was that new versions of both were released at that time and there were few experiences of its adoption and assessment (El Emam & Briand, 1997), so its suitability for small enterprises (C1) and its adoption cost (C2) were unknown. Both could be national standards (C3) and are specific for software development organizations (C4). ISO/IEC 12207 is defined as a set of pro-

Table 1. Model comparison

Model	C1	C2	C3	C4	C5
ISO 9000	Yes	Yes	Yes	No	No
CMM /CMMI	Yes	No	No	Yes	Yes
ISO/IEC 12207	?	?	Yes	Yes	Yes
ISO/IEC 15504	?	?	Yes	Yes	No

cesses (C5), but in the case of ISO/IEC 15504, a specific software process reference model is not addressed (C5).

The conclusion of this analysis was: None of those models fulfills all criteria. As a consequence, the Mexican government decided to develop the national standard for software development and maintenance MoProSoft® (Oktaba, Alquicira Esquivel, Su Ramos, Martínez Martínez, Quintanilla Osorio, Ruvalcaba López, et al., 2003) and its process assessment method EvalProSoft (Oktaba, Alquicira Esquivel, Su Ramos, Palacios Elizalde, Pérez Escobar, & López Lira Hinojo, 2004). The basic requirements for their definition were meeting the criteria C1 to C5 as well as ISO/IEC 15504 Part 2 conformance. Not everyone agreed with this decision; the declaration that no available standards was useful and the development of one standard in Mexico was incomprehensible for some people. The model in Spanish was named "*Modelo de Procesos para la Industria de Software*" (MoProSoft) and resumes the well known practices of other models and standards, offering a new process structure, some new process documentation elements, more precise process relationship, and explicit process improvement mechanisms.

MODEL'S PROCESS STRUCTURE

To define the structure of the process model, first we analyzed the structure of the software development enterprise. Even the micro-enterprise (with less than 10 people) has a top management group which makes decisions about the direction of the business. Also, it has a middle management group which is responsible for project and resource procurement and control. Finally, there exists an operation group which develops projects using assigned resources. The members of those groups recognize their responsibilities through assigned roles. Roles have vertical authority alignment and horizontal collaboration relationship between

them. Based on those observations, we decided to group our processes in three categories: top management, management, and operation. The purpose is to provide specialized processes for each functional group. Figure 1 presents the MoProSoft category and process structure by means of unified modeling language (UML) package diagram.

The top management (TM) category contains practices related to business management. Provides the directions for the processes of the management category and receives reports from them. This category contains a business management process (TM1). The management category (MAN) includes process, project, and resource management practices which are aligned with business goals of top management category. The MAN category provides elements for the performance of operation category processes, receives and evaluates the information generated by those processes, and informs the results to the top management

Figure 1. Process categories

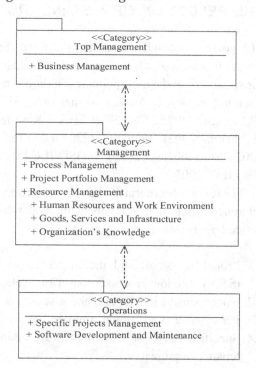

category. Process management (MAN1), project management (MAN2), and resource management (MAN3) are the processes that set up the MAN category. The resource management process includes three subprocesses: human resources and work environment (MAN3.1); goods, services, and infrastructure (MAN3.2); and organization knowledge (MAN3.3). The operations category (OPE) addresses the practices of software development and maintenance projects. This category performs the activities using the elements provided by the management category and delivers the reports and the generated software products. The OPE category contains the specific projects management process (OPE1) and the software development and maintenance process (OPE2).

PROCESS DOCUMENTATION PATTERN

The process pattern is a framework of elements needed to document a process. It contains three sections: general process definition, practices, and tailoring guidelines. The general process definition includes process name, category, purpose, abstract of process activities, goals, goals indicators, quantitative objectives for goals, responsibility and authority roles, subprocesses (if any), related processes, inputs, outputs, internal products, and bibliographical references. The practices section identifies the roles involved in the process and the training required, describes detail of activities associating them to the process goals and to the roles involved, includes a UML activity diagram, describes product's verifications and validations required, lists the products that should be incorporated into the organization knowledge base, identifies the infrastructure resources necessary to support activities, exemplifies process measurements for each goal indicator, as well as recommended training practices, exceptional situation management, and the use of lessons learned. The tailoring guidelines suggest

the possible process modifications which should not affect the achievement of process goals.

Standards and Model Used

After the structure and the documentation pattern were set, processes were defined by Mexican software process improvement experts through the rearrangement, summary, and compilation of the following standards:

- CMMI (Chrissis et al., 2003)
- ISO 9000 quality management systems (ISO, 2000)
- ISO/IEC 12207 software life cycle processes (ISO/IEC, 2002)
- ISO/IEC 15504 software process assessment (ISO/IEC, 2003)
- ISO 10006 guidelines for quality management in projects (ISO, 2003)

MoProSoft coverage studies to these standards are available.

Process Relationships

The main contribution of MoProSoft is its systematic approach, establishing relationships among processes, products, and roles. These features speed up the model implementation and reduce the cost of it. The relationships among processes are based on product interchange and role participation. Each output product generated by the process is explicitly identified as the input product in one or more processes. The internal products are "consumed" by the same process that has generated them. The process relationship based on role participation means that some roles of one process participate in activities of other processes. For example, the person responsible for the business management role participates in the validation of the process plan activity of the process management process. This participation is defined in the process activity description.

Process Improvement

The process improvement is explicitly included in the model through the process management process. The purpose of this process is to establish the organization processes based on the required processes identified in the strategic plan, as well as defining, planning, and implementing the corresponding improvement activities. The strategic plan is developed by the business management process which assures that the process improvement program complies with the organization business goals.

Each process has defined goal indicators and establishes the measurement practices for them. Periodic results of these measurements and suggested improvements for the process are reported to the process management process. Based on the reports of all processes, the quantitative and qualitative process performance report is elaborated and delivered to the business management process.

Process Assessment

The process assessment method EvalProSoft, based on requisites of ISO/IEC 15504 Part 2, was developed. The process reference model for the assessment is MoProSoft. It allows companies to evaluate the capability level of each process. Additionally, we defined the organization maturity level in terms of the maximum capability level achieved by all processes.

Pilot Experience

In 2005, we ran four pilots in small enterprises with a typical profile of the Mexican software industry. The purpose of the pilots was to evaluate MoProSoft easiness and usefulness as a software process model for small companies and the cost of the assessment method EvalProSoft. We conducted the initial assessments to establish the base line capabilities of the enterprise processes. The result was "classic" between 0 and 1. During the next six months, our consultants were coaching the companies in MoProSoft tailoring and adoption. Finally, we applied the second assessment to each company. All enterprises achieved 1.08 average increment of the capability level of all processes. Table 2 contains the average capability level increment by process category.

Table 3 shows for each company the number of employees total improvement effort in hours

Table 2. Capability level increment by category

Category	Increment
TM	1.00
MAN	1.20
OPE	0.75
Global	1.08

Table 3. Effort and improvement data by enterprise

Enterprise	Employees	Total effort in hours	Effort per person	Average improvement
A	17	479	28.18	1.00
B	8	199	24.88	1.00
C	17	628	36.94	1.56
D	29	221	7.62	0.78
Average	18	383	21.28	1.08

and effort per person. The last column includes the average capability improvement per process. It is interesting to observe the relation between the effort per person and the average process improvement. Company C has invested the biggest number of hours per person and achieved the biggest increment in process improvement. The average employee number was 18, and the average effort per person was of 21.28 hours during six months.

CMMI THROUGH MOPROSOFT

MoProSoft is made up of good practices as well as other models like CMMI; then when a company is adopting MoProSoft, it is also implementing requirements of others models. Mexican companies are specially interest in adopting MoProSoft as a first step to achieve a CMMI level. We prepared a formal study of MoProSoft coverage of level 2; Table 4 shows the results.

Consensus among Mexican SPI experts is that when a company has a low maturity level. MoProSoft is a good model to start learning to improve; after reaching level three, the company is prepared to switch toward CMMI L3.

MoProSoft As a Mexican Standard

The pilots of MoProSoft and EvalProSoft confirmed that both fulfill C1-C5 criteria mentioned in the second section of this chapter. Due to the results of this experiment, the Ministry of Economy decided to formalize MoProSoft and EvalProSoft as the Mexican standard for software

Table 4. MoProSoft coverage of CMMI L2

Coverage of CMMI L2	Percentage
Fully	67%
Largely	10%
Partially	17%
Not Covered	6%

development. An evaluation unit staffed with trained people to perform the evaluations was set; the challenge now is to improve the software process maturity level of Mexican companies through MoProSoft adoption. It requires a huge amount of effort in training and deployment, and it also requires a coordinated approach of government and industry.

MoProSoft As a Basis for an ISO Standard

Meanwhile, we were invited by the WG24 of ISO/IEC JTC1 SC7, where life cycle profiles and guidelines for use in very small enterprises are being developed, to present the Mexican program; after doing so, they decided to take MoProSoft as a basis to develop their life cycle profiles. This recognition for the work done compiling several ISO standards to create MoProSoft and EvalProSoft was unexpected. We also realized that small companies around the world, even in Europe and the U.S., have the same needs as Mexican companies. Thus, we hope that our model will be useful for them too. The first profile, based on MoProSoft, may be released in the next couple of years, and our local model will become a global one.

ACKNOWLEDGMENT

We would like to acknowledge the contribution to the MoProSoft and EvalProSoft definition of Claudia Alquicira Esquivel, Angélica Su Ramos, Gloria Quintanilla Osorio, Mara Ruvalcaba López, Francisco López Lira Hinojo, Maria Julia Orozco, Alfonso Martínez Martínez, Maria Elena Rivera López, Yolanda Fernández Ordoñez, Miguel Ángel Flores Lemus, Carlos Pérez Escobar, Jorge Palacios Elizalde, Cecilia Montero Mejía, and Alfredo Calvo. Also, we want to extend very grateful thanks to SGA, ARTEC, MAGNABYTE, and E-Genium companies for their enthusiasm and dedication during the experiment. Finally, we would like to thank the Ministry of Economy of Mexico for the confidence and the support for this project. This chapter has been developed inside the project "Process Improvement for Promoting Iberoamerican Software Small and Medium Enterprises Competitiveness – COMPETISOFT" (506AC287) financed by CYTED (Programa Iberoamericano de Ciencia y Tecnología para el Desarrollo).

REFERENCES

Chrissis, M.B., Konrad, M., & Shrum, S. (2003). *CMMI guidelines for process integration and product improvement* (SEI Series in Software Engineering). Addison-Wesley.

El Emam, K., & Briand, L. (1997). *Costs and benefits of software process improvement.* (International Software Engineering Network tech. rep. no. ISERN-97-12).

ISO. (2000). *ISO 9000:2000 quality management systems: Requirements.*

ISO. (2003). *ISO 10006:2003 quality management systems: Guidelines for quality management in projects.*

ISO/IEC. (2002). *ISO/IEC 12207:1995 information technology: Software life cycle processes* (Amd. 1).

ISO/IEC. (2003). *ISO/IEC 15504 software process assessment* (part 2).

Konrad, M., Chrissis, M.B., Curtis, B., & Paulk, M. (2002). *A report on the May 2002 CMMI Workshop: Adoption Barriers and Benefits for Commercial Software and Information Systems Organization* (Special rep. no. CMU/SEI-2002-SR-005).

Oktaba, H., Alquicira Esquivel, C., Su Ramos, A., Martínez Martínez, A., Quintanilla Osorio, G., Ruvalcaba López, M., López Lira Hinojo, F., Rivera López, M.E., Orozco Mendóza, M.J., Fernández Ordoñez, Y., & Flores Lemus, M.A. (2003). *MoProSoft v. 1.3 Por Niveles De Capacidad De Procesos.* Secretaría de Economía. Retrieved December 14, 2007, from http:// software.net.mx

Oktaba, H., Alquicira Esquivel, C., Su Ramos, A., Palacios Elizalde, J., Pérez Escobar, F., & López Lira Hinojo, F. (2004). *EvalProSoft v1.1.* Secretaría de Economía.

Secretaría de Economía. (2004). *Estudio del nivel de madurez y capacidad de procesos de la industria de tecnologías de información.* Retrieved December 14, 2007, from http://software.net.mx

SEI. (1995). *The capability maturity model: Guidelines for improving the software process* (SEI Series in Software Engineering). Addison-Wesley.

Chapter IX
Agile SPI:
Software Process Agile Improvement—A Colombian Approach to Software Process Improvement in Small Software Organizations

Julio A. Hurtado
University of Cauca Colombia, Colombia

Francisco J. Pino
University of Cauca Colombia, Colombia

Juan C. Vidal
University of Cauca Colombia, Colombia

César Pardo
University of Cauca Colombia, Colombia

Luís Eduardo Fernández
University of Cauca Colombia, Colombia

ABSTRACT

This chapter presents Agile SPI, a framework in which the main goal is to motivate small and medium size enterprises (SMEs) towards improving and certifying their software development processes. This framework was born in the SIMEP-SW project where a software process improvement model for supporting process improvement in the Colombian software industry context was built. We present Agile SPI, its origin, development, principles, architecture, main components, and the initial experiences.

INTRODUCTION

Nowadays, the software industry represents an important economical activity; it offers different possibilities for business and it aims to be a great opportunity for developing countries. In Latin American countries, the software industry is usually immature; companies face an undisciplined process and that means quality is unpredictable (Mayer&Bunge, 2004). Not only will it be impossible to plan and manage quality without a mature environment, but also when we achieve it, we will not know why and we could not repeat it (Hurtado, Pino, & Vidal, 2006). The Latin American software industry has grown smoothly, so the generation of strategies for achieving the software process improvement (SPI) environment that would allow organizations to take advantage of effective software processes. Software quality assurance through software process improvement is one of the strategies software companies could engage in with two goals: the first one is to improve the quality process so that they can get into a new market, and the second one is the need for their processes, like administrative units, to become more efficient and effective (Pino, Garcia, Ruiz, & Piattini, 2006).

One of the characteristics of the Latin American software industry is that it is mainly formed by small and medium size enterprises (SMEs). Most of these companies did not have a defined software process improvement project basically due to the great initial investment required and the disadvantage of their personnel competitiveness on the software process areas. The special characteristics of small companies cause that processes improvement programmes must be applied of a way particular and visibly different from the typical way the great organizations do it, this is not as simple as the fact to consider these programmes as versions to minor scale of great organizations (Richardson, 2001; Storey, 1982).

Agile SPI (Hurtado et al., 2006) is a framework SPI based on a strategy for institutionalization the software process in the small organizations context. For the process to be sustained, process behaviour needs to be integrated into the organization's culture. A process is institutionalized when it is followed consistently and performed naturally by everyone involved in performing the process activities. This will happen when the SME has in place a framework for software process improvement appropriate, for that reason Agile SPI is composed by three components:

- Two light models, a light reference model and an evaluation model, with a set of processes which are typically used by the Colombian small software organizations.
- Agile process for supporting a project SPI. A process SPI model for guiding a SPI program of way agile. A process definition model for supporting the implementations of improvements.

In the context of the SIMEP_SW[1] project, a pilot experience was carried out in order to validate the theoretical results of this research. Some programs SPI in a Colombian software development companies was implemented according to the guidelines suggested by Agile SPI. The results were analysed for validating our model and improving it.

In the second section is presented the background. The third section presents the Agile SPI origins including a description of the SIMEP-SW project and its developing. Agile SPI, its principles, architecture and main components are presented in the fourth section. The study cases are presented in the fifth section. Finally, the sixth section presents the main conclusions and describes perspectives.

BACKGROUND

The software industry is characterised for a fast product innovation but not by the process refinement. Software process improvements are required to increase the productivity of software companies. Generally, it is the aim to increase the quality of the produced software and to keep budget and time. Quality models for software process improvements were developed in context of large organisations and multinational companies. In the Latin American software industry, there are many problems in a SPI efforts because they are based on models created for others contexts (geographical, human, sizes of organizations, technologies used, process users and others factors). In some countries like Colombia, most of the organizations are small, with undisciplined behaviour, ad hoc process and absence of process focus. The same situation is presented in most of the countries of the world, even in development countries exists a great capacity in small enterprises. The models and technologies associated to the process must be adapted to the organization's needs. The quality models usually do not consider the factors of success for the companies, such as profitability, competitiveness, strategy of market and satisfaction of users (Conradi & Fuggetta, 2002).

The traditional frameworks focuses the efforts for the discipline and the risk reduction. Nowadays, the software products looks for the competitiveness: faster, better, and cheaper. Inside the focus of SPI models, Conradi and Fuggetta (2002) present three differences: process assessment, process refinement, and process innovation. Models like CMMI contribute to assessment and refinement focus, however the Quality Improvement Paradigm (QIP) contributes to innovation focus through the reuse concept. Printtzel and Conradi (2001) presented a taxonomy in order to compare the SPI frameworks based on some causal relations between process quality and process quality. They compare CMMI, ISO, ISO/IEC 15504, QIP, Experience Factory (EF), Gode Question Metric (GQM), and Software Process Improvement for better Quality (SPIQ). This strategy was important for defining the causal relations for Agile SPI.

Latin American countries have been concerned in recent years about software quality and development processes in their own industry, becoming as a main feature in increasing product quality (Bedini, Llamosa, Pavlovic, & Steembecker, 2005). For example, the "MoProSoft" model from Mexico and the "MR.MPS" from Brazil, amongst others that could be mentioned.

In Mexico, the MoProSoft model has been developed - "Modelo de Procesos para la Industria de Software" (Oktaba, 2005) (Processes Model for the Software Industry). This model is based on ISO 9001:2000, ISO/IEC 15504-2:1998 y CMM. MoProSoft aims to provide the software industry in Mexico with a model based on the best international practices. This model is at the same time easy to understand, simple to apply and economical to adopt. It seeks to assist organizations in standardizing their practices, in the assessment of their effectiveness and in the integration of ongoing improvement. MoProSoft defines three process categories: organizational, management, and operation. It specifies three parts for each process categories: a general definition, practices, and a guide for adjustments. A tenet of its improvement strategy is that the organization should establish its own strategy for the setting up of the processes defined by the model. The processes should evolve in alignment with the suggestions for improvement. The organization's strategic plan will be reached with increasingly ambitious goals being set all the time. In this way the organization can reach maturity progressively, by this ongoing and continual improvement in its processes.

In Brazil, the MPS.BR project (Weber, Araújo, Rocha, Machado, Scalet, & Salviano, 2005) has been developed. Its basis lies in ISO/IEC 12207:2002, CMMI e ISO/IEC 15504:2003. The MPS.BR project has two models: a Reference Model for the software improvement process–MR_MPS along with a Business Model for the software improvement process– MN_MPS. MN_MPS defines the elements and interactions involved in the certification of the organization by implementing MR_MPS in two ways: first one for an organization and second one for a group of organizations together (thus managing to make it more affordable for SMEs). MR_MPS is made up of maturity levels, along with an assessment model. The maturity level is organized in two dimensions: capability and process. The process maturity is classified into seven levels: optimized, managed quantitatively, defined, almost completely defined, partially defined, managed, and partially managed. Process areas are attributed to each maturity level based on the levels of CMMI. This is so as to ensure a gradual and fully appropriate implementation in Brazilian SMEs. The implementation level of the practices, associated with each process area, is evaluated by means of indicators.

In the previous models have been set out explicitly no improvement strategy for guiding an improvement process. Agile SPI improvement strategy is based on providing the organization with an agile process which supports the basis for addressing a SPI Program.

In Blowers and Richardson (2006); Garcia, Graettinger, and Kost (2006); Scott, Jeffery, Carvalho, D'Ambra, and Rutherford (2001); Wangenheim, Weber, Rossa Hauck, and Trentin (2006), among others, are observed others related efforts to software process improvement in small software organizations.

Agile SPI was developed inside to SIMEP-SW project (An Integrated System for the Improvement of Software Development Processes), between the 2004 to 2006 years, supported by the University of Cauca, Colciencias and some Small enterprise of South Colombian.

Agile SPI - Process is an agile process of software processes improvement, which can be used as guide for the implementing of a software process improvement program in SMEs. Agile SPI - Process takes as premise the precepts of the Agile Manifesto and the requirements for a light SPI, which have been adapted to the necessities of a software processes improvement program for small software enterprises. These are:

1. The highest priority is to satisfy the client's necessity through the early and continuous delivery of significant improvements to the development process because of Agile SPI - Process provides a light and agile process of software processes improvement.

2. There are not stable requirements of improvement. For this reason, the diagnosis is a key phase. Even so, requirements of improvement that arise will be prioritized and welcomed as it is feasible to carry out them.

3. To give frequently improvements of the software process.

4. An improvement program with Agile SPI - Process should be based on the effective collaboration among the consultants, the improvement group, the top management, the development group, the SQA group, marketing and other dependences related with the SPI project.

5. To build projects around motivated individuals toward the improvement of individual, group, and organizational processes. To give them the opportunity and the support that they need and to offer to them trust so that they carry out the tasks.

6. The most efficient and effective form of communicating round trip information inside an improvement team is through face-to-face conversation.

7. The maturity of process, as the average performance of the projects, should be the main measure of the progress improvement. The base measurements to measure the performance are the productivity and the quality.

8. Agile SPI - Process promotes the sustained development. The work must be continuous and indefinite.

9. Agile SPI - Process promotes a technical and management infrastructure, appropriate to support the process improvement.

10. Agile SPI - Process promotes the conformation of a dynamic organizational infrastructure, based on objectives, not in control strategies.
11. Agile SPI - Process promotes the continuous learning as a key discipline. The objective of this discipline is to allow knowing the work, to meditate about this and to adjust the work through short and concise iterations.
12. Agile SPI - Process promotes the effective conformation of the teams proposed by its infrastructure, it worries about the quality of the human work to carry out.

Agile SPI aims to support process improvement for the Colombian software industry. Its main goal was to motivate small and medium size companies towards improving and certifying their development processes. The framework must include practical recommendations for process implementation, in order to facilitate their internalisation by a person when following the process and institutionalisation by organizations when everyone follows the common process and the process discipline is enforced, and also it should consider a tool for process definition. In the context of the SIMEP-SW project, a pilot experience was carried out in order to apply the theoretical results of this research. Inside these project researchers of University of Cauca and some small enterprise worked for to analyse, design, and proof the different models and strategies for improve the local industry in the Popayán and Cali cities. Some strategies was adopted in addition to the Agile Model, requirements for a company to achieve a maturity level CMMI using: agile practices, adoption of reuse strategies like software product line and adoption of agile methods for implementing some practices, and a collaborative focus for improve the humans process. The most important contribution of SIMEP-SW project was its participation in the project Competisoft Project[2]. This new project supported by CYTED aims "To increase the competitiveness level of the Latin American Software SMEs by means of the creation and diffusion a methodologic framework.

Framework Agile SPI for Software Process Improvement

Agile SPI is a framework based on models lightweight, international standards, agile improvement, and agile practices. Agile SPI promotes an improvement with lacking of agility, promotes the agility with quality and recognizes in the innovation the most promissory source for the improvement of all the aspects that involves a process: people, methods, techniques, and tools. The SMEs will be able to create its processes, if these do not exist, following its principles and needs, or will be able to follow the cycles and the models, if it is supporting a process previously defined and wants to improve it. The improvement focuses in the quality of the product and the productivity of the organization, from which to organize by disciplines it aims towards the securing of the quality of the product and that to maintain the process agile and to innovate in their components is the principles that move the productivity. The discipline give reliability in the process, a mature process offers to certain degree of reliability on the accomplishment of a project in the organization as far as the reach of its goals of quality and costs. The agility and the innovation are present to support the feature in which the traditionally mature processes never will consider, under this approach the process must be agile with the purpose of being able to be reconciled to a SME with its time and resource restrictions. And of course, the process must be defined and institutionalised, and prudentially controlled.

Agile SPI Architecture

Agile SPI is an integral model for the Software Process Improvement that exhibits the following characteristic: the main focus is SME. In this kind of organisations there are a great interest in innovating as far as products or services, but not as far as the organization processes. The processes are ad-hoc, light or chaotic, there is not great motivation in improving this aspect. Agile SPI was created like a framework for supporting improvement in software SME. Usually, the quality assurance is more focused to the test than to have a complete program of quality control. In the best of the cases the quality assurance is focused to control processes instead of facilitating its improvement. The academy is looking for new forms of development, nevertheless is more focused in the technologies than in the processes or methodologies. The improvement of process is considered a remote work, reaching for a great companies. It isn't known that the improvement is possible from teams and its members up to enterprise level. The universities that distribute the work related to the improvement show the models of quality, their interpretation and all the required infrastructure to do it, this can motivate to work to improve the state-of-the-art, but it don't to change the state of the practice.

The Agile SPI architecture has been influenced by the structure of models defined by SEI and ISO, but considering others quality models of processes well-known internationally. Agile SPI

structure has a main components of an improvement program: an improvement guide and models for supporting, Agile SPI - Light Quality Model and Agile SPI - Light Metrics Model. There are two dynamic elements of the static structure: the conceptual model Framework SPD (Software Process Definition) and the improvement process. The Figure 1 depicted the Agile SPI architecture.

Due to the context SME, Agile SPI is a complete framework (it is not a model that says what makes lack, but like complementing the process). It is functional, its application facilitate the complete operation of an improvement program. It search be understandable, to guarantee his learning and application: therefore it is simple and clear. It aims to be usable, that implies that the strategy must be clear, intuitive, flexible and adjustable to the needs. It aims to motivate, that implies that the improvements must be visible in short periods, it is necessary the sufficient motivation to guarantee that the improvement project has continuity. It aims to implement a model for applying in the SME, that is to say, to apply the model must be viable (economically) and feasible (attainable). The flexibility of Agile SPI is based on its models independence. Agile SPI can be used in different contexts with several models.

The framework Agile SPI presents the following components:

Figure 1. Agile SPI architecture

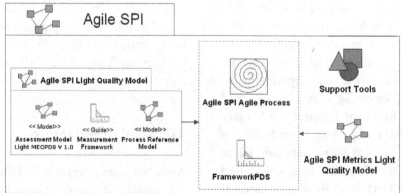

- A guide for an improvement program called Agile SPI Process. It is a process that guides the efforts of a SME towards the adjustment of a software process adequate to its necessities. This process is the framework of reference for the management of the improvement projects, the framework includes a method, models, infrastructure, techniques, and the tools of support.
- A light quality model for Agile SPI. Agile SPI Light Quality Model integrated process and product, and that guides the organization of the people and the teams, the disciplines and the areas of work associated to the definition, application and improvement of the process towards a defined maturity level. Defining a set of processes which are typically used by the Colombian SME's. It allows to identify and diagnose problems of the industry as far as the process and that allows to planning the improves according to a process reference model.
- A light measurement model for Agile SPI. Agile SPI Light Measurement Model allows to measure: the performance of the process in the projects in which it is applied, to improve the estimations of the projects through the measurement of the effort, the maturity of the this and improvement of the process within the framework of a program SPI.
- A conceptual and technological frame for the definition, visualization and application of processes, Agile SPI - Conceptual Framework. This conceptual frame is based on metamodel SPEM - Software Process Engineering Metamodel, this frame is the conceptual base on which SPI and the tools of support are supported to all the models of Agile SPI. This conceptual framework allows to relate elements of process, with the elements of the quality model, with the model of evaluation, the measurement model. For example, the disciplines concept is a separating element of areas of the process and the structure of Agile SPI are defined based on this concept.

Agile SPI Focused on Disciplines and Process Components

Agile SPI allows to organize an improvement project, very integrated with the development projects, and each organizational and technical change is to handle through an experience with the purpose of visualizing in an isolated way, if the improvement really has been done. The improvement project follows a process of defined by Agile SPI - Agile Process, this is organized by small iterations, in which the different disciplines participates in a greater or smaller degree of intensity. Agile SPI is based on the concept of discipline like representative areas of process like approach of assurances. In the approach of refinement of the process Agile SPI defines the concept of capacity, which usually measures the quality degree of a discipline with respect to a quality model or process model. See Figure 2.

Agile SPI define three dimensions for improvement: capability, innovation, and agility with the following causal relationship:

- F1 (Discipline)→F2 (Capacity)→ Quality(Process)→ Quality (Product)
- F1' (Component Process)→F2'(Innovation in Component)→Quality (Process) → Quality (Product)
- F1'' (Discipline)→F2''(Agility on Discipline)→Performance(Process)→Productivity (Project).
- F1'''(Component Process)→F2''' (Learning in component)→Quality (Process) && Performance (Process)→Quality (Product) & Productivity (Project).

Therefore F1 + F1'+ F1''+ F1''' ⇔ Quality(Product) & Productivity (Project)

Figure 2. Example of discipline in Agile SPI framework.

```
Discipline Evaluation from Agile SPI Process( e.g. apply to Discipline ABC.)
Apply to Process Component: {Description - Artifacts - Roles - Workflow }
   Disciplina ABC
Based on Quality Model Component:{Description, Goals, Practices, Measurement ,
   verification } Disciplina ABC.
With Evaluation Component: { Measurement, verification } Disciplina ABC.
Measurement Component: {Productivity, defects} Disciplina ABC.
   Composed by:
             {Roles: Evaluator - Artifacts: Referent Quality Models and sub
             artifacts, evaluation plans, evaluation results, training
             requirements -   Roles: evaluator - Workflow: Define evaluation
             objective, planning evaluation, execute evaluation}
```

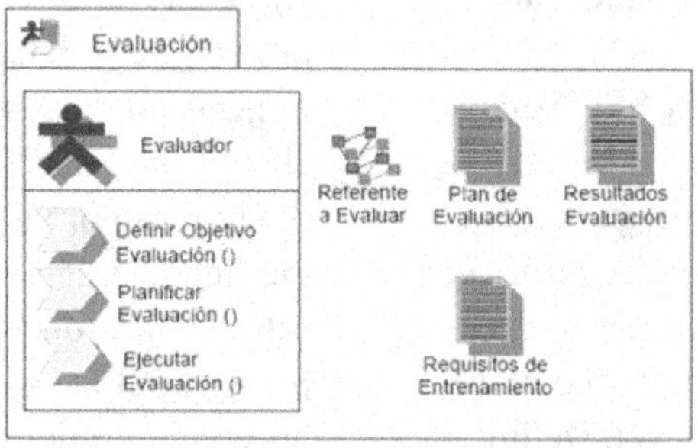

The process components are created, evolved and replaced according to the results of the evaluation and the priorities of each organization. The improvement is visualized by disciplines and components of process. The improvements are organized by iterations that lean in the technology of processes to manage the configuration of process.

The Agile SPI: Process Life Cycle

Agile SPI – Process is an agile and light process of software processes improvement, which can be used as guide for the execution of a software processes improvement program in small and medium enterprises (SMEs). Light because enterprises like the SMEs which possess certain characteristics as: low resources, light processes, small human resource, limited economic availability, and so forth, need a model that supports an improvement program that consider the real characteristics of their industry, besides offering quick results in their improvement programs.

Agile SPI – Process is an iterative and incremental process is based on improvement cases, which has the feature of throwing quick results of improvement because it allows to create mini improvement programs that include improvement cases inside a global improvement program. The improvement cases are atomic units of improvement in the processes areas that have been selected to be improved either because the enterprise follows a certification or because for it its priority is to improve a specific process.

Obtaining quick improvement results will allow in consequence to the improvements to be visible from the early phases of the improvement project, more agile and quicker as the mini improvement programs finish depending on the prioritize criteria that the enterprise has defined previously. This seeks to maintain the personnel's motivation toward the improvement program, through permanent improvement results, removing the risks of the project in the first phases, to focus the major effort in the areas that the enterprise considers more important for its business. The life cycle is highly influenced by the iterative and incremental life cycle models present in many development processes such as RUP, XP, Scrum, among others; since the improvement projects cover extensive requirements and they impact the whole organizational structure of any enterprise, some characteristics of these models have been adapted to create a complete, agile, and less bureaucratic improvement process and sensitive to the related activities with the management (meetings, documents, infrastructure, etc.).

Agile SPI – Process allows the parallelism between iterations or improvement programs, being very advantageous because improvements can be developed in processes areas where an evident independence exists. In the certification processes, the appraisal before the beginning of an improvement program is very important, since this allows estimating which processes areas the enterprise has and which is their maturity level. Currently many tools exist with which the process areas of an enterprise can be appraised according to a particular quality model, for example: CMMI (SEI, 2002) in its continuous or staged version, ISO/IEC 15504 (ISO_15504-2, 2004; ISO_15504-5, 2006), ISO 9001-2000 (ISO_9001, 2000), and others. In this aspect Agile SPI – Process can be used independently of the quality model and evaluation method, for example this it can be used if a continuous or staggered CMMI has been selected or if the choice is ISO 15504.

Agile SPI – Process also includes, documents, and explains a set of disciplines to any improvement process that can be applied in smaller or bigger measure in each one of the phases in which several iterations can be developed, for this we were based on the Software Development Unified Process. When we identify in Agile SPI – Process the disciplines to be developed in each one of the improvement process phases, we are assuring that personnel involved in the improvement program will be able to visualize in major

detail the behaviours and activities that should be developed inside an improvement program. We have considered as vital disciplines in any improvement program: Training, Improvement Management, Evaluation, Analysis, Design, Installation, Process Configuration Management and Learning.

The Agile SPI - Process Phases

Agile SPI - Process describes a process of software processes improvement in five phases, next we will see each one of them:

The Figure 3 presents to Agile SPI – Process phases: installation, diagnostic, formulation, improvement, and revision of the program.

- **Phase 1 —Installation:** This is the beginning phase for Agile SPI - Process. Motivation should exist in the organization to undertake a plan of improvement of its processes. In this phase a proposal of improvement is created based on the business needs, which will help to guide to the organization through each one of the following phases, this proposal must be approved by the management to guarantee this way the assignment of the necessary resources for the improvement project. During this phase some objectives also are defined, which are established from the enterprise needs. Besides a feature very important in Agile SPI - Process is offering a guide in the improvement of software processes, also provides a management infrastructure, which describes the way in which committed people are or-

Figure 3. Agile SPI: Process phases modeled under SPEM

(1). Installation (2). Diagnostic (3). Formulation. (4). Improvement (5). Revision

ganized inside the improvement effort; this infrastructure organizes the improvement effort keeping in mind a management team (MT), a processes technology team (PTT), and improvement teams (ITs); these teams have been influenced by the infrastructure proposed by IDEAL, complementing it with the creation of effective groups proposed by the methodology TSP (Team Software Process), adapted by Agile SPI - Process like TSPI (Team Software Process Improvement) and some of the features in the administration of a project using the SCRUM methodology.

- **Phase 2—Diagnostic:** In this phase, a program has already begun toward the improvement of processes and the work that here is realized is fundamental for the realization of the following phases. An appraisal is realized to know the general state of the enterprise processes, besides an analysis of the results that will allow establishing the priority of the improvement cases, allowing this way to create one of the main products of this phase known as "improvement general guide or plan."

- **Phase 3—Formulation:** In this phase, the most high-priority cases of improvement (1 or 2) are taken to improve according to the results of the appraisal made in the previous phase and the planning of a first improvement iteration is realized, this with the purpose of finding a measure of the effort that serves as base for the estimate of the effort that the rest of the improvement project will take to carry out.

- **Phase 4 —Improvement:** In the improvement phase of Agile SPI - Process the whole effort of the improvement cases is managed based on the estimate made in the improvement execution plan created in the previous phase and consequently the plans corresponding to the different iterations of the process areas to improve or to create

are developed. A document should exist where it is registered the execution of the test pilots, the evaluation of the new process areas or the new improvement that has been realized. If the pilot plans have been developed satisfactorily it is necessary to create acceptance and institutionalisation plans of the new processes in the enterprise.

- **Phase 5 —Revision:** In this phase, a feedback is made before starting the beginning phase again. In this phase all the learned lessons and the metrics developed to measure the accomplishment of the objectives serve like knowledge base or source of information for people involved in the following improvement cycle. With all the gathered information the realized work should be evaluated and all the elements related with the execution of the program SPI should be corrected or adjusted, how for example the established infrastructure, the used methods, the communication channels and if the solutions to the identified problems were the appropriate ones.

Iterations in Agile SPI - Process and Their Correspondence with the SCRUM Development Process

Iteration in Agile SPI - Process is a mini cycle improvement that allows advancing the development and management of a set of improvement cases in an independent way. The iteration is the integrative concept between phases and disciplines. The phases can be decomposed in time and space (teams) for iterations, and an iteration, being itself a guide of improvement, is defined starting from a set of disciplines according to the phase where it is and to the characteristics of the improvement project. Iterations in Agile SPI - Process is a very important part in the Software Processes Improvement because this way independent improvements can be developed, and so to deliver quicker improvements. The key resides in developing iterations in areas that are independent of others, this way the work in them can be achieved in parallel, and the work of improvement that in them is developed doesn't cause problems; nevertheless it is necessary to keep in mind that a dependence can exist among areas, in that case it is necessary to study which is the impact that could create a improvement case and based on this to order the way of how improvements will be developed in the other improvement cases.

The iterations for the improvement cases in the diagnostic, formulation, and improvement phases can be developed in a similar way to the Scrum development process with its sprints, in each one of them there are three phases: pregame, game, and postgame, which we have called them pre-improvement, improvement, and post-improvement.

Improvement cases can be seen as Sprint Backlog (Improvement Requirements List), which have been divided in smaller improvement tasks, and these in their entirety and respective correspondence would conform a specific area that would be seen as a prioritised list of features required by the improvement, which has been obtained

thanks to the appraisal achieved to the enterprise; in relation to the SCRUM development process this list of features is created starting from the client's requirements and is called Product Backlog (Initial Improvement Requirements List).

In Figure 4 is showed how the iterations in Agile SPI - Process are developed. In the pre-improvement phase the appraisal discipline is developed for the creation of the product accumulation or delay registry (initial improvement requirements list). After prioritising the areas to improve, an improvement requirements list is created through the evaluation of each area, which allows defining an order for each one of the improvement iterations to execute. It is important the assistance of dependences net to order in a detailed way the improvements to achieve in the selected areas. The dependences net allow identifying the improvement cases or the number of iterations to develop for each area. The improvement cases are the activities that compose the area.

After identifying the improvement cases that compose the area and ordering them through dependences net, the next is the analysis and design

Figure 4. Iterations in Agile SPI – Process

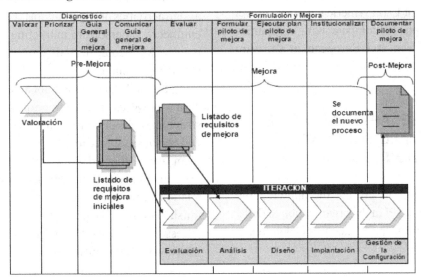

of the new or improved process and its respective installation and documentation.

Agile SPI - Process also adapts and proposes techniques and practices for the teams conformation and management, it exemplifies the net of dependences that can exist between areas or practices that they compose depending of the quality model and the way of treating this characteristic. It also documents and identifies the milestones and workproducts resultants of these and it proposes some control and management templates for the improvement process, all this inside a guide that doesn't seek to be an extensive model but a friendly, easy to use, and agile process of software processes improvement independent of the quality model and evaluation methods, and the most important: adapted to the characteristics of the Colombian software industry and in general Latin America.

At the moment, Agile SPI - Process is in its verification stage, we are achieving improvement programs in some small enterprises of our region, which have demonstrated from the beginning a great interest to improve their processes after they knew the advantages that it can bring to the quality of their products, as well as the benefit of having an international certification. With this process for the software processes improvement we seek to help to the enterprises not only of our region but also of Latin America to reach a level that allows them to compete with companies like the American and European in software development.

STUDY CASE: APPLYING AGILE SPI IN A SMALL SOFTWARE ORGANIZATION

This section aims to present the applying the framework Agile SPI in the organization SIDEM Ltda (http://www.sidemltda.com) - Colombia.

SIDEM Ltda.

Sidem Ltda. is an organization in Cauca's Valley, from the Cali City, Colombia. This organization is dedicated to production, integration, maintenance, supporting and consulting of Information Systems, using multiplatform design to support the constant challenges of productive processes.

Nowadays, Sidem Ltda. account with more of 300 clients in Colombia, using his management and financial solution. These solutions allowed to this organization to be classified by the "Cámara de Comercio de Occidente" like enterprising industrialists of the Cauca's Valley and to position itself like one of the best organizations in the Colombian south.

Experience with SIDEM Ltda.

Previous View to the Software Improvement Process

At the beginning six years ago, Sidem Ltda. was a small organization with four people, which one developed several activities. There were not defined roles or positions in a specific way and the software process was not documented. Two years ago, Sidem Ltda. is growing because account with 18 persons: one person is in charge to assign activities of client support, 11 development engineers, 2 persons in marketing and management area, 2 people in quality area, and 2 persons in management jobs.

In Sidem Ltda there are not areas defined in a clear way, we just found defined one organizational structure of the organization with some activities and persons assigned to them, overlapping among them and without documents. For that reason, there are chaos and immaturity process without relation. Almost all the time, the activities are not finished in time, budget and quality, because it is necessary to attend other problems and activities, which wastes too much time.

As a first step, Sidem Ltda created a Quality Team composed by 2 people. This team was created because:

- Defining software development activities
- Madding documents about development process
- Establishing control activities on the development process.

But, due to problems inside Sidem Ltda, the Quality Team finished madding another activities and that first effort was lost.

Any way, we founded another effort for improving process. Sidem Ltda there was implemented two projects with adoption UP Methodology and UML. The results obtained were a very good results for the team project. These results showed a better management and planning of the activities.

Initial Phase

First, we made an install meeting with Sidem Ltda. The Sidem manager presented the organization and necessities. Also, he was concerned about immature process, bad development methodologies, problems with estimating time and cost and chaos generated in management and development of projects.

The SIMEP-SW Team explained that an improvement project could be one of the most important solutions and decisions that Sidem Ltda should take and support. Consequently, the organization decided to initiate an improvement project based on the components of the Framework Agile SPI.

The SIMEP-SW Team proposed: 2 researchers to develop the appraisal on CMMI, 1 researcher in charged to obtain the development process implicit in the organization and 2 researchers in charge to manage all the Improvement Program based on Agile SPI Process, 1 researcher as a leader team.

At the same way, Sidem Ltda assigned an Improvement Team, working as a management bridge for supporting all the necessities during the Improvement Program. Fits, schedules, meetings, and necessary material in each meeting program. Each meeting should be programmed with two weeks before, with the objective of having a suitable management time.

When the two teams were ready for starting activities, we started a training about:

- Bases of Agile SPI Process.
- Reference Model CMMI.
- Presenting study cases.

After of training to the people, the SIMEP-SW Team prepared a plan or proposal of improvement with: objectives of improvement, the identified necessities of business, the necessary resources, roles and people, strategies in the development of the objectives, a schedule of work, and possible risks in the course of the project. Finally, we presented the improvement program to Sidem Ltda and we installed it.

Diagnose Phase

In order to know the current state of Sidem Ltda the SIMEP-SW Team made an appraisal in Level 2 CMMI, using SPQA Web Tool, which we would obtain an overview in the process capacity. With this process baseline, we could apply evaluations more detailed. In according to the results and recommendations generated by SPQA.WEB Tool:

- In a general way, acceptable requirement management. Then it is necessary an improvement of this area because this allows to collect and to control requirements, and to avoid deviations throughout the development of products.
- Project Planning, Project tracing and subcontract management are in a low degree of implementation. In consequence, the

organization cannot control its development processes.

- Quality Assessment, configuration management and metrics are not implemented in the organization.

With the appraisal results, it was established a meeting with the objective to obtain the areas that should be improve. Finally, we obtained the next conclusion:

CMMI Engineering Area

- First Iteration: Management Requirements and Development Requirements.
- Second Iteration: Technical Solution and Product Integration.
- Third Iteration: Validation and Verification

Later, we began the training activities about:

- CMMI Engineering Area
- Management Requirements and Development Requirements

The work product about to improvement program was updated and new dates were specified. We planned evaluation activities in process areas selected. With the evaluation results, we designed a improvement plan based on the priorities selected by Sidem Ltda. Consequently, we generated a work product, which was communicated in all the organization, the objective was to establish a feeling of responsibility in the areas selected.

Formulation Phase

Nowadays, the Improvement Project in the organization Sidem Ltda is in this phase.

Once we made formulation of improvement cases, we will prepare the design of improved process. We will implement pilot proof. After studying of the impact, if the improvement is positive and advisable for the Sidem Ltda Process, we will deployment in formal way all of the new improved process.

This study case presents the results of one first stage or cycle for the first period of a improvement project. In this study case until now the deployment of Agile SPI Process has been made during eight weeks. Two weeks for Installing, two weeks in diagnose phase and four weeks for the formulation phase. We hoped that the Improvement Project will continue and that always represent one of the primary targets of the Sidem Ltda.

Learned Lessons

The following lessons have been learned as a result of application Agile SPI Process:

- The management leader must agree in applying Agile SPI - Process and promoting.
- Communicate to all organization about the applying Agile SPI - Process.
- Develop tasks in a smooth way.
- It is important to obtain results quickly to maintain motivation in the improvement program.
- The improvement process must be planned, be managed and the necessary resources for their development are due to assign.
- Good communication between organization team leader and improvement team leader.
- If the personnel available in the organization is limited, then to make sure that parity in the assigned work exists.
- There is a confusion between processes and structure.
- The organization not always knows clearly his processes.
- Many organizations have a implicit process, it is necessary to document.
- Training about modelling of the business process and the development process.
- It is not necessary planning objectives of improvement that will not be carried out.

- If an improvement first cycle has not all support and commitment, it is better to choose not to generate negative experiences in organization with unsuccessful improvement programs.
- The improvement process does not have to be left, to be suspended, or diminished because of other events, this it must be considered of greater or equal importance than the projects or diverse situations that can be presented in the organization.

CONCLUSIONS AND PERSPECTIVES

The software process in the organizations requires evolution and maturity to approach to its different stakeholders and continues improvement and Assessment. Therefore, they have arisen different kinds of Frameworks normally named like Quality Models and Improvements methods for supporting SPI strategies. In this paper we had presented Agile SPI, a framework based on models lightweight, international standards, agile improvement, and agile practices. Agile SPI is mainly influenced by the SMEs, the agile manifest, Conradi-Fuggetta thesis, and the existent and well-know models. Agile SPI includes a flexible infrastructure based on Discipline concept of SPEM and define five contexts for applying itself. The initial improvement is measured by the product quality and the project productivity, and then by the process capability and agility. Agile SPI is differenced of others Frameworks due and this is complete respect to the models, is flexible due a permits the inclusion of other models and was designed for SME industry. Agile SPI respect to other Latin-American initiatives is different because include a improvement model. This model permits apply the framework to an improvement program.

ACKNOWLEDGMENT

This work has been funded by the following projects: SIMEP_SW financed by Colciencias and University of the Cauca; COMPETISOFT (506AC287) financed by CYTED and MECENAS (PBI06-0024) granted by the "Junta de Comunidades de Castilla-La Mancha."

REFERENCES

Bedini, A., Llamosa, A., Pavlovic, M., & Steembecker, K. (2005). *Quality software map of South America*. In *Proceedings of the 1st International Research Workshop for Process Improvement in Small Settings*, Pittsburgh, PA (pp. 216-227).

Blowers, R., & Richardson, I. (2006). The capability maturity model (SW and integrated) tailored in small indigenous software industries. In *Proceedings of the 1st International Research Workshop for Process Improvement in Small Settings*, Pittsburgh, Carnegie Mellon University (pp. 175-181).

Conradi, R., & Fuggetta, A. (2002, July/August). Improving software process improvement. *IEEE Software, 19*(4), 92-99.

Garcia, S., Graettinger, C., & Kost, K. (2006). *Proceedings of the 1st International Research Workshop for Process Improvement in Small Settings, 2005* (Special report CMU/SEI-2006-SR-001), Pittsburgh, Software Engineering Institute. Retrieved December 14, 2007, from http://www.sei.cmu.edu/pub/documents/06.reports/pdf/06sr001.pdf

Hurtado, J., Pino, F., & Vidal, J. (2006). *Software process improvement integral model: Agile SPI* (Tech. Rep. No. SIMEP-SW-O&A-RT-6-V1.0). Popayán, Colombia, Universidad del Cauca-Colciencias. ()

ISO_15504-2. (2004). *ISO/IEC 15504-2:2003/ Cor.1:2004(E). Information technology: Process assessment, Part 2: Performing an assessment.* Geneva: International Organization for Standardization.

ISO_15504-5. (2006). *ISO/IEC 15504-5:2006(E). Information technology: Process assessment, Part 5: An exemplar process assessment model.* Geneva: International Organization for Standardization.

ISO_9001. (2000). *ISO 9001:2000. Quality management systems: Requirements.* Geneva: International Organization for Standardization.

Mayer&Bunge. (2004). *Panorama de la Industria del Software en Latinoamérica.* Brasil: Mayer&Bunge Informática LTDA. Retrieved December 14, 2007, http://www.mbi.com. br/200409_panorama_industria_software_america_latina.pdf

Oktaba, H., (2005). *Modelo de Procesos para la Industria de Software - MoproSoft - Versión 1.3, Agosto de 2005. NMX-059/01-NYCE-2005.* Ciudad de México: Organismo Nacional de Normalización y Evaluación de la Conformidad - NYCE. Retrieved December 14, 2007, from http://www.normalizacion-nyce.org.mx/php/ loader.php?c=interes.php&tema=21

Pino, F., Garcia, F., Ruiz, F., & Piattini, M. (2006). A lightweight model for the assessment of software processes. In *Proceedings of the European Systems & Software Process Improvement and Innovation (EuroSPI 2006),* Joensuu, Finland (pp. 7.1-7.12).

Printzell, C., & Conradi, R. (2001). *A taxonomy to compare SPI frameworks.* Paper presented at the Software Process Technology 8th European Workshop (EWSPT 2001), Witten, Germany (Vol. 2077, pp. 217-235). Springer.

Richardson, I. (2001, September). Software process matrix: A small company SPI model. *Software Process: Improvement and Practice, 6*(3), 157-165.

Scott, L., Jeffery, R., Carvalho, L., D'Ambra, J., & Rutherford, P. (2001). Practical software process improvement: The IMPACT Project. In *Proceedings of the Australian Software Engineering Conference* (pp. 182-189).

SEI. (2002). *CMMI for systems engineering/ software engineering* (Version 1.1). Pittsburgh: Software Engineering Institute (SEI). Retrieved December 14, 2007, from http://www.sei.cmu. edu/cmmi/

Storey, D. J. (1982). *Entrepreneurship and the new firm.* Croom Helm.

Wangenheim, C. G. v., Weber, S., Rossa Hauck, J. C., & Trentin, G. (2006, January). Experiences on establishing software processes in small companies. *Information and Software Technology,* pp. 1-11.

Weber, K., Araújo, E., Rocha, A., Machado, Scalet, D., & Salviano, C. (2005). Brazilian software process reference model and assessment method. *Computer and Information Sciences, 3733,* 402-411. Berlin/Heidelberg: Springer.

ENDNOTES

[1] SIMEP_SW: An Integrated System for Software Process Improvement

[2] COMPETISOFT (Process Improvement for Promoting Iberoamerican Software Small and Medium Enterprises Competitiveness) project financed by CYTED.

Chapter X
Agile Practices In Project Management

John Gómez
Ericsson Chile, Chile

Alejandro Núñez
Practia Consulting S.A, Chile

ABSTRACT

This chapter introduces agile project management as a way to improve the processes for software development in small organizations. The chapter contains a description of the main concepts and techniques used along with practical recommendations for their application in real situations. The chapter also analyzes the relationship between these practices and recognized process improvement models like the CMMI and the PMI PMBOK and presents case studies to illustrate implementation.

INTRODUCTION

Most of the reasons behind failure in software projects lie in the lack of sound project management practices. The results of many industry studies and surveys show that the absence of appropriate strategies for scope management, risk handling, or project planning are frequently found in challenged projects.[1] For that reason, process improvement (PI) initiatives start with the project management discipline. For example, the maturity level 2 of the Capability Maturity Model Integration (CMMI®[2]) model is focused on the development of basic project management capabilities (CMMI Product Team, 2006, p. 55). This means that although an organization should improve the project management and the engineering process, beginning with the first one may allow it to obtain better results.

Nevertheless, starting process improvement is an overwhelming endeavor no matter the size or nature of the organization. The improvement initiatives have to compete with "delivery projects" that always seem to be more important (or urgent) especially from the business user's point of view. The benefits of a PI initiative are usually difficult to perceive or measure in the short term. This causes the organization motivation to decline progressively and lead the initiative to failure. This situation is even worse for small or medium organizations where resource limitations are higher. Small and medium organizations must approach process improvement in a way that benefits are realized sooner.

Another aspect of PI projects that reinforces the situation previously described is that many times PI teams replace the absence of good practices with over-engineered processes where formalism and control exceed what is needed due the nature of the work on the project or organization. Managers, users, and practitioners start to perceive these new processes as obstacles and not as tools and refer to the new way of doing things as bureaucratic, rigid, or heavy-weight. Product quality may be improved (initially), but team productivity and motivation remain low which is going to impact product quality in the long run. Also, team focus deviates from reaching project objectives to blindly follow procedures. Small and medium organizations are also more affected by this situation since usually their environments (team size, product size, project duration, cost, etc.) are smaller, and over-engineered methods may have a greater impact on project delivery.

The application of agile practices for project management addresses these common problems and may allow an organization (especially small and medium ones) to manage effectively a process improvement initiative. The development of project management capabilities facilitates the establishment of the environment to control not only project delivery but also the improvement project itself. The agile approach (by definition lighter and goal-oriented) may reduce the effort (and cost) and contribute to realize benefits sooner, keeping high morale and motivation. Our intent is to describe briefly how agility is understood and applied within the project management context and how this may benefit a process improvement initiative.

There has been a lot of discussion between agile and traditional methods authors and supporters. We do not adhere to any of them, and our purpose is not to contribute to any side of that polemic. What we see is that the limits known as the usual home grounds for agile and traditional methods are blurring creating environments where no one of them is enough or complete. A mixed approach is needed to find the best solution. Also, as many other disciplines, agile project management (APM) may be enhanced by a proper use of tools. Choosing the right tool and deciding how to use it is not easy, so we created a special section to make some recommendations on that subject.

Agile Project Management

Origin of APM

APM has its roots in the agile methodologies for software development created specially during late 1990s and publicly formalized as a movement with the formation of the Agile Alliance and subsequent publication of the Agile Manifesto (see Figure 1. *Manifesto for Agile Software Development*) in 2001 (Beck et al., 2001). Every agile method adheres to the declaration of values and principles stated in the manifesto, but the

Figure 1. Manifesto for Agile Software Development

Manifesto for Agile Software Development

We are uncovering better ways of developing software by doing it and helping others do it.

- Through this work we have come to value:
- Individuals and interactions over processes and tools
- Working software over comprehensive documentation Customer collaboration over contract negotiation Responding to change over following a plan

That is, while there is value in the items on the right, we value the items on the left more.

---

approach to deliver the solution varies from one to another; however, since agile methodologies are designed to handle a product development project, project management practices are present in most cases. We took our main references from the work of Jim Highsmith who recently published a book on agile project management, the SCRUM method created by Ken Schwaber and Jeff Sutherland, and the Crystal Clear method developed by Alistair Cockburn.

Since its official birth in 2001, agility has grown beyond software development, and one of these areas is project management. This means not only that practices that were initially used for software development projects are currently applied for nonsoftware projects but also that there is an ongoing effort within the agile community to improve and extend the current state of the practice. The formation of the Agile Project Leadership Network (APLN[3]) and the publications of books on agile project management like the one from Highsmith (2004) mentioned before showed that work.

Agility Defined for Project Management

For the purpose of the chapter agility in project management is defined by:

- Keeping the team focused on reaching project goals oriented by customer objectives

- Use of a risk-oriented approach to accomplish project goals based on frequent delivery of functional solutions
- Creating and maintaining a healthy environment for team interaction and development, enhancing self-management, transparency, and visibility
- Use of balanced project management processes to allow the appropriate mix of flexibility and control, enhancing team productivity

The APLN also published a declaration of values and principles of agile and adaptive approaches to project management (see Figure 3. *Declaration of Interdependence*). Note how for APLN the appropriate term is "leadership" and not management. We talk about this topic later when discussing the role of the project manager in an agile environment.

Life Cycle of an "Agile-Managed" Project

There are three major phases of an agile managed project:

- Initiate phase, where product vision is defined, initial scope is established, a high level plan is elaborated, and the team and environment are set up.

Figure 2. Agile project life cycle

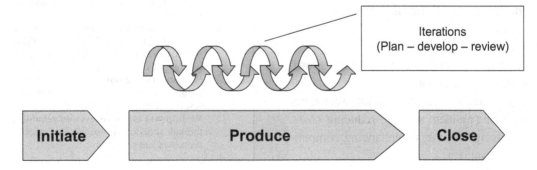

- Produce phase, which is conformed by a successive set of iterative and incremental deliveries of functional product that ends in a product release.
- Close phase, which ends the project and gathers lessons learned.

The produce milestone may be divided into more than one release and each release in more than one milestone to establish different levels of control. The most important concept on this stage is the iterative-incremental approach that aims to reduce risk and uncertainty by delivering fully functional portions of the product to the customer. Every iteration has an internal cycle of plan (reviewing and updating scope and high-level plans and elaborating a detailed plan for the iteration), develop (building functional increments of the product), and review (team self-assessment on project performance and customer reviews of the product). In the next section, we will be seeing practices that fit into this life cycle.

Agile Project Management Practices

Product and Project Envisioning

Establishing a shared vision is critical in an agile environment. This is based on the belief that people work better when they are motivated for the long-term effects of the job. This is done by making the team realize the benefits that the project results will bring to the customers and the performing organization. A product or project vision statement is declared using workshops as team-building tools. Defining the product vision must include:

- Description of customer needs, motivations, or problematic situations
- Expected benefits or value added to customer business (problem solving, reducing costs, increasing revenue, or enhancing competitive advantage)

- Expected benefits for the organization performing the project

Highsmith (2004) suggests the use of a technique called the product vision box, where the team and customer representatives participate in a workshop to design the box that will contain the product. The team designs the front and back of the box and defines a set of statements that should be on the box to help sell the product. This may end with an "elevator test statement" containing the product vision (Chapter VI). For Crystal, this is part of a workshop is called "The Exploratory 360°." The product/project vision is defined in project initiation but is reviewed and communicated along the project to assure that objectives are still on target and that the team is oriented by those goals. The project vision normally ends with some charter of the project that contains

Figure 3. Declaration of Interdependence

Declaration of Interdependence

Agile and adaptive approaches for linking people, projects and value

We are a community of project leaders that are highly successful at delivering results. To achieve these results:

- [ ] We **increase return on investment** by making continuous flow of value our focus.
- [ ] We **deliver reliable results** by engaging customers in frequent interactions and shared ownership.
- [ ] We **expect uncertainty** and manage for it through iterations, anticipation, and adaptation.
- [ ] We **unleash creativity and innovation** by recognizing that individuals are the ultimate source of value, and creating an environment where they can make a difference.
- [ ] We **boost performance** through group accountability for results and shared responsibility for team effectiveness.
- [ ] We **improve effectiveness and reliability** through situationally specific strategies, processes and practices.

the product vision, business objectives, project organization, and environment definitions.

Environment Setup

Enhancing team interaction is one of the goals of an agile managed project. This practice refers to establishing the environment when interaction happens. Environment definition covers essentially:

- **Interaction rules:** Agile methodologies are oriented by principles and values. These two, in combination with the product/vision, have a function within the agile environment: they allow team self-management. In agile environments many decisions on how to accomplish the work are left to the team who uses this rules to keep the work oriented to goals.
- **Processes and tools:** Agile teams should select the processes and tools that allow them to accomplish the objectives. A methodology workshop may be conducted to decide on this topic that results in a set of roles, practices, work products, and tools that the team will use on the project.
- **Physical environment:** Co-location is frequently suggested in many forms within agile environments to facilitate communication and interaction. This can be seen explicitly as a practice in extreme programming (XP) (Beck, 2000, chap. 13) and slightly modified with the osmotic communication property of Crystal Clear (Cockburn, 2005, p. 24). Face-to-face conversation is the most effective way of communication and the physical environment must facilitate that. Also the environment is designed to promote transparency, so it is common to use dashboards with task or feature cards where critical information like issues or progress are published and made visible to the whole team. A very good description of this practice is the information radiators

strategy in Crystal Clear (Cockburn, 2005, p. 54). In projects with virtual teams, other collaborative tools are available and frequently used. The use of these kinds of tools will be commented on later.

Scope Management Strategy

Scope creep is one of the most common causes related to project failure, so strategies to handle this are a must. The degree of uncertainty is key in defining an adequate strategy for scope management. Uncertainty leads to change, and agile teams recognize that change is unavoidable and even beneficial. In that sense, change requests are allowed anytime in pursuit of maximizing the value that a customer may get for the product. Anyway, implementing changes as they are requested leads exactly to scope creep, so there must be some sort of change control. This is how it works:

- Scope is established using backlogs of scope elements. A scope element is a requirement (functional and nonfunctional), feature, use case, user story, defect, or change request.
- Changes to scope elements are received anytime but added at the end of the backlog.
- At the beginning of each iteration, the backlog is prioritized to decide which elements are to be developed during the iteration. Change requests are in the backlog so the customer has the chance to include them for the next iteration if they are considering more important that previous elements.

Engagement rules are established at the beginning of the project to manage customer expectation, and roles are defined to accomplish the scope management tasks. Normally, a customer representative owns the backlog and is in charge of prioritizing. This customer representative act also as an official provider of scope definitions.

This way, uncontrolled changes from unofficial channels are prevented.

With this approach, the customer does not have to wait too long to include a change if he/she really wants it. When the time of prioritizing comes, many change requests are dismissed because they add little to no value compared to other features previously defined. Iteration duration is critical to the success of this strategy. The iteration duration establishes the "lag" or "waiting time" for the customer to introduce changes to the project. A high change rate suggests a shorter iteration time. Anyway, sometimes changes are critical and must be included right away. When this situation happens, there is no sense to continue the iteration: the iteration is stopped and a new iteration is planned.

The backlog is usually maintained with as little detail as possible to facilitate updates. Scope elements definition may be detailed some more with feature cards or use cases/user stories descriptions. Detail information is usually added only for elements to be developed in the next iteration. Scope definition is also complemented with release or milestone plans. At the beginning of the project, the initial scope is established and release or milestone plans are elaborated to organize the project within a schedule. A release or milestone plan is usually a high level plan that describes which scope elements will be developed for each release or milestone. Release and milestone plans are based on the backlog and are reviewed and updated each iteration. This subject will be covered next.

Layered Planning

The focus on the planning process is to keep it the most cost-effective as possible. According to the scope management strategy, there are scope elements that are really committed (the ones that will be developed the current iteration) and others that are not. Detailed planning for items not committed or with low priority may be a waste.

However, there should be a mechanism to elaborate a schedule for the whole project. A common misunderstanding of agile projects is that since changes are always allowed, the project is not able to commit for a fixed date. This is not true. A finish date is required to organize the work. This seems to be a paradox but has a simple solution. At the beginning of the project, an initial scope is established, and with that initial scope, a project plan is elaborated. This plan is kept at high level and its purpose is to establish a base schedule with some levels (or layers) of control. A large project with more than one delivery (release) to production environment may be organized by releases (every six months or more). A release is an organized set of scope elements associated with a date in the schedule. This primary level of control may be decomposed into a second one (milestones, from one to three months) that are also defined in terms of scope elements and dates. The work to accomplish a milestone is then divided in iterations (from one week to one month). The iteration is the minimum unit of work and is where the scope management strategy is fully applied. The iteration work is fixed, and the team is able to focus on that work. Then, predictability for the iteration work is higher, and detailed planning is cost-effective. The plans for the primary (releases) or secondary (milestones) layers are reviewed and updated each iteration.

Iteration planning is usually done in workshops where the customer and the whole team interact. This workshop is present in most of the agile methods (Beck, 2000; Cockburn, 2005; Scwhaber, 2004) and usually works like this:

- During the first part of the workshop, the customer representative explains the scope elements to be developed during this iteration.
- The team raises technological or environmental issues that may affect priorities which are adjusted.

- Based on previous performance results, the team estimates the effort to develop the scope elements. Restriction analysis (resource availability, risk identification, etc.) are incorporated to the estimations to allow contingencies. Based on estimation, the scope for the iteration is agreed and committed. The whole team participates in the estimations, produced taking into account the complexity and size of the requirement, using a relative scale and assigning "points." This way, the simplest requirement takes one point and so on. The concept of relative scale refers to a predefined set of the amount of points that a requirement may get: 1, 2, 3, 5, 8, 13, 20, 40, 80 (Cohn, 2004, chap. 8). This kind of scale facilitates discussion among team members considering that for more complex or larger requirements uncertainty is higher and may reveal the need for further information or more decomposition.
- The team takes scope elements and breaks them down into tasks; tasks are assigned and effort is estimated. Task estimation is verified against scope element estimation to verify consistency.
- Resource load is reviewed and leveled.
- Team decides on task dependencies and sequencing and defines priorities. Tasks for the first day of work are agreed on and communicated.

The planning workshop is usually time boxed (Schwaber & Beedle, 2002).[4] The tasks are listed in another backlog. To facilitate control, tasks are always mapped to scope elements. This allows the team to keep the focus on the commitments for the iteration.

Frequent Inspection

The purpose of frequent inspection is to detect any obstacles before they can cause a major impact on project goals. The frequency of the inspection is left to be decided by the team, but most of the agile methods detect and remove obstacles on a daily basis. There are two more objectives of frequent inspection: set up a space for team interaction and

Figure 3. Burn-down chart

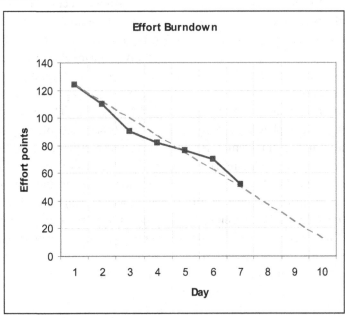

communication and provide visibility on work progress to the team and project stakeholders. There are two main strategies related to frequent inspection: daily team meetings and daily task re-estimation and burn-down charts.

In the daily team meeting, the whole team gathers together for a maximum of 15 minutes with the main purpose of detecting any obstacles that may prevent the team from accomplishing the iteration goal. Each member of the team participates in the meeting, answering three questions:

- What tasks was I working on since the previous daily meeting?
- What tasks am I going to be working on until the next daily meeting?
- What obstacles or problems are or may be on the way?

No other subjects are allowed at the meeting, and problems are scheduled for further discussion later, commonly right after the meeting. Many soft aspects are related to this meeting: the team usually forms a circle (of peers) and is standing up. When a team member speaks, everyone else is listening. No interruptions are allowed, but questions may be asked to clarify some subject. The team leader conducts the meeting but only to keep the focus and register issues. Issues are registered for further action. It is expected that a defined response action must be in place for every issue before the next meeting.

The second strategy is to re-estimate the remaining effort of every not-completed task daily. Based on the daily information of total remaining effort, a "burn-down" is calculated. This information is graphically represented in "burn-down" charts as seen in Figure 4. Burn-down chart. In the figure, the blue/continuous line is plotted between the points of total remaining effort for each day. The trend of this line represents the "velocity" of the team. This actual velocity may

be compared against an ideal or planned velocity (the red-dashed line) to obtain daily information about progress and make performance forecasts. The graphics may be interpreted as follows:

- If at any given point, the actual velocity line is over the planned velocity line, the team is advancing slower than expected; probably, there are issues impeding the team progress or maybe the team underestimates the work to be done, so adjustments may be needed.
- If the actual velocity line is below the planned velocity line, the team is advancing faster. Assumptions may have changed, or the team overestimates effort.

With the value of actual velocity, the team is able to forecast its performance and make adjustments to assure that it will meet the iteration objectives. Burn-down information is public, and graphics are printed and published in a dashboard or any other place that everyone can see.

Product Review

Product review is present in agile environments with different techniques. For software projects, the use of automated unit testing linked to a disciplined procedure is frequent. Therefore, customer involvement in reviews is required and techniques like acceptance testing, technical reviews, or customer focus groups are common (Highsmith, 2004, chap. 8). These customer reviews occur normally at the end of every iteration. In SCRUM, there is a practice named sprint (iteration) review, the main focus of which is to review the product developed during the sprint; the sprint review is a meeting time boxed to three or four hours where the team presents the product to the product owner and other stakeholders. Defects and change requests are added to the product backlog to be prioritized at the next sprint (Schwaber, 2002, p.

54). The purpose of this practice is to show the actual progress on the product development and allow the customer to make changes and recommendations if the product does not match stated requirements and expectations.

Team and Environment Tuning

Not only is the product reviewed to verify conformance to requirements and expectations; the performance of the team is also evaluated. At defined moments or at the end of every iteration, the team meets and reflects on its performance trying to find essentially what things worked well (and should be maintained), what did not (and should be adjusted or removed), and what improvements may be made to the team interaction or environment to enhance performance. In SCRUM, this is called the sprint retrospective (Schwaber, 2002, p. 54). Crystal Clear named it the reflection workshop (Cockburn, 2005, p. 65).

Time Boxes

The use of time boxes has a wide range on agile environments and that is why we decided to include a special part on this technique. A time box is a fixed duration time frame assigned to an event in the project. The most important time box is for iterations: once the iteration starts, the finish date is not changed. Time boxes are also applied for the daily meetings and the planning and reflection workshops.

Role of the Agile Project Manager

First of all, it is appropriate to state that the word "manager" is rarely used in agile environments to refer to the person that conducts the project planning and execution. Team self-management is a fundamental concept of agile projects, and having that in mind, there is no place for a traditional "project manager." Instead, the agile project manager's main responsibilities are:

- Facilitating team interaction, removing obstacles from the path of the team to allow goal accomplishment and enhance performance
- Coaching and serving as change agents, promoting the values and principles, and encouraging discipline on the defined processes and rules
- Leading the team by keeping the team focus on customer objectives and the defined product vision and project goals
- Coordinating the work, helping in decision making and problem solving

One of the most interesting aspects of this role is the difference between self-management and self-direction. For authors like Highsmith (2004), agile teams are self-managed since they organize their own work and decide how to accomplish the goals. However, the team is not self-directed: there is a leader that keeps the work on track of the vision and objectives (Chapter III).

Figure 5. Agile vs. Traditional PM paradigms

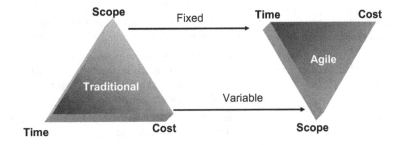

Relating APM and Traditional PM Models

Agile vs. Traditional Paradigms for Managing a Project

Figure 5[5] shows the way the triple-restriction of projects is managed in agile and traditional environments. From the agile point of view, traditional project management aims to maintain the scope fixed by strict control of changes. When a scope is committed, the project tries to deliver it allowing some variations of time and cost. If the scope changes significantly, then the time and cost are adjusted. In an agile project, the time restriction is fixed (using time boxes), and the scope is allowed to change in benefit of the customer objectives, which is facilitated by the prioritizing practice in the scope management strategy.

Agile Project Management and the CMMI[6]

The CMMI model is one of the most important references in process improvement, especially for the software development industry. The CMMI establishes a set of recognized best practices for product development at the project and organizational contexts. The model is organized in 25 process areas, six of them dedicated to project management. Therefore, there is a cross-sectional focus on project management for the maturity level 2 and capability levels 1 and 2. That is why we decided to comment on the relationships between the CMMI and APM. We are not trying to prove that an organization may achieve a CMMI maturity or capability level using agile practices. Our purpose is to show how the agile practices

Exhibit 1.

Process Area	Specific Goal	Compatibility of Agile Practices
Requirements Management	SG1 Manage requirements	In an agile environment, there is a defined scope management strategy. There is a documented backlog of scope elements. Understanding is assured by the definition of official providers and the customer involvement in the development. Commitments are made and established in the iteration plan. Normally, there is traceability between scope elements and tasks. Changes are managed.
Project Planning	SG1 Establish estimates	Scope is established trough the development of the scope elements backlog and the release/milestone plan which also contains the defined lifecycle. Rationale for estimations is present and usually scope elements receive an assignation of attributes of size and complexity. Effort estimation is realized at ROM for the project and detailed for each iteration.
	SG2 Develop a project plan	Explicit planning of some parameters is missing (i.e., data management) and may be analyzed for each project. A schedule, budget, and resource plan exists. There are artifacts that represent the planning process.
	SG3 Obtain commitment to the plan	Planning is usually made at workshops when the customer participates. Resource leveling occurs by iteration.
Project Monitoring and Control	SG1 Monitor project against plan	During the daily meeting, issues that may cause deviations are detected. During iteration planning, the parameters for the whole project are reviewed and adjusted. Progress is analyzed daily using burn-down charts.
	SG2 Manage corrective action to closure	Issues detected are analyzed and a corrective action should be initiated as soon as possible.

continued on following page

Exhibit 1. continued

Process Area	Specific Goal	Compatibility of Agile Practices
Integrated Project Management	SG1 Uses the project defined process	Normally, at the beginning of the project, a process is defined to manage the project. This process is reviewed at the end of every iteration and adjusted. Estimations are adjusted using velocity data of previous iterations or projects. Lessons learned are gathered and shared among teams.
	SG2 Coordinate and collaborate with relevant stakeholders	Stakeholders are identified and its participation defined from the beginning of the project.
	SG1 Prepare for risk management	The priorities and the choosing of life cycle are driven by project risks.
Risk Management	SG2 Identify and analyze risks	Risks are identified and monitored as potential blocks in the daily meetings.
	SG3 Mitigate risks	Potential blocks are detected and preventive actions initiated using the same rationale as issues.

we commented are related to some key elements of the project management discipline on the CMMI model. The table shows the goals process areas of the project management category until maturity level 3. Supplier management was out of the scope of this work, so the supplier agreement management process area was not included; instead the requirements management process area was included due its relevance to the project management discipline; although for the CMMI, it belongs to the engineering category.

Note how there are many agile elements that give some level of support to the specific goals of this process areas. Considering the nature of the SCAMPI method is difficult to affirm that an organization may achieve a capability or maturity level using only agile practices. In most cases, a refinement or addition is needed. Further, in this chapter, we comment on a case were a CMMI level 3 organization used some agile practices in a project without sacrificing the CMMI implementation.

Agile Project Management and the Project Management Body of Knowledge (PMBOK[7])

The PMBOK (Project Management Institute, 2004) is recognized as one of the top standards in the project management profession. As many traditional methods are usually misunderstood as heavyweight processes that are unsuitable for small environments, the PMBOK contains a series of best practices that are recognized as successful for a wide range of projects, and it is not expected that every one of them should be applied for every project. One statement says that quality should be planned into the project from the beginning and defining adequate processes is part of that definition. The adequate processes should address the objectives and nature of the project and this does not mean that every practice in the PMBOK is adequate for every case.

We can start analyzing compatibility with the groups of processes of project management

Exhibit 2.

Knowledge Area	Compatibility of Agile Practices
Scope management	Scope is defined using the scope elements backlog and the release plan, which when combined are equivalent to the WBS. The scope management strategy is defined from the beginning of the project and most of its rules (prioritizing as a key one) are performed every iteration.
Time management	Activity definition and dependency analysis for sequencing occur every iteration. There is not usually a bar (Gantt) chart or network diagrams to show the schedule. Also, techniques like resource leveling, theory of constraints, and rolling wave planning are frequently applied in agile environments. Schedule control also uses time boxes and is supported by burn-down charts.
Cost management	ROM (rough order of magnitude) estimations occur at initiation. Detailed task effort estimations occur every iteration. Effort control is based on daily re-estimation and burn-down charts.
Risk management	The whole life cycle of the project and the priorities are driven by project risk. Quantitative risk analysis is not commonly used. Mitigation occurs at the project level with time boxing and prioritization and at the iteration level with definition of corrective and preventive actions to avoid or remove obstacles
Quality management	Adequate processes are selected at the beginning of the project. Normally, there are quality control techniques in place like acceptance testing, product reviews, or customer focus groups.
Human resource management	The team is the most important factor in agile environments. Ground rules are explicitly established at the beginning of the project and maintained along the way. Team development is enhanced with reflection on causes of good or bad performance. The daily meeting allows for team management and interaction.
Communications management	The PMBOK states that the best way of communication is the face-to-face conversation which is also an agile principle. Communication is key on agile environments and frequently promoted through the workshops, daily meetings, and even the physical environment (i.e., with information radiators). Stakeholder identification and analysis is also conducted.
Integration	Chartering occurs at the beginning of the project by establishing a vision of the product and the project. The project is managed with integrated perspective of the scope, release plan, and iteration plans, which are maintained consistently through the project.

in the PMBOK (initiating, planning, executing, monitoring and controlling, and closing) and the agile project life cycle. The process groups do not happen in a cascade in the project; instead they occur many times in different project phases. In an agile project, initiating and closing are related to the initiate and close phases, and the produce phase are continuous cycles of planning, executing and monitoring, and controlling the iterations. For that reason, most of the planning processes occur every iteration. The following table shows some compatibility of agile practices within the context of PMBOK areas:

Lessons Learned (Tales From the Trench)

Managing a Project Without a Gantt Chart

Power Games Co. (PGC) is a small game development studio[8] with just three years on the market. PGC works for larger game publishers developing small products oriented to the casual gamer segment. A typical project at PGC takes about six months with a team of five to six people integrated by designers and engineers. In the game industry, the product are built incrementally. This is explained since most of the features need to be tested to prove not only that the software works as specified but also that the gaming experience is fun. PGC delivers a product increment each month or so. The culture is informal, and people are very talented.

PGC has a product manager who is in charge of all projects, and from previous work experiences, she firmly believes that the best way to eliminate risk or uncertainty is to plan up-front the activities with as much detail as possible. The team writes a project plan and produces a detailed schedule of the whole project tasks. Preparing this plan usually takes from two to three weeks. The team is not very comfortable with this way of doing things that, by the way, does not seem to be consistent with the culture and the iterative product development cycle; however, it seems to work for PGC: products are delivered on time and usually exceeding customer expectations. Publishers give PGC bigger contracts which implies developing more exciting games and making people feel happy. There are no complaints.

This success opens new opportunities for PGC, and one shows up quickly: a very important publisher contracts PGC for a new game. This project is different from any other PGC has executed in the past. It is a nine-month project that requires at least 15 people; most of the visual design of the game has to be outsourced and the game involves the use of technology that is unknown to people at PGC. Another challenge rises up: contract and franchise negotiations took almost two months, but the delivery dates remain fixed. A nine-month project is now a seven-month one. The product manager decides to start planning the project right away, as usual: the team takes about three weeks to build a detailed schedule with fine-grained tasks for the seven months of the project plotted in a Gantt chart. The first production iteration starts, and three weeks later (one before the first delivery), the project is completely challenged. Tasks seem to be advancing, but no real progress is visible. Team interaction is difficult: status

meetings are held weekly but are not effective. Morale is very low. By this time, many tasks in the schedule do not make sense anymore, and the schedule has to be updated. This sole fact worries the team a lot because they know that it may take at least a week.

It is evident that the management approach is not working in this case, and a change is needed. The team decides to use an agile approach. First, the team is divided into three mini-teams of five people each. Each team has an assigned leader and is self-sufficient in terms of the required skills; this means that each team has at least a game designer, an illustrator, an animator, and a programming engineer. The product is also divided into two major components and assigned to the first two teams. The third team receives the responsibility of integrating the game. Regarding the planning process, considering the business and technology uncertainty, it is recognized that full up-front planning is not useful so a high-level milestone plan is prepared, and it is defined that detailed planning will be conducted iteratively. The iteration's duration is established in two weeks. Every iteration will start with a planning session when the scope is analyzed and tasks are identified and estimated. Tasks will be re-estimated daily, and progress will be reported with burn-down charts. Each team will hold daily inspection meetings. Team leaders will hold a daily meeting too. Agile principles and philosophy are communicated to the team, and ground rules are established. To support this transition, a coaching strategy is launched.

The results for this project improve significantly. After the first iteration pitfall, commitments with the customer are always fulfilled on time. Technology issues are common, but they are handled by the team and the product is delivered with high quality levels. There is also another big gain: people at the company have acquired competencies to lead a team and manage a project. The company feels more confident in taking bigger and more challenging projects. There is a paradox in this case that must be noticed. What we can call a natural agile environment (small new product developed iteratively by a co-located team of highly talented people) was performing well using a traditional method. However, when they needed to scale-up, agile practices supported that better.

Mixing Approaches

Real Insurance Corp. is a large CMMI maturity level 3 company for which the project management methodology is based on the PMI framework. IT projects are managed using a strong matrix organization and the project management discipline is supported by the establishment of a project management office (PMO). There are senior project managers with more than eight years of experience. The company wants to develop two products for a business unit. The first one is a traditional product that is going to be re-engineered in a 12-month project that is partially outsourced. The second one is a new product which is going to be based in the framework developed for the first one. This second project will start three months before the first one ends and is planned to last about nine months (the first release in the sixth month). The first project starts and is challenged from the beginning: deliveries are always late; the primary supplier is changed twice and deliveries are normally rejected. The progress is very slow and schedules change frequently. The second project starts as planned by the ninth month of the first one with a six-person team. After two months, the first project is cancelled. A quality assurance audit is then conducted on the second project, but no significant methodology issues are detected. Knowing that this project was going to use components developed for the first one (that are not ready), six more people are added to the team. The team struggles trying to use the portions of components previously built, but the first partial delivery is late and rejected. This fact raises alarms to IT management which has been highly

committed to the business unit since the first project failure. Now its three months to the first release, and the team realizes that it is less costly to stop trying to work around the half-developed components and start from scratch.

The decision was to include some agile practices to facilitate team interaction and improve morale. Scope management artifacts were maintained but change control procedures were slightly modified to allow fixed scope iterations. The scope of the first release was renegotiated by prioritizing items. The work was divided into four fixed-duration iterations: the first three finishing with a fully functional increment of the product and the fourth dedicated only to refinements and tuning. The project schedule was updated, leaving only milestones and high-level descriptions. The formal estimation method was maintained, but estimations were reviewed according to the defined iteration plan. Iteration planning workshops were conducted to create task backlogs. Daily meetings and burn-down charts were used. The main project management artifacts, like the project charter and project plan, were updated to reflect these changes. The project status reports required weekly by the PMO were maintained and also the risk management processes. Nevertheless, the main focus was not the process itself. A detailed communication plan was put in place and a coaching program was launched to facilitate change. The team was trained in agile principles and values, and workshops to establish ground rules were conducted. The team was co-located. The customer was involved in the methodology changes, and the acceptance testing plans were modified to fit the new approach.

The first iteration was the most difficult. The planning workshop lasted almost three days (not the day that was expected for the three-week iteration). Initially, the 12-person team was separated into two functional groups which was believed to be the most appropriate approach, but this was confusing for the people who decided to create groups by architecture layer. Initial daily meetings were also longer than expected. After a week, the first integrations started with some suffering, but by the end of the second week, the team solved most of the problems allowing them to finish the iteration on time. Due the slow procedures to release a product to the acceptance testing environment, the result of the first iteration was presented in the development environment. Despite the customer's surprise, there was not too much to see but the team was able to accomplish a goal and deliver for the first time on the project a product that was functional. The team interaction improved a lot, but some political factors were present always and required a lot of attention along the project. The next iterations were less difficult but not exempt of challenges. The team was able to finish the development of all functionalities committed for the first release two weeks before the deadline, which was normally considered too short. However, since acceptance testing was conducted incrementally too, the first release went to production on time. Quality assurance reviews were conducted on the project, and no deviations from the CMMI process were noted. The management approach and practices were registered as lessons learned and made part of the organizational process assets.

Software Tools for APM

Software tools have been around us, helping to achieve goals since the beginning of the computer age. We can easily recall the different approaches to word processing of the late 1980s, the endless race of database engines of the mid-1990s, and the overpopulation of support software for whatsoever one may like in the present day. We may remember many enterprise resource plans (ERPs), customer relationship management (CRMs), operating systems (OSs), information managers, to-do lists, reminders, Web development, CAD tools, 3D modelers, and so on, but something amazing has revealed, in the continuous (and chaotic) race towards the future, that project management has

received help from project management support packages. The offer is wide: they come in many flavors and some are more appealing to some clients (organizations) than to others. We will try to give a perspective of the present status of agile-focused project management tools or, to put it in the right way, tools that can be used to assist agile project management, and possibilities of their use in agile organizations, giving hints of alternate uses and warnings when risks are identified. In our search, we have recognized four flavors in which tools fit:

- Plan-based/traditional
- Wiki
- Web (2.0)
- Methodology-specific

As tools evolve and are fed with industry trends, new ideas, or customer feedback, they start to share some inspiration, leading ultimately to the fact that no tool can be allocated exclusively to one of these flavors, but the most influential one will represent its type. We will approach these tools with APM in mind, trying to relate their specific functions to components of APM.

Plan-based/Gantt Chart-Driven Software Tools

This is maybe the most overcrowded segment of consideration. There are many tools available, ranging from feature rich and quite expensive packages to free Gantt drawers. All these tools seem to have a strong bond to the traditional paradigm of project management, but some allow a degree of flexibility to adapt to the principles of APM.

Primavera Project Planner (Primavera) and MS Project (Microsoft) are the top of mind tools for many people, both are being used for a long time, and are the "de facto" standard for certain industries. Both tools are usually perceived as Gantt drawing tools, but they are feature rich and very helpful giving assistance to the project manager. For product and project envisioning, Primavera Project Planner offers embedded forums on which the envisioning can take place as text post. These posts are published inside the application and are visible for all project members. Another possibility is to put the envisioning documents shared and access them through the embedded file manager. MS Project allows shared documents using project server's collaboration abilities.

For the layered planning, both tools use the traditional planning, so it is possible to specify milestones for the releases and some referential tasks to give a view of the project as a whole. Due to the inherent volatility of the tasks to be performed on an iteration, its inclusion on these tools would result in task/resource administration overhead. A parallel tool to maintain the feature list, task list, and estimations would be recommended. It must be said that a XP (template/extension) is available for MS Project on the Microsoft Web site (http://www.microsoft.com). Both products have an issue manager (in the case of Project, using Project server's collaboration capabilities) that allows tracking issues that might rise during product development.

Some other tools that have the same focus but with different implementations are eGroupware and TUTOS, both Web based, both open source. Each of these collaborative tools have a project module in which tasks and milestones are added with explicit task precedence and assignment. It is able to form a Gantt chart from the data set. Again, changing the content to be developed on the iterations can be a painful experience, especially when page loading time matters.

Wiki

Wikis have radically transformed the collaborative documentation works as we know them; its simplicity of concept has allowed many different implementations on many languages and platforms. Some people are using wikis as a project documentation repository; others are integrating tools around wikis to enhance planning and collaboration capabilities. Inside this group, the numbers point to open source as the most common licensing method. Among the best qualified applications is Trac (Edgewall Software), a software development project management tool with configuration management capabilities. Trac consists on a wiki integrated to an issue tracker and a subversion repository viewer for configuration management.

During the life cycle of the project, the wiki functions will allow the product and project envisioning development and organization in a collaborative way. Using the tool configurations, it is possible to define expected releases for the product. For each planned release, the project members have the chance to link any issue (or requirement) to any release, in such a way that the project features are organized based on the release in which they are expected. The wiki pages can act as concentrators, allowing linking from documentation to issues, change sets, files, including past versions of the project files (stored in a subversion server). The issue tracker provides configurable reports to check the project status according to the defined tasks.

A very lightweight alternative is TiddlyWiki and its branches, particularly d3, an implementation of GTD (Getting Things Done) by David Allen. D3 is a stand-alone wiki with the advantage of having certain tiddlers (wiki pages) with special behaviors, like projects or tasks that can be tracked as pending or checked as completed. Each tiddler has tags that will give us another way to search for them. Although this is not an APM tool, the flexibility that modern wikis give can empower a tool to handle more complex tasks. In this case, for the early stages of the project, the wiki inherent features can be very useful for the envisioning and project setup. Each task resides in a context; for our use, each context will be a release. In that way, a release will have many tasks that fulfill it. Using the task review, it is possible to see a list of all tasks pending, associated to its particular release. In this case, we can use tags to assign the tasks to a particular team member. Any issue can be inserted into an issues context for its tracking.

Web

In the last year, the Internet community has seen the blooming of the Web 2.0 trend, the principles of which try to serve as a group of guidelines for Web applications towards a better user experience, where collaboration and social interactions are very strong concepts and tend to take applications out of the desk and onto the Net. Web 2.0 has brought some fresh air into project management tools, and some companies are actively working towards a better and more agile project management tool, and the results so far look promising.

Maybe the best example for this category comes with BaseCamp (37 signals), a Web application (service) for project management with an appealing user interface and simple but highly effective design. A BaseCamp project is a group of task lists, milestones, messages, and files. Its use for an APM project would be as follows: For envisioning, messages or files can contain the envisioning results that, in later phases, will become a major input for the planning; the release plan would consist of milestones marking approximate dates for each release; features are created in the form of task lists containing the actions to be performed in order to achieve the feature. Each feature can be assigned to a particular release, so it is possible to have a wide vision of the tasks needed to complete each release. This service was thought to handle many projects simultaneously and has access control features to give specific permissions to administrators, project members, and clients.

An open source clone is available under the name ProjectPier; it presents the same functionality of BaseCamp, with a less polished user interface. This tool can be installed into an organization's intranet (beating some of the fears that rise when one thinks of maintaining projects on the Web) and allows tagging for any element that is created. Although it is in active development, its available version has enough to carry a full project.

Stepping away from Web 2.0 and back to the traditional Web tools, another important referent is TargetProcess which can be used as a service or downloaded and installed in the organization's intranet. Its design denotes a profound knowledge of agile practices for project management and tries to cover the software life cycle in full. It has a user stories management module with mass import capabilities (from comma separated values files [CSV]), layered planning for releases and iterations, effort planning helpers, and team velocity estimation. It also includes per release burn-down charts based on the planning and daily status report. Additionally, it integrates its own bug tracking and test definition tools.

Methodology-Specific

Many of the APM tools available have a strong focus on a particular methodology. Among the more popular are Scrum and eXtreme Programming. In some cases, as we have seen in the past categories, we will notice mixtures of them. In this category, we discuss some tools with a scope limited to the methodology that may help to institutionalize their practices.

Wikiscrum is an open source wiki, adapted to support the Scrum project management methodology. Inside of a wiki page, the planned sprints are listed along the product backlog. Each sprint is clickable, leading to the task list for that sprint, having the opportunity to attach new tasks to it or to the product backlog, assigning the effort estimations for each task and the specific project member involved. One noticeable aspect of this tool is the charting capabilities included to show the burn-down chart for each sprint, based on the daily estimation variations for that sprint's tasks. These are very basic but enough to get a team on track.

IceScrum is a basic tool for Scrum that lacks advanced functionality like planning support or resource estimating but achieves good works on giving order to releases, sprints, features, and tasks. It has security management that allows the daily review of the project, based on the team information about tasks. It is currently on active development.

On the road of eXtreme Programming, Xplanner is an open source tool made to simplify the project management using eXtreme Programming. The early stages of the project are supported in the way of a user stories management module; these user stories can be assigned to each planned iteration and, from these iterations, can be linked the tasks to perform. Among other aspects, the integration queue can be highlighted as a specific help for the project team, along with its time tracking module with special support for the tracking of pairs, like in pair programming.

CONCLUSION

The application of agile principles and value will continue its expansion to other disciplines. The next step from the project management point of view is the use of agile practices in multiproject environments and even more important in portfolio management. The portfolio management discipline by nature have many similarities with the agile context: a close relationship with business goals, prioritizing opportunities and enhancing resource productivity. Application of concepts like time boxes is starting at the project portfolio level in some companies, and we can expect many other applications in the next years.

We told before about the polemic raised between supporters of agile and traditional methods. For us, much of that discussion was based on misunderstandings. Many times, misusing a method is far more harmful than not having any. This is true for traditional and agile methodology implementations. A misunderstanding on the traditional planning paradigm may lead to the belief that fine-grained (one or two hour's tasks initiating 10 months from today) schedule elaboration is appropriate. A misunderstanding of the agile paradigm may lead to not having any plans at all.

Also it has been said that agile and traditional paradigms have home grounds where their principles and practices are appropriate, but outside of that zone, they are no longer valid. We agree that there is not any single method that may be applied to every context: there are no silver bullets. However, we do not believe that home grounds are mutually exclusive. In today's environments, the characteristics are crossing those limits. In those environments, neither agile nor traditional methods are able on their own to provide the best solution. The most effective solution is obtained by taking the best the two worlds can offer for that specific context. We truly believe that organizations may benefit from knowing how to apply best practices for their process improvement initiatives no matter the origin or philosophy behind them.

REFERENCES

Beck, K. (2000). *Extreme programming explained: Embrace change*. Boston: Addison-Wesley.

Beck, K., Beedle, M., van Bennekum, A., Cockburn, A., Cunningham, W., & Fowler, M., et al. (2001). *Manifesto for agile software development*. Retrieved December 16, 2007, from http://www.agilemanifesto.org

CMMI Product Team. (2006). *CMMI for development* (version 1.2, CMMI-DEV v1.2, SEI Tech. Rep. No. 06.tr.008). Pittsburgh: Software Engineering Institute, Carnegie Mellon University.

Cockburn, A. (2005). *Crystal clear: A human powered methodology for small teams*. Pearson Education Inc.

Cohn, M. (2004). *User stories applied for agile software development*. Addison-Wesley.

Highsmith, J. (2004). *Agile project management: Creating innovative products*. Addison-Wesley.

Project Management Institute. (2004). *A guide to the project management body of knowledge* (3rd ed.).

Schwaber, K. (2004). *Agile project management with Scrum*. Microsoft Press.

Schwaber, K., & Beedle, M. (2002). *Agile software development with Scrum*. Upper Saddle River, NJ: Prentice Hall.

ENDNOTES

[1] The Chaos Report and Chaos Chronicles 1994, 1998, 2000, 2004, Standish Group (www.standishgroup.com)

[2] CMMI is a Service Mark of the Software Engineering Institute at the Carnegie Mellon University

[3] For more information on the APLN, please visit http://www.apln.org

[4] Time boxing is commented on later. Scrum suggests a full day planning for a 30 day iteration.

[5] This graphic, although common in agile sources, was adapted from the DSDM Consortium site (http://www.dsdm.org)

[6] We are using the CMMI-DEV version 1.2 as reference (CMMI Product Team, 2006)

[7] PMI and PMBOK are trademarks of the Project Management Institute in the United States and other countries

[8] The names of the companies are fictional

Chapter XI
COMPETISOFT:
An Improvement Strategy for Small Latin–American Software Organizations

Hanna Oktaba
Facultad de Ciencias, National Autonomous University of Mexico, Mexico

Francisco J. Pino
University of the Cauca, Colombia

Mario Piattini
Alarcos Research Group, University of Castilla-La Mancha, Spain

Félix García
Alarcos Research Group, University of Castilla-La Mancha, Spain

Claudia Alquicira
Ultrasist, Mexico

Francisco Ruiz
Alarcos Research Group, University of Castilla-La Mancha, Spain

Tomás Martínez
Alarcos Research Group, University of Castilla-La Mancha, Spain

ABSTRACT

From the beginning of the 21st century onwards, the software engineering community (industry and researchers) has expressed a special interest in software process improvement (SPI) for small and medium enterprises (SMEs). This growing interest is due to the fact that the software industry in most countries has an industrial backcloth, made up mainly of small and medium software organisations which favour the growth of their national economies. In order to fortify these kind of organisations, efficient strategies, practices, or guides to tailor SPI to their size and type of business are needed. Therefore, in this chapter, the COMPETISOFT project is presented. The COMPETISOFT project's main aim is to provide the software industry in Latin America with a reference framework for software process improvement and certification, which will enable it to be more competitive in the global market.

INTRODUCTION

From the beginning of the 21st century onwards, the software engineering community (industry and researchers) has expressed a special interest in software process improvement (SPI) for small and medium software enterprises (SMEs). This is evidenced by the growing number of articles that deal with the topic of SPI in SMEs which can be seen in the analysis of the trends in publications concerning this subject (e.g., Pino, Garcia, & Piattini, 2006) and also in the appearance of a great number of standards and proposals related to SPI for SMEs. It is important to emphasize the work of the Software Engineering Institute (SEI) and International Organization for Standardization (ISO) in order to that their standards can be applied in these types of organizations:

- The International Process Research Consortium (IPRC) from the SEI is carrying out a research initiative into process improvement in small settings as one of its high-priority topics. The term "small settings" includes small teams, small projects, small organizations, and small businesses.
- The ISO has formed the SC7-WG24 workgroup in order to develop software life-cycle profiles and guidelines for use in very small enterprises.

Interest in SPI in SMEs is growing due to the fact that these companies are an extremely important cog in the gears of the economy of many nations in the world. The software industry in most countries has an industrial backcloth, made up mainly of small software organisations which favour the growth of national economies. Such companies face serious problems as they reach maturity however, as in many cases there is no common software development process known to a given firm, which leads to chaotic performance affecting the whole organization (Batista & Figueiredo, 2000) and, obviously,

its products. This situation is especially critical in Latin America's incipient software industry, with its problems of lack of competitiveness and consequent limitations of growth (Mayer&Bunge, 2004). Therefore, in order to fortify this kind of organization, efficient strategies, practices, and/or guides to tailor software process improvement to their size and type of business are needed.

Currently, the COMPETISOFT project is being developed with the aim of providing Latin-American countries with a reference framework for the improvement and certification of their software processes which will help them to be more competitive in the global market. This project deals with the creation of the software reference process, assessment, and improvement models adapted to the characteristics of the software industry in Latin America, which is mainly composed of small-sized enterprises. The COMPETISOFT approach is based on models which have previously shown their practical usefulness, such as MoProSoft, EvalProSoft, and Agile SPI, among others.

In this chapter, the current convergence of efforts to improve the software industry in Latin American countries is reported in the context of the COMPETISOFT project. First, we summarize the related works, and then the COMPETISOFT project is presented with a description of its scope and characteristics. Finally, conclusions are drawn and future work is described.

RELATED WORKS

In literature, diverse proposals and initiatives are to be found that address the tailoring of assessment and improvement initiatives for the special characteristics and problems of small and medium-sized enterprises, for instance, related to:

- The process reference model. MoProSoft (Oktaba, 2006), MR-MPS (Weber, Araújo, Rocha, Machado, & Salviano, 2005), among others. With regard to SEI models, some representative tailoring proposals are reported in different studies (e.g., Batista & Figueiredo, 2000; Blowers& Richardson, 2006; Coleman, Larsen, Shaw, & Zelkowitz, 2005; Serrano, Montes de Oca, & Cedillo, 2006; among others).

- The process assessment method. Some methods adapted to ISO 15504 for SMEs are SPINI (an approach for SPI initiation) (Mäkinen, Varkoi, & Lepasaar, 2000), TOPS (Toward Organised Processes in SMEs) (Bucci, Campanai, & Cignoni, 2001), MARES (Anacleto, Wangenheim, Salviano, & Savi, 2004), and RAPID (Rapid Assessment for Process Improvement for Software Developed) (Rout, Tuffley, Cahill, & Hodgen, 2000), which are based on ISO/IEC 15504:1998. In this last proposal, developed by the Australian Software Quality Institute, the scope of the assessment is limited to eight key processes (requirements elicitation, software development, configuration management, quality assurance, problem resolution, project management, risk management, and process establishment), and the assessment model only includes questions relating to levels 1 to 3. The model was applied to 22 small Australian software development firms, 15 of which reported some improvements in their processes.

- The process improvement guide or model. PROCESSUS (Horvat, Rozman, & Györkös, 2000), MESOPyME (Calvo-Manzano, Cuevas, San Feliu, De Amescua, & Pérez, 2002), and IMPACT (Scott, Jeffery, Carvalho, D'Ambra, & Rutherford, 2001), among others.

With regard to Latin American initiatives, the following proposals deserve special attention:

- The MARES method (Método de Avaliação de Processo de Software) has been developed in Brazil. It is based on capability dimension from ISO/IEC 15504:2003, Part 5: An Exem-

plar Process Assessment Model: MARES, a set of guidelines for conducting 15504-conformant software process assessments, and focuses on small companies. MARES is not just another method but rather a set of well-structured guidelines for conducting 15504-conformant software process assessments in small companies. MARES provides guidance for identifying target process profiles and selecting high-priority processes to assess an organization on the basis of its business goals and model (concerning its product, revenue, services, and implementation strategies) as well as its process maturity and growth stage. It also adapts a growth pattern model to represent a small company's evolution from its existence (focusing on it becoming a viable business) to its survival (negotiating between expenses and sales income) to its success (growing in size and profitability).

- The MSP.BR project (Weber et al., 2005), another Brazilian initiative, is based on ISO/IEC 12207:2002, CMMI, and ISO/IEC 15504:2003, and comprises two models for the software improvement process: a reference model (MR mps) and a business model (MN mps). The maturity level is organised in two dimensions: capability and process, with process maturity divided into seven levels: optimized, managed quantitatively, defined, almost completely defined, partially defined, managed and partially managed. There are 21 process areas attributed to each maturity level based on the levels of CMMI. The aim is to ensure a gradual and fully appropriate implementation of the model in Brazilian SMEs.

- The SIMEP-SW ("An Integrated System for the Improvement of Software Development Processes") (Hurtado, Pino, & Vidal, 2006) is a proposal developed in Colombia. It integrates elements from improvement to capability, process, and assessment models, which are internationally recognized but tailored to the specific characteristics of Colombian SMEs. The main result of the SIMEP-SW Project is Agile SPI (Software Process Agile Improvement) (Hurtado et al., 2006), the main components of which are: (1) agile process: an agile process which guides the process improvement programme; (2) light quality model: a lightweight capability and assessment model of productive process; (3) framework PDS: a conceptual and technical element to support processes; and (4) light metrics quality model: a lightweight model of measurements for the productive process.

- The Mexican government promoted the MoProSoft project together with a corresponding method for process assessment, EvalProSoft (Oktaba, 2004) with the aim of providing the Mexican software industry with a model based on the best international practices whilst being easy to understand, simple to apply, and economical to adopt. It sought to assist organizations in standardizing their practices in the assessment of their effectiveness and in the integration of ongoing improvement. This model builds on the well-known practices of SW-CMM, ISO 9000:2000, PMBOK, and others and offers a new process structure, some new process documentation elements, a more precise process relationship, and an explicit process improvement mechanism. Trials of MoProSoft and EvalProSoft in four Mexican companies confirmed the suitability of the model for SMEs with low maturity levels, borne out by the improvements achieved and the low cost of process adoption. In August 2005, MoProSoft was approved as a Mexican standard NMX-059-NYCE-2005. In a Bangkok meeting in May 2006, the ISO/IEC JTC1 SC7 Working Group 24 decided to use the Mexican standard as a basis for the development of profiles and guidelines for very small enterprises (VSE).

THE COMPETISOFT APPROACH

In 2005, several researchers and practitioners from different Latin-American countries recognized the importance of an improvement and certification framework for SMEs and under the direction of Professors Hanna Oktaba and Mario Piattini suggested the COMPETISOFT project to CYTED (Programa Iberoamericano de Ciencia y Tecnología para el Desarrollo, Ibero-American Science and Technology Development Programme), which was created in 1984 for multilateral scientific and technological cooperation and is supported by 21 Latin-American countries plus Spain and Portugal. The CYTED program has the objective of contributing to the harmonious development of the Ibero-American region by establishing cooperation mechanisms between university research groups, research and development (R&D) institutes, and innovative companies in the countries involved, with a view to obtaining scientific and technological results transferable to productive systems and social politics.

The research method applied in the definition, refinement, and application of the COMPETISOFT model is action research (A-R), which is a collaborative research method merging theory and practice. A-R is focused on building new knowledge through the identification of solutions to real problems, which is achieved by the intervention of researchers in the real world of practitioners and by the results of this experience being equally beneficial to both groups. The application of A-R is based on continual feedback between the researchers and the companies involved. Figure 1 provides a summary of the A-R application.

The participants in the COMPETISOFT project could be grouped into two main categories:

- Researchers, from the following universities: National Autonomous University of Mexico, Mexico; New University of Lisbon, Portugal; University of São Paulo, Brazil; University of the Andes, Venezuela; Federico Santamaría

University, Chile; National University of Comahue, Argentina; University of Castilla-La Mancha, Spain; International SEK-ICAPI University, Ecuador; University of the Cauca and EAFIT Colombia; University of Information Technology, Cuba; Institute of Technology, Costa Rica; National University of La Matanza, Argentina; Catholic University of the Maule, Chile; University of the Republic, Uruguay; and Pontifical Catholic University, Peru.

• Critical Reference Group: a representative group of the problem to be solved which participates in the research process, although less actively than the researchers themselves. In the COMPETISOFT project this reference group is composed of three main types of organizations: a national standards body, the Argentinian IRAM (Argentinian Institute for the Standardization and Certification); a government body, the Government of the Neuquén region in Argentina and SMEs such

as the Spanish firms Enxenio and Technical Systems of the Spanish Lottery, Ultrasist of Mexico, MV Systems of Ecuador, and Parquesoft Popayán of Colombia.

To develop the COMPETISOFT project, we studied different Latin-American initiatives such as MoProSoft, MPS.BR, and Agile SPI. The Spanish methodology METRICA v3, which is promoted by the Spanish Ministry of Public Administration, was also considered, as it too seeks to achieve the improvement of software processes and products. A general overview of COMPETISOFT is given in Figure 2.

As Figure 2 shows, we developed COMPETISOFT by borrowing heavily from well-known process reference models intended for small companies, especially MoProSoft. In fact, COMPETISOFT can be conceived as an evolution of the MoProSoft model with all the experience in software process development and improvement gained by researchers and practitioners during

Figure 1. Action-Research application to the COMPETISOFT project

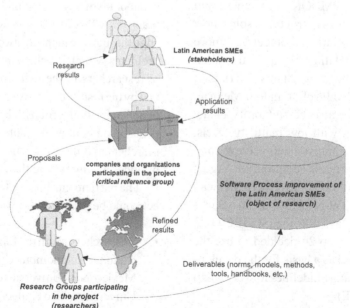

the COMPETISOFT project. The main objective is to develop the new process reference and evaluation model, which enhances MoProSoft and EvalProSoft, and a new process improvement model based on Agile SPI.

The processes of the three models are documented by means of a process pattern with the aim to be more intuitive and easy to use by SMEs. Figure 3 shows the metamodel on which the process pattern is based.

THE COMPETISOFT PROCESS REFERENCE MODEL

The COMPETISOFT process reference model is based on MoProSoft. The processes are organized in three categories: top management, management, and operation. Its purpose is to provide specialized processes for each functional group of the software development enterprise. Figure 4 presents the MoProSoft category and process structure in the form of a unified modeling language (UML) package diagram.

The proposed COMPETISOFT Process Reference Model improvements and refinements are the following:

- **Business management process:** We need to include virtual enterprise management and intercompany connectivity. Nowadays, these are increasingly important topics for companies participating in clusters or virtual nets, and key requirements to guarantee the survival of SMEs in today's marketplace.
- **Process management process:** We need to improve quality assurance and internal and external assessments. We have developed a self-assessment questionnaire that could help SMEs in their first contact with the assessment and improvement of their process maturity.
- **Project management process:** We have to include a set of measures and indicators for different maturity levels. Another critical point to be tackled here is the improvement of estimation techniques, a fundamental need of SMEs but one that is difficult to understand and apply in these settings.
- **Resource management processes:** We need to emphasize the importance of reusability by means of the development of a knowledge base to be populated with experiences structured according to the processes in the process reference model. To this end, other similar experiences, as reported in Kurniawati and

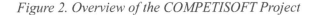

Figure 2. Overview of the COMPETISOFT Project

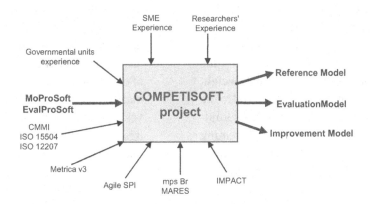

Figure 3. COMPETISOFT process pattern

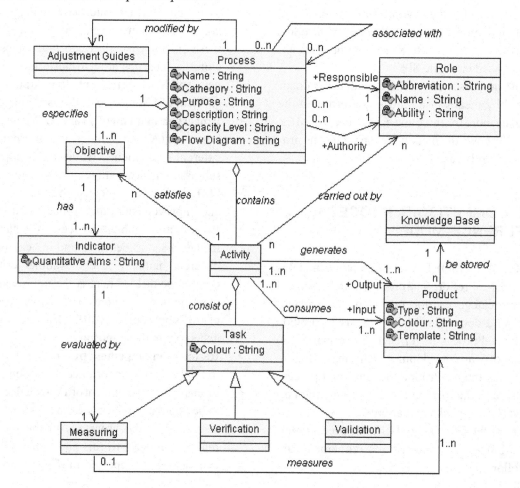

Jeffery (2006), will be considered. Indeed, COMPETISOFT gives great importance to the experience base from the outset and at all organizational levels, regardless of the quality of the components stored in that base, as they may all be useful. We also recognize the value of a more formal yet still lightweight method of experience elicitation suited to the use of a small organization, providing guidance and structure to assist users in creating more experiences for the base. Other important issues to address are documentation and configuration management.

- **Development and maintenance process:** We consider it very important to separate this process into two parts. The nature and characteristics of development and maintenance are very different, and many of the techniques, tools, methodologies, and so forth, of development are not directly applicable to maintenance. Indeed, many SMEs have to develop pure software maintenance projects, so it is very important for them to apply specific maintenance methodologies. In this respect, the COMPETISOFT approach will adapt the MANTEMA maintenance methodology

Figure 4. MoProSoft Process categories and process names.

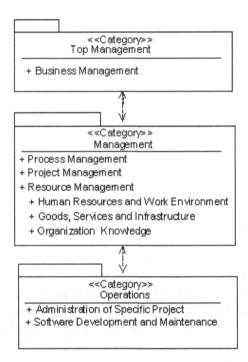

(Polo, Piattini, & Ruiz, 2002) to the special characteristics of SMEs.

Besides the improvements proposed for specific processes, two aspects common to all processes will be the incorporation of free and open-source tools, a key element for SMEs to reduce costs, and the development of specific techniques for the improvement of software usability.

THE COMPETISOFT EVALUATION MODEL

The COMPETISOFT evaluation model is based on the EvalProSoft which fulfills the standard ISO/IEC 15504:2004. Figure 5 presents the EvalProSoft structure.

The proposed COMPETISOFT assessment model improvements and refinements are the following:

- **Measures:** We need to define a set of measures to evaluate the performance and capability of software processes. The aim is to help SMEs carry out their own internal assessments by reducing subjectivity and making the process more formal. The measures are grouped into two main types:
  - ○ The "capability measure" to evaluate process capability (from level 1 to 5) on the basis of the process attribute's indicators (PAIs) from ISO/IEC 15504-5:2006 (E).
  - ○ The "performance measure," based on some of the elements defined in MoProSoft, to evaluate process performance.
- **Instruments:** We need to build the collection of instruments to support the measurement process related to the measures proposed. There must be an instrument for each attribute of the capability dimension and for all the MoProSoft processes in the process dimension.
- **Tools:** We need to develop a software tool to support the application of process performance and capability evaluation instruments.

THE COMPETISOFT IMPROVEMENT MODEL

The COMPETISOFT improvement model is based on Agile SPI (Hurtado et al., 2006). Its purpose is to provide a guide for the carrying out a programme of software process improvement in small and medium companies. The aim is to provide SMEs with a software improvement framework that uses the process reference and evaluation models previously described and, furthermore, to provide improvement infrastructure, techniques, and tools to support improvement programs.

This model integrates some basics of the agile paradigm, and the IDEAL® (McFeeley,

Figure 5. COMPETISOFT Evaluation Model

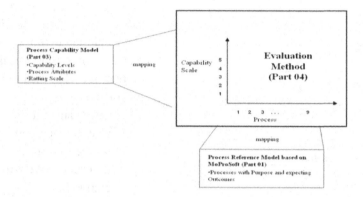

1996) model has also been considered for its development. The improvement process life cycle is highly influenced by the iterative and incremental approaches of many methodologies such as rational unified process (RUP), extreme programming (XP), Scrum, and so forth. As improvement projects usually cover many requirements and affect the whole organisation, some characteristics of these proposals have been adapted to build a complete improvement model which is agile, less bureaucratic, and is sensitive to management activities (meetings, documentation, infrastructure, etc.).

The model defines an iterative and incremental process consisting of five phases: (1) installation, (2) diagnosis, (3) formulation, (4) improvement, and (5) programme review. Furthermore, it includes a set of disciplines which can be applied in the different phases: (1) training, (2) SPI management, (3) evaluation, (4) result analysis, (5) design, (6) implementation, (7) process configuration management, and (8) learning. By discovering the disciplines that can be used in each phase, the people involved in SPI will always know how to proceed. Moreover, the model is based on improvement cases as it allows companies to create mini-improvement programmes in the context of an overall improvement programme in order to obtain fast results. Improvement cases are atomic

improvement units of the processes selected to be improved. Fast results will allow the visualization of improvements from the early phases in the improvement project, with the consequent motivation of the SPI staff. This mitigates possible risks from the beginning and allows personnel to focus their efforts more on the most important business areas for the company.

This model is currently being applied in some small software development companies in Spain and Colombia. The feedback and experience obtained by researchers and practitioners with the application of improvement programmes during the COMPETISOFT project will be used to refine and improve the SPI model.

CONCLUDING REMARKS AND FUTURE WORK

In this chapter, the COMPETISOFT project has been presented, which constitutes a binding force of different SPI proposals with the aim to increase the competitivity of SMEs in Latin America by means of a methodological framework suited to their special characteristics. This framework establishes the necessary elements to guide SPI initiatives in SMEs in an economical way, that is, in a short period of time with few resources.

The methodological framework is composed of three models: a process reference model which describes good practices for the development of software, an evaluation model in order to perform an assessment that allows generating a quantitative score which characterizes the process capability, and an model for guiding process improvement that will provide guidelines for the carrying out of improvements inside of processes of the organization.

One of the strategies of the COMPETISOFT project has been the analysis of existing offers which have demonstrated success in SMEs. Thus, COMPETISOFT is highly influenced by proposals such as MoProSoft, EvalProSoft, and Agile SPI. It is important to highlight that the framework proposed will reach a much higher level than if countries develop frameworks individually, and this will contribute to their integration and lead to the creation of a Latin-American software engineering community with good scientific standing. As future work, the COMPETISOFT framework will be refined and improved on the basis of feedback and lessons learned with the current application of the process reference, evaluation, and improvement models in the different companies involved in the project.

ACKNOWLEDGMENT

This work has been developed inside the projects: "Process Improvement for Promoting Ibero-American Software Small and Medium Enterprises Competitiveness – COMPETISOFT" (506AC287) financed by CYTED (Programa Iberoamericano de Ciencia y Tecnología para el Desarrollo), MECENAS" (PBI06-0024) granted by the "Junta de Comunidades de Castilla-La Mancha" of Spain and ESFINGE (TIN2006-15175-C05-05) financed by Dirección General de Investigación of the Ministerio de Educación y Ciencia of Spain.

REFERENCES

Anacleto, A., Wangenheim, C. G. v., Salviano, C. F., & Savi, R. (2004). A method for process assessment in small software companies. In Proceedings of the 4th International SPICE Conference on Process Assessment and Improvement (SPICE 04), Portugal (pp. 69-76).

Batista, J., & Figueiredo, A. (2000, December). SPI in a very small team: A case with CMM. Software Process: Improvement and Practice, 5(4), 243-250.

Blowers, R., & Richardson, I. (2006). The capability maturity model (SW and integrated) tailored in small indigenous software industries. In Proceedings of the 1st International Research Workshop for Process Improvement in Small Settings, Pittsburgh, Carnegie Mellon University (pp. 175-181).

Bucci, G., Campanai, M., & Cignoni, G. A. (2001). Rapid assessment to solicit process improvement in SMEs. Software Quality Professional, 4(1), 33-41.

Calvo-Manzano, J. A., Cuevas, G., San Feliu, T., De Amescua, A., & Pérez, M. (2002, November). Experiences in the application of software process improvement in SMES. Software Quality Journal, 10(3), 261-273.

Coleman, K., Larsen, P., Shaw, M., & Zelkowitz, M. (2005, November). Software process improvement in small organizations: A case study. IEEE Software, pp. 68-75.

Horvat, R. V., Rozman, I., & Györkös, J. (2000, March). Managing the complexity of SPI in small companies. Software Process: Improvement and Practice, 5(1), 45-54.

Hurtado, J., Pino, F., & Vidal, J. (2006). Software process improvement integral model: Agile SPI (Tech. Rep. No. SIMEP-SW-O&A-RT-6-V1.0).

Popayán, Colombia, Universidad del Cauca-Colciencias.

Kurniawati, F., & Jeffery, R. (2006). The use and effects of an electronic process guide and experience repository: A longitudinal study. Information and Software Technology, 48(7), 566-577.

Mäkinen, T., Varkoi, T., & Lepasaar, M. (2000). A detailed process assessment method for software SMEs. In Proceedings of the 7th European Software Process Improvement Conference (EuroSPI 2000)(pp. 1.14-1.26). Copenhagen, Denmark.

Mayer, & Bunge. (2004). *Panorama de la Industria del Software en Latinoamérica* (p. 97). Brasil: Informática LTDA.

McFeeley, R. (1996). IDEAL: A users guide for software process improvement (Handbook CMU/SEI-96-HB-001). Pittsburgh: Software Engineering Institute, Carnegie Mellon University. Retrieved January 1, 2008, from http://www.sei.cmu.edu/publications/documents/96.reports/96.hb.001.html

Oktaba, H. (2004, March). Método de Evaluación de procesos para la industria de software - EvalProSoft (Versión 1.1, NMX-I-006/(01 al 04)-NYCE-2004). México City: Organismo Nacional de Normalización y Evaluación de la Conformidad (NYCE). Retrieved January 1, 2008, from http://www.normalizacion-nyce.org.mx/php/loader.php?c=interes.php&tema=21

Oktaba, H. (2006). MoProSoft®: A software process model for small enterprises. In Proceedings of the 1st International Research Workshop for Process Improvement in Small Settings, Pittsburgh, Carnegie Mellon University (pp. 93-101).

Pino, F., Garcia, F., & Piattini, M. (2006, April). Revisión sistemática de mejora de procesos software en micro, pequeñas y medianas empresas. Revista Española de Innovación, Calidad e Ingeniería del Software (REICIS), 2(1), 6-23.

Polo, M., Piattini, M., & Ruiz, F. (2002, November). Using a qualitative research method for building a software maintenance methodology. Software Practice and Experience, 32(13), 1239-1260.

Rout, T., Tuffley, A., Cahill, B., & Hodgen, B. (2000). The RAPID assessment of software process capability. In Proceedings of the 1st International Conference on Software Process Improvement and Capability Determination (pp. 47-56).

Scott, L., Jeffery, R., Carvalho, L., D'Ambra, J., & Rutherford, P. (2001). Practical software process improvement: The IMPACT Project. In Proceedings of the Australian Software Engineering Conference (pp. 182-189).

Serrano, M., Montes de Oca, C., & Cedillo, K. (2006). An experience on implementing the CMMI in a small organization using the team software process. In Proceedings of the 1st International Research Workshop for Process Improvement in Small Settings, Pittsburgh, Carnegie Mellon University (pp. 81-92).

Weber, K., Araújo, E., Rocha, A., Machado, S. D., & Salviano, C. (2005). Brazilian software process reference model and assessment method. Computer and Information Sciences, 3733, 402-411. Berlin/Heidelberg: Springer.

Chapter XII
SPI Long–Term Benefits:
Case Studies of Five Small Firms

Aileen Cater-Steel
University of Southern Queensland, Australia

Terry Rout
Griffith University, Australia

ABSTRACT

The contribution of small enterprises to the software industry is marked, but the level of understanding of the ways in which they can survive, grow, and improve is limited. In particular, there has been a lack of information on the long-term outcomes of process improvement initiatives in small firms. Building on the basis of a study of assessment-based improvement in 23 small and medium size organizations, we have undertaken a follow-up meeting with each company approximately five years following the original assessment. The results show that changes made in an organisation, driven by a framework of model-based improvement, can have long-term impacts even in small organisations; it appears, however, that there is no necessary link between success in implementing improvement and survival of the organisation. The results provide insight into the extent to which improvement actions can reinforce overall success for the small business.

INTRODUCTION

Faced with an enormous choice of methods, tools, and techniques, software development managers need evidence that their investment in new practices will produce benefits (Fenton, Pfleeger, & Glass, 1994; Wood, Daly, Miller, & Roper, 1999).

Unfortunately, many approaches are adopted 'based on anecdotes, gut feelings, expert opinion and flawed research, not on careful, rigorous software engineering experimentation' (Fenton et al., 1994, p. 87). Therefore, researchers are urged to undertake evaluative research involving realistic projects with sufficient rigour to ensure that any benefits identified are clearly derived from the concept in question (Fenton et al., 1994). Although past studies have indicated factors which inhibit adoption of software process improvement (SPI), empirical research on SPI in small firms is largely lacking. Recently, research into capability maturity model integration (CMMI) adoption by small units in large companies has been undertaken (Garcia, Graettinger, & Kost, 2005), but there are fundamental differences between small software firms (i.e., where the owner is an operator) and small enterprises (which may be a small unit in a much larger business). Consequently, there is insufficient knowledge about which innovations are effective and which factors influence their adoption. It is vital to understand the processes currently used and to evaluate the effectiveness of process improvement programs, or investments in SPI are wasted (Mustonen-Ollila & Lyytinen, 2003). This research provides evidence of the long-term outcomes of software process innovation in five small software development firms.

A retrospective review of participants in a SPICE-based process improvement program considered the long-term impact of the program on five small firms. After establishing the need to evaluate the long-term effects in small firms, this chapter presents a detailed account of the experiences of five small firms. Recently, retrospective reviews of the SPI outcomes were held with five of the firms that participated in the Rapid Assessment for Process Improvement for software Development (RAPID) program. After describing the methodology, this report considers the long-term impact of the RAPID program on five small firms five years since it was conducted. For each firm, changes in the business are summarised, then the major outcomes of the program, as reported at the follow-up meetings are reviewed to determine progress subsequent to the follow-up meetings. The firms are then compared and contrasted, and conclusions are presented.

PROCESS IMPROVEMENT IN SMALL ENTERPRISES

Recent research has raised doubts about whether traditional SPI models (assessment based) are appropriate for small software development organisations. This study is a response to demands for more research to evaluate the long-term effectiveness of assessment-based SPI programs within small development firms (Brodman & Johnson, 1997; Kautz, 1998).

Significant benefits have been shown to derive from process improvement programs, both in software and systems engineering (Gibson, Goldenson, & Kost, 2006) and in conventional manufacturing (Repenning & Sterman, 2001). Long-term studies in manufacturing organisations have identified problems and issues in maintaining improvement initiatives over long periods; a variety of issues have been identified, including the 'Improvement Paradox': significant improvements in productivity may lead to production outstripping market demand, with consequent adverse impacts on the firm's survival. The previous studies we have identified relate almost entirely to large organisations and predominantly outside the software domain. There have been few reports on the long-term benefits that may have been derived from improvement initiatives in the domain of systems and software engineering (Fenton et al., 1994). In particular, few if any long-term studies on the impact of improvement initiatives in small enterprises have been reported.

Recently, plans were announced for the conduct of follow-up studies on participants in the SPIRE Project (SPIRE, 1998) in Europe. The approach we have taken in our retrospective analysis is quite different from that proposed in the Irish study (Sanders & Richardson, 2005b), and in the longer term a comparison of the findings from the two studies will be of value. This work answers the call to evaluate the implementation of a culture of improvement in organisations which took part in improvement programs long enough ago to call these long-term benefits, in particular in small firms, a part of the software community for which few statistics exist (Sanders & Richardson, 2005a).

Small Firms are Different

As early as 1992, Johnson and Brodman reported that the cost of CMM implementation was prohibitive for small firms. They summarised problems experienced by 200 small businesses throughout the U.S. in using the capability maturity model (CMM): 'documentation overload; unrelated management structure; inapplicable scope of reviews; high resource requirements; high training costs; lack of needed guidance; unrelated practices' (Brodman & Johnson, 1997, p. 661). This view of SPI methodologies being beyond the reach of small companies has been echoed since by many researchers (Bucci, Campanai, & Cignoni, 2001; Grunbacher, 1997; Kautz, 1998; Larsen & Kautz, 1997; Pfleeger, Jeffery, Curtis, & Kitchenham, 1997; Pringle, 2001; Richardson & Ryan, 2001; Wilkie, McFall, & McCaffery, 2004; Working Group 24, 2006). Furthermore, Fayad and Laitinen (2000) question whether the traditional SPI models, based on the U.S. defense scenario of large bespoke projects, are appropriate for today's smaller, newly founded software development firms which are aiming at the software package mass market. Organisational behaviour and management literature establishes that small organisations are different from larger organisations in terms of formalisation, centralisation, complexity, and personnel ratios (Daft, 1998). Furthermore, research has highlighted other characteristics of small firms compared to large firms:

- Small organisations have a flat structure and are managed by their owners in an organic, free-flowing, personalised management

style that encourages entrepreneurship and innovation, less formalised decision-making structures and procedures, and more freedom for employees to depart from the rules (Attewell & Rule, 1991; Daft, 1998; Johns, Dunlop, & Sheehan, 1989; O'Regan & Ghobadian, 2004).

- Uncertainty, evolution, and innovation play a greater role in small firms (Storey, 1994).
- All the critical management decisions such as finance, accounting, personnel, purchasing, processing or servicing, marketing and selling are made by one or two persons, without the aid of internal specialists, and with specific knowledge in one or two functional areas (Johns et al., 1989).
- Small firms are averse to consultants and reluctant to seek external help (Cragg, 2002, p. 277).
- The personal involvement of employees in small firms encourages motivation and commitment because the employees identify with the company's mission (Daft, 1998).
- Small organisations have the advantage of being responsive and flexible (Daft, 1998; Grover & Teng, 1992; King, 1996).
- Compared to larger firms, small firms neglect training (Voss, Blackmon, Cagliano, Hanson, & Wilson, 1998).
- In small firms, much of the work is coordinated through direct supervision and mutual adjustment (Mintzberg, 1983).
- Small firms have faster employment growth rates and generate more new jobs than giant ones (Attewell & Rule, 1991).

The differences between small and large software engineering organisations were highlighted in recent research by Laporte, April, and Renault (2006) who found the priorities and concerns for firms with more than 20 employees differed greatly from small firms. Therefore, small firms should not be considered to be scaled down versions of large firms (Richardson, 2002; Storey, 1994), and it is clear that process improvement models, such as the SW-CMM, which were developed for large software contractor firms, may not be appropriate for small firms. Much of the IT research to date is biased towards large corporations (Attewell & Rule, 1991) and does not take into account issues relating to small organisations.

BACKGROUND TO THE RETROSPECTIVE

In 1999-2000, 22 small software development firms participated in a software process improvement program sponsored by Software Engineering Australia (SEA) of Queensland, Australia. The programme was designed to address many of the factors that had been claimed to adversely affect the adoption of assessment-based improvement by small enterprises. Process assessment is typically seen as requiring intensive use of resources. Wiegers and Sturzenberger (2000) point out that many organizations have developed small-scale assessment approaches to support improvement projects in between full scale assessments, and a similar strategy is described by Natwick, Draper, and Bearden (1999). The SPIRE Project (SPIRE, 1998) highlighted the importance of assessment in improvement projects for small and medium size enterprises and correctly identifies the need for a specific approach to such assessment. The approach they select, however, while adequately diagnostic, does not claim to be conformant with the international standard, and the results are seen as applicable within the organization, with only limited applicability of comparisons such as benchmarking. A key issue for many small and medium size companies is the ability to obtain meaningful and reliable evaluations of capability with limited investment of time and resources. The Rapid Assessment for Process Improvement for software Development (RAPID) was developed to address this need. The RAPID method was purely designed for process improvement

and is not intended to be adopted for supplier management.

RAPID defines an approach to assessment that delivers consistent evaluations of process capability based upon an intensive investigation of the operations of the organisation. The approach is based upon the following principles. The assessment is conducted within a one-day time frame to minimise the cost and investment of time and resources required by small to medium sized companies.

The assessment is based upon an assessment model of limited scope, with a standard set of eight processes (drawn from ISO/IEC TR 15504-5, 1998):

- Requirements elicitation
- Software development
- Configuration management
- Quality assurance
- Problem resolution
- Project management
- Risk management
- Process establishment.

The high-level software development process (ENG.1) is assessed as a whole without disaggregation into its component processes. The competence and experience of the assessors is seen as of primary importance. A team of two assessors with experience in performing full-bodied assessments based upon ISO 15504 is used for a RAPID assessment. Competency is focused on assessors who have completed training as ISO/IEC 15504 assessors, with formal education relevant to the field of software engineering, and experience in the performance and management of software development.

Data collection is limited to the single technique of moderated discussion by performers of the processes—the management team and other members of the organisation. The generation of ratings of capability is performed by a process of consensus-gathering involving all of the participants in the discussion, rather than by judgement of the assessors. Restricting the assessment to one day rather than a more intense three-to-four day assessment, enables small organisations to participate in a process capability assessment. Most organisations are willing to invest a day of their time and resources without feeling the impact of the assessment on their commitments. It also allows the cost of the assessment to be constrained.

RAPID was developed specifically for small organisations; however, it has been successfully performed in larger organisations, and it seems that it has strong potential for performance of snapshot assessments on projects within the larger organisation. By restricting and fixing the scope of the assessment to the eight processes, it is possible to quickly provide benchmarking information for organisations assessed using RAPID. The RAPID process improvement initiative provided each firm with a one-day on-site process assessment; then about 10 months later, a follow-up meeting was held to determine the extent to which the assessment recommendations had been implemented (Rout, Tuffley, Cahill, & Hodgen, 2000). At the follow-up meetings, many of the firms expressed the view that the RAPID assessment had provided an accurate profile of their strengths and weaknesses, and also realistic and worthwhile recommendations. However, for many, the recently defined processes were too new to be adequately assessed at the time of the follow-up meeting. Detailed outcomes from the RAPID initiative have been previously reported by Cater-Steel, Toleman, and Rout (2006).

Data Collection: Retrospective Interviews

To conduct the retrospective interviews, a questionnaire was developed to ensure that the data would be collected in a standard format to enable collation and comparisons. The first part of the questionnaire contained general questions about the performance of the firm since the assessment, the impact of the RAPID program on the firm, and the sponsors' perceptions about the value of SPI. The second part of the questionnaire contained specific questions for each firm based on the prioritised actions from the initial assessment report and the review of these actions at the follow-up meeting.

Each retrospective interview was conducted face-to-face between one of the authors and one representative from each firm with a duration of 30 minutes to 1 hour. Each interview was transcribed from audio recording and validated with the respondent. Figure 1 presents a timeline illustrating the participation of each of the five firms in the three stages of this study.

For competitive reasons, the firms wish to remain anonymous, but are probably typical of many of the myriad of small software development firms in Queensland. In this chapter, the firms are referred to as Firm A to Firm E. The basic characteristics of the five firms at the time of the initial study are summarised in Table 1.

Between January 2005 and May 2006, five retrospective face-to-face interviews were conducted between one of the authors and one representative from each firm. These are their stories.

Figure 1. Timeline of initial assessments, follow-up meetings, and retrospective interviews

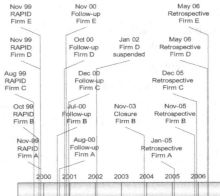

Table 1. Capability levels and outcomes at follow-up meetings

Firm	Staff FTE	Year Founded	RE	SD	CM	QA	PR	PM	RM	PE	Outcome at Follow-up Meeting (12 months)
A	10	1984	1	1	1	0	0	0	0	0	Lost key staff. GST big impact
B	10.5	1992	3	2↑	1↑	2	1	2	0↑	1↑	Improved 4 processes a total of 4 levels
C	16	1990	2	1	1	1	1	1	0	0	Adopted new methodology. Too new to assess
D	3.5	1994	1	1	2	0	1	1	1	0	Disrupted by break-in at premises. Reduced operation.
E	3.5	1985	2	1	1	1	0	1	0	2	Some changes implemented

Note: Staff full-time equivalent (FTE) and capability levels are as at initial assessment and arrows indicate increase in level of capability.

CASE A

Firm A has been in business for about 20 years and develops a software package for the agricultural sector. It does not undertake custom development. In November 1999, when the initial assessment was conducted, the firm employed 10 full-time staff and was enjoying a sales growth phase due to the introduction of the Australian Government's Goods and Services Taxation legislation (GST). By the time of the follow-up meeting in August 2000, the number of staff employed almost doubled, but subsequently—at the retrospective interview—dropped back to the same level as at the time of the assessment. The retrospective interview was conducted in January 2005 with one of the firms' software developers. The respondent had commenced employment at Firm A subsequent to the follow-up meeting and was unable to answer many of the questions directly related to the RAPID program. Since the initial assessment the firm had coped with major staff changes: at least three key developers had left the firm.

At the initial assessment in November 1999, the project management planning process existed for the major releases of the product, but activities to achieve the plans were only tracked informally. The first step to improve the project management process involved the use of MS Outlook to record the staff assignment of tasks related to six projects. At the time of the follow-up meeting in August 2000, actual effort was not being recorded. At present, the firm is finding MS Project useful for managing projects and actual effort is being recorded. The firm recognises that the hours recorded are not entirely accurate as the developers are often interrupted to perform technical support tasks when they are scheduled to work on new projects or enhancements for the new release of the core product.

In 1999, the firm was in the process of developing a help-desk system to manage client registration, despatches, and to record problem reports. This system was successfully implemented by the time of the follow-up meeting, but it was intended to further develop the system to track problem reports through to their resolution in new versions or releases. Due to the loss of senior staff and the need to focus resources on products for sale, rather than for internal use, no further development was undertaken on the in-house developed system. A more workable solution was found by implementing a problem tracking system called Mantis—an open source Web-based bug tracking system to track issues raised, issues with existing products, feature requests from clients, and the status of the fixes in relation to the firm's development schedule. Due to the small number of developers involved and effective personal communication, there is no need to have a formal interface from Mantis to the help-desk system.

The firm has also added a component to development projects to assist in troubleshooting. EurekaLog is integrated with Delphi's IDE and builds applications with the capability to intercept every exception and trace a detailed log from the start of the application to the point where an exception was raised. The client is prompted to send an e-mail with the problem report to the support team, where the problem can be identified and quickly resolved. At the initial assessment, a coherent process was found to be in place for configuration management, and it has continued to improve since the follow-up meeting. The firm experienced some problems with MS Visual SourceSafe and tried FreeVCS for a time because it behaved more seamlessly in a Dephi environment. One identified improvement since the follow-up meeting is that all the help files, release documents, and technical support documents are now under version control with SourceSafe.

The need for a more formalised testing process was identified as a major issue at the initial assessment and treated as a high priority in the recommendations. The firm employed a tester to develop test cases and record test logs in a MS Access database, but this person was gradually diverted to a technical support role and has since left the firm. Rational Robot (test automation tool) was implemented for regression testing and as a first step towards using the Rational Rose suite.

Staff attended Rational Robot training in Sydney, and a test suite was developed for the core product. After this, the firm decided to develop a new version of the core product to provide a new 'look and feel,' using components to give themes capability to the product. When themes were added, every single form in the project had changed its reference. Consequently, the regression tests no longer functioned, as the objects sought were no longer referenced in the same way. After adding the themes capability, the developers also found some problems with Rational Robot not correctly recognising the state of some of the properties, causing more time to be spent in investigating incorrect test results. Management decided it was not worth the cost to build a new suite of regression tests in Rational Robot, and the ongoing costs to maintain a licence for the product were not justified and so the firm discontinued its use.

At the time of the retrospective interview, testing is still considered to be an area where improvements could be made but market and financial concerns and lack of resources make it infeasible to address at this time. Internal testing is performed to the extent resources allow, and key clients are successfully involved in Beta testing. It was stated at the follow-up meeting that Visio would be used to ensure that documentation of the software modules was available to the new staff. This did not eventuate, but reverse engineering was tried to extract unified modeling language (UML) from the program code. Unfortunately, this attempt was abandoned as the documents produced were unreadable.

As well as improvements resulting from the assessment, other processes have changed with the firm adopting a more agile approach to development. This change in methodology came about as a direct result of the interest of a new staff member. Now there is less documentation done at the start of each project, and the development is done in shorter cycles. The firm has found many advantages from this approach: the managers can see the product as it is developed; they can provide more input as they are not working from abstract specifications and designs; they are able to respond to market pressures, and can tailor the features to be included in response to the market. The firm has adopted a virtual machine environment using VMWare. This allows preservation of the total build environment, a consistent hardware environment for development, the ability to test new development components, and restoration of the development environment in the case of hardware failure to a development machine.

CASE B

Firm B was founded in 1992 to commercialise an information systems development methodology developed by the owner/manager. Its principal business was the delivery of professional services to the government and semigovernment sector; most projects involve database solutions, with an emphasis on Ingres applications. Firm B also developed several software products, all specialised tools supporting Ingres development and maintenance; these were marketed to a limited degree. Firm B showed strong growth and employed 10 full-time staff and one contractor at the time of the initial assessment. Most projects were 12 to 18 months duration. Firm B's quality management system (QMS) was based upon ISO 9001 and it was central to the company's operations.

The initial RAPID assessment was performed in October 1999 and revealed that Firm B had a remarkably mature process for a small business. The principal business of the organisation focused around a well-defined process, based upon the firm's methodology and quality manual. There was excellent control of initial project requirements, and changes over the course of a project were well handled, though on an individual project basis. Firm B effectively addressed financial risks through undertaking work on a 'time and materials' basis. Project management was limited in scope but effective.

As a result of relatively rapid growth in the years prior to the assessment, Firm B faced problems in ensuring consistent application of its defined process across the life cycle. Many of its approaches to project management, while appropriate to its current environment, were limited in their use in less well-controlled environments. There was a need for a thorough review of the quality management system, to ensure that it retained its usefulness in a changing business environment. Firm B also needed to take more advantage of its strengths by developing effective measures for monitoring performance in terms of both productivity and product quality.

The follow-up meeting was held July 2000 and established that the changes implemented by Firm B impacted the capability of four of the target processes: software development; configuration management; risk management; and process establishment (as shown in Table 1). Many of the changes were too new to have impact at the time of the follow-up meeting. However, the configuration management tool and error-tracking software had made it easier to manage multiple developer projects, and testing had been enhanced in terms of efficiency and quality.

At the follow-up meeting, Firm B considered the assessment provided valuable motivation to review and improve the software development process. The assessment provided the impetus to make available resources to address the action items from the assessment report. Staff at Firm B also considered the assessment results to have provided evidence of their software process capability and therefore provided competitive advantage in formal tenders. Finally, the strengths highlighted in the assessment report improved the morale of the team by providing positive feedback about the value of process improvement. Firm B was convinced the improvement actions resulting from the assessment would return great value in the future by ensuring it was better placed to bid for large projects.

Towards the end of 2003, although Firm B was performing well, the owner/manager decided he no longer wished to continue with the business. He became bored after 12 years in the same role and felt he needed a new challenge. As efforts to sell the firm did not produce a buyer, he closed the doors in November 2003. The owner/manager assisted staff to find alternative employment and is now employed in a senior IT position in a large organisation.

The retrospective interview was held in November 2005 and focused on the 3.5-year time period from the follow-up meeting in mid-2000 to the closure of the firm in November 2003. During this time, Firm B continued to develop in terms of earnings. Although post-Y2K was a difficult period, Firm B maintained its position in the market releasing new products at the start of 2003. All the RAPID recommendations were implemented and impacted to a limited extent on the business processes and methods and in a positive way on the financial results.

Prior to the follow-up meeting in July 2000, Firm B undertook a major review and update of the development methodology. It became more flexible; for example, the methodology relating to modeling has been extended to include object-oriented (OO) concepts and UML. A hands-on workshop was designed and conducted to train all staff in the enhanced methodology. Also, all templates were updated to reflect changes. Every staff member was given responsibility for auditing part of a project for conformance against the quality plan. As well as sharing the workload for conducting audits, this process provided valuable training for all staff by giving them a different perspective of the QMS, and encouraged all staff to suggest future improvements. From the nonconformances found, it was concluded that the quality plan needed to be more rigid. Subsequent to the follow-up meeting, further updates were performed on the methodology. As well as the workshops, postworkshop reviews were conducted to check the effectiveness of the workshops.

The area most impacted by the RAPID program related to preventative and corrective actions. The standard templates relating to these areas were updated and refined on an ongoing basis.

As Firm B was restricted by the client's quality process, it was considered impossible to fully control the quality process. However, the follow-up meeting revealed some procedures had been improved, for example, those relating to the initial process with the client and also documentation of the clients' variation requests. The development of a risk assessment and management procedure had a major impact on the quality management system and necessitated changes to procedures including testing, contract review and planning, and requirements control. A process for developing new procedures had been defined, and a template was developed and included in the quality manual to be used for all new procedures.

At the time of the follow-up meeting, the impact of ISO 9000:2000 had not yet been analysed as it was not considered high priority at that time. However, during the retrospective interview, it was found that Firm B did gain certification to ISO 9000:2000, being one of the first Queensland IT firms to achieve this milestone. In relation to configuration management, procedures for SourceSafe were updated and dispersed through mentoring. The duties of code librarian were allocated to one staff member on a part-time basis.

As the development environment depends on the client's requirements, it varies on a project-by-project basis. Therefore, Firm B decided it was not possible or desirable to implement a common development environment at Firm B. However, at the time of the follow-up meeting, documentation had been improved by compiling registers of hardware and software. It was considered essential to maintain a diverse range of operating systems to provide necessary test environments. Also, a variety of development tools was considered appropriate to suit individual developers and therefore maintain productivity. Further efforts in this area after the follow-up meeting saw the establishment of registers for loaned equipment, configurations, and documentation. After implementing the RAPID recommendations, the CEO decided that there was little value in further efforts due to the small size of the firm.

At the follow-up meeting, the opinion was expressed that the most valuable recommendation from the assessment was the need to develop a global change request and problem resolution system. Consequently, a lot of effort was directed into extending the customer database to include a global change request system and comprehensive document register. Also, a software package had been introduced to help track and manage bugs and issues. Subsequent to the follow-up meeting, Firm B actually developed a new product for sale as well as for their internal use—Enterprise Client Management (ECM). ECM proved to be extremely successful in the market. It included a project administration tool with change request management and impact analysis.

At the time of the follow-up meeting, Firm B was considering how to collect and analyse measurement data. Statistics from previous projects were used to produce estimates. Subsequent to the follow-up meeting, the importance of collecting and analysing measurement data was addressed as part of the development of ECM. ECM enabled the extraction of key performance indicators, recorded information about responsiveness to issue resolution and change requests, and facilitated the compilation of comprehensive reports.

CASE C

Firm C at the time of the initial RAPID assessment was a growing software development organisation catering to the inventory management of large capital items. They had developed a tailorable system to manage the acquisition, procurement, supply, and implementation of their inventory items and spare parts. The product had been installed in a number of sites, and the field support

and installation were provided by consultants employed by the company. Twelve months after the initial assessment, Firm C had adopted a new development methodology that allowed a more appropriate model to be used throughout the development environment, rather than adhering to the traditional 'waterfall' model. This has enabled the firm to introduce a more considered approach to issues like software design and advanced project management techniques. Work had also commenced on the adoption of a more thorough configuration management practice, which can be tailored to individual site installations.

The company confirmed at the follow-up meeting that the rapid assessment had afforded considerable value to their company, not only in providing an objective opinion of their current development environment, but also in providing legitimisation of the established development activities. The assessment was also viewed as providing an initial point for creating a 'mentoring' role in implementing selected improvement activities.

At the long-term retrospective interview, Firm C shows a pattern of evolution towards a larger organisation, with the small business employing strategies for growth. At the time of the initial assessment, 4 of the 14 staff were actively involved in product development. Seven years later, when the retrospective interview was conducted, the firm had changed its trading name, and now employed over 30 staff; however, its basic product domain was the same, although extended.

In the initial assessment, seven action items were identified, and the follow-up meeting showed that positive steps had been taken in respect of five of these. The critical actions involved the adoption of an explicit project-based approach to development, with both methodological and tool-based support. At the time of the retrospective interview, this action was still seen as critical to the survival of the firm through difficult market periods, and remained the basis for the product development approach:

I think it was a very big plus to move to multi-disciplinary project-based teams rather than discipline teams so that team members could identify much more with the project. I guess that the other major thing...is the project management structure, where everybody gives their estimates and re-validates or calibrates those estimates on a regular basis, and so we are able to know how the project is performing. (owner/manager Firm C)

From the retrospective interview, three dominant themes emerge as key factors in the survival and success of the company:

- The availability of additional working capital led to expansion of market opportunities;
- The company was strongly affected by the 'dot com crash' of 2003, and the lack of market demand for one of the key 'strategic' product lines was a cause of some frustration. However, the proven strength of the basic product set, and the company's proactive approach to product improvement provided strengths to weather the variations in the market;
- The company had progressively implemented organisational infrastructure to support continuing improvement. Executive management groups focusing on both product quality and process effectiveness had become established and operated on a continuing basis.

CASE D

Firm D specialised in developing process control systems for manufacturing firms. The three full-time staff were skilled in client-server and real-time systems as well as object-oriented methodologies. The initial assessment was held in November 1999 and found the firm used a strong engineering philosophy with a professional approach to requirements gathering and analysis. The software development processes, based on Rational Unified Process (RUP) and UML, were sound but could be enhanced by minor improvements in work product management. Software was developed as part of a system integrated with hardware and procedures. The standard development environment included Visual Basic, Java, and C++ with increasing use of HTML, Active Server Pages, and scripting languages.

Configuration management was performed informally with Visual SourceSafe used to manage source code during development and after release. Scope for improvement in software quality assurance was recognised with the need for quality objectives, targets, and audits. However, clients were not prepared to invest in quality assurance. Other risks identified were the requirements for evolutionary development with high visibility to and participation by the client. Also, changes to the technology required significant investment to stay current or ahead of the competition. It was recognised that significant re-use in software development was a key to meeting market demands for faster availability and lower cost. After the initial assessment, the recommendations from the assessors were implemented and the business developed in terms of earnings. The project initiation process was defined based on ISO 12207 and streamlined. The concept of offering a money-back guarantee to clients was seriously considered but not implemented as the clients were satisfied with the current time and materials contracts. A new custom product was developed and successfully implemented for a client. However, Firm D found it difficult to market its services and failed to generate new leads for additional projects. Estimating procedures were improved with actual records of effort fed back to improve the estimates. A basic document repository was established using Sharepoint Web pages.

At the initial assessment, it was recognised that the major risks for the company related to developing the business and winning new development contracts. Firm D experienced cash flow problems associated with large projects as payment for completed work lagged three months behind payments to staff for their development efforts. As a result, insufficient effort was invested in gaining new business. At the time of the follow-up meeting, October 2000, the number of full-time staff had reduced to one. A personal issue with a staff member of a key client resulted in the loss of major contracts. The administrative staff member of Firm D was sacked for dishonesty and one of the developers left the firm and took some clients with him. One of the partners was not prepared to invest in business development and marketing and also left Firm D. Disheartened by the impact of these 'betrayals' and faced with excessive travel commitments and a growing family, the remaining principal decided in January 2002 to put the company on hold rather than employ additional staff. Currently, he is contracting to large firms in the area of quality assurance and project management. The principal of Firm D realises that although robust software processes are important, it is vital to back them up with excellent business processes and is looking forward to resurrecting the firm in a few years.

CASE E

At the time of the initial assessment in November 1999, Firm E provided specialised Unix, Windows, and new technology (NT) based applications for the mining industry, based on developing relational databases of geophysical data using Ingress, Progress, and Oracle. The applications developed provided geological, mining, and related expertise in the technical and commercial aspects of the mining industry. Firm E showed excellent capability in requirements gathering, due to the expertise of the managing director. Whilst software development was very strong, it was noted that implementation of proper testing procedures and traceability procedures, together with actual implementation of the defined process, would improve this capability rating greatly. Project management, configuration management,

and problem resolution processes all showed good capability. Project management could be improved with adequate tracking and configuration management with proper planning. Problem resolution relies heavily on an organisational developed tool, and by managing this process its capability would improve.

The two weak areas identified were quality assurance and risk management. There was a basis and a culture for quality assurance within Firm E with informal reviews and checklists in place. Implementation of the checklists and proper recording of the QA activities would improve this process. Risk management could be improved by formalising, planning, documenting, and monitoring the risks involved with projects. Other opportunities for improvement were noted: the need for proper tracking of actual effort on project tasks; lack of planning and definition in configuration management activities; and lack of formalised testing procedures and traceability between specifications, design, and implementation.

In November 2000, the follow-up meeting found an early warning system for cost and scheduling variations was in place with actual task effort tracked. Testing had been improved with the implementation of QA checklists. At the time of the retrospective interview in May 2006, Firm E had diversified into developing software for a financial planning company and the agricultural sector with two new major clients and a number of smaller clients. Recently, Firm E has changed its focus from the Unix/4GL environment to dot net. As an outcome of the RAPID program, Firm E staff revisited how they assemble their standards and working processes and were able to establish a useful knowledge base related to the new processes. The focus is on quality improvement of methods and processes, followed by personal skills and tools. Staff members are working towards Microsoft certified solution developer MCSD certification and have identified a range of productivity tools for dot net development. Firm E has implemented Gemini, a Web-based comprehensive change request system that not only records and enables prioritisation of work requests, but also keeps track of working notes, actual effort, and completion records. Gemini provides the facility for clients to log new issues and to check the status of outstanding requests.

However, the firm had come perilously close to financial disaster. Firm E had partnered with a large company to bid for a complex system for a material handling facility at a shipping port. After Firm E had committed excessive resources to develop a prototype system over a six-month time period, it became clear that the partner firm was not developing the complementary equipment. The purchaser recognised that Firm E's proposed system was superior to the competition but the contract was not awarded to Firm E on account of the poor performance of the partner firm.

The owner/manager of Firm E is convinced of the benefits of SPI:

These days the whole changing infrastructure of software engineering and software development is such that unless you have a documented software quality process I don't think you're going to survive. I truly don't. There's so many fly-by-nighters, which is where some of our work comes from because we get it third-hand, people have

had two or three attempts at it and it's just been a disaster and they come to us.

However, he commented that certain aspects of the process are more easily implemented in larger organisations compared to smaller firms. The owner/manager of Firm E has recently become aware of CMMI, and he believes it has a very valid place in terms of software development, but he feels the RAPID program goes further and impacts broadly on the firm's relationship with the clients, the business model, and future planning. The RAPID program accomplished two purposes:

it gave us the guidelines, and some very specific areas to look at, some specific processes, which in themselves were very valuable, but also it gave us the incentive, being involved in something like this, and the potential to be involved in a process improvement program.

ANALYSIS AND DISCUSSION

In the analysis, we do not wish to deal with the cases in a linear fashion but focus on common themes across the cases. Table 2 summarises

Table 2. Firm characteristics at time of retrospective study

Characteristic	Firm				
	A	B	C	D	E
Operational Status	✓	X	✓	X	✓
Impact of non-SE events	Stable	Lifestyle MD	+Capital	Staffing issues	Commercial partner
Business growth	0	↓	↑	↓	↓
Staff growth	0	0	14→35	4→1	4→2
Implemented recommendations	✓	✓✓	✓✓	✓	✓✓
Other improvements	Agile		Improvement infrastructure		
Overall satisfaction with RAPID program	✓	✓✓	✓✓	✓	✓✓

the positions of the five firms as seen in the retrospective interviews. Three of the companies have survived, though with different growth patterns; the reasons for nonsurvival of the two closed businesses were quite different. External events (outside the domain of software engineering practices) had a significant impact on four of the five companies.

All of the interviewees remained strongly supportive of the benefits of the RAPID program, two owner/managers maintaining this view even after the company ceased to operate. In two cases, the focus on improvement initiated by the RAPID program provided an ongoing stimulus to business survival and growth. All surviving companies had initiated improvements outside the scope of the original RAPID recommendations. The increasing availability of open source tools such as Mantis (Firm A) and Gemini (Firm E) provide small firms with a low-cost option to improve communications with clients by Web-based problem/enhancement logging and tracking.

The Value of Improvement

The bulk of research performed to date focuses on factors influencing the initiation of SPI in small business. There is very limited data on longer term effects and ongoing evolution of SPI programs; this is the direct focus of our current studies. This study confirms the view of Keating, Oliva, Repenning, Rockart, and Sterman (1999) that improvement programs are tightly coupled to other functions and processes in the firm, and to the firm's customers (Firm E), suppliers, competitors, and capital markets (Firm C)—our results indicate a further two key factors, the firm's staff (Firm D), and commercial partners (Firm E).

A theme that emerges from these retrospective studies is that the improvement initiative helped to support the survival of those companies which were still operating five years after the initial assessment. The improvements realised by implementing the RAPID recommendations were seen as important, even by the firms that did not survive. Three of the five firms stated that the improvements were critical in supporting the company's ability to deal with significant external turbulence in the business environment, changes in the marketplace, and problems with staff and commercial partners.

Survival Depends on Owner/Manager

From the retrospective interviews, it is clear that SPI success depends on the motivation of the owner/manager and their plans for the firm's future. In Australia, only 33 percent of all small businesses survive more than 10 years (ABS, 2004). Firms B and D are interesting cases in that their closure was caused by lifestyle concerns rather than market forces. In fact, for many small organisations, their existence is dependent on the motivations of the owner/manager, and their continued existence may depend on lifestyle decisions taken by the owner. Given this, traditional views of 'success' and 'failure' can be seen as not applying to many small firms, and caution should be applied in trying to assign issues of organisational survival to 'failure' to adapt to the business environment.

These interviews indicate that one of the competencies required by owner/managers is an understanding of the strategic importance of process improvement throughout the organisation. There is an emphasis on a long-standing commitment to improvement as a driving strategy for the success of the business; this issue should be considered as one of the key competencies for the owner/manager.

Government Support Essential for SMEs

Small companies need external assistance as they have scarce resources and limited possibilities to keep up-to-date with the state-of-the-art research and practice (Kautz, 1998). The RAPID program would not have happened without government funding to SEA for the assessments. SEA also offered training and opportunities for small software developers to network.

This constitutes an obvious opportunity for effective government support. Many national governments have recognized that their local software development industry is made up of a myriad of small firms and have provided funding for SPI programs, for example, results from government funded projects have been reported from Ireland (SPIRE project/SPIRE, 1998) and Science Foundation Ireland (Blowers & Richardson, 2005); Brazil MARES project (Anacleto, von Wangenheim, Salviano, & Savi, 2004); Italy (Bucci et al., 2001); Chile, Brazil, and Colombia (Bedeni, Ardlia, Pavlovic, & Steembecker, 2005); and Hong Kong (Leung, Goh, & Lui, 2005).

Challenges Faced by Small Software Firms

The need for software engineering standards tailored to small firms has been recognised by ISO/IEC JTC 1/SC 7 at its meetings in Brisbane (2004), Finland (2005), and Bangkok (2006). A standard recently developed in Mexico (Ministry of the Economy, 2005) has been selected by Working Group 24 as an input document for the development of profiles and guides for firms with less than 25 staff (Laporte, Renault, Alexandre, & Uthayanaka, 2006). In 2005, WG24 conducted a survey of very small enterprises (VSEs) to explore their use of ISO/SC7 standards and the associated challenges (Working Group 24, 2006). The five case studies presented here support the findings of the WG24 survey that small software firms are different in many respects from development groups in large organisations.

The retrospective interviews highlight the critical role of the owner/manager in the small enterprise supporting the view of Johns et al. (1989) that all the critical management decisions

such as finance, accounting, personnel, purchasing, servicing, marketing, and selling are made by one or two persons, without the aid of internal specialists, and with specific knowledge in one or two functional areas. It has been found that the owner/manager needs to have a broad high-level skill set including competencies in finance, marketing, and human resource management; it is this issue, as much as anything else, that differentiates the small software engineering firm from the internal software development unit of a large organisation.

Problems with staff or partners can have a devastating impact in a small firm, as happened in Firm D. In small firms, attention needs to be paid to the business processes. Some of the owner/managers of small software development firms find this difficult because they are software engineers first and business managers second.

Some factors that have attracted much attention by researchers in respect to SPI adoption by small software development groups in large firms do not appear to be issues for small firms. These include senior management commitment, organisation politics, and communication within the development group. Earlier researchers have asserted that only a handful of companies are ready for SPI 'because their software health is so bad (that is if they have any development process at all)' (Smith, Fletcher, Gray, & Hunter, 1994, p. 207). Despite the low initial process capability shown in Table 1, all firms exhibited a concerted effort to implement the recommendations from the initial assessment. Although all firms continued to implement process improvement initiatives after the follow-up meeting, surprisingly, Firm B, the firm with highest capability, is no longer in business.

CONCLUSION

In the conventional view, small firms aim to develop into large firms; this is similar to the concept of an individual having a 'job for life.' In fact, many small firms exist due to the motivation of one individual—the owner/operator. The future existence of the firm depends on the lifestyle decisions taken by this individual.. Given this, traditional views of 'success' and 'failure' can be seen as not applying to many small firms, and caution should be applied in trying to assign issues of organisational survival to 'failure' to adapt to the business environment.

The long-term study has shown that changes made in an organisation, driven by a framework of model-based improvement, can have long-term impacts even in small organisations. Even where specific initiatives are lost, as a result of failure to effectively institutionalise the changes, the positive impact of change may remain and have a long-term impact on the way that the organisation does its business.

We can also see, however, that there is no necessary link between success in implementing improvement and survival of the organisation. One of the firms in this study was the most successful of the five in implementing improvements and in using these improvements to satisfy business objectives; but at the end of the day, it is no longer in business. Concepts of success and failure for small enterprises need to be re-examined, especially where the role of the business owner is active rather than simply the supplier of capital.

Government sponsored programs are essential to help small firms improve their software processes. Sponsored assessments as well as low-cost training courses are required. As well as software engineering support, small firms may need government sponsored training to improve the management of marketing, capital investment, human resources, and risk.

This chapter attempts to highlight the importance of long-term studies of improvement in small enterprises. The initial focus identified by Sanders and Richardson (2005b) has been the impetus for the study, and the results demonstrate the value of the research. Our results provide insight into the small enterprise environment and into the extent to which improvement actions can reinforce overall success for the small business.

ACKNOWLEDGMENT

The authors recognise the contribution of colleagues at the Software Quality Institute of Griffith University who participated in developing the RAPID method and in conducting the RAPID assessments and follow-up meetings.

REFERENCES

ABS. (2004). 8127.0 characteristics of small business, Australia. Retrieved January 1, 2008, from http://www.abs.gov.au/ausstats/abs@.nsf/b06660592430724fca2568b5007b8619/8ceaee35da67c721ca256ff20005a042!OpenDocument

Anacleto, A., von Wangenheim, C. G., Salviano, C. F., & Savi, R. (2004). Experiences gained from applying 15504 to small software companies in Brazil. In *Proceedings of the International SPICE Conference on Process Assessment and Improvement* (pp. 33-37), Lisbon, Portugal.

Attewell, P., & Rule, J. B. (1991). Survey and other methodologies applied to IT impact research: experiences from a comparative study of business computing. In K. Kraemer (Ed.), *The information systems research challenge: Survey research methods* (Vol. 3, pp. 299-315).

Bedeni, A. G., Ardlia, A. L., Pavlovic, M., & Steembecker, K. (2005, October 19-20). *Quality software map of South America.* Paper presented at the International Research Workshop for Process Improvement in Small Settings, Pittsburgh, Pennsylvania, USA.

Blowers, R., & Richardson, I. (2005, October 19-20). *The Capability Maturity Model (SW and Integrated) tailored in small indigenous software industries.* Paper presented at the International Research Workshop for Process Improvement in Small Settings, Pittsburgh, Pennsylvania, USA.

Brodman, J. G., & Johnson, D. L. (1997). A software process improvement approach tailored for small organizations and small projects. In *Proceedings of the International Conference on Software Engineering* (pp. 661-662). Boston: IEEE CS.

Bucci, G., Campanai, M., & Cignoni, G. (2001). Rapid assessment to solicit process improvement in small and medium-sized organisations. *Software Quality Professional, 4*(1), 33-41.

Cater-Steel, A. P., Toleman, M. A., & Rout, T. (2006). Process improvement for small firms: An evaluation of the RAPID assessment-based method. *Information and Software Technology, 48*(5), 323-334.

Cragg, P. B. (2002). Benchmarking information technology practices in small firms. *European Journal of Information Systems, 11*(4), 267-282.

Daft, R. L. (1998). *Essentials of organization theory and design.* Cincinnati, OH: South-Western College Publishing.

Fayad, M. E., Laitinen, M., & Ward, R. P. (2000). Software engineering in the small. *Communications of the ACM, 43*(3), 115-118.

Fenton, N., Pfleeger, S. L., & Glass, R. L. (1994). Science and substance: A challenge to software engineers. *IEEE Software, 11*(4), 86-95.

Garcia, S., Graettinger, C., & Kost, K. (2005). *Introduction.* Paper presented at the First International Research Workshop for Process Improvement in Small Settings, Pittsburgh, Pennsylvania.

Gibson, D. L., Goldenson, D. R. & Kost, K. (2006) *Performance Results of CMMI-Based Process Improvement.* CMU SEI

Grover, V., & Teng, J. T. C. (1992). An examination of DBMS adoption and success in American organisations. *Information and Management, 23,* 239-248.

Grunbacher, P. (1997, September 1-4). *A software assessment process for small software enterprises.* Paper presented at the EUROMICRO 97 New Frontiers of Information Technology, Proceedings of the 23rd EUROMICRO Conference, Budapest, Hungary.

ISO/IEC TR 15504-5. (1998). *Information technology: Software process assessment, Part 5: An assessment model and indicator guidance* (No. ISO/IEC TR 15504-5:1998(E)).

Johns, B. L., Dunlop, W. C., & Sheehan, W. J. (1989). *Small business in Australia: Problems and prospects* (3rd ed.). Sydney: Allen and Unwin.

Johnson, D. L., & Brodman, J. G. (1992). Software process rigors yield stress, efficiency. *Signal,* pp. 55-57.

Kautz, K. (1998). Software process improvement in very small enterprises: Does it pay off? *Software Process: Improvement and Practice, 4,* 209-226.

Keating, E. K., Oliva, R., Repenning, N. P., Rockart, S., & Sterman, J. D. (1999). Overcoming the improvement paradox. *European Management Journal, 17*(2), 120-134.

King, W. R. (1996). Achieving global strategic advantage. *Information Systems Management, 13*(4), 57-60.

Laporte, C. Y., April, A., & Renault, A. (2006). *Applying ISO/IEC software engineering standards in small settings: Historical perspectives and initial achievements.* Paper presented at the SPICE 2006 Conference, Luxembourg.

Laporte, C. Y., Renault, A., Alexandre, S., & Uthayanaka, T. (2006). Applying software engineering standards in very small enterprises. *ISO Focus, International Organisation for Standardisation*, pp. 36-38.

Larsen, E. A., & Kautz, K. (1997). Quality assurance and software process improvement in Norway. *Software Process: Improvement and Practice, 3*(2), 71-86.

Leung, H., Goh, J., & Lui, Y. (2005, October 19-20). *CMM Fast Track (CMMFT) Programme for Hong Kong SME software companies.* Paper presented at the International Research Workshop for Process Improvement in Small Settings, Pittsburgh, Pennsylvania, USA.

Ministry of the Economy. (2005). *NMX-059-NYCE-2005 information technology: Software models of processes and assessment for software development and maintenance* (Parts 1-4). Mexico: Ministry of the Economy.

Mintzberg, H. (1983). *Structure in fives: Designing effective organizations.* Englewood Cliffs: Prentice Hall.

Mustonen-Ollila, E., & Lyytinen, K. (2003). Why organisations adopt information system process innovations: A longitudinal study using diffusion of innovation theory. *Information Systems Journal, 13*, 275-297.

Natwick, G., Draper, G., & Bearden, L. (1999, October). Software mini-assessments: process and practice. *Crosstalk: The Journal of Defense Software Engineering,* pp. 10-14.

O'Regan, N., & Ghobadian, A. (2004). Testing the homogeneity of SMEs: The impact of size on managerial and organisational processes. *European Business Review, 16*(1), 64-77.

Pfleeger, S. L., Jeffery, D. R., Curtis, B., & Kitchenham, B. (1997). Status report on software management. *IEEE Software, 14*(2), 33-43.

Pringle, L. (2001, Summer). Size does matter: Improvement for SMEs. *Software (SEA National),* pp. 4-7.

Repenning, N. P. & Sterman, J. D. (2001). Nobody ever gets credit for fixing problems that never happened: Creating and sustaining process improvement. *California Management Review, 43*, 64-88.

Richardson, I. (2002). Software process improvements in very small companies. *Software Quality Professional, 4*(2), 14-22.

Richardson, I., & Ryan, K. (2001). Software process improvements in a very small company. *Software Quality Professional, 3*(2), 23-35.

Rout, T. P., Tuffley, A., Cahill, B., & Hodgen, B. (2000). *The rapid assessment of software process capability.* Paper presented at the 1st SPICE 2000 International Conference on Software Process Improvement and Capability dEtermination, Limerick, Ireland.

Sanders, M., & Richardson, I. (2005a). *Research into long-term improvements in small to medium-sized organisations using SPICE as a framework for standards.* Limerick, Ireland: Department of Computer Science and Information Systems, University of Limerick.

Sanders, M., & Richardson, I. (2005b). *What happened after SPI assistance in Ireland?* Paper presented at the 4th International SPICE Conference on Process Assessment and Improvement, Klagenfurt, Austria.

Smith, W. L., Fletcher, R. I., Gray, E. M., & Hunter, R. B. (1994). Software process improvement: The route to software quality? In M. Ross, C. A. Brebbia, G. Staples, & J. Stapleton (Eds.), *Software quality management II* (Vol 1: Managing Quality Systems, pp. 193-211). Southampton Boston: Computational Mechanics Publications.

SPIRE. (1998). *The Spire Handbook: Better, faster, cheaper software development in small organisa-*

tions. Dublin: Centre for Software Engineering, DCU Campus.

Storey, D. J. (1994). *Understanding the small business sector*. London: Routledge.

Voss, C., Blackmon, K. L., Cagliano, R., Hanson, P., & Wilson, F. (1998). Made in Europe: Small companies. *Business Strategy Review, 9*(4), 1-19.

Wiegers, K. E., & Sturzenberger, D. C. (2000). A modular software process mini-assessment method. *IEEE Software*, pp. 62-69.

Wilkie, F. G., McFall, D., & McCaffery, F. (2004). *The centre for software process technologies: A model for process improvement in geographical regions with small software industries*. Paper presented at the Software Engineering Process Group, Orlando, FL, USA.

Wood, M., Daly, J., Miller, J., & Roper, M. (1999). Multi-method research: An investigation of object-oriented technology. *Journal of Systems and Software, 48*(1), 13-26.

Working Group 24. (2006, September). Public site of the ISO/IEC JTC1/SC7 Working Group 24. Retrieved January 1, 2008, from http://profs.logti. etsmtl.ca/claporte/English/VSE/index.html

Chapter XIII
An Incremental Functionality–Oriented Free Software Development Methodology

Oswaldo Terán
ENDITEL; Centro de Micro Electrónica y Sistemas Distribuidos and Centro de Simulación y Modelos, Universidad de los Andes, Venezuela

Johanna Alvarez
CENDITEL, Venezuela

Blanca Abraham
CEMISID Universidad de los Andes, Venezuela

Jose Aguilar
CENDITEL; Centro de Micro Electrónica y Sistemas Distribuidos, Universidad de los Andes, Venezuela

ABSTRACT

This chapter presents a methodology used as reference model for a free software factory that is part of the National Centre for Free Technologies in Venezuela. This centre is oriented at promoting free software development for serving mostly the public sector in order to promote endogenous development and technologic autonomy. Under this strategy, strengthening the software small and medium size enterprises and cooperatives, by allowing them to participate in different projects (improving their know-how) and providing them with a methodology for increasing their capabilities and software quality, is necessary and urgent. This methodology plans the development process incrementally, based on a prioritisation of the software functionalities development in accordance to the functionalities risks, development urgency, and dependencies. It combines aspects of the two styles of free software development, namely cathedral and bazaar. The development process is centralised, in essence collaborative, and continuously allows source code release.

INTRODUCTION

The Free Software Factory (FSF) of CENDITEL (Venezuelan national centre for promoting free technologies) has been conceived and created as part of the efforts of the Venezuelan State aiming at increasing endogenous development and technological sovereignty. In particular, it intends to strengthen the national software sector, especially the small and medium software enterprises (including the cooperatives), by allowing them to access the technology and participate in the software market, on one hand, and to increase their capabilities and software quality, on the other hand.

Two styles exist for developing free software: the cathedral style and the bazaar style. In the cathedral mode, software is developed from a unified *a priori* project that prescribes all the functions and the features to be incorporated in the final product. Programmers' work is centrally coordinated and supervised in order to assure the integration of various components. On the other hand, in the bazaar style, software emerges from an unstructured evolutionary process. Starting from a minimal code, groups of programmers add features and introduce modifications and patches to the code. There is no central allocation of different tasks; developers are free to develop a given program in directions they favor.

This chapter presents an attempt at building a free software development methodology having many characteristics of the cathedral style but keeping certain principle of the bazaar mode. The methodology has been developed at a public organisation which responds to public sector free

software necessities and requirements that must be satisfied in a limited time period. Because of this, it is necessary to adopt the cathedral mode of work while taking key advantages of the bazaar style. For instance, it is allowed that developers from outside the organisation contributes with software coding, testing, and so forth; these external developers do not follow a centrally controlled process; and the software code is made public as soon as it is tested.

This methodology assumes an organisational structure oriented towards specific processes. The processes dedicated to software development are:

- *Process # 1*: Free Software Project Management
- *Process # 2*: Specific Project Administration
- *Process # 3*: Free Software Application Development

Actions to be carried out in these processes are classified in steps and activities. In particular, steps and activities in the third process are implemented by the following six phases. This methodology has taken ideas from diverse software development methodologies, methods, and models such as the extreme programming method (Beck, 2004), the rational unified process (Kruchten, 2000; Pollice, 2001; Probasco, 2000), the watch method (Montilva, 2004; Montilva, Hamzan, & Ghatrawi, 2000), and the model of processes for software development (MoProSoft) (Oktaba et al., 2005). Due to the fact that these models and methods, except extreme programming, have been proposed proprietary software development, it has been necessary to adapt the hints, ideas, or procedures taken from them to the free software development needs.

The methodology to be proposed has been validated at the FSF of the Foundation for Science and Technology of the Mérida State in Venezuela (FUNDACITE-Mérida). This factory has permitted us to understand better, empirically, the real needs of a free software development process and has also been a source of interesting ideas. The proposed structure will allow planning and control activities which are required in the management and administration of software projects. In addition, the free software application development process is iterative and incremental, in terms of the software application functionalities. On the other hand, the design of the application is based on component architecture, which allows software reuse. Each process will be explained in detail in the main body of this chapter. For facilitating each process, some free software tools will be suggested.

FREE SOFTWARE DEVELOPMENT METHODOLOGY

Process # 1: Free Software Project Management (FSPM)

This process is responsible for managing all projects being carried out by the organisation, that is, both internal projects (projects for the organisation) and external projects (projects for other organisations) are managed. Specifically, in this process, a "service offer" for the project to be developed is generated. This offer must include a conceptualisation, a description, and a (general) development plan for the project, as well as the definition of the free software license. Figure 1 shows the steps as a workflow for the FSMP process. Subsequently, these steps will be described.

Figure 1. Free software project management process

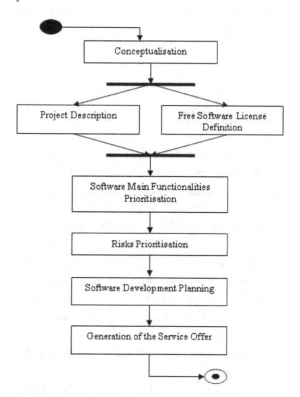

a. **Conceptualisation**

Description: Specific user needs and/or problems must be identified in order to define the scope of the project. In case of a high complexity of the project, for instance, the scope of the problem goes beyond a software need and involves organisational issues, methodologies such as technologic prospective and strategic planning, and/or tools such as fish bone (a technique commonly used in operation research and in quality control) are recommended. In this case, the study would suggest a set of solutions and organisational changes, of which software needs would be only part of the whole answer.

People Responsible: According to free software philosophy, all people associated with the project (project manager, project administrator, developers, users, and so forth) must be involved from the very early stages of it, even when new actors can be incorporated to any phase of the project.

Techniques: Prospective analysis, strategic planning, or any other useful technique.

Products: (1) Client/user's needs and/or problems; (2) scope of the project.

b. **Project Description**

The main point in this phase is to achieve a detailed description of the project. Each actor must analyse the client's need and problem, as well as the project's scope, in order to contribute to the description of the project.

People Responsible: Clients, users, project manager, project administrator, developers, assessors and other people interested in the project participation.

Products: Project description document.

c. **Free Software License Definition**

Description: In this step, the free software license to be adopted for the development is defined. It might be the case that a license from the market satisfies the client requirements and then is chosen or, in case that there is not an existent license matching the user's requirements, a new license is defined.

People Responsible: Clients, users, project manager, project administrator, assessors.

Products: Project license.

d. **Software Main Functionalities Prioritisation**

Description: In this step, the goal is to describe and classify the software functionalities in accordance with the implementation urgency required by the client.

People Responsible: Clients.

Products: Functionalities prioritised.

e. **Risk Prioritisation**

Description: To identify, prioritise, and associate the risks to software application functionalities. The risks are prioritised in accordance to their impact on the application development.

People Responsible: Clients, users, project manager, project administrator, developers, assessors, and other people interested in the project.

Products: Risks prioritised.

f. **Software Development Plan**

Description: To build the development plan, the implementation order of the functionalities of the application must be established, in accordance to the functionality priorities defined by the client, and the risks prioritised associated to the functionalities. This must allow determining the number of cycles or iterations required for the development of the application. A cycle is responsible for developing a certain number of functionalities (taken into account their priority order). A development plan can be modified after an iteration, as a result of work reorganisation, in line with the dynamic of the project.

People Responsible: Project manager, project administrator, and developers.

Products: Development plan.

g. **Generation of the Service Offer**

Description: The service offer is completed in this step. It specifies all important issues of the project, such as the goal, scope, and description of the project; the development plan; the due dates for deliverables; the work team; the project cost; and the operation platform.

People Responsible: Project manager, clients.

Techniques and Tools: Service offer forms.

Note: In accordance to the chosen software license, the products achieved in this process must be published in a collaborative development platform. This will facilitate the interested people access to the software products and their documentation.

Process #2: Administration of Specific Projects (ASP)

The administration of specific projects leads the developer team of a software application (it is assumed that a software application development corresponds to a software project). In this sense, each software project must have at least one project administrator. The project administrator is responsible for organising and planning the activities corresponding to each iteration defined in the development plan. Additionally, the project administrator must assure the software quality, manage the system configuration, and the collaborative technical platform, as well as supervise and control the project development and the administration of subcontracts. Figure 2 shows the main steps as a workflow for the ASP process. Subsequently, these steps will be described.

Figure 2. Process for the Administration of Specific Projects

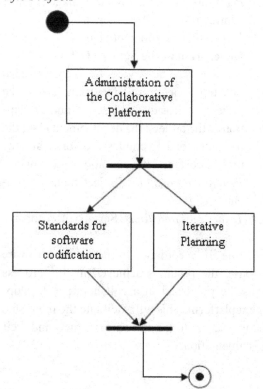

a. **Administration of the Development Collaborative Platform**

Description: The processes related to the ASP phase are facilitated by using a collaborative platform. A software developing team has its own necessities; accordingly it is important to select the correct tool for collaborative software management considering such necessities. In this phase, the collaborative platform is set up. The collaborative platform permits any interested person to collaborate with and share ideas, source code, documentation, testing, and so forth. This is a very important aspect of the free software development. However, as part of the administration of this platform, the project administrator must approve and then publish the software versions and the associated documentation in accordance with the free software license assumed.

People Responsible: Project administrator.

Tools: GFORCE, and so forth.

Products: Collaborative development server.

b. **Standard for Software Codification**

Description: This step establishes the standards for code generation and for the documentation to be used during the software development. These standards allow a quick and simple reading of the code, facilitating the work of the whole group, including the client, the user, and other actors.

People Responsible: Project administrator.

Products: Coding and documentation standards.

c. **Iterative Planning**

Description: The activities of the iteration to be carried out in accordance with the functionalities to be developed are planned. After an iteration is performed, the next iteration is planned and takes into account functionalities that could not be implemented and problems found during the previous iteration.

People Responsible: Project administrator.

Techniques: Gantt, Pert/CPM

Tools: Planner, GFORCE, XPTracker, Source-Forge, and so forth.

Products: Plan for the iteration to be developed.

Note: Products accomplished in this process must be placed at the collaborative platform in accordance with the adopted free software license.

Process #3: Free Software Application Development

The software application is constructed by the sequence of iterations or cycles in an incremental and iterative way, allowing that users and clients can check the advances of the work and give feedback useful for improving the development and testing processes. The methodology presents a general reference framework or structure for the activities to be planned at each iteration of this process (see Figure 3). In each cycle, one activity receives the main attention while the others are secondary. The whole set of functionalities is developed during the cycles.

Any person can access and execute the source code stored in the collaborative platform. In this way, everyone can contribute to the project. Experiences show that the more people use and test the software, the more quickly the errors and bugs will be found and solved.

It is important to mention that during the software application construction, not only must the code be published but also all associated documentation. In this manner, new programmers and collaborators can be easily incorporated. As mentioned earlier, the code and associated documentation publication depends on the software license established. Next, in Figure 3, the development phases carried out during this process will be presented.

a. **Application Domain Analysis**
    Description: This phase is considered one of the most important in the software development process, since the domain environment and context where the application will operate are analysed and understood. Such analysis is carried out in the first iteration but can be upgraded in the subsequent iterations. The

Figure 3. Free software development process

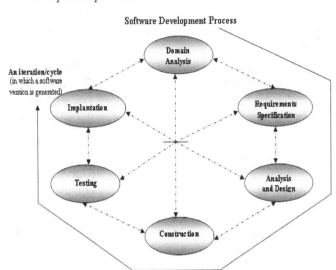

activities workflow for this phase is shown in Figure 4. Following this figure, the main activities will be described.

◦ ***Domain Description***

Description: Establishes and validates the application domain and its organisational scope.

People Responsible: System analyst internal to the developer organisation, users, clients, programming team. In this chapter, the phrase "*internal to the organization*" means a person who works for the organization that develops the software, as opposed to "external to the organization," which means a person who is not actually working for the developer organization.

Techniques: Domain engineering, interviews, revision of documents, and bibliography.

Products: Domain application definition.

Figure 4. Steps for the application domain analysis phase

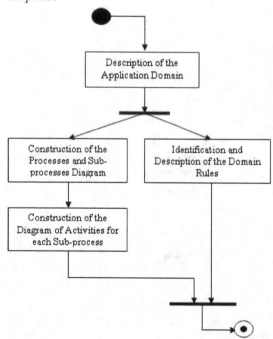

◦ ***Construction of the Processes and Subprocesses Diagram***

Description: This activity must identify processes and subprocesses related to the application domain, as well as events associated to all these, in order to generate the domain processes and subprocesses diagram. Finally, this diagram must be validated.

People Responsible: System analyst (internal to the organisation), users, clients.

Techniques: The processes diagram given by UML.

Tools: Umbrello, ArgoUML, caseUML.

Products: Domain processes and subprocess diagram.

◦ ***Construction of the Diagram of Activities for Each Subprocess***

Description: Generates and validates the activities diagram for each subprocess.

People Responsible: System analyst (internal to the organisation), users, clients.

Techniques: Activities diagram offered by UML.

Tools: Umbrello, ArgoUML, caseUML.

Products: Subprocess activity diagrams.

◦ ***Identification and Description of the Domain Rules***

Description: Domain rules regulating the application domain must be identified and studied.

People Responsible: System analyst (internal to the organisation), users, clients.

Techniques: the activities diagram offered by UML.

Tools: Umbrello, ArgoUML, caseUML.

Products: Subprocess activity diagrams.

b. **Requirements Specification**

Description: In this phase, the functionalities to be developed in the planned iteration are specified, and the nonfunctional requirements are defined or upgraded. Generally, the nonfunctional requirements are defined in the early iterations. The requirement specification document will be upgraded from iteration to iteration. It is important to notice that in this phase the user or the client can modify, change, include, or eliminate requirements and risks, which, in turn, might entail updates of the development plan. The activities workflow for this phase is shown in Figure 5. Following this figure, the main activities for this phase will be described.

° ***Description of Requirements Related to the Actual Iteration***

Description: A detailed description of the functional requirements for the present iteration is generated, and the nonfunctional requirements are defined or upgraded. These will allow generating and validating the requirements definition document. It is important to mention that only the definition

Figure 5. Steps for the requirements specification

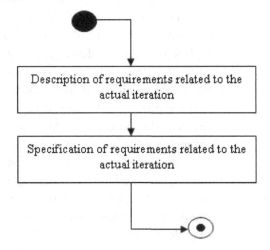

of such requirements related to the present iteration are validated, since those requirements related to previous iterations were validated during the corresponding iterations.

People Responsible: System analyst (internal to the organisation), users, clients.

° ***Specification of Requirements Related to the Actual Iteration:***

Description: To create or upgrade the requirements specification document, including the use cases describing the functional requirements associated with the actual iteration. In this methodology, it is understood that the requirements specification is made in terms of diagrams and textual descriptions of the use cases. Only the specification of those requirements associated to the present or actual iteration must be verified and validated in this step.

People Responsible: System analyst (internal and/or external to the organisation), users, clients.

Techniques: the use cases diagram offered by UML.

Tools: Umbrello, ArgoUML, caseUML.

c. *Analysis and Design*

Description: In this phase, the specification of requirements is translated into a design specification, based on a set of architectonic views, which represent the system architecture. In this phase also, the user interfaces and databases are designed. The application architecture, like the requirements, is enriched or upgraded as the subsequent iterations are carried out, since each iteration add functionalities to the software application been developed. All this gives flexibility to the design, permitting that change in the client's viewpoint about desired functionalities be taken into account without great difficulties.

Figure 6. Steps for the analysis and design phase

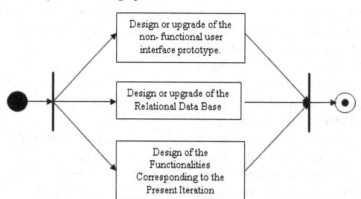

The activities workflow for this phase is shown in Figure 6. Afterwards, the main activities are going to be described.

° **Design or Upgrade of the Nonfunctional User Interface Prototype**

Description: Create or update the nonfunctional user interface prototype. This design includes the hierarchic diagram of windows, taking into account the user requirements. This design must be validated.

People Responsible: System analyst (internal or external to the developer organisation), programmers, users, clients.

Tools: UX, DIA.

Products: Design of the nonfunctional user interface prototype.

° **Design or Upgrade of the Relational Database:**

Description: The database design document is generated or upgraded. This document must contain the diagram entity/relation and the relational scheme, for the actual iteration. For these diagrams, the entities of the database and their attributes, as well as the primary and the foreign keys, must be defined. The entities of the database are identified by using the use cases for the present iteration. Finally, the database administrative procedures (i.e., backup, security, recovery, etc.) must be defined, and the database design document must be validated.

People Responsible: System analyst (internal and external to the organisation), programmers.

Techniques: Normalisation formulas.

Products: Entity relation diagrams.

° **Design of the Functionalities Corresponding to the Present Iteration**

Description: The architectonic views must be generated or upgraded. It is constituted by the logic, the implementation, the behaviour, and the conceptual views. The logic view is defined by the class diagrams of the software application. It is created or upgraded by: (a) deriving from the use cases (associated to the actual iteration) the objects of the application, (b) generating the sequence diagrams for the "methods" or functions involved in the realisation of the use cases for the actual iteration. The implementation view is generated or upgraded from the components diagrams. The behaviour view is created or upgraded from the interaction relations among the components. The conceptual view is defined or upgraded from the use case diagrams corresponding to the actual iteration.

People Responsible: System analyst (internal or external to the organisation).

Techniques: Class, components, and interaction diagrams

Tools: Umbrello, ArgoUML, caseUML.

Products: Architectonic view of the software application.

d. **Construction**

Description: For the actual iteration or cycle, the user interface, the database, and the functionalities of the application are constructed or upgraded in this phase. For that, the software application source code for the actual version is developed. The activities workflow for this phase is shown in Figure 7. Afterwards, the main activities of this phase will be described.

  ° **Collecting Reusable Free Software:**

Description: Reusable free software components, abstract data type, classes, functions, and whole systems, useful for the software application, are searched for and collected.

People Responsible: Programmers (internal and/or external to the organisation). This is the first activity where external programmers participate in the software development.

Tools: Some are available at Web sites such as www.fsl.funmrd,gov.ve, freshmeat.net, sourceforge.net, and so forth.

  ° **Construction or Upgrading of the User Interface U/S**

Description: The reusable user interface components corresponding to the design of the interface associated to the actual iteration are adapted and, when required, those of the previous iterations are upgraded.

People Responsible: Programmers (internal and/or external to the organisation).

  ° **Construction or Upgrading of the Database**

Description: Build or upgrade the database using information from the database design document for the actual iteration. Additionally, components of the user interface must be integrated along the database.

Figure 7. Steps for the construction phase

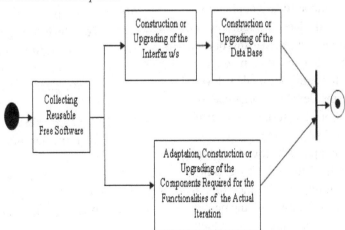

People Responsible: Programmers (internal and/or external to the organisation).

Techniques and Tools: Web sites like www.fsl.funmrd,gov.ve, freshmeat.net, sourceforge.net, and so forth.

○ ***Adaptation, Construction, or Upgrading of the Components Required for the Functionalities of the Actual Iteration***

Description: For the components, abstract data types, classes, and functions requited for the functionalities of the actual iteration: (a) adapt those reusable already collected, (b) construct those that could not be found, (c) update those useful from previous iterations.

People Responsible: Programmers (internal and/or external to the organisation).

Tools: Some are available at Web sites such as www.fsl.funmrd,gov.ve, freshmeat.net, sourceforge.net, and so forth.

e. **Testing**

Description: In this phase, the unitary, integration, functional, and nonfunctional tests, for the components corresponding to the functionalities associated to the actual iteration, are designed or upgraded, and applied. The nonfunctional tests are applied only in the last version of the software application, which is obtained in the last iteration. The installation tests are also designed in this phase, but are applied in the implantation phase. It is important to say that code modified by developers external to the developer organisation must also be appropriately tested. Only after these tests are successfully completed can the project administrator publish the code. Figure 8 shows the workflow for this phase. Since this figure sufficiently explains each step, in the text following the figure, only the people responsible, techniques, tools, and products

Figure 8. Steps for the testing phase

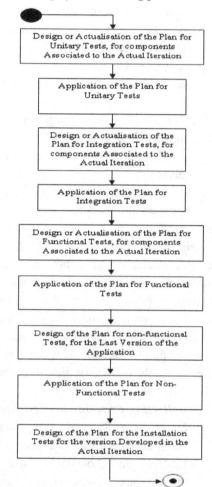

for a test design/upgrade or for a test application will be specified.

○ **Test design/upgrade:**

People Responsible: Tester (internal and/or external to the organisation).

Techniques: White and black box tests.

Products: Test plans.

○ **Test application:**

People Responsible: Tester (internal and/or external to the organisation).

Tools: Test, Check, Junit, Cppunit.

Products: Test reports.

Figure 9. Steps for the installation phase

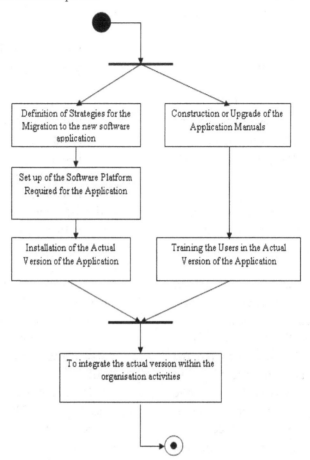

f. **Implantation**

In this phase, the actual iteration version is released to the client so that the client can validate this version while other functionalities are developed in the next iterations. The migration strategies towards the new application are defined, the user is trained for using the delivered version, the actual version is installed, the installation test is applied, and the software application manuals are generated or upgraded, and verified. Finally, the actual version of the software application is integrated along with the organisation activities. Figure 9 shows the workflow for this phase. Given that the figure sufficiently explains each step of this phase, a detailed description for each step will not be given. However, it is important to mention that: (a) the people responsible for these steps are programmers and testers (both internal to the developer organisation) and (b) the main products of this phase are the system manuals, the training material, and the installation test reports for each installed version.

STUDY CASE

The presented methodology has been shaped and updated recently and has been implanted partially only in two projects. The implantation process will continue during the present year (2007) in order to apply the whole methodology to all projects. The two projects involved in the implantation process until now are:

1. The Dis-centralised Administrative System.
2. The Automation of the FSF. This means the automation of the free software project management, administration of specific projects, and software application development processes.

The Dis-centralised Administrative System had already been started and was entering the test phase at the moment the methodology began implantation. Because of this, until now, the methodology has been applied in this project only for part of the software application development process, more specifically, for the unitary tests of the test step. On the other hand, since the automation of the FSF is still in course, the methodology has been applied up to the point the project has reached at present. However, the methodology has been applied from the beginning of the project. The following processes of the methodology have been implanted: the free software project management, administration of specific projects, and some aspects of the software application development process. Next, details about the application of the methodology to both of these projects will be presented.

Case 1: Automation of the Free Software Factory

Process # 1: Free Software Project Management

a. **Conceptualization**
Results of carrying out this step are summarised in a set of filled templates, which are stored in the GForge server (see Alvarez, 2007, sections 1 and 2). These templates show

needs and problems, and scope of the project of implementation of the FSF. Those problems and needs include:

○ Lack of a database of digitalised templates for documenting the development processes.
○ The dynamics of the demand requires urgent development.
○ Need of a knowledge base for learned lessons.

The scope of the project delimitates the system to be developed in terms of which processes and which steps will be covered.

b. **Project Description**
This gives an overview of how the automation of the FSF project is being carried out.

c. **Free Software License Definition**
There is not any licence defined for this project. All material developed in this project will be available from the GForge server.

d. **Software Main Functionalities Prioritisation.**
All functionalities to be covered by the automation system of the factory were defined and prioritised. Results of this phase are presented in Alvarez (2007, section 3). Among these functionalities, we have:

○ Digitalise the functionalities and the risks prioritisation templates.
○ Select analysis and design tools.
○ Choose testing tools.
○ Automate the project plan template.
○ Integrate templates and design tools.
○ Integrate design and programming phases (generation of automatic code)
○ Develop a knowledge base.

These functionalities received a weight, as the methodology states.

e. **Risk Prioritisation**
At this step, the more important development risks were defined (see Alvarez, 2006, section 4 for more details). Among these risks, we have:

○   Scarcity of free automation tools and FSF's development team's lack of knowledge and capacities for building, design, and test tools for free software development.

○   Few people dedicated at testing and short experience in testing.

○   Low experience in following methodologies.

As above, a weight is associated to these risks.

f.   **Development Priorities Definition**

A prioritisation of the functionalities was performed (Alvarez, 2006, section 5), by following this formula:

Total functionality F_1 weight = ($\sum VR_i$ para F_1) * PR + VF_1 * PF , where,

○   the VR_i are the risks for the functionality F_1;

○ VF_1 is the weight for the functionality F_1;

○   PR and PF are the relative weights-of-the-factors, in this case, between the total sum of risk weights, factor 1, and the functionality weight, factor 2.

Following this procedure, one of the most important functionalities resulted to be automated design and testing facilities. Tools for these tasks were selected from those available on the Internet.

g.   **Software Development Plan**

This plan presents the development schedule, indicating the functionalities to be developed at each iteration; there were seven defined iterations after considering the functionality dependencies, size of the development team, and the functionalities development prioritisation (for more details, see Alvarez, 2007, section 5).

h.   **Generation of the Service Offer**

The service offer indicates (Alvarez, 2007, section 6), for instance:

○   The offer proposal: to develop a system to automate the free software development processes.

○   The project scope: to automate in some degree, by integrating and digitalising (and in some cases completely automating, when the complexity of these tasks allows it) tools for implementing the FSF.

○   The release schedule (to the client).

Process #2: Administration of Specific Projects

a.   Administration of the Collaborative Platform.
     GForce was installed as the collaborative Platform.

b.   Standards for software codification.
     The codification standard is being defined at present.

c.   Iterative planning.
     This step is performed by using a GForce scheduling facility (Alvarez, 2007, section 7).

Process #3: Software Application Development

The software application development process consists basically on programming on top of GForge, in order to adapt it and add functionalities, to permit carrying out the software development activities required by the FSF processes. Some of the adaptations already implemented are:

•   Digitalisation of templates, among which we have: client's needs and problems; scope of the project; service offer; test plan; test reports.

•   Automation of the project plan.

Case 2: Dis-Centralised Administrative System

Process #3: Software Application Development

As mentioned previously, for this project, the methodology has been implanted to perform the unitary test plan (Alvarez, 2007, section 8).

CONCLUSION

The presented methodology pretends strengthening the software national sector, especially the small and medium software enterprises (including the cooperatives), by allowing them to access the technology and participate in the software market through a collaborative development of software for the public administration (main goal of the FSF), on one hand, and to increase their capabilities and software quality, on the other hand.

In this sense, the development process presents certain specific characteristics and numerous advantages (as it is stated in the methodology). As said before, a fundamental aspect is the collaborative development by iteration: a particular development group may enter or leave to collaborate at any iteration in accordance to the group interests. Additionally, the software developments and upgrades coming from any involved group are open to the community via a collaborative platform. Consequently, the development groups get benefits from a methodological framework, which establishes the ways and moments for participation, forms to recovery versions of the development, development rules and tools, and so forth. All these practices on the bases of the development framework allow any small or medium enterprise to share/communicate with partners in the free software development community, in accordance with the free software development philosophy. The proposed methodology has been partially validated at the FSF of the Foundation for Science and Technology of the Mérida State in Venezuela (FUNDACITE-Mérida). In addition, this factory has permitted to understand better, empirically, the real needs of a free software development process and has also been a source of ideas.

ACKNOWLEDGMENT

This chapter has been developed inside the project: "Process Improvement for Promoting Iberoamerican Software Small and Medium Enterprises Competitiveness – COMPETISOFT" (506AC287) financed by CYTED (Programa Iberoamericano de Ciencia y Tecnología para el Desarrollo)

REFERENCES

Alvarez, J. (2007). *Resumen del avance de la aplicación de la metodología desarrollada para la Fábrica de Software Libre* (Tech. Rep. No. 001-2007). Fundacite, Merida: Fábrica de Software Libre. Retrieved December 17, 2007, from http://www.funmrd.gov.ve/drupal/files/technicalReportJohanna.pdf

Alvarez, J., Aguilar, J., & Teran, O., et al. (2006). *Metodología para el Desarrollo de Software Libre: Buscando el Compromiso entre Funcionalidad y Riesgos* (Tech. Rep. No. 001-2006). Fundacite, Merida, Venezuela: Fábrica de Software Libre.

Beck, K. (2004). *Extreme programming explained: Embrace change* (2nd ed.). Addison-Wesley Professional.

Corredor IIMI. (2006). *Evaluación de MoProSoft como alternativa metodológica de organización de empresas de desarrollo y mantenimiento de software.* Tesis de Pregrado, Escuela de Ingeniería de Sistemas-Universidad de Los Andes, Mérida, Venezuela.

Kruchten, P. (2000). *The rational unified process: An introduction* (2nd ed.). Addison-Wesley.

Montilva, J. (2004). Desarrollo de Aplicaciones Empresariales: El Método WATCH. Mérida, Venezuela: Jonás Montilva.

Montilva, J., Hamzan, K., & Ghatrawi, M. (2000, July). The watch model for developing business software in small and midsize organizatios. In *Proceedings of the IV World Multiconference on Systemics, Cybernetics and Informatics (SCI'2000)*, Orlando, FL.

Oktaba, H., Alquiara, C., Su, A., Martinez, A., Quintarilla, A., Ruvalcaba, M. (2005). *Modelo de Procesos para la Industria de Software* (MoPro-Soft, Versión 1.3). México. Retrieved December 16, 2007, from http://www.software.net.mx

Pollice, G. (2001). *Using the rational unified process for small projects: Expanding upon eXtreme programming* (White Paper TP 183). Rational Software.

Probasco, L. (2000). *The ten essentials of RUP: The essence of an effective development process* (White Paper TP177). Rational Software.

Chapter XIV
How to Align Software Projects with Business Strategy

Gustavo Ricardo Parés Arce

Instituto Tecnológico y de Estudios Superiores de Monterrey Campus Santa Fe , Mexico

ABSTRACT

Small and medium-sized enterprises (SMEs) are facing a great challenge that consists of using all the opportunities technology can offer in order to help improve their productivity, geographical reach, and reinvent or complement their business models. Those companies that are not capable of using technology in order to become more competitive will face new threats because nowadays SME companies need to compete with companies not only in the same geographic area, but also need to compete with new products and services that change business rules faster than ever. The main purpose of this chapter is to provide a methodological framework to promote strategic alignment and improve execution through a better communication and understanding about IT projects that will help entrepreneurs and managers to make better IT investment decisions in order to offer a competitive edge to their companies through a better management of the strategic IT portfolio.

INTRODUCTION

Small and medium-sized enterprises (SMEs) are facing a great challenge nowadays because of all the great and new opportunities they have to use technology to improve their productivity, geographical reach, and reinvent or complement their business models. It is also true that there are also new threats because nowadays SME companies need to compete with companies not only in the same geographic area, but also need to compete with new products and services that change business rules faster than ever; and those companies that are not agile enough to change will face big problems in the long term.

According to Venkatraman and Henderson (1998), the information revolution challenges the traditional business logic in three distinct yet interdependent vectors: (1) the customer interaction vector, which deals with the new challenges and opportunities for company-to-customer interactions; (2) the asset configuration vector that focuses on firms' requirements to be virtually integrated in a business network; and (3) the knowledge leverage vector is concerned with the opportunities for leveraging diverse sources of expertise within and across organizational boundaries. Today, e-business enables what could be called virtual organizing, and the consequences are new forms of doing business; those companies that do not consider and understand these proposed vectors will not take full advantage of technology to boost a competitive advantage.

Today, the world is smaller and faster than ever. The small accounting firm in Texas that used to do tax returns for a medium-sized company in Houston might be competing with accounting firms in California, Nevada, or even outside the U.S. This is because many accounting firms are using new technology like Web-based workflow software, voice-over IP communications, or video conferencing to eliminate the geographic barriers, and these companies could be as far away as Bombay, Manila, or Shanghai.

Technology can be a really important business drive and a critical tool (Rathnam, Johnsen, & Wen, 2004) if it is used to leverage the most relevant business opportunities of every company. That is why the topic of software project alignment with business strategy should be a core discussion within all SME executive teams. To lead a better discussion and to standardize the process of software project alignment and prioritization, this chapter will provide a practical framework to identify, rank, and align the projects in order to achieve a greater strategic impact through the selection and execution of appropriate projects.

A challenge facing the SME is the lack of sufficient resources to be able to accept all projects or even to execute some of them simultaneously because of scarce financial, human, or technological resources. SMEs should focus all their efforts on becoming more profitable through operational excellence, superior customer satisfaction, or

whatever core competence they count on; but they need to have the clear understanding that IT is a really important tool, and if it is not used correctly, this could cost them an opportunity that the competition might be willing to take advantage of. In simple terms, it means that the SME should have a clear understanding of which project to execute first and what impact it could have on the business if that project fails or is delayed, and which projects to postpone since some companies might want to implement a critical project when there is less business impact due to business cycles. You do not want your point of sales terminals having technical troubles during your peak month of sales. Another case might be when companies modify their business models, for example, changing to a pure e-business strategy for a particular product, and if the people are not trained, the customers are not informed, and the operating procedures are not clear, you might want to postpone the project.

As might be clear to you, there are many factors to consider as to which project to execute first. Managers should not make decisions based only on financial aspects like the project cost or its net present value (NPV), or based only on a strategic reason if the company cannot afford its cost, or if it is not the right time to choose that project. According to the work of Barbara Farbey and colleagues (Farbey, Targett, & Land, 1994), the search for a single technique that can deal with all IT investment projects is fruitless. That is why we provide a framework that includes five different perspectives that will help managers and company owners make better investment decisions regarding IT investments. The decisions about which information systems projects should be implemented are frequently determinant of business performance and are not only able to change the competitive positioning of the companies but also can modify the competitive structure of the industry, especially when a particular industry relied heavily on the use of information systems (Laurindo, 2006). The main objective of this chapter is to explain the importance of software project alignment, and to explain and provide a practical framework that can be used by many different managers of different business types and with different educational backgrounds.

BACKGROUND

In this chapter, we will explain how to align software projects with business strategy, but first of all, I will start with a common background regarding the basic concepts we will be using from now on to have a clear understanding.

Strategy

The first important aspect we should consider is that defining a good strategy is only the beginning of a long road. According to a cover article in *Fortune Magazine* in 1999, the emphasis made on strategy and vision led to the wrong belief that the only thing needed to succeed was to have the right strategy (Kaplan & Norton, 1996). One of the most important things is to have a defined strategy in order to be able to focus all company efforts on achieving a competitive advantage We will say that successful companies must have a clear strategic focus on what they should do to be more competitive; moreover, it is very important that this strategic focus be translated into clear statements that can be called strategic needs or objectives. Let us take a look, for example, at the three generic strategies proposed by Michael Porter (1982):

1. Leadership in global costs
2. Differentiation
3. Focus

The management team might choose as the main strategic focus to follow a differentiation strategy in which the company must develop new products and services, and offer them to a particu-

lar niche of customers that expect personal and high quality treatment. If you are able to express what the strategic needs for this scenario are, for example, one strategic need might be to develop and implement a new set of customized services aimed at targeting the highest income customers; another might be to develop internal processes and tools to offer superior customer service. Thus, at this point, we have:

- **Strategic Focus:** Follow a differentiation strategy based on developing new products and services to satisfy high income, excellent-service-demanding customers.
- **Strategic Need 1:** Develop and implement a new set of customized services aimed at targeting the highest income customers.
- **Strategic Need 2:** Develop the internal processes and tools to offer superior customer service.

Note: If you are familiar with strategy maps, you may have already seen that strategic needs are the elements contained in each perspective; you might want to classify them according to the four different perspectives (Financial, Customer, Internal Process, Learning and Growth); but for the purpose of this chapter, we will not focus our discussion on the balanced scorecard methodology.

What could happen if, as we have just seen, you do not communicate your strategic focus on to all of your employees? Some of them may think that the company is pursuing leadership on a global cost strategy, and instead of making an effort to give superior treatment to your customers, they now think they must save every possible cent in order to be better employees. The same thing might happen with IT projects if efforts are not aligned, nor will execution nor added value be present at your company. This is why, after the management team has developed the strategy, it is crucial to explain this strategy to everyone in the company;

if people do not know or understand the strategy, they will not be able to execute it.

Therefore, it makes no sense at all to have a well-defined strategy if no one knows about it. One of the most common concerns of the IT staff is that many times they are not well informed of the strategy, its execution, and how IT should respond to some strategic needs. The IT department often works long hours to finish some projects, only to realize that when the project is finished, it is not that important anymore. And there is another project that is even longer, more complex, and more important to the company that they need so that they can accomplish the sales volume needed. This is why the framework we will discuss later on acknowledges this gap in communication and reinforces some tasks so as to avoid or at least decrease the size of the gap. This framework will depend on the strategic focus definition and the strategic needs statement to rank and prioritize different IT projects so that they make sure they are aligned with the strategy.

Even the largest companies started small; many of them were able to grow through the years because they sustained their effort on what is called a strategic intent (Hamel & Prahalad, 2005). The strategic intent is a concept that captures the spirit of entrepreneurship because it points out that some huge companies at their beginning had a disproportionate ambition related to their resources and capabilities. Nevertheless, they were able to translate this ambition or obsession to become better, faster, different, and more efficient through an active management process that includes focusing the organization attention on the essence of winning. The strategic intent needs all employees to know and understand what the company wants to accomplish in order to ensure alignment and the development of important competences because it sets a target that deserves personal effort and commitment. SMEs have scarce resources and a great ambition to win; just do not forget that if you do not guide your efforts and invest your resources wisely, you might not survive in the long

term. But if you are able to develop and maintain a set of strong core competences on which your company is the best, you will be able to have a competitive advantage that will help you grow even on competitive markets.

Execution

Now that we have conveyed the idea that first, it is crucial to have a defined strategy; second, it is necessary for everyone in the company to understand it and identify how they can contribute with their work toward accomplishing the strategy execution; and third, it is necessary to define some important concepts regarding the execution, I would like to take some concepts from a book titled *Execution* (Bossidy & Charan, 2002) where some really clear ideas are provided concerning the problems that arise between strategy formulation and its execution.

Some important topics mentioned in the first chapter agree with one of our previous discussions and state that it is often believed that when a company does not accomplish its goals, it is usually due to bad strategic direction set by the executive team, when in fact, strategies fail more often because they are not executed properly. Things that should be done never get done, and this may be because the organizations are not capable, or their leader underestimates the challenges their companies are facing, or both. Without a proper execution, innovation is unmanageable and confusing, people cannot accomplish precise goals, and change is deterred from the very beginning. No company can fulfill all its commitments unless its leaders practice the discipline of execution on every level. Execution must be a part of the strategic process; it is the missing ingredient between aspirations and results. Many of us are able to explain execution in our own way; thus, it is difficult to give a complete definition as to what it is and how it is done, which is why we will take other definitions from the reference book.

Execution Is a Discipline and an Integral Part of the Strategy

People often think that execution is the tactical aspect of the business. This is the first mistake, because tactics are important for the execution, but execution is not tactics. Execution is a core element of the strategy and it helps to shape it, which is why no strategy should be considered without taking into account the organizational abilities that execute them. Execution is the systematic process of discussing, regularly and seriously, the how and the what, to answer questions, follow up thoroughly, and ensure personal accountability. You cannot demand high levels of execution if your employees do not know the strategy on a detailed level so that they know how they can participate, or if the business leaders do not care or know about the business restrictions or environmental challenges that the company is facing. Business leaders and employees alike must discuss, understand, and evaluate difficulties and redraw the strategic path that should be followed to ensure the proper execution. The heart of execution is based on three processes: the personal process, the strategic process, and the operational process.

Execution Is the Principal Task of Business Leaders

Many executives and business leaders like to think that they do not need to know about the trivial details of implementation and that their position allows them to forget about the small things. This can be very dangerous because if they do not understand the context, they may make inaccurate predictions about the precise execution level to accomplish. Business leaders must be involved personally and profoundly in the business because execution demands a full comprehension of the business, its people, and its environment.

Business leaders should be paying close attention to their people and their teams; they should be asking the right questions at the right moment to prevent problems, or at least to help solve them; the dialogue should be at the core of the organizational culture. If everyone knows the strategy and what they must do, it is the leader's role to ask questions to assess what advances have been made and help the people understand the best course of action to take.

Execution Must be a Fundamental Part of an Organizational Culture

Execution must be embedded at the heart of your organizational culture, but to be a part of it, it should be aligned with your compensation system, your performance evaluation system, and also a part of the company values, philosophy, corporate policies, and norms of conduct. The discipline of execution will not work unless people are practicing it every day. Everyone should be following this discipline, and with time, you should be able to perceive different attitudes and better performance.

Alignment

At this point, we have analyzed the importance of strategy and execution; now we will take a look at another important aspect to consider which is alignment. What happens when you have two people traveling on a boat and each one of them has an oar; one person wants to go to the left and the other one wants to go to the right. Unless they work together and make a decision on where to go, they will not move. Now imagine that a company is a large boat with hundreds of people holding its oars; if there is no clear direction (strategy) on where to go, everyone may be working really hard to make the boat move, but if everybody is trying to move the ship in opposite directions, it will not move.

Now imagine there is a defined strategy or a clear direction on where to go and only four of the five different areas of the boat have been informed of the direction. The boat will probably move, but the area that does not know the direction it is going in will still be working very hard to make the boat move and will probably slow down the movement of the boat instead of making it go faster. If you now inform this last area of the direction and you communicate to the five different areas, the boat will more likely move faster. This may be a very basic example, but I find it really illustrative that alignment means using all your available resources to work towards a common goal and achieving it faster and better. Now imagine that the boat is your company and the five areas are your different functional departments (Human Resources, Information Technology, Sales, Accounting, and Operations). What happens when the IT department is trying to move in a different direction than sales? I am pretty sure you want all your efforts to be focused on the most profitable projects, the ones that will enable your company to become more competitive.

We also need to understand alignment as another process that goes hand in hand with strategy and execution. As already seen, they are all related; so when you have no alignment, you have poor execution; when you have no strategy, there is even less alignment and execution. Any company that wants to achieve synergy must be well communicated and coordinated; the executive team must be concerned and fully accountable to make sure there is general alignment in the organization. And to ensure that, there should be a formal process for alignment, just as there is budgeting and it should be an integral part of the management yearly cycle. This alignment process must be cyclical and the approach must be from the top down.

To do this, there should be an explicit alignment component in the management process; the execution of the strategy requires the highest level of integration and a work team between different areas and organizational processes. We can see that execution managers play a very important role in the process of alignment. But they must

be very aware that the people who must execute the strategy are the people at all levels of the organization, starting with the customer service representatives, the sales force, the call center operators, and many others throughout the company. It is important not only to help employees see how they can contribute to the strategy, but if they are not motivated to change or act according to the strategy, nothing positive will happen. That is why personal performance indicators and incentives must be designed in such a way that they contribute to motivating the people to work according to the strategy. As we discussed previously, the organizational culture must be concerned with execution, but if there is no alignment, great execution from some areas might not help at all if they are executing something that is not according to the overall strategy.

To implement an explicit alignment component, you could refer to the work of Henderson and Venkatraman. They propose that the inability to realize value from IT investments is, in part, due to the lack of alignment between the business and IT strategies of organizations. They propose a strategic alignment model that is based on two main concepts; the first is strategic fit and the second functional integration. These authors group multivariate relationships on four dominant alignment perspectives:

- **Perspective one—Strategy execution:** This perspective is anchored on the notion that a business strategy has been articulated and is the driver of both organizational design choices and the design of IT infrastructure.
- **Perspective two—Technology transformation:** This alignment perspective involves the assessment of implementing the chosen business strategy through appropriate IT strategy and the articulation of the required IT infrastructure and processes.
- **Perspective three—Competitive potential.** This alignment perspective is concerned with the exploitation of emerging IT capabilities to

impact new products and services, influence the key attributes of strategy, and develop new forms of relationships.

- **Perspective four—Service level:** This alignment perspective focuses on how to build a world-class IT service organization. This requires an understanding of the external dimensions of IT strategy with corresponding internal design of the IT infrastructure and processes.

The strategic alignment model is an interesting reference model in order to understand and implement better alignment processes in your company. Keep in mind that in order to implement it, you need to focus the IT function from an internal orientation toward one of strategic fit where the business context or external forces need to be taken in consideration. Another important consideration is that different companies and different stages on each company might need to consider different alignment perspectives, ones that best suit the business conditions and organizational objectives.

The framework proposed in this chapter not only considers that entrepreneurs and managers should have different alignment perspectives, but also it is important to deal with the main issues of why a business strategy and IT strategy gap exists. According to the research done by Rathnam, Johnsen, and Wen (2004), some of the reasons why gaps exist are:

- Poor strategy development, management, and communication
- No general accepted framework for business strategy
- Lack of strategic focus within organizations
- No strategy management process
- IT not involved in business strategy development process
- Business areas unwilling to include IT in strategy discussions

- IT investments are not linked to corporate strategy

As you can see, some of the common issues have to do with the lack of a common framework to assign priorities to IT projects, based on communication, understanding of the strategy, and collaboration. You will find the ranking methodology proposed in this chapter very useful in minimizing the alignment gaps between business and IT strategy.

IT Projects

First, I would like to define what I understand as project, and then we will focus on some of the characteristics that make IT projects different from other types of projects. A project is a planned activity different from day to day tasks, and its purpose is to change, improve, or adapt the company to new challenges or circumstances. Some of the characteristics that distinguish projects can be summarized as follows, according to Hughes and Coterrel (2002):

- Nonroutine tasks are involved
- Planning is required
- Specific objectives are to be met or a specified product or service is to be created
- The project has a predetermined time span
- Work involves several specialists
- Work is carried out in several phases
- The resources available for use on the project are constrained
- The project is large or complex

After reading some of the project characteristics, we now have the clear understanding that projects involve planned change developed by a team of people with different specialties who work together to overcome different challenges to accomplish a specific objective. Our first impression might be that IT projects are more or less the same as any other project and this is true; but we need to pay very special attention to some of the particularities that were pointed out by Fred Brooks (Hughes & Coterrell, 2002):

- **Invisibility:** Software or the progress of many other IT projects cannot be seen as tangible milestones in contrast to the construction of a building, where people can see how they build each floor. Many times, IT projects will not show a perceptible advance until they are almost finished. That is why it is really important for the management team to give continuous follow up to make sure that the project is advancing as promised. Another reason to include different milestones of testing and functionality verification is that IT projects are really abstract and there may be a misinterpretation of a definition. If nobody makes sure the progress is carried out with the proper functionality, it would then be more time consuming and expensive to correct any mistake.

- **Complexity:** Software products are more complex than any other engineered artifacts because they have embedded business rules, validations, and different restrictions that might be very simple as a whole but are as complicated as an airline reservation system. Software products handle and process a lot of information according to many different rules, which is why there should always be a good set of definitions behind any software project.

- **Conformity:** Traditionally, people worked with items they could see and mold; these physical systems and physical materials are very different from software components, databases, and telecommunication networks. The physical systems might also have had some complexity, but that complexity was governed by physical laws that were consistent. Software developers have to conform and understand their tasks after obtaining the requirements from human

clients. And it is not just that individuals may be inconsistent, but organizations and processes might be defined and interpreted differently even among the same group of people defining the requirements. One of the most important phases of any IT project is to do extensive and precise requirement documentation and approval by the main users prior to starting the coding phase.

- **Flexibility:** The ability to adapt the software is seen as one of its strengths. However, this means that in the software system where there is interface with a person or another system, the software should be able to accommodate to other components and needs. This means that the software systems are likely to be subject to a high degree of change. It is normal to adjust a requirement definition in any phase of a project, but keep in mind that if you constantly modify the scope and functionality of a software project, you will end up with higher costs and your deadline will not be met.

MAIN THRUST OF THE CHAPTER

Issues

Software engineers, software architects, programmers, and even IT project managers focus most of their time and effort on understanding, documenting, and managing isolated projects or requirements. Many times, the projects or requirements are attended to on a first in, first out basis, or depending on the hierarchy and urgency of the soliciting area. But IT departments are known for saying "yes" to almost all projects that are authorized by the business units. There is often even a deadline for finishing the project, but very few times do IT departments ever reject projects of this kind or question the real business value of a particular project. There is always significant pressure on the IT areas to execute the software projects in a timely and accurate manner. But unfortunately, one of the most important problems regarding IT has to do with the lack of alignment between the business strategy and the projects developed by IT. Apparently, only some mature companies enforce the active participation of the IT department in the formulation of corporate strategy and corporate goal setting. If the IT staff does not participate from the onset, they will not be able to distinguish between a set of projects, which ones should be done first, and which ones should not be done at a certain time.

Nowadays, no one can question the business value of IT; in recent years, many companies have expanded their business by focusing primarily on an e-business strategy. The ability of these companies to leverage the appropriate IT project at a specific time is a crucial aspect of business. Unfortunately, many small and medium-sized enterprises that are successful today do not think technology is relevant to their strategy; therefore their IT staff role is to obey orders given by sales or division managers. These types of companies should ask themselves what will happen to them in 15 years if they do not reinvent their business models, their managerial practices, and assign proper resources to their IT projects. The first approach companies use is to implement some of the best practices recommended by known orga-

nizations like the Project Management Institute, but many times they fall short due to a lack of understanding of the different challenges faced by IT project managers.

Solutions and Recommendations

The next section of the chapter presents a practical solution to help your company obtain greater value from its IT projects. First, we will explain the general processes that you should follow in order to promote a better alignment between the strategy and the IT projects. These processes deal with different aspects such as how to link the strategic process with the IT projects, and how to communicate between top management and functional employees, and how their work and decisions must be based on a ranked IT project portfolio. Finally, you must understand that this is a dynamic process, and project rankings might vary depending on the particular context of the company.

Project Alignment with Strategy Is a Process, Not a Milestone

The general process consists of seven principal steps that are explained in the following paragraphs:

Figure 1. General processes for project alignment with strategy

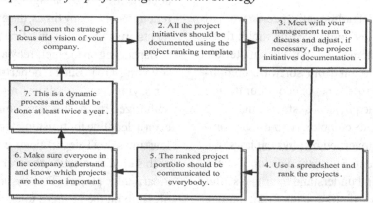

1. You need to document the strategic focus and vision of your company. You should use the same defined strategy in your strategy definition process; it is important to point out that you should be able to write down from three to seven strategic needs to be fulfilled in order to accomplish your strategy. This is the most important aspect; without a strategic definition, nothing else can be done. You cannot align your projects with the strategy if you do not have a clear idea of it. In other words, you must clearly define the following in terms of the strategy:
   - Strategic focus and vision (strategy map optional).
   - From three to seven strategic needs written down as simple statements.

2. All the project initiatives should be documented using the project ranking template; this template contains the information needed in order to give different ranking positions to the projects according to five dimensions included in the template. (Remember this is a baseline framework; after you understand the concepts and relationships used in it, you can adopt it to your particular needs.)

3. Meet with your management team and any other key people needed to discuss and adjust, if necessary, the project initiatives documentation. All project ranking templates should be filled in using the same strategic needs and point assignment mechanism.

4. Use a spreadsheet and rank the projects according to the framework explained in the following pages. The management team should take a look at the project rank and make the final adjustments according to new information or corrections.

5. After the project ranking process has been finished, the ranked project portfolio should be communicated to everybody in the company and/or any others involved in the risk. You should also provide the information of how and why the projects were ranked that way. This will be of great help to the many people who are usually left out of the strategy definition process so that they understand the strategy.

6. Make sure managers, project leaders, and everyone in the company understand and know which projects are the most important and guide your decision-making process based on the priorities presented in the project ranking. If possible, also align compensation systems based on the accomplishment of the projects.

7. Remember this is a dynamic process and should be done at least twice a year; most likely, the projects' relative position will change, but the most important thing is that it be done repeatedly.

Framework

As already stated, the framework must be used in the process of ranking the projects, a process where management must gather key users in order to assure that the projects are documented properly and management understands the scope, cost, reach, and impact of each project. The framework will provide two artifacts (a project ranking template filled out for each project and a spreadsheet with the total results of all ranked projects) that will be invaluable for the task of prioritizing the different IT projects.

The Basic Logic Behind the Framework

The main idea of this framework is to provide a practical tool for SMEs in order to help them prioritize their different projects so that they can focus on working on the most profitable and convenient projects. The basic idea consists of analyzing the projects on five different dimensions relevant to all SMEs; each dimension bears weight on the final result. The best project in each dimension will receive the maximum amount of points possible for that dimension, and the projects that have more points will be ranked accordingly.

Figure 2. Five dimensions used to rank the IT project portfolio

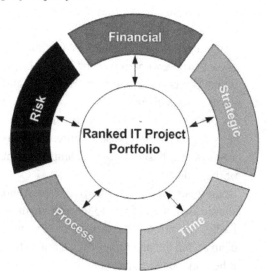

Financial Dimension

This dimension will measure the effectiveness of each project to generate wealth for the company. To assess each project, two elements should be considered: first, the net present value generated by the project, and second, the total cost of the project. If you need further information on how to calculate it, refer to project evaluation literature. As you might know, there are several indicators we can use to rank the projects. For the purposes of this chapter, we will only use the NPV, which in our opinion is the best one to use; we would like to keep our framework simple and effective. If you consider you need to use other indicators like internal rate of return, payback period, or others, please feel free to include it in your analysis.

It is well known that investment analysis tools such as payback period (PP), return on assets (ROA), and return on investment (ROI) are weak because they do not take into consideration the time value of money (Blanchard & Babrycky, 1990). A definition of the net present value is included to stress its benefits and that is why we

enforce its usage for the ranking methodology. Let's look at this definition, taken from Wikipedia (2006): "The net present value (or NPV) is a standard method in finance of capital budgeting used in the process of planning and evaluating different investment options." If you use the NPV method to analyze an investment option, you should accept it if the present value of all cash inflows minus the present value of all cash outflows (including the initial investment) is greater than zero. The rule of thumb is that you should not accept a project if its NPV is negative because it would affect the wealth of the company. If you have two mutually exclusive projects of the same initial total investment cost, you should choose the one that has a greater NPV. Every day, SMEs face the challenge of obtaining additional financing to invest in new projects and support everyday operations. Because financing is scarce or very expensive, companies should use every dollar they have wisely.

It is really important to point out that each different project, due to its nature or its total cost, can be financed in different ways. For example, some projects may be financed by using financial resources such as past year earnings or excess working capital, while others will probably need financing of a different nature, including loans, strategic alliances, private capital, or any other sources available to the company. Taking this into consideration, each project should be discounted at its own particular discount rate for the project to calculate the NPV.

If all your projects are being financed the same way and the discount rate for all of them is the same, you can then use the same one for all your projects; this is what happens more often with larger companies. But using the same discount rate for all projects is not recommended if they have different types of discount rates because the discount rate is a key element in the calculation of the NPV.

1.   Calculate the discount rate (r) for each project.

Figure 3. Financial dimension ranking template section

Financial Dimension	
Total cost (TC):	Discount rate (r): %
Net present value (NPV):	Payback period (PP):
Internal rate of return (IRR):	Sources of financing:

2. Calculate the total cost (TC) of the project and its cash flows for the entire project.

3. Calculate the net present value for the project and other financial indicators such as the internal rate of return or the payback period if you consider it necessary.

4. Fill out the section on the Financial Dimension of the Project Ranking Template.

5. After you have finished doing the first four steps, and the financial dimension section of the template has been properly filled out for all the projects, you will need to use a spreadsheet to do the following steps:

    ◦ In one column write, down the name of each project using a different row for each project.

    ◦ In the next column, write down the total cost of each project, and make sure to use the row corresponding to the project.

    ◦ In the third column, write down the net present value of each project.

    ◦ Use the next column to rank the projects; the project with the greatest NPV should be ranked first, using the same logic rank for all the projects. Remember that a smaller NPV means that the project will not be as profitable, and a negative NPV implies that the project will affect wealth or it will cause the company to lose money.

6. After all projects have been ranked on the spreadsheet, you should assign the corresponding amount of points to each project using the following formula:

    a. The project ranked first will receive the maximum amount of points; we recommend giving 50 points to the project with the greatest NPV, and from that base, give fewer points to the other projects with less NPV. The framework calculates the points using the following formula:

Points = (x/ranking position) => where x is the number of points. For the purpose of this example, it will be 50 and the ranking position will be the relative position received for each project after its ranking. For the project with the greatest NPV, the formula would look like this:

Points = 50/1 = 50

Using this formula, the best projects will receive many more points than the others to stress the importance of choosing the most profitable projects.

Strategic Dimension

This is a key perspective by which projects must be analyzed because even though two projects may have the same NPV, the purpose of one of them may be to enhance business opportunities and the other to optimize the payroll. In the beginning, you might think that if they have the same NPV they might be equally as good, but now think again. To ensure execution and a better strategic alignment, all resources should be focused on sum efforts and accomplish the strategy. If you have two projects with the same NPV, as we have already seen, you need to take into consideration which one of them is going to give you a competitive advantage; the projects that are more aligned with your strategy are the ones that will help your company achieve a competitive edge. As we have seen earlier in this chapter, SMEs should have a strategic focus and they should be able to express that strategic focus on strategic needs. A strategic need is a statement that describes one or several particular aspects of the strategic focus.

In order to assign points to each project:

1. Define the strategic focus of your company.
2. Write down from three to seven strategic needs of your company to execute the strategy (it is not recommended to have less than three or more than seven).
3. On the strategic dimension part of the Project Ranking Template, fill in all the strategic needs in the first column, using one row for each strategic need.
4. Assess according to the project scope and objectives, if the project has a direct, indirect, or null impact on each of the strategic needs, then in the last column write down how the project is having an impact.
   a. For each strategic need that the project has direct impact on, you should assign 10 points, for each indirect impact, 5 points, and 0 points for no impact at all.
   b. Remember that for all projects, you should use the same number and description of strategic needs; this means

that if you used a set of four strategic needs to rank a project, you should use the same set of strategic needs to rank all the other projects; otherwise, the framework will not make sense.

5. Total the points corresponding to this section and write the total on the template in the space provided in the upper part of the dimension table.

Time Dimension

This dimension will take into consideration, once the project is finished and implemented, how much time will be needed for it to have a strong impact on company productivity and income. In other words, imagine that you know that in three or five years you will need a state-of-the-art mobile phone, Web-based extranet for your sales force, but at this point in time you need to increase the functionality of your customer relationship management system in order to be integrated with your accounting system. This would enable your company to reduce in half the time you need to close your accounting cycle and can save your company 30% of your accounting expenses. Furthermore, it would improve the accuracy of your customer information. The first project might have a greater NPV, a greater strategic impact, but its impact may not be noticeable for the following two years. By that time, you could have saved a lot of money integrating your systems and focusing your accounting and financial staff on making more

Figure 4. Strategic dimension ranking template section

Strategic Dimension Directly = 10 points Indirectly = 5 points No= 0 points			Total=
Strategic need	Satisfied by project?	How?	
	Directly Indirectly No		
	Directly Indirectly No		

effective use of the financial resources instead of doing tasks that do not add value to your company at this particular time. Small and medium-sized enterprises must understand that timing is very important; if you fall behind on something important and your competition does not, you will lose your competitive edge and could lose a lot of money. It is important to build a sound basis for the future, but if your company does not take care of the present, there may be no future.

This does not imply that companies should not consider long-term projects; it is just as important to point out that you should first execute and implement those projects that will help you increase or maintain your income in order to have enough resources to invest in other projects to develop new business opportunities or future trends. Even though the total length of the project will not add or subtract points, this information will be important in a scenario where you have two projects which, when implemented, will have an immediate positive impact on the business value; but one project will last 14 months and the other 5 months. If you could choose between these projects, you might prefer the second one that takes 5 months so that you can start adding value to your business as soon as possible.

1. In the section of total length of project, write down in calendar months how long it will take from its initial planning to its functional roll out to be implemented.
2. The second row will ask you what will happen to your business after the project is rolled out.

In other words, once the project is finished and operational, how long it will take to provide a tangible positive business impact? The sooner the project has a positive impact on the company, the better it will be for the company; that is why the short term will add more points than the long term.

3. After marking down if the project will have an impact in the short, medium, or long term, check how many points should be assigned to this dimension and write the number in the upper right hand corner.

Process Dimension

In this dimension, we will determine if the projects have influence on the core business processes of the company or if they just have impact on some back office processes. Small and medium-sized enterprises need to improve their value creation processes to the maximum level of efficiency. For example, think about a restaurant which might have the best inventory management system, as well as a state-of-the-art payroll system, but if the restaurant has to do the billing by hand, it will take that much longer and errors will occur more often. This will affect the smaller customer satisfaction experience. It would be better to have a great billing system, and maybe outsource the payroll and have a regular inventory management system that is verified by a very good acquisition and food quality process. Remember that most of the processes in any company are carried out by humans, and you need to be very careful when

Figure 5. Time dimension ranking template section

Time Dimension Short term = 20 points Medium term = 10 points and Long term = 5 points		Total=
Total length of project:	( ) months	
After implementation, when is it going to have a real business impact?	Short term (1 to 6 months) Medium term (6 to 18 months) Long term (more than 18 months)	

you choose which processes will be automated to increase the value proposition of the company. It is crucial to identify in your strategy which processes are the most important to be developed in the company to be able to sustain the value proposition that will translate into accomplishing the financial goals. There is a cause-effect relationship among the customer value proposition, the business process management, the company know-how, and the ability to be a profitable company. If the company cannot deliver a product or service on time or offer quality, the company will not have any value added that will enable it to increase its market position and value.

An IT project will be better for your company if it can be used by several of your core business processes, and even more so if that project improves the productivity and functionality of the process. This means that the project is relevant to improving the competitiveness and supports the strategy of the company. The core business processes that you include on the ranking template must be aligned with the strategic focus and needs used in the strategic dimension.

1. After analyzing your strategic focus and needs, you must define a set of processes that are important to consider. You should separate the front end processes from the back end processes. This framework will assign more points to the business processes that help the company generate income. Fill in the template in each row with the processes.

2. Mark the checkbox if the project will be used by the process in that row. Go to the next column in the same row.

3. Mark the checkbox if the project will increase the productivity of the process in that row. Go to the next column in the same row.

4. Mark the checkbox if the project will add new functionality or flexibility to the process defined in that row.

5. Do the same for each process.

6. After you finish, you should add two points for each checkbox marked on the business processes, and 1 point for the ones checked for the staff area or back office processes. Total everything and write down the result in the upper right hand corner.

Risk Dimension

Many people might be unfamiliar with this dimension, but many times projects fail because nobody took any time to analyze the risk through self assessment. But let us take a minute to look at a

Figure 6. Process dimension ranking template section

Process Dimension Each box marked = 2 points for **BU** and 1 point for Staff				Total =
		Project used by?	Improves productivity?	Adds new required functionality?
Business Units Processes **(BU)**	Sales			
	Operations			
	Customer service			
	Claims attention			
Staff Area Processes **(Staff)**	Human Resources			
	Information Technology			
	Finance			
	Purchase			

definition of risk: A risk denotes a potential negative impact on an asset or some characteristic of value that might arise from some present process or from some future event. If we are analyzing different projects that will affect our company, we must assess how this project could affect, in a negative way, the company, its customers, employees, or owners. Now let us think about a project that has a great NPV, an almost immediate positive impact on efficiency and an important strategic impact, but there is a huge risk that the project can not be delivered on time. And since quality is needed to assure a successful business, this project involves a huge financial resource commitment and needs to core business processes to be redefined. Different managers may have different attitudes toward risk, but you should make sure that management risk aversion or risk seeking criteria should be clearly defined and assessed. This will also be different from industry to industry and from company to company. It is very important that the management team asks the right questions in order to properly assess the risk. There are some sample questions on the project ranking template which can be used, but it would be better if you tailor that section to your particular needs.

First, you need to make a risk assessment of your organization regarding the relevant topics your particular company might be facing. If your company is in the financial industry, the risks might be very different from those of a construction company. On the ranking template, we provide some examples that could be a useful guide, but we strongly recommend identifying and measuring the most important risks concerning the implementation of the IT projects.

Once you identified the relevant risks to consider in this point analysis, you should write them down; in each row, you should write down the risk as a simple yes/no question. You may write down as many identifiable risks as you want; just consider that the ranking framework consists of a weighted result among the five dimensions. If you do not adjust the point scale and add many rows either on the risk dimension, strategic dimension, or the process dimension, the predominant dimension on weighing the projects will become the one that has more elements, and it might not be what we want to do. Another important aspect is that you might want to form the questions either in a positive or negative way. For some questions, it might be better to answer "yes" and for others, it might be better to answer "no." Make sure you do not mix your questions; you must assign points to all of them, whether you answer "yes" or "no," but try to avoid mixing them because it will cause confusion.

Figure 7. Risk dimension ranking template section

Risk Dimension		Total =
Does the company have the appropriate infrastructure to support the project?		Yes No
Does the company have sufficient financial resources to pay for the project without affecting the business operations?	Yes No	
Does the company have the appropriate people to plan, develop, and execute the project effectively?		Yes No
Does the company have the required process maturity to implement the project in the short term?		Yes No
Does this project affect any regulatory compliance?		Yes No

Considerations about Dimension Pondering

So far, we know that there are five dimensions we need to consider in order to apply our framework, but it is important to point out that depending on the particular weight we assign to each one, the resulting ranked project portfolio could be different. For example, if your company is with scarce financial resources, you would like those projects with greater NPV and with the shortest time of implementation to be ranked at the top of the project portfolio. One disadvantage of assigning a great weight to the financial perspective is that you might exclude some strategic projects that might have a very low or even negative NPV in the short term, but that could be the projects that will create a competitive advantage in the long term.

On the other hand, imagine that you have an unlimited amount of financial resources and you want to develop some strategic core competences in order to achieve a long term competitive advantage; in this scenario, you do not really care too much about if the project will be implemented and in use in two months or two years. You know that these projects might need several years of effort and loss before you see the final results.

Let us take a look at three different strategies proposed in order to give you a starting point on how to ponder the different dimensions according to your own particular needs (Figure 8).

The first strategy, the one proposed in the column named W1, has a simplistic approach and a starting point on which you might give the same weight (20%) to all dimensions, and

Figure 8. Proposed pondering strategies

Dimension	W1	W2	W3
Financial	20%	40%	10%
Strategic	20%	10%	40%
Time	20%	35%	10%
Process	20%	10%	30%
Risk	20%	5%	10%

start tuning after several iterations. According to the particular needs of your company, your own management expertise and the context you will learn that maybe there are some dimensions that are most important for your company in a particular moment of time.

The second strategy, in the column named W2, will be suitable for those companies who are on a growing phase and have a considerable pressure for cash and liquidity; in this case, those projects that have a greater NPV and a shorter implementation and impact time on the revenue will be ranked at the top. Remember that your company might use one or two years for this strategy (W2), but in the long term, it could be useful to think also in the long term.

The third strategy, in the column named W3, gives a lot of importance to the strategic and process dimension. For mature companies with the ability to invest money and think on a long term competitive advantage, this is a good pondering strategy because those projects that will need maybe 20 months to be finished and that will have at the beginning a negative return might become a core and strategic system three years from now. According to McFarlan (1984), managers must not be to efficiency-oriented in IT resource allocation. They must encourage creativity in research and development and should not permit the use of simplistic rules to calculate desirable IT expense levels. And his sustaining argument to support this is that the technology has given the organization the potential for forging sharp new tools that can produce lasting gains in market share. But remember this strategy applies to those companies that can afford at any particular time to invest on the medium and long term, small companies on a growing phase with scarce money should not use this third strategy.

Now you can create as many pondering strategies as you like; these three examples are just to give a brief explanation of how to use and understand the different mixes of the five dimensions and to point out that according to the different ponderings the resulting ranked IT project portfolio could be different.

CONCLUSION

We have seen that there are several important aspects in order to align the software project management with the business strategy. The principal ones are the strategy definition and communication process, the execution as a discipline to be followed by everyone in the company, alignment as a process of summing efforts in order to achieve results on a more efficient way. Finally, we tried to take all these concepts and give them a sense through a practical framework to be implemented in SMEs in order to help them achieve greater business success; its implementation can be useful in any country because it was designed to improve general processes of the software development process and it allows the adoption of particular needs.

As there is a changing environment, you must have in mind that the communication of your strategy, training, and a cultural change are fundamental aspects that will leverage positive change throughout your organization. The alignment of software projects is a process that should be repeated as many times as necessary according to your company's particular needs. For example, a company on a mature industry of low growth could apply the framework only one or two times a year; on the other hand, an e-business company on a fast growing market might prefer to apply the framework every two months. The framework is very flexible, and you can customize it to your own particular needs, not only on how often you use it, but also on how do you assign more or less importance to any particular dimension according to your own personal needs.

Another important aspect is that you should document properly all your project ranking templates; it is a very valuable part of the framework, and many times it is a task that nobody likes to do, but we have seen huge IT projects fail due to a bad focus, unmanaged scope, and a lack of strategic alignment, especially when we mention enterprise resource planning systems where its implementation affects directly the many of the critical business processes (Sullivan, 2005). Both the CEO and CIO should be the project sponsors of the project ranking framework, because if they are not committed to have a defined strategy, to follow up and participate on a cultural change that will enforce execution and to facilitate communication among the different areas, the framework will not be as useful. Top management should have an active participation on the follow up and enforcement of the process.

It is really important to invest in projects that will generate greater business value to the company; unfortunately those types of projects could come up just a week after you had communicated your annual plan; do not be afraid to rank it among all other projects, and if it is a new project ranked on the top three projects, communicate it to the company. Information technology people do not like to change projects, nor priorities, especially when they have started already, but if you have a documented and consistent explanation of why it is important to the company, they will embrace the change easily, and the company could generate a greater value.

There is a group of companies that have been very successful on the process of implementing strategic information systems. Those companies can participate in a very complex world, facing even larger competitors. The key to success is to invest wisely in order to achieve operational excellence, flexibility, and use information to take the correct decisions. I am confident that after you start applying these concepts to your company, you will be find a great value and you will be able to customize the framework to your own particular needs; I hope you start soon and you find the framework useful.

ADDITIONAL RESOURCES AND EXAMPLES

Please visit the following Web page (http://www.tiparalapyme.com/project_ranking/) in order to find some tools including the project ranking template in Word (.doc) and Rich Text Format (.rtf), as well as the spreadsheet templates to rank the results of all the projects.

You can also download some complete examples of the framework as well as tutorials and additional resources in order to help you get started.

REFERENCES

Bossidy, L., & Charan, R. (Eds.). (2002). *Execution: The discipline of getting things done.* Mexico: Aguilar.

Farbey, B., Targett, D., & Land, F. (1994). Matching an IT project with an appropriate method of evaluation: A research note on "Evaluating investments in IT." *Journal of Information Technology, 9*, 239-343.

Hamel, G., & Prahalad, C.K. (2005). Strategic intent. *Harvard Business Review, 83*, 148-161.

Hughes, B., & Cotterell, M. (2002). *Software project management.* Berkshire, UK: McGraw-Hill.

Kaplan, R., & Norton, D. (Eds.). (1996). *The balanced scorecard: Translating strategy into action.* Barcelona: Gestión 2000.

Laurindo, F.J.B., & Moraes, R.O. (2006). IT projects portfolio management: A Brazilian case study. *International Journal Management and Decision Making, 7*(6), 586-603.

McFarlan, W.E. (1984). Information technology changes the way you compete. *Harvard Business Review, 62*(3), 98-103.

Porter, M. (Eds.). (1982). *Competitive strategy: Techniques for analyzing industries and competitors.* Mexico: Macmillan.

Rathnam, R.G., Johnsen, J., & Wen, J.H. (2004). Alignment of business strategy and IT strategy: A case study of a Fortune 50 financial services company. *Journal of Computer Information Systems, 45*, 1-7.

Sullivan, L. (2005). ERPzilla: 10 ERP deployments show that megaprojects are standing strong—though they've changed in focus and function. *InformationWeek.* Retrieved December 17, 2007, from http://www.informationweek.com/showArticle.jhtml?articleID=165700832

Venkatraman, N., & Henderson, J. (1998). Real strategies for virtual organizing. *Sloan Management Review, 40*(1), 33-48.

GENERAL REFERENCES

Bardhan, I., Bagchi, S., & Sougstad, R. (2004). Prioritizing a portfolio of information technology investment projects. *Journal of Management Information Systems, 21*(2), 33-60.

Chang, R.Y. (2005). What's your strategic alignment quotient? *Chief Learning Officer, 4*(8), 20.

Erlanger, L. (2005). The next step: IT portfolio management. *InfoWorld, 27*(33), 35.

Flaig, J.J. (2005). Improving project selection using expected net present value analysis. *Quality Engineering, 17*(4), 535-538.

Henderson, J.C., & Venkatraman, N. (1993). Strategic alignment: Leveraging information technology for transforming organizations. *IBM Systems Journal, 32*, 472-481.

Merlyn, V., & Morrison, B. (2003). Director's guide to exploiting the business value of IT. *Directorship, 29*, 11-15.

Peppard, J., & Ward, J. (2005). Unlocking sustained business value from IT investments. *California Management Review, 48*(1), 52-70.

Poland, W.B. (1999). Simple probabilistic evaluation of portfolio strategies. *Interfaces, 29*(6), 75-83.

ANNEX 1: PROJECT RANKING TEMPLATE

Project Ranking Template

Project name:	
Objective:	
Main goals:	

Financial Dimension	
Total cost (TC):	Discount rate (r): %
Net present value (NPV):	Payback period (PP):
Internal rate of return (IRR):	Sources of financing:

Strategic Dimension Directly = 10 points Indirectly = 5 points No= 0 points			Total=
Strategic need	Satisfied by project?	How?	
	Directly Indirectly No		
	Directly Indirectly No		
	Directly Indirectly No		

Time Dimension Short term = 20 points Medium term = 10 points and Long term = 5 points		Total=
Total length of project:	( ) months	
After implementation, when is it going to have a real business impact?	Short term (1 to 6 months) Medium term (6 to 18 months) Long term (more than 18 months)	

Process Dimension Each box marked = 2 points for **BU** and 1 point for Staff			Total =3	
		Project used by?	Improves productivity?	Adds new required functionality?
Business Units Processes (BU)	Sales			
	Operations			
	Customer service			
	Claims attention			
Staff Area Processes (Staff)	Human Resources			
	Information Technology			
	Finance			
	Purchase			

Risk Dimension	Total =	
Does the company have the appropriate infrastructure to support the project?	Yes	No
Does the company have sufficient financial resources to pay for the project without affecting business operations?	Yes	No
Does the company have the appropriate people to plan, develop and execute the project effectively?	Yes	No
Does the company have the required process maturity to implement the project in the short term?	Yes	No
Does this project affect any regulatory compliance?	Yes	No

Chapter XV
A Model to Classify Knowledge Assets of a Process–Oriented Development

Raquel Anaya
Departamento de Informática y Sistemas, Universidad EAFIT, Columbia

Alejandra Cechich
Departamento de Ciencias de la Computación, Universidad Nacional del Comahue, Argentina

Mónica Henao
Departamento de Informática y Sistemas, Universidad EAFIT, Columbia

ABSTRACT

Knowledge assets are knowledge regarding markets, products, technologies and organizations, that a business needs to own and that enable its business processes to generate profits. Today, how to model knowledge assets is a concern of the organizational modeling community; mostly because consensus on a knowledge asset model is far from achieved. This chapter is aiming at identifying a model to characterize knowledgeable assets and their relationships in a software organization. Generally speaking, knowledge assets represent intellectual capital for a software organization and support the whole organizational process. The model proposed here is an initial step towards defining knowledge management as a transversal process at the organization. An instantiation of the model is illustrated through a case study in a real software company that recognizes the value of knowledge as a tool to support and improve the organizational strategies.

INTRODUCTION

The term "software process improvement" (SPI) groups all those activities aiming at improving processes in software organizations. SPI models, such as capability maturity model integration, or CMMI (Chrissis, Konrad, & Shrum, 2005), and MoProSoft (Oktaba et al., 2003), offer a general guide about the goals and best practices that should be adopted by the organization in order to define a standard, controlled, and monitored process. For this purpose, many research lines around software processes have emerged.

Metaprocesses have been used to study the particular characteristics of the software process and to express the relevant questions to be asked at a conceptual level (Nguyen & Conradi, 1994; Ruiz, García, Piattini, & Polo, 2002; Senge, 1990). For example, the SPEM (Software Process Engineering Metamodel) is a specification defined by the OMG[1] that describes a concrete software development process or a family of related software development processes (Senge, 1990). Additionally, several research efforts have investigated on how to describe software processes precisely by using knowledge representation techniques and process-centred software engineering environments (PSEEs) (Dingsøyr, 2003; Dingsøyr & Røyrvik, 2003; Liao, Qu, & Leung, 2005). They add logic rules to the processes so as to provide appropriate management of information. But most of the existing PSEEs only focus on the life cycle models oriented to the development processes and omit software process models. There are also some SPI tools that can help improve the processes by providing many functions, such as document management. However, the usage of these tools and environments is limited, due to their lack of flexibility, so their reusability and extensibility are limited.

To develop software is an example of "knowledge work" proposed by Peter Drucker (1993) because the software process engineering's "value is (...) created by 'productivity' and 'innova-

tion.'" One of the latest tendencies to improve the software process is knowledge management, a field that provides concepts and tools to manage organizational knowledge (Ruiz et al., 2002; Scharmer, 1996), and it is also related to creating "learning organizations" in software engineering: "learning software organizations" (Dingsøyr, 2003). Knowledge is defined by Davenport and Prusak (1998) as:

a fluid mix of framed experience, values, contextual information, and expert insight that provides a framework for evaluating and incorporating new experiences and information. It originates and is applied in the minds of knowers. In organizations, it often become embedded not only in documents or repositories but also in organizational routines, processes, practices, and norms.

Knowledge can be tacit or explicit and may embody high-level company policies; a customer sets the way of doing business or even know-how about technical methods such as standard design methods. Tacit knowledge refers to that knowledge that is embedded in individual experience and includes insights, perceptions, intuition, and skills that are highly personal and hard to formalize, making them difficult to communicate or share with others. Explicit knowledge is knowledge that has been articulated in formal language and can easily be transmitted among individuals. All those can be assets that share a common intent; they are meant to support organizational processes.

Another new approach is organizational learning, a field of study of the organization and representations of experiences have been defined in such a way that learning can be retrieved and used for solving a new problem (Brown & Duguid, 1991; Scharmer, 2001). A learning organization is "an organization skilled at creating, acquiring, and transferring knowledge, and at modifying its behaviour to reflect new knowledge and insight" (Garvin, 1993). This approach funds on designing rationale of systems (Concklin, & Begeman, 1988;

McGarry et.al., 1994), organizational memories (Staab, Studer, & Sure, 2002), and experience stimulation and externalization (Fischer, Lindstaedt, Ostwald, Scneider, & Smith, 1996).

The application of knowledge management to the software process is an active field (Dingsøyr, 2003; Dingsøyr, & Conradi, 2002; Dingsøyr, & Røyrvik, 2003; Hansen, Nohrian, & Tierney, 1999; Henninger, 2001; Holz, 2003). The main reason to managing knowledge in software engineering is that it is a human and knowledge intensive activity, and knowledge-intensive work can be improved by managing knowledge better. Whether you are an information system architect or designer, or a business process analyst or manager, the success of your work depends on the degree of your understanding of organizations, processes, methods, standards, and so forth. Unfortunately, learning from experience demands tailoring to specific domains and environments, which is suppose to reflect the specifics of the company in general and the projects in particular. The knowledge generated within an organization to specialize existing techniques represents a significant asset. For example, knowing how unified modeling language (UML) diagrams are represented is knowledge we can find in textbooks; however understanding how those diagrams should be used to create a specific application is a different kind of knowledge that comes from the organizational context.

During process execution, new knowledge is created to meet development needs that are unique to the project. This new knowledge can be synthesized and packaged to create new knowledge resources. The newly formed knowledge is then used as the basis for new product development. Additionally, the desire of higher productivity and higher quality of use has strongly influenced the supporting technologies for classifying and retrieving this information generated in a software development project.

CMMI proposes, in the OPD[2] practice, the use of an organization's process asset library to support organizational learning. Several efforts

in building these libraries, such as the STARS programme (STARS, 2006), show us the potential advantage of these libraries to support the software process knowledge in small and medium software enterprises. In a previous work (Anaya, Londoño, & Hurtado, 2006), we have introduced a first model to represent software process knowledge. This model is based on the notions of process-oriented development, which funds in turn on several baselines that represent the core disciplines (requirements, analysis and design, testing, configuration management, etc.). In a specific project, the baselines are configured with prescriptive assets that guide the execution of an activity. It allows enriching every process' practice with experience gained in its application. Accomplishing this requires the ability of representing both knowledge categories and associated experiences.

This chapter is aiming at identifying a model to characterize the knowledgeable assets and their relationships in a software organization. Generally speaking, knowledge assets represent the capital of these companies to support all the processes. The model proposed is an initial step oriented to define the knowledge management as a transversal process at the organization (Anaya, Cechich, & Henao, 2006). The organization of this chapter is as follows. The next section discusses background and related work that support the proposal. The third section describes the model that characterizes the knowledge asset in a software organization; and the fourth section briefly introduces results from a case study. Finally, the last section draws some conclusions and future work.

BACKGROUND AND RELATED WORK

Organizational learning applied to software processes has focused on capturing, storing, and reusing such organizational knowledge emphasizing the importance of creating experience-based methodologies (Hansen et al., 1999; Henninger, 2001; Nour, Holz, & Maurer, 2000). In many of these approaches, a tool is required to support the *experience factory*. This concept represents a group of people interacting with a tool to reuse experiences, which are consolidated, validated, and classified in an experience repository (Hansen et al., 1999; Henninger, 2003). An experience-based methodology is supported in the quality improvement paradigm (QIP) proposed for NASA by McGarry (Mentzas, Apostolou, Abecker, & Young, 2003), which consists of an iterative process of six steps. The steps, performed within projects, are: (1) characterize project goals, (2) set goals, (3) choose a process, (4) execute, (5) analyze results, and (6) package the results of analysis.

Generally, tools explore experience-based repositories that allow the definition of a case-based organizational memory. To use it, people first create project instances to be customized by using knowledge from the repository. Second, a set of activities to carry out the project is defined. Then, activities are executed and tailored to reuse knowledge. It allows choosing options to any activity and storing results, which in turn populate the repository. Some tools facilitate articulation between organizational knowledge and experience-based software development techniques. For example, BORE (Building an Organizational Repository of Experience) (Hansen et al., 1999; Henninger, 2003) combines a work breakdown structure with repository tools to create a framework for designing software process methodologies and repositories for capturing knowledge artifacts. BORE is supported by an experience-based methodology, which includes several steps such as project instantiation, domain creation, project execution, and so forth.

Henniger (2003) defined the experience-based knowledge life cycle, shown in Figure 1. At the product creation, knowledge is both created by and used within the specific context of a software development organization. In the analysis phase,

the new knowledge can be synthesized and packaged to create new knowledge resources. Our proposal builds upon the basic ideas of BORE in order to define the asset knowledge management process of a software organization.

Another approach, based on the different experience-related materials encountered in an organization (Landes, Schneider, & Houdek, 1999), proposes a classification of the documents with respect to their maturity, which range from raw context-specific documents to experiences and lessons learned. This classification would help understand how these documents should be collected, analyzed, validated, and so forth. In essence, this approach expresses the fact that all information may be valid as an experience, no matter what particular format or medium is used to support it. As another example, processes in the DARPA's STARS programme (STARS, 2006) can be modeled using several notations, such as English, diagrams, and process modeling languages. Process definition technologies are categorized into different layers, meaning that lower levels represent definition technologies that could be used for describing more details of the same process step represented more abstractly by a technology in a higher level. The degree of formality associated with a defined process will indicate the possibility of being supported by a tool.

Although knowledge models vary, normally a process has a set of practices that guides the software production. Then, searching similarities among processes and practices has recently becoming a matter of interest for the research community. For example, software processes are expressed at a conceptual level by using ontologies (Mentzas et al., 2003). (Iria, Ciravegna, Cimiano, Lavelli, Motta, Gilardoni, & Mönch, 2004), which assist in evaluating SPI models such as CMMI; or ontologies are considered as a basis for indexing experiences from an experience base (Dingsøyr, 2003; Rouvellou et al., 2000).

As another example, the SPEM (2006) metamodel takes the object-oriented approach and uses UML as specification language. This specification is structured as a UML profile and provides a complete MOF-based metamodel. This approach facilitates exchange with both UML tools and MOF-based tools/repositories. The SPEM's basic model is conformed by *roles* that interact or collaborate by exchanging *work products* and triggering the execution, or enactment, of certain *activities*. Each activity uses or produces work products. Each role is responsible for the work products that it generates. The overall goal of a process is to bring a set of work products to a well-defined state. Besides, SPEM defines *guidance* elements, which may be associated with ModelElements "to provide more detailed information to practitioners about the associated ModelElement. Possible types of Guidance depend on the process family and can be for example: Guidelines, Techniques, Metrics, Examples, UML Profiles, Tool mentors, Checklist, Templates" (SPEM, 2006). This work takes the basic semantic of the SPEM's metamodel about roles, activities, work products, and their relationship. However, the model we propose in this chapter has been extended with two main goals in mind: (1) to characterize some process' elements as process assets that represent useful capital for reuse; we will especially emphasize experience assets as key elements in an experience-based development process and (2) to integrate other knowledge assets that represent important intellectual capital for a software organization. For this last goal, we have reviewed some works that characterize the organization's knowledge assets.

CHARACTERIZING KNOWLEDGE ASSETS

Unlike information, knowledge is less tangible and depends on human cognition and awareness. *Knowledge assets* are the knowledge regarding markets, products, technologies, and organizations that a business owns or needs to own and which enable its business processes to generate profits. In Mentzas et al. (2003), "Knowledge assets are the resources that organizations wish to cultivate," but they are different from other organizational resources.

There are different typologies about knowledge assets. Mentzas et al. present Know-Net

Figure 1. The experience-based knowledge life cycle (Henninger, 2003)

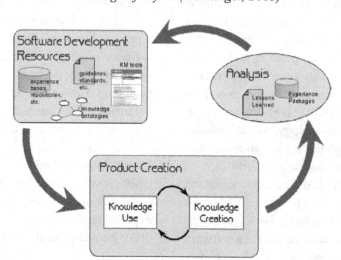

knowledge assets: human knowledge assets that generate organizational capabilities; structural knowledge assets that generalize the human capabilities; and market knowledge assets that gauge the products and services of the company. Dingsøyr (2003) introduces similar concepts but names them differently: human capital, relational capital, and structural capital. Human capital is about people's capabilities to work in the organization, their knowledge, skills, and experience; this capital is increased by socialization and internalization. Relational capital represents the organizational knowledge related with external relations such as market, organizational customers, and business partners and competitors; this capital is increased by socialization. Structural capital (named infrastructural capital, too) is about organizational capabilities needed to achieve the functional requirements (process, policies, etc.), infrastructure included is able to qualify and maintain the human capital (systems, hardware, and software). At the same time, structural capital is the organizational capability, including transmitting and saving intellectual materials.

Knowledge can be seen in different refinement levels, which can be understood as different knowledge maturity. These levels of knowledge correspond to what Nonaka and Takeuchi (1995) call the "ontological dimension." This dimension is referred to as the social interactions that begin at the individual level and then by communication between groups and organizations let knowledge expand and grow. Another dimension is the epistemological dimension, referred to as the knowledge type, specifically to explicit and tacit knowledge and the way that they can be transformed into the other (explicit to tacit, tacit to explicit).

Following the process or product approaches in knowledge management and according to the software engineering activities, knowledge needed and produced during the software process can be classified as a "product" or a "process." The first implies that knowledge is a thing that can be located and manipulated as an independent object that it is possible to capture, distribute, measure, and manage. This approach mainly focuses on products and artifacts containing and representing knowledge. It allows reuse of knowledge. The second "process" or "personalization" approach focuses on the creation of communities of interest or practice or experts, to share knowledge between the community members. It is linking people so that tacit knowledge can be shared. In a software process development, both the process and the product approaches are applied to support the identifying, managing, and leveraging of knowledge through better management of the organization's knowledge (Figure 2).

Knowledge in software engineering would be classified into categories: organizational knowledge, management knowledge, technical knowledge, and knowledge of the domain. The organizational and management category represents knowledge about policies and strategies around the company. Most of this knowledge is stable during the company's life, like a mission, vision, and so forth. Technical and domain knowledge represents the critical knowledge in a software organization; the first one is about skills to do some activities or tasks during the software process, related with methods and technologies appropriate to the organization and to the particular project. This knowledge is dynamic and changes frequently, but it can be explicitly related with standards and patterns. The knowledge domain is the specific domain which the software is about. This knowledge changes between projects. It is obtained from static and dynamic sources during the elicitation process. Usually this knowledge is represented by diagrams, models, libraries, and frameworks.

MODELING KNOWLEDGE ASSETS

Our contribution is in identifying those typical aspects of a software development process by pursuing pertinent questions like: What aspects

Figure 2. Product and process approaches of knowledge asset management

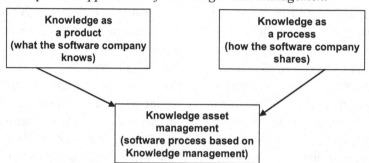

are needed? Which affects impact the components of a software process? How and when should they be used (and reused)? Consequently, knowledge has multiple relationships with other entities highly relevant to modeling processes. Knowledge assets are generated and used by work units and require resources (e.g., infrastructure, people); depend on a context (e.g., a particular application domain, a client, supporting technology); and are produced, validated, and updated by people. At the same time, knowledge assets enable users to deal with different issues by addressing key knowledge aspects. We distinguish the following types of knowledge assets in the model (Figure 3), which address several issues: what knowledge is available (conceptual base), how it was used (rationale, process), why it should be used (rationale, business), skills needed to apply it (profile), how it should be controlled (control), and what organizational infrastructure and resources are necessary to apply it (infrastructure):

- Rationale Assets. One of the main challenges during the instantiation of a knowledge-based development is the clarification of design decisions, experiences, guidelines, and so forth. These elements share an interesting feature: they all must be useful to look at since they enable us to learn something from our previous actions and decisions. This information is collected from the diverse activities that constitute a software development process

and categorized by identifying their maturity level, that is, their degree of institutionalization and the amount of analysis involved. This "rationale part" should be documented emphasizing the purpose and intended group of readers of the experience. Another essential element is the description of the context in which the experience was gained. Properly documenting rationale is critical because people make decisions in complex environments and they involve trade-offs. For example, explicitly documenting architecture decisions can provide a concrete direction for implementation and serve as an effective tool for communication. In our model, rationale assets are kept simple to allow us to instantiate classification according to different subjects from business- to code-level. In this way, we provide a skeleton (metamodel) to be "filled" by particular rationale classifications such as the ontology for object-oriented (OO) micro-architectural design knowledge introduced in Garvin (1993). Guidelines and criteria for composing software development processes from process assets are another example.

- Process Assets. They include complete definitions of life cycle processes, process elements, and generic process architectures; and they are assembled by following appropriate rationale and documented through a Process Asset Library (PAL) such as the STARS project suggests (Staab et al., 2002). Conceptually, every project has a project-specific PAL. It serves as a source of process assets when a project is planned and its process is defined. Note that a complete process definition may be a very complex specification of process requirements, a variety of interrelated process models, and process code. For example, workflow models might be used to describe the steps to transform project inputs into products. Particularly, process base lines would help us to describe recurrent steps able to be reused by a particular process. For example, we might reuse typical processes including their links (requirements elicitation, architecting, coding, etc.), when discussing variations of software development life cycles. Under this conception, a software development process will be considered a set of process-related steps, which must be assembled to instantiate a given case. Similarly, organizational processes will be depicted based on base lines that would facilitate the use of defined

processes. It will promote collaboration and teamwork by making the process' activities, roles, responsibilities, and dependencies visible to all personnel.

- Infrastructure Assets. Tailoring a process requires identifying resources needed and the infrastructure required to implement their activities. It embodies knowledge about the work units, work groups, and the basic skills and competences required by the different processes and domains. In a software organization, the work environment should be designed to maintain working conditions that allow individuals to concentrate on their tasks and motivate the group work. The knowledge about the adoption of external tools (as CASE tools, CVS, infrastructure frameworks) or about the tool developed internally (as intranet) represents an important asset for the organization. The organization of group works becomes another valuable asset. How are people arranged so they con-

Figure 3. Knowledge asset model

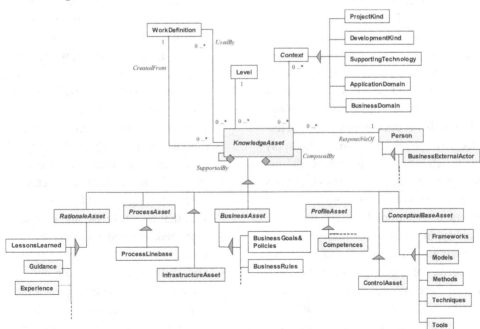

stitute teamwork? How do they communicate with each other? Knowledge about possible communication paths allows us to identify the formal and informal structure on which communication flows. Generally speaking, an enterprise has its own formal communication channels called communicating flows or vectors (Ciamberlani & Steimberg, 1999). They can be (1) upward and downward vectors, allowing hierarchical communication as command-reporting channels; (2) horizontal vectors, allowing communication among people on the same hierarchical level; these vectors have the goal of improving organizational development by increasing internal cohesion and facilitating management processes; and (3) transversal vectors, allowing communication among people of different areas that are not connected by the hierarchical network. Considering these flows, there is a great variety of messages to be used by communication processes. For instance, task messages are involved in new or changing tasks, maintenance messages are related to routine work, and human messages have a direct impact on motivation.

- Business Assets. Represent the business knowledge about the client's organization. Developers must understand the purpose of the business, the current practices of the business, and the IT strategy of the client company. To do so, business knowledge should be explicitly documented. Some of this knowledge is represented by models that apply practices such as business process modeling. An enterprise model, for example, models both the structural business entities and the current (and dynamic) business practices. Particularly, business rules may be one of the following: definitions of business terms, data integrity constraints, mathematical and functional derivations, logical inferences, processing sequences, and relationships among facts about the business. These types

of business rules are examples of metadata, where semantic validation is based on current practices that are dynamic in the sense that they depend on changing regulations. Business rules are the dynamic for the sentences that are found in the language of business. The best way to identify business rules is to look at the organization from its customers' point of view. Thus, a good enterprise model reflects a concise understanding of the structural qualities of the business plus dynamic regulations (Oktaba et al., 2003). Another practice that contributes to know the client organization is the enterprise architecture modeling. An enterprise architecture (EA) is a framework that provides a common context both for diagnosing the need of change and for managing the process of change oriented by a strategic technology (Marques & Sousa, 2004). The EA helps capture the global vision of all perspectives such as business, information system, and technical perspectives.

- Profile Assets. It embodies knowledge about the skills and competences of the human resource. This asset should help improve the organization by increasing the capability of individuals and aligning their motivation with that of the organization. It should help retain human assets (i.e., people with critical knowledge and skills) within the organization. With the level of productivity differences evidenced during software development processes, individual and team skills become strategic competitive assets. Since knowing skills and competences is crucial, its modeling, managing, and storing are important aspects of this asset. Staffing should be designed in such a way that talent, skills, and competences are recruited, selected, and assigned to tasks. Recruiting involves identifying the knowledge and skill requirements for open positions; selection involves developing a list of qualified candidates, defining a selection strategy, evaluating candidates, and selecting the most qualified candidate; and assignment involves orienting selected candidates to the organization and ensures their successful transition into their positions. Storing profile assets additionally helps us to measure individual productivity, provide productivity feedback, and enhance productivity continuously. Training is designed to ensure that all individuals have the adequate skills required to perform their tasks. Training involves identifying the skills and competences required to perform the tasks and ensuring that needed training is given. Finally, profile assets are useful elements when compensation is designed. It includes defining a compensation strategy where evaluations are based on skills and competences, among other aspects.

- Control Assets. Every element of a project, from software products to business processes (or even control processes), must be under control. We should take appropriate steps to ensure that those elements, which we are responsible for addressing, are defined and controlled. To achieve this control, we must deal with several ways of controlling, that is, testing software pieces, measuring quality attributes, and so forth. Whenever a product is elaborated, or a process defined and executed, the affected plans, work products, and activities are adjusted to remain consistent and under control. Control assets should provide adequate visibility about how elements should be controlled. It implies that the different versions of the element are known (i.e., version control) and changes are incorporated in a controlled manner (i.e., change control). Examples of elements to be controlled are estimations (size, effort, time, etc.), product's quality attributes, process workload, training procedures, schedules, expenditures, and so forth. Control assets help us identify how those elements should be controlled. It implies also identifying suitable combinations of concep-

tual base assets such as testing techniques, measurement methods, and so forth.

- Conceptual Base Assets. The act of placing a knowledge asset within a context requires additional knowledge about methods, techniques, and so forth. This conceptual base supports the most diverse activities involved in software development, process design, business modeling, an so forth. Examples of frameworks might include well-known object-oriented frameworks, quality evaluation frameworks, and so on. Models and methods embody a large list of current software engineering methods, project management (i.e., estimation methods), and so forth. Finally, techniques and tools make the support more specific. They can be used along with many different methods, models, and frameworks. Of course, combinations are possible and this is precisely the point here. As a conceptual base asset, knowledge is categorized in such a way that the combination allows us to choose the best conceptual base for a particular endeavour. The state-of-the-art and the state-of-the-practice are taken into account to reach the best solution.

Now, let us go deeper into the relationships of our knowledge asset structure. First, several knowledge assets, which recursively compose complex structures, might support a particular knowledge asset. For example, an elicitation technique (conceptual asset) may support an elicitation process (process asset); a business rule (business asset) may support a decision (rationale asset); a tool (conceptual asset) may support a technique (conceptual asset), and so on. Second, several knowledge assets might compose a particular knowledge asset. The meaning behind this recursive composition is that a knowledge asset potentially needs the realization of a set of knowledge assets in order to be modeled. For example, a lesson learned (rationale asset) may need other previous lessons learned to support a decision; a technique (conceptual base asset) may need other techniques to get proper results; and so forth.

On the other hand, every knowledge asset reaches a maturity level that varies depending on the asset's evolution. Like growing versions, assets become mature after several stages of inception, elaboration, evaluation, and institutionalization. Depending on the kind of asset, these steps will be arranged as an iterative incremental process, a whole-unit process, and so forth. Our model makes this situation explicit by associating a maturity level to each knowledge asset, which should be temporally assigned to a particular level. Similarly, a person should be responsible for producing, evaluating, and making decisions on a particular knowledge asset. Of course, people may be responsible for different assets (i.e., business external actors may be responsible for business rules, business goals, etc.), but we would expect that a particular asset would be the responsibility of only one person.

Knowledge assets are strongly related to the domain in which they are intended to be used. This situation led us to associate different kinds of contexts, following the diverse views when analyzing a problem. A well-defined domain might be expected to identify knowledge assets that should be reused or relocated to another domain, or engaged fully in the structure of the domain. To do so, we consider a context as a set of aspects that might influence the conceptualization of a particular asset. Those aspects will consider: (1) project kind, which embodies organizational projects such as business reengineering, as well as software development projects such as Web system development; (2) development kind, which addresses existing approaches to project development, such as outsourcing; (3) supporting technology, which identifies the diverse available platforms and technology such as JavaBeans, .NET, and so forth; (4) application domain, which

identifies a domain area such as health care, judicial, and so forth; and (5) business domain, which helps categorize a business endeavour such as business-to-business, business-to-consumer, and so forth.

Finally, knowledge assets are created from work definitions, which describe the work performed in a process that produces one (or more than one) work product. It may be a piece of software, a piece of information, a document, a model, source code, and so on. At the same time, knowledge assets are used by work definitions to produce themselves and their products. In this way, work definitions become the source and destination of knowledge assets. They are elaborated from activities following their diverse phases and life cycles; and they are consumed by activities of the same or different phases. The validity of combinations depends on the work operation constraints defined by an operational model.

A CASE STUDY

As a first empirical validation, our knowledge asset model was tested during a bottom-up process carried out at the AvanSoft organization in Colombia. This is an 80-person software development company, which is currently standardizing its software process. To initiate the validation, we gathered information from different areas of the company during six months. We focused on how knowledge assets were defined and used by the different stakeholders. First, our enquiries addressed some basic aspects, such as how knowledge assets contribute to adding value; how knowledge is represented; and so forth. Then, we went deeper into details gathering more specific information.

After this process, we analyzed and arranged the information according to our model, producing two kinds of results. First, we refined the model and updated it to make some assets more clear. Second, we instantiated the model aiming at testing its effectiveness. Some results of the instantiation are as follows:

1.   AvanSoft instantiates the *knowledge asset maturity level* concept by defining a three-level maturity model.

     a.   The first level involves information from a particular project, where people start to collect and reuse their own experiences. Knowledge is embedded in applications or made explicit through spreadsheets.

     b.   The second level involves information to be applied in more than one project; for example, common guidelines, standards, or practices. A supporting tool helps manage models even considering versioning.

     c.   The third level involves general knowledge organized through a common repository. It includes supporting systems for the projects, reusable models, metrics and indicators, and so on.

2.   AvanSoft instantiates the *profile asset* (particularly competences) by classifying competences and skills into two categories depending on the source of the tacit knowledge. It could be gathered from *internal referents* such as the organization's personnel or from *external referents* such as advisers. These assets can dynamically evolve according to the different profiles.

3.   AvanSoft instantiates the *infrastructure asset* by explicitly specifying an organizational structure and an organizational strategy driven by key aspects. Additionally, a learning strategy complements the supporting elements of the competence infrastructure. It defines guidelines to model and store knowledge, including learning tools, bibliographic assets, and so on. The role assignment programme is supported by information from skill requirements, recruit-

ment processes, and training programmes and plans. The workload is organized by projects and reinforces component reuse, architectural modeling, and technology development. The work units are divided into two categories: main work units (adding value) and supporting work units.

4.   AvanSoft intstantiates the *process asset* by classifying knowledge into base lines that include information from other assets such as standards, lessons learned, guides, methods and techniques, supporting tools, innovative ideas, metrics, process layouts, and so forth. These assets are classified as external referents (i.e.,well-accepted methods and techniques); internal referents (i.e., knowledge about how to use a particular method such as UML); elaborations (i.e., lessons learned, decisions, measures, etc.); and deliverables (i.e., artefacts to be reused).

5.   AvanSoft instantiates the *rationale asset* by storing information produced by the R&D (research and development) area, which is in charge of supporting the development projects. It is also in charge of leading specific research. Information related to work products is stored to be shared and used as a reference for evaluating the impact of changes. Decisions leading to adopting a new technology are also documented as organizational assets.

6.   AvanSoft instantiates the *conceptual base asset* by providing bibliographic references that address explicit knowledge. They are stored as conceptual support. Additionally, there is a reference to different technologies adopted by the organization such as XML to metadata definition, PHP and Java as programming languages, PKADS (Portable Knowledge Asset Development System) to manage knowledge assets, and so on.

The instantiations above were quite easy to find; however, we also found some interesting considerations from our case study. First, we believe the key success factor for applying the model has been the engagement of the company in implementing a software process improvement program. It allowed us to identify information from clear defined processes, where decisions about how to document knowledge were already done. This fact could lead us to a first consideration: *"a knowledge asset modeling requires organizational engagement to successfully identify assets."*

Second, in designing our model, we tried to balance simplicity and expressiveness of information with knowledge needed to support various software development processes. Under these constraints, we dealt with several limitations. For example, how is information effectively shared among projects? Is there any way of measuring similarity among processes and identify knowledge reuse? How should we document each assessment in order to be easily understood and reused? Our model has shown to be flexible enough to cover all knowledge assets required by the case study; however, further analysis is needed to provide guidelines on the effective use of the model. This fact would lead us to a second consideration: *"effectiveness of reusing assets strongly depends on the way knowledge is represented"* (we assume here two representation aspects: how to document knowledge and how to associate the adequate information for each process).

Third, using our model allowed us to easily spread a common vocabulary among stakeholders. This fact facilitated discussions reaching commitment after relatively less time. Although the company had already implemented a knowledge asset development system, information was populated without taking care of relationships and structure. Now, mostly because of having a documented and visible model, understanding knowledge interactions on strategic business processes was faster. This fact lead us to a third consideration: *"having a supporting knowledge model helps improve communication and un-*derstanding of processes, "* and we believe this is true in spite of the way knowledge is actually documented (consideration two).

Finally, it seems that knowledge assets management programmes are exclusively addressed by large organizations. However, also small and mid-ranged organizations are turning their views into the advantages of reusing knowledge, as our case study shows. The key point here is to provide companies with a practical and expressive way of modeling and reusing knowledge. In our case study, the organization found out that they could tailor our model based on the company's operational context. This is a first (and promissory) step to continuing refining and validating the model. We finally would like to say *"a tailorable knowledge asset model helps to create a sustainable SPI culture in knowledge management and bring lasting benefits to the companies."*

CONCLUSION AND FUTURE WORK

One of the main challenges during the creation of an experience repository is collecting and classifying information. In this chapter, we have introduced a model that characterizes knowledge assets of a software development organization. The model includes both technical and managerial perspectives in order to pinpoint the intellectual capital relevant at software organizations. Additionally, thinking of improving software processes, we have focused on knowledge assets as resources to be defined and managed. The model aims at classifying assets in such a way that they can be reused through different processes, software- and/or organization-oriented.

The model should be supported by experience-based software development. In this context, the *rationale assets* are key elements to share previous actions and decisions. These assets become mature after several stages and represent valuable candidates to be shared between software companies. Currently, we are defining a special case of rationale (lessons learned), going deeper into the elements that will be building blocks in defining and reusing lessons.

Our model constitutes a first step towards a unified knowledge base to be shared by organizations all over Ibero-America. To achieve this goal, there is still much work to do. We identify here several lines that we synthesize in three groups: the process, the architecture, and the practical approaches.

The process: The model should provide a systematic process to classify, retrieve, and update the asset. Besides, the model's process should provide guidelines about the particular treatment for the diverse kinds of assets. As a starting point, we have defined a first structure for knowledge management as a transversal process (Anaya et al., 2006). We are currently refining this structure to specialize the different treatments.

The architecture: It is necessary to define the repository that will contain the entire knowledge asset. Attending their scope, the knowledge assets can be useful to a specific software project, a particular organization, or many software organizations. In Anaya et al., 2006, we have defined a first repository structured in three packages: the *Project Asset Repository,* which contains the assets relevant to a specific project; the *Organizational Asset Repository*, which contains the organization's assets that represent both particular knowledge and project experiences that have been generalized; and the *Public Asset Repository,* which contains the assets useful to all software organization. This repository will be populated in a cooperative effort by many software organizations.

Practical: Finally, it is necessary to explore several environments and tools that support process- and knowledge-based environments as well as the current experience of software organizations. This perspective represents a practical approach that will explore the acceptance of our model in the Ibero-American context.

ACKNOWLEDGMENT

Our work was developed under research projects at the EAFIT University, Colombia; the research project 04/E059 at the GIISCo Research Group (http://giisco.uncoma.edu.ar), University of Comahue, Argentina; and the project: "Process Improvement for Promoting Iberoamerican Software Small and Medium Enterprises Competitiveness – COMPETISOFT" (506AC287) financed by CYTED (Programa Iberoamericano de Ciencia y Tecnología para el Desarrollo).

REFERENCES

Anaya, R., Cechich, A., & Henao, M. (2006). *Enfoque integrado de la Gestión del Conocimiento en el modelo de procesos de Competisoft* (Technical Report). Competisoft Project.

Anaya, R., Londoño, L., & Hurtado, J. (2006). Una Estrategia para Elevar la Competitividad de las Industrias de Software PYMES. In *Proceedings of the 9th Workshop Iberoamericano de Ingeniería de Requisitos y Ambientes Software* (IDEAS), La Plata, Argentina.

Brown, J., & Duguid, P. (1991). Organizational learning and communities-of-practice: Toward a unified view of working, learning, and innovation. *Organizational Science, 2*(1), 40-57.

Chrissis, M.B., Konrad, M., & Shrum, S. (2005). *CMMI: Guidelines for process integration and product improvement.* Addison-Wesley.

Ciamberlani, L., & Steimberg, L. (1999). *Comunicación para la transparencia.* Granica Ed.

Concklin, P., & Begeman, M. (1988). gIBIS: A hypertext tool for exploratory policy discussion. *Transactions of Office Information Systems, 6*(4), 303-331.

Davenport, T., & Prusak, L. (1998). *Working knowledge: How organizations manage what they know*. Boston: Harvard Business School Press.

Dingsøyr, T. (2003). *Knowledge management in medium-sized software consulting company: An Investigation of intranet-based knowledge management tools for knowledge cartography and knowledge repositories for learning software organizations*. Norwegian University of Science and Technology.

Dingsøyr, T., & Conradi, R. (2002). A survey of case studies of the use of knowledge management in software engineering. *International Journal of Software Engineering and Knowledge Engineering, 12*(4), 391-414.

Dingsøyr, T., & Røyrvik, E. (2003). An empirical study of an informal knowledge repository in a medium-sized software consulting company. In *Proceedings of the International Conference on Software Engineering*. IEEE.

Drucker, P. (1993). *Post-capitalist society*. Oxford, MA: Butterworth Heinemann.

Fischer, G., Lindstaedt, S., Ostwald, J., Scneider, K., & Smith, J. (1996). Informing system design through organizational learning. In *Proceedings of the International Conference on Learning Sciences* (pp. 52-59).

Garvin, D. (1993, July-August). Building a learning organization. *Harvard Business Review,* pp. 78-91.

Hansen, M., Nohrian, N., & Tierney, T. (1999). What's your strategy for managing knowledge? *Harvard Business Review.*

Henninger, S. (2001). Turning development standards into repositories of experiences. *Software Process Improvement and Practice, 3*(6), 141-155.

Henninger, S. (2003). Tool support for experience-based methodologies. In *Proceedings of the 4th International Workshop on Advances in Learning Software Organizations* (LNCS 2640, pp. 44-59). Springer-Verlag.

Holz, H. (2003). *Process-based knowledge management support for software engineering*. Doctoral Dissertation, University of Kaiserslautern, Germany.

Iria, J., Ciravegna, F., Cimiano, P., Lavelli, A., Motta, E., Gilardoni, L., & Mönch, E. (2004). Integrating information extraction, ontology learning and semantic browsing into organizational knowledge processes. In *Proceedings of the EKAW Workshop on the Application of Language and Semantic Technologies to Support Knowledge Management Processes, at the 14th International Conference on Knowledge Engineering and Knowledge Management.*

Landes, D., Schneider, K., & Houdek, F. (1999). Organizational learning and experience documentation in industrial software projects. *International Journal of Human-Computer Studies, 51,* 643-661.

Liao, L., Qu, Y., & Leung, H. (2005). A software process ontology and its application. In *Proceedings of the Workshop on Semantic Web Enabled Software Engineering (SWESE), at the 4th International Semantic Web Conference.* Retrieved December 17, 2007, from http://www.mel.nist.gov/msid/conferences/SWESE/accepted_papers.html

Marques, C., & Sousa, P. (2004). A method to define an enterprise architecture using the Zachman framework. In *Proceedings of the 2004 ACM Symposium on Applied Computing* (pp. 1366-1371).

McGarry, F., et.al. (1994). *Software process improvement in the NASA Software Engineering Laboratory* (Tech. Rep. No. CMU/SEI-95-TR-22). Department of Computer Science, University of Maryland, College Park, MD 20742.

Mentzas, G., Apostolou, D., Abecker, A., & Young, R. (2003). *Knowledge asset management: Beyond the process-centred and product-centred approaches.* Springer. ISBN 1-85233-583-1.

Nguyen, M., & Conradi, R. (1994). Classification of meta-processes and their models. In *Proceedings of the 3rd International Conference on the Software Process* (pp. 167-175).

Nonaka, I., & Takeuchi, H. (1995). *The knowledge-creating company.* Oxford University Press.

Nour, P., Holz, H., & Maurer, F. (2000). Ontology-based retrieval of software process experiences. In *Proceedings of the ICSE Workshop on Software Engineering over the Internet.*

Oktaba, H., et al. (2003). Modelo de Procesos para la Industria de Software: MoProSoft Por Niveles de Capacidad de Procesos.

Rouvellou, I., et al. (2000). Extending business objects with business rules. In *Proceedings of the Technology of Object-Oriented Languages and Systems (TOOLS 33).* IEEE Press.

Scharmer, C. (1996, February 23). *Knowledge has to do with truth, goodness, and beauty: Conversation with Professor Ikujiro Nonaka.* Tokyo. Retrieved December 17, 2007, from http://www.dialogonleadership.org/Nonaka-1996cp.html, 07/6/2006

Scharmer, C. (2001). Self-transcending knowledge: Organizing around emerging realities. In I. Nonaka & D. Teece (Eds.), *Managing industrial knowledge: Creation, transfer and utilization* (pp. 68-90). Thousand Oaks: Sage Publications.

Senge, P. (1990). *The fifth discipline: The art and practice of the learning organization.* London: Random House.

Staab, S., Studer, R., & Sure, Y. (2002). Knowledge processes and meta processes in ontology-based knowledge management. In C. Holsapple (Ed.), *Handbook on knowledge management.* Springer.

STARS. (2006). *Conceptual framework for reuse processes.* Retrieved December 17, 2007, from http://www2.umassd.edu/swpi/STARS/Process-Concepts/pcsum.html

ENDNOTES

[1]   Object Management Group
[2]   Organizational Process Definition

Chapter XVI
Practical Application of a Software Development Framework in an Accountant Office

Alicia Mon
La Matanza National University, Argentina

Marcelo Estayno
La Matanza National University, Argentina

Patricia Scalzone
La Matanza National University, Argentina

ABSTRACT

The present chapter exposes the definition and practical application of a framework in the system area of an organization. Due to the total lack of the process, this framework has permitted us to generate the need of the implementation of a definite process model for software development. The described framework has been applied in a study case, just as has been done in other opportunities by different organizations with similar characteristics. This work provides the possibility of applying the framework slowly against an improvised and indefinite process, in which a methodology, a process model, and a collection of techniques and tools converge. These elements are advisable for small- and medium-sized software development companies and would facilitate their way to implement an integral process model which would continuously improve.

INTRODUCTION

This chapter describes the experience of a framework implementation in the IT area of a company where the absence of a formal process has permitted it to generate the need of the introduction of a clearly-defined process model for software development. This case study intends to show how a software development process is influenced by the organizational structure of a company, its culture, and the way it grows. This framework has been applied to an accounting company, the core business of which is the advice and consulting of economic results management and impact for companies with different business activities. This company was selected for this example because it fulfills the most important characteristics of a small and medium enterprise: a single owner, who has been first growing in the main areas of need, and then in other complementary areas of the "business core" moved by the needs produced by the growing company.

The enterprise has been covering different functions, moved by the dynamic of a growing company, creating structures like a group of islands, without any connection among them. At the management level, this produced the need to define an ordering process; for this, the whole enterprise was committed to a business focused quality certification system while leaving behind the IT area, considering it secondary and making no emphasis on its organization.

The process definition for the development area that is presented here allows companies to progressively put a work model into practice opposite an indefinite and improvised process, where a methodology, a process model, and a collection of techniques and recommended tools for small and medium enterprises or software development areas converge and which would facilitate the road for the initial implementation of an integral continuous improvement process model.

COMPANY DESCRIPTION

The main activity of the company is the administration and valuation of business assets, especially the analysis of fixed assets, financial assets, warehouses, supplies, procurement, reliable valuations, and corporative contacts. It has its own software development area which provides all the systems for the internal management of the company and the data administration for its customers. The company, based on the acquired experience in this area, started to sell the internally developed software products as management products for other companies, together with consulting and training services of the products. The company has a payroll of 50 people, with a team of eight developers in the IT area who are in charge of the system resources management, software development, and technical support to the company.

DESCRIPTION OF THE EXPERIENCE

The company had accomplished the ISO 9001:2000 certification for the quality management systems of its processes (ISO 9001, 2000); the IT management office was in charge of a developer who had an empiric training in software development and who had developed the first information system for the company. This developer had wide and vast experience in the problem domain but had poor knowledge in software development project management. The company was growing in customers and services; its software had limited customization options and there was no application of a clearly defined process or a work methodology, despite the fact that the company was certificated by ISO regulations.

New team development members were assigned with tasks based on required features and not based on roles within the development team.

All this showed the lack of project and human resources planning. The certification process of the company did not mean better work in the software development field because the certification did not enter the organizational culture of the company and it was only exhibited as a guarantee stamp. In this way, there were more and more consecutive product versions to maintain falling into chaotic development status. The quality certification obtained by the company was not enough to organize the IT area because the certification process did not penetrate organizational culture and it was only exhibited as a guarantee stamp. In this way, there were more and more consecutive product versions to maintain resulting in a chaotic software development process.

Based on the wide experience of the company in this business, its software developments started to get a position in the market. But the demand called for system improvements that included Web graphic interfaces, distributed databases, and all the progresses of new technology. To make this possible, a migration and a reengineering of the existing products were extremely necessary. The software products for internal use of the company and the applications for the customers were developed in Visual Basic as a programming language without components, with a poor architecture, and with almost no possibilities to escalate. The needed upgrades required to pass to a Web environment, taking into account that such applications with their numerous versions, had to continue delivering services and meeting the changes required by the customers until the replacement took place.

The main goal to accomplish rested on getting the necessary information to determine which processes were missing, to determine improvement goals, to define the critical processes and to define the methodology to be used, to prepare an improvement plan applicable to the company and to determine the necessary resources, and finally, to check the efficiency of the application.

ACTIVITIES DEVELOPMENT

The development team initiated the improvement request when they noticed that the actual work process was unmanageable as time went by. They had in mind their need to be organized and to grow in order to improve their developments. The improvement activity started by making certain changes inside the work team with the purpose of creating a process "culture" adapting tools which would facilitate the software development recognized by the market with the hardness of formality but taking the most dynamic version that was possible. Consequently, the first step was a training in subjects related to documentation on the basis of the unified modeling language (UML) (Booch, Jacobson, & Rumbaugh, 2003a). Then, a theoretical training was necessary, which made easier the awareness of the need of its application.

The development team was guided in order to detect its own weaknesses and needs. Simple and reachable guidelines were stated, which produced the following changes: roles reassignment, definition of documentation data sheets with all-known Office tools commonly used by the team, and it was decided to start by the requirements phase quickly observing some first results. As a consequence, it was decided to advance one more step in the training cycle and due to the characteristics of the company and the IT team, the Software Development Unified Process was adopted in an agile version (Larman, 2004), which allowed them to have a quick training and to start implementing a simple and relatively informal process. This process gradually became a rigorous process capable of pass more specific certifications.

The main characteristic of the selected process is that it is based on an iterative and incremental project life cycle. This life cycle is perfect to enhance the productivity of the area, mainly when there are limited human resources to support the workload. This life cycle increases the use of the existing resources as best as possible avoiding idle roles when waiting for the precedent activity to be completed. The most difficult part of it is to truly achieve the iterations (Boehm, 1988) without the need of using a waterfall methodology.

The success of this approach was based on the gradual advance, making each member take a role in a natural way, understanding the existing restrictions, and visualizing a future favorable change when including a clearly-defined and established process. In this way, the team will not advance isolated but jointly. The action items realized as the initial framework were the following:

1. Roles were defined.
2. Templates of documents, reports, and so forth were proposed.
3. A case tool was selected in order to help the team.
4. A requirement list was made.
5. A risks list was made, and the risks were prioritized because the process was risk-driven.
6. The vision document of the project was elaborated with the participation of the whole team in the definitions.
7. Requirement specification was made using the use case model, which made the initial definition of the functional testing possible. *The use cases found were widened with a state transition diagram and an activity diagram.

The system architecture was defined, highlighting the most important points to include and the person accountable to make each component.

- A components diagram of the architecture was designed.
- A sequence diagram was designed in order to discuss and inform how the interaction between components would be made or more precisely between objects.

Quality rules were established in order to write code.

Iterations were planned (Booch, Jacobson, & Rumbaugh, 2003b) according to logic and to the quantity of members of the team in order to be as short as possible. For each iteration:

- Each use case involved was specifically detailed.
- Necessary objects to make the data model and the logical model of classes were designed.
- Some additional sequence diagrams were made to observe the interaction among the objects.
- Selected use cases were codified.
- Unit tests were made.
- Functional tests were made according to the specifications.
- Integration tests were made.

Migration of data was made with a test in parallel.

It was put into effect.

Figure 1 shows the activity diagram made as a framework.

Figure 1. Activity diagram

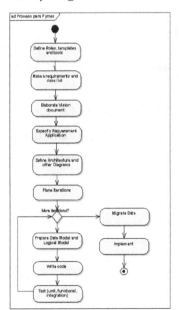

ROLES DEFINITION

The development area had eight developers who had the same function without taking they experience as a skill variable. The development of new applications was mixed with the maintenance of the existents. The IT manager also worked hands-on as a developer, mainly on database administration, so poor attention laid to the management of the different activities.

With the need to define roles, the "team of peers" model was adopted. This model was proposed by the Microsoft Solution Framework (MSF) (Haynes, Robin, Paschino, Short, Kazmi, Oikawa, et al., 2002) in its version for the development of agile applications. The main characteristic of MSF is the communication and the work by consent putting aside the traditional hierarchical model. This was easily adapted since the team was small and willing to change.

The first task in the roles definition was to separate the development activities from the tasks of analysis and knowledge acquisition, adding another person to the team who would receive the training to work in the area. The project leader was differentiated and the architecture of the application started to gain importance in order to identify this role among the peers. From that activity, the following roles were defined (Figure 2).

Once the differentiation of the functions and the definition of the roles were made, the focus was

Figure 2. MSF team model

on separating the existing activities of correction and maintenance of the actual systems from the new applications that had to be developed. This caused some differences among the peers because everybody wanted to work under the new methodology, but then they reached an agreement and they understood that all the roles had important aims and that each aim contributed to achieve the global objective regardless of the assigned project. This first impulse began to organize the activities, the order in which they had to be done, and the generated work from the division of the roles, functions, and aims clearly defined for each member of the team. The aims that are defined for each role are shown in Figure 3.

Figure 3. Roles and aims line-up

Team role		Goal
Product management	⟹	Satisfied customers
Program management	⟹	Delivery within project constraints
Development	⟹	Delivery to product specifications
Testing	⟹	Release after addressing all known issues
Architecture	⟹	Organizational structure of the application well defined
Release Operations	⟹	Smooth product deployment

Generated Process: Roles, functions, and goals definition. The model of the team work used is well adapted to small- and medium-sized companies of software development, especially those which have no definite process included. This way of making up the team and working by consent produces decompression and a better work dynamic in small groups where normally a constant need of change arises.

DEFINITION OF DOCUMENTS TEMPLATES, REPORTS, AND SO FORTH

The need of organizing the activities generated compelled the need for documenting. It was essential to organize the change requests and the new requests for the existing applications. A memo with a simple format which users had to fill in and send by e-mail was designed in order to start with this documentation. Each memo was registered in a simple sheet with the request priority and the person responsible for making the change with the estimated delivery date.

Then, other documents were added, classifying the ones that were compulsory and the ones that could be used under exception conditions. Model templates of the unified process (Booch, Jacobson, & Rumbaugh, 2003b) and Microsoft Solution Framework (Getchell, Hargrave, Haynes, Lubrecht, Kazmi, Oikawa, et al., 2002) were used, adopting the necessary changes for the company. From that point in time, a template was created to register the minutes of the meeting in order to document each interview of knowledge acquisition with the users. An example of the minutes of meeting template is shown in Figure 4.

Generated Process: Definition of simple documentation to formalize the initial process. The incorporation of written documents made that the dynamic of the work and the communication between the development team and the users changed; and it modified the IT manager's office image outstandingly. From those registers, the users started to suggest improvements for the defined templates.

SELECTION OF A CASE TOOL

When the work team was trained in UML (Booch et al., 2003a), diagrams were designed with the computing drawing tool of the company. But when it was considered that it was tidier to store everything together, it was decided to select a case tool which was efficient under determined parameters and had an affordable cost. It was decided to work with the enterprise architect (Sparx Systems, 2006). First, tests with the trial version were made and when it was understood that the complete tool was needed, the product was acquired to work in a shared way and also to make the necessary reengineering.

Figure 4. Meeting draft copy

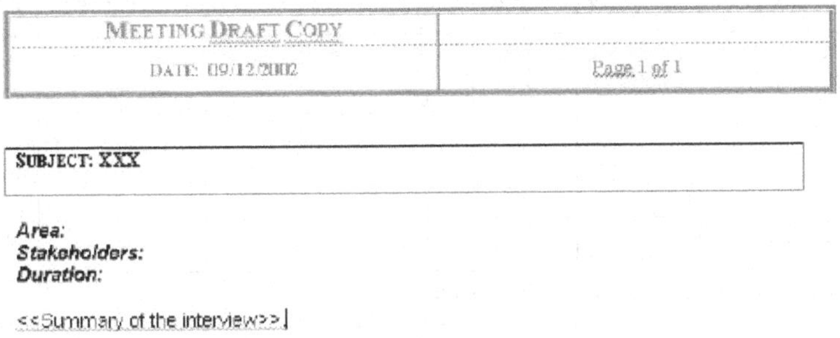

MEETING DRAFT COPY	
DATE: 09/12/2002	Page 1 of 1

SUBJECT: XXX

Area:
Stakeholders:
Duration:

<<Summary of the interview>>

Generated Process: Case tool incorporation for projects development and management. The selection of an unique tool requires the determination of the structure to be used in order to organize all the projects in the same way (for example, the one used in this case was Model of 4+1 Views, of Kruchten, 2000).

LIST OF REQUIREMENTS CONSTRUCTION

As part of the incorporation of documents, the list of requirements began with them being registered in a spreadsheet, with just the enumeration of the users' requests. This list became gradually important and it became the base for the definition of the project vision. Figure 5 shows the template used as a list of requirements.

Generated Process: Essential and initial documentation of requirements. The incorporation of a template to register the requirements improved the understanding of them and was the base to define the vision of the project.

CONSTRUCTION OF A RISK LIST

A simple list with the main risks detected for each project was made and they were organized by priority according to the process of risks management (Robin, Preedy, Campbell, Paschino, Hargrave, Born, et al., 2002), indicating the mitigation and contingency plan. The results were incorporated in the following schedule. In this way, the measuring and monitoring of each development improved considerably. A sample of the template made for the risks evaluation is shown in Figure 6.

Figure 5. List of requirements template

			List of Requirements			
Date	Area	Application/ Component	Required by:	Description	Receipted by:	Priority

Figure 6. Risks assessment template

Risk Assessment Template									
#	Risk Statement		(Scale)	(Scale)					
	Condition	Consequence	Probability	Impact	Exposure	Mitigation	Contingency	Triggers	Assignee
1			0	0	0				
2			0	0	0				
3			0	0	0				
4			0	0	0				
5			0	0	0				
6			0	0	0				
7			0	0	0				
8			0	0	0				
9			0	0	0				
10			0	0	0				
11			0	0	0				
12			0	0	0				
13			0	0	0				

Generated Process: Identification, record, and risks analysis. The elaboration of a risk list made possible to identify, evaluate, give priority, and define the monitoring with the incorporation of the risks to the schedule and cost of the project.

Elaboration of the Project Vision Document

The vision document was the first significant milestone after the training. It showed the organization that the distribution made in training and consultancy in the area gave positive results taking into account that since there was no process culture existed, the fact of "not writing lines of code" did not mean neither a waste of time nor investment. The construction of this document took a bit more than a month. It was shown to the organization stating that, if in 10 days there was no answer, it would be considered approved. Before the deadline, one of the interested persons saw that his/her objective was not reflected in the document and, not by chance, that it belonged to the area that had had less participation in the process of knowledge acquisition. Then, after three weeks, the vision of the project was finished, including all the areas involved. It was the first time that there was a discussion based on a written document and not about a codified application, which made the discussion easier and allowed for saving time on the definitions. The index of the first vision document made is shown in Figure 7.

The model of the document is based on a template and analyzed through a revision history. This register made possible the control of all the interaction that the vision document had during its production. The monitoring of the production process of the document has been registered as shown in Table 1.

Generated Process: Elaboration of the vision document. This document helped to define the scope of the projects, including the functional features and the nonfunctional features. The revision history helped to control the interaction generated

Figure 7. Index of the vision document

Table of Contents

1. Introduction 5
   - 1.1 Purpose
   - 1.2 Definitions, Acronyms and Abbreviations
   - 1.3 References
2. Positioning 6
   - 2.1 Business Opportunity
   - 2.2 Problem Statement
3. Stakeholder and User Descriptions 6
   - 3.1 Stakeholder Summary
   - 3.2 User Summary
   - 3.3 User environment
4. Product Features 9
   - 4.1 Functional Features
     - 4.1.1 Feature XX
     - 4.1.2 Feature YY
   - 4.2 Functional constraints
5. Precedence and Priority 10
6. Other Product Requirements 10
   - 6.1 Deployment environment
   - 6.2 Development environment
   - 6.3 Performance Requirements
7. Documentation and Training Requirements 10
   - 7.1 User Manual
   - 7.2 Online Help

Table 1. History of checking

Revision History

Date	Version	Description	Author
<28/Mar/03>	<1.0.x>	Draft	Silvia
<15/Abr/2003>	<1.1>	1st. Review	Patricia
<29/Abr/2003>	<1.2>	2nd. Review	Pablo
< 02/May/2003>	<1.3>	3rd. Review	Luis
<15/May/2003>	<1.4>	4th. Review	Oscar
<22/May/2003>	<1.5>	5th. Review	Patricia
<29/May/2003>	<1.6>	6th. Review	Review Victor and Patricia
<10/Jun/2003>	<1.7>	7th. Review	Oscar

during its production. Once its importance was detected, the vision document was considered compulsory inside the organization.

APPLICATION REQUIREMENTS SPECIFICATION

Once the list of requirements was defined, the actors and their functions were found. This was shaped in a use case diagram and a functional map which allowed quick positioning in the application to define the responsible role and the relationship between the different actors. A brief description was written for each of the defined use cases to specify their scope and to understand if all the requirements and their priorities had been considered. The analysis model was completed with a state-transition diagram (also known as states machine) to represent the different states through which an entity or subsystem goes from a condition or given state. Finally, an activity diagram was elaborated to visualize the interaction between sections or activities not to be informatized. Figure 8 shows an example of the use case diagram elaborated, where each use case has been represented with an oval.

Generated Process: Application requirements specification. The representation of the functional requirements through a use case diagram allowed the identification of the actors and their description as well as the analysis of their relationships.

DEFINITION OF THE APPLICATION ARCHITECTURE

Once the well known functional and nonfunctional requirements were obtained, understood, and documented, an architecture meeting was held and all the members of the team attended it. With the technological platform defined, the architecture of the application was shaped. The proposals came from the most experienced developers, but the decision on the architecture was made with the

Figure 8. Use cases diagram

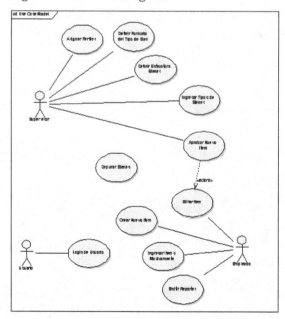

consent of all the attendants, strengthening the implemented equipment model.

The definition of the components diagram was jointly developed based on a draft of the possible components of the application, on a whiteboard, drawing and erasing until obtaining a components diagram which had the consent of all the members of the team. Different colors were used to identify the persons who would be the developers responsible for the implementation of the components. In this way, each participant perfectly knew his/her role, his/her goal, and which other component he/she was going to communicate to, the one he/she depended on, and which was the global goal to reach, with no ambiguities. On the other hand, this joint work allowed the participants to organize the name spaces needed to work on the defined platform. Figure 9 shows an example of the components diagram.

The sequence diagrams were also drawn in the same meeting, on a whiteboard, to discuss and define how the interaction between the previously detected components would be and to prove, in a theoretical way, if they were properly defined.

Generated Process: Definition of the application architecture. The discussion and joint definition of the different architecture options with the participation of all the working team allowed them to have the knowledge needed to start with the development of the application.

DEFINE QUALITY RULES FOR CODING

To start with the development of the application, very simple writing code rules were set, without resorting to many theoretical concepts but applying the coherence. The goal was to define simple rules and that all the developers knew them. It was decided to use the Pascal casing rating for

Figure 9. Component diagram

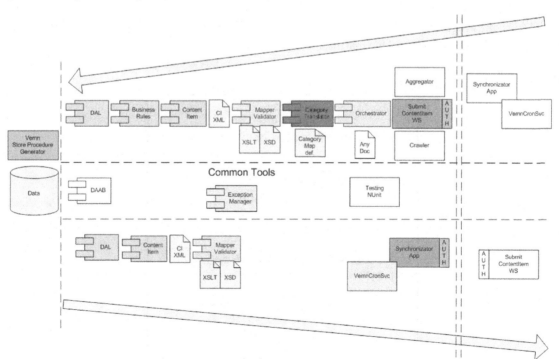

class names, methods, and file names and Camel casing for member names and parameters of the methods. It was also decided to discuss the code clearly, so that any programmer who had to read it could easily understand it. Besides, the code had to start with the name of the programmer, starting date, use case name, and due date. Moreover, as the development moved forward, it was going to be updated with the date of the changes, name of the petitioner, and name of the programmer assigned. Figure 10 shows an example of the code rating used.

Generated Process: Definition of code quality rules. The simple rules allowed all the developers to know and understand them and to be able to easily apply them to obtain a reusable code easy to understand for any member of the team.

ITERATIONS PLANNING

The definition and planning of the development was a very complex task. It was almost impossible to understand the way in which to work or the benefit of doing the iterations planning, if they would constantly require changes in the database, in the classes, in the components and that the each

iteration would discover new functionalities. The basic resolution sequence took a classic working plan on a cascade basis (Royce, 1970).

It was decided to do the iterations according to the development team working on the project, to the functional requirements, and to the technology used. Now, therefore, if there were three developers, the functional requirements were grouped so that in iteration, the team could finish all together with an application deliverable and then present it to the testing area. Each of these iterations originated a new version of the application which was registered and controlled with an automated tool. To understand the iterations, the MSF processes model (shown in Figure 11) was the reference.

In the iterations planning process, once the use cases for each iteration had been selected, were registered in a form which allowed to the estimation and control of each of the activities to be done for each use case. Once the iteration finished, the generated delays were documented or otherwise, the spare time. As a result, it was possible to obtain information to statistically analyze future quantities and estimates. Figure 12 shows the efforts template used for the record of estimates per use case.

Figure 10. Source code rating

```
public class SampleClass
{
        private int _var = 0;

        public int Var
        {
            get { return _var; }
            set { _var = value; }
        }

        bool VerifyCompanyName ( string
companyName )
        {
            if ( companyName != "" )
            {
                return true;
            }
        }
```

Figure 11. MSF process model

Figure 12. Efforts template

Use Case	Complexity (1,2,3,4,5)	Requirements	Analysis	Design	Implementation	Test	Delay
Use Case							

To the end of grouping the features for iteration, the use cases were prioritized, the selected ones were specified, and at the same time, the data model and the class model were completed together with the user interface. To specify the use cases, it was decided to use case specification templates according to the structure presented in Table 2.

Developmental prototypes of user interface were developed, revised, modified, and arranged with the users. In addition, the documentation process was enhanced since the prototypes were attached to the corresponding documents for each use case. The use of prototypes was very useful for understanding the problem between the developers and the users. Figure 13 shows an example of the user interface prototype used.

Sequence diagrams were developed to model the use cases at a second level of detail so that the programmers had more specifications to assign a code. In these diagrams, it was possible to see the interaction between the detected objects. At the beginning, one sequence diagram was developed

Table 2. Use case specification structure

Name		
Brief Description		
Flow of Events		
	Activation	
	Basic Flow	
	Alternative Flows	
Special Requirements (non functional)		
Preconditions		
Post conditions		
Extension Points		

Figure 13. User interface prototype

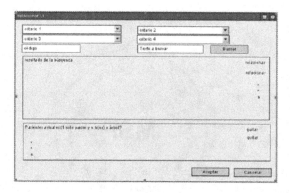

Figure 14. Sequence diagram

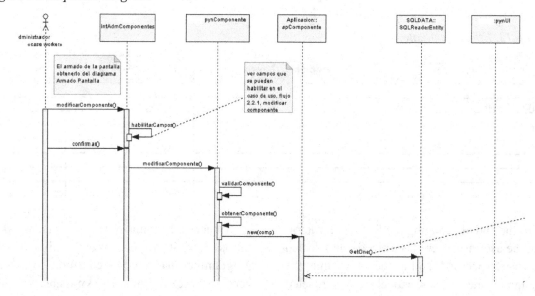

for each case. Later on, it was decided that it was not appropriate to devote so much time to define diagrams which did not directly disclose what was coded but that it would be more beneficial to use them only to pose the ideas and to assign the final design to the developer. Figure 14 shows an example of the sequence diagram used.

The classes model was defined as the sequence diagrams for each analyzed use case was designed, adding the new methods, properties, or new emerged classes.

Here is an example of a class diagram developed in Figure 15.

The database construction and documentation process was done as follows: the data model was written directly on the chosen database motor and then the model was imported to the case tool used for its documentation. A little portion of the entity relation diagram (ERD) is shown is Figure 16.

Each programmer had to test the code before enabling the functional test. These would be the unit tests starting in a rudimentary way until

Figure 15. Class diagram

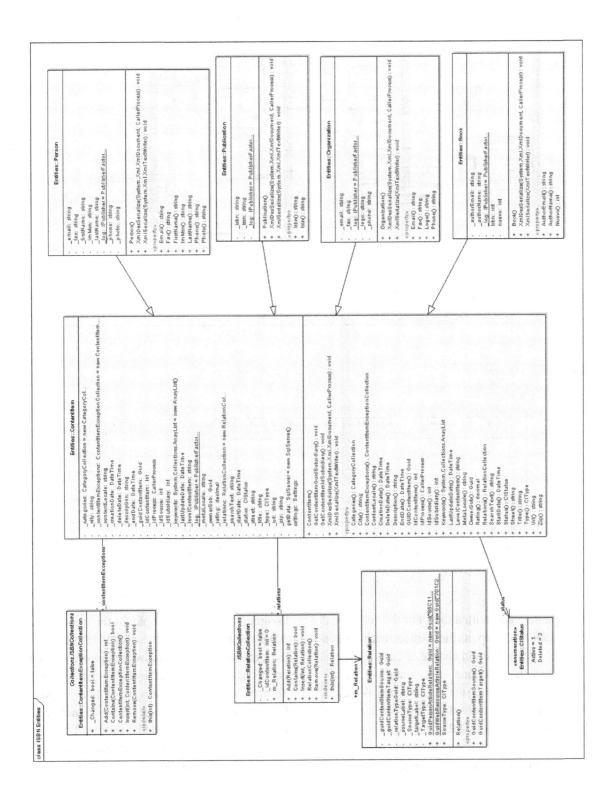

Figure 16. Entity relation diagram

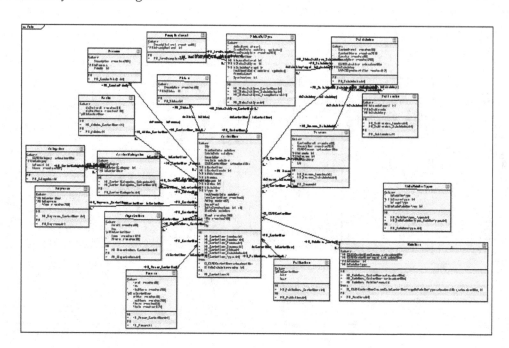

Table 3. Test cases

TC ID #	Scene	Existing Unit	Desired Unit	Expected Result	T1	T2	T3
CB1	1st scene Successful search	T	V	Data filled in the previous screen			
CB2	2nd scene No coincidence	I	n/a	Returns to step 1. Basic flow			
CB3	3rd scene Re-search	T	I	Returns to step 1. Basic flow			
CB4	4th scene Cancelled search	T	I	Does not find a desired unit. End Use Case			

being automated with a tool. For the functional tests, a specific role with the team format had been defined. The person in charge of each team had to analyze the functional specification of the use cases and to elaborate the test scenario. A matrix was developed to record the test cases and the possible variations as Table 3 shows.

A report of errors was created, where the errors were arranged in order in a spreadsheet and where

assigned to different people for their correction. After the functional tests resulted satisfactorily, the integration tests started with the corresponding creation of data lots and the record of their results. To pretend that the data were real, an importer from the previous application was generated to import the data that could be migrated.

Generated Process: Iterations planning. In order to be able to plan the development, little iterations were defined according to the development team who would take care of each one and the effort and each development task done were documented. The process had to be clear and defined to facilitate the control and the documentation and to use the resources of a small team efficiently.

DATA MIGRATION

Once 60% of the application was developed, a migration of the data from the previous system was made and a test instance was started by the end users. Since the development aim was to replace one existing application which was working, there was an attempt to migrate as much data as possible so that the users could make their tests in an already known context. The migration was made with the tools provided by the chosen motor database and a parallel with the previous application was kept to generate the confidence that was needed since this new product had to be sold to big national and international corporations.

Generated Process: Data migration. The users made tests with already known data, trying to simulate real situations, generating more confidence and responsibility over them.

START-UP

With the start-up of the application and with the delivery of the first stable version to the client, the team started to relax. After two weeks, a meeting was held, where the functioning of the application and the things learned during all the generated initial process were highlighted, focusing on the strengths and discussing how to improve the weaknesses.

Generated Process: Start-up of the application, analysis and revision of the things learned with all the development team. This process was the future knowledge basis for the enhancement

of the whole of the process applied.

ELABORATED FRAMEWORK STRUCTURE

The initial framework generated throughout this real case allowed the definition and the enhancement on the software development processes in a small IT area which did not have any structure or definition of their processes. The activities of the initial framework generated in this case have been systematized as shown in Table 4, 5, and 6

CONCLUSION

The study case hereby presented has allowed us to elaborate an initial framework which would help us to define and enhance the processes of the software development in a small IT area which did not have any structure or definition of their processes. It did not have documentation, it did not record versions control, it did not emphasize the requirements or the risks, and its development activity started directly with the coding. From this point of view, there is no such thing as team work to accomplish a common goal, and there is no alignment with the strategic plan.

The activities developed in this case show the progressive implementation of an initial framework, previous to the application of a processes model or a quality standard. This initial framework generates a first structuring for a small organization which was in a chaotic state regarding the development of their products, with no organizational structure at all, an undefined and extemporaneous process, but certified under an international quality standard regulating the business processes of the company.

In the foregoing framework, we find a methodology, a process model, and a collection of techniques and rules recommended for small and middle sized companies or software development areas which facilitate the implementation of an integral process model of continuous enhancement. The work objective was to organize the IT area and make it adopt a controlled process culture like the rest of the organization, and modify its image so it could be valued before other company areas. The aim of the work was to organize the IT area of the company and to modify its image so it could be appraised before the other departments and not to be considered as a waste of money for the company but as a business generator together with the "core business" of the company.

The results obtained were satisfactory with the progressive introduction of a controllable process in the organization, modifying the cultural situation and transforming the weaknesses in challenges, where each little improvement will become a success with the passing of time. Regarding its adoption by the IT area, this gradual process offered a successful experience. It also leveled off the way for the adoption of any quality model.

ACKNOWLEDGMENT

This chapter has been developed inside the project: "Process Improvement for Promoting Iberoamerican Software Small and Medium Enterprises Competitiveness – COMPETISOFT" (506AC287) financed by CYTED (Programa Iberoamericano de Ciencia y Tecnología para el Desarrollo).

REFERENCES

ISO 9001. (2000). *Sistemas de gestión de la calidad: Requisitos.*

Boehm, B. (1988). A spiral model for software development and enhancement. *IEEE Computer, 21*(5), 61-72.

Booch, G., Jacobson, J., & Rumbaugh, I. (2003a). *The unified modeling language.* Addison-Wesley.

Booch, G., Jacobson, J., & Rumbaugh, I. (2003b). *The unified software development process.* Addison-Wesley.

Getchell, Hargrave, Haynes, Lubrecht, Kazmi, Oikawa, Paschino, Robin, Short. (2002, June). MSF Process Model v. 3.1. Retrieved December 17, 2007, from http://www.microsoft.com/msf

Haynes, Robin, Paschino, Short, Kazmi, Oikawa, Getchell, Hargrave, Lubrecht, Huber, Vukcevic, Leocadio, Rocha, Santello, Schimpl. (2002, June). MSF Team Model v. 3.1. Retrieved December 17, 2007, from http://www.microsoft.com/msf

Kruchten, P. (2000, July). *The rational unified process: An introduction* (2nd ed.). Addison-Wesley.

Larman, C. (2004). *Agile and iterative development: A manager's guide.* Addison-Wesley.

Sparx Systems. (2006). Enterprise architect user's guide. Retrieved December 17, 2007, from http://www.sparxsystems.com.au

Robin, Preedy, Campbell, Paschino, Hargrave, Born, Huber, Haynes, Kazmi, Oikawa, Getchell. (2002, June). MSF Risk Management Discipline v. 1.1. Retrieved December 17, 2007, from http://www.microsoft.com/msf

Royce, W.W. (1970, August). Managing the development of large software systems: Concepts and techniques. In *Proceedings of Wescon.*

Chapter XVII
Estimate of Effort in Software Implementation Projects

María Julia Orozco Mendoza
Ultrasist, Mexico

Evaristo Fernández Perea
Ultrasist, Mexico

Claudia Alquicira Esquivel
Ultrasist, Mexico

ABSTRACT

This document contains a proposal for project estimation of software implementation to be used in a Mexican SME business (small and middle size companies). This method, named Ultrasist Use Case Points (UsistUCP), is based on the Use Case Point (UCP) estimation method, developed in 1993, along with the object-oriented methods, by Gustav Karner (1993). We start by explaining the use case point estimation method; then we will develop the UsistUCP proposal, specifying its differences with the original method (UCP). To make a comparative analysis between these two methods, we take one case under study to be estimated based on these two methods and then we will provide the corresponding conclusions.

INTRODUCTION

Ultrasist is a Mexican company with more than 10 years of experience integrating computing technology in the business process of its clients with consultancy and systems implementa-tion. Ultrasist was the first SME in Mexico to achieve capability maturity model (CMM) level 4. Ultrasist has established as its quality policy the implementation of IT systems that meet their clients' needs. For this, Ultrasist has developed a framework to implement systems based on the best practices, leading-edge technologies, and international standards. This frame includes a series of processes that cover the whole software's life cycle and support processes, including a process to review project's feasibility and software estimation to quote the effort required. This process has been perfected for five years and is based on the historic database of real projects of 10 years.

The feasibility process takes into account three main aspects before making the decision to carry out a project. First, we seek a clear description of the objectives in order to choose the best solution option, for which we analyze feasibility in the following three main items:

1. **Operational feasibility:** In the operational feasibility, we establish if the proposed solution is within the business lines, that is, if it is aligned with the company's strategic objectives.
2. **Technical feasibility:** In the technical feasibility, we analyze if the proposed solution can be implemented with the available human resources and if there is the necessary infrastructure.
3. **Economic feasibility:** This consists of estimating the effort needed to implement the project and be able to conclude if the project is profitable for the organization. The size and effort required to implement it are also estimated in this item, considering the scope being identified.

This document focuses on the third item referring to the economic feasibility.

We start by explaining the use case point estimation method; then we will develop the UsistUCP proposal, specifying its differences with the original method: use case point (UCP). To make a comparative analysis between these two methods, we take one case under study to be estimated based on these two methods and then we will provide the corresponding conclusions.

BACKGROUND

The size of software is one of the main factors to determine the effort needed to design any system. Several models have been proposed to estimate size; one of the most famous is the COCOMO model. However, one of the most widespread techniques to estimate size of systems is the function points analysis. This technique is based on the number of inputs, outputs, queries, files, and interfaces. To know all these attributes, we need to have enough information of the system and/or applications to be designed, but for new implementations, generally there is only an initial list of requisites that in most cases is quite general. Both models are identified as top-down estimate proposals.

Another type of estimate proposal is bottom-up, in which an estimate is made by dividing the software under implementation by the main applications or units. Each application is then classified as simple, average, and complex based on certain criteria. For each classification, a standard effort for coding and tests is defined, named designing effort. This standard designing effort can be based on data from previous similar projects, available internal guidelines, or a combination of both. Both proposals, top-down and bottom-up, require information on the project, size (top-down), and a list of tasks (bottom-up) (Jalote, 2002).

This document describes the UsistUCP method, developed by Ultrasist to estimate the effort in projects considering the use case analysis, which combines both proposals (top-down and bottom-up). Our method originated in the UCP original method and was gradually modified based on our experience. We share our experience so that it can be used by other organizations, specifically the SMEs, as their activities are dynamic and feasible to perform, and this is quite evident with the successful establishment of our company.

USE CASE POINT ESTIMATION METHOD

This method is divided into two parts: the first one measures the system's functionality based on the use case model and will be named unadjusted use case point (UUCP). The second part takes into account the technical factors involved in the development of the functionality and environmental factors. The use case points are the result of the UUCPs and technical and environmental factors, which correspond to an estimate of the system size. Additionally, the productivity required, which may be obtained from the organization's historic data, must be associated per use case point.

Unadjusted Use Case Points

1. Identify actors and classify them according to Table 1.
2. Identify the use case and analyze them according to Table 2.
3. Add the three weights of actors and use cases in order to obtain the UUCPs.

If no additional information on environmental and technical factors is available, the UUCPs may be used to estimate the size.

1. Determine the technical complexity factor with the following formula:

$$TCF = 0.6 + (0.01)*(\text{sum of factors}*Wi)$$

Factors (Fi) will be assigned values from 0, 1, 2, 3, 4, and 5, where zero means that the factor is irrelevant and 5 that the factor is essential.
The Wi weight values will be assigned according to Table 3.

1. Determine the environmental factor with the following formula:

$$EF = 1.4 + (-0.03)*(\text{sum of factors}*Wi)$$

Values of Wi weights will be assigned according to Table 4.
Factors (Fi) will be assigned values from 0, 1, 2, 3, 4, and 5, where zero means that the factor is irrelevant and 5 that it is essential.

Table 1. Actor weights

Complexity	Definition	Weight (W)
Simple	An actor is considered simple if it represents another system with a defined application programming interface.	1
Average	An actor is considered average if: 1. An interaction with another system is through some protocol. 2. A human interaction with a terminal line.	2
Complex	An actor is considered complex if interaction is through a graphic user interface.	3

Table 2. Use case weights

Complexity	Definition	Weight (W)
Simple	If there are 3 or less transactions including optional ways.	5
Average	If there are from 3 through 7 transactions including optional ways.	10
Complex	If there are more than 7 transactions including optional ways.	15

Table 3. Technical factors

Factor	Definition	Weight (W)
F1	Distributed systems	2
F2	Application with performance objectives	1
F3	End user efficiency (online)	1
F4	Complex internal processing	1
F5	Reusability, the code must be available for reuse in other applications	1
F6	Installation ease	0.5
F7	Easy use, usable	0.5
F8	Portable	2
F9	Changeability	1
F10	Concurrent	1
F11	With especial security features	1
F12	Provides direct access to third parties	1
F13	User training facilities	1

Table 4. Environment factors

Factor	Definition	Weight (W)
F1	Known object-oriented technology	1.5
F2	Part-time staff	-1
F3	Analysis capability	0.5
F4	Application experience	0.5
F5	Object-oriented experience	1
F6	Motivation	1
F7	Difficult programming language	-1
F8	Stable requirements	2

1. Determine the UCPs as the result of unadjusted use case points, the technical complexity factor, and the environmental factor.

$$UCP = UUCP*TCF*EF$$

Estimate Method Based on Ultrasist Use Case Points

Estimates of software cost and effort will never be an exact science. There are too many variables (human, technical, environmental, policies) that can affect the software cost and final effort for implementation of a system (Pressman, 2002). There are many possible options to make such estimates; some of them require a deeper knowledge of the project, which is lacking when preparing a proposal or a bidding. For instance, the use case point estimate technique needs that we already have the detailed use cases in order to calculate the complexity of each of them (see Table 2). This data may imply an effort of weeks and even of a couple of months (depending on the project's size), which in most cases the client is not willing to provide until it has a total estimate of the system. Due to the above, the UsistUCP estimate method becomes valuable.

The UsistUCP method starts by identifying the use cases at a general level. There are two ways for this: one is the formal method that seeks that the client contracts the business process designing,[1] before estimating the effort (from which the cost derives) of the software implementation. Consequently, the use cases are identified naturally and in detail. The second method is to identify the use cases empirically and in a short period of time. For this, Ultrasist relies on its most experienced analysts. What is important here is to turn the client's initial requirements into general use cases, and historic data from prior projects, converted into Excel formulae, will do the rest to obtain the project's estimated effort.

To identify use cases, the expert analysts take into account the requisites provided by the client, from where the analyst identifies components, such as subsystems, modules, screens, reports, programs, and files. With each standard component being identified and based on the criteria provided in Table 5, use cases and their complexity are recognized. The following examples will aid understanding this concept.

For each identified catalog, one simple use case (1) is considered; for a screen or a report involving a master–detail[2] that involves registries, cancellations, and changes, three average use cases (2) are considered; any use case that cannot classified in practical terms is considered complex (3).

Once the complexity has been assigned to each use case, we obtain the first effort estimate (unadjusted use cases) for each phase of the implementation life cycle, including management of the project and quality assurance (SQA) (see Table 6).

Values in each cell are filled out according to the organization's average historic data from previous projects for each complexity of the use case. If this information is not available, we can start with opinions from experts or with the Program Evaluation and Review Technique (PERT) method.[3] What is interesting in this method is that the more information on projects available, the more the estimate values approach the organization's reality. Up to now, we have an initial estimate of the effort required to design the system based on the functionality needed. However, we have not considered issues such as technology, the client, and resources that will be variables affecting the implementation length. The following section includes these variables in the estimate.

Table 5. Use case classification

Use Case Type	Classification Criteria	Complexity
Simple	The Use Case is considered as a simple part of the work if it uses a simple user interface and touches only a single database entity.	1
Average	The Use Case is more difficult; it involves more interface design and touches two or more database entities.	2
Complex	The Use Case is very difficult; it involves a complex user interface or processing and touches 3 or more database entities	3

Table 6. Effort by phases of the project and complexity of the use case based on the organization's historic data

Use Case	Complexity	Project Managm.	SQA	Tests	Analysis	Design	Programming	Implementation	Total
Use Case 1	1	0.5	0.20	1.5	3	2.5	6	1.75	15.6
Use Case 2	2	1	0.25	3	6	7	12	1.75	32
Use Case 3	3	2	0.5	6	12	13	18	2	55

Adjusted Use Cases

To adjust an estimate, complexity is considered in two aspects: complexity of each phase of the life cycle and the project complexity.

Complexity by Phase of the Life Cycle

In this case, the complexity factors are considered within a range from zero to three, depending on the project's context. Factor 1 means that activities of the phase or project established in the organization's process will be carried out. When any of the activities in the phase are omitted, the factor is less than one, and if it has agreed to carry out activities additional to those established, then the value to be considered will be from one to three. For instance, if during the analysis phase, it is agreed that no prototype will be carried out, the factor considered is 0.8; or otherwise, if it is agreed to carry out a prototype with functionality, then we have a factor of 1.2.

Complexities in phases must be defined according to the organization's history. For instance, for the programming phase, as long as the organization has experienced programmers and components to be reused, then the phase will remain unadjusted and thus the assigned value will be on Table 7, which shows the Ultrasist values for the programming phase.

It is necessary to document the criteria used in order to create history records of estimates in the project, as shown in Table 8.

The adjusted estimate by phase (AEP) is determined by adding the value of each cell of

Table 7. Complexity factors (Ultrasist) for the programming phase

Language	Extra Complexity Factor
Java	1.5
.Net	1.5
Power Builder	1.2
Visual Basic	1.2

Table 8. Documentation of criteria used for the project

Considerations Taken into Account for the Estimate by Phase:
Programming will be made in Java; since there is a team of young programmers, a complexity factor of 1.5 was assigned for the programming phase
The system must be installed in three locations of the client, for which a complexity of 3 was assigned to the introduction phase

Table 9. Adjusted effort by complexity in each phase of the life cycle

Use Case	Complexity	Project Managm.	SQA	Tests	Analysis	Design	Programming	Imple-mentatio	Total
Use Case 1	1	0.5	0.2	1.5	3	2.5	6	1.75	15.6
Use Case 2	2	1	0.25	3	6	7	12	1.75	32
Use Case 3	3	2	0.5	6	12	13	18	2	55
Subtotal		3.5	0.95	10.5	21	22.5	36	5.5	102.6
Complexity by phase		1	1	1	1	1	1.5	3	
Total		3.5	0.95	10.5	21	22.5	54	16.5	129

each phase multiplied by the phase complexity factor. Table 9 shows the complexity x phase, in accordance with the considerations taken in Table 8.

PROJECT COMPLEXITY

The project complexity (PC) takes into account risk factors, regardless the life cycle phases, for instance, a new product, the client's business rules, and the new members of the work team, among others, are unknown. The complexity factors are considered within a range from one to three, where one means no risk and three is the highest risk element.

Table 10 shoes an example of the project complexity, where PC is equal to the average of complexities being identified.

The total estimate of the project (UsistUCP) is obtained with the following equation:
UsistUCP = PC*AEP

Where:
UsistUCP = Ultrasist Use Case Point
AEP = Adjusted Estimate by Phase
PC= Project Complexity

Table 11 shows the column of the UsistUCPs obtained based on the project complexity obtained in Table 10.

We do not need a big system to make the estimates; a simple spreadsheet, as shown in Table 11, containing the history of prior projects in formulae, will suffice. So, once designed, each proposal may be used with the following steps:

1. Record the name and complexity of each use case
2. Enter the complexity by phase
3. Enter (in an independent cell) the complexity by project.

In Ultrasist, the effort associated to factors of complexity by phases will be considered in the work schedule, while the effort corresponding to the project complexity will be used by the project's

Table 10. Project complexity

Project Complexity (PC)	1.3
New client	2
Known Business	1
Experienced Team Work	1

Table 11. Adjusted effort by project complexity (Complexity = 1.3)

		Hours-Man								
Use Case	Complexity	Project Managm.	SQA	Tests	Analysis	Design	Programming	Implementatio	Total	Project Complexity
Use Case 1	1	0.5	0.2	1.5	3	2.5	6	1.75	15.6	
Use Case 2	2	1	0.25	3	6	7	12	1.75	32	
Use Case 3	3	2	0.5	6	12	13	18	2	55	
Subtotal		3.5	0.95	10.5	21	22.5	36	5.5	102.6	
Complexity x phase		1	1	1	1	1	1.5	3		
Total		3.5	0.95	10.5	21	22.5	54	16.5	128.95	167.635

manager to control the identified risks or new contingencies that may arise. For more complex projects, we suggest, as an initial step, to identify the subsystems or services. In this case, use cases of each subsystem are reviewed.

Application of the Ultrasist Use Case Points (UsistUCP) Calculation for a Case under Study

The case under study that will serve as basis for the estimation with the two methods described (UCP and UsistUCP) is a spare part store. The use cases were obtained from the following sales process:

For the time being, many business processes are carried out manually; the clients seek in printed catalogs available in an area within the store. Catalogs include the description and unique price number of the product. The client fills out a purchase order from the selected catalog and writes down the product's unique number and the amount before handing it over to one of the store's responsible parties in charge of registering the order. The responsible party checks that there are products for each item in the order and assigns a

price to each. Once all the order's lines have been checked, the order total price is calculated.

The client picks up the order at the cash desk, where the cashier records data of the payment (cash or credit card) for the order with a unique number of transaction, registry number, date and time, for accounting purposes. A receipt is prepared and given to the client. The receipt includes data of the transaction, the quantity, price and total value for each product, and the total amount paid. Also, a supply ticket is prepared showing the number of the product and the quantity for each line in the order for the warehouse person, who is in charge of gathering the products until the order is complete and sends it to dispatch. The dispatcher work is to ensure that the client receives the products and stamps the seal reading "received" on the client's receipt.

The other use cases are described similarly. Table 13 shows the complexity for use cases obtained from calculating transactions according to Table 2. This is seen in the use case "Register a purchase order," described in Table 12, which has a complexity of 3 and was obtained by counting the steps in the use case description (11), including optional ways and referring to Table 2, in which,

Figure 1. Use cases in a spare part sale store

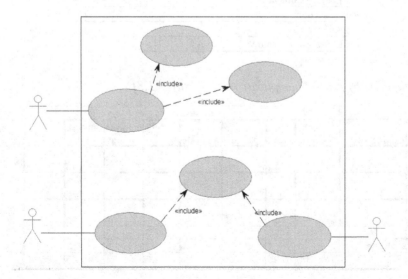

Table 12. Description of one use case

	Register a Purchase Order
Description	Register a purchase order based on the application filled out by the client.
Normal Sequence	1. The system shows the following general order data: Order number, date and name of the dispatcher. 2. The user looks for the client (see the corresponding use case). 3. The system shows data of the client: Name, Address (Street, District, Zip Code), telephone. 4. For each spare part indicated in the application: 5. The user looks for the spare part (see the corresponding use case). 6. The system shows the description, price and unique number of the product. 7. The user enters the quantity required of the product. 8. The system checks that there are products (A1) 9. Once all the lines in the order have been checked, the system determines the total order price.
Optional Ways	A1 • If the product is not available, the system sends the message "There are no products available for this item" • and deletes the line from the order.

Table 13. Application of complexity criteria to the case under study

Number	**Use Case**	**Complexity**
1	Register a purchase order	3
2	Look for the client	2
3	Look for spare parts	2
4	Register payments	3
5	Check the order	1
6	Provide the order	2

Table 14. Effort estimate (in hours) by each phase for the example under study (unadjusted use case)

Use Case	Complexity	Hours-Man							Total
		Project Managm.	SQA	Tests	Analysis	Design	Programming	Imple-mentatio	
Register a Purchase Order	3	2	0.5	6	12	13	18	2	53.5
Look for the Client	2	1	0.25	3	6	7	12	1.75	31
Look for Spare Parts	2	1	0.25	3	6	7	12	1.75	31
Register Payments	3	2	0.5	6	12	13	18	2	53.5
Check the Order	1	0.5	0.2	1.5	3	2.5	6	1.75	15.45
Provide the Order	2	1	0.25	3	6	7	12	1.75	31
Subtotal		7.5	1.95	22.5	45	49.5	78	11	**215.45**

for use cases with more than 10 transactions, complexity is of 3.

Then, the effort calculation is made in hours by phase in these use cases. A spreadsheet includes the effort data in hours by phase of the project, depending on the complexity. This is shown in Table 14, where, for instance for a simple use case for the analysis phase, 3 hours are used; 6 hours are used for an average use case and 12 hours for a complex use case. The effort of these six use cases is 228.45 hours. These are the unadjusted use case points.

The next step is to obtain the adjusted effort according first to the complexity by phase. Table 15 shows the complexity by phases considered in this example, which, for the programming phase is 1.5, and for the implementation phase is 3. The reasons for this is that programming will be per-

formed in Java[4] and the system must be installed in three locations of the client. This information must be documented as shown in Table 8.

Table 16 shows the adjusted effort by phase taking into account values in Table 15.

Once the adjusted effort by phase has been obtained, we will consider for the project a factor of 1.3 according to the criteria of Table 10. Table 17 shows the project's total effort, which is 359 hours-man.

When concluding each project, comparisons of the initial estimate with the real estimate must be made in order to adjust future estimates, for each increase, phase, and when completing the project, which will allow the organization to obtain estimates more precise every time; that is, historic data of the organization are generated.

Table 15. Example of values of complexity by phase

Complexity by phase	
Analysis	1
Design	1
Programming	1.5
Implementation	3
Tests	1
Project Management	1

Table 16. Adjusted effort by phase

Use Case	Complexity	Hours-Man							Total
		Project Managm.	SQA	Tests	Analysis	Design	Programming	Implementatio	
Register a Purchase Order	3	2	0.5	6	12	13	18	2	53.5
Look for the Client	2	1	0.25	3	6	7	12	1.75	31
Look for Spare Parts	2	1	0.25	3	6	7	12	1.75	31
Register Payments	3	2	0.5	6	12	13	18	2	53.5
Check the Order	1	0.5	0.2	1.5	3	2.5	6	1.75	15.45
Provide the Order	2	1	0.25	3	6	7	12	1.75	31
Subtotal		7.5	1.95	22.5	45	49.5	78	11	215.45
Complexity x phase		1	1	1	1	1	1.5	3	
Total		7.5	1.95	22.5	45	49.5	117	33	276.45

Table 17. Adjusted effort by project complexity

| Use Case | Complexity | Hours-Man | | | | | | | Total | Project Complexity |
		Project Managm	SQA	Tests	Analysis	Design	Programming	Imple-mentatio		
Register a Purchase Order	3	2	0.5	6	12	13	18	2	53.5	
Look for the Client	2	1	0.25	3	6	7	12	1.75	31	
Look for Spare Parts	2	1	0.25	3	6	7	12	1.75	31	
Register Payment	3	2	0.5	6	12	13	18	2	53.5	
Check the Order	1	0.5	0.2	1.5	3	2.5	6	1.75	15.45	
Provide the Order	2	1	0.25	3	6	7	12	1.75	31	
Subtotal		7.5	1.95	22.5	45	49.5	78	11	**215.45**	
Complexity x phase		1	1	1	1	1	1.5	3		
Total		7.5	1.95	22.5	45	49.5	117	33	**276.45**	**359.385**

APPLICATION OF THE UCPS CALCULATION FOR THE CASE UNDER STUDY

For the example in Figure 1, users represent a kind of complex actor given that these are persons using the system through a graphical interface.

UAW = 1 X 3 = 3.

The factor of the unadjusted use case weight is obtained in Table 18; based on the number of transactions, the rating will be applied like the complexity in UUCP (see Table 2).

The UUCPs are then determined:

Table 18. Factor of the unadjusted use case weight (UUCW)

Number	Use Case	Weight Factor
1	Prepare invoice	3
2	Check the client	2
3	Enter the order	2
4	Separate the products	2
5	Reduce the inventory	1
	UUCW	10

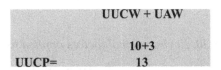

$$UUCP = \frac{UUCW + UAW}{} = \frac{10+3}{13}$$

Technical factors are assigned a value of 3 so that these have little influence on the estimate (see Table 19 for the example under study).

Similarly, environmental factors are assigned a value of 3 so that these have little influence on the estimate (see Table 20 for the example under study).

The adjusted use case points are as follows:

$$UPC = 12.18 \quad \frac{UUCP*TCF*EF}{13*1.05*0.725}$$

According to Karner (1993), the use case point average is among 15 and 30 hours.

Effort = UPC*30= (12.18)*30= 365.4

By comparing the two methods, we can see in Table 21 that the unadjusted UsistUCP result is lesser than the original method, and when the adjustment is made, estimates may be similar or higher than in Ultrasist because environmental

Table 19. Technical factors applied for the example under study

	Technical Factors		Influence	Influence * Weight
Factor	Description	Weight	(0,3,5)	
1	Distributed system	2	3	6
2	Response adjectives	2	3	6
3	End-user efficiency	1	3	3
4	Complex processing	1	3	3
5	Reusable code	1	3	3
6	Easy to install	0.5	3	1.5
7	Easy to use	0.5	3	1.5
8	Portable	2	3	6
9	Easy to change	1	3	3
10	Concurrent	1	3	3
11	Security features	1	3	3
12	Access for third parties	1	3	3
13	Special training required	1	3	3
			Tfactor	45
			TCF	**1.05**

Table 20. Environmental factors applied for the example under study

	Environmental Factors		Influence	Influence*Weight
Factor	Description	Weight	(0,3,5)	
1	Familiar with process	1.5	3	4.5
2	Application experience	0.5	3	1.5
3	Object-oriented experience	1	3	3
4	Lead analyst capability	0.5	3	1.5
5	Motivation	1	3	3
6	Stable requirements	2	3	6
7	Part-time workers	-1	3	-3
8	Difficult programming language	2	3	6
			Efactor	22.5
			EF	**0.725**

Table 21. Comparison of the two methods

Estimate	UCP	UUCP
Unadjusted	390	215.45
Adjusted	365.4	359.4

factors can be handled based on the organization's nature. That is, the UsistUCP method can take into account factors that approach more to reality of each organization, with the advantage that factors of the original method may be included. Another difference is that the effort is based on the organization's historic data, more than on statistics of the industry.

TRENDS

Measurement institutes such as the International Function Point Users' Group (IFPUG) and United Kingdom Software Metrics Association (UKSMA) are still working with estimates made by points per feature, but for those UML technically object-oriented organizations, use cases lead development, therefore UCP (use case point) should be the measurement unit. It is worth creating a history that may allow the method to be more assertive with the object used as reference for small and middle size companies (SMEs).

CONCLUSION

The UCP method assumes that we have detailed use cases at the level of transactions. Generally, the client is not willing to invest in this activity. Once points are obtained, these must be multiplied by the productivity to obtain the effort. A company that does not record history lacks this information. With UCP, there are predefined technical and environmental factors available to make the adjustments.

The UsistUCP method relies on use cases at the general level. The productivity estimate may be made by opinion of experts and Program Evaluation and Review Technique (PERT) reference. Like in the UCP method, estimate adjustments are also made, but unlike the original method, the complexity of each phase and the project complexity are taken into account. Factors of adjustments

are not predefined, which gives the organization flexibility to define its own factors. What is valuable in this method is that it refines every time in order to reduce deviations in the estimate based on the metrics history and organization's idiosyncrasy. Based on this method, our organization has established the quantitative goal of 5% to 15% of deviation of real effort from the estimated effort. Once the required effort has been identified, the size (number of use cases) and the project's cost can also be obtained by multiplying the effort obtained by the hourly cost of the organization.

ACKNOWLEDGMENT

This chapter has been developed inside the project: "Process Improvement for Promoting Iberoamerican Software Small and Medium Enterprises Competitiveness–COMPETISOFT" (506AC287) financed by CYTED (Programa Iberoamericano de Ciencia y Tecnología para el Desarrollo).

REFERENCES

Karner, G. (1993). *Resource estimation for objectory projects*. Retrieved December 17, 2007, from http://www.bfpug.com.br/

Jalote, P. (2002). *Software project management in practice*. Addison-Wesley.

Pressman, R. S. (2002). *Ingeniería de Software un enfoque práctico* (R. Ojeda Martín, V. Yagüe Galaup, I. Morales Jareño, & S. Sánchez Alonso, Trans., 5th ed.). Madrid, Spain: McGraw-Hill.

ENDNOTES

[1]   Designing of the business is beyond the scope of this article. This is performed in Ultrasist when the client does not have identified requisites.

2   For example, a master obtains general infor-
     mation from an order and details of products
     associated to the order.

3   PMBook
4   The value of 1.5 is obtained from Table 6
     (historic data Ultrasist)

Chapter XVIII
Improving Resource Management:
Lessons from a Case Study in a Middle-Range Governmental Organization

Juan M. Luzuriaga
Poder Judicial de la Provincia de Neuquén, Argentina

Rodolfo Martínez
Poder Judicial de la Provincia de Neuquén, Argentina

Alejandra Cechich
GIISCo Research Group, Universidad Nacional del Comahue, Argentina

ABSTRACT

In organizational studies, resource management is the efficient and effective deployment of an organization's resources when they are needed. Such resources may include financial resources, inventory, human skills, production resources, or information technology. Usually small organizations have to carry out these activities themselves because they cannot yet afford part- or full-time help. However, they should always ensure that policies that conform to current regulations are applied. This is especially true for middle-ranged governmental organizations. In this chapter, we discuss a case study where resource management was addressed through recommendations of a process improvement model called MoProSoft. We illustrate the resource management procedure and we draw some lessons learned from the case study.

INTRODUCTION

While there is an increasing benefit of software process improvement in terms of producing high quality software, the adoption in software development has resulted in limited success for many efforts. There are many instances in which process assessment is at best wasteful and at worst counterproductive (Leung, 1999; Saiedian, 2003). Of particular concern is the comparison of a real world organizations' practices against the idealized recommendations of an improvement model. As more and more organizations embark on software process improvement, the question most frequently asked preceding any commitment to investment is what tangible and intangible benefits can be expected. Generally speaking, there is a perception in small to medium software developers that process improvement models such as CMMI (Capability Maturity Model Integration) or ISO/IEC 15504 (Helfat & Raubitschek, 2000) are developed and are relevant only for large organizations. Then, benefits must be scarce and highly costly when applying them to small organizations (Demirörs et al., 1998; Tuffey, Grove, & McNair, 2004).

The correct implementation of any improvement initiative is an important undertaking. In this context, COMPETISOFT (2006) is a process improvement project set up through seed funding from the CyTED organization (CyTED), an Ibero-American organization aiming at supporting science and technology development in Latin America, Spain, and Portugal. In 2006, CyTED funded this project for small to medium software developments. The initial phase involved, among other things, conducting a number of assessments and experiences in implementing improvement practices. It included selecting participating organizations where investigate about the advantages and pitfalls of applying such improvement practices.

As the judicial system of the Province of Neuquen, Argentina, a medium governmental organization that produces software has previous experience in process improvement activities such as Metrica V.3; there was a concern about new programs oriented to small/medium organizations. Particularly, it was interesting to them to analyze the organization's perception of what a process improvement project involves in order to manage resources. With this concern in mind, the organization set the following goals that it wishes to realize by participating in a process improvement program:

1. Improve efficiencies within the resource acquisition practices
2. Improve productivity
3. Reduce critical dependency of subjective evaluations
4. Set operational policies and procedures to evaluate and acquire resources

This chapter discusses the results of a case study focusing on the conduct of a process improvement project in this medium-sized governmental organization mentoring to improve the capability of the organization's resource acquisition processes (Luzuriaga, Martínez, & Cechich, 2006). The activities centered on the recommendations of the Mexican model MoProSoft (Oktaba et al., 2003), providing a basis for developing management practices, which were implemented over a period of six months, and finally determining the improvements realized over that time frame. We discuss lessons learned and highlight benefits and drawbacks of implementing improvement from the case study.

RESEARCH PROJECT

There is a considerable diversity of recent proposals to address organizational research (Clegg & Ross-Smith, 2003; Czarniawska, 2003), ranging from modest attempts at enhancing "managerial implications" sections of scholarly articles to calls for better cooperation between scholars and practitioners to radical manifestos for the redesign of academia (Ghoshal, 2005; Gosling & Mintzberg, 2004; Mintzberg, 2004; Pfeffer, 2005).

Some of them argue that the application of complexity science holds the promise of a unified organizational theory rich enough to provide a framework to study both the dynamic interactions among heterogeneous agents and the phase transitions in organizations. And some others argue for an increase in complexity of models and suggest that simulation can provide useful theoretical insight through the study of artificial simplified replicas of the "real world" by building thousands of interacting dynamic "agent models" that each simulate the behavior of a particular social entity, and then observing over long cycles the effects of interplay between those models (Brown & Eisenhardt, 1997; Helfat & Raubitscheck, 2000).

On the other hand, the *design driven organization science* is a substream of the *action research* and it has recently been brought to the forefront (Boland & Collopy, 2004; Romme & Georges, 2003; Romme, Georges, & Endenburg, 2006). It is based on the simple observation that organizations "out there in the real world" engage in design on a daily basis: they design new products and services, new organizational structures, processes and procedures, and so forth. On these lines, the methodology used for our research was the action research paradigm. Action research entails the analysis of direct intervention of the researcher (Gill & Johnson, 1997). We applied the traditional action-research five-phase cyclical process-based approach as defined by Susman and Evered (1978) and Baskerville (1997) for our research project. Using this approach allowed us to perform the role of assessor in the process-improvement program detailed in this chapter. It also provided us with the objectivity and structure to effectively perform our work. It was based on a client-system infrastructure, which is the collaborative agreement reached between the client (organization) with whom the research is being carried out and the

researchers. This agreement defined the boundaries of the research area. The initial diagnosing was where the underlying causes and reasons for change were collaboratively defined. In the following state, the activities required to bring about that change were collaboratively planned. This was followed by a phase where those activities were performed. Additionally, a collaborative evaluation was carried out and the effectiveness of the actions employed was researched. This was followed by a learning procedure, where the lessons learned from the activities as a whole were directed to the client.

ORGANIZATION BACKGROUND

According to Mintzberg (2004), an organization typically embodies administrative units that provide services to itself, such as a cafeteria, mailroom, legal counsel, public relations, and so forth. These are called the *support staff*. The Informatics Area (IA) of the Judicial System of Neuquén (JSN) is a department supplying computing services to a judicial governmental organization, and it is specifically oriented to assist final users in using software applications. Therefore, IA is a typical support staff for the organization. The IA is a service area that supports other departments in charge of administering justice. Similarly to IA, there are other service areas inside the organization such as the General Administration Area in charge of dealing with finances and acquisition processes; or the School of Training in charge of supporting training needs of the entire organization. Despite the hierarchical structure of most of the areas, service areas are transversal to the organization and support any level of the structure. Besides, the IA is not a complete software development area by itself: it needs other areas to accomplish specific processes such as supplier administration and purchases. Figure 1 shows these relationships.

Figure 1. Relationships between areas in JSN

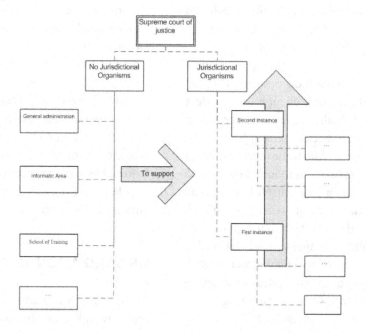

The IA is divided into four areas as follows: technology, operations, development, and logistics. They work collaboratively to support users and customers in their diverse needs. For example, among other responsibilities, the development area is currently in charge of developing a new software system to administer the judicial procedure. This new system must satisfy the needs of customers and users and replace the current and operational system. One of the goals of the technology area is the evaluation and implementation of new technologies for supporting the software system, managing resources, and supporting decision making. The operations area assists users through a help desk that keeps continuous communication with users by receiving their claims and proactively responding when needs are detected. Finally, the logistics area is in charge of coordinating, distributing, replacing, and installing workstations, and analyzing all users' needs that require informatics as assistance to daily work.

The IA is related to other departments of the JSN acting as a link between detecting users'

needs and implementing software solutions, and additionally participating in other activities such as service and good acquisition, training, and so forth. Despite that IA is not currently adopting any model or recommendation for improvement, it is engaged in implementing certain activities that allow controlling internal processes and dynamically analyzing them under a continuous improvement framework.

ORGANIZATION MOTIVATION

Every activity coordination task in which the human factor takes part to reach predefined goals should be performed in a systemic way and according to good practices. In this way, a good organization will not only be characterized by the arrangement of its activities but also by its management and control. With these statements in mind, in 2005, the JSN elaborated the organization's strategic plan (2005-2007), which defines guidelines clearly detailing the level of relevance of informatics inside the management of the processes.

Previously, before 2005, the IA was only in charge of one task: the implementation of a software system developed by a third party and supported by the SCO UNIX © platform. Because of that, the arrangement of people into areas was quite different in those days. People were focused on implementing third-party developments; and all support was addressed to this activity. Consequently, there was no "development area." Now, based on the strategic plan, a set of goals and objectives addressed the replacement of the software system aiming at adopting new technologies and improving user attendance. The accomplishment of these goals and objectives involved the development or creation of specific areas of the IA and, of course, setting their internal goals.

Defining the areas was a relatively easy task. Based on the different goals, scope, and information, networks were designed. The main intent was to keep every process under control. The hard part was to make a decision about "which people should be assigned to which area," that is, *taking resources into account* to get the best distribution. A good starting point was trying to understand the motivation behind each person to accomplish a particular activity, whether he/she was comfortable with his/her work, what expectations he/she had, and most importantly, in which way he/she was relating (communicating, interchanging, etc.) with other people. At this point, our challenge was clear: we had to organize people into a group capable of accomplishing the goals and objectives of the strategic plan. This group of people would constitute one of the "resources" that the IA should count on to develop the strategic plan. We considered taking a reference model to resource management as a good starting point. That was our connection to software process improvement (SPI) models and particularly to MoProSoft.

RESEARCH QUESTIONS

The case study was carried out within the IA, employing 35 people. The questions researched in this project included:

- Can a resource management model work within a medium governmental organization?
- Do a process improvement model make a meaningful contribution, or does it add unnecessary levels of bureaucracy?
- Does the MoProSoft's resource management work?

IMPROVING RESOURCE MANAGEMENT

Basically, the argument behind the CMM's improvement approach is that as the organization standardizes software processes and the developers learn techniques, the time required to accomplish development tasks will reduce and the productivity and the quality of the product will improve. However, there is some evidence supporting that software process improvement models such as the CMM and ISO 9001 (2000) are not suitable for small software developing companies (Cattaneo, Fuggeta, & Lavazza, 1995; Demirörs et al., 1998). In general, they face organizational, cultural, financial, and technical obstacles. In terms of organizational problems, one company with only a few projects probably cannot access an infrastructure of services and advice; it is more difficult to staff complex projects with sufficient expertise; and usually interactions are quite informal. Moreover, the competitive environment of most small companies is such that survival depends on having an extreme performance draw. In this context, the basic problem is to undertake enough management practices to ensure short-term results and long-term survival.

To compound this concern, there are claims that the idealized list of CMM's practices has not been proven to work (Fayad & Laitinen, 1997). While the individual practices themselves are of unquestionable value, the documentation and associated recommendations are not so useful for small organizations. Particularly, resource management, which implies diverse aspects such as staffing and knowledge management, is addressed by CMM as a direct management responsibility (including providing technical direction and administering the personnel) and embedded into the different practices. For example, as part of planning (level 2), changes in staffing and other software costs that affect software commitments are negotiated with the affected groups and then documented. Similarly, the actual and projected use of the project's critical computer resources are tracked and compared to the estimates for each major software component as documented in the software development plan. As another example, as part of organization process focus (level 3), long-term plans and commitments for funding, staffing, and other resources are established. Similarly, technical and management lessons learned are documented and stored in the organization's library of software process-related documentation. Resource management spreads among different recommendations of ISO 9001. For example, it requires that purchased products conform to their specified requirements. This includes the assessment of potential subcontractors and verification of purchased products. Knowledge management is not explicitly addressed, but ISO 9001 requires that records be collected and maintained, making them easily available.

In sum, by using CMM or ISO 9001, the management of the cost, staffing, and other resources is tied to the tasks of the project's defined software process. Then, visibility turns into one questionable matter, and ease-of-use particularly hinders applicability at small-range organizations.

To overcome this problem, several efforts have addressed software process improvement for small organizations (Laitinen, Fayad, & Ward, 2000). More recently and oriented to Latin-American organizations, the MoProSoft (Oktaba et al., 2003) model has been introduced aiming at improving software development and maintenance practices in middle-range organizations. To do so, the model is based on the following criteria:

1. Elaborate a process' structure according to the structure of the organization, splitting practices into three levels: business management, project management, and operational management.
2. Emphasize the role of the business management level in promoting good practices for strategic planning, its assessment, and continuous improvement.
3. Consider the project management level a supplier of resources, processes, and projects, as well as the main responsibility of evaluating the achievement of the organization's strategic goals.
4. Consider the operational level a developer of software development and maintenance projects.
5. Clearly and consistently integrate the elements needed to define processes and their relationships.
6. Integrate the elements needed to manage projects into only one process.
7. Integrate the elements of product software engineering into one framework, which additionally includes supporting processes such as verification, validation, documentation, and configuration control.
8. Emphasize the importance of *resource management*, particularly those that constitute the organizational knowledge such as measurements, lessons learned, experiences, and so forth.
9. Base the process on the ISO 9000:2000 standard (ISO/IEC 9001-1, 2000) and CMM V1.1 (CMM). Use the ISO/IEC 15504 Software Process Assessment standard (Helfat & Rau-

bitschek, 2000) as a general framework and incorporate practices from other models such as project management body of knowledge (PMBOK) and software engineering body of knowledge (SWEBOK).

Note that MoProSoft (item 8 above) explicitly emphasizes the importance of resource management, which embodies organizational knowledge. Management here is focused on capturing, storing, and reusing such organizational knowledge. To be more specific, the following section further describes resource management in MoProSoft.

OVERVIEW OF RESOURCE MANAGEMENT IN MOPROSOFT

The main purpose of the resource management (RM) area is providing the organization with human resources, infrastructure, and supplier records; and administrating the knowledge base of the organization. The main goal of the RM area is to support the activities towards achieving the *Strategic Plan*'s goals. The main activities involved in the RM area are as follows (Figure 1):

- **Resource planning:** It receives information from the *Strategic Plan* and *Acquisition and Training Plan* of processes and projects. As a result of this activity, the following plans are produced: *Human Resources and Working Environment Operative Plan*; *Goods, Services and Infrastructure Operative Plan*; and *Organizational Knowledge Operative Plan*.
- **Tracking and oversight:** It establish adequate visibility into actual progress so management can take effective actions on every subprocess by considering information from the *Available Human Resource Report*, the *Training and Working Environment Report*, the *Goods, Services and Infrastructure Report*, and the *Organizational Knowledge-Base Status*

Report. Corrective Actions take place when deviations are detected. *The Quantitative and Qualitative Report* is produced from the reports previously mentioned and includes information about available and acquired resources according to the *Communication and Implementation Plan*. Finally, based on the *Process Measurement Plan*, the *Measurement and Improvement Recommendation Report* is generated.
- **Technology trends analysis:** It performs several analyses to determine viability and adequacy of new technologies using the *Strategic Plan* as a guideline. As a result, the *Technology Proposal Report* is produced.

The activities listed above are then instantiated to support the different processes that constitute the RM area. It comprises three subprocesses:

1. GES 3.1: Human Resources and Working Environments. It is in charge of supplying human resources according to the profiles required by the roles played in the organization; and evaluating working environments.
2. GES 3.2: Goods, Services and Infrastructure. It is in charge of selecting suppliers of goods, services, and infrastructure, which must satisfy the acquisition requirements of processes and projects.
3. GES 3.3: Organizational Knowledge. It administers the organizational knowledge base that stores information and products produced by the organization.

The following section describes a case study aiming at improving the resource management by using the subprocesses and activities introduced in this section as guidelines. The case study is limited to the first two subprocesses (GES 3.1 and GES 3.2) since the third one (GES 3.3) is currently under development.

THE RESOURCE MANAGEMENT PROJECT

After identifying the organization's motivation (as introduced in the second section of this chapter) and the research questions (also stated in the second section), we proceed by elaborating a plan execution according to the RM recommendations of MoProSoft.

From the *Strategic Plan* of the Judicial System for 2005-2007, which includes purchasing software for the administration, and from the steps in Figure 2, we started the activities *A1: Resource Planning* and *A3: Technology Trends Analysis* in parallel. The results of those activities would help us state the resources needed by the Strategic Plan Execution: software and hardware to be acquired, modification of the internal organization, and definition of a training program.

To do so, *Activity A3* included the evaluation of technology tools for the development of information systems. Because of the nature of the source information, the tools should be able to manage text documents efficiently. Detecting suitable tools involved searching on the Internet to collect information about the state-of-the-practice of the different required technologies. We analyzed the available tools on the marketplace, considering aspects such as cost, learning time, known uses, and so forth. "Communities" (set of organizations sharing experiences on a particular tool) were taken into account to perform the analysis. In this way, several distributed and geographically dispersed organizations were visited to gather information about experiences, lessons learned, and recommendations. After evaluating the alternatives, the *Technology Proposal* recommended migrating the supporting software platform to the Lotus Notes/Domino© technology. It was the documental database finally selected.

Activity A1 produced the *Human Resource and Working Environment Operative Plan*, which was developed by planning staffing of the Informatics Department of the JSN, distributing work stations, assigning roles, and evaluating the needs of hardware, software tools, furniture, and rooms. Similarly, to elaborate the *Acquisition and Training Plan*, we developed technical specifications for software tools, hardware, and training courses. Then, the General Administration Area of the JSN was in charge of effectively purchasing goods and services by following rules depicted for governmental acquisitions. Taking this plan as an input, we started to define the working teams, rearranging the staff, which consisted of three senior analysts, two senior programmers, two junior programmers, and three domain experts as consultants.

Staffing and evaluation of personnel were not precisely easy tasks considering that the JSN was not supporting any software improvement program or certifying quality in any way. Assigning people to roles, as required by MoProSoft, consequently needed evaluation through interviews and by using tools such as the MBTI (Myers-Briggs Type Indicator) to identify suitable candidates and line them up according to the Strategic Plan's goals.

Roles of the resource management process were assigned to three managers, who were in charge of the Informatics Area, Software Development Area, and Training Area, respectively. After analyzing expertise and background of the personnel, we designed a Training Plan that included basic knowledge about the MoProSoft model, the Lotus Notes tool, and the judicial system. The plan consisted of a 20-hour course of MoProSoft; three courses of Lotus Notes (60 hours) that included several case studies for analysis; and lectures about the judicial system, which consisted of two-hour meetings twice a week for three months.

As part of *Activity A2*: *Tracking and Oversight*, we redefined the information to be stored to include specific background and expertise of the personnel. This information was considered to evaluate personnel and to produce the *Measures and Improvement Recommendations*.

Figure 2. Resource management activity flow

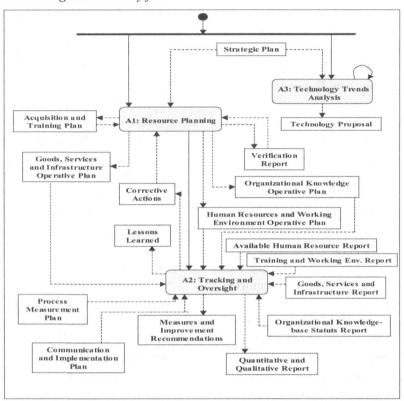

To produce the *Available Human Resources Report*, information about previous positions, studies (precollege, college, and postgraduate), training, group work skills, and previous evaluations were added to every person's record. Then, the *Training and Working Environment Report* was built based on multiple-choice questionnaires that included:

- Interpersonal relationships and teamwork skills to design work groups.
- Work schedule distribution based on different preferences (full- or part-time; flexible time)
- Available technology and tools to support daily work. This subject allowed us to identify the minimal needs for each workstation, such as Internet connection to access knowledge bases, e-mail, operative system versioning, and so forth.
- Furniture and room were redesigned to adapt to teamwork. People were grouped into four-person groups to facilitate discussions, and a meeting room was made available to improve oral communication. A whiteboard was used as a common space for communicating news and advances.

Finally, regarding *Measures and Improvement Recommendations*, we should note that measuring time showed the importance of keeping acquisition procedures under control. From our experiences, time for acquisition of technology largely exceeded estimations, which hindered the overall schedule and negatively impacted on motivation.

ANALYSIS AND EVALUATION

The use of the MoProSoft model made a substantial contribution to the success of the resource management initiative outlined in this research. We first addressed the need for a clear understanding of the initiative. Once that had been determined, goals and objectives were put in context with the objectives and business strategy of the organization. Then, the diagnosing allowed a baseline of the existing process and facilitated the development of recommendations and improvements. As one of the most important consequences, our preliminary experience impacted directly on the control practices of the organization. Although a decision on changing the structure is still under consideration, the new practices for acquiring resources and training were immediately adopted. Learning from our experiences provided an excellent opportunity to evaluate what has been achieved and identify lessons learned. However, at the same time we found out great benefits, we faced some problems. The following sections briefly address some of them.

Benefits

- **Staffing and working environment pPlanning.** Developing both plans at the same time was a very positive experience. It made strengths easier to detect, which came from increasing motivation and improving the working environment. Overall, participants agreed that the quality of working conditions had improved. They believed they were facing fewer problems and that the increased stability in their working environment was giving them more confidence (see the survey's results in the fifth section).
- **Goods recording.** The Judicial System of Neuquén centralizes recording through a particular area, which is in charge of registering only patrimonial goods. To apply the MoProSoft model, we had to create a database

to store the internal products required by the model. It allowed us to control any technical device and improve corrective and preventive maintenance.

- **Internal product recording.** Information required by the MoProSoft model proved useful and convenient to quantitatively and qualitatively analyze processes. It additionally allowed us to extend the information recorded by the organization. Participants agreed they have a better understanding and awareness of how the organization develops software and acquire resources (see the survey's results in the fifth section).

Difficulties

- **Role assignment.** It was difficult to accomplish because the quality improvement program was limited to some areas of the organization. Interrelations among different areas would need a whole discussion of roles; therefore, for our case study, roles of management process' activities were played by personnel of the Informatics Area and by a training specialist.
- **Goods, services, and infrastructure selection.** Considering that the main intent was to select suppliers who could satisfy the acquisition requirements of processes and projects, we faced the problem of constraining selection because of the needs of hiring by the state's laws. Consequently, we could not evaluate different suppliers, and this situation seems common and recurrent to many governmental organizations.
- **Quality system implementation.** All activities of the MoProSoft model need information as input or produce information as output (in the way of reports or plans). One of the problems we faced during the implementation was to implement the resource management process without a supporting tool, which would help accomplish administration of

versioning, tracking, oversight, and so forth. To make implementation feasible, we consider the development of a supporting tool to assist the MoProSoft model absolutely necessary.

Lessons Learned

- **Consequences of not being prescriptive.** Because MoProSoft is a reference model, it makes following recommendations more difficult and applies them in governmental institutions. The lack of specificity about "how" to do certain activities and the inexistence of modeling frameworks forced us to hire experts in implementing quality improvement programs. It might be a common situation derived from the descriptive character of many improvement models.
- **Availability of human resources.** Because the IA is mostly a service-oriented area, it requires focusing on rationally assigning resources to the different scheduled tasks, avoiding deviations due to attending rush and unexpected requirements. This is a permanent debate between considering the "important" and "the urgent." People in charge of implementing a quality model or in charge of running a project must not ignore this situation. It requires continuous management to assure the right assignment of resources.
- **Acquisition of technological resources.** Governmental entities suffer an excessive bureaucracy as a result of the huge number of checkpoints a technology acquisition procedure must pass. However, time is a key factor for this kind of organization, and this situation led us to avoid delays through specific supervision of the acquisition's status. It implied the creation of a new role, called "acquisition procedure supervisor," who was in charge of tracking the technology acquisition procedure. Because of this new role, we could keep all acquisition terms under control.

- **Measurement.** It is important to know that following a quality model includes incorporating activities, which might be not so well understood and in consequence, they might induce wrong schedule estimations. It is necessary to store the measures, deviations, and causes in a knowledge base as a reference for future projects, and as way of supporting continuous improvement. We should know that not having previous experience in implementing a quality model might produce considerable deviations to our planned schedule.

A PRELIMINARY SURVEY

This survey was conducted over a three-month period. The survey was distributed via the JSN e-mail network to 35 members of the IA. They all responded on a 5-point Likert scale (strongly agree, agree, neutral, disagree, and strongly disagree). Fortunately, there was no empty answer and we received responses from the 35 members of the IA. We are aware that optimal survey design should take into account several factors such as population sampling, questionnaire design, and mode of data collection. There are many reasons for the variations in survey quality and, in many cases, it arises from not attending carefully those factors. However, our intent was only to collect a preliminary impression from participants after applying our improvement effort. In this sense, the survey collected feedback about people's feeling regarding improvements of quality of work life; ability to communicate; and organization acquisition efficiency. To better understand these categories, they were further detailed as Table 1 shows. We did not go deeper into quantitative measures because of our main intent: to gather a preliminary impression about possible improvements. Our questionnaire formed the basis to capture respondent's impressions. Of course, these categories do not aim at constituting a framework to evaluate improvements. Far from this, they are only a way of starting to bring participants' opinions into our research. Only in this context, the following results must be interpreted.

Figure 3 shows bar charts of the responses to some relevant questions in the survey; respondents generally agreed in regard to the three categories (even though the concentration of data is around the "neutral" response, there were many respondents who "agreed" and no respondent who "disagreed"). These findings show that participants of our improvement program agreed that quality of working life, communication, and acquisition procedures had in principle improved. However, by looking at the figures more carefully, we distinguished some differences. For example, quality of work life seemed better because of the findings of less pressure/crisis and more stable work environment. But at the same time, people seemed to be working a similar number of overtime hours and dealing with a similar number of problems/crisis (without discussing here complexities of the different problems/crisis). Then, it seemed that the resource management improvement program had positively impacted on motivation and working conditions, but it could not satisfactorily deal with preventing causes of problems/crisis.

Organization communication had mainly improved across projects, but it kept neutral for communication upwards to and downwards from managers. The standardization in processes had facilitated easier communication among project teams. They shared resources without the overhead of adapting to new resource management and procedures as well. This is supported by the following respondent's comments: "...much greater transparency of resource management among teams" and "...uniformity across the procedures." However, communication to/from managers was not specially affected. Finally, the ability to acquire resources had clearly improved because of both a better ability to recruit new staff and a better understanding of how the organization acquires goods and services.

The results of this survey may not be generalizable as they reflect the experience of a single organization. The survey only highlights some benefits in resource management improvement and suggests that the realization of these benefits is important and should be further investigated. Although validation and replication of the survey are still open issues, the results collected might be used as a baseline on which to gauge the extent of improvement to higher quality levels. Of course, our results are just qualitative expressions. It was not our intent to quantify expressions such as "greater transparency of resource management" or "uniformity across procedures." These expressions were used to support a decision on agreement just as a qualitative judgment.

Table 1. Benefit groupings

Benefit	Defined by
Improved quality of work life	Fewer overtime hours
	Fewer problems/crisis
	More stable work environment
	Less stress/pressure
Improved organization communication	Improved communication upwards to management
	Improved communication downwards from management
	Improved communication across projects
Improved ability to acquire resources	Improved ability to recruit new staff
	Improved understanding of how the organization acquires goods and services

Response to Research Questions

In summary, the MoProSoft model provided a good framework for improving resource management within the governmental medium-sized organization we researched. That stated, we would stress that the model should be tailored to fit the needs of the organization utilizing it. The need of tailoring mostly comes from complying with state's regulations for acquisition. In spite of this, the recommendations for management, supervision, and support provided by the MoProSoft model encouraged effective resource management. Of course, the degree of effectiveness depends on the interpretation and application of guidelines across the organization. However, to be effective, the model requires the establishment of a supporting system. It took too long to set plans and document reports. Keeping them effectively up-to-date may turn the system into a bureaucratic set of practices that hinder the model's intent and motivation. But we are not suggesting here that it should be a quick fix program. The MoProSoft's resource management model actually works and offers a simple view of the process.

CONCLUSION AND FUTURE WORK

The main objective of our project was to investigate whether the recommendations of a resource management model, MoProSoft, in this case, would be useful to a governmental medium-sized organization. However, as the comments from the survey and the analysis indicate, many difficulties must be overcome to consider the process effective. We must be aware that the resource management efforts are guided by rather than prescribed by

Figure 3. A preliminary survey

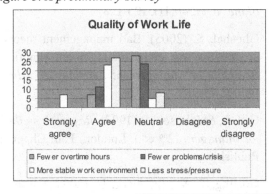

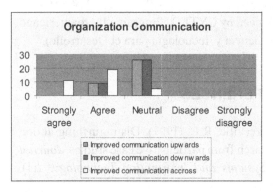

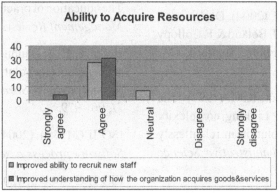

the model. It implies tailoring, which there is also a concern among the organization's software professionals in terms of what they perceive as an application of an improvement model.

The results of the survey may not be generalizable as they reflect the experience of a single organization. Further research should be carried out to extend and replicate the study in a number of governmental organizations to provide more generalizable results. Also, further research is recommended to be carried out now that the organization is familiar with a resource management model. The experiences collected by this case study should be used as a baseline on which to gauge the extent of improvement.

ACKNOWLEDGMENT

This chapter has been developed inside the project: "Process Improvement for Promoting Iberoamerican Software Small and Medium Enterprises Competitiveness–COMPETISOFT" (506AC287) financed by CYTED (Programa Iberoamericano de Ciencia y Tecnología para el Desarrollo).

REFERENCES

Baskerville, R.L. (1997). Distinguishing action research from participative case studies. *Journal of Systems and Information Technology, 1*(1), 25-24.

Boland, R. J., & Collopy, F. (2004). Design matters for management. In R. J. Boland & F. Collopy (Eds.), *Managing as designing*. Stanford, CA: Stanford University Press.

Brown, S. L., & Eisenhardt, K.M. (1997). The art of continuous change: Linking complexity theory and time-paced evolution in relentlessly shifting organizations. *Administrative Science Quarterly, 42*, 1-34.

Cattaneo, E., Fuggetta, A., & Lavazza, L. (1995). *An experience in process assessment*. In *Proceedings of ICSE'95* (pp. 115-121). IEEE Computer Society Press.

Clegg, S. R., & Ross-Smith, A. (2003). Revising the boundaries: Management education and learning in a postpositivist world. *Academy of Management Learning & Education, 2*, 85-98.

Competisoft. (2006). Retrieved December 17, 2007, from http://alarcos.inf-cr.uclm.es/competisoft/

Czarniawska, B. (2003). Forbidden knowledge: Organization theory in times of transition. *Management Learning, 33*, 353-365.

Demirörs, E., et al. (1998). Process improvement towards ISO 9001 certification in small software organizations. In *Proceedings of ICSE'98* (pp. 435-438). IEEE CS Press.

Fayad, M., & Laitinen, M. (1997). Process assessment considered wasteful. *Communications of the ACM, 40*(11), 125-128.

Ghoshal, S. (2005). Bad management theories are destroying good management practices. *Academy of Management Learning & Education, 4*, 75-91.

Gill, J., & Johnson, P. (1997). *Research methods for managers* (2nd ed.). London: Paul Chapman Publishing.

Gosling, J., & Mintzberg, H. (2004, Summer). The education of practicing managers. *MIT Sloan Management Review*, pp. 19-22.

Helfat, C. E., & Raubitschek, R. S. (2000). Product sequencing: Coevolution of knowledge, capabilities and products. *Strategic Management Journal, 21*, 961-979.

ISO/IEC 15504. (2004). *Information technology: Software process assessment standard*.

ISO/IEC 9000-1. (2000). *Quality management and quality assurance standard*.

Laitinen, M., Fayad, M., & Ward, R. (2000, September/October). Software engineering in the small [Special issue]. *IEEE Software.*

Leung, H. (1999). Slow change of information system development practice. *Software Quality Journal, 8*(3), 197-210.

Luzuriaga, J., Martínez, R., & Cechich, A. (2006). Mejora en la Gestión de Recursos: Experiencias hacia la Aplicación de un Estándar IberoAmericano. In *Proceedings of the 7th Argentine Symposium on Software Engineering (ASSE)*, 35 JAIIO, Mendoza, Argentina.

Mintzberg, H. (2004). *Managers not MBAs: A hard look at the soft practice of management and management development.* London: FT Prentice Hall.

Oktaba, H., et al. (2003). *Modelo de Procesos para la Industria de Software: MoProSoft Por Niveles de Capacidad de Procesos.*

Pfeffer, J. (2005). Why do Bad Management Theories Persist? A Comment on Ghoshal'. *Academy of Management Learning & Education, 4*, 96-100.

Romme, A., & Georges, L. (2003). Making a difference: Organization as design. *Organization Science, 14*, 558-573.

Romme, A., Georges, L., & Endenburg, G. (2006). Construction principles and design rules in the case of circular design. *Organization Science, 17*, 287-297.

Saiedian, H. (2003). Practical recommendations to minimize software capability evaluation risks. *Software Process Improvement and Practice, 8*, 145-156.

Susman, G., & Evered, R. (1978). An assessment of the scientific merits of action research. *The Administrative Science Quarterly, 23*(4), 101-114.

Tuffley, A., Grove, B., & McNair, G. (2004). SPICE for small organizations. *Software Process Improvement and Practice, 9*, 23-31.

Compilation of References

Aaen, I., Bøtcher, P., & Mathiassen, L. (1997). Software factories. In L. Mathiassen (Ed.), *Reflective systems development* (Vol. II, pp. 407-433). Aalborg, Denmark: Aalborg University, Institute for Electronic Systems, Department of Computer Science. Retrieved December 5, 2007, from http://www.cs.auc.dk/~larsm/Dr_Techn/Volume_II/17.pdf

ABES⁴-Associação Brasileira das Empresas de Software. (2006a). *Blumenau (SC) faz esforço para formar mão-de-obra*. Retrieved December 12, 2007, from http://www.abes.org.br/templ3.aspx?id=232&sub=21

ABES-Associação Brasileira das Empresas de Software. (2006b). *TCS diz que Brasil não tem técnicos para cumprir meta de exportação*. Retrieved December 12, 2007, from http://www.abes.org.br/templ3.aspx?id=232&sub=19

ABES-Associação Brasileira das Empresas de Software. (2006c). *Mercado brasileiro de software – panorama e tendências*. Retrieved December 12, 2007, from http://www.abes.org.br

Abrahamson, E. (1991). Managerial fads and fashions: The diffusion and rejection of innovations. *The Academy of Management Review, 16*(3), 586-612.

ABS. (2004). 8127.0 characteristics of small business, Australia. Retrieved January 1, 2008, from http://www.abs.gov.au/ausstats/abs@.nsf/b06660592430724fca2568b5007b8619/8ceaee35da67c721ca256ff20005a042!OpenDocument

Ad Hoc Report. (2004, May). Software engineering standards for small and medium enterprises. ISO/IEC JTC1/SC7 /N3060. Retrieved December 12, 2007, from http://www.jtc1-sc7.org/

Ahonen, J.J., Forsell, M., & Taskinen, S.K. (2002). A modest but practical software process modeling technique for software process improvement. *Software Process Improvement and Practice, 7,* 33-44.

Akao, Y. (1990). QFD: Integrating customer requirements into product design. Portland, OR: Productivity Press.

Aktouf, O. (1998). *La administración entre tradición y renovación*. Cali: Artes Gráficas Univalle-Gaëtan Morin Éditeur.

Allen, P., Ramachandran, M., & Abushama, H. (2003, November 6-7). PRISMS: An approach to software process improvement for small to medium enterprises. In *Proceedings of the 3rd International Conference on Quality Software (QSIC '03)* (pp. 211-214). Dallas, Texas.

Alvarez, J. (2007). *Resumen del avance de la aplicación de la metodología desarrollada para la Fábrica de Software Libre* (Tech. Rep. No. 001-2007). Fundacite, Merida: Fábrica de Software Libre. Retrieved December 17, 2007, from http://www.funmrd.gov.ve/drupal/files/technicalReportJohanna.pdf

Alvarez, J., Aguilar, J., & Teran, O., et al. (2006). *Metodología para el Desarrollo de Software Libre: Buscando el Compromiso entre Funcionalidad y Riesgos* (Tech. Rep. No. 001-2006). Fundacite, Merida, Venezuela: Fábrica de Software Libre.

Alvesson, M. (2004) Knowledge Work and Knowledge-Intensive Firms, New York: Oxford University Press.

Anacleto, A., von Wangenheim, C. G., Salviano, C. F., & Savi, R. (2004). Experiences gained from applying 15504 to small software companies in Brazil. In *Proceedings of the International SPICE Conference on Process Assessment and Improvement* (pp. 33-37), Lisbon, Portugal.

Anacleto, A., Wangenheim, C. G. v., Salviano, C. F., & Savi, R. (2004). A method for process assessment in small software companies. In Proceedings of the 4th International SPICE Conference on Process Assessment and Improvement (SPICE 04), Portugal (pp. 69-76).

Anaya, R., Cechich, A., & Henao, M. (2006). *Enfoque integrado de la Gestión del Conocimiento en el modelo de procesos de Competisoft* (Technical Report). Competisoft Project.

Anaya, R., Londoño, L., & Hurtado, J. (2006). Una Estrategia para Elevar la Competitividad de las Industrias de Software PYMES. In *Proceedings of the 9th Workshop Iberoamericano de Ingeniería de Requisitos y Ambientes Software* (IDEAS), La Plata, Argentina.

Associacao Brasileira de Normas Técnicas. (1997). *NBR ISO/IEC 12207/1997 Tecnologia de Informação—Processos de ciclo de vida de software*. Brazil.

Associacao Brasileira de Normas Técnicas. (2002). *NBR ISO 19011 Diretrizes para auditorias de sistema de gestão da qualidade e/ou ambiental*. Brazil.

Asterion. (2005). Tríptico: Preludio. *Zahir blog*. Retrieved December 5, 2007, from http://www.zonalibre.org/blog/zahir/archives/081847.html

Attewell, P., & Rule, J. B. (1991). Survey and other methodologies applied to IT impact research: experiences from a comparative study of business computing. In K. Kraemer (Ed.), *The information systems research challenge: Survey research methods* (Vol. 3, pp. 299-315).

Aubert, N. (1994). Du systeme disciplinaire au systeme managinaire: L'emergence du management psychique. In J.P. Bouilloud & B.P. Lécuyer (Eds.), *L'invention de la gestion. Histoire et pratiques* (pp. 119-136). Paris: L'Harmattan.

Aubert, N., & Gaulejac, V. d. e (1993). *El costo de la excelencia: del caos a la lógica o de la lógica al caos?* Barcelona: Paidós.

Basili, V. R., Caldiera, G., & Rombach, H.D. (1994). The experience factory. In J.J. Marciniak (Ed.), *Encyclopedia of software engineering* (Vol. 1, pp. 469-476). New York: John Wiley & Sons. Retrieved August 5, 2006, from http://wwwagse.informatik.uni-l.de/pubs/repository/basili94c/encyclo.ef.pdf

Basili, V., & Rombach, D. (1998). The TAME project: Towards improvement-oriented software environments. *IEEE Transactions on Software Engineering, 14*(6), 758-773.

Basili, V., & Weiss, D. (1984). A methodology for collecting valid software engineering data. *IEEE Transactions on Software Engineering, 10*(6), 728-738.

Basili, V., Caldiera, G., & Rombach, D. (1994a). Goal question metric paradigm. In J. Marciniak (Ed.), *Encyclopedia of software engineering* (vol. 1, pp. 528-532). New York: Wiley.

Basili, V., Caldiera, G., & Rombach, D. (1994b). The experience factory. In J. Marciniak (Ed.), *Encyclopedia of software enginering* (vol. 1, pp. 469-476). John Wiley & Sons.

Baskerville, R.L. (1997). Distinguishing action research from participative case studies. *Journal of Systems and Information Technology, 1*(1), 25-24.

Batista, J., & Figueiredo, A. (2000, December). SPI in a very small team: A case with CMM. Software Process: Improvement and Practice, 5(4), 243-250.

Beck, K. (2000). *Extreme programming explained: Embrace change*. Boston: Addison-Wesley.

Beck, K. (2004). *Extreme programming explained: Embrace change* (2nd ed.). Addison-Wesley Professional.

Beck, K., Beedle, M., van Bennekum, A., Cockburn, A., Cunningham, W., & Fowler, M., et al. (2001). *Manifesto for agile software development*. Retrieved December 16, 2007, from http://www.agilemanifesto.org

Becker-Kornstaedt, U. (2001). Towards systematic knowledge elicitation for descriptive software process modeling. In *Proceedings of the 3rd International Confer-*

ence on Product Focused Software Process Improvement (PROFES) (pp. 312-325). Germany.

Becker-Kornstaedt, U., Hamann, D., & Verlage, M. (1997). Descriptive modeling of software processes (IESE-Report 045.97/E). Germany: Fraunhofer Institute IESE.

Bedeni, A. G., Ardlia, A. L., Pavlovic, M., & Steembecker, K. (2005, October 19-20). *Quality software map of South America.* Paper presented at the International Research Workshop for Process Improvement in Small Settings, Pittsburgh, Pennsylvania, USA.

Bedini, A., Llamosa, A., Pavlovic, M., & Steembecker, K. (2005). *Quality software map of South America.* In *Proceedings of the 1st International Research Workshop for Process Improvement in Small Settings*, Pittsburgh, PA (pp. 216-227).

Ben-Ari, M. (1998). *The software factory.* Paper presented at 10th Annual Workshop of the Psychology of Programming Interest Group, PPIG 1998, Knowledge Media Institute, Open University, UK. Retrieved December 5, 2007, from http://www.ppig.org/papers/10th-benari.pdf

Bertaux, D., & Singly, F.d. (1997). *Les Récits de vie: perspective ethnosociologique* (Collection 128, 122). Paris: Nathan.

Bezerra, C.I.M., Carneiro, D.M.R., Nibon, R.T., Carneiro, R.M.R., & Araújo, S.A. (2006). *Capacitação em melhoria de processo de software: uma experiência da implantação do SW-CMM em um grupo de pequenas empresas.* Ministério de Ciência e Tecnologia (MCT). Retrieved December 12, 2007, from http://www.mct.gov.br/upd_blob/2641.pdf

Biro, M., Messnarz, R., & Davison, A.G. (2002). The impact of national cultural factors on the effectiveness of process improvement methods: The third dimension. *Software Quality Professional, 4*(4), 34-41.

Black, R. (2002). *Managing the testing process.* Wiley Publishing Inc.

Blowers, R., & Richardson, I. (2005, October 19-20). *The Capability Maturity Model (SW and Integrated)*

tailored in small indigenous software industries. Paper presented at the International Research Workshop for Process Improvement in Small Settings, Pittsburgh, Pennsylvania, USA.

Blowers, R., & Richardson, I. (2006). The capability maturity model (SW and integrated) tailored in small indigenous software industries. In *Proceedings of the 1st International Research Workshop for Process Improvement in Small Settings*, Pittsburgh, Carnegie Mellon University (pp. 175-181).

Blowers, R., & Richardson, I. (2006). The capability maturity model (SW and integrated) tailored in small indigenous software industries. In Proceedings of the 1st International Research Workshop for Process Improvement in Small Settings, Pittsburgh, Carnegie Mellon University (pp. 175-181).

Boehm, B. (1988). A spiral model for software development and enhancement. *IEEE Computer, 21*(5), 61-72.

Boehm, B. (2006). A view of 20th and 21st century software engineering. In D. Osterweil, D. Rombach, & M.L. Soffa (Eds.), *Proceedings of the 28th International Conference on Software Engineering ICSE '06* (pp. 12-29). New York: ACM Press.

Boje, D.M. (1999). The storytelling organization game. Retrieved December 5, 2007, from http://business.nmsu.edu/~dboje/between.html

Boland, R. J., & Collopy, F. (2004). Design matters for management. In R. J. Boland & F. Collopy (Eds.), *Managing as designing.* Stanford, CA: Stanford University Press.

Booch, G., Jacobson, J., & Rumbaugh, I. (2003a). *The unified modeling language.* Addison-Wesley.

Booch, G., Jacobson, J., & Rumbaugh, I. (2003b). *The unified software development process.* Addison-Wesley.

Bossidy, L., & Charan, R. (Eds.). (2002). *Execution: The discipline of getting things done.* Mexico: Aguilar.

Briand, L., Differding, C., & Rombach, H.D. (1996). Practical guidelines for measurement-based process improvement. *Software Process: Improvement and Practice, 2,* 253-280.

Brodman, J. G., & Johnson, D. L. (1997). A software process improvement approach tailored for small organizations and small projects. In *Proceedings of the International Conference on Software Engineering* (pp. 661-662). Boston: IEEE CS.

Brooks, F. P. (1995). *The mythical man-month: Essays on software engineering.* Reading, MA: Addison-Wesley.

Brown, J., & Duguid, P. (1991). Organizational learning and communities-of-practice: Toward a unified view of working, learning, and innovation. *Organizational Science, 2*(1), 40-57.

Brown, S. L., & Eisenhardt, K.M. (1997). The art of continuous change: Linking complexity theory and time-paced evolution in relentlessly shifting organizations. *Administrative Science Quarterly, 42,* 1-34.

Bryman, A. (1989). *Research methods and organizational studies.* England: Urwin Hyman Ltd.

Brynjolfsson, E. (1994). Information assets, technology, and organization. *Management Science, 40*(12), 1645-1662.

Brynjolfsson, E., & Hitt, L.M. (2000). Beyond computation: Information technology, organizational transformation and business performance. *The Journal of Economic Perspectives, 14*(4), 23-48.

Brynjolfsson, E., & Hitt, L.M. (2003). *Computing productivity: Firm-level evidence* (MIT Sloan Working Paper 4210-01, eBusiness@MIT Working Paper 139). Cambridge, MA: MIT Sloan School of Management. Retrieved December 5, 2007, from http://ebusiness.mit.edu/erik/cp.pdf

Bucci, G., Campanai, M., & Cignoni, G. (2001). Rapid assessment to solicit process improvement in small and medium-sized organisations. *Software Quality Professional, 4*(1), 33-41.

Bucci, G., Campanai, M., & Gignoni, G.A. (2000). *Rapid assessment to solicit process improvement in SMEs.* In Annals from EuroSPI 2000: European Software Process

Improvement. Retrieved December 12, 2007, from http://www.iscn.at/select-newspaper/assessments/italy.html

Bueno, C. (2000). QS9000: Calidad en la diversidad. *Revista Mexicana de Sociología, 62*(3), 29-49.

Burnstein, I. (2003). *Practical software testing: A process-oriented approach.* New York: Springer.

Burr, V. (2003). *Social Constructionism.* London: Routledge.

Bush, M. (1995). *The capability maturity model: Guidelines for improving the software process* (SEI Series in Software Engineering). Carnegie Mellon University, Software Engineering Institute. Addison-Wesley.

Byrnes, P., & Phillips, M. (1996). *Software capability evaluation* (Version 3.0: Method description (SCE V3.0), CMU/SEI-96-TR-002). USA: Carnegie Mellon University, Software Engineering Institute. Retrieved December 12, 2007, from http://www.sei.cmu.edu/pub/documents/96.reports/pdf/tr002.96.pdf

Calvo-Manzano, J. A., Cuevas, G., San Feliu, T., De Amescua, A., & Pérez, M. (2002, November). Experiences in the application of software process improvement in SMES. Software Quality Journal, 10(3), 261-273.

Calvo-Manzano, J.A., et al. (2002). *Experiences in the application of software process improvement in SMES. Software Quality Journal, 10,* 261-273.

Carmel, E., & Bird, B.J. (1997). Small is beautiful: A study of packaged software development teams. *Journal of High Technology Management Research, 8*(1), 129-148.

Carrillo, J., & Lara, A. (2005). Mexican maquiladoras: New capabilities of coordination and the emergence of new generation of companies. *Innovation: Management, Policy & Practice, 7*(2/3), 256-273.

Cater-Steel, A. P., Toleman, M. A., & Rout, T. (2006). Process improvement for small firms: An evaluation of the RAPID assessment-based method. *Information and Software Technology, 48*(5), 323-334.

Cattaneo, E., Fuggetta, A., & Lavazza, L. (1995). *An experience in process assessment.* In *Proceedings of ICSE'95* (pp. 115-121). IEEE Computer Society Press.

Cellule Interfacultaire de Technology Assessment CITA. (1997). *Utilisation des Systèmes d'Information Inter-Organisationnels [SIO] par les PME Belges* (SIO Research Report). Cita-Computer Sciences Department, University of Namur.

Chrissis, M.B., Konrad, M., & Shrum, S. (2003). *CMMI guidelines for process integration and product improvement.* Addison-Wesley.

Chrissis, M.B., Konrad, M., & Shrum, S. (2006). *CMMI: Guidelines for process integration and product improvement.* Addison-Wesley.

Ciamberlani, L., & Steimberg, L. (1999). *Comunicación para la transparencia.* Granica Ed.

Cignoni, G.A. (1999). Rapid software process assessment to promote innovation in SME's. In *Proceedings of Euromicro 99*, Italy.

Clarke, T., & Clegg, S.R. (1998). *Changing paradigms. The transformation of management knowledge for the 21st century.* London: Harper and Collins Business.

Clegg, S. R., & Ross-Smith, A. (2003). Revising the boundaries: Management education and learning in a postpositivist world. *Academy of Management Learning & Education, 2*, 85-98.

Clegg, S.R., & Hardy, C. (1996). Organizations, organization and organizing. In S. Clegg, C. Hardy, & W. Nord (Eds.), *Handbook of organization studies* (pp. 1-28). Thousand Oaks, CA: Sage.

CMMI Product Team (2001a). *Capability Maturity Model Integration (CMMI)* (Version V1.1 CMMI for systems engineering and software engineering (CMMI-SE/SW, V1.1): Continuous representation CMU/SEI-2002-TR-001). USA: Carnegie Mellon University, Software Engineering Institute. Retrieved December 12, 2007, from http://www.sei.cmu.edu/cmmi/models/v1.1se-sw-cont.doc

CMMI Product Team. (2001). *Appraisal requirements for CMMI* (Version 1.1 (ARC, V1.1), CMU/SEI-2001-TR-034). USA: Carnegie Mellon University, Software Engineering Institute. Retrieved December 12, 2007, from http://www.sei.cmu.edu/pub/documents/01.reports/pdf/01tr034.pdf

CMMI Product Team. (2006). *CMMI for development* (version 1.2, CMMI-DEV v1.2, SEI Tech. Rep. No. 06.tr.008). Pittsburgh: Software Engineering Institute, Carnegie Mellon University.

CMMI. (2002). CMMI for systems engineering and software engineering (CMMI-SE/SW, V1.1): Continuous representation (CMU/SEI-2002-TR-001). Software Engineering Institute.

Coallier, F. (2003). *International standardization in software and systems engineering. Crosstalk, Journal of Defense Software Engineering*, 18-22.

Cockburn, A. (2005). *Crystal clear: A human powered methodology for small teams.* Pearson Education Inc.

Cohen, L. (1995). *Quality function deployment: How to make QFD work for you.* USA: Addison-Wesley.

Cohn, M. (2004). *User stories applied for agile software development.* Addison-Wesley.

Coleman, K., Larsen, P., Shaw, M., & Zelkowitz, M. (2005, November). Software process improvement in small organizations: A case study. IEEE Software, pp. 68-75.

Competisoft. (2006). Retrieved December 17, 2007, from http://alarcos.inf-cr.uclm.es/competisoft/

Concklin, P., & Begeman, M. (1988). gIBIS: A hypertext tool for exploratory policy discussion. *Transactions of Office Information Systems, 6*(4), 303-331.

Conradi, R., & Fuggetta, A. (2002, July/August). Improving software process improvement. *IEEE Software, 19*(4), 92-99.

Corredor IIMI. (2006). *Evaluación de MoProSoft como alternativa metodológica de organización de empresas de desarrollo y mantenimiento de software.* Tesis de Pregrado, Escuela de Ingeniería de Sistemas-Universidad de Los Andes, Mérida, Venezuela.

Cragg, P. B. (2002). Benchmarking information technology practices in small firms. *European Journal of Information Systems, 11*(4), 267-282.

Curtis, B., Kellner, M.I., & Over, J. (1992). Process modeling. *Communications of the ACM, 35*(9), 75-90.

Cusumano, M.A., & Selby, R.W. (1997). How Microsoft builds software . *Communications of ACM, 40*(6), 53-61.

Czarniawska, B. (2003). Forbidden knowledge: Organization theory in times of transition. *Management Learning, 33*, 353-365.

Daft, R. L. (1998). *Essentials of organization theory and design.* Cincinnati, OH: South-Western College Publishing.

Daskalantonakis, M. (1994, July). Achieving higher SEI levels. *IEEE Software,* pp. 17-24.

Davenport, T., & Prusak, L. (1998). *Working knowledge: How organizations manage what they know.* Boston: Harvard Business School Press.

Demirörs, E., et al. (1998). Process improvement towards ISO 9001 certification in small software organizations. In *Proceedings of ICSE'98* (pp. 435-438). IEEE CS Press.

Denning, P.J. (1998). Computer science and software engineering: Filing for divorce? *Communications of the ACM, 41*(8), 128.

DiMaggio, P.J., & Powell, W.W. (1983). The iron cage revisited: Institutional isomorphism and collective rationality in organizational fields. *American Sociological Review, 48*(2), 147-160.

Dingsøyr, T. (2003). *Knowledge management in medium-sized software consulting company: An Investigation of intranet-based knowledge management tools for knowledge cartography and knowledge repositories for learning software organizations.* Norwegian University of Science and Technology.

Dingsøyr, T., & Conradi, R. (2002). A survey of case studies of the use of knowledge management in software engineering. *International Journal of Software Engineering and Knowledge Engineering, 12*(4), 391-414.

Dingsøyr, T., & Røyrvik, E. (2003). An empirical study of an informal knowledge repository in a medium-sized software consulting company. In *Proceedings of the International Conference on Software Engineering.* IEEE.

Drucker, P. (1993). *Post-capitalist society.* Oxford, MA: Butterworth Heinemann.

Dunaway, D.K., & Masters, S. (2001). *CMM-based appraisal for Internal process improvement* (CBA IPI, Version 1.2: Method description CMU/SEI-2001-TR033). USA: Carnegie Mellon University, Software Engineering Institute. Retrieved December 12, 2007, from http://www.sei.cmu.edu/pub/documents/01.reports/pdf/01tr033.pdf

Dybå, T. (2000). Improvisation in small software organizations. *Software, 17*(5), 82-87.

Dybå, T. (2001). *Enabling software process improvement: An investigation of the importance of organizational issues* (NTNU 2001:101, IDI Report 7/01). Unpublished doctoral dissertation, Norwegian University of Science and Technology, Trondheim, Norway. Retrieved December 5, 2007, from http://www.idi.ntnu.no/grupper/su/publ/phd/dybaa-dring-thesis-2001.pdf

Dybå, T. (2002). Enabling software process improvement: An investigation of the importance of organizational issues. *Empirical Software Engineering, 7*(4), 387-390.

Dybå, T. (2003). Factors of software process improvement success in small and large organizations: An empirical study in the Scandinavian context. *ACM SIGSOFT Software Engineering Notes, 28*(5), 148-157.

Dybå, T. (2005). An empirical investigation of the key factors for success in software process improvement. *IEEE Transactions on Software Engineering, 31*(5), 410-424.

Dybå, T., Kitchenham, B.A., & Jorgensen, M. (2005). Evidence-based software engineering for practitioners. *Software, 22*(1), 58-65.

El Emam, K., & Briand, L. (1997). *Costs and benefits of software process improvement.* (International Software Engineering Network tech. rep. no. ISERN-97-12).

Electronic Industries Alliance. (1998). *Systems engineering capability model appraisal method EIA/IS-731.2*. Electronic Industries Alliance, Engineering Department.

Enriquez, E. (1992). *L'Organisation en analyse*. Paris: Presses Universitaires de France.

Ensmenger, N.L. (2001a). *From "black art" to industrial discipline: The software crisis and the management of programmers*. Unpublished doctoral dissertation, University of Pennsylvania.

Ensmenger, N.L. (2001b). The "question of professionalism" in the computing fields. *IEEE Annals of the History of Computing, 23*(4), 56-74.

Ensmenger, N.L. (2003). Letting the "computer boys" take over: Technology and the politics of organizational transformation. *International Review of Social History, 48*(Supplement), 153-180.

Ensmenger, N.L., & Aspray, W. (2000). Software as labour process. In U. Hashagen, R. Keil-Slawik, & A.L. Norberg (Eds.), *Proceedings of the International Conference on History of Computing: Software Issues* (pp. 139-165). New York: Springer-Verlag.

e-Quallity. (2006). *Prueba de Software: una Definición*. Retrieved December 12, 2007, from

ESSI. (1994, February). *IBERIA, LAE, SPIE: Software process improvement and experimentation* (ESSI Project No. 10344).

European Commission. (2005). *The new SME definition. User guide and model declaration*. Europe: Enterprise and Industry Publications.

Farbey, B., Targett, D., & Land, F. (1994). Matching an IT project with an appropriate method of evaluation: A research note on "Evaluating investments in IT." *Journal of Information Technology, 9*, 239-343.

Fayad, M. E., Laitinen, M., & Ward, R. P. (2000). Software engineering in the small. *Communications of the ACM, 43*(3), 115-118.

Fayad, M., & Laitinen, M. (1997). Process assessment considered wasteful. *Communications of the ACM, 40*(11), 125-128.

Fenton, N., Pfleeger, S. L., & Glass, R. L. (1994). Science and substance: A challenge to software engineers. *IEEE Software, 11*(4), 86-95.

Fischer, G., Lindstaedt, S., Ostwald, J., Scneider, K., & Smith, J. (1996). Informing system design through organizational learning. In *Proceedings of the International Conference on Learning Sciences* (pp. 52-59).

Fortuna, R.M. (1988, June). Beyond quality: Taking SPC upstream. *Quality Progress, 21*(6), 23-28.

Fundação para o Prêmio Nacional da Qualidade. (2002). *Critérios de Excelência—O estado da arte da gestão para a excelência do desempenho e aumento da competitividade*. Brazil: FPNQ (National Foundation for Quality Award). Retrieved December 12, 2007, from http://www.fpnq.org.br

Fundação para o Prêmio Nacional da Qualidade. (2002). *Instruções para Candidatura - Prêmio Nacional da Qualidade—2003*. Brazil: FPNQ (National Foundation for Quality Award). Retrieved December 12, 2007, from http://www.fpnq.org.br

Gabbar, H.A. (Ed.). (2006). *Modern formal methods and applications*. Berlin-Heilderberg: Springer-Verlag.

Galin, D. (2004). *Software quality assurance, from theory to implementation* (1st ed.). Pearson, Addison-Wesley.

Garcia, S. (2005). *Thoughts on applying CMMI in small settings*. Presentation to Montréal SPIN.

Garcia, S., Graettinger, C., & Kost, K. (2005). *Introduction*. Paper presented at the First International Research Workshop for Process Improvement in Small Settings, Pittsburgh, Pennsylvania.

Garcia, S., Graettinger, C., & Kost, K. (2006). *Proceedings of the 1st International Research Workshop for Process Improvement in Small Settings, 2005* (Special report CMU/SEI-2006-SR-001), Pittsburgh, Software

Engineering Institute. Retrieved December 14, 2007, from http://www.sei.cmu.edu/pub/documents/06.reports/pdf/06sr001.pdf

Garshol, L.M. (2006). *BNF and EBNF: What are they and how do they work?* Retrieved December 12, 2007, from http://www.garshol.priv.no/download/text/bnf.html#id1.1

Garvin, D. (1993, July-August). Building a learning organization. *Harvard Business Review*, pp. 78-91.

Gergen, K.J. (1996). *Realidades y relaciones. Aproximaciones a la construcción social.* Barcelona: Paidos.

Getchell, Hargrave, Haynes, Lubrecht, Kazmi, Oikawa, Paschino, Robin, Short. (2002, June). MSF Process Model v. 3.1. Retrieved December 17, 2007, from http://www.microsoft.com/msf

Ghoshal, S. (2005). Bad management theories are destroying good management practices. *Academy of Management Learning & Education, 4*, 75-91.

Gibson, D. L., Goldenson, D. R. & Kost, K. (2006) *Performance Results of CMMI-Based Process Improvement.* CMU SEI

Gill, J., & Johnson, P. (1997). *Research methods for managers* (2nd ed.). London: Paul Chapman Publishing.

Glass, R.L. (2006). The Standish report: Does it really describe a software crisis? *Communications of the ACM, 49*(8), 15-16.

Goffman, E. (1993). *La presentación de la persona en la vida cotidiana.* Buenos Aires: Amorrortu.

Gosling, J., & Mintzberg, H. (2004, Summer). The education of practicing managers. *MIT Sloan Management Review*, pp. 19-22.

Greenfield, J., & Short, K. (2003). Software factories: Assembling applications with patterns, models, frameworks and tools. In R. Crocker & G.L. Steele (Eds.), *Companion of the 18th Annual ACM SIGPLAN Conference on Object-Oriented Programming, Systems, Languages, and Applications* (pp. 16-27). Anaheim, CA: ACM Press.

Gresse von Wangenheim, C. (2002). *Planning and executing GQM based software measurement* (Tech. Rep. No. LQPS001.01E). Sao Jose, Brazil: UNIVALI.

Gresse von Wangenheim, C., Anacleto, A., & Salviano, C.F. (2006, January/February). Helping small companies assess software processes. *IEEE Software, 23*(1), 91-98.

Gresse von Wangenheim, C., Hoisl, B., & Wüst, J. (1995). *A process model for GQM based measurement* (Tech. Rep. No. STTI-95-04-E). Software Technology Transfer Initiative, University of Kaiserslautern, Germany.

Gresse von Wangenheim, C., Punter, T., & Anacleto, A. (2003). Software measurement for small and medium enterprises: A Brazilian-German view on extending the GQM method. Retrieved December 12, 2007, from http://www.sj.univali.br/prof/Christiane%20Gresse%20Von%20Wangenheim/papers/ease2003.pdf

Gresse von Wangenheim, C., Weber, S., Hauck, J.C.R., & Trentin, G. (2006). Experiences on establishing software processes in small companies. *Information and Software Technology, 48*, 890-900.

Griss, M.L., & Wendtzel, K.D. (1994). Hybrid domain-specific kits for a flexible software factory. In H. Berghel, T. Hlengl, & J. Urban (Ed.), *Proceedings of the 1994 ACM Symposium on Applied Computing 1994* (pp. 47-52). Phoenix: ACM Press.

Grover, V., & Teng, J. T. C. (1992). An examination of DBMS adoption and success in American organisations. *Information and Management, 23*, 239-248.

Grunbacher, P. (1997, September 1-4). *A software assessment process for small software enterprises.* Paper presented at the EUROMICRO 97 New Frontiers of Information Technology, Proceedings of the 23rd EUROMICRO Conference, Budapest, Hungary.

Hackman, J.R., & Wageman, R. (1995). Total quality management: Empirical, conceptual, and practical issues. *Administrative Science Quarterly, 40*(2), 309-342.

Haigh, T. (2001). The chromium-plated tabulator: Institutionalizing an electronic revolution, 1954–1958. *IEEE Annals of the History of Computing, 23*(4), 75-104.

Hamel, G., & Prahalad, C.K. (2005). Strategic intent. *Harvard Business Review, 83*, 148-161.

Hansen, J.E., & Thomsen, C. (2004). *Enterprise development with visual studio: NET, UML, and MSF.* New York: Apress.

Hansen, M., Nohrian, N., & Tierney, T. (1999). What's your strategy for managing knowledge? *Harvard Business Review.*

Hauser, J.R., & Clausing, D. (1988, May-June). The house of quality. *Harvard Business Review*, 63-73.

Haynes, Robin, Paschino, Short, Kazmi, Oikawa, Getchell, Hargrave, Lubrecht, Huber, Vukcevic, Leocadio, Rocha, Santello, Schimpl. (2002, June). MSF Team Model v. 3.1. Retrieved December 17, 2007, from http://www.microsoft.com/msf

Heckman, S.J. (1983). Weber's ideal type: A contemporary reassessment. *Polity, 16*(1), 119-137.

Helfat, C. E., & Raubitschek, R. S. (2000). Product sequencing: Coevolution of knowledge, capabilities and products. *Strategic Management Journal, 21*, 961-979.

Henninger, S. (2001). Turning development standards into repositories of experiences. *Software Process Improvement and Practice, 3*(6), 141-155.

Henninger, S. (2003). Tool support for experience-based methodologies. In *Proceedings of the 4th International Workshop on Advances in Learning Software Organizations* (LNCS 2640, pp. 44-59). Springer-Verlag.

Herrera, E.M., & Trejo Ramirez, R.A. (2003). A methodology for self-diagnosis for software quality assurance in small and medium-sized industries in Latin America. *The Electronic Journal on Information Systems in Developing Countries, 15*(4), 1-13.

Hibberd, F.J. (2005). *Unfolding Social Constructionism*, New York: Springer.

Highsmith, J. (2004). *Agile project management: Creating innovative products.* Addison-Wesley.

Hodgson, D.E. (2004). Project work: The legacy of bureaucratic control in the post-bureaucratic organization. *Organization, 11*(1), 81-100.

Holz, H. (2003). *Process-based knowledge management support for software engineering.* Doctoral Dissertation, University of Kaiserslautern, Germany.

Horvat, R. V., Rozman, I., & Györkös, J. (2000, March). Managing the complexity of SPI in small companies. Software Process: Improvement and Practice, 5(1), 45-54.

http://www.e-quallity.net/def.php

Hualde, A. (2003). ¿Existe un modelo maquilador?: Reflexiones sobre la experiencia mexicana y centroamericana. *Nueva Sociedad, 186*. Retrieved December 5, 2007, from http://www.iztapalapa.uam.mx/amet/debate/modelomaquilador.html

Hualde, A. (2004, August). *Proximity and transborder networks in the US Mexican border: The making of a software cluster.* Paper presented at the *4th Congress on Proximity Economics: Proximity*. Marseille: Université de la Méditerranée, Groupe de Recherche Dynamiques de proximité. Retrieved December 5, 2007, from http://139.124.177.94/proxim/viewabstract.php?id=82

Hughes, B., & Cotterell, M. (2002). *Software project management.* Berkshire, UK: McGraw-Hill.

Humphrey, W.S. (1989). *Managing the software process.* USA: Addison-Wesley Publishing Company.

Hurtado, J., Pino, F., & Vidal, J. (2006). *Software process improvement integral model: Agile SPI* (Tech. Rep. No. SIMEP-SW-O&A-RT-6-V1.0). Popayán, Colombia, Universidad del Cauca-Colciencias. ()

Hurtado, J., Pino, F., & Vidal, J. (2006). Software process improvement integral model: Agile SPI (Tech. Rep. No. SIMEP-SW-O&A-RT-6-V1.0). Popayán, Colombia, Universidad del Cauca-Colciencias.

Iberle, K. (2002). But will it work for me? In *Proceedings of the Pacific Northwest Software Quality Conference*, Portland, WA.

IEEE Computer Society. (2004). *Guide to the software engineering body of knowledge (SWEBOK)*. Los Alamitos, CA.

Ilavarasan, P.V., & Sharma, A.K. (2003). Is software work routinized? Some empirical observations from Indian software industry. *The Journal of Systems and Software, 66*(1), 1-6.

Institute of Electrical and Electronic Engineers. (1990). *IEEE Std 610.12-1990. IEEE Standard glossary of software engineering terminology*. Los Alamitos, CA.

Iria, J., Ciravegna, F., Cimiano, P., Lavelli, A., Motta, E., Gilardoni, L., & Mönch, E. (2004). Integrating information extraction, ontology learning and semantic browsing into organizational knowledge processes. In *Proceedings of the EKAW Workshop on the Application of Language and Semantic Technologies to Support Knowledge Management Processes, at the 14th International Conference on Knowledge Engineering and Knowledge Management.*

ISO 9001. (2000). *Sistemas de gestión de la calidad: Requisitos.*

ISO. (2000). *ISO 9000:2000 quality management systems: Requirements.*

ISO. (2003). *ISO 10006:2003 quality management systems: Guidelines for quality management in projects.*

ISO/IEC 12207. (1995). *Information technology: Software life cycle processes*. Geneva, Switzerland: International Organization for Standardization/International Electrotechnical Commission.

ISO/IEC 15288. (2002). *Systems engineering: Systems life cycle process*. Geneva, Switzerland: International Organization for Standardization/International Electrotechnical Commission.

ISO/IEC 15504. (2003-2005). *Information technology: Process assessment* (Part 1-5). Geneva, Switzerland: International Organization for Standardization/International Electrotechnical Commission.

ISO/IEC 15504. (2004). *Information technology: Software process assessment standard.*

ISO/IEC 15504-2. (2003). *Information technology: Process assessment* (Part 2: Performing an assessment). Geneva, Switzerland: International Organization for Standardization/International Electrotechnical Commission.

ISO/IEC 17799. (2005). *Information technology: Security techniques* (Code of practice for information security management). Geneva, Switzerland: International Organization for Standardization/International Electrotechnical Commission.

ISO/IEC 9000-1. (2000). *Quality management and quality assurance standard.*

ISO/IEC 90003. (2004). *Software engineering: Guidelines for the application of ISO 9001:2000 to computer software*. Geneva, Switzerland: International Organization for Standardization/International Electrotechnical Commission.

ISO/IEC 9001. (2000). *Quality management systems: Requirements*. Geneva, Switzerland: International Organization for Standardization/International Electrotechnical Commission.

ISO/IEC JTC1/SC7 N3288. (2005, May). *New work item proposal: Software life cycles for very small enterprises*. Retrieved December 12, 2007, from http://www.jtc1-sc7.org/

ISO/IEC TR 10000-1. (1998). *Information technology: Framework and taxonomy of international standardized profiles* (Part 1: General principles and documentation framework, 4th ed.). Geneva, Switzerland: International Organization for Standardization/International Electrotechnical Commission.

ISO/IEC TR 15504-5. (1998). *Information technology: Software process assessment, Part 5: An assessment model and indicator guidance* (No. ISO/IEC TR 15504-5:1998(E)).

ISO/IEC. (2002). *ISO/IEC 12207:1995 information technology: Software life cycle processes* (Amd. 1).

ISO/IEC. (2003). *ISO/IEC 15504 software process assessment* (part 2).

ISO/IES 9126 (1991). *Information technology: Software product evaluation, quality characteristics and guidelines for their use.*

ISO_15504-2. (2004). *ISO/IEC 15504-2:2003/ Cor.1:2004(E). Information technology: Process assessment, Part 2: Performing an assessment.* Geneva: International Organization for Standardization.

ISO_15504-5. (2006). *ISO/IEC 15504-5:2006(E). Information technology: Process assessment, Part 5: An exemplar process assessment model.* Geneva: International Organization for Standardization.

ISO_9001. (2000). *ISO 9001:2000. Quality management systems: Requirements.* Geneva: International Organization for Standardization.

ISO9001 mapping to CMMI. http://www.sei.cmu.edu/ cmmi/adoption/iso-mapping.html

ISOTR19759-05. (2005). *Software engineering body of knowledge: Technical report ISO/IEC PRF TR 19759.* Geneva, Switzerland: International Organization for Standardization/International Electrotechnical Commission.

IThe International Organization for Standardization and the International Electrotechnical Commission (ISO/IEC) (2006). *ISO/IEC 15504-5:2006 Information technology—Process Assessment—Part 5: An exemplar Process Assessment Model.* Suisse, Geneve: ISO.

ITMark. (2006). Retrieved December 12, 2007, from http://www.esi.es/en/main/iitmark.html

ITS (Instituto de Tecnologia de Software). (2006a). *Institucional.* Retrieved December 12, 2007, from http://www.its.org.br/default.aspx?portalid=LJFKQN UL&navid=351

ITS (Instituto de Tecnologia de Software). (2006b). *TQI conquista CMMI nível 2.* Retrieved December 12, 2007, from http://www.its.org.br/default. aspx?pagid=EMMCUMUL

Jalote, P. (2002). *An integrated approach to software engineering* (2nd ed.). Narosa Publishing House.

Jalote, P. (2002). *Software project management in practice.* Addison-Wesley.

Johns, B. L., Dunlop, W. C., & Sheehan, W. J. (1989). *Small business in Australia: Problems and prospects* (3rd ed.). Sydney: Allen and Unwin.

Johnson, D. L., & Brodman, J. G. (1992). Software process rigors yield stress, efficiency. *Signal,* pp. 55-57.

Johnson, D.L., & Brodman, J.G. (1998). Applying the CMM to small organizations and small projects. In *Proceedings of the 1998 Software Engineering Process Group Conference,* Chicago, IL.

Johnson, G., Scholes, K., & Sexty R.W. (1989). *Exploring strategic management.* Englewood Cliffs, NJ: Prentice Hall.

Jones, C. (2000). *Software assessments, benchmarks, and best practices.* USA: Addison-Wesley.

Jorgensen, P. (2002). *Software testing: A craftman's approach.* CRC Press.

Juran, J.M. (1992). *A Qualidade desde o Projeto—Novos Passos para o Planejamento da Qualidade em Produtos e Serviços* (N. Montigelli Jr., Trans.). Brazil: Pioneira Thomson Learning.

Kaplan, R., & Norton, D. (Eds.). (1996). *The balanced scorecard: Translating strategy into action.* Barcelona: Gestión 2000.

Karner, G. (1993). *Resource estimation for objectory projects.* Retrieved December 17, 2007, from http://www. bfpug.com.br/

Kasunic, M. (2005). *Designing an effective survey* (Handbook CMU/SEI-2005-HB-004). Software Engineering Institute.

Kautz, K. (1998). Software process improvement in very small enterprises: Does it pay off? *Software Process: Improvement and Practice, 4,* 209-226.

Keating, E. K., Oliva, R., Repenning, N. P., Rockart, S., & Sterman, J. D. (1999). Overcoming the improvement paradox. *European Management Journal, 17*(2), 120-134.

Keir, M. (1918). Scientific management simplified. *Scientific Monthly, 7*(6), 525-529.

Kellner, M.I., Becker-Kornstaedt, U., Riddle, W.E., Tomal, J., & Verlage, M. (1998). Process guides: Effective guidance for process participants. In *Proceedings of the 5th International Conference on the Software Process* (pp. 11-28).

King, W.R. (1996). Achieving global strategic advantage. *Information Systems Management, 13*(4), 57-60.

Ko, R., & O, J. (2002). *HKSQS model: An implementation tool for CMM.* Paper presented at the SEPG Conference on Tour.

Kohan, S. (2003). **QuickLocus**: *Proposta de um método de avaliação de processo de desenvolvimento de software para pequenas organizações.* Master's dissertation, Instituto de Pesquisas Tecnológicas, São Paulo, Brazil.

Konrad, M., Chrissis, M.B., Curtis, B., & Paulk, M. (2002). *A report on the May 2002 CMMI Workshop: Adoption Barriers and Benefits for Commercial Software and Information Systems Organization* (Special rep. no. CMU/SEI-2002-SR-005).

Kruchten, P. (2000). *The rational unified process: An introduction* (2nd ed.). Addison-Wesley.

Kruchten, P. (2003). *Introdução ao RUP.* Rio de Janeiro: Ciência Moderna.

Kuhn, T.S. (1971). La estructura de las revoluciones científicas. Argentina: Fondo de Cultura Económica.

Kurniawati, F., & Jeffery, R. (2006). The use and effects of an electronic process guide and experience repository: A longitudinal study. Information and Software Technology, 48(7), 566-577.

Laitinen, M., Fayad, M., & Ward, R. (2000, September/October). Software engineering in the small [Special issue]. *IEEE Software.*

Land, S.K. (1997, June 1-6). Results of the IEEE survey of software engineering standards users. In *Proceedings of the Software Engineering Standards Symposium and Forum: Emerging International Standards (ISESS 97),* Walnut Creek, CA (pp. 242-270).

Landes, D., Schneider, K., & Houdek, F. (1999). Organizational learning and experience documentation in industrial software projects. *International Journal of Human-Computer Studies, 51,* 643-661.

Laporte, C. Y., April, A., & Renault, A. (2006). *Applying ISO/IEC software engineering standards in small settings: Historical perspectives and initial achievements.* Paper presented at the SPICE 2006 Conference, Luxembourg.

Laporte, C. Y., Renault, A., Alexandre, S., & Uthayanaka, T. (2006). Applying software engineering standards in very small enterprises. *ISO Focus, International Organisation for Standardisation,* pp. 36-38.

Laporte, C.Y., & April, A. (2006a, January). Applying software engineering standards in small settings: Recent historical perspectives and initial achievements (CMU/SEI-2006-Special Report-001). In *Proceedings of the 1st International Research Workshop for Process Improvement in Small Settings* (pp. 39-51). Software Engineering Institute, Carnegie Mellon University.

Laporte, C.Y., April, A., & Renault, A. (2006, May 4-5). Applying ISO/IEC software engineering standards in small settings: Historical perspectives and initial achievements. In *Proceedings of the SPICE Conference,* Luxembourg (pp. 57-62).

Laporte, C.Y., Papiccio, N.R., & Trudel, S. (1998). *A software factory for the Canadian government Year 2000 Conversion Program.* Paper presented at Software Process Improvement 98, Monte Carlo. Retrieved December 5, 2007, from http://www.lrgl.uqam.ca/publications/pdf/701.pdf

Laporte, C.Y., Renault, A., Desharnais, J.M., Habra, N., Abou El Fattah, M., & Bamba, J.C. (2005, May 27-June 1). Initiating software process improvement in small enterprises: Experiment with micro-evaluation framework (SWDC-REK). In *Proceedings of the International Conference on Software Development,* University of Iceland, Reykjavik, Iceland (pp. 153-163).

Larman, C. (2004). *Agile and iterative development: A manager's guide.* Addison-Wesley.

Larsen, E. A., & Kautz, K. (1997). Quality assurance and software process improvement in Norway. *Software Process: Improvement and Practice, 3*(2), 71-86.

Laurindo, F.J.B., & Moraes, R.O. (2006). IT projects portfolio management: A Brazilian case study. *International Journal Management and Decision Making, 7*(6), 586-603.

León-Carrillo, L.V. (2005). Caracterización de la Prueba de Software. *Software Gurú, 1*(5), 49.

León-Carrillo, L.V. (2005). *La Especificación de un "Process Definition Language"* (Reporte interno). Guadalajara, Mexico: e-Quallity.

León-Carrillo, L.V., Ruelas-Minor, E., & Castillo-Hernández, A. (2004). *Métricas de Proyecto y de Proceso* (Internal Report). Guadalajara, Mexico: e-Quallity.

Lethbridge, T.C., Sim, S.E., & Singer, J. (2005). Studying software engineers: Data collection techniques for software field studies. *Empirical Software Engineering, 10*(3), 311-341.

Leung, H. (1999). Slow change of information system development practice. *Software Quality Journal, 8*(3), 197-210.

Leung, H., Goh, J., & Lui, Y. (2005, October 19-20). *CMM Fast Track (CMMFT) Programme for Hong Kong SME software companies.* Paper presented at the International Research Workshop for Process Improvement in Small Settings, Pittsburgh, Pennsylvania, USA.

Lewerentz, C., & Rust, H. (2000). Are software engineers true engineers? *Annals of Software Engineering, 10*(1-4), 311-328.

Liao, L., Qu, Y., & Leung, H. (2005). A software process ontology and its application. In *Proceedings of the Workshop on Semantic Web Enabled Software Engineering (SWESE), at the 4th International Semantic Web Conference.* Retrieved December 17, 2007, from http://www.mel.nist.gov/msid/conferences/SWESE/accepted_papers.html

Ludewig, J. (1996). Software engineering: Why it did not work. In A. Brennecke & R. Keil-Slawik (Eds.), *History of software engineering* (pp. 25-27). Dagstuhl Seminar, Paderborn University. Retrieved December 5, 2007, from http://citeseer.ist.psu.edu/rd/0%2C229833%2C1%2C0.25%2CDownload/http://coblitz.codeen.org:3125/citeseer.ist.psu.edu/cache/papers/cs/2159/ftp:zSzzSzftp.dagstuhl.dezSzpubzSzReportszSz96zSz9635.pdf/history-of-software-engineering.pdf

Luzuriaga, J., Martínez, R., & Cechich, A. (2006). Mejora en la Gestión de Recursos: Experiencias hacia la Aplicación de un Estándar IberoAmericano. In *Proceedings of the 7th Argentine Symposium on Software Engineering (ASSE)*, 35 JAIIO, Mendoza, Argentina.

Madhavji, N.H, Holtje, D., Hong, W., & Bruckhaus, T. (1994). Elicit: A method for eliciting process models. In *Proceedings of the 3rd International Conference on the Software Process* (pp. 111-112).

Mahoney, M.S. (1990). The roots of software engineering. *CWI Quarterly, 3*(4), 325-334. Retrieved December 5, 2007, from http://www.princeton.edu/%7Emike/articles/sweroots/sweroots.pdf

Mahoney, M.S. (2004). Finding a history for software engineering. *Annals of the History of Computing, 26*(1), 8-19.

Maia, J.A. (2005). *Construindo softwares com qualidade e rapidez usando ICONIX.* Retrieved December 12, 2007, from http://www.jugmanaus.com

Mäkinen, T,, Varkoi, T., & Lepasaar, M. (2000). *A detailed process assessment method for software SMEs.* Annals from the EuroSPI 2000: European Software Process Improvement. Retrivied December 12, 2007, from http://www.iscn.at/select-newspaper/assessments/tampere.html

Mäkinen, T., Varkoi, T., & Lepasaar, M. (2000). A detailed process assessment method for software SMEs. In Proceedings of the 7th European Software Process Improvement Conference (EuroSPI 2000)(pp. 1.14-1.26). Copenhagen, Denmark.

Marques, C., & Sousa, P. (2004). A method to define an enterprise architecture using the Zachman framework.

In *Proceedings of the 2004 ACM Symposium on Applied Computing* (pp. 1366-1371).

Martin, S. (2002). *Business process improvement.* McGraw-Hill.

Martins, A.F., & Von Wangenheim, C.G. (2002). *Caracterização da gestão de conhecimento em micro e pequenas empresas de software.* LQPS - UNIVALI - CES VII, São José, SC, Brasil.

Mauss, M. (1970). *The Gift: Forms and Functions of exchange in Archaic Societies,* London: Routledge.

Mauss, M. (2002[1924]) *Essai sur le don,* Retrieved May12, 2006, from http://socioeconomie.free.fr/MAUSS/essai_sur_le_don.pdf

Mayer&Bunge. (2004). *Panorama de la Industria del Software en Latinoamérica.* Brasil: Mayer&Bunge Informática LTDA. Retrieved December 14, 2007, http://www.mbi.com.br/200409_panorama_industria_software_america_latina.pdf

Mazur, G. (1994, November). QFD for small business: A shortcut through the "maze of matrices." *Transactions from the 6th Symposium on Quality Function Deployment,* Michigan (pp. 375-386).

McFall, D., Wilkie, F.G., McCaffery, F., Lester, N.G., & Sterritt, R. (2003, December 1-10). Software processes and process improvement in Northern Ireland. In *Proceedings of the 16th International Conference on Software & Systems Engineering and their Applications,* Paris, France. ISSN: 1637-5033.

McFarlan, W.E. (1984). Information technology changes the way you compete. *Harvard Business Review, 62*(3), 98-103.

McFeeley, B. (1996, February). *IDEALSM: A user's guide for software process improvement* (Handbook CMU/SEI-96-HB-001). Software Engineering Institute, Carnegie Mellon University.

McFeeley, R. (1996). IDEAL: A users guide for software process improvement (Handbook CMU/SEI-96-HB-001). Pittsburgh: Software Engineering Institute, Carnegie Mellon University. Retrieved January 1, 2008, from http://www.sei.cmu.edu/publications/documents/96.reports/96.hb.001.html

McGarry, F., et.al. (1994). *Software process improvement in the NASA Software Engineering Laboratory* (Tech. Rep. No. CMU/SEI-95-TR-22). Department of Computer Science, University of Maryland, College Park, MD 20742.

McIlroy, M.D. (1969). Mass produced software components (and discussion panel). In. P. Naur & B. Randell (Eds.), *Software engineering: A conference sponsored by the NATO Science Committee.* Garmisch, Germany: NATO Scientific Affairs Division. Retrieved August 15, 2006, from http://homepages.cs.ncl.ac.uk/brian.randell/NATO/nato1968.PDF

Meijaard, J., Brand, M.J., & Mosselman, M. (2005). Organizational structure and performance in Dutch small firms (SCALES-paper N200420). Netherlands: EIM Business and Policy Research: Scientific Analysis of Entrepreneurship and SME. Retrieved December 5, 2007, from http://www.eim.net/pdf-ez/N200420.pdf

Members of the Assessment Method Integrated Team. (2001). *Standard CMMI appraisal method for process improvement* (SCAMPI, Version 1.1: Method definition document CMU/SEI-2001-HB-001). USA: Carnegie Mellon University, Software Engineering Institute. Retrieved December 12, 2007, from http://www.sei.cmu.edu/pub/documents/01.reports/pdf/01hb001.pdf

Mentzas, G., Apostolou, D., Abecker, A., & Young, R. (2003). *Knowledge asset management: Beyond the process-centred and product-centred approaches.* Springer. ISBN 1-85233-583-1.

Microsoft Corporation. (2003). *Microsoft solutions framework version 3.0 overview.* Retrieved December 12, 2007, from http://download.microsoft.com/download/2/3/f/23f13f70-8e46-4f44-97f6-7dfb45010859/MSF_v3_Overview Whitepaper.pdf

Miller, D., & Hartwick, J. (2002). Spotting management fads. *Harvard Business Review, 80*(10), 26-27.

Miller, J.P. (1970). Social-psychological implications of Weber's model of bureaucracy: Relations among expertise, control, authority, and legitimacy. *Social Forces, 49*(1), 91-102.

Ministerio da Ciencia e Tecnologia. (2001). *Quality and productivity of the Brasilian software sector* (in Portuguese). Brazil: Ministerio da Ciencia e Tecnologia.

Ministry of the Economy. (2005). *NMX-059-NYCE-2005 information technology: Software models of processes and assessment for software development and maintenance* (Parts 1-4). Mexico: Ministry of the Economy.

Mintzberg, H. (1975). The manager's job: Folklore and fact. *Harvard Business Review, 53*(4), 49-61.

Mintzberg, H. (1979). *The structure of organizations.* Englewood Cliffs, NJ: Prentice Hall.

Mintzberg, H. (1983). *Structure in fives: Designing effective organizations.* Englewood Cliffs: Prentice Hall.

Mintzberg, H. (2004). *Managers not MBAs: A hard look at the soft practice of management and management development.* London: FT Prentice Hall.

Mintzberg, H., & Westley, F. (2001). Decision making: It's not what you think. *MIT Sloan Management Review, 42*(3), 89-93.

Moe, N.B., Dingsoyr, T., & Johansen, T. (2002). Process guides as software process improvement in a small company. In *Proceedings of the EuroSPI Conference* (pp. 177-188). Germany.

Mondragon, O.A. (2006). Addressing infrastructure issues in very small setting. In *Proceedings of the 1st International Research Workshop for Process Improvement in Small Setting* (pp. 5-11).

Montaño, L. (2005). ¿Qué son los estudios organizacionales?, conference presented at the *Coloquio Internacional: Los Estudios Organizacionales en México: Una Década de Investigación, formación y vinculación*, Universidad Autónoma Metropolitana – Iztapalapa, September 27th, 2005, Mexico City.

Montilva, J. (2004). Desarrollo de Aplicaciones Empresariales: El Método WATCH. Mérida, Venezuela: Jonás Montilva.

Montilva, J., Hamzan, K., & Ghatrawi, M. (2000, July). The watch model for developing business software in small and midsize organizatios. In *Proceedings of the IV World Multiconference on Systemics, Cybernetics and Informatics (SCI'2000)*, Orlando, FL.

MST (Ministry of Science and Technology). (2001). *Pesquisa nacional de qualidade e produtividade no setor de software brasileiro – Caracterização das organizações.* Retrieved December 12, 2007, from http://www.mct.gov.br/index.php/content/view/4913.html

Mugler, J. (2004). The configuration approach to the strategic management of small and medium-sized enterprises. In *Proceedings of the Budapest Tech Jubilee Conference.* Budapest: Budapest Tech. Retrieved December 5, 2007, from http://www.bmf.hu/conferences/jubilee/Mugler.pdf

Mustonen-Ollila, E., & Lyytinen, K. (2003). Why organisations adopt information system process innovations: A longitudinal study using diffusion of innovation theory. *Information Systems Journal, 13*, 275-297.

Mutafelija, B., & Stromberg, H. (2003). *ISO 9001:2000 – CMMI v1.1 Mappings.* Pittsburgh, PA: Carnegie Mellon University, Software Engineering Institute. Retrieved December 5, 2007, from http://www.sei.cmu.edu/cmmi/adoption/pdf/iso-mapping.pdf

Myers, G. (1979). *The art of software testing.* John Wiley & Sons.

Nakano, D.N., & Fleury, A.C.C. (1996). Métodos de Pesquisa na Engenharia de Produção (CD-ROM). In *XVI ENEGEP—Encontro Nacional de Engenharia de Produção, Annals.* Piracicaba: UNIMEP/ABEPRO.

Natwick, G., Draper, G., & Bearden, L. (1999, October). Software mini-assessments: process and practice. *Crosstalk: The Journal of Defense Software Engineering,* pp. 10-14.

Naur, P., & Randell, B. (Eds.). (1969). *Final report from software engineering: A conference sponsored by the NATO Science Committee.* Garmisch, Germany: NATO Scientific Affairs Division. Retrieved December 5, 2007, from http://homepages.cs.ncl.ac.uk/brian.randell/NATO/nato1968.PDF

Nguyen, M., & Conradi, R. (1994). Classification of meta-processes and their models. In *Proceedings of the 3rd International Conference on the Software Process* (pp. 167-175).

Nielsen, P.A., & Pries-Heje, J. (2002). A framework for selecting an assessment strategy (pp. 185-198). In L. Mathiassen, J. Pries-Heje, & O. Ngwenyama (Eds.), *Improving software organizations from principles to practice*. USA: Addison-Wesley.

NMX-059-NYCE. (2005). *Information technology-software-models of processes and assessment for software development and maintenance* (Part 1: Definition of concepts and products, Part 2: Process requirements (MoProSoft), Part 3: Guidelines for process implementation, Part 4: Guidelines for process assessment (EvalProSoft)). Mexico Ministry of Economy.

Nonaka, I., & Takeuchi, H. (1995). *The knowledge-creating company*. Oxford University Press.

NORMAPME. (2006). Retrieved December 12, 2007, from http://www.normapme.com/

Nour, P., Holz, H., & Maurer, F. (2000). Ontology-based retrieval of software process experiences. In *Proceedings of the ICSE Workshop on Software Engineering over the Internet*.

O'Regan, N., & Ghobadian, A. (2004). Testing the homogeneity of SMEs: The impact of size on managerial and organisational processes. *European Business Review, 16*(1), 64-77.

Oktaba, H. (2004, March). Método de Evaluación de procesos para la industria de software - EvalProSoft (Versión 1.1, NMX-I-006/(01 al 04)-NYCE-2004). México City: Organismo Nacional de Normalización y Evaluación de la Conformidad (NYCE). Retrieved January 1, 2008, from http://www.normalizacion-nyce.org.mx/php/loader.php?c=interes.php&tema=21

Oktaba, H. (2006). MoProSoft®: A software process model for small enterprises. In Proceedings of the 1st International Research Workshop for Process Improvement in Small Settings, Pittsburgh, Carnegie Mellon University (pp. 93-101).

Oktaba, H., (2005). *Modelo de Procesos para la Industria de Software - MoProSoft - Versión 1.3, Agosto de 2005. NMX-059/01-NYCE-2005*. Ciudad de México: Organismo Nacional de Normalización y Evaluación de la Conformidad - NYCE. Retrieved December 14, 2007, from http://www.normalizacion-nyce.org.mx/php/loader.php?c=interes.php&tema=21

Oktaba, H., Alquiara, C., Su, A., Martinez, A., Quintarilla, A., Ruvalcaba, M. (2005). *Modelo de Procesos para la Industria de Software* (MoProSoft, Versión 1.3). México. Retrieved December 16, 2007, from http://www.software.net.mx

Oktaba, H., Alquicira Esquivel, C., Su Ramos, A., Martínez Martínez, A., Quintanilla Osorio, G., Ruvalcaba López, M., López Lira Hinojo, F., Rivera López, M.E., Orozco Mendóza, M.J., Fernández Ordoñez, Y., & Flores Lemus, M.A. (2003). *MoProSoft v. 1.3 Por Niveles De Capacidad De Procesos*. Secretaría de Economía. Retrieved December 14, 2007, from http:// software.net.mx

Oktaba, H., Alquicira Esquivel, C., Su Ramos, A., Palacios Elizalde, J., Pérez Escobar, F., & López Lira Hinojo, F. (2004). *EvalProSoft v1.1.* Secretaría de Economía.

Oktaba, H., et al. (2003). Modelo de Procesos para la Industria de Software: MoProSoft Por Niveles de Capacidad de Procesos.

Organisation for Economic Co-operation and Development. (2002). *OECD small and medium enterprise outlook 2002*. Paris: OECD Publications Service.

Osterweil, L.J. (1987, March). Software processes are software too. In *Proceedings of the 9th International Conference of Software Engineering*, Monterey, CA (pp. 2-13).

Parnas, D.L. (1998). *Software engineering: An unconsummated marriage*. Paper presented at McMaster University, Hamilton, Ontario, Canada. Retrieved December 5, 2007, from http://www.cs.utexas.edu/users/software/1998/parnas-19981208.pdf

Parquesoft Brief. (2006). Cali, Colombia: Parquesoft.

Patton, R. (2006). *Software testing*. Sams Publishing.

Paulk, M. (1998). Using the CMM in small organizations. In the *Joint 1998 Proceedings of the Pacific Northwest Software Quality Conference and the Eighth International Conference on Software Quality*, Portland, Oregon (pp. 350-361).

Paulk, M., Curtis, B., Chrissis, M.B., & Weber, C. (1993, February). Capability maturity model for software (Version 1.1, CMU/SEI-93-TR-24, DTIC No. ADA263403). Software Engineering Institute.

Paulk, M.C., Weber, C.V., Curtis, B., Chrissis, M.B., et al. (1995). *The capability maturity model: Guidelines for improving the software process.* USA: Addison-Wesley.

Pfeffer, J. (2005). Why do Bad Management Theories Persist? A Comment on Ghoshal'. *Academy of Management Learning & Education, 4*, 96-100.

Pfleeger, S. L., Jeffery, D. R., Curtis, B., & Kitchenham, B. (1997). Status report on software management. *IEEE Software, 14*(2), 33-43.

Pino, F., Garcia, F., & Piattini, M. (2006, April). Revisión sistemática de mejora de procesos software en micro, pequeñas y medianas empresas. Revista Española de Innovación, Calidad e Ingeniería del Software (REICIS), 2(1), 6-23.

Pino, F., Garcia, F., Ruiz, F., & Piattini, M. (2006). A lightweight model for the assessment of software processes. In *Proceedings of the European Systems & Software Process Improvement and Innovation (EuroSPI 2006)*, Joensuu, Finland (pp. 7.1-7.12).

Pinto, J.K., & Mantel, S.J. (1990). The causes of project failure. *IEEE Transactions on Engineering Management, 37*(4), 269-276.

PMBOK. (2006). Project management body of knowledge. Retrieved December 12, 2007, from http://www.pmi.org/publictn/pmboktoc.htm

Pollice, G. (2001). *Using the rational unified process for small projects: Expanding upon eXtreme programming* (White Paper TP 183). Rational Software.

Polo, M., Piattini, M., & Ruiz, F. (2002, November). Using a qualitative research method for building a software maintenance methodology. Software Practice and Experience, 32(13), 1239-1260.

Porter, M. (Eds.). (1982). *Competitive strategy: Techniques for analyzing industries and competitors.* Mexico: Macmillan.

Pressman, R. S. (2002). *Ingeniería de Software un enfoque práctico* (R. Ojeda Martín, V. Yagüe Galaup, I. Morales Jareño, & S. Sánchez Alonso, Trans., 5th ed.). Madrid, Spain: McGraw-Hill.

Pressman, R.S. (2002). *Software engineering: A practitioner's Approach* (6th ed.). McGraw-Hill.

Pringle, L. (2001, Summer). Size does matter: Improvement for SMEs. *Software (SEA National)*, pp. 4-7.

Printzell, C., & Conradi, R. (2001). *A taxonomy to compare SPI frameworks.* Paper presented at the Software Process Technology 8th European Workshop (EWSPT 2001), Witten, Germany (Vol. 2077, pp. 217-235). Springer.

Probasco, L. (2000). *The ten essentials of RUP: The essence of an effective development process* (White Paper TP177). Rational Software.

Project Management Institute. (2000). *A guide to the project management body of knowledge.*

Project Management Institute. (2004). *A guide to the project management body of knowledge (PMBOK guide).* Newton Square, PA.

Project Management Institute. (2004). *A guide to the project management body of knowledge* (3rd ed.).

Rathnam, R.G., Johnsen, J., & Wen, J.H. (2004). Alignment of business strategy and IT strategy: A case study of a Fortune 50 financial services company. *Journal of Computer Information Systems, 45*, 1-7.

Rational Unified Process. (2004). *IBM Rational.*

Reed, M. (1996). Organizational theorizing: A historically contested terrain. In S. Clegg, C. Hardy, & W. Nord (Eds.), *Handbook of organization studies* (pp. 25-50). Thousand Oaks, CA: Sage.

Repenning, N. P. & Sterman, J. D. (2001). Nobody ever gets credit for fixing problems that never happened: Creating and sustaining process improvement. *California Management Review, 43*, 64-88.

Resolutions. (2005, May). Presented at the JTC1/SC7 Plenary Meeting (ISO/IEC JTC1/SC7 N3274), Helsinki, Finland.

Revankar, A., Mithare, R., & Nallagonda, V.M. (2006). Accelerated process improvements for small settings. In *Proceedings of the 1st International Research Workshop for Process Improvement in Small Setting* (pp. 117-126).

Richardson, I. (2001). Software process matrix: A small company SPI model. *Software Process: Improvement and Practice, 6*, 157-165.

Richardson, I. (2002). Software process improvements in very small companies. *Software Quality Professional, 4*(2), 14-22.

Richardson, I. (2002). SPI models: What characteristics are required for small software development companies? *Software Quality Journal, 10*, 101-114.

Richardson, I., & Ryan, K. (2001). Software process improvements in a very small company. *Software Quality Professional, 3*(2), 23-35.

Robin, Preedy, Campbell, Paschino, Hargrave, Born, Huber, Haynes, Kazmi, Oikawa, Getchell. (2002, June). MSF Risk Management Discipline v. 1.1. Retrieved December 17, 2007, from http://www.microsoft.com/msf

Romme, A., & Georges, L. (2003). Making a difference: Organization as design. *Organization Science, 14*, 558-573.

Romme, A., Georges, L., & Endenburg, G. (2006). Construction principles and design rules in the case of circular design. *Organization Science, 17*, 287-297.

Rosa, A. d.e la. (2000). La micro, pequeña y mediana empresa en México: Sus saberes, mitos y problemática. *Revista Iztapalapa, 20*(48), 183-220. Retrieved December 5, 2007, from http://148.206.53.230/revistasuam/iztapalapa/include/getdoc.php?rev=iztapalapa&id=656&article=667&mode=pdf

Rout, T. P., Tuffley, A., Cahill, B., & Hodgen, B. (2000). *The rapid assessment of software process capability.* Paper presented at the 1st SPICE 2000 International Conference on Software Process Improvement and Capability dEtermination, Limerick, Ireland.

Rouvellou, I., et al. (2000). Extending business objects with business rules. In *Proceedings of the Technology of Object-Oriented Languages and Systems (TOOLS 33).* IEEE Press.

Royce, W.W. (1970, August). Managing the development of large software systems: Concepts and techniques. In *Proceedings of Wescon.*

Rozenberg, G., & Salomaa, A. (Eds.). (1997). *Handbook of formal languages.* Berlin-Heilderberg: Springer-Verlag.

Saiedian, H. (2003). Practical recommendations to minimize software capability evaluation risks. *Software Process Improvement and Practice, 8*, 145-156.

Sanders, M., & Richardson, I. (2005a). *Research into long-term improvements in small to medium-sized organisations using SPICE as a framework for standards.* Limerick, Ireland: Department of Computer Science and Information Systems, University of Limerick.

Sanders, M., & Richardson, I. (2005b). *What happened after SPI assistance in Ireland?* Paper presented at the 4th International SPICE Conference on Process Assessment and Improvement, Klagenfurt, Austria.

SC7 Secretariat Presentation. (2005, May 25). ISO/IEC Advisory Group Planning Meeting, Helsinki, Finland.

SC7 Secretariat Presentation. (2006, May). Bangkok, Thailand.

Scharmer, C. (1996, February 23). *Knowledge has to do with truth, goodness, and beauty: Conversation with Professor Ikujiro Nonaka.* Tokyo. Retrieved December 17, 2007, from http://www.dialogonleadership.org/Nonaka-1996cp.html, 07/6/2006

Scharmer, C. (2001). Self-transcending knowledge: Organizing around emerging realities. In I. Nonaka & D. Teece (Eds.), *Managing industrial knowledge: Creation, transfer and utilization* (pp. 68-90). Thousand Oaks: Sage Publications.

Schulmeyer, G.G., & McManus, J.I. (Eds.). (1993). *Total quality management for software*. New York: Van Nostrand Reinhold.

Schwaber, K. (2004). *Agile project management with Scrum*. Microsoft Press.

Schwaber, K., & Beedle, M. (2002). *Agile software development with Scrum*. Upper Saddle River, NJ: Prentice Hall.

Scientific American. (1994). *Software's chronic crisis*. Retrieved December 12, 2007, from http://www.cis.gsu.edu/~mmoore/CIS3300/handouts/SciAmSept1994.html

Scott, L., Jeffery, R., Carvalho, L., D'Ambra, J., & Rutherford, P. (2001). Practical software process improvement: The IMPACT Project. In *Proceedings of the Australian Software Engineering Conference* (pp. 182-189).

Scott, L., Jeffery, R., Carvalho, L., D'Ambra, J., & Rutherford, P. (2001). Practical software process improvement: The IMPACT Project. In Proceedings of the Australian Software Engineering Conference (pp. 182-189).

Scott, L., Zettel, J., & Hamann, D. (2000). Supporting process engineering in practice: An experience based scenario. In *Proceedings of the Conference on Quality Engineering in Software Technology (CONQUEST)* (pp. 160-169), Germany.

Scott, W.R. (1992). *Organizations: Rational, natural, and open systems*. Englewood Cliffs, NJ: Prentice Hall.

Secretaría de Economía. (2004). *Estudio del nivel de madurez y capacidad de procesos de la industria de tecnologías de información*. Retrieved December 14, 2007, from http://software.net.mx

SEI. (1995). *The capability maturity model: Guidelines for improving the software process* (SEI Series in Software Engineering). Addison-Wesley.

SEI. (2001a, September). Capability Maturity Model® (SW-CMM®) for software. Retrieved December 14, 2007, from http://www.sei.cmu.edu/cmm

SEI. (2001b, September). CMMI publications and transition materials. Retrieved December 14, 2007, from http://www.sei.cmu.edu/cmmi/publications/pubs.html

SEI. (2001c, September). CMMI product suite. Retrieved December 14, 2007, from http://www.sei.cmu.edu/cmmi/products/products.html

SEI. (2001d). CMMI tutorial. Retrieved December 14, 2007, from http://www.sei.cmu.edu/cmmi/publications/stc.presentations/tutorial.html

SEI. (2002). *CMMI for systems engineering/software engineering* (Version 1.1). Pittsburgh: Software Engineering Institute (SEI). Retrieved December 14, 2007, from http://www.sei.cmu.edu/cmmi/

Senge, P. (1990). *The fifth discipline: The art and practice of the learning organization*. London: Random House.

Serrano, M., Montes de Oca, C., & Cedillo, K. (2006). An experience on implementing the CMMI in a small organization using the team software process. In Proceedings of the 1st International Research Workshop for Process Improvement in Small Settings, Pittsburgh, Carnegie Mellon University (pp. 81-92).

Sharp, H., & Robinson, H. (2004). An ethnographic study of XP practice. *Empirical Software Engineering, 9*, 353-375.

Sievers, B. (1994). *Work, death, and life itself: Essays on management and organization*. Berlin: Walter de Gruyter.

Simon, L. (2002). *Le management en univers ludique: Jouer et travailler chez UbiSoft, une entreprise du multimédia à Montréal (1998-1999)*. Doctoral thesis, École des Hautes Études Commerciales, Université de Montréal, Montréal, Canada.

Sinclair, B. (2003). Can Mexico develop a software maquiladora industry? *Infoamericas Tendencias Latin American Market Report, 38*. Retrieved December 5, 2007, from http://tendencias.infoamericas.com/article_archive/2003/038/038_industry_analysis.pdf

Smith, J., & McKee, P. (2001). Troubled IT projects: Prevention and turn around (IEE Professional Applications of Computing Series, 3). England: MPG Books.

Smith, W. L., Fletcher, R. I., Gray, E. M., & Hunter, R. B. (1994). Software process improvement: The route to software quality? In M. Ross, C. A. Brebbia, G. Staples, & J. Stapleton (Eds.), *Software quality management II* (Vol 1: Managing Quality Systems, pp. 193-211). Southampton Boston: Computational Mechanics Publications.

Software Engineering Institute. (1997). *Introduction to the capability maturity model: Participant notebook.* USA: Carnegie Mellon University, Software Engineering Institute.

Software Engineering Institute. (n.d.). *Improving processes in small settings: A research initiative of the SEI's IPRC.* Retrieved December 12, 2007, from http://www.sei.cmu.edu/iprc/iprc-overview.pdf

Software Engineering Standards Commitee of the IEEE Computer Society (1991). *IEEE STD 610-90 IEEE Standard Computer Dictionary.* United States: IEEE.

Software Technology Park Foundation. (2006). Retrieved December 12, 2007, from http://www.parquesoft.com

Sparx Systems. (2006). Enterprise architect user's guide. Retrieved December 17, 2007, from http://www.sparxsystems.com.au

SPIRE. (1998). *The Spire Handbook: Better, faster, cheaper software development in small organisations.* Dublin: Centre for Software Engineering, DCU Campus.

Staab, S., Studer, R., & Sure, Y. (2002). Knowledge processes and meta processes in ontology-based knowledge management. In C. Holsapple (Ed.), *Handbook on knowledge management.* Springer.

STARS. (2006). *Conceptual framework for reuse processes.* Retrieved December 17, 2007, from http://www2.umassd.edu/swpi/STARS/ProcessConcepts/pcsum.html

Stewart, M. (2006, June). The management myth. *The Atlantic Monthly, June,* pp. 80-87. Retrieved December 5, 2007, from http://www.edst.educ.ubc.ca/courses/EADM532/Stewart.management.myth.pdf

Storey, D. J. (1982). *Entrepreneurship and the new firm.* Croom Helm.

Storey, D. J. (1994). *Understanding the small business sector.* London: Routledge.

Sullivan, L. (2005). ERPzilla: 10 ERP deployments show that megaprojects are standing strong—though they've changed in focus and function. *InformationWeek.* Retrieved December 17, 2007, from http://www.informationweek.com/showArticle.jhtml?articleID=165700832

Susman, G., & Evered, R. (1978). An assessment of the scientific merits of action research. *The Administrative Science Quarterly, 23*(4), 101-114.

Tassey, G. (2002, May). *The economic impacts of inadequate infrastructure for software testing* (Final Report). National Institute of Standards & Technology.

Teles, V.M. (2004). *Extreme programming.* São Paulo: Novatec.

Thai Quality Standard. (2005, March). Association of Thai Software Industry presentation to the Special Working Group Meeting, Bangkok, Thailand.

Thayer, R.H. (Ed.). (1997). *Software engineering project management.* Piscataway, NJ: Wiley-IEEE Computer Society Press. Retrieved December 5, 2007, from http://media.wiley.com/product_data/excerpt/08/08186800/0818680008.pdf

The International Organization for Standardization and the International Electrotechnical Commission (ISO/IEC) (2004). *ISO/IEC 15504-1:2004 Information technology—Process assessment—Part 1: Concepts and vocabulary.* Suisse, Geneve: ISO.

The International Organization for Standardization and the International Electrotechnical Commission (ISO/IEC) (2003). *ISO/IEC 15504-2:2003 Information technology—Process assessment—Part 2: Performing an assessment.* Suisse, Geneve: ISO.

The International Organization for Standardization and the International Electrotechnical Commission

(ISO/IEC) (2004a). *ISO/IEC 15504-3:2004 Information technology—Process assessment—Part 3: Guidance on performing an assessment.* Suisse, Geneve: ISO.

The International Organization for Standardization and the International Electrotechnical Commission (ISO/IEC) (2004b). *ISO/IEC 15504-4:2004 Information technology—Process assessment—Part 4: Guidance on use for process improvement and process capability determination.* Suisse, Geneve: ISO.

Traxler, F. (2005). Firm size, SME and business interest associations: A European comparison. In F. Traxler (Co-ord.), *Small and medium sized enterprises and business interest organisations in the European Union.* Europe: European Commission, DG Employment. Retrieved December 5, 2007, from http://www.ueapme.com/docs/projects/Project%20Business%20Associations/study_final.pdf

Tsoukas, H., & Hatch, M.J. (2001). Complex thinking, complex practice: The case for a narrative approach to organizational complexity. *Human Relations, 54*(8), 979-1013.

Tuckman, A. (1994). The yellow brick road: Total quality management and the restructuring of organizational culture. *Organization Studies, 15*(5), 727-751.

Tuffley, A., Grove, B., & McNair, G. (2004). SPICE for small organizations. *Software Process Improvement and Practice, 9,* 23-31.

Turner, J.R., & Müller, R. (2003). On the nature of the project as a temporary organization. *International Journal of Project Management, 21,* 1-8.

Van de Ven, A.H., & Poole, M.S. (2005). Alternative approaches for studying organizational change. *Organization Studies, 26*(9), 1377-1404.

Varkoi, T., & Mäkinen, T. (1999). Software process improvement network in the Satakunta region: SataSPIN. In *Proceedings of the EuroSPI'99,* Pori, Finland.

Venkatraman, N., & Henderson, J. (1998). Real strategies for virtual organizing. *Sloan Management Review, 40*(1), 33-48.

Ventura-Miranda, M.T., & Peñaloza-Báez, M. (2006). *MoProSoft: modelo de procesos de software hecho en México.* Retrieved December 12, 2007, from http://www.enterate.unam.mx/Articulos/2006/marzo/moprosoft.htm

Voss, C., Blackmon, K. L., Cagliano, R., Hanson, P., & Wilson, F. (1998). Made in Europe: Small companies. *Business Strategy Review, 9*(4), 1-19.

Wangenheim, C. G. v., Weber, S., Rossa Hauck, J. C., & Trentin, G. (2006, January). Experiences on establishing software processes in small companies. *Information and Software Technology,* pp. 1-11.

Watson, T.J., Jr., & Petre, P. (1990). *Pai, Filho & CIA. A História da IBM* (M.C. Fittipaldi, Trans.). Brazil: Editora Nova Cultural Ltda.

Weber, K., Araújo, E., Rocha, A., Machado, S. D., & Salviano, C. (2005). Brazilian software process reference model and assessment method. Computer and Information Sciences, 3733, 402-411. Berlin/Heidelberg: Springer.

Weber, K., Araújo, E., Rocha, A., Machado, Scalet, D., & Salviano, C. (2005). Brazilian software process reference model and assessment method. *Computer and Information Sciences, 3733,* 402-411. Berlin/Heidelberg: Springer.

Wiegers, K. E., & Sturzenberger, D. C. (2000). A modular software process mini-assessment method. *IEEE Software,* pp. 62-69.

Wilkie, F. G., McFall, D., & McCaffery, F. (2004). *The centre for software process technologies: A model for process improvement in geographical regions with small software industries.* Paper presented at the Software Engineering Process Group, Orlando, FL, USA.

Wilkie, F.G., McFall, D., & McCaffery, F. (2005, April 27-29). The express process appraisal method. In *Proceedings of 5th International SPICE Conference (SPICE 2005),* Klagenfurt, Austria (pp. 27-36). Austrian Computer Society. ISBN 3-85403-190-4.

Winter, M., & Smith, C. (2006). *Rethinking project management (EPSRC Network 2004-2006)* (Final Report). United Kingdom: Engineering and Physical Sciences

Research Council. Retrieved December 5, 2007, from http://www.mace.manchester.ac.uk/project/research/management/rethinkpm/pdf/final_report.pdf

Wood, M., Daly, J., Miller, J., & Roper, M. (1999). Multi-method research: An investigation of object-oriented technology. *Journal of Systems and Software, 48*(1), 13-26.

Working Group 24. (2006, September). Public site of the ISO/IEC JTC1/SC7 Working Group 24. Retrieved January 1, 2008, from http://profs.logti.etsmtl.ca/claporte/English/VSE/index.html

Yin, R.K. (1994). *Estudo de Caso—Planejamento e Métodos* (D. Grassi, Trans.). Brazil: Bookman Companhia Editora.

Zahran, S. (1998). *Software process improvement.* USA: Addison-Wesley.

Zavala, J. (2004, February). ¿Por qué fracasan los proyectos de software? Un enfoque organizacional. Paper presented at *Congreso Nacional de Software Libre 2004*. February 11th, 2004, Mexico City. , Retrieved December 5, 2007, from http://www.consol.org.mx/2004/material/63/por-que-fallan-los-proy-de-soft.pdf

Zavala, J. (2006). *Dinámica organizacional en el área informática de una organización pública de México.* Unpublished master's dissertation, Universidad Autónoma Metropolitana–Iztapalapa, Mexico City, Mexico.

About the Contributors

Dr. Hanna Oktaba has a PhD in computer science from the University of Warsaw, Poland, 1982. She has been professor of computer science at the Universidad Nacional Autónoma de México (UNAM) since 1983. She was part of the group that founded the Mexican Society of Quality for Software Engineering (AMCIS), where she has played major roles ever since. She has been in charge of the MoProSoft and EvalProSoft projects for the Mexican government program PROSOFT since 2002. MoProSoft is a software process model for micro and small software development organizations, and EvalProSoft is a process assessment method based on ISO/IEC 15504-2; both documents were accepted as Mexican national standards in August 2005. She was distinguished by the Software Engineering Institute (SEI) as a member of the International Process Research Group (IPRC) whose purpose is to define the process research roadmap for the next 10 years. She has been the technical director of the COMPETISOFT project, funded by CYTED, since January 2006. The general purpose of this project is to enhance competitiveness through process improvement in small and medium Ibero-American software companies; the project comprises 23 groups from 13 countries.

Dr. Mario Piattini has a MSc and PhD in computer science from the Technical University of Madrid and an MSc in psychology from the UNED. He is a certified information system auditor and a certified information security manager by ISACA (Information System Audit and Control Association). He is a professor in the Department of Computer Science at the University of Castilla-La Mancha in Ciudad Real, Spain. As the author of several books and papers on software engineering, databases, and information systems, he leads the ALARCOS research group of the Department of Information Systems and Technologies at the University of Castilla-La Mancha. His research interests are software process improvement, database quality, software metrics, software maintenance, and security in information systems. Since January 2006, he has been the general director of the COMPETISOFT project. He may be contacted at: Escuela Superior de Informática, Paseo de la Universidad 4, 13071-Ciudad Real, Spain, or Mario.Piattini@uclm.es.

* * *

Blanca Abraham is a system engineer (Cum-Laude) with a master's in computer science from the University of Miami and a PhD student of the University of Los Andes. She has been working as a software manager for the last five years in Fundacite, Merida, Venezuela. During this time, she contributed to the implementation of important projects like the Free Software Factory of CENDITEL at the Center of Informatics Security and the Free Software Academy of Venezuela. Blanca worked as a professor at the University of Los Andes, she has had scientific publications in national and international journals, and now she is working as a software implementation leader of a company in the United States. She may be contacted at +58-416-2447111 or blanca@funmrd.gov.ve.

Jose L. Aguilar received a BS in system engineering in 1987 (Universidad de los Andes-Venezuela), a MSc in computer science in 1991 (Universite Paul Sabatier-France), and a PhD in computer science in 1995 (Universite Rene Descartes-France). He was a postdoctoral research fellow in the Department of Computer Sciences at the University of Houston (1999-2000). He is a titular professor in the Department of Computer Science at the Universidad de los Andes. He has published more than 200 papers and five books in the field of parallel and distributed systems, computational intelligence, science and technology management, and so on. Dr. Aguilar has been a visiting research professor at different universities and laboratories, the coordinator or inviting research in more than 20 research or industrial projects, and the supervisor for more than 20 master's and doctoral theses. He may be contacted at +58-416-2447111 or aguilar@ula.ve.

Simon Alexandre is currently in charge of the Software Quality Research Team at CETIC, an ICT research center in Belgium. He has been a scientific collaborator in the software engineering department of the Computer Institute of the University of Namur since 2001. His interests are software process assessment and improvement techniques for small and medium enterprises, agile methodologies, automation of software product quality analysis and open source development processes. He received his MS in informatics from the University of Namur. He is a member of the ISO/IEC-SC7 working group 24, which is tasked with developing profiles and guidelines for software life cycles used in very small enterprises.

Claudia Alquicira Esquivel holds a master's in computer science from the Universidad Nacional Autónoma de México. She has worked on ISO 9000:2000 for several software organizations in their process improvement programs: SW-CMM, CMMI, and MoProSoft. She participated as the main editor of MoProSoft and EvalProSoft. MoProSoft is a software process model for micro and small software development organizations, and EvalProSoft is a process assessment method based on ISO/IEC 15504-2. Both model and method were accepted as the national standard for software process improvement. Currently, she is a team member of the COMPETISOFT project.

Johanna Alvarez has a BSc in systems engineering from the University of Los Andes in Venezuela. Her dissertation thesis pertained to a multi-agent based simulation model of a forest reserve from a social perspective, where she characterizes land holding size distributions, achieving the highest qualification and a publication mention. Afterwards, Miss Alvarez worked in projects for the oil industry and the foundation for science and technology in Mérida State, related with data management and information systems. She has also led the elaboration and implementation of a software development methodology at the Free Software Factory of the Venezuelan Centre for Free Technologies. He may be contacted at +58-416-2749992 or jalvarez@funmrd.gov.ve.

Raquel Anaya has a PhD in informatics from the Polytechnic University of Valencia, Spain. She is a titular professor and head of the Software Engineering Research Group at the EAFIT University of Medellín, Colombia. She is working in aspect-oriented software developed approaches and software process improvement. She coordinates the engineering group of the COMPETISOFT project.

Aileen Cater-Steel is a senior lecturer in information systems at the University of Southern Queensland (USQ) Australia. Her current research interests are software process improvement for small firms and IT service management. She has also published research related to IT governance, software development standards, organizational and national culture, and electronic commerce. Prior to her university appointment, Aileen worked in private and government organizations where her career progressed from programmer, systems analyst, and project manager to IT manager.

Alejandra Cechich is an associate professor and head of the GIISCo Research Group (http://giisco. uncoma.edu.ar) at the University of Comahue, Argentina. Her interests are centered on conceptual modeling, software quality, and component technology and their use in the systematic development of software systems. She holds a European PhD in computer science from the University of Castilla-La Mancha, Spain, and an MSc in computer science from the University of South, Argentina.

Ivanir Costa has a PhD in production engineering from the Polytechnical School of São Paulo University (USP) and a master's in production engineering for the University Paulista (UNIP). As an invited professor and coordinator of courses of after-graduation in SENAC University Center and titular professor of the University Paulista (UNIP). He has 36 years of experience in computer science with emphasis in software engineering and software quality, acting mainly in software development, development methodology, software production, and software factory.

Marcelo Gustavo Estayno is a specialist in software engineering, information systems, and social psychology. Currently, he is the director of postgrade at the National University of La Matanza. Formerly, he was the dean of engineering and technological investigations in the Department of National University of La Matanza in Argentina and titular professor at three national universities. He has led a software engineering group, investigated and directed several projects Consultant PNUD (ONU for development program). SAP application consultant. Manager and consultant in several and different privates companies. He is the author of a number of papers, manuals, and a lot more besides articles about the new technologies, client/server, market reality, an others, published in several magazines.

Valerio Fernandes del Maschi has specialized in information technology since 1985 with emphasis in software development, quality and software engineering, and IT project management. He has worked in companies such as EP3M Enterprise Project Management, and Warehouse Consultoria e Sistemas as a consulting independent, and PRODESP. At the moment Valerio is a Msc Student in Engineering of the Production - Engineering/Production of Software, with certification PMP® ID: 226689 for the PMI® - Project Management Institute the USA. Pos Graduated "Lato Sensu" the MBA Management of Projects – PMI framework - IBTA - Nov/2004; Specialist in Systems of Information – PRODAM - 1985; and Bachelor in Administration with Specialization in Analysis of Systems - FASP - 1984. Currently as Senior Manager of Projects - PMO Head, in software development, outsourcing and infrastructure applying quality models like CMMI, RUP, COBIT and ITIL. He's a teacher in IT and Project Management Master Courses at FGV, FAAP, SENAC, IBTA.

Evaristo Fernández has a master's in IT from the Universidad Nacional Autónoma de México with 10 years of experience in object-oriented analysis and design. He has expert knowledge in the business by using techniques such as Catalyst and BPMN, applied to financial sectors, the government, and medical and retail services. He has given object-oriented analysis and design courses to different companies. He is a member of the Ultrasist's assessing committee to obtain SW-CMM level 4. He is presently in charge of the project's office and a member of Ultrasist's processes group.

Luis Eduardo Fernández is an engineer in computer science from the University of Cauca. He is a member of the IDIS Research Group. His research interest is software processes improvement in small companies.

Félix García is a lecturer at the University of Castilla-La Mancha (UCLM). His research interests include business process management, software processes, software measurement, and agile methods. He holds a MSc and PhD from the UCLM in computer science and is a member of the ALARCOS Research Group of that university, specialized in information systems, databases, and software engineering. He may be contacted at Escuela Superior de Informática, Paseo de la Universidad 4, 13071-Ciudad Real, Spain, or Felix.Garcia@uclm.es.

SuZ García is a senior member of the technical staff at the Software Engineering Institute of Carnegie Mellon University in Pittsburgh, PA, USA. She currently works in the Integrating SW Intensive Systems initiative. Her research in this area is focused on creating processes, tools and techniques to support complex systems of systems engineering. From June 2001 to Oct 2006, she worked in the technology transition research area, with 3 of those years focused specifically on transition support of process improvement for small settings. From Nov 1997-May 2001, she was the Deployments Manager for aimware, Incorporated's US customers, focusing on using technology to accelerate organizational improvement. The 5 years prior to this were spent at the SEI working in various capacities on all the Capability Maturity Models the Institute was involved in. She spent the previous 12 years in multiple improvement-related roles at Lockheed Missile and Space Co. She is co-author of CMMI Survival Guide: Just Enough Process Improvement, a book that focuses on the skills and practices needed to establish and support process improvement programs in small and other constrained-resource settings. Education: BA, Ergonomics, 1980 from University of California, Santa Barbara; MS, Systems Management, 1988 from University of Southern California.

John Gómez is a project management professional certified by the Project Management Institute and works as a project office manager for service delivery at Ericsson Chile. John has more than 15 years of experience in software development projects as programmer, designer, architect, and project manager. For the last three years, John has collaborated with and leads projects and process improvement initiatives based on agile methodologies and traditional models like ISO 9001:2000 and the CMMI. He has also authored articles, papers, and lectures on agile topics, including the Latin-American edition of the SEPG conference in 2004, 2005, and 2006.

Mónica Henao-Cálad has a PhD in informatics from the Universidad Politécnica de Valencia, Spain; a MSc on technology management from the Universidad Pontificia Bolivariana, Colombia; and a BS on systems engineering from the Universidad EAFIT, Colombia. He is a research professor at the Computer

Engineering Department in the Universidad EAFIT. She has been invited professor at the Universidad Politécnica de Valencia, Spain, and part of various research projects. He has written several papers related to knowledge-based systems, knowledge management, and concept maps. Professor Henao-Cálad is currently the chair of the Systems Engineering Program at EAFIT University.

Julio A. Hurtado is an engineer in electronics and telecommunications from the University of Cauca, Colombia. He is a member of the IDIS Research Group; a specialist in software development from the University San Buenaventura, Colombia; a PhD student of computer science in the University of Chile; and an assistant professor at the Electronic and Telecommunications Engineering Faculty at the University of Cauca, Popayán (Colombia). His research interest is software processes improvement in small companies.

Sarah Kohan has a bachelor's in computing science from the Instituto de Matemática e Estatística–Universidade de São Paulo and a master's in software engineering from the Instituto de Pesquisas Tecnológicas in São Paulo, Brazil. She is an auditor for ISO 9001:2000 and GoodPriv@cy, international standards for data protection and privacy management requirements. Mrs. Kohan has experience in projects, application software development as well as in compiler and operational systems software development. In recent years, she has participated in software quality programs in training as well as software development process evaluation and implementation activities through the Fundação Carlos Alberto Vanzolini from Escola Politécnica at Universidade de São Paulo. She was a co-author of the Reference Norm NRY2k–Year 2000 Bug (December, 1998) and of the OnLine Privacy Reference Norm–NRPOL (June, 2000) and respectives evaluation methods, both published by Fundação Carlos Alberto Vanzolini. She teaches quality courses at the IT Project Management specialization program from the same foundation.

Claude Y. Laporte is a professor at the École de Technologie Supérieure (ÉTS), an engineering school where he teaches graduate and undergraduate courses in software engineering. His research interests include software process improvement in small and very companies and software quality assurance. He received a master's in physics from the Université de Montréal and a master's in applied sciences from the École Polytechnique de Montréal. He is the editor of an ISO/IEC-JTC1 SC7 working group tasked to develop software life cycle profiles and guidelines for use in very small enterprises. He is a member of IEEE, PMI, INCOSE, and l'Ordre des Ingénieurs du Québec (Professional Association of Engineers of the Province of Québec).

Luis Vinicio León-Carrillo received a BS in systems engineering from ITESO University (Instituto Tecnológico y de Estudios Superiores de Occidente) in 1989; in 1995, he received the equivalent to a MS from the Technische Universität Clausthal in Germany, where he is currently a PhD candidate with a dissertation on software testing. Mr. León-Carrillo is a faculty member of the Department of Electronics, Systems, and Informatics at ITESO University and co-founder of e-Quallity, a specialized firm in software testing, where he has headed its research and development team. He is the president of the Western Chapter of AMCIS (Asociación Mexicana de Calidad en Ingeniería de Software) and member of the editorial board of *Software Guru*, a specialized Latin American IT magazine.

Hareton Leung is an associate professor of the Department of Computing at the Hong Kong Polytechnic University and serves as the director of the Software Development and Management Lab. Dr. Leung has conducted research in software testing, software maintenance, quality and process improvement, and software metrics. He currently serves on the editorial board of *Software Quality Journal* and *Journal of the Association for Software Testing*. In 1995, Dr. Leung co-founded the Hong Kong Software Process Improvement Network (HKSPIN) to promote software process and quality improvement in Hong Kong. Prior to joining HK PolyU, Dr. Leung held team leader positions at BNR, Nortel, and GeneralSoft Ltd. He is also an accomplished industry consultant. His clients include large- and medium-sized organizations and government departments throughout Hong Kong and China.

Alexandre de Lima Esteves has a BSc in computer science and is currently a MSc student in industrial engineering for software production, Microsoft certified solution developer for Microsoft .NET, and Microsoft certified application developer for Microsoft .NET. He has spent more than 11 years working for IT with deep domain in software factory management and as a team mentor/coach for the software development process. Nowadays, his motivation has been to create correspondence between the industrial engineering field and the software engineering field by applying techniques identified in the industrial engineering field such as lean manufactory, kaizen, Toyota production system, and theory of constraints to the software engineering field. Those techniques have been implemented in a Brazilian software factory in addition to elaborating the strategic planning for a software company.

Ms. Yvette Lui is a technical consultant in the CMMFT Programme and was instrumental in writing the process guides under this program. She was a certified software quality analyst (CSQA), trained in the SEI Challenge Program (Motorola, based on CMM® v.1.1), and had conducted about 30 gap analyses for Motorola Semiconductors (Hong Kong) and Hong Kong software SMEs (small to medium enterprises). At the time of this writing, she was the manager of the Software Development and Management Laboratory under the Department of Computing in the Hong Kong Polytechnic University. She holds a BA (Hons, computing studies), and an MBA (Warwick, UK).

Jorge Luis Pirolla is attending the MBA course of industrial engineering at Paulista University (UNIP). He is also a technologist who graduated from São Judas Tadeu University (USJT). Currently, he is a university teacher of computer science subjects (structure of database, development of systems guided to objects and software processes), besides acting as an IT consultant. He was a development manager of software products related to educational management, as well as a coordinator of systems developed for the stell mill area.

Juan M. Luzuriaga is head of the Informatics Department at the Judicial System of the Province of Neuquén, Argentina. He is also an adjunct professor and member of the GIISCo Research Group at the University of Comahue, Argentina. His interests are focused on requirements engineering, conceptual modeling, and software process improvement. He graduated in computer science and holds a specialization in auditing quality systems.

Rodolfo Martínez is in charge of the Software Development Department at the Judicial System of the Province of Neuquén, Argentina. He is also an assistant professor and member of the GIISCo Research Group at the University of Comahue, Argentina. His interests are focused on requirements engineering, conceptual modeling, and software process improvement. He graduated in computer science and holds a specialization in auditing quality systems.

Tomás Martínez is a MSc of computer science at the University of Castilla-La Mancha (UCLM). He is a PhD student at the ALARCOS Research Group of that university. His research interests are software process improvement, software process lines, and aspect-oriented software. He may be contacted at Escuela Superior de Informática, Paseo de la Universidad 4, 13071-Ciudad Real, Spain, or Tomas.Martinez@uclm.es.

Mauro de Mesquita Spinola has a bachelor's in electronic engineering from the Instituto Tecnológico de Aeronáutica, a master's in applied computing from Instituto Nacional de Pesquisas Espaciais, and a PhD in computing engineering from Escola Politécnica at University of São Paulo (EPUSP). He is a professor in the Production Engineering Department at EPUSP. He has more than 20 years of experience in software projects and has worked for companies like INPE, Itauplan, FDTE, and Philco. He has been researching software for more than 15 years, particularly software quality and has been taking part in CMM/CMMI implementation projects in manufacturing and financial enterprises, including process evaluation. He teaches several extension courses in fields like information technology and software quality. He is the coordinator at eLabSoft where he conducts research on software factories and software process.

Alok Mishra is assistant professor of computer engineering at Atilim University, Ankara, Turkey. He has a PhD in computer science (software engineering) and a master's in computer science and applications and human resource management. His areas of interest and research are software engineering, information systems, information and knowledge management, and object-oriented analysis and design. He has extensive experience of distance and online education related to computers and management courses. He has published articles, book chapters, and book reviews related to software engineering and information systems in refereed journals, books, and conferences, including *International Journal of Information Management, Government Information Quarterly, Behaviour and Information Technology, Public Personnel Management, European Journal of Engineering Education,* and *International Journal of Information Technology and Management.*

Deepti Mishra is an assistant professor of computer engineering at Atilim University, Ankara, Turkey. She earned her PhD in computer science (software engineering) and master's in computer science and applications. Her areas of interest and research are software engineering, database management, and data warehousing.

Alicia Laura Mon is director of the Computer Science MSc of National University of La Matanza and professor in several national universities. She is the invited professor of the Technical University of Madrid MSc in software engineering. She has received the National Research Award "Jose Antonio Balseiro." She has a master's in software engineering and is a PhD student of the UPM and DEA of the UCM, Spain. She is the author of a number of papers; her last book, *A Software Process Model Handbook for Incorporating People's Capabilities,* has been published by Springer. She is a member of the program committees of several international congresses and of the Quality in Technology of the Information Sub-Committee (Argentine Institute of Normalization).

Alejandro Núñez is a computer engineer and works as a senior consultant for process improvement at Practia Consulting S.A. His experience as a software project leader has allowed him to incorporate open source principles and tools into small and medium sized companies, helping teams to collaboratively work from requirements, plan, build, test, and deploy in an efficient and learning-focused way.

María Julia Orozco Mendoza is a mathematician with a master's in computer science. She has been developing systems for the different life cycles for 20 years and has worked with programs to improve software engineering processes in several organizations. She assisted in the development of the Mexican Official Standard for "MoProSoft" software development. She was a member of the Mexican Association for the Quality in Ingenerate de Software's board of directors. She belongs to the Competisoft project working team where 13 countries participate to define a model to improve software development in Latin America. She presently works as a technical director in Ultrasist and is responsible for the improvement project which took the company to become the first Mexican PYME to reach SW-CMM level 4; she is in charge of the project to obtain CMMI level 5.

César Pardo is an engineer in computer science from the University of Cauca. He is a member of the IDIS Research Group. His research interest is software processes improvement in small companies.

Gustavo R. Parés Arce obtained a MBA from the ITESM Campus at Mexico City, participating in an international exchange program with the Pontificia Universidad Católica de Chile; he also holds a bachelor's in management information systems from the ITESM Campus at Mexico City where he also participated an exchange program with the University of Illinois at Urbana-Champaign. He teaches two courses at the ITESM Campus Santa Fe that focus on how to use technology to increase the competitiveness and efficiency of small- and medium-sized enterprises. He has published different articles and technical notes on different forums in the USA, Canada, Russia, China, Mexico, Colombia, and Peru. He is the responsible editor for the technology section of the magazine *Microempresa Mexicana*. He is the founder of the Web site www.softwarepyme.com and an active advocate of the use of technology as a strategic tool for companies to achieve a long term competitive advantage.

Marcelo Schneck de Paula Pessôa has a bachelor's in electronic engineering and master's and PhD from Escola Politécnica at University of São Paulo (EPUSP). He is a professor at the Production Engineering Department at EPUSP. Has more than 30 years of experience in computer science, automation and telecommunications, and has worked for companies like Cosipa, Siderbrás, and the Research Center at Telebrás. He has been an active member in ABNT's Center of Software Lifecycle Management Study and participates in the creation of local and international standards for software development representing Brazil at international meetings. He is a coordinator at eLabSoft where he conducts research on software factories and software process. He also participates in research regarding IT strategy.

Francisco J. Pino is a lecturer at the Electronic and Telecommunications Engineering Faculty at the University of Cauca in Popayán (Colombia). He is a member of the IDIS and ALARCOS Research Group. His research interest is software processes improvement in small companies. He is currently a PhD student of computer science at the University of Castilla-La Mancha (UCLM) in Spain. He may be contacted at University of Cauca, Street 5 N. 4 – 70 – Popayán, Colombia, or fjpino@unicauca.edu.co.

Alain Renault is a project leader at the Henri Tudor Public Research Center–Luxembourg. He is a 1984 software engineering graduate. After nine years in the industry as a software engineer, he returned to university, where he contributed to the development of OWPL (SPI framework and micro-evaluation for SME). He has been working on SME projects for the past eight years, recently focusing on security and service management. He is a member of an ISO/IEC-SC7 working group tasked to develop software life cycle profiles and guidelines for use in very small enterprises.

Terry Rout is an associate professor in the School of Information and Communications Technology at Griffith University, Queensland, Australia, and leads the process assessment and improvement group within the Software Quality Institute at the university. He is the overall project editor for *ISO/IEC 15504: Process Assessment*. He has led the efforts of the SQI to transition process assessment improvement and assessment approaches into Australian industry. He is a charter member of the International Process Research Consortium, established by the Software Engineering Institute to develop a roadmap for future research directions in process modeling and improvement.

Francisco Ruiz is an associate professor in the Department of Information Technologies and Systems at the University of Castilla-La Mancha, Spain. He received his PhD in computer science from the UCLM and a MSc in sciences from the Complutense University of Madrid. He has been dean of the Faculty of Computer Science and Computer Services CEO's in the UCLM between 1985 and 2000. He has also worked in private companies as analyst-programmer and project manager. His current research interests include business processes modeling and measurement, software measurement, software process technology, and methodologies for planning and managing of software projects. He has written more than 50 international publications, including two books, 10 chapters, 21 articles in refereed journals, and 22 communications in congresses and conferences. He has been a member of more than 20 scientific program committees. He belongs to several international scientific and professional associations (IEEE Computer Society, ACM, ISO JTC1/SC7, EASST). He may be contacted at francisco.ruizg@uclm.es.

Patricia Alejandra Scalzone has a bachelor's in systems analysis from Buenos Aires University. Founding partner of VEMN Systems, Argentine company of Consultancy and Software Applications Development, high technologies specialist, with 15 years of trajectory. Project Manager, specialist in software development process for the Small and Medium Enterprise. Educational College teacher at La Matanza National University, expositor, awarded by Microsoft like Most Valuable Professional (MVP).

Luciano Soares de Souza is a professor and coordinates the course of Technology in Automation and Robotics at the University Paulista (UNIP) at São Paulo, Brazil, where he also serves as a systems analyst in the Department of Information Technology. He is a graduate in computer science and a MSc student of production engineering at the University Paulista.

Oswaldo R. Terán has a degree in systems engineering and a MSc in applied statistics in Venezuela, and a PhD in computational modeling at the Manchester Metropolitan University, UK. He has been a lecturer and researcher at the Operations Research Department and at the Simulation and Modelling Centre of the University of Los Andes since 1992. Mr. Terán has been the planning and development manager at FUNDACITE-Mérida since 2003, where he has participated in diverse projects related with software development, prospective and planning. He has been a member of the Scientific Committee of international workshops in Social Simulation and Artificial Intelligence and is involved in international software development projects such as COMPETISOFT. He may be contacted at +58-274-4164406 or oteran@ula.ve.

Ana Vázquez is an electronic systems engineer with 15 years of experience in software development and implementation of quality systems. Recently, she finished the successful implementation of a quality system compliant with CMMI L4 in a Mexican company; now she is working in the evolution of this system to CMMI L5. Acknowledged by the Project Management Institute (PMI) as a distinguished reviewer of PMBoK 2000 version, she has designed and given courses based on this body of knowledge in several forums. She had a major role in the design of the Mexican software development standardization strategy based on ISO/IEC 15504 and in the management of the project to pilot the Mexican Software Development Process Model (MoProSoft) document, which was taken as base for the Mexican standard for software development. In 2006, she was the head of the delegation for plenary and interim meetings of ISO/IEC JTC1 SC7, where the Mexican standard was selected as base for the development of the international standard in charge of WG24 "Lifecycle Profiles for VSE (Very Small Enterprises)."

Wilson Vendramel is a graduate in systems information, postgraduate in administration and software engineering, and a student in a mastery course in production engineering; professional experience as Specialist Systems in IBM Brazil acting with on activities the Outsourcing, project and development of Software and database implementation; university professor of some institutions in the state of São Paulo, teaching mainly disciplines as Software Engineering, Analysis and Project of Systems, Database Project and Systems Information.

Juan Carlos Vidal has a PhD in computer science from the University of Chile and is an engineer in Electronics and Telecommunications at the University of Cauca. He is a member of the IDIS Research Group and a titular professor at the Electronic and Telecommunications Engineering Faculty at the University of Cauca in Popayán (Colombia). His research interests are mobile agents, distributed systems, information retrieval on the Web, and software processes improvement.

Jesús Zavala-Ruiz has been a member of the Association for Computing Machinery (ACM) since 2000, a member of the Organization Studies Researchers Mexican Network (Red Mexicana de Investigadores en Estudios Organizacionales, REMINEO) since 2006, and a member of the A-typical Work Research Group (Colectivo de Estudios de Trabajo A-típico, CESTA) based on Universidad Autónoma Metropolitana (UAM), Mexico, since 2006. Mr. Zavala holds an irrigation engineering bachelor's degree from the Universidad Autonoma Chapingo, Mexico. He has a certificate in computer science and holds a master's in organization studies at UAM. Currently, he studies his doctorate in organization studies at UAM, Mexico City. He actively participates in the software community and in consulting. His main interests are skilled professionals, consulting firms, software firms, organization modeling, software project management and new management approaches using software engineering, clinical sociology, and human sciences. He can be reached by e-mail at jzavalaruiz@gmail.com and jzr@xanum.uam.mx.

Index